Look Smarter Than You Are with Oracle Enterprise Planning Cloud

interRel Consulting

1st Edition

interRel Press, Arlington, Texas

Look Smarter Than You Are with Oracle Enterprise Planning Cloud

interRel Consulting

Published by:
    interRel Press
    A Division of interRel Consulting Partners
    1000 Ballpark Way, Suite 304
    Arlington, TX 76011

All rights reserved. No portion of this book may be reproduced or transmitted in any form or by any means, electronic or mechanical, including photocopying, recording or by any information storage retrieval system without the express written consent of the author or interRel Press except for the inclusion of brief quotations in a review.

Copyright © 2016-Present by interRel Consulting
1st edition
Printed in the United States of America

Library of Congress Cataloging-in-Publication Data
interRel Consulting
Look Smarter Than You Are with Oracle Enterprise Planning Cloud

interRel Consulting 1st ed.
    p. 557 cm.
    Includes index.
978-1-329-84553-4

Trademarks
Various trademarked names appear throughout this book. Rather than list all the names and the companies/individuals that own those trademarks or try to insert a trademark symbol every time a trademarked name is mentioned, the author and publisher state that they are using the names only for editorial purposes and to the benefit of the trademark owner with no intention of trademark infringement.

This book is dedicated to astronaut Mark Watney.

Your story was an inspiration to us all.

Thanks to you, we will never give up hope

even when we're in serious trouble.

ABOUT THE AUTHORS

This book is an interRel collaboration of many, many people. Primary authors are:

Opal Alapat (interRel Oracle EPM Cloud Specialist, Oracle ACE Associate, ODTUG Board of Directors)

Opal refuses to date herself, so all she'll say is that she's been wandering around in the EPM and BI space for over 15 years...and something about how side ponytails need to be back in style again. Since joining interRel, Opal has been immersed in all things Oracle EPM/BI Cloud. She's been writing, speaking, and training on Cloud technologies, as well as working with Oracle product development on future releases. When not evangelizing Cloud, Opal enjoys working on her second (volunteer) job, ODTUG, as well as being a complete goofball at home, and eating her way through Dallas' new and exciting cuisines. Visit Opal's blog at http://womaninepm.com/ or follow her on Twitter at @opal_EPM.

Tracy McMullen (interRel Director of Product Strategy, Oracle ACE Director, OAUG Planning Domain Lead)

Tracy, a.k.a. Goddess of all things Oracle EPM and now Oracle EPM Cloud, has been leading the development of EPM and Data Warehousing applications for over 15 years. She helped co-write the Oracle Essentials certification exams with Oracle for Hyperion Planning, Hyperion Financial Management, Essbase, and Data Relationship Management. As if those achievements weren't enough, she's also a certified Project Management Professional (PMP). She's a regular speaker, instructor, mentor, proponent of women in technology, and visionary leader. She currently holds the title for most Hyperion books authored by a single person. Her strong technical background is complimented by comprehensive practical experience, a skill important not only on the job but at home as well where she manages her kids on a daily basis (ok, she attempts to, but with moderate success). Tracy calls interRel "home" and has been there for 10+ years. She is currently the Director of Strategic Projects. Follow Tracy on Twitter at @TracyAMcMullen1.

Edward Roske (interRel CEO, Oracle ACE Director)

Edward, the leader of the vast interRel empire, was hit by the Hyperion cupid waaaaaay back in 1995. When he saw his first demo of Arbor Essbase (as it was known at the time), he quit his job to become a full-time Essbase consultant. He then went on to become one of the world's first Essbase certified consultants. He was also one of the first people in the world to become certified in Hyperion Planning. In May of 1997, Edward co-founded interRel Consulting. He has been the CEO of interRel ever since, growing the company to a multi-million dollar firm that spans coast to coast. Edward still keeps his technical skills sharp and you can find him evangelizing Oracle EPM and BI (and now Oracle EPM and BI Cloud), as well as billing on customer projects. Edward continues to be a regular speaker at conferences and he's known for his humorous slant on boring technical information. In the last ~20 years, Edward has spoken to over 10,000 people in 15+ countries across 5 continents. Visit Edward's blog at http://looksmarter.blogspot.com/ or follow him on Twitter at @ERoske.

Cathy Son (interRel Associate Consultant)

Cathy was fortunate enough to discover the amazing, ever-changing world of EPM and BI shortly after graduating from UCLA. She was even more fortunate to be on this journey with interRel from the beginning. Since joining interRel a couple of years ago, she has been involved in various types of projects and has been one of the first to implement Enterprise Planning Cloud applications. She hopes that readers find this book to be an insightful and invaluable start to their Oracle Cloud journey! Follow Cathy on Twitter at @Hyp4Me!

ABOUT INTERREL CONSULTING

Founded in 1997, interRel Consulting is the longest-standing Hyperion partner dedicated solely to implementing Oracle EPM/BI solutions for Fortune 500 and mid-size companies, and is the only three-time winner of Oracle's specialized Partner of the Year for BI and EPM. The company is an eight-time Inc. 5000 honoree committed to education with a platform that includes 10+ books in its best-selling technical reference series, "Look Smarter Than You Are with Hyperion," free, twice-weekly webcasts, the free-access video education platform, Play it Forward, on YouTube, and multi-track Oracle EPM/BI Solutions Conferences across the U.S. and Canada. Home to three Oracle ACE Directors and three Oracle ACE Associates, interRel frequently participates in Oracle Technology Network international tours in developing markets. To learn more about interRel Consulting, please visit www.interRel.com.

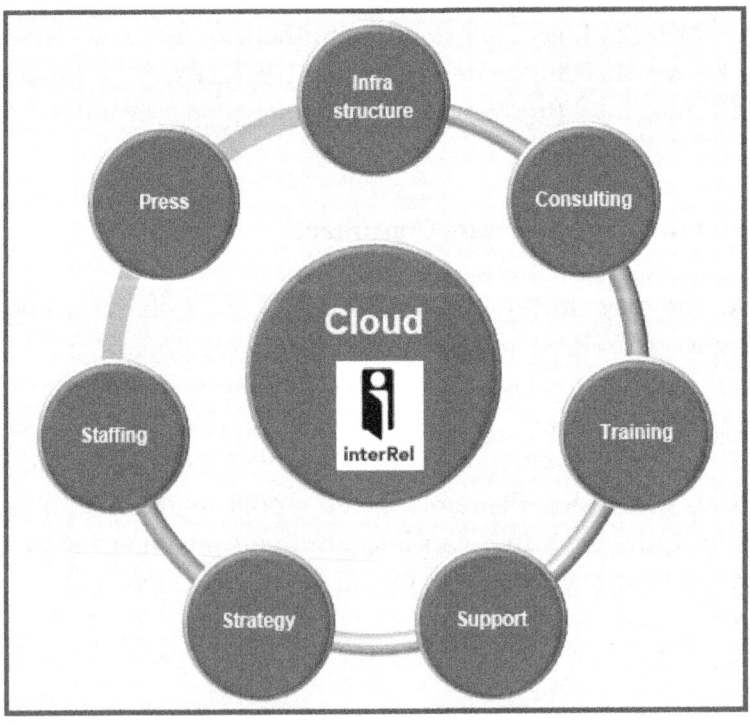

ACKNOWLEDGEMENTS

If we were to thank all of those who assisted us in the creation of this book, we would have to not only personally mention hundreds of people but also several companies and one or two federal agencies (though we will give a special shout-out to those wacky guys over at the Internal Revenue Service: keep it real, yo!). Suffice to say, if this book stands tall, it is only by balancing on the heads of giants.

Thank you to the following individuals who provided significant contributions to this book (content, proofing, and more):

Kurt Mayer – Kurt has been living and breathing Reporting & Analysis, Business Intelligence, and Data Integration for over 30 years – the last 13 years of which he has enjoyed working in the Oracle EPM/BI space. As a Consultant at interRel, he specializes in the design and delivery of data integration and modeling solutions on Hyperion EPM, Planning, and OBIEE projects. When he doesn't have his head in the Cloud, he enjoys a little wind therapy riding his Harley around Southeast Texas.

Pete Puskar – Pete is an EPM professional with over eight years of Hyperion consulting experience. He specializes in building complex data and metadata integration solutions with FDM, FDMEE, ODI, and DRM. As Senior Integration Lead at interRel, his primary responsibility is to drive the overall implementation strategy for data integration, as well as lead the design, oversight, and delivery of integration projects. His secondary responsibility is to challenge anyone within shouting distance of the arcade at interRel HQ.

Summer Watson – With 15 years in the EPM industry, Summer Watson now uses her expertise to support/train all kinds of users in the EPM space. She helps to resolve customer issues that range from infrastructure to end-user, and from server logs to Smart View retrievals. You've got a problem, she will solve it. You can follow her support tips and tricks at http://epmsxsw.com/.

Thank you to Syed Raziuddin, Tanya Shringapure and Ceca Bridges for their efforts in helping this book come to fruition.

We also want to thank some folks from Oracle whose help was invaluable in writing this book: Al Marciante, Gabby Rubin, Shankar Viswanathan, Mark Rinadli, Steve Liebermensch, Tom Lefebvre, Toufic Wakim, Karen Imber, Joshua Torres, and David Respaldiza.

We give our sincerest gratitude to all the people above, and we hope that they feel that this book is partly theirs as well (just without the fame, glory, and most importantly, the royalties).

DISCLAIMER

This book is designed to provide supporting information about the related subject matter. It is being sold to you and/or your company with the understanding that the author and the publisher are not engaged by you to provide legal, accounting, or any other professional services of any kind. If assistance is required (legal, expert, or otherwise), seek out the services of a competent professional such as a consultant.

It is not the purpose of this book to reprint all of the information that is already available on the subject at hand. The purpose of this book is to complement and supplement other texts already available to you. For more information (especially including technical reference information), please contact the software vendor directly or use your on-line help.

Great effort has been made to make this book as complete and accurate as possible. That said, there may be errors, both typographic and in content. Therefore, use this book only as a general guide and not as the ultimate source for specific information on the software product. Further, this book contains information on the software that was generally available as of the publishing date. Please note that Oracle Cloud products are ever-changing and some differences are likely to be found between this book and the current versions of the Cloud products.

The purpose of this book is to entertain while educating. The authors and interRel Press shall have neither liability nor responsibility to any person, living or dead, or entity, currently or previously in existence, with respect to any loss or damage caused or alleged to be caused directly, indirectly, or otherwise by the information contained in this book.

We've included a parody storyline to go along with the educational Cloud content - a parody on a recent book and movie. No real clients were harmed in the making of this book

If you do not wish to abide by all parts of the above disclaimer, please stop reading now and return this book to the publisher for a full refund.

TABLE OF CONTENTS

PROLOGUE: THE EPM MARTIAN 1

CHAPTER 1: INTRO TO THE EPM CLOUD 3
    THE DARK DAYS OF SERVERS 3
    THE CLOUD 5
    ORACLE ENTERPRISE PLANNING CLOUD 7
    BUSINESS INTELLIGENCE CLOUD/DATA VISUALIZATION CLOUD . 9
    ENTERPRISE PERFORMANCE REPORTING CLOUD 10
    ACCOUNT RECONCILIATION CLOUD 12
    FINANCIAL CONSOLIDATION & CLOSE CLOUD 12
    CLOUD GONE WILD 13
    HYBRID IMPLEMENTATION APPROACH 13

CHAPTER 2: LAUNCH INTO THE CLOUD 15
    CLOUD.ORACLE.COM 15
    CLOUD ROLES, PRIVILEGES, & RESPONSIBILITIES 18
    ORACLE CLOUD – MY ACCOUNT 19
    ORACLE CLOUD – MY SERVICES 20
    CLOUD ACTIVATION PROCESS 22
    USERS IN THE CLOUD 29
    MANAGE & MONITOR YOUR CLOUD INSTANCE 36
    LOGGING A CLOUD SUPPORT CASE 39

CHAPTER 3: INTRO TO ORACLE ENTERPRISE PLANNING CLOUD 41
    INTRO TO ORACLE ENTERPRISE PLANNING CLOUD 41
    USER INTERFACES 41
    NAVIGATE THE SIMPLIFIED UI 42
    MEMBER SELECTION IN THE SIMPLIFIED UI 49
    NAVIGATE THE WORKSPACE UI 52
    COMPARING THE INTERFACES 56
    APPLICATIONS & PLAN TYPES DEFINED 57
    VISION APPLICATION DESIGN 59

CHAPTER 4: BUILD AN APPLICATION 62

CREATE AN APPLICATION 62
DIMENSIONS EXPLAINED 66
BUILD SCENARIO DIMENSION 74
REFRESH THE DATABASE 77
BUILD VERSION DIMENSION 81
ACCOUNT DIMENSION EXPLAINED 84
CREATE SMART LIST 90
BUILD ACCOUNT DIMENSION 92
VIEW & ADD YEARS TO YEARS DIMENSION 97
VIEW PERIOD DIMENSION & ENABLE DTS 98
VIEW HSP_VIEW DIMENSION 100
CREATE CUSTOM PRODUCT DIMENSION 100
IMPORT & EXPORT DIMENSIONS 102
USE EXCEL TO UPDATE DIMENSIONS 109
ATTRIBUTE DIMENSIONS 115
SET PLAN TYPE DEFINITIONS 121
ASO PLAN TYPES 124
VARIABLES 129

CHAPTER 5: INTEGRATE DATA 133

INTEGRATION OPTIONS OVERVIEW 134
IMPORT DATA WITH THE SIMPLIFIED UI 136
EXPORT DATA WITH THE SIMPLIFIED UI 142
INTRO TO DATA MANAGEMENT 145
LOAD DATA FILE USING DATA MANAGEMENT 149
EXPORT DATA USING DATA MANAGEMENT 209
SYNC DATA WITH DATA MANAGEMENT 222
OTHER DATA MANAGEMENT CONCEPTS 227
SYNC DATA WITH DATA MAPS 228
AUTOMATE DATA INTEGRATION 234
REST API 234

CHAPTER 6: CALCULATE DATA 237

INTRO TO CALCULATION MANAGER 237
CREATE BUSINESS RULE IN GRAPHICAL MODE 241
CREATE GRAPHICAL RULE WITH A SCRIPT COMPONENT 246
CREATE BUSINESS RULE IN SCRIPT MODE 250
DEPLOY BUSINESS RULE 256

Launch Business Rule 257
View Business Rule Status 258
Assign Business Rule to Form 260
Export Data Using a Business Rule 262
ASO Plan Type Business Rules 264

CHAPTER 7: CREATE USER INTERFACES 267

Data Forms 267
Smart Forms 310
Valid Intersections 313
Action Menus 319
Tasks 321
Dashboards 324
Financial Reports 328
Ad Hoc Grids & Dynamic Reports 352

CHAPTER 8: ASSIGN SECURITY 364

Native Groups 365
Set Enterprise Planning Cloud Application Security ... 368
Assign Member Access 370
Assign Form Access 373
Assign Business Rule Access 374
Assign Task List Access 374
Allow Tablet Access 376

CHAPTER 9: AUTOMATE & MIGRATE 378

Job Scheduler 378
EPM Automate 390
Application Management 415
Application Migration 417

CHAPTER 10: END USER ACTIVITIES 427

Navigate Simplified UI 427
Review Dashboards 427
Follow Tasks 428
Input Plans 430
Everything's Under a Menu 433
Select Smart List Values 435

ENTER TEXT & DATES 435
REFRESH A DATA FORM 436
SAVE A DATA FORM 436
SHORTCUT KEYS 437
AUTOSAVE & UNDO 437
ADJUSTMENTS & DATA SPREADING 438
ATTACHMENTS, COMMENTARY, & DETAIL 442
FORMATTING 448
VIEW MEMBER FORMULAS 449
ANALYZE 450
USE SMART FORMS 455
RUNNING BUSINESS RULES 456
APPROVALS 458
RUN REPORTS 458
SETTINGS 460
ALLOW USERS TO ADD MEMBERS ON THE FLY 463
PREDICTIVE ANALYTICS 474
PLAN IN EXCEL USING SMART VIEW 475
RETAIN EXCEL FORMATTING / CUSTOM STYLES 481
MOBILE SUPPORT 484

CHAPTER 11: SANDBOXING 486

SANDBOXING 486

CHAPTER 12: MAINTAIN & SUPPORT 497

MANAGE PLAN TYPES 497
CHANGE HISTORY / AUDIT TRAIL 503
MAINTENANCE AND NOTIFICATIONS 505
DELETE APPLICATION 508
APPLICATION SETTINGS 509
ACADEMY & LEARNING MORE 510

EPILOGUE: THE EPM MARTIAN 511

APPENDIX: *LOOK SMARTER THAN YOU ARE WITH ESSBASE* HIGHLIGHTS 512

INTRO TO ESSBASE 512
BLOCK STORAGE DATABASE 520
AGGREGATE STORAGE DATABASE 527

HYBRID AGGREGATION 528
COMPARING ESSBASE DATABASE OPTIONS 528
DIMENSION ORDER FOR BSO PLAN TYPE 531

INDEX 533

Prologue:
The EPM Martian

LOG ENTRY: SOL 10, Entry 1

I'm pretty much screwed.

That's my considered opinion. Screwed, and not in a good way.

Nine sols into what should be the best EPM implementation of my life, and it's turned into a complete nightmare.

For the record... the EPM implementation didn't die on Sol 9. Certainly the rest of my team thought it did, and I can't blame them. And they'll be right eventually.

So, where do I begin?

Oracle EPM Cloud. Oracle reaching out to send customers to the Cloud and expand the horizons of companies beyond traditional servers...blah, blah, blah. First Hyperion introduced System 9 creating a common workspace for all of the EPM products. They got accolades, fame, and a lovely Solutions conference in their honor. Oracle then bought Hyperion and improved the EPM solution to its current "Business Analytics" state. They got a press release and a boxed lunch at OpenWorld.

Implementing a best practice EPM solution for the Vision Company, a subsidiary of the global-dominating Juggling Wolverines Enterprises. Well, that is my mission. Okay, not mine per se. Project Commander McMullen was in charge. I was just one of her crew along with Strategic Architect Joe Aultman, Consolidations Specialist Terrance Walker, Infrastructure Architect Jason Novikoff, and Reporting Analyst Sandy Nozaki-Gonzalez. Actually, I was the lowliest member of her crew, Edward Roske. I would only be "in command" of the mission if I were the only remaining person.

What do you know? I'm in command.

It was a ridiculous sequence of events that led to me and the project almost dying. My client, Vision, needed an EPM solution. They were on board and ready to move forward before the IT roadblocks started. The hardware was too expensive. It would be costly to upgrade in the future. IT resources at Vision were scarce. So the project was not approved and the Vision finance and ops team were left without an EPM solution.

On top of that, I was somehow catapulted into the vast expanse which is the Cloud. Now I'm stranded. Why couldn't I be stranded on Mars where they don't have any clouds? Hence, the "I'm screwed" complaint. Really it was Vision that was screwed.

So that's the situation. I have no way to communicate with i.n.t.e.r.R.e.l or Earth. Everyone thinks the project is dead.

But it isn't... Somehow I have to make this work in the Cloud for the Vision Company. If the budgeting and forecasting portion fails, they can't make decisions and the project will die. If the reporting portion fails, Vision won't be able to find the critical information to pinpoint the source of the problem and the project will die. If I can't consolidate and close the books, the company will die.

So yeah. I'm screwed. Oh well. Maybe someday a good-looking, A-list actor like Matt Damon will play me in the movie version of my story...

Chapter 1:
Intro to the EPM Cloud

THE DARK DAYS OF SERVERS

This is hard to believe, but in the not too distant past when companies wanted to implement enterprise software they had to call up a computer manufacturer, describe the exact specifications of the computer they wanted, and then wait a few weeks for the machine to be assembled and shipped to the company. Now manufacturers – in an attempt to make computers built from off-the-shelf commodity parts sound more impressive – call these computers "servers."

When I started doing Hyperion back in the '90s, all we had was Essbase and it really didn't require much of a server. The servers back then often had a single CPU and, frankly, were less powerful than the average modern-day smartphone. The good news about this is that a so-called server could be bought by a CFO and placed under her desk without IT ever realizing it. One of these under-the-desk servers was powerful enough to host an entire finance department's implementation of Essbase.

Essbase grew up really quickly and servers did too. By the turn of the century when Essbase 7 came out, most companies had data centers at their corporate headquarters. These "data centers" were basically a lot of raised, air conditioned floors housing all of the company's servers. Even though it was just a room of chilled computers off in the basement, IT realized that calling them data centers would make them sound more impressive. (Notice the tendency people have of "making things sound more impressive than they really are.")

Around 2004, Hyperion released System 9. It was an enterprise-class suite of EPM (Enterprise Performance Management) and BI (Business Intelligence) tools and it took a trained professional to install System 9 on one or more servers. By this time, most enterprise-class products couldn't be installed by mere mortals.

At about the same time, IT departments realized that having a data center in the company's headquarters wasn't the best use of corporate office space, so they started to move their data centers off-site. Users would still access the servers as before, but they were now only connected to the corporate servers by – for lack of a better way to put it – really long cables. This is also about the time users stopped knowing where the servers were actually physically located. IT wasn't pleased when they realized that no one actually cared where the servers were physically located.

In mid-2007, Oracle bought Hyperion (now rebranded to "Oracle EPM") and helped turn it into a truly enterprise-class product (Hyperion only thought they had one, but looking back, System 9 was really pitiful compared to what exists now).

With the onslaught of the Great Recession shortly after, IT departments were being forced to cut costs. One of the ways to lower spending was to move their data centers even farther away – preferably near a waterfall (hydroelectric power is cheap) and somewhere cold (to lower the air conditioning needs).

Since most companies couldn't afford to go buy their own building in Norway (in my mind all modern data centers are in Norway, surrounded by little villages straight out of *Frozen*), they started having other companies manage their data centers. So now we had data centers attached to our users by virtual cables and it turned out that no one really cared how their computers talked to the servers as long as it worked.

Now jump ahead several years. In the days after the Great Recession, smartphones became a standard extension of people's hands. The web became the default place to go for information. Applications installed on computers started to become a thing of the past. And flying cars finally became available.

(That last sentence actually isn't true. Despite being promised flying cars since I was a kid, there still aren't flying cars. To be honest, it really annoys me that we'll have self-driving cars before flying cars…but I digress.)

In other words, we became comfortable with storing our information remotely because we could then access it any time from any device. We no longer have any idea where our servers are, who owns them, or how the magic happens that lets us talk to the servers. For all we know, there aren't even physical servers out there and it turns out that no one really cares.

So to make it sound more impressive, we decided to call these far away servers owned by no one in particular that house data and run applications…

> ```
> LOG ENTRY: SOL 11, Entry 1
>
> Okay. I've had a good night's sleep and things
> don't seem as hopeless as they did yesterday. Thinking
> about this Cloud revolution helped me to feel a little
> hopeful about my situation. First, I guess I should
> explain how the Cloud works.
> ```

THE CLOUD

Yes, that's right. The "Cloud" is just a cool way of saying servers that are really far away that we don't own. Or to put it a different way, the Cloud is software and services that run on the internet.

Pause for a moment and look down at your smartphone. (It's probably in your hand, in your pocket, or at worst, within arm's reach.) Notice the applications you use most: email, messages, weather, browser, etc. Each one of these is a Cloud application. Your email isn't really stored on your phone: it's on a far flung server somewhere. Your messages are bouncing all around people's servers that you couldn't locate even if you wanted to. The weather app is accessing data stored someplace else. The browser is pulling up information stored around the world. And so on. *Your smartphone is a Cloud-access device.*

As consumers, we're completely comfortable with the Cloud. We don't think we understand the Cloud, but that's just because people have been trying to make us think the Cloud is some complicated thing that can only be understood by rocket surgeons. (I blame the movie *Sex Tape* for this, but I tend to blame that movie for a lot of what's wrong in the world.)

The Cloud has a lot of benefits. Companies no longer have to buy servers. No one has to install (and then patch forever) software on the servers. There's no need to manage the server because *it's now someone else's problem.*

At the time I'm writing this, some IT departments who should know better are afraid of the Cloud (which is weird because those same people in IT are comfortable with their whole personal life being on the

Cloud). Is our data secure in the Cloud? What if the Cloud crashes? Is the software in the Cloud any good? Will it slow things down to put them in the Cloud?

A lot of this is fear of the unknown, and, speaking from the standpoint of someone who may not make it through this alive, I have a lot of that fear myself. I know I shouldn't be scared: Cloud companies should be a whole lot better at security than I am. They are better at making sure things shouldn't crash than I am, and they are probably running their Cloud products on far faster servers than I could ever hope to buy... but nonetheless, I'm filled with uncertainty and doubt. Plus the idea that I'm no longer owning my software but rather renting it by the month is a little unnerving (though I do lease my car and rent my apartment).

Note!

Cloud Terminology:
- Cloud – software and services that run on the Internet; Physical infrastructure (servers) in massive data centers all over the world
- SaaS (Software as a Service) – software licensing and delivery model
  o Software is licensed on a subscription basis – "pay as you grow"
  o Centrally hosted, limiting additional hardware
  o Accessed via thin client or web browser

Cloud Benefits

The Cloud provides a number of benefits to companies including facilitating the expansion to new geographies, products, or departments. Lower software fees could be found with a SaaS model. IT costs are absolutely reduced with less personnel and equipment required. Related to EPM, the EPM Cloud can accelerate EPM adoption within your organization. An intuitive user interface means reduction in training costs. The Cloud allows companies to focus on analytics vs. software support. A final bonus is that upgrades and patches are automatically applied (no more waiting for the latest and greatest version).

Oracle Cloud offerings are available via a monthly subscription with self-service sign-up, instant provisioning, self-service management and self-service monitoring.

Cloud Challenges & Considerations

The Cloud is not without some challenges including security management, target and source integration, defining new strategies between IT and the business, what to do with existing software investments and compliance and reliability concerns.

```
LOG ENTRY: SOL 11, Entry 2

Is the Cloud "ready" for me? Is it ready for
i.n.t.e.r.R.e.l to implement or Vision Company to use?
I think that it's not a matter of if I'll be using the
Cloud, but rather when. It seems like it's coming faster
than anyone expected, so maybe it won't kill me after
all.
With that comforting knowledge, I took stock of
what's in the Cloud for Oracle EPM and BI and here's
my situation.
```

ORACLE ENTERPRISE PLANNING CLOUD

In 2014, Oracle rolled out its first EPM Cloud product and they called it Planning and Budgeting Cloud Service (PBCS). In the early days of the Cloud, companies took their on-premise (also known as "on-premises" by contrarian grammarians or "on-prem" by people in too much of a hurry to utter an extra syllable) products and released limited versions of those products on the Cloud. In Oracle's case, they took Hyperion Planning (which had been around since 2001 and had thousands of companies using it), installed it on some Oracle Exalytics servers, changed the front-end a little, and called it PBCS. Recently Oracle has slightly rebranded the solution as Oracle Enterprise Planning Cloud. They offer two pricing scenarios: Planning and Budgeting pricing option which is the original PBCS solution (with no prebuilt frameworks) and Enterprise Planning pricing option which contains prebuilt frameworks to support the entire enterprise wide planning function.

Oracle sells this product through the SaaS model: Software as a Service. As I mentioned earlier, you pay by the month to use the software instead of paying a huge amount up front to own the software (and then still having to pay a monthly amount to Oracle to support the software).

Enterprise Planning Cloud provides, as the name implies, planning and budgeting solutions over the web. You can still use Excel to access the information if you'd like (through a free Oracle tool called Smart View), but in general, you're probably using a web browser on a computer or tablet.

Oracle wasn't sure if companies were ready for a Cloud-based EPM solution, but in less than 2 years after the launch of PBCS, over 750 companies had bought it, making it the #1 Cloud-based budgeting product in the world.

Oracle does love a winner, so that product went from being a limited use version of Hyperion Planning to a product that surpassed its on-premise elder in functionality and usability in the summer of 2015.

The Enterprise Planning pricing option within Oracle Enterprise Planning Cloud is a world-class Cloud solution that balances built-in best practice, configurable frameworks with high flexibility. Pre-release, this solution was referred to as Enterprise Planning Budgeting Cloud Service (EPBCS) but the current naming convention is Enterprise Planning.

At its core, it leverages the robust Planning and Budgeting Cloud technology which provide familiar features for powerful analytics, dashboarding, reporting, predicting, and planning. A number of pre-configured, best-in-breed frameworks are delivered with the Enterprise Planning solution and can save customers time when implementing solutions for:

- Financials planning including income statement, balance sheet and cash flow (with driver based or direct input for revenue and expense planning)
- Workforce planning
- Capital assets planning
- Project financial planning

Customers can upgrade their planning framework to suit their needs as their business grows. It's easy to use and easy to maintain through its wizards and intuitive interfaces. It allows customers to spend more time running the business and less time maintaining planning processes. It fits both finance and operational needs by offering scalability to evolve with the business, in addition to transparency and control. The federated architecture allows for operational independence and an aligned planning solution.

In addition, it supports both Cloud and hybrid Cloud deployments by allowing for a number of data management options, single sign-on, and a robust API. Oracle Enterprise Planning Cloud follows the Software as a Service (SaaS) license model.

BUSINESS INTELLIGENCE CLOUD/DATA VISUALIZATION CLOUD

In September 2014, Oracle released the next Cloud product in the Oracle Business Analytics space: BICS (Business Intelligence Cloud Service). Technically, it's an Oracle BI product (not EPM) but it's in the same family at Oracle and delivers analytics and reporting over the web. It's similar to Enterprise Planning Cloud in that it took an existing on-premise product, OBIEE (Oracle Business Intelligence Enterprise Edition) and ported it to the Cloud.

It is a different animal than Enterprise Planning Cloud, though, because while Enterprise Planning Cloud delivers application ready functionality, BICS is more of a platform waiting for you to build your own solutions on top of it. As such, it is not considered to be a SaaS solution, but rather PaaS (Platform as a Service). PaaS is sometimes priced per user and for a set amount of storage. In the case of BICS, Oracle does both. They charge you a monthly fee per user and then they also charge you a flat monthly fee for the underlying Oracle Database Schema Service (sometimes called DBaaS or DataBase as a Schema).

Like PBCS before it, BICS quickly started adding functionality that its on-premise version (OBIEE) did not have. Later, one of these awesome features, Visual Analyzer, became available on its own outside of BICS. In November 2015, Oracle started selling DVCS (Data Visualization Cloud Service), which was cheaper than BICS (since it was a subset of BICS) and didn't require a separate fee for the underlying database. Data

Visualization Cloud Service focuses on the Visual Analyzer (VA) feature from BICS. DVCS allows users to upload and blend data files and then visualize the data in multitude of graphical presentations. Users can then share insights and "tell a story" using "story teller mode". Just think... No more death by PowerPoint! Keep discussions interactive and present! DVCS is fully mobile supported and requires 50% fewer clicks to create dashboards (when compared to competitor's tools and BICS Answers and Dashboards).

```
LOG ENTRY: SOL 11, Entry 3

   Some BI purists will wonder why we are talking
about "BI" in an "EPM" book. The divide of BI vs. EPM
has always irked Project Commander McMullen. Each
involves solutions to help users make better decisions
and they will always go hand in hand.
```

ENTERPRISE PERFORMANCE REPORTING CLOUD

Users have been asking to explain their numbers since, roughly, the beginning of time. When the first tax collector came to the first pharaoh to show him that the expected tax revenue fell short of projections, pharaoh had him beheaded before he could explain that tax revenue was down due to a series of plagues befalling the country. Sadly, the idea that narration should accompany the numbers died with him (and all subsequent tax collectors who simply showed pharaoh the numbers and never getting a chance to explain them).

Yes, my knowledge of ancient times apparently is limited to the existence of pharaohs, tax collectors, beheadings, and plagues... and I'm not totally sure there were beheadings. But my point is still valid: the world needs narration. Numbers alone don't tell the whole story and in July 2015, Oracle released Enterprise Performance Reporting Cloud (EPRCS) to solve that problem (and hopefully end future metaphorical corporate beheadings).

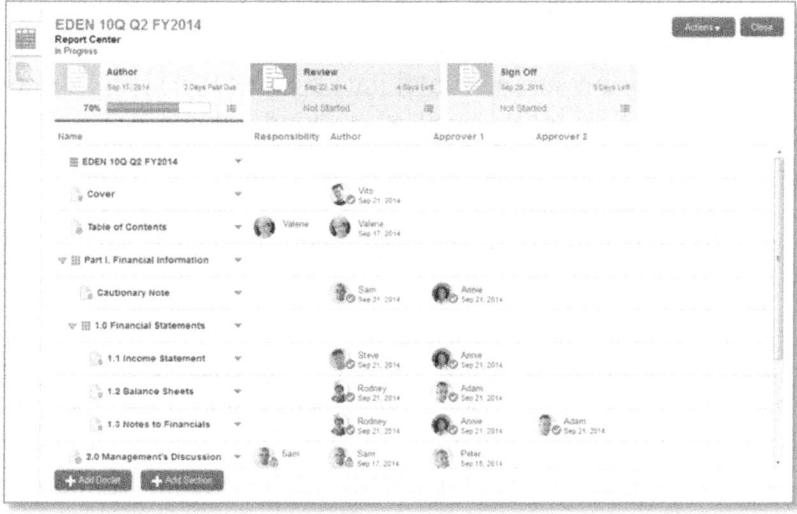

Enterprise Performance Reporting Cloud is not only Oracle's solution for narrative reporting, it's also their first Oracle EPM product to only exist in the Cloud. Created from day one to be a Cloud solution (and not a port of an on-premise product), EPRCS lets users author report packages, distribute them, and collect commentary on the packages no matter where the data (or the user, for that matter) resides. Like Enterprise Planning Cloud, EPRCS is sold using a SaaS model.

ACCOUNT RECONCILIATION CLOUD

Oracle Account Reconciliation Cloud is a purpose-built Cloud-based solution that manages, supports, and improves the global account reconciliation process. Leveraging the capabilities of the current release of on-premise Account Reconciliation Manager (ARM), it reduces risk and increases efficiency by leveraging prebuilt reconciliation formats and automating certain reconciliation tasks. Customers can also choose to create their own custom solutions. Built upon best practices for global reconciliation, this solution provides an intuitive interface, interactive and real-time dashboards, and instant visibility into the reconciliation process. Collaboration is driven by role-based tasks and work areas, signoffs, and approvals. Oracle Account Reconciliation Cloud provides flexible balance mapping rules, rule-based thresholds, workflow and audit capabilities, and reporting, monitoring, and analysis. It can integrate data from ERP and EPM systems and supplemental data sources like spreadsheets and databases. Oracle Account Reconciliation Cloud follows the Software as a Service (SaaS) license model.

FINANCIAL CONSOLIDATION & CLOSE CLOUD

Oracle Financial Consolidation and Close Cloud (FCCS) is a new, enterprise-wide Cloud solution that provides a best-practice consolidation solution to optimize the close cycle. This is NOT "HFM on the Cloud". FCCS is a newly architected alternative end-to-end consolidation solution delivered on the Cloud. It can be implemented quickly and with less stress and maintenance by providing out of the box functionality. It gives customers visibility into the entire close, consolidation, data collection and management, workflow, audit, monitoring, reporting, and lights-out processes. In addition, it can connect to core source systems and comes prebuilt with cash flow, balance sheet, and income statement reporting. It supports IFRS, GAAP, and Multi-GAAP so that customers can feel confident and secure with their regulatory compliant solution. Some of the common business processes included include full currency support, intercompany eliminations, equity eliminations, adjustments, and detailed data tracking. It can also integrate with Microsoft Office and Enterprise Performance Reporting

Cloud (EPRCS). Oracle Financial Consolidation and Close Cloud follows the Software as a Service (SaaS) license model.

CLOUD GONE WILD

And Oracle didn't stop there. At OpenWorld 2015, they announced that they would be the first company in the world to have a complete EPM suite in the Cloud. Starting early in 2016, they began to roll out Cloud products faster than any company before or since. Other products likely coming soon to the EPM Cloud include:

- **EssCS** (Essbase Cloud) – takes Essbase, the greatest BI cube technology ever, into the Cloud
- **PCMCS** (Profitability & Cost Management Cloud) – allocates and analyzes profitability & cost data by customer, location, product, and more
- **TPRCS** (Tax Provisioning & Reporting Cloud) – manages the collecting, calculating, and distributing of tax information
- **DMCS** (Dimension Management Cloud) – manages hierarchies and roll ups across the organization

Within three years of launching their first EPM Cloud product, Oracle will have a complete suite of Cloud solutions.

HYBRID IMPLEMENTATION APPROACH

I was skeptical. What if a company had an on-premise solution and wasn't ready to move their entire EPM suite? Would they be able to go entirely to the Cloud overnight? Luckily, Oracle EPM Cloud was designed to work with the Oracle on-premise solutions. So let's say a company wanted to put part of their EPM / BI strategy into the Cloud and leave part of it in their data center. This is called a "hybrid" solution and there are a number of ways it can play out:

- If your company has existing on-premise EPM tools, they can keep using those and deploy new products into the Cloud. For instance, maybe they've been using HFM for years for financial consolidation. They can still implement Enterprise Planning

Cloud for forecasting and share the data with HFM using tools like FDMEE (Financial Data Quality Management Enterprise Edition).
- If your company likes the Oracle EPM Cloud products, but is more comfortable with the on-premise products, they can pay for servers and software up-front for the on-premise solutions and pay-as-they-go for the Cloud products.
- If your company wants the production data to stay on-premise, they can still use the Cloud for developing applications. As long as you're on a fairly recent version of the equivalent on-premise product, the Cloud and on-premise applications can be migrated back and forth.
- If your corporation has divisions or departments around the world, you don't have to put all of them onto one platform. Your corporate headquarters might use on-premise Essbase while your remote offices use EssCS (Essbase on the Cloud).

The most likely scenario is that a company starts off with on-premise products and then migrates them over time to the Cloud. As IT departments get tired of being hacked, get annoyed at users begging for newer versions, and get pressured to stop spending so much money up-front, the Cloud adoption at your company will take off like a Martian rocket.

> **LOG ENTRY: SOL 11, Entry 4**
>
> **Knowing all of this about the Cloud... I think this could maybe work. My project and I just might make it through alive. I'll just have to EPM the bits out of this thing.**

Chapter 2:
Launch Into the Cloud

> LOG ENTRY: SOL 11, Entry 5
>
> A launch of the N.A.S.A. space shuttle is complicated, involving hundreds of people, rocket boosters, propulsion systems, abort systems and more.
>
> Would launching Vision's Cloud instance prove to be as involved? As intense? Could I fail before I even started?
>
> Thankfully I have my "Launching into the Cloud" Manual, created by i.n.t.e.r.R.e.1 Cloud Specialist Opal Alapat, which documents how to get started, roles and responsibilities, and more. With this resource and all of the documentation at https://cloud.oracle.com, what could go wrong?
>
> 10, 9, 8, 7, 6, 5, 4, 3, 2, 1...

CLOUD.ORACLE.COM

The main place that you need to go to first get started with the Cloud is https://cloud.oracle.com. This site is a one stop shop for all Oracle Cloud customer service subscription needs:

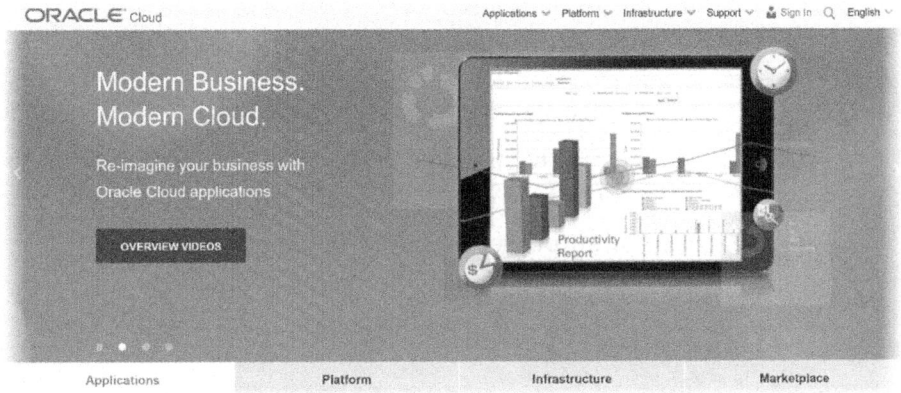

First I'll share some helpful terminology to understand how the Oracle Cloud environment is setup.

Term	What	Where To Manage
Account	Unique customer account May have a single identity domain with many Oracle Cloud services or many identity domains with many Oracle Cloud services May have many Oracle Cloud services Manage account in My Account where you create identity domains, monitor account status and designate other account administrators	Email to activate; My Account
Identity domain	Controls the authentication and authorization of the users who can sign into an Oracle Cloud service May have one or many Oracle Cloud Services Cannot be changed after activation	My Account
Service	Software offering in Oracle Cloud A service will belong to a single identity domain Multiple services may belong to the same identity domain (called a Service Association)	My Services

Look Smarter Than You Are with Enterprise Planning Cloud   17

Term	What	Where To Manage
Service Instance	An instance of a Cloud Service Account could have one or more service instance (for example, you may have 3 different service instances of Enterprise Planning Cloud for different lines of business in your organization)	My Services
Service Name	Service name is the name assigned to the Service that must be unique within the identity domain Cannot be changed after activation	My Services

Now I have understand some of the terminology, I'm ready to take a look at this bad boy.

To navigate to the Oracle Cloud,
1. Navigate to cloud.oracle.com.
2. Select *Applications >> Oracle Enterprise Planning Cloud*.
3. Click *Sign in*.

You will see a dashboard of options that is role-based. You will see options to manage *My Account, My Services, My Home and Identity Self Service*, and *Application Services Notifications*:

Chapter 2: Launch Into the Cloud

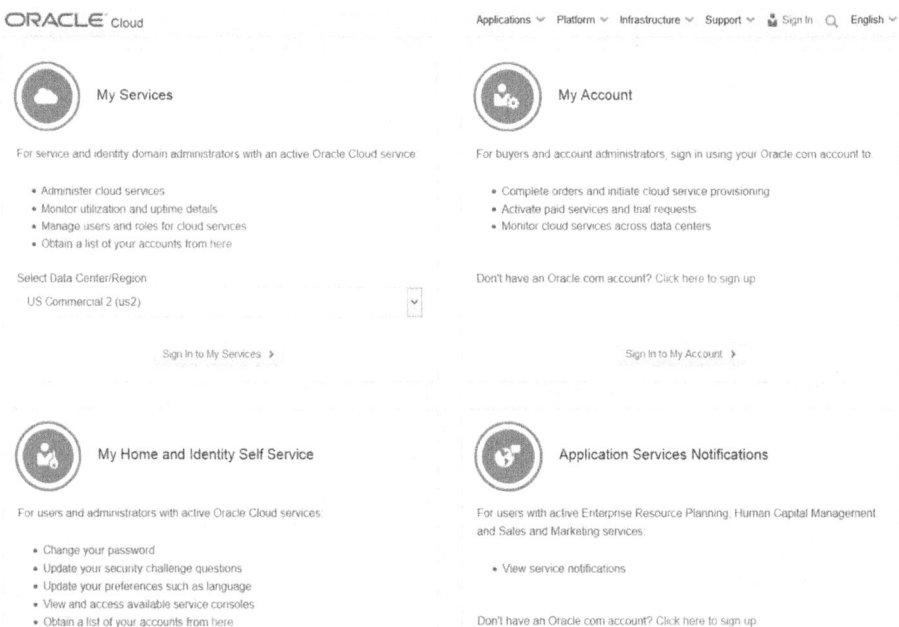

Before we jump into each of these options, let's define the Cloud user roles, privileges and responsibilities.

CLOUD ROLES, PRIVILEGES, & RESPONSIBILITIES

The Cloud supports the following user roles:

Role	Description
Buyer	Makes the initial purchase
Designates the account administrator
Upsizes, updates, and terminates the paid subscription
Note: If you are purchasing more than one Cloud subscription, you may want to consider having the same buyer for all subscriptions

Role	Description
Account Administrator	Uses the My Account section of cloud.oracle.com to activate the Oracle Cloud Services Monitors the status of services Reviews utilization
Identity Domain Administrator	Manages the administrative functions within an identity domain, just like a Service Administrator Uses the My Services section of cloud.oracle.com Adds, removes, and manages users who have access to the services (this is the main difference between this role and the Service Administrator)
Service Administrator	Manages the administrative functions within an identity domain Uses the My Services section of cloud.oracle.com
User	Works within one or more Cloud Services Their service and application role is assigned to them within an identity domain Uses the My Home and Identity Self Service link You can have different types of users: Application Administrators, power users, and end users

Depending on your organization, your Account Administrator, Service Administrator, and Identity Domain Administrator may be the same person. Think through these roles and assignments before activating and setting up your Cloud environment.

ORACLE CLOUD – MY ACCOUNT

The My Account section of cloud.oracle.com allows customers to monitor services for their entire account, across data centers and identity domains. Here, Account Administrators can view information about all of your active, expired, and pending services. This is where you also activate new services, view a dashboard with the status of each of the environments that you have access to, and manage certain administrator accounts.

My Account URL:

https://myaccount.cloud.oracle.com/mycloud/faces/dashboard.jspx

Username: Use your Oracle account user name
Password: Use your Oracle account password

Note! The My Account ID and password is tied to the Oracle.com ID and password. Your My Services ID and password is NOT tied to the Oracle.com ID and password. So your My Account password and My Services password *could be different*. Try to keep these in sync.

The Account Administrator will have access to the dashboard in My Account, which enables them to view metrics and uptime information of the Cloud services. Besides activating the service, the Account Administrator can add Identity Domain Administrators and additional Account Administrators after the service is provisioned.

ORACLE CLOUD – MY SERVICES

The My Services section of cloud.oracle.com allows Service Administrators and Identity Domain Administrators to manage and monitor all services within a single identity domain. This is where you will do the majority of Cloud management after the services have been activated.

Identity Domain & Identity Domain Administrator

The Cloud service must belong to an identity domain. Identity domains control authentication and authorization, i.e. who can log in and the services they can access once they log in. Identity Domain

Administrators can create new users and define which Cloud services they can access.

> If you have different domains for each Cloud instance, do not choose the option to "SAVE" the Cloud domain when prompted by your Internet browser. Otherwise, it will be challenging to change the saved cloud domain information when you want to switch. In recent Cloud versions, you will see an option to change the domain:

Note!

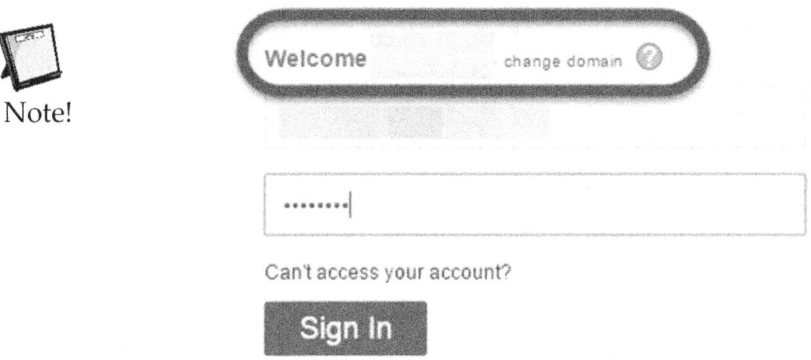

Once you define the Identity Domain Id, you cannot change it. You can change the *Identity Domain Name* under *My Account >> Identity Domain Administration*:

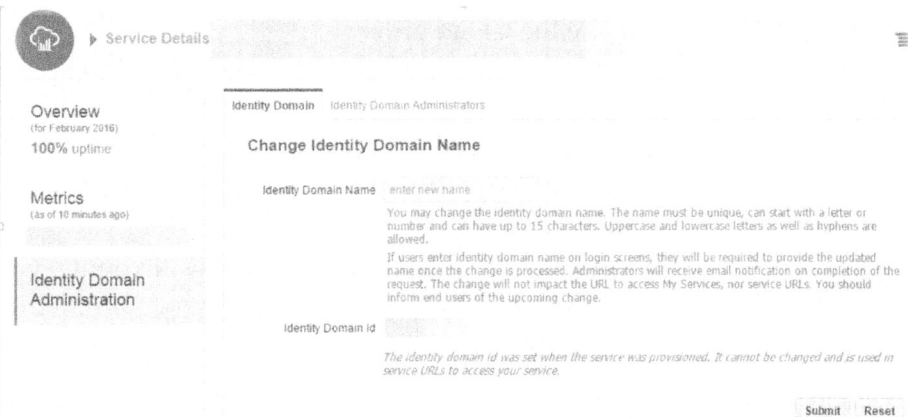

Service Administrator

The Service Administrator has the rights to monitor and manage the service. After activating the service, the Identity Domain Administrator can designate and assign other Service Administrators.

You will use My Services to add and manage user access to the service, monitor your service status, and view current and historical usage data.

My Services URL (available after the Cloud service is activated):

https://myservices.usx.oraclecloud.com/mycloud/yourdomain/faces/dashboard.jspx

Username: Use your My Services account username
Password: Use your My Services account password

CLOUD ACTIVATION PROCESS

The general process from initial order to being able to actively use the system is as follows:

Who	What	Where
Buyer	Place the Cloud order	Oracle Sales Team; Communicate to Oracle who the Account Admin should be
Account Administrator	Account activation, access and service details. Account Administrators do not have access to the specific Cloud services	My Account
Identity Domain Administrator	Create user accounts and roles	My Services

Look Smarter Than You Are with Enterprise Planning Cloud 23

Who	What	Where
Service Administrator	Create service instance Configure, manage and monitor services	My Services
User (with application admin assignment)	Build the application & load data	Enterprise Planning Cloud URL
User (power user)	For example, create reports and analyses	Enterprise Planning Cloud URL
User	Use the application	Enterprise Planning Cloud URL

After the order is received by Oracle, Oracle will send an email to log into cloud.oracle.com as the Account Administrator and complete the order (note, your emails may look slightly different as Oracle is continually evolving this process):

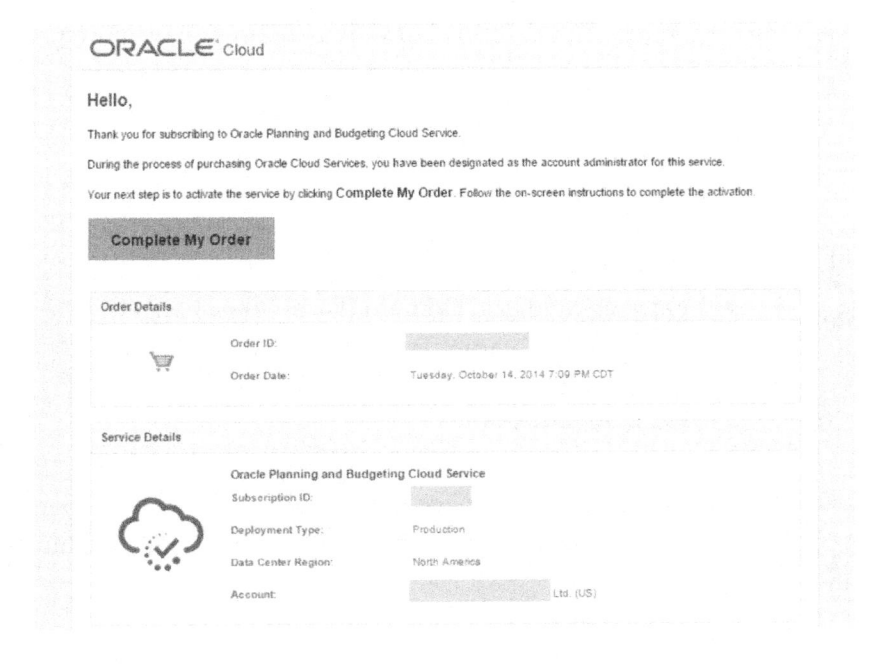

ORACLE Cloud

Hello,

Thank you for subscribing to Oracle Planning and Budgeting Cloud Service.

During the process of purchasing Oracle Cloud Services, you have been designated as the account administrator for this service.

Your next step is to activate the service by clicking Complete My Order. Follow the on-screen instructions to complete the activation.

[Complete My Order]

Order Details

Order ID:
Order Date: Tuesday, October 14, 2014 7:09 PM CDT

Service Details

Oracle Planning and Budgeting Cloud Service
Subscription ID:
Deployment Type: Production
Data Center Region: North America
Account: Ltd. (US)

Log in with your Oracle.com account or create one if you don't have one yet:

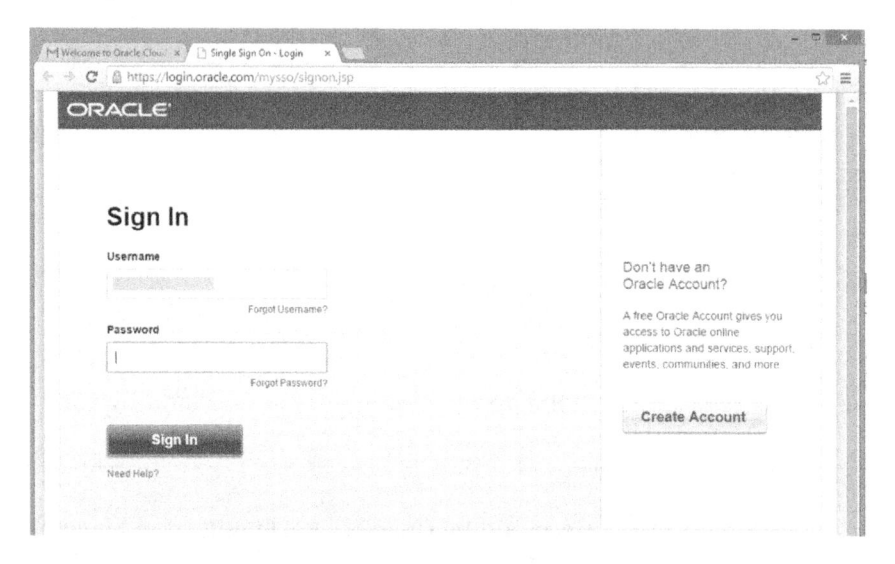

You will then complete the *Assign Service Details* form. You'll create the Identity Domain name and administrator. Again, the Identity Domain controls the authentication and authorization of the users who can sign into an Oracle Cloud service. It may contain one or more Cloud services.

Note!

Recommendations on Identity Domain naming conventions:
- The Identity Domain ID and Name should be something easy to remember
- Once created, the Domain ID can't be changed
- The Domain Name can be changed
- Users will need to enter it when signing onto the service

Next you will create the service name. The service name is Service name is the name assigned to the service that must be unique within the identity domain.

Look Smarter Than You Are with Enterprise Planning Cloud   25

Recommendations on Service Name naming conventions:

- Service Name should be something product or project related such as a project acronym
- Once created, it can't be changed
- The service name will display in the service dashboard and is used as part of the URL to access the service
- The suffix "-test" will be automatically included in the pre-production instance name and URL:

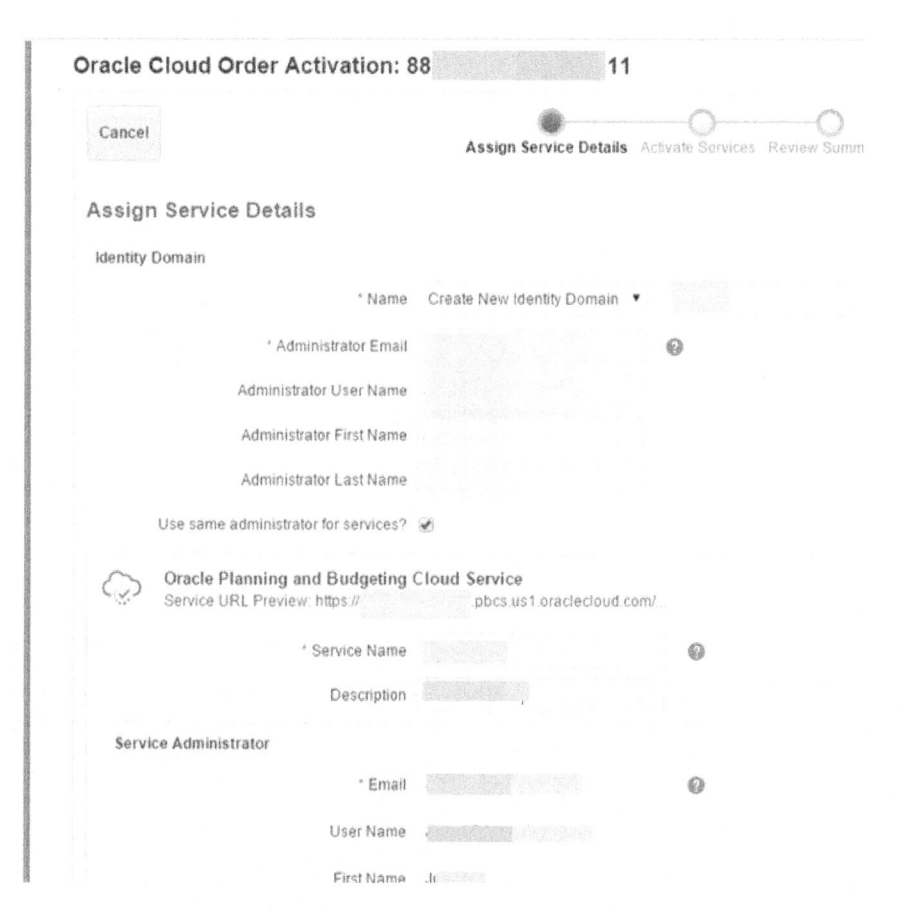

Note!

```
Oracle Cloud Order Activation: 88            11

Cancel                          Assign Service Details  Activate Services  Review Summ

Assign Service Details

Identity Domain

                    * Name    Create New Identity Domain ▼

        * Administrator Email

        Administrator User Name

        Administrator First Name

        Administrator Last Name

Use same administrator for services? ✓

    Oracle Planning and Budgeting Cloud Service
    Service URL Preview: https://         .pbcs.us1.oraclecloud.com/

                * Service Name

                   Description

Service Administrator

                      * Email

                   User Name

                   First Name
```

Both the domain and the service name will become part of the URL:

https://domainname-servicename.pbcs.xx.oraclecloud.com

Review the service details and click *Activate* when ready:

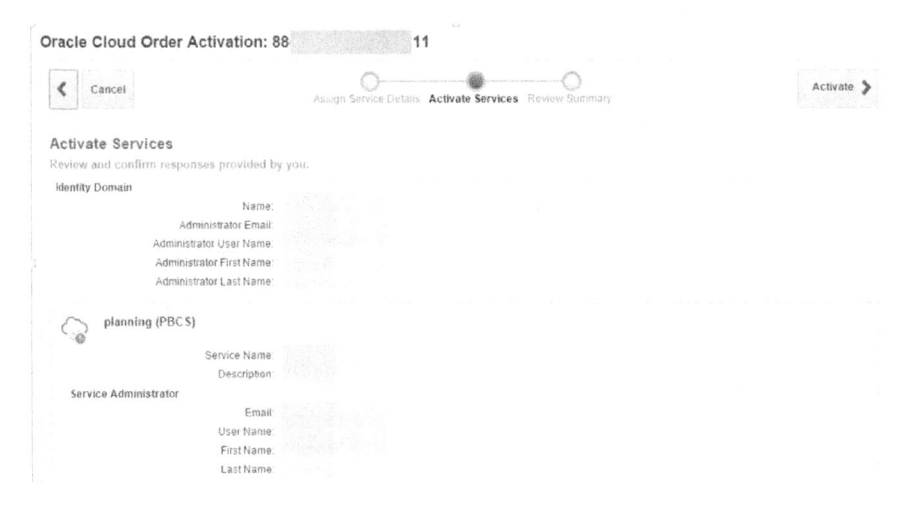

The final step is to review the summary of the Activation process:

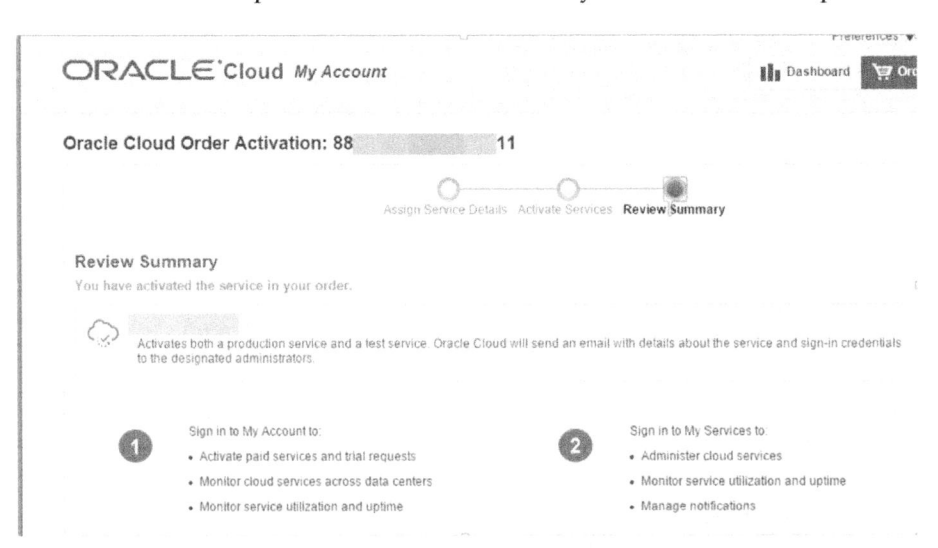

From the *Orders* tab you can monitor the status of the order. For example, below, I see *Show: Activation in Progress*:

As the activation process continues, you can see the status of each instance on the Dashboard:

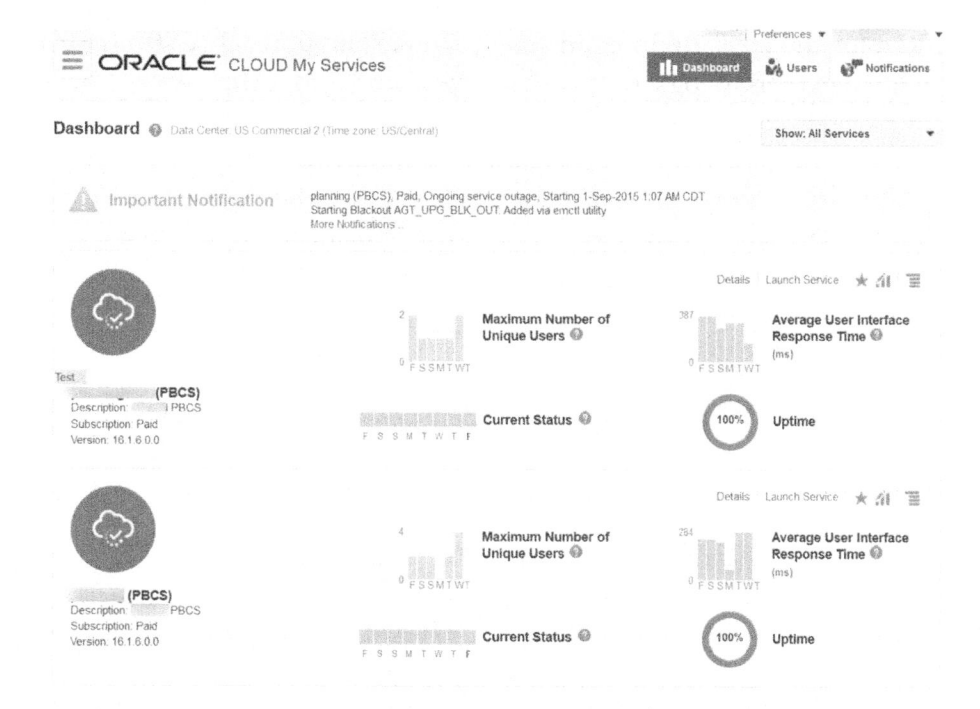

Once the service is activated, the Dashboard displays the uptime and status of each instance (Pre-Production and Production). This dashboard is accessible at https://myaccount.cloud.oracle.com.

Once the service is activated, Oracle will send two emails to the Account Administrator. One email will contain connection details for the

Production instance and a temporary password for the identity domain. The second email will contain the same information for the Pre-Production instance.

Note! With your Cloud subscription, you get two environments: a Pre-Production and Production instance. In Enterprise Planning Cloud, each instance may have a single application.

Both the Account Administrator and Identity Domain Administrator (if different people) receive a "Welcome to Oracle Cloud" email. Additional details are included within this email including the URLs for the subscription and the Customer Support ID (CSI) number (you'll need this to log a case with Oracle Cloud Support).

Subscription ID vs. Customer Support ID

Note! The Subscription ID is necessary if you need to make changes to your subscription. Your Customer Support ID is necessary if you need to log a support case for the Cloud.

My Services Administration Details

Use **My Services** to monitor your service status, view current and historical usage data, manage user access to My Services, and manage the services assigned to you.

If you will not be performing these duties, add the appropriate person.

My Services URL: https://myservices.us2.oraclecloud.com/mycloud/faces/dashboard.jspx

Identity Domain:

Service Details

planning (Oracle Planning and Budgeting Cloud Service)

Click the **Service URL** to sign in to this Oracle Planning and Budgeting Cloud Service.

Deployment Type: Production

Service URL: https://   pbcs.us2.oraclecloud.com/workspace

Identity Domain:

Data Center: US Commercial

Subscription ID:

Look Smarter Than You Are with Enterprise Planning Cloud

Next, you will log into the My Services URL provided by Oracle via email or the link from the Oracle Cloud dashboard using the temporary password in the email. You'll change your password and enter the security question responses when prompted.

A sample My Services URL is as follows:

https://myservices.usx.oraclecloud.com/mycloud/faces/dashboard.jspx

From the Dashboard get the URL of the Enterprise Planning Cloud service. A sample URL is below:

https://servicename-domainname.pbcs.usx.oraclecloud.com/HyperionPlanning

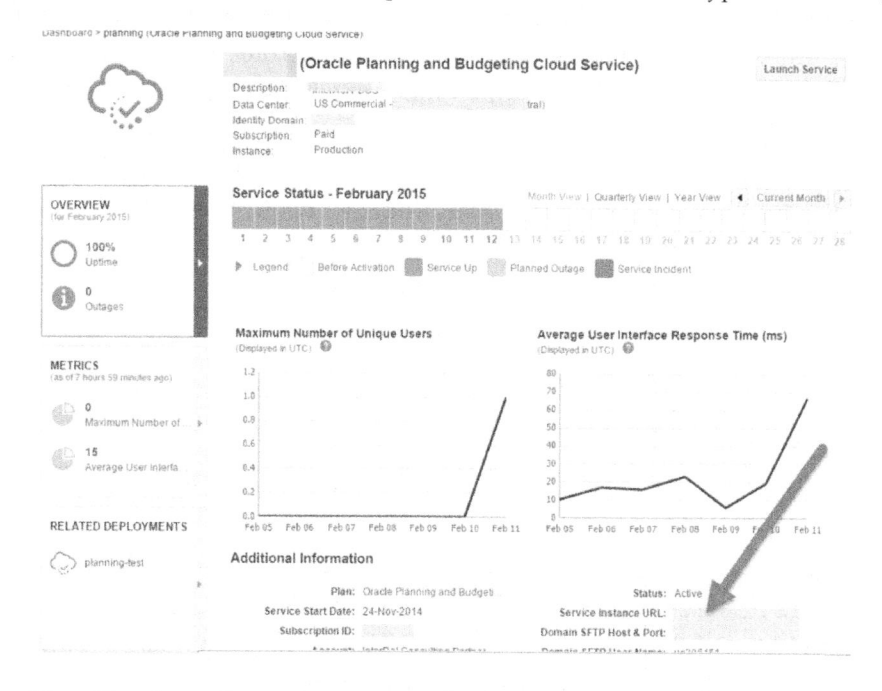

The Cloud configuration is complete, but now I need to add users!

USERS IN THE CLOUD

Create Users in the Cloud

Users can only be created and provisioned by the Identity Domain Administrator through Oracle Cloud My Services. Each Cloud service will have its own set of roles in addition to Identity Domain Administrator and Service Administrator.

Note! The processes below are described for Enterprise Planning Cloud, but they are similar across all Oracle EPM Cloud tools. One obvious difference is that the pre-defined roles will differ between technologies.

Before I do anything in the Cloud, I need to set up the users in the Cloud who will be creating and testing the application. I can come back later and add end users at any point. I will set up the users in My Services. Note, other Cloud services will have different roles but the basic role assignment process for users will be the same steps taken here.

Note! For Enterprise Planning Cloud, users cannot be created within the Enterprise Planning Cloud Workspace or within the Simplified Interface. For those familiar with Shared Services and on-premise Hyperion Planning, creating users is different in the Cloud.

Enterprise Planning Cloud Specific Roles

Within Enterprise Planning Cloud there are only five different roles. The table below briefly describes the roles available.

Role	Description
Identity Domain Administrator	Creates users and assigns roles in Oracle Cloud My Services (as mentioned before)
Service Administrator	Functional administrator for an application

Role	Description
Power User	Grants some functional administrator rights such as creating and maintaining forms, Smart View worksheets, business rules, task lists and FRS reports; control approvals process; this is like the Interactive User role in on-premise Hyperion Planning
Planner	Enters data through forms and Smart View, performs ad hoc analysis and drills through to source system
Viewer	Grants view-only access through forms and Smart View

To create users in My Services,

1. If you aren't already there, go to *https://cloud.oracle.com/sign-in*.
2. In the My Services section, select the appropriate Data Center / Region:

My Services

For service and identity domain administrators with an active Oracle Cloud service:

- Administer cloud services
- Monitor utilization and uptime details
- Manage users and roles for cloud services
- Obtain a list of your accounts from here

Select Data Center/Region

US Commercial 2 (us2)

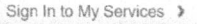

Sign In to My Services ›

3. Click *Sign in to My Services*.
4. Click on *Users*:

5. Click *Add* to create new users.

Note! If the Add, Import, and Export buttons are not available, the user who is logged in has not been granted access to perform those actions.

6. Complete the necessary fields:

```
        * First Name  Jerry
         * Last Name  Seinfield
             * Email  [      ]interrel.com
Use email as user name  ☑
      Manager Email  [      ]interrel.com
```

7. In the Simple Role Selection section, select the appropriate service and check *Service Administrator* or *Other Roles*:

```
▲ Simple Role Selection

Identity Domain Administrator  ☐
                      Service  planning(PBCS)  ⌄   »
                               ☐ Service Administrator
                               ☑ Other Roles
```

Choose options if required to define the user as another Identity Domain Administrator or Service Administrator.

Look Smarter Than You Are with Enterprise Planning Cloud 33

8. After checking the *Other Roles* option, click the arrow to move the selection to the right. Deselect the roles that will not be assigned to the user:

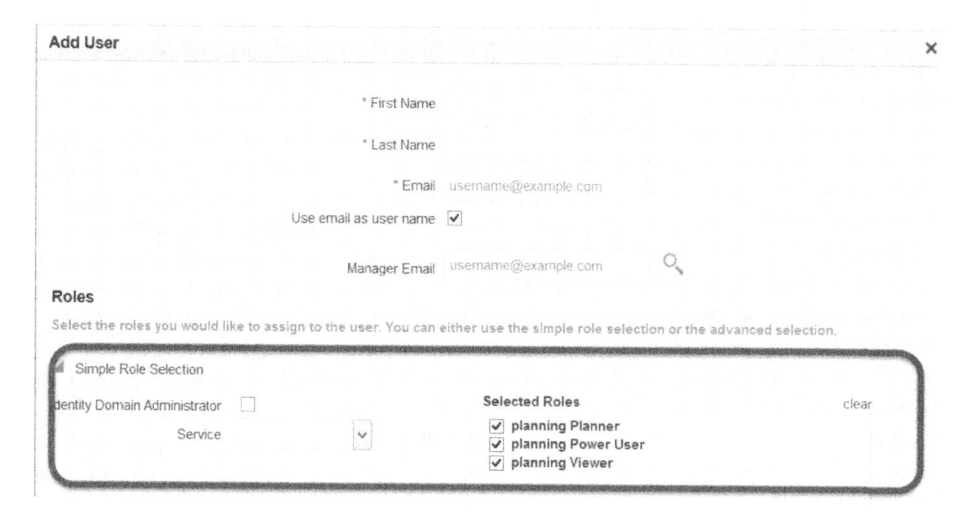

Add User

* First Name
* Last Name
* Email username@example.com
Use email as user name ✓
Manager Email username@example.com

Roles

Select the roles you would like to assign to the user. You can either use the simple role selection or the advanced selection.

Simple Role Selection

Identity Domain Administrator ☐
Service

Selected Roles   clear
✓ planning Planner
✓ planning Power User
✓ planning Viewer

Alternatively, the Identity Domain Administrator can go to *Advanced Role Selection* and select users that way.

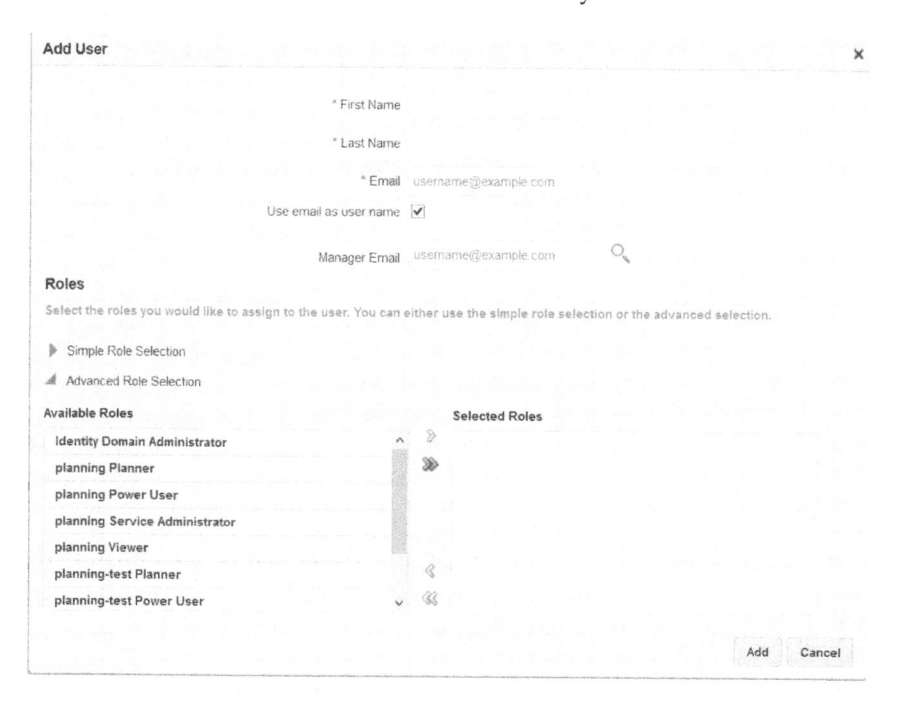

Add User

* First Name
* Last Name
* Email username@example.com
Use email as user name ✓
Manager Email username@example.com

Roles

Select the roles you would like to assign to the user. You can either use the simple role selection or the advanced selection.

▷ Simple Role Selection
◢ Advanced Role Selection

Available Roles

Identity Domain Administrator
planning Planner
planning Power User
planning Service Administrator
planning Viewer
planning-test Planner
planning-test Power User

Selected Roles

Add   Cancel

9. Click *Add*.

After the user has been created, a confirmation email will be sent to the user's email address.

The Identity Domain Administrator can sort users by roles or by name:

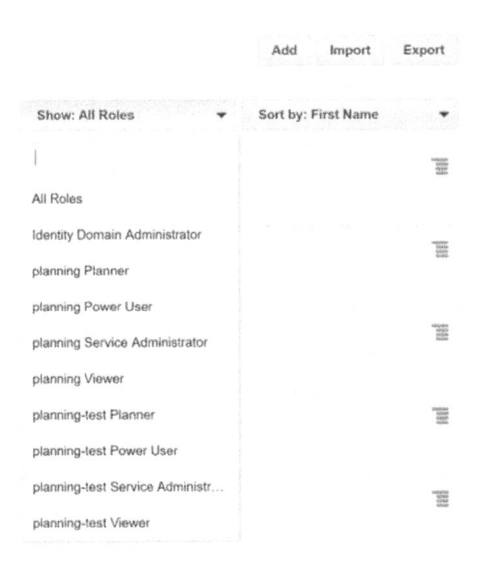

```
                    Add      Import    Export

Show: All Roles  ▼       Sort by: First Name  ▼

|                                           ☰
All Roles
Identity Domain Administrator
                                            ☰
planning Planner
planning Power User
planning Service Administrator              ☰
planning Viewer
planning-test Planner                       ☰
planning-test Power User
planning-test Service Administr...
                                            ☰
planning-test Viewer
```

Identity Domain Administrators can also modify users, reset passwords, manage roles and remove users in My Services:

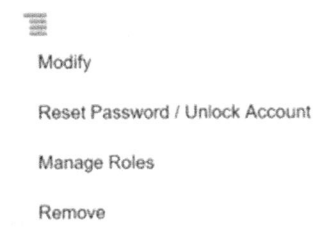

☰
Modify

Reset Password / Unlock Account

Manage Roles

Remove

Import Users

Oracle Enterprise Planning Cloud provides a way to import users using a flat file in My Services. In my example below, I'm going to import users into Enterprise Planning Cloud.

Look Smarter Than You Are with Enterprise Planning Cloud 35

First, I'm going to export the users to get the format of the file.
1. In My Services, click *Users* then *Export*.
2. Save the file and click *OK*.

I now have the template for creating an import file for users. I can use the exported file template and insert in my new users for import. You will define the user name, title and role.

3. Add the following users to the file (Jerry has already been added and the title is irrelevant at this point):

First Name	Last Name	Title	Role
Jerry	Seinfield	VP of Sales	Viewer
Cosmo	Kramer	International Sales Manager – Hardware	Planner
Elaine	Benes	Domestic Sales Manager – Hardware	Planner
George	Costanza	International Sales Manager – Services & Other	Planner
Larry	David	Domestic Sales Manager – Services & Other	Planner
Susan	Ross	Director of Sales – Hardware	Viewer
Frank	Costanza	Director of Sales – Services & Other	Viewer

4. Save as a CSV file.
5. Under Users in My Services, click *Import* then *Browse* to select the file.
6. Click *Import*. A notification will appear at the top of the page:

ORACLE CLOUD My Services   Dashboard Users Notifications

Import request PBCS_VISION_Security.csv has been submitted for processing. Oracle Cloud will send you an email with results of your import.

7. Check the email for results.
8. Once the users have been imported, assign roles by clicking the *Action* icon next to the user, then click *Manage Roles*:

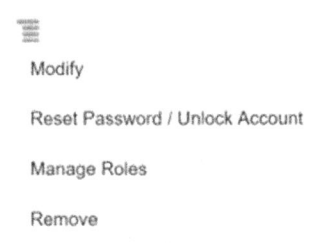

   Modify

   Reset Password / Unlock Account

   Manage Roles

   Remove

9. Refer to the table above for roles. Move the desired roles to the right panel.
10. Click *Save*.

MANAGE & MONITOR YOUR CLOUD INSTANCE

Monitor Service Status

To monitor the status of your Cloud Service,
1. Sign in to My Services and the dashboard will display:

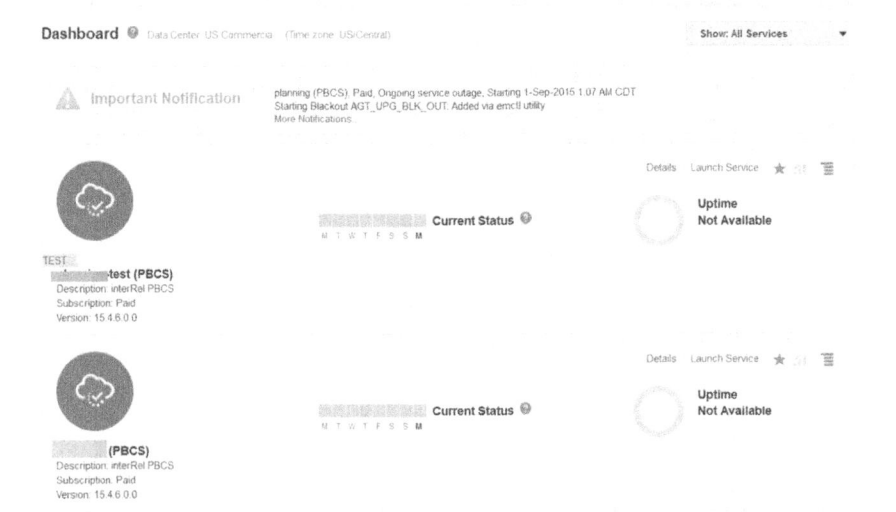

2. Click the service name to open the details page for the service.

The Overview page contains the Overview tile displaying the current month and year, the percentage of time the service was up during the month, and the number of service outages that occurred:

Monitor Usage Metrics

To monitor the usage metrics and see who has logged into the Cloud, click on the *Metrics* tile.

The Metrics page contains *Historical Usage* metrics which display the usage data in the form of a graph that is collected per day for the current service for the past seven days (by default). The *Latest Usage* metric (at the bottom) shows a snapshot of the last set of metrics collected and when those metrics were collected:

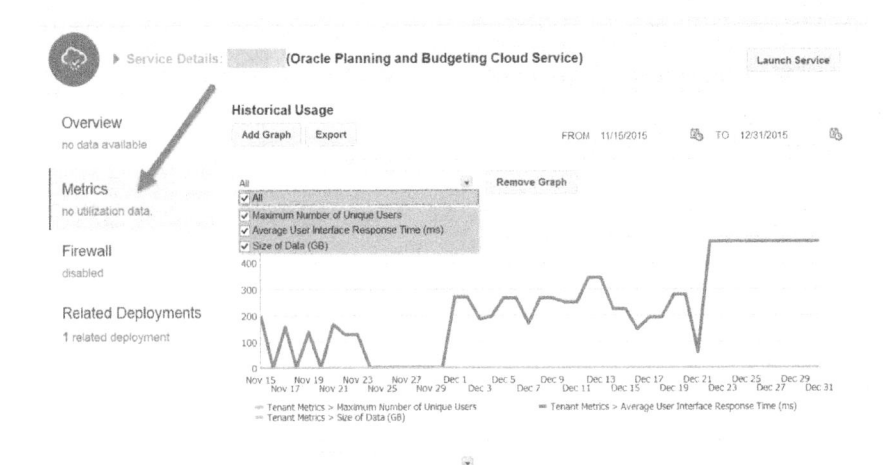

Monitor Notifications

To monitor the notifications from Oracle about your cloud services,

1. Sign into My Services. You will be logging directly into your specific cloud tool.
2. Click *Notifications*:

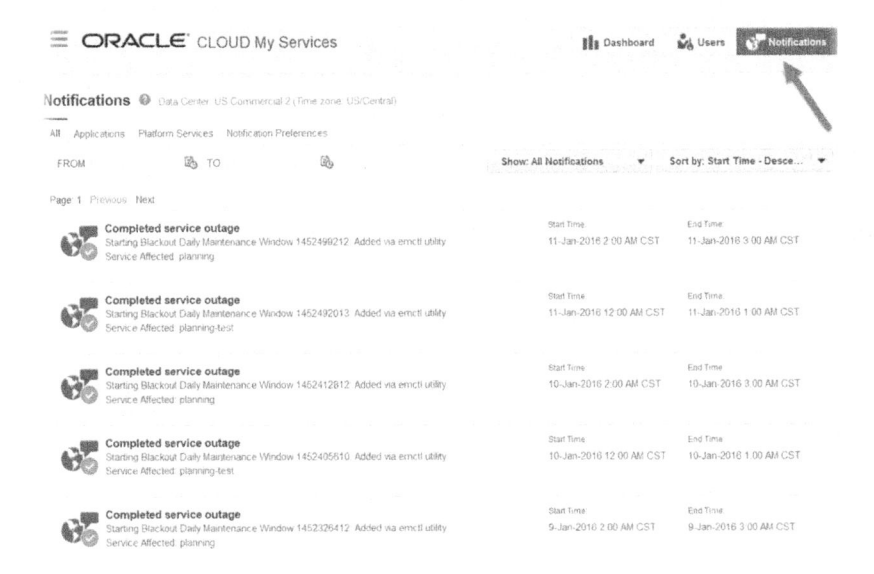

The My Services Notifications page lists all of the notifications related to the services and displays the following information:

- Name of the Oracle data center where the services are located
- Name of the identity domain to which the services belong
- Three page tabs:
    - **All** – displays all notifications for the services
    - **Applications** – displays only the notifications for the Oracle Software as a Service (SaaS) applications
    - **Platform Services** – displays only the notifications for the Oracle Platform as a Service (PaaS) services
    - **Notification Preferences** – displays the notification preferences (you can receive notifications via email or SMS)

Perform Operations on Services

You can access the My Services application and then drill down to the service details page to perform the following operations:

- Launch service
- Create firewall rules
- View and access related deployments

The *Manage Associations* option in the service details page allows administrators to manage associations between certain types of services. *Service Association* allows different Cloud services to communicate with each other (e.g., Business Intelligence Cloud Service also comes with Oracle Database Cloud Service; these two services are associated together and can share information across services).

LOGGING A CLOUD SUPPORT CASE

To log a case for your Cloud instance, go to http://support.oracle.com/. Choose the *Cloud Support* portal. You can also log a case from My Services.

To use My Oracle Support (MOS),
1. Register your Company with your Customer Service ID (CSI). This was provided in the "Welcome to Oracle Cloud" email that your Account Administrator received after you activated the order.
2. Enter names and emails of all people who need access to MOS, including partners and consultants who may log cases on your behalf.

You should be ready to log a Cloud support case. For more information, you can watch this Cloud Support Webcast: *Essentials Webcast: Oracle Cloud Support (Doc ID 1555872.1)*, which can be found at the following URL:

https://support.oracle.com/epmos/faces/DocumentDisplay?id=1555872.1&displayIndex=1

```
LOG ENTRY: SOL 11, Entry 6

    Success! Launching into Oracle Cloud was WAY
easier than launching a space shuttle. The Vision
Oracle Enterprise Planning Cloud instance is now in the
Cloud and ready for development!
    ...
    Now what?
```

Chapter 3: Intro to Oracle Enterprise Planning Cloud

> LOG ENTRY: SOL 11, Entry 7
>
> My first mission in the Cloud is to implement Oracle Enterprise Planning Cloud. I'll worry later about the reporting, dashboarding, and consolidating. That will be whole different set of log entries.
> For now I have a purpose: Vision needs to implement a sales forecasting solution in just sols. So that is what I'm going to do.

INTRO TO ORACLE ENTERPRISE PLANNING CLOUD

Oracle Enterprise Planning Cloud (the product formerly known as Planning and Budgeting Cloud Service or PBCS) is a centralized, Cloud-based planning, budgeting, and forecasting solution. Never fear Excel gurus, Microsoft Office integration is also possible with Enterprise Planning Cloud. Features include: easy to use user interface, powerful calculation capabilities, central, secured repository, approvals and process management, flexible modeling, Predictive Analytics, powerful reporting and analysis, task lists, and more. You can do both Top-down (Target) and Bottom-up planning, as well as have multiple versions for iterative planning cycles.

USER INTERFACES

Enterprise Planning Cloud utilizes two user interfaces, the Workspace UI which is similar to the on-premise Hyperion Planning user interface and the Simplified UI (new with the first release of Enterprise Planning Cloud).

The same tasks can be achieved in the Simplified UI and standard Workspace, with few exceptions. The Simplified UI was first developed for tablets, and therefore, has a minimalist look-and-feel and intuitive navigation:

To access the Simplified UI, enter the Enterprise Planning Cloud URL ending in *oraclecloud.com/HyperionPlanning* into your web browser. To access the standard Workspace interface, enter the Enterprise Planning Cloud URL ending in *oraclecloud.com/workspace*.

Note! Check out the latest documentation for supported browsers. We have found FireFox to be the most stable browser for Enterprise Planning Cloud. In this book, we are using the latest version of FireFox (v45.x) for all functionality tests and screen shots.

NAVIGATE THE SIMPLIFIED UI

The Home screen of the Simplified UI for Enterprise Planning Cloud will display upon login:

Look Smarter Than You Are with Enterprise Planning Cloud   43

[Oracle Vision home screen showing icons: Dashboards, Tasks, Plans, Rules, Approvals, Reports, Console, Settings, Academy, Navigator]

> **Note!** If you are logging in for the very first time, no applications have been created yet. You will see an initial screen prompting you to create an application.

From here you can access:

- **Dashboards** – a listing of dashboards created for users and, if provisioned, the ability to create new dashboards:

[Dashboards screen showing navigation bar and a list with one entry: FY14 Actual Sales, Modified 12/30/15 admin]

- **Tasks** – task lists created to guide users through a process; will include dashboards and plans (or data forms):

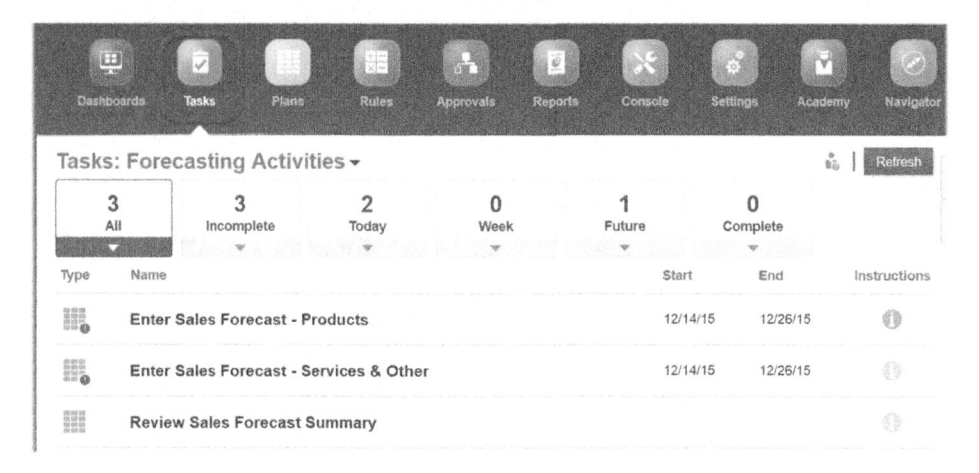

[screenshot: Tasks: Forecasting Activities toolbar showing Dashboards, Tasks, Plans, Rules, Approvals, Reports, Console, Settings, Academy, Navigator icons]

Tasks: Forecasting Activities ▼						Refresh
3 All	3 Incomplete	2 Today	0 Week	1 Future	0 Complete	
Type	Name			Start	End	Instructions
	Enter Sales Forecast - Products			12/14/15	12/26/15	
	Enter Sales Forecast - Services & Other			12/14/15	12/26/15	
	Review Sales Forecast Summary					

- **Plans** – a listing of simple data forms, composite forms, ad hoc grids, and Smart Forms:

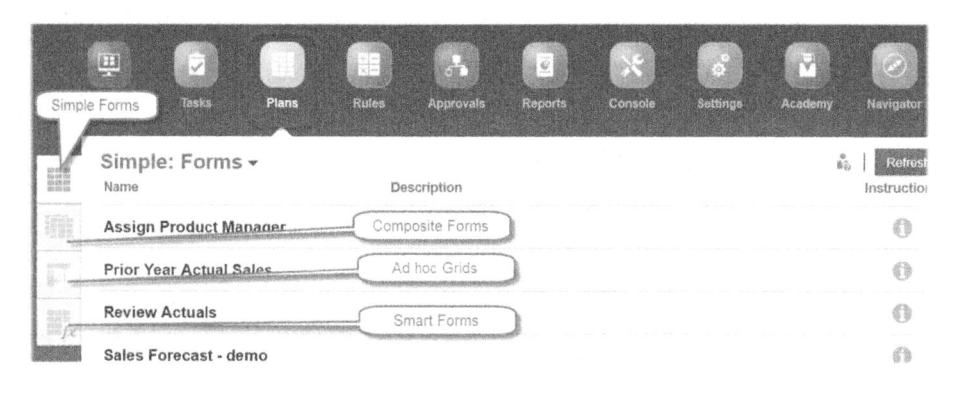

[screenshot: Simple Forms panel with toolbar]

Simple: Forms ▼		Refresh
Name	Description	Instructio
Assign Product Manager	Composite Forms	
Prior Year Actual Sales	Ad hoc Grids	
Review Actuals	Smart Forms	
Sales Forecast - demo		

Look Smarter Than You Are with Enterprise Planning Cloud   45

- **Rules** – rules to launch (to create business rules, you will go to Calculation Manager via *Navigator >> Administer >> Rules* in the Simplified UI):

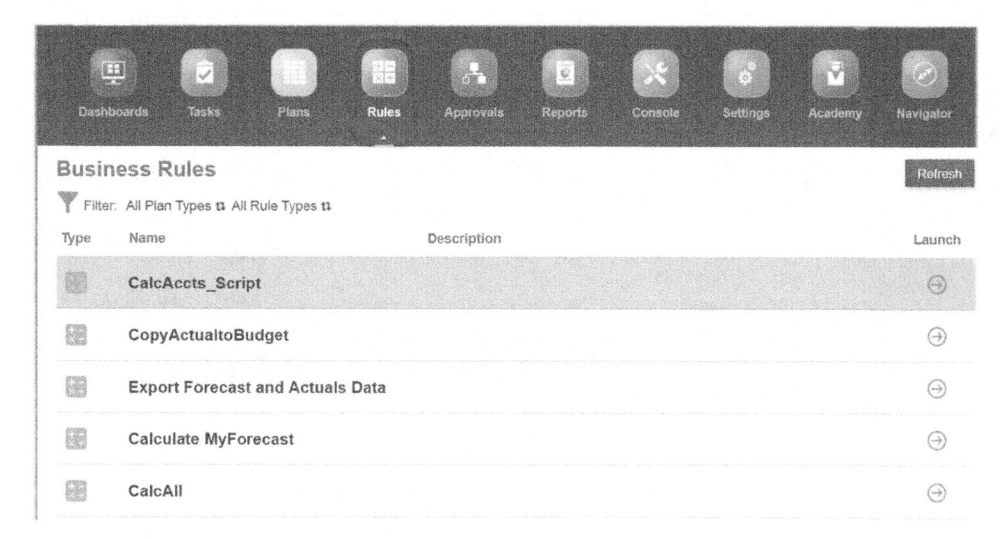

Business Rules

Type	Name	Description	Launch
	CalcAccts_Script		→
	CopyActualtoBudget		→
	Export Forecast and Actuals Data		→
	Calculate MyForecast		→
	CalcAll		→

Filter: All Plan Types ⁞ All Rule Types ⁞

- **Approvals** – review and approve plans:

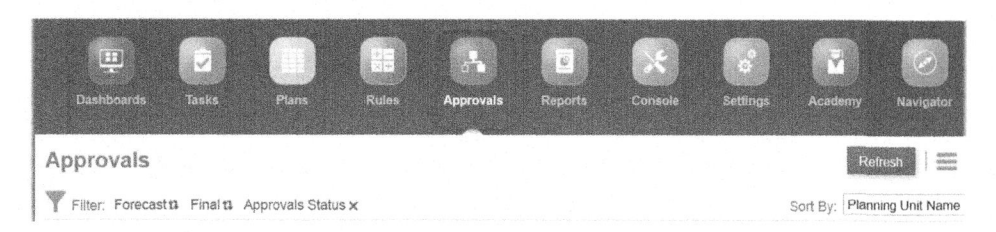

Approvals

Filter: Forecast ⁞ Final ⁞ Approvals Status ✗   Sort By: Planning Unit Name

- **Reports** – run reports in either HTML or PDF format:

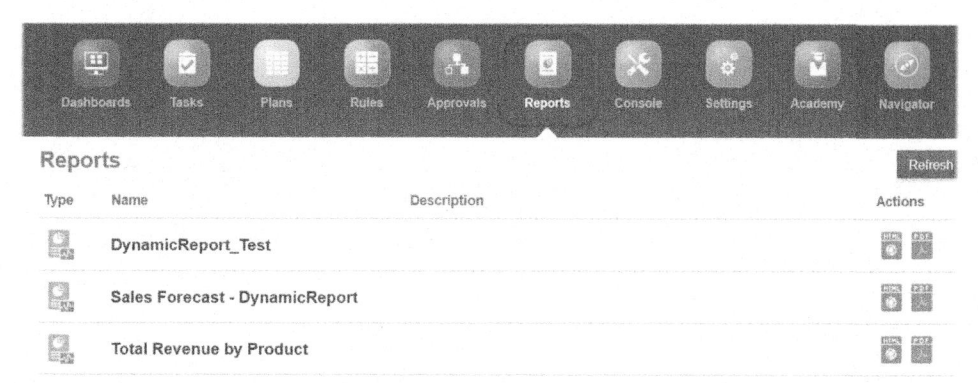

Reports

Type	Name	Description	Actions
	DynamicReport_Test		HTML PDF
	Sales Forecast - DynamicReport		HTML PDF
	Total Revenue by Product		HTML PDF

- **Console** (for administrators) – the central hub of creating and managing the Enterprise Planning Cloud application

In the *Console >> Application* section, administrators can view quick metrics on the overall application.

In the *Actions* menu for the Application, administrators can *Import Data* and *Export Data* (this is data, not dimensions), *Refresh Database* for any changes, *Remove Application* (delete the application), define *Maintenance Times*, access the *Inbox / Outbox Explorer* (a handy place for getting files to and from the Cloud), and *Manage Sandboxes*:

The *Plan Types* tab under Application allows administrators to view and create Plan Types. The *Dimensions* tab allows administrators to view dimensions, set the dimension order and dense / sparse settings, and import / export dimensions:

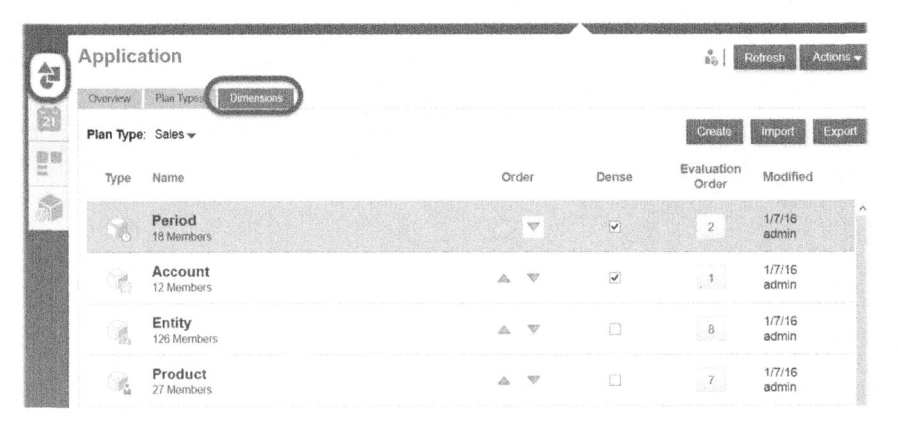

To view dimension properties, click on the dimension (although this will only show you the top level dimension member). To access and view all of the members in the Dimension Editor, you will go to *Navigator >> Dimensions* to jump to the dimension editor.

To access Jobs, choose the *Calendar* icon and you can view recently run jobs, upcoming jobs, and schedule new jobs (to run rules, import data and metadata, export data and metadata, refresh the database, and push data from one plan type to another):

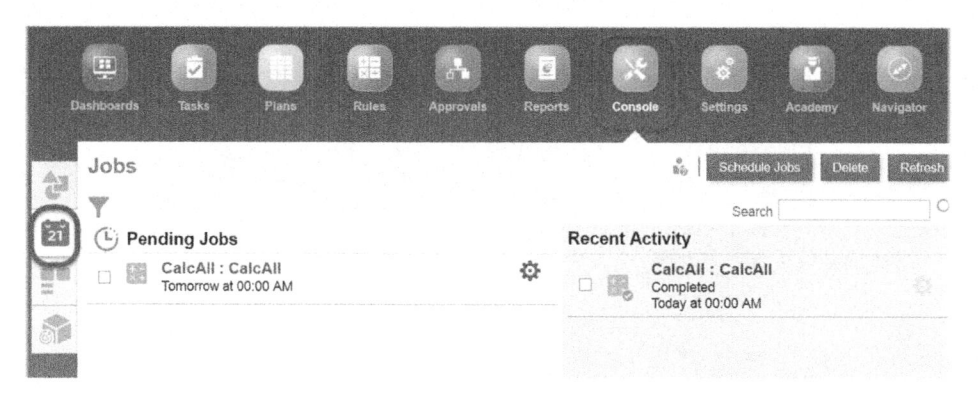

Click the *Valid Intersections* icon to view, create, and maintain valid intersections for the application (more on this later):

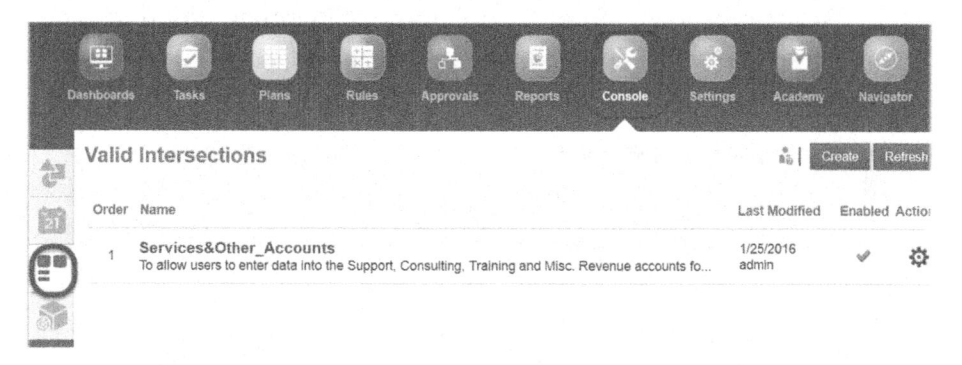

Click the *Data Maps* icon to define, update, and run mappings that will push data from one plan type to another plan type within the Enterprise Planning Cloud application:

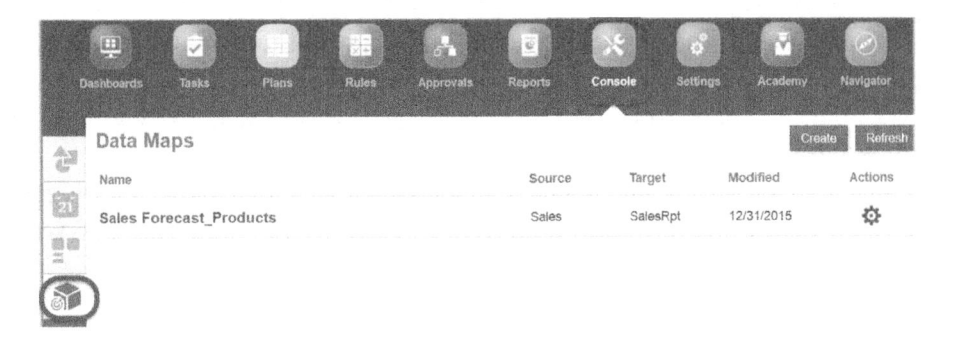

48   Chapter 3: Intro to Oracle Enterprise Planning Cloud

- **Settings** – users set preferences and admins define application defaults:

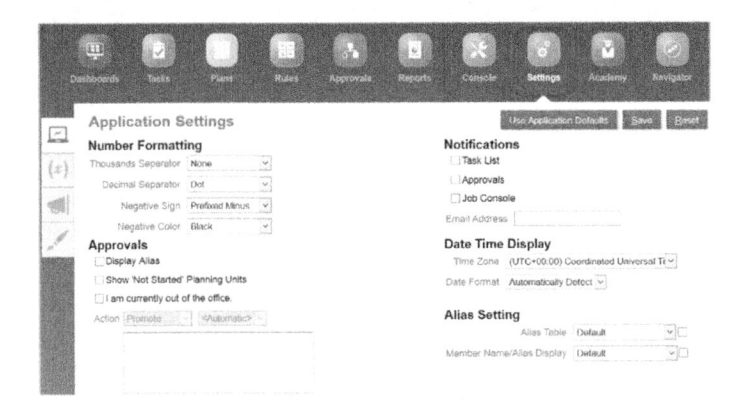

- **Academy** – learn more about Enterprise Planning Cloud
- **Navigator** – this link will take you to almost every administrative task that is not available in *Console*:

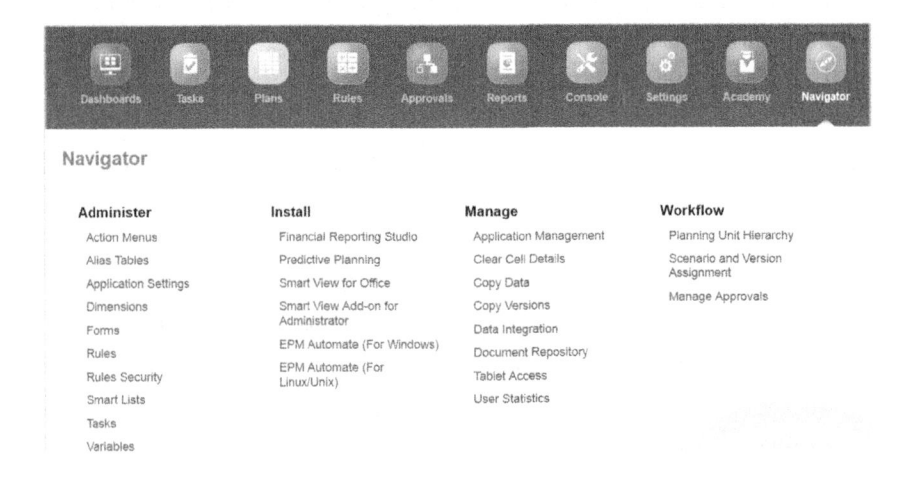

Note! As Oracle adds more features into the Console, this Navigator section will change (items could be removed from Navigator and added elsewhere in the Simplified UI).

MEMBER SELECTION IN THE SIMPLIFIED UI

The Simplified UI has a member selector that you will use throughout Enterprise Planning Cloud. It has a common look and feel across the various Enterprise Planning Cloud components. Once your application is built and you have dimensions and members, users and administrators will use the member selection window to select desired member or members. Enterprise Planning Cloud has revamped this feature to be compatible with the web browser interface.

The member selector allows planners to select dimension members as necessary for the planning process. For instance, you can select members for data forms or Financial Reports. Only valid members will be selectable to the user, based on a combination of security and valid intersection rules.

The member selector has three basic sections:
1) Search box
2) Hierarchy navigation columns
3) Settings menu

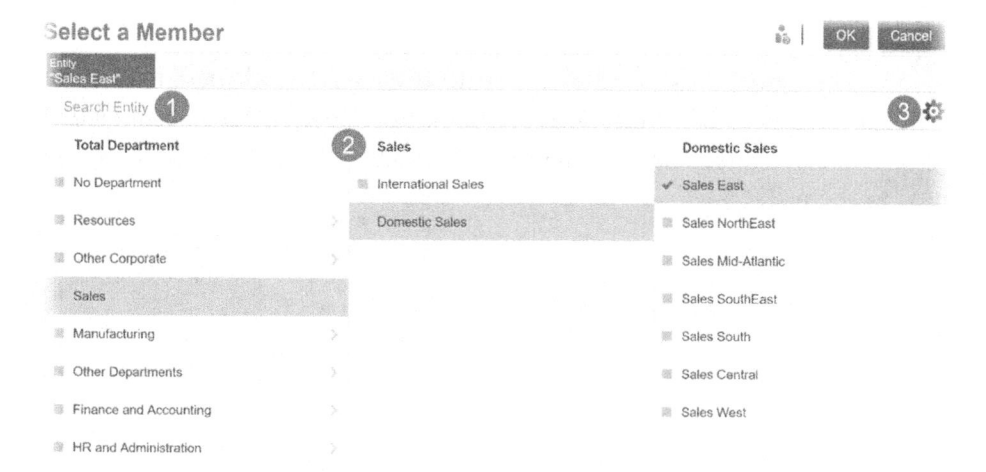

Select a Member

Entity
"Sales East"

Search Entity ①   ③ ⚙

Total Department	② Sales	Domestic Sales
☐ No Department	☐ International Sales	✓ Sales East
☐ Resources	Domestic Sales	☐ Sales NorthEast
☐ Other Corporate		☐ Sales Mid-Atlantic
Sales		☐ Sales SouthEast
☐ Manufacturing		☐ Sales South
☐ Other Departments		☐ Sales Central
☐ Finance and Accounting		☐ Sales West
☐ HR and Administration		

The search box allows planners to search for a specific member within the dimension. All or part of the member or alias can be used. Also, one or more words can be used. In addition, advanced wildcard searches are allowed. Wildcard searches can include the following types of characters:

- ? – to match any single character
- * – to match zero or multiple characters
- # – to match any single number (0-9)
- **[list]** – match any single character within a list of characters; a dash can be used to represent a range
- **[-list]** – match any single character not found within a list of characters; a dash can be used to represent a range

The hierarchy navigation columns are the drill downs into the dimension. This is read left to right, top to bottom. In the previous screen shot, the "Sales" member is highlighted. This then opens the children of Sales into another column. Since the "Domestic Sales" child is also highlighted, the children of Domestic Sales are shown in the third column. Clicking on a member name indicates drill down on the member. Selecting the checkbox to the left of the member name actually selects the member. "Sales East" is checked, therefore, it is the member selected. You can confirm this by looking at the dimension name in the top left of the member selector window – "Sales East" is the member shown there, which indicates selection.

The *Settings* menu allows you to filter, sort, and display various types of members within the hierarchy navigation columns. Settings that toggle, or can be used in conjunction with other settings, have checkmarks next to them:

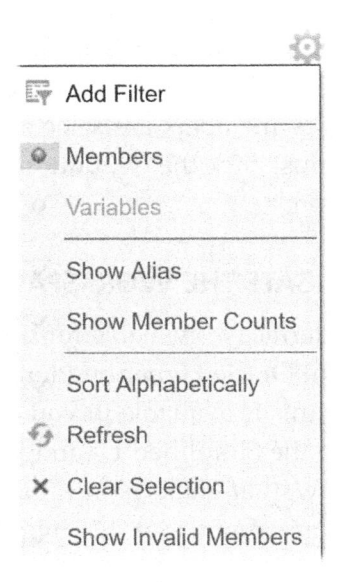

Look Smarter Than You Are with Enterprise Planning Cloud   51

```
            Add Filter
            Members
            Variables
            Show Alias
            Show Member Counts
            Sort Alphabetically
            Refresh
         X  Clear Selection
            Show Invalid Members
```

Filtering options include the following. This allows users to filter all members for a given dimension based on relationship functions, specified attributes, member level, or member generation:

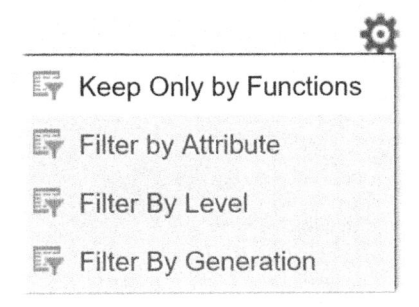

```
            Keep Only by Functions
            Filter by Attribute
            Filter By Level
            Filter By Generation
```

Display options include displaying the member name or alias and/or member counts for each parent member. Members that are considered invalid due to valid intersection rules will be suppressed.

Sort options include sorting alphabetically. However, this alphabetical sort is limited to sorting only the member names. Aliases will not be sorted even if they are selected for display purposes.

The *Clear Selection* option will clear the current members that are checked. It does not clear the current member selected for the dimension.

Finally, the *Show Invalid Members* option displays all members that are suppressed due to valid intersection rules. These members are displayed only, and cannot be selected. This option is helpful to understand why certain members are not available for selection.

Once the necessary members are selected by checking the boxes next to them, planners must click the *OK* button in the upper right-hand corner to confirm selection.

NAVIGATE THE WORKSPACE UI

A second user interface is available for users. This is the "legacy" Workspace interface from Oracle Hyperion Planning used in on-premise implementations. While this is available to you today, Oracle's direction is to move everything to the Simplified UI and I suspect this Workspace User Interface will go away at some point. Still I'll wander through it because occasionally as an administrator, I might need to jump over to this interface.

When you log into the Workspace URL, you'll land at the Home screen (as an administrator):

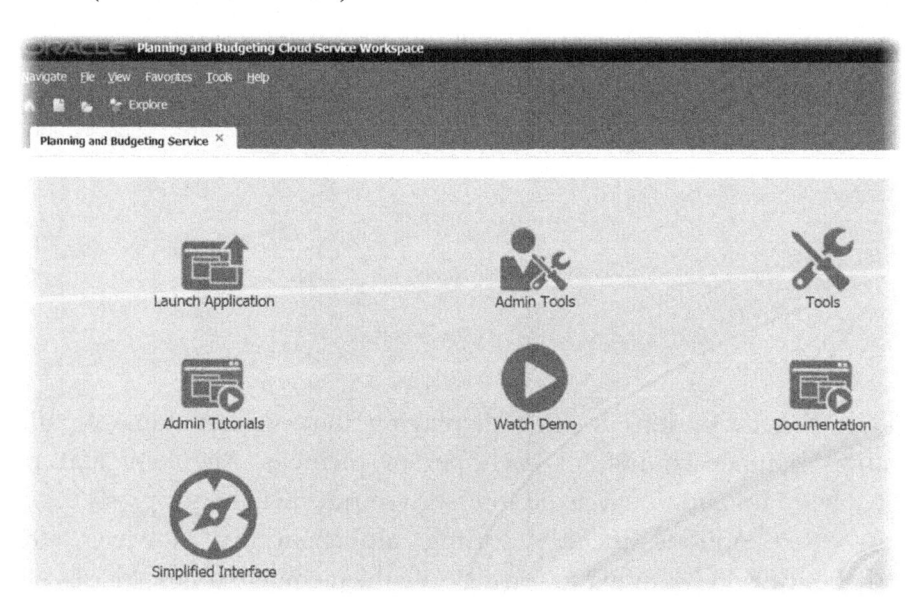

You can launch the application within Workspace or you can switch to the Simplified Interface. If you launch the application in Workspace, you'll see the interface resembling the on-premise Planning interface:

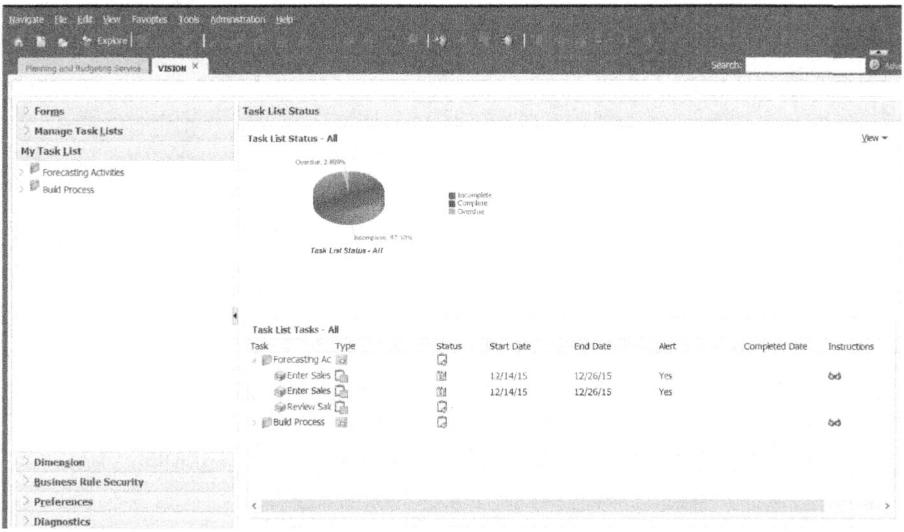

While this works fine, you might want to try to do most activities in the Simplified UI. Oracle's overall direction is to build new functionality into the Simplified UI. Many new features are not supported in the Workspace UI.

Within Workspace, administrators can access the Admin Tools:

- **Delete Application** – where users delete the existing application
- **Application Management** – where users can import and export the application (the entire application or specific components), Calculation Manager business rules and other objects, Financial reporting objects, and Data Management objects; this is also where users can create native groups and assign users to those groups
- **Desktop Installs** – where users can download and install needed client desktop software
- **Maintenance Time** – where administrators set the daily maintenance time and shows the last patch applied:

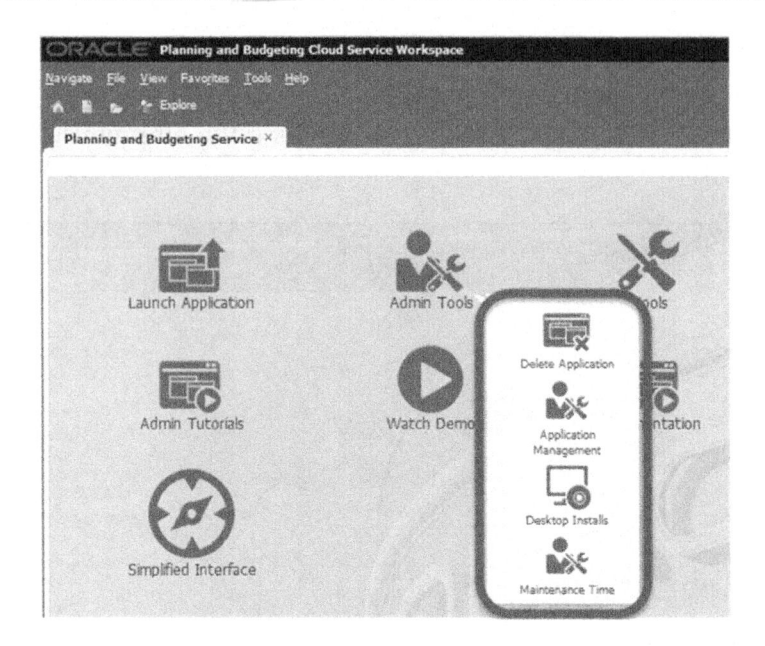

Depending upon provisioning, users can access Tools:

- **Explore** – repository where reports and other objects are stored in the Workspace
- **Calculation Manager** – where users define business rules and calculations
- **Desktop Installs** – where users download any needed client software, like Smart View
- **Data Integration** – where users can build interfaces to load data and execute data loads via Data Management (note, it is a little confusing that the *Data Integration* option takes you to "Data Management"):

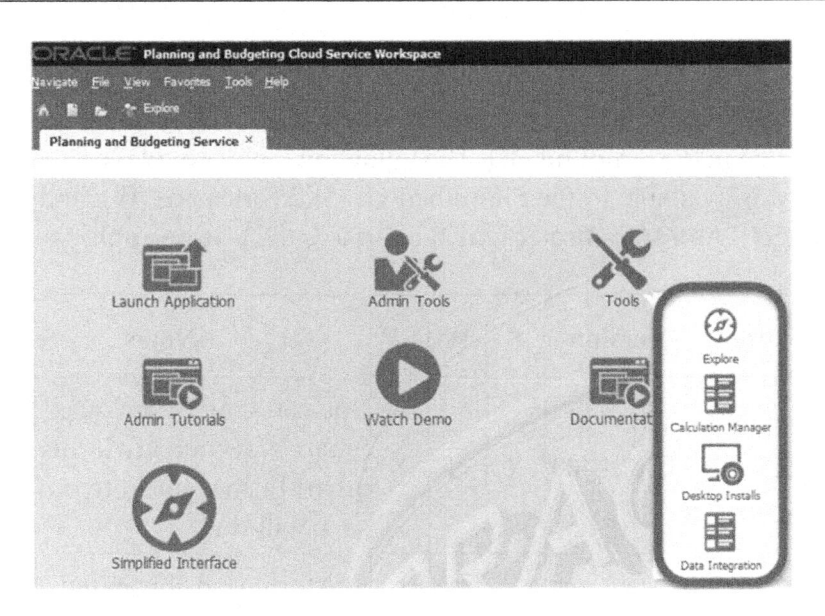

Look Smarter Than You Are with Enterprise Planning Cloud   55

To learn more, watch the *Admin Tutorials*, *Demos*, and review the *Documentation*:

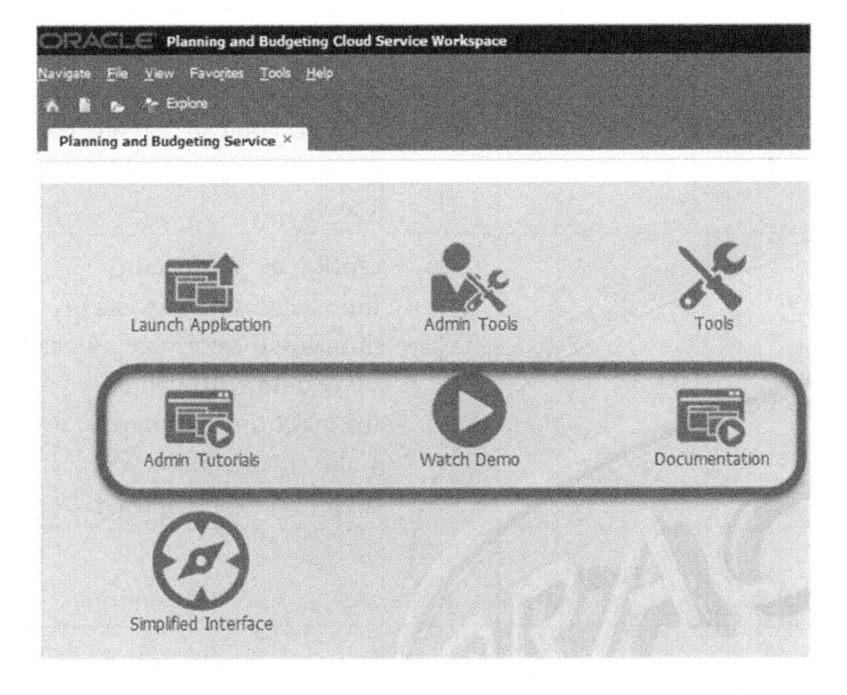

COMPARING THE INTERFACES

Several of the new features in Enterprise Planning Cloud are only supported in the Simplified UI. The following table provides an overview of what is available in the Simplified UI (S), Workspace (W), and Smart View (SV). An "X" indicates which interfaces the feature applies to.

Feature	Version	S	W	SV	Notes
Smart Push	11.1.2.4.400	X	X	X	You can't push data maps from Smart View but any forms with Smart Push enabled to run on save will run.
Smart Form	11.1.2.4.400	X		X	The form is visible in the Workspace UI but cannot be opened.
Sand-boxing	11.1.2.4.400	X			Sandbox functionality is available in Smart View (you can ad hoc and update a sandbox, though you can't create, delete, or publish data from Smart View).
Valid Intersections	11.1.2.4.400	X		X	Option to create valid intersection only exists in Simplified Interface. You can view data with valid intersections in Smart View. Valid intersections will NOT display in Workspace UI.
Job Scheduler	11.1.2.4.400	X			
Dynamic Reports	11.1.2.4.400	X	X	X	Dynamic reports are created in the Simplified UI but can be

Feature	Version	S	W	SV	Notes
					opened and viewed in Workspace UI and Smart View.
Autosave & Undo	11.1.2.4.400	X			
Keyboard Shortcuts	11.1.2.4.400	X			
Print Supporting Detail	11.1.2.4.400	X	X		
Adding Formulas & Cascading	11.1.2.4.400			X	This is a Smart View feature.

Note: S = Simplified UI, W = Workspace, SV = Smart View

APPLICATIONS & PLAN TYPES DEFINED

An Enterprise Planning Cloud application contains dimensions, data, business rules, and interfaces to meet a specific set of planning needs. You can have one application, per environment, per instance for Enterprise Planning Cloud.

Within the Enterprise Planning Cloud: Planning and Budgeting application, you can have up to seven plan types (or databases or models). A plan type is a grouping of related dimensions, data, interfaces and business rules to meet a specific planning need.

You can design the plan types to meet planning and forecasting needs. You might create a Summary plan type that consolidates data from a custom revenue plan type, custom workforce plan type and custom capital expense plan type. You might have a separate revenue details plan type with actuals details:

```
                    ┌─────────────────┐
                    │  Summary Plan   │
                    │      Type       │
                    └────────┬────────┘
          ┌──────────────────┼──────────────────┐
┌─────────┴────────┐ ┌───────┴────────┐ ┌───────┴────────┐
│   Revenue Plan   │ │   Workforce    │ │ Capital Expense│
│      Type        │ │  Expense Plan  │ │   Plan Type    │
│                  │ │      Type      │ │                │
└────────┬─────────┘ └────────────────┘ └────────────────┘
         │
┌────────┴─────────┐
│  Revenue Details │
│     Plan Type    │
└──────────────────┘
```

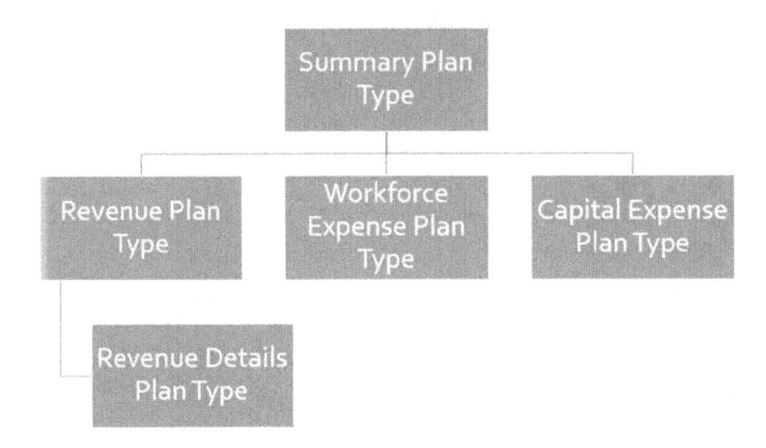

Note! The Enterprise Planning Cloud: Planning and Budgeting licensing option does *NOT* include the out of the box Workforce and Capex planning functionality / modules. You can build your own plan types with this logic and interfaces.

A pricing offering for Oracle Enterprise Planning Cloud, called Enterprise Planning pricing option (sometimes referred to as EPBCS), DOES include prebuilt Financials, Workforce, Projects and Capex frameworks / processes.

Enterprise Planning Cloud utilizes a multi-dimensional database called Essbase to store the numerical data. Each plan type will have one Essbase database. The Essbase database could be block storage (BSO) databases, aggregate storage (ASO) databases, or in the future, a hybrid aggregation mode database. More on this later and if you are new to Essbase, please review the Appendix on Essbase at the end of the book.

The Planning and Budgeting pricing option allows one application per environment. Each application may have up to three block storage option (BSO) plan types. You may also have the same number of ASO plan types as you have BSO plan types plus one (so this means potentially up to seven plan types within an application). In future versions, BSO plan types can be designed to utilize hybrid aggregation mode. This is important to know when you are designing your application.

The Enterprise Planning licensing option provides prebuilt frameworks for financials, workforce, capex, and projects. Each one of those frameworks will be its own plan type. You also have the standard three BSO and 4 ASO plan types in addition to the prebuilt frameworks. That is up to 11 plan types in one Enterprise Planning Cloud application!

The Enterprise Planning Cloud application and plan type names are limited to a maximum of eight characters.

Each application and plan type will have a number of components:

- **Dimensions** – hierarchies of related master data or metadata
- **User Interfaces** – data forms for entering plan data over the Web or in Excel with Smart View, task lists, dashboards and more
- **Business Rules** – objects that are executed to perform pre-defined calculation logic or other operations on data; common business rules include those to roll up data from base data to totals, perform allocations from upper level data to lower levels, perform driver based calculation logic, copy data and clear data

Some Enterprise Planning Cloud components may be used across plan types:

- **Task Lists** – guided steps to complete a process
- **Composite Data Forms** – combination view of one or more simple data forms

VISION APPLICATION DESIGN

To meet the sales forecasting needs for Vision I'm going to create an application with two plan types: Sales (BSO) and SalesRpt (ASO):

Vision

Sales Plan Type (BSO)   **SalesRpt Plan Type (ASO)**

The Sales plan type will capture forecast from end users by product and entity. Because I'm so excited about the hybrid capabilities, I'm going to design one of the plan types as a *hybrid plan type* (BSO with all upper level sparse members dynamic) even though hybrid is not actually supported yet (as of April 2016). Don't try this at home folks, because I'll repeat, hybrid is not supported (yet). Still I want to show you the steps to making a BSO plan type into a hybrid plan type so you'll know. Once hybrid is supported and I've set up the plan type properly, I don't have to have any additional aggregation business rules; all upper level members automatically roll up.

Pausing for a moment for a mini-technical deep dive into why I might choose hybrid plan type over BSO and ASO plan types in the future (for more details check out the Appendix in this book or *Look Smarter Than You Are with Essbase*).

Option	Consideration
The issue with BSO	• Large sparse dimensions can't be dynamically calculated • Stored sparse dimensions increase aggregation time and database size
The issue with ASO	• Specifically designed for databases with large sparse dimensions • Missing key BSO calculation engine elements (e.g., allocations, driver based calculations)

The case for Essbase hybrid aggregation	• Combines BSO functionality with ASO performance • Keeps the use of BSO calculation elements while enabling the use of more (and larger) sparse dimensions • Reduces the database footprint • Improves performance

End users will forecast Units and List Price. I will create a member formula that will calculate revenue for the accounts based on units multiplied by rates. Data will be loaded using Data Management and then product manager smart list assignments will also be loaded using the Simplified UI. To finish it off, a business rule will be created that will seed forecast data based on loaded actuals data.

The SalesRpt plan type will provide more detailed actuals reporting by product, entity, and customer. I'll push the forecast data from the Sales plan type to the SalesRpt plan type. No calculations are required for the SalesRpt data and this is a more detailed cube with extra dimensions, so I'm going to create this as an ASO plan type.

```
LOG ENTRY: SOL 11, Entry 8

    Not a bad application design, I don't mind saying.
This  design  uses  some  best  practices  and  will
illustrate most of all of the Enterprise Planning Cloud
features and functions.
```

Chapter 4: Build an Application

> **LOG ENTRY: SOL 11, Entry 9**
>
> Now that I have my design for the Vision application, I'm ready to build the application. Fist bump myself for starting this exciting journey! And I was so worried just a few hours ago...

Note! The steps in this book and screen shots are based on the Simplified UI and Enterprise Planning Cloud version 15.11.65.

CREATE AN APPLICATION

Enterprise Planning Cloud will guide you through the process to create an application. Use the application creation wizard to create the planning and budgeting application.

Note! For most of this chapter, I tried to use the Simplified UI. Most of the steps demonstrated in this book can also be done in the Planning and Budgeting Cloud Service Workspace.

Note! To follow along the build process, please email info@interrel.com for sample metadata and data files. You can also request an export of this application to import into your environment for testing and learning.

To create an application,
1. Enter the URL for the Simplified UI or in the Enterprise Planning Cloud Workspace click the *Simplified Interface* icon, as shown below:

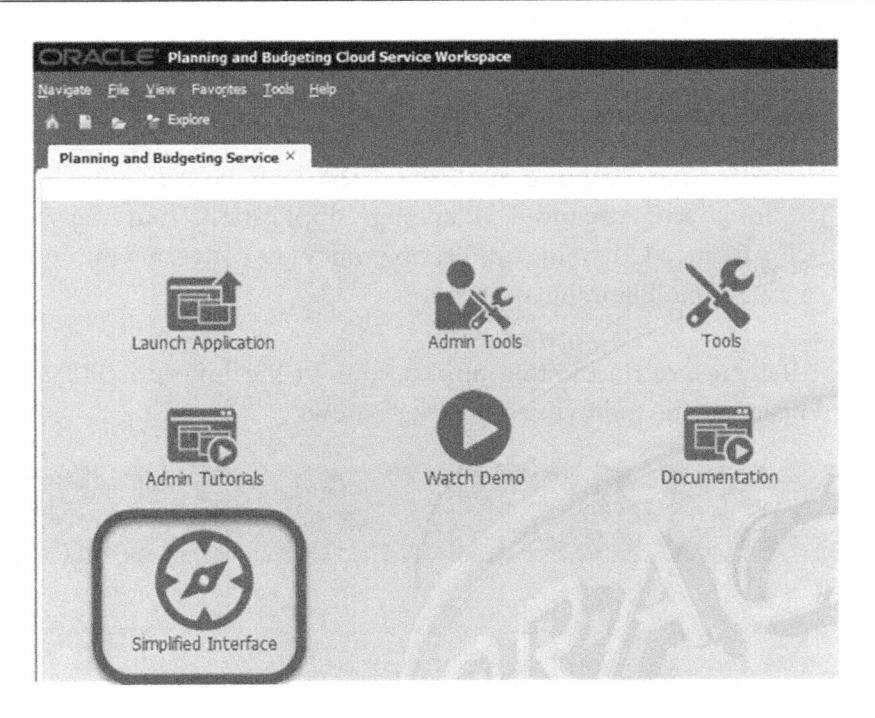

The Simplified UI provides three options at the beginning of application creation: Sample Application, Simple Planning, and Advanced Planning. The Enterprise Planning Cloud Workspace interface will not provide these options. Below is a summary of these three options:

- **Sample Application** – this is self-explanatory; a sample application will be created for administrators and users to explore
- **Simple Planning** – this application type will only have one plan type (or database) and can hold up to 20 dimensions. MDX (a syntax/language for defining logic) is supported for member formulas only which tells me this is an ASO plan type. Features NOT available include: business rules, mapped reporting cube, copy data, copy version, exchange rates, and currency conversion
- **Advanced Planning** – this application type initially creates 1 BSO and 1 ASO plan type with the option to add more plan types. There are 7 total plan types possible: 3 BSO plan types, 1 ASO plan type for each BSO plan type (for reporting purposes, although they don't have to be mapped directly), plus 1 extra ASO plan type for plan type consolidation purposes. An Advanced Planning

application has the functionality of a Simple Planning application with the addition of business rules and custom calendars

Note! A Simple Planning application can later be converted into an Advanced Planning application, but an Advanced Planning application cannot be converted into a Simple Planning application.

If there are no existing applications in the Enterprise Planning Cloud instance, the following screen will show:

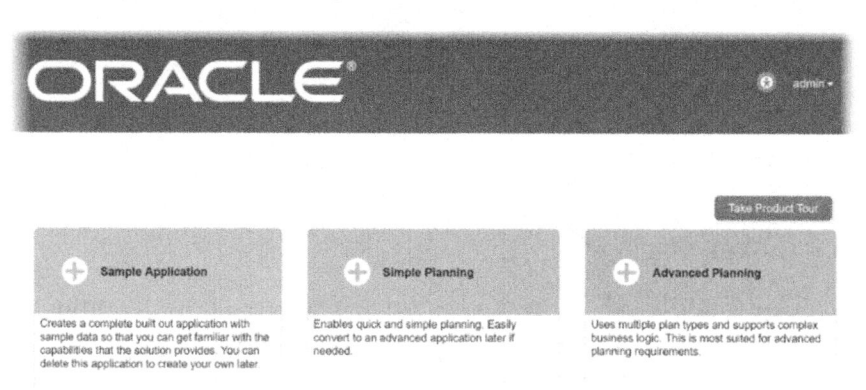

2. Click *Advanced Planning*.
3. Enter a name and description for the application. I will call the application "VISION". Click *Next*.
4. Now fill in the application details:
   a. Select the appropriate calendar and currency options according to application requirements.
   b. You can check *Enable rolling forecast for this application* if you would like to automatically create a rolling forecast and specify the period duration. For these steps, I am NOT going to enable it mainly so I can show you how to add this later during application build (in case you want to add to an existing application).
   c. Check *Enable Sandbox* to allow users to create their own sandboxes as they work on their plans. I'll check the

Look Smarter Than You Are with Enterprise Planning Cloud   65

option to enable sandboxes for this application. Note – you cannot enable or disable sandboxes once the application has been created.

d. Name the BSO and ASO Plan Types. As mentioned before, I'll name our BSO database "Sales" and our ASO database "SalesRpt":

Our planning frequency is	Weekly **Monthly** Quarterly
Select a start and end year	2010 To 2020
Fiscal Year First Month	January
Weekly Distribution	Even Distribution
	☐ Enable rolling forecast for this application
Rolling Forecast Period Duration	1
Our main currency is	USD United States of America dollar
We use more than one currency	☐
Enable Sandbox	☑
Plan Type : BSO	Sales
Plan Type : ASO	SalesRpt

Notice that I'm creating one BSO plan type and one ASO plan type for this application. I mentioned earlier that a third option that will be available soon: hybrid aggregation. However, hybrid aggregation is not a formal option in the application creation wizard. The reason why is because a hybrid aggregation plan type is really just a BSO plan type with the sparse dimensions set to dynamically calculate. So if you want to utilize the hybrid aggregation functionality (in the future), choose BSO. This will make more sense as I go along; the patience will pay off. Also, please review the Appendix on Essbase at the end of the book for more information.

5. Click *Next*.
6. Review and confirm the application details. Then click *Create*.
7. Wait for the application to create successfully. Click *OK*:

Application Creation Status
Application created successfully.

OK

```
LOG ENTRY: SOL 13, Entry 1

     Well, that's done. I would celebrate, but
recognizing that I only have a short time to complete
this application, I had better move onto the next
phases.
     I went through the crew's things. Hey - when you
are stranded in the Cloud, everything is up for dibs.
Surely Project Commander McMullen's iPad had some
good movies to entertain myself while stranded in the
Cloud.
     Full seasons of Glee and Smash? Seriously? Why
couldn't it be Breaking Bad or The Sopranos? I only
have musical comedies to watch?
     Well, I guess I won't complain; it's something.
Finn and Rachel it is.
```

DIMENSIONS EXPLAINED

Data is organized within an Essbase database (or plan type) into dimensions, or groupings of related data elements in a hierarchical format. To oversimplify, a dimension is something that can be put into the rows or columns of your report or data form like "Periods", "Accounts", "Entities", or "Products". Different databases have different dimensions. In Enterprise Planning Cloud, dimensions and dimension properties can be edited manually in the dimension editor or imported via a flat file. I will build the dimensions using both methods.

Note! Standard dimensions will already exist in the application (Period, Years, Account, Entity, Scenario, and Version). The HSP_View dimension is created when sandboxes are enabled. To create a new custom dimension, click ✢, but remember that they cannot be deleted once created.

Dimension Types & Member Properties

A dimension can be assigned a dimension type which enables specific functionality and member properties for time and financial intelligence within Enterprise Planning Cloud. Valid dimension types for Enterprise Planning Cloud applications include:

- Accounts
- Time
- Country
- Attribute

Enterprise Planning Cloud will assign the Accounts, Time, and Country dimension types by default. The Country dimension type is used for the multi-currency modules, if that option is chosen during the application creation.

Dimensions also have their own properties in addition to dimension types. In most cases, these properties are applicable for all members, as well as top-level dimension nodes. These properties govern how the member will be displayed to the end user, calculated (if applicable), reported, and more. These are described in the following sections:

Alias

The Alias property provides an alternate name or description for the member. This property is viewed by end users and is assigned by an alias table. You can use multiple alias tables to store different member names for end users to use in planning and reporting. For instance, you might want to have an alias table for "English" and another for "Spanish" so your users can practice their Español when looking at members in forms and reports.

Data Type

Members in Enterprise Planning Cloud may have a specific data type assigned: Unspecified, Currency, Non Currency, Percentage, Smart List, Date, and Text. I'll further define these data types when discussing the Accounts dimension:

Data Storage

The Data Storage property tells Essbase how the member should be stored back in Essbase. Valid data storage options include:

```
Data Type   Unspecified                    ∨
            Unspecified
            Currency
            Non Currency
            Percentage
            SmartList
            Date
            Text
```

- **Store** – stores the data value with the member
- **Dynamic Calc and Store** – does not calculate the data value until a user requests it, but stores the data value immediately after the retrieval; this type was designed to be used for infrequently calculated formulas
- **Dynamic Calc** – does not calculate the data value until a user requests it, and then discards the data value
- **Never Share** – does not allow members to be shared implicitly; Enterprise Planning Cloud creates a lot of "Never Share" members by default so that you can easily send information into summary members for "Target" versions
- **Shared** – shares data between two or more members
- **Label only** – creates members for navigation and grouping and doesn't calculate data at this level; these members (e.g., "Statistical Accounts") usually won't make sense from a logical consolidation standpoint:

Data Storage Store

> Store
> Dynamic Calc and Store
> Dynamic Calc
> Never Share
> Shared
> Label only

When should you set a member to *Store* in Enterprise Planning Cloud? When you will need to load data or input data to that member. Set a member to store if that member has a large number of children. Most of the time, your large sparse dimensions will be set to Store. (What is a sparse dimension? I'll address this later because it's a somewhat advanced topic.) You may also set dense members with member formulas to store so that a calculation occurs at a level 0 member and then aggregates for all dimensions. I'll do this for my Vision application in just a bit.

In most cases, use the *Dynamic Calc* property for your variances, ratios, averages, and other formulas. You can also set upper level members of a hierarchy to *Dynamic Calc* when those members have just a few children. Oftentimes you set upper levels of the Accounts and Time dimensions (and other dense dimensions) to *Dynamic Calc* to help reduce your database size.

I recommend sticking to *Dynamic Calc* over *Dynamic Calc and Store* unless you have little used sparse members with very complicated formulas.

You should assign *Never Share* to a member that is the only child of its parent (or could potentially be the only child of its parent). Essbase has a built-in feature called "Implicit Sharing", a mischievous gremlin of a function that can cause confusion in your Essbase databases. Essbase tries to be smart for us in this case. When a parent only has one child, the data values for both the parent and the child will always be the same, right? So Essbase decides to only store one value, the child value, which reduces your database size. But this causes issues in loading or inputting data for the parent, who dynamically pulls the data value from the child.

When should you use *Label Only*? Use *Label Only* for members like Scenario, Ratio, or Drivers, whose sole purpose in life is to organize the dimension and hierarchy: members for which it never makes sense to add their children together. A member marked as *Label Only* will automatically pull the value of its first child when referenced. Because of this, when you make a member Label Only, you will often make its first child have a plus (+) consolidation operator and the other children have a tilde (~) to designate that only the first child is rolling to the member (more on consolidation properties in the next section). This is entirely to help indicate what's going on in Essbase to a user who might not know that a Label Only member pulls the value from its first child. For example, it makes no sense to add Actual and Budget members together, so you flag the Scenario dimension as *Label Only*.

Valid for Plan Type

As discussed, a single Enterprise Planning Cloud application may have multiple plan types or databases. Depending on the dimension, a dimension (or member) may or may not be required for all plan types. The Administrator has some flexibility in defining the dimensions and members that are valid and available in the plan types. You can specify how the member should roll up within the hierarchy using the Consolidation property once a member is assigned to one or more plan types.

For the Years and Period dimensions, all members are assigned to all plan types. The administrator cannot change this assignment (the option isn't available), but other dimensions can be changed..

You can, however, assign the consolidation property. What's the consolidation property?

Consolidation Operators

Consolidation properties, also known as consolidation operators, tell Essbase how to roll up the members in the outline. Valid consolidation operators for Enterprise Planning Cloud include:

- Addition (+)
- Subtraction (-)
- Multiplication (*)
- Division (/)
- Percent (%)
- Ignore (~)
- Never (^)

Note! Never (^) will not aggregate a member up across any dimension in the Essbase database (e.g., prices, index) while Ignore (~) will not aggregate a member up the dimension in which it resides. However, Ignore will aggregate for all other dimensions (e.g., Product, Customer).

Two Pass

The two pass member property tells Essbase to "come back and calculate this member at the end." Why is this important? Let's look at an example.

The Accounts dimension is calculated first (I'll explain shortly), which means that Profit % is calculated based on the input Sales and Profit members. Once I roll up the Time dimension, the monthly Profit % is added together and placed in Q1, as shown below:

	Jan	Feb	Mar	Q1
Profit	100	100	100	300
Sales	1000	1000	1000	3000
Profit %	10%	10%	10%	30%

Hmmm... something's not right there. I want Profit % to re-calculate after the quarter and year totals for Profit and Sales have been calculated.

Tag the Profit % member with the two pass calculation property:

Data Storage Store
Two Pass Calculation ☑

Now Essbase knows to circle back to calculate the correct percent after it's finished calculating everything else:

	Jan	Feb	Mar	Q1
Profit	100	100	100	300
Sales	1000	1000	1000	3000
Profit %	10%	10%	10%	10%

UDAs

You can create user defined attributes (UDAs) for members on the UDA tab. UDAs provide a way to tag multiple members for analysis, calculations, or data loading. For example, say you want to perform a 10% bonus calculation for all managers managing "Large" markets and a 5% bonus calculation for all managers managing "Small" market accounts. While UDAs can be used to pinpoint those managers for calculating these bonuses, what they can't do is easily give a subtotal for "Large" and "Small" markets – alternate hierarchies or attributes would be a better solution to meet this requirement.

Member Formulas

Because Enterprise Planning Cloud sits on top of Essbase, I have an amazingly powerful calculation engine at my electronic fingertips. One way to build in calculations for Enterprise Planning Cloud is through member formulas. These are calculated back in Essbase.

Conditional operators allow for tests based on criteria. An Essbase member formula to calculate "Commission" might use these conditional checks:

```
IF (Sales > 1000)
     Sales * .02;
ELSE
     10;
ENDIF
```

In English-speak, if Sales is greater than 1000, then Commission is equal to Sales times two percent; otherwise, Commission is equal to 10.

Mathematical functions define and return values based on selected member expressions. These functions include most standard statistical functions. An example of a mathematical function would be the standard formula for a Variance calculation for Actual and Budget data:

```
(Actual-Budget)/Actual;
```

Mathematical functions can be used in Essbase member formulas. The member formula for the "Market Share" member uses an index function:

```
Sales % @PARENTVAL (Markets, Sales);
```

In other words, Market Share is equal to the Sales for the current member as a percent of the current member's parent data value for the Markets dimension.

The member formula for the member "Mar YTD" uses a financial function:

```
@PTD(Jan:Mar);
```

The member formula for "Payroll" shows you an example of how to use conditional or Boolean criteria:

```
IF (@ISIDESC (East) OR @ISIDESC (West))
     Sales * .15;
ELSEIF (@ISIDESC(Central))
     Sales * .11;
ELSE
     Sales * .10;
ENDIF
```

To put it in English, for all of the members under and including East and West, Payroll is equal to Sales times 15 percent. For all members under and including Central, Payroll is equal to Sales times 11 percent. For all other members Payroll is equal to Sales times 10 percent.

Note! Essbase member formulas must end with semicolons. If the member name has spaces in it, you must enclose the member name in double quotes.

Now that you are fully fluent in basic Enterprise Planning Cloud dimension types and member properties, let's turn our attention to building out the all of the dimensions, beginning with Scenario.

BUILD SCENARIO DIMENSION

The Scenario dimension in an Enterprise Planning Cloud application is used to apply and track different planning methods, as well as create new forecasts. Scenarios can be associated with different time periods and exchange rates. Start period, start year, end period, and end year are Scenario properties that control data form entry. You can also build calculated members into the Scenario dimension to perform variance analysis.

The Scenario dimension will be built manually using the dimension editor.

To build the Scenario dimension,
1. Navigate to *Dimensions* under *Navigator >> Administer*:

2. Select *Scenario* from the drop-down menu:

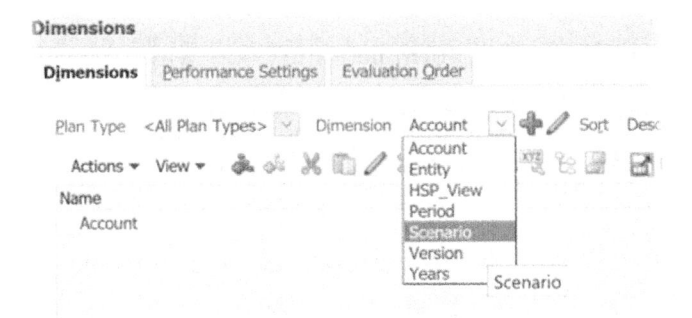

Look Smarter Than You Are with Enterprise Planning Cloud   75

3. Under Actions, use (Add Child) to add new Scenario members.

4. Members can be edited by first selecting the member to edit and then clicking the ✏ icon found directly above the dimension name in the hierarchy tree, or clicking *Edit* under Actions.

Note! There is another Edit icon that is next to the dimension drop-down. This edits the entire dimension and not a specific dimension member.

5. Add (or edit) the following members and properties to the Scenario dimension:

Member Name	Start Yr.	Start Period	End Yr.	End Period	Data Storage	Process Management	Data Type
Plan	FY15	Jan	FY16	Dec	Never Share	Y	Unspecified
Actual	FY10	Jan	FY20	Dec	Never Share	N	Unspecified
Forecast	FY15	Jan	FY16	Dec	Never Share	Y	Unspecified
Plan Comments	FY10	Jan	FY20	Dec	Never Share	N	Text
Variance	FY10	Jan	FY20	Dec	Dynamic Calc	N	Unspecified

* If the property is not noted above, accept the default value.

Note! You'll notice that Scenario members have been created in the application by default, including Plan, Actual, Forecast and Variance. Edit the properties of those members to match the table above.

Edit Member : Plan

Member Properties | UDA | Member Formula

Name	Plan
Description	
Alias Table	Default
Alias	
Start Yr.	FY15
Start Period	Jan
End Yr.	FY16
End Period	Dec
Include BegBal as Time Period	☑
Enabled for Process Management	☑
Exchange Rate Table	<None>
Hierarchy Type	Not Set
Data Storage	Never Share
Two Pass Calculation	
Plan Type	Sales — Addition / SalesRpt — Addition
Data Type	Unspecified
Smart Lists	<None>
Enable for Dynamic Children	☐
Number of Possible Dynamic Children	10
Access Granted to Member Creator	Inherit

Note! You can copy an existing scenario member and its properties to a new scenario member using the (Copy Scenario) icon:

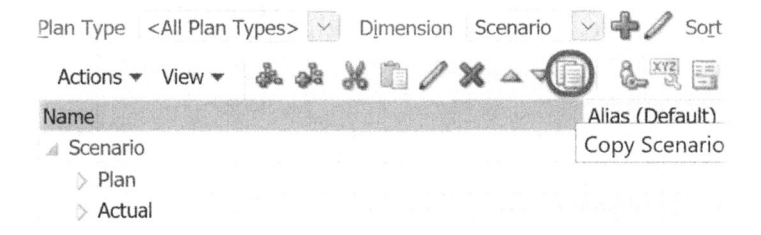

Plan Type <All Plan Types> Dimension Scenario Sort

Actions ▼ View ▼

Name	Alias (Default)
▲ Scenario	Copy Scenario
▷ Plan	
▷ Actual	

If you need users to input data into the BegBalance member, make sure to check the option *Include BegBal as Time Period* for the Scenario member:

Edit Member : Plan	
Member Properties UDA Member Formula	
Name	Plan
Description	
Alias Table	Default
Alias	
Start Yr.	FY15
Start Period	Jan
End Yr.	FY16
End Period	Dec
Include BegBal as Time Period	✓
Enabled for Process Management	✓
Exchange Rate Table	<None>
Hierarchy Type	Not Set
Data Storage	Never Share
Two Pass Calculation	
Plan Type	Sales ✓ Addition
	SalesRpt ✓ Addition

6. Now delete existing Scenario members that are not needed by selecting the member and clicking ✖.

REFRESH THE DATABASE

Any time you make a change to a dimension or member within a dimension, you will need to "Refresh the Database." This means pushing changes that you make in the Enterprise Planning Cloud UI to the underlying Essbase database.

To refresh the database,
1. In the Simplified UI, go to *Console*.
2. Select the *Application* tab and select *Actions >> Refresh Database*:

3. Click *Create*, select options, and then click *Refresh Database*:

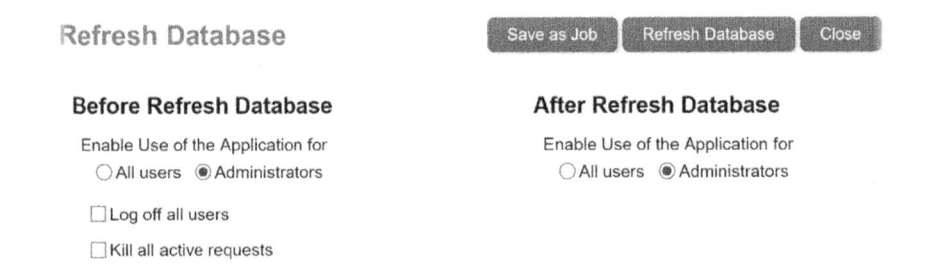

You can optionally save this Refresh Database as a job that can be scripted during a nightly process. You can define options to log off users and/or administrators while the refresh is occurring (this is a recommended practice).

4. At the warning message, click *Refresh Database* and wait for the following message:

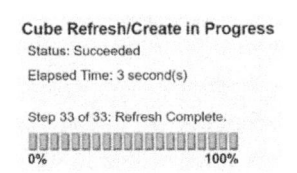

Look Smarter Than You Are with Enterprise Planning Cloud 79

5. Click *Finish* and then *Close* twice. The Refresh is complete.

Note! Refresh the database when there are any metadata or security changes that need to be pushed to Essbase.

Vision Company needs variance calculations for Actual and Plan. To take advantage of the Essbase calculation engine, I'm going to build calculations into the database via a member formula. A member formula is a calculation formula that is assigned to a member in a dimension.

To edit the Variance member in the Scenario dimension,
1. Go back into the dimension editor and select the *Scenario* dimension.
2. Edit the *Variance* member to match the following properties (be sure that the Data Storage is set to *Dynamic Calc*):

Edit Member : Variance

Member Properties | UDA | Member Formula

Name	Variance
Description	
Alias Table	Default
Alias	
Start Yr.	FY10
Start Period	Jan
End Yr.	FY20
End Period	Dec
Include BegBal as Time Period	☐
Enabled for Process Management	☐
Exchange Rate Table	<None>
Hierarchy Type	Not Set
Data Storage	Dynamic Calc
Two Pass Calculation	☐
Plan Type	Sales ✓ Addition
	SalesRpt ✓ Addition
Data Type	Unspecified
Smart Lists	<None>
Enable for Dynamic Children	☐
Number of Possible Dynamic Children	10
Access Granted to Member Creator	Inherit

Although listed as options, properties like *Start Year* and *End Period* are not applicable for this member because it is dynamically calculated. Users will not be submitting data for Variance.

3. Click the *Member Formula* tab and enter the following formula:

```
@VAR(Actual, Plan);
```

Edit Member : Variance

Member Properties | UDA | **Member Formula**

Plan Type   Default
Data Storage   Dynamic Calc
Solve Order   0
Enter Member Formula   @VAR(Actual, Plan);

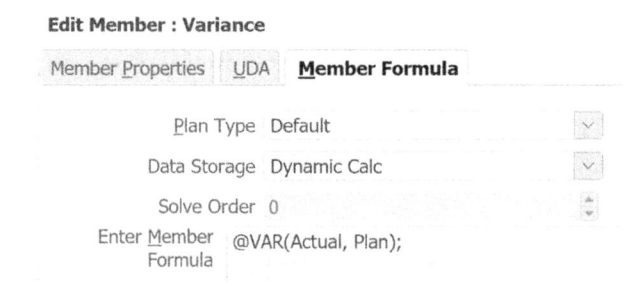

4. *Validate* the formula to ensure that the syntax clears, then click *Save*.
5. Now add a "Variance %" member using the same member properties as the Variance member and enter the following formula:

```
@VARPER(Actual, Plan);
```

6. Go back to *Console* to refresh the database.

The @VAR and @VARPER are just two of the many Essbase functions. See the Essbase Technical Reference for all of the Essbase calculation functions and examples.

Here's what I am left with for the Scenario dimension (ignore the Security column for now):

Name	Alias (Default)	Description	Security	Start Period	Start Yr.	End Period	End Yr.	Exch. Table
Scenario								
> Plan			View	Jan	FY15	Dec	FY16	
> Actual			View	Jan	FY10	Dec	FY20	
> Forecast			View	Jan	FY15	Dec	FY16	
> Plan Comments				Jan	FY10	Dec	FY20	
> Variance				Jan	FY10	Dec	FY20	
> Variance %				Jan	FY10	Dec	FY20	

BUILD VERSION DIMENSION

The Version dimension is used to differentiate between different drafts of Budget and Plan data. You can model possible outcomes based on more optimistic or less optimistic assumptions like Best Case and Worst Case, or use Version to manage the dissemination of Plan data like Internal and External.

The Version dimension and its members are independent of Scenario members, and Version members are available to all Scenario members. This is because Version and Scenario are two distinct dimensions in the application.

Versions are either defined as Target or Bottom Up. Target versions allow data entry at any level in the hierarchy of dimensions. If data is entered at higher levels, business rules can be created to allocate data down to lower levels. The Enterprise Planning Cloud Administrator has access to create these business rules. In addition, you can copy one Target version to another, which will copy data for all levels and members.

Note! Approval tasks are not allowed for Target versions.

Bottom Up budgets only allow data entry at the bottom members of every dimension (Level 0 members). Summary members are display-only and aggregate from bottom level members. You can copy data from one Bottom Up version to another.

If *Enable Sandbox* was checked during the application creation wizard, one "Sandboxes" member will be created automatically in the Version dimension. When a sandbox is created by a user, a new member will be added under the Sandboxes member (e.g., – "Sandbox1"). The data in Sandbox1 will be stored at the intersection of Sandbox1 and the HSP_View member "SandboxData" (more on the HSP_View dimension later).

To build the Version dimension,
1. Navigate to the dimension editor and select *Version* from the drop-down menu.
2. Add (or edit) the following members and properties to the Version dimension (rename BU Version_1 to Pass1 and add Pass2):

Member Name	Storage	Version Type	Consolidation
Pass1	Never Share	Standard Bottom Up	Ignore
Pass2	Never Share	Standard Bottom Up	Ignore
Final	Never Share	Standard Bottom Up	Ignore

Note! Check the box for *Enabled for Process Management* to allow the version to be subject to approvals. Check the box for *Enable Sandboxes* to allow users to create their own sandboxes in the application for the selected version (more on sandboxing at the end of the mission):

Look Smarter Than You Are with Enterprise Planning Cloud 83

Name	Pass1
Description	
Alias Table	Default
Alias	
Type	Standard Bottom Up
Enabled for Process Management	☑
Enable Sandboxes	☑
Hierarchy Type	Not Set
Data Storage	Never Share
Two Pass Calculation	☐
Plan Type	Sales — Ignore
	SalesRpt — Ignore
Data Type	Unspecified
Smart Lists	<None>
Enable for Dynamic Children	☐
Number of Possible Dynamic Children	10
Access Granted to Member Creator	Inherit

The resulting Version dimension should look as follows:

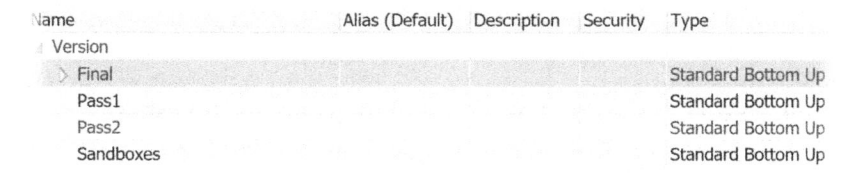

Name	Alias (Default)	Description	Security	Type
Version				
> Final				Standard Bottom Up
Pass1				Standard Bottom Up
Pass2				Standard Bottom Up
Sandboxes				Standard Bottom Up

Note! Enterprise Planning Cloud automatically creates "Base" and "What if" as children of the Final version. If you do not wish to use these members in your application, simply delete them using ✖.

3. Edit "Final" and check the option to *Enable sandboxes*:

[Screenshot of Dimensions / Edit Member: Final dialog showing Member Properties tab. Fields include Name: Final, Alias Table: Default, Type: Standard Bottom Up, Enabled for Process Management (checked), Enable Sandboxes (checked, circled), Data Storage: Never Share, Plan Type: Sales/Ignore and SalesRpt/Ignore, Data Type: Unspecified, Smart Lists: <None>, Number of Possible Dynamic Children: 10, Access Granted to Member Creator: Inherit.]

4. Refresh the database to push the changes to Essbase.

ACCOUNT DIMENSION EXPLAINED

The Account dimension houses the metrics for the database. While almost every application will have an Account dimension, what the dimension contains will vary greatly:

- A **financial planning** application will have accounts for income statement, balance sheet, and sometimes cash flow.
- An **inventory planning** application will have measures for beginning inventory, ending inventory, additions, returns, adjustments, and so forth.
- A **sales planning** application will have measures for sales dollars, units sold, and average sales price.

- A **human capital or workforce planning** application will have metrics for payroll, unemployment, payroll taxes, sick days, vacation days, years of employment, and so on.

The Account dimension is the most important dimension in any application since it lets you define what metrics you're going to plan and analyze. You can safely expect every Account dimension to be unique for each plan type.

Before I build the Account dimension, I'll review a few of the Account-specific properties.

Source Plan Type

As the administrator, you can define which accounts are valid for which plan types. If an account is valid for more than one plan type, a source plan type must be specified. This is where the data will be stored. The other plan types will reference that data value using the @XREF function. The plan types valid for a member are determined by the plan types assigned to the parent.

Variance Reporting

The Variance Reporting property (also known as Expense Reporting in Essbase circles) is a simple flag that tells downstream calculations and reports whether a positive variance is good or bad. If you're over your target on revenue, everyone is happy. Of course, the opposite is true when you spend too much on office supplies. Well, not everyone will be upset, but you don't want to be making enemies in the Finance Department when it comes time for them to cut you the bonus check for those positive-variance revenues, right?

Let's walk you through an example. If you budget $1,000,000 in revenue and you make $1,100,000, that's a favorable variance of $100,000. Expenses are quite the opposite: if you budget $1,000,000 in marketing expenses and you spend $1,100,000, that's an unfavorable variance of $100,000. In general, you want expense data to have lower actuals than budget.

To allow for this, Planning (and Essbase) uses a property called Variance Reporting. Tag all of your expense accounts with "Expense" and Essbase will calculate the variance correctly when using the @VAR or

@VARPER functions. Essbase will show a positive variance when Actual data is higher than Budget for revenue or metric accounts. Essbase will show a negative variance for those expense accounts tagged with the Variance Reporting property of "Expense":

	Jan	FY2007	
	Actual	Budget	Variance
Net_Rev	100	75	25
Op_Expense	100	75	-25
Op_Income	#Missing	#Missing	#Missing

The Variance Reporting property should be set to Expense for all measures where budget should be higher than actual.

There is also a "Non-Expense" property. This tags the Account as not an Expense. Essbase will calculate the variance by subtracting the budgeted amount from the actual amount to determine the variance.

If you choose an Account Type of *Saved Assumption* (more on this later), you can specify the Variance Reporting property. If you choose any of the other account types, the Variance Reporting property will be automatically assigned (though it can be changed). Note, I will discuss account type in just a moment.

Time Balance Property

The Time Balance property is only available in the Account dimension, and is used to tell Planning / Essbase how a given member should be aggregated up the Time dimension.

For example, should Headcount for January, February, and March be added together for Q1 (Quarter 1)? This definitely wouldn't make sense:

	Actual	FY2007			
	Jan	Feb	Mar	Q1	Q2
Headcount	100	125	122	347	#Mis

In most cases, you want Q1 to equal the March headcount (though some might want the average across the periods), or in other words, the last headcount in the period. To get Planning to do this, you tag Headcount with the *Balance* option (in Essbase circles this is known as "Time Balance Last" or "TB Last") so that it will take the last member's value when aggregating time.

Depending on your requirements, you could also assign *First* or *Average*. Here is Q1's headcount, now nicely equaling its last child, Mar (short for March):

	Actual	FY2007			
	Jan	Feb	Mar	Q1	Q2
Headcount	100	125	122	122	#M

What if I have just closed January? Showing the March headcount wouldn't be accurate because March is blank. A second property associated with Time Balance, called "Skip", allows us to define how I handle missing and zero values. In this example, I would want to ignore any blanks (or #Missing). So I set the Headcount account's Time Balance option to *Balance* and then set the Skip option to *Missing*.

Now Q1 will correctly show the January value:

	Actual	FY2007			
	Jan	Feb	Mar	Q1	Q2
Headcount	100	#Missing	#Missing	100	#M

Another example of Time Balance utilization is for inventory analysis members:

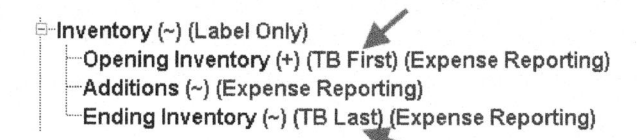

```
⊟-Inventory (~) (Label Only)
   ├─Opening Inventory (+) (TB First) (Expense Reporting)
   ├─Additions (~) (Expense Reporting)
   └─Ending Inventory (~) (TB Last) (Expense Reporting)
```

"Fill" is another Time Balance option that will automatically "fill" or distribute the parent value to all of its descendants. The "Weighted Average" Time Balance option will provide a weighted daily average accounting, with or without Leap Year.

Account Type

The Account Type property will dictate how an account will flow over time and how the account's sign will calculate when performing variance calculations. Each account member will be assigned an account type:

- **Expense** – Flow and Expense
- **Revenue** – Flow and Non-Expense
- **Asset** – Balance and Non-Expense
- **Liability** – Balance and Non-Expense
- **Equity** – Balance and Non-Expense
- **Saved Assumption** – User Defined Time Balance and User Defined Variance Reporting

The "Saved Assumption" account type is often used to store drivers like headcount, square feet, or units sold. Once Saved Assumption is selected, you define variance reporting and time balance properties for the member.

Data Type

The Data Type property determines how values are stored in account members and, if multi-currency is used, the exchange rates used to calculate values. Valid data type options include Unspecified, Currency, Non Currency, Percentage, Smart List, Text, and Date.

An account member with a data type of "Text" allows users to enter free-form text comments or information for the account at the intersection of other dimension members. For example, if your Capital Expense application has an account called "Asset Model Number", users can input a specific model number by item.

Hierarchy Type

I'll discuss the Hierarchy Type member property shortly when we get to the ASO plan type section. This property does not apply for block storage plan types.

Exchange Rate Type

The Exchange Rate Type is only enabled if Data Type is set to *Currency* and the application is multi-currency. It includes the following options:

- **Average** – uses account's average exchange rate
- **Ending** – uses account's ending exchange rate
- **Historical** – uses account's exchange rate that was in effect when the earnings for a "Retained Earnings" account were earned or the assets for a "Fixed Assets" account were purchased (for example)

Smart Lists

Simply put, Smart Lists are customized drop-down menus that users can access within data forms. Smart Lists allow administrators to control a list of values for users to select. Users may not type in the cell of a member that is of a Smart List type. You can create a data element as a Smart List in an Enterprise Planning Cloud application, in place of a regular dimension (which helps with performance and database size). Once you've created a Smart List, you can use its values in member formulas:

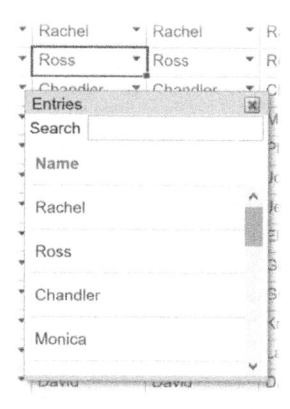

I'm going to go ahead and create the Smart List first so it will be available when I create dimensions later.

CREATE SMART LIST

To create a Smart List,
1. Click *Navigator*:

2. Under Administer, click *Smart Lists*.
3. Under Actions, click *Create* to add a new Smart List:

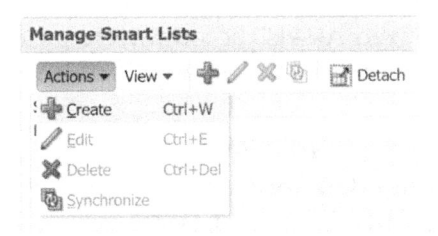

4. Name the Smart List. It can't have any spaces or special characters. Also type in the Label, the text to be displayed to users once the Smart List is selected. Labels can have spaces and special characters. I will create a Smart List for the Product Managers in Vision Company.
5. Select the Display Order, #Missing Drop-down Label, and #Missing Form Label:

Look Smarter Than You Are with Enterprise Planning Cloud   91

```
Manage Smart Lists
Edit Smart Lists : Product_Manager
Properties  Entries  Preview

              * Smart List  Product_Manager
                   * Label  Product Manager
             Display Order  ID
   #Missing Drop Down Label
        #Missing Form Label  Form Setting
    Automatically generate ID ☐
```

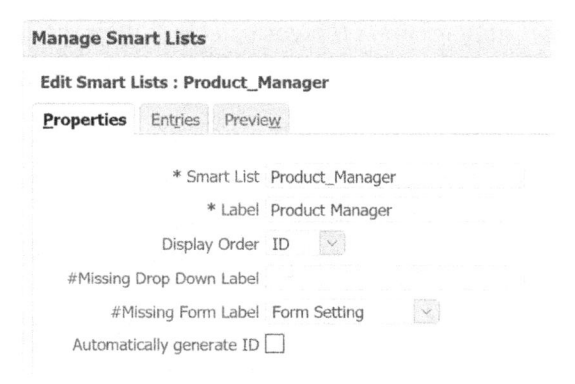

You can define the following parameters for Smart Lists:

- **Smart List** – unique name of the smart list; can only contain alphanumeric and underscore characters, no special characters or spaces
- **Label** – display text when the smart list is selected
- **Display Order** – determining factor for how the smart list entries will be ordered: by ID, name, or label
- **#Missing Drop Down Label** – text to be displayed when the value for a smart list entry is #Missing
- **#Missing Form Label** – determines whether or not the smart list #Missing setting or the form #Missing setting governs what displays for #Missing values
- **Automatically generate ID** – have the system generate the unique numbers that control the order of the smart list entries; if this is checked, the sort order cannot be customizable

6. Check *Automatically generate ID* to have the system generate the numeric ID for each entry in the Smart List. Leaving this unchecked will allow ID values to be customized.
7. Click the *Entries* tab.
8. Click ✚ to add entries to the Smart List.
9. Type in the required Name and Label fields.

As I mentioned above, the *Label* is the text displayed to users and it will auto-populate with the value entered into the Name field. If the option to *Automatically generate ID* was selected, then the ID field will also auto-populate.

10. Create the following entries for the Product_Manager Smart List.
11. Once finished, click the *Preview* tab.
12. If all looks good, click *Save*:

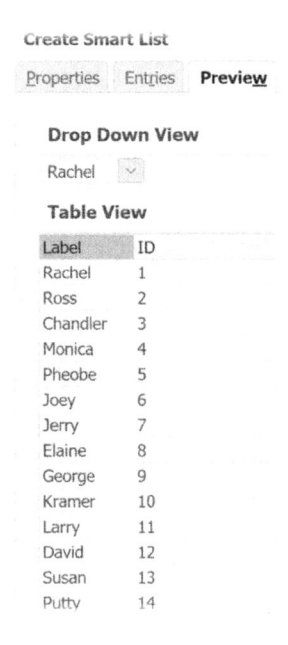

Create Smart List

Properties   Entries   **Preview**

Drop Down View

Rachel

Table View

Label	ID
Rachel	1
Ross	2
Chandler	3
Monica	4
Pheobe	5
Joey	6
Jerry	7
Elaine	8
George	9
Kramer	10
Larry	11
David	12
Susan	13
Putty	14

Our Smart List can now be assigned to a member in a dimension. Back to the Account dimension; it's time to build!

BUILD ACCOUNT DIMENSION

To build the Account dimension,
1. Navigate to *Dimensions* under *Navigator >> Administer*.
2. Select *Account* from the dimension drop-down menu.
3. Click (Add Child).
4. Type "Statistics" for the member name and set properties to match the following:

Look Smarter Than You Are with Enterprise Planning Cloud 93

Name	Statistics
Description	
Alias Table	Default
Alias	
Account Type	Saved Assumption
Variance Reporting	Non-Expense
Time Balance	Flow
Skip	None
Exchange Rate Type	No Rate
Source Plan Type	Sales
Hierarchy Type	Dynamic
Data Storage	Label only
Two Pass Calculation	
Plan Type	Sales ☑ Ignore SalesRpt ☑ Ignore
Data Type	Unspecified
Smart Lists	<None>
Enable for Dynamic Children	☐
Number of Possible Dynamic Children	10
Access Granted to Member Creator	Inherit

5. Under "Statistics", add and set properties for the following "children" members (members placed under the Statistics member):

Member Name	Account Type	Source Plan Type	Data Storage	Consolidation	Data Type
Units	Saved Assumption	Sales	Store	Ignore	Unspecified
List Price	Saved Assumption	Sales	Store	Ignore	Currency
Average Price	Saved Assumption	Sales	Dynamic Calc	Ignore	Currency

If the property is not noted in the table, accept the default value.

Now that the "Statistics" hierarchy is complete, let's add a "Total Revenue" hierarchy to the Account dimension.

6. Select the *Account* dimension name and click (Add Child).
7. Type "4001" as the member name and "Total Revenue" as the alias. Set the properties according to the following:

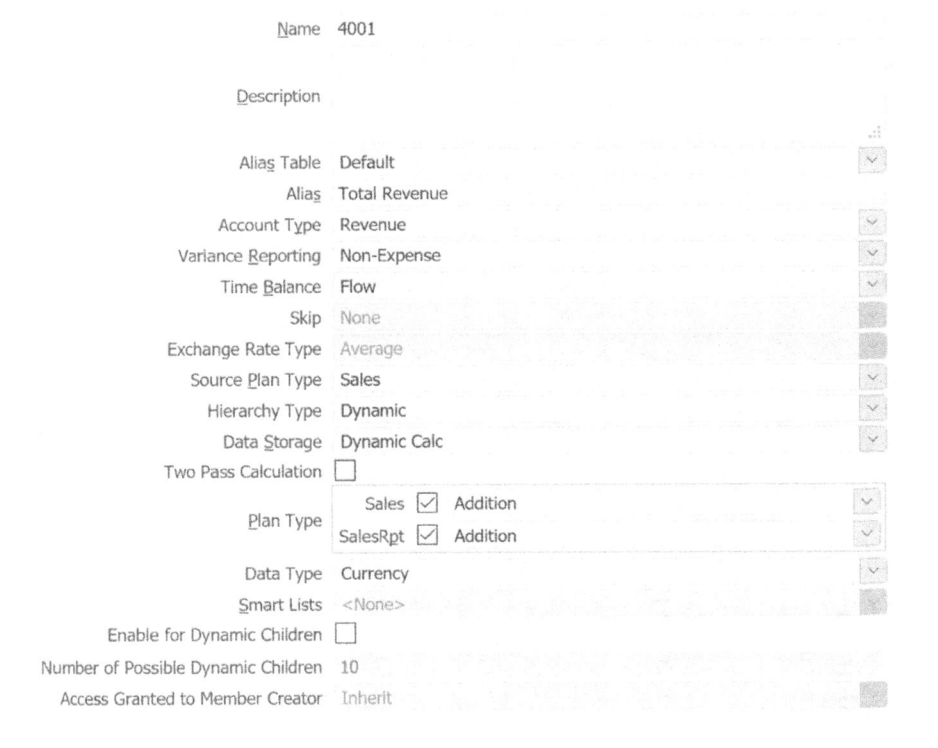

Name	4001
Description	
Alias Table	Default
Alias	Total Revenue
Account Type	Revenue
Variance Reporting	Non-Expense
Time Balance	Flow
Skip	None
Exchange Rate Type	Average
Source Plan Type	Sales
Hierarchy Type	Dynamic
Data Storage	Dynamic Calc
Two Pass Calculation	☐
Plan Type	Sales ☑ Addition
	SalesRpt ☑ Addition
Data Type	Currency
Smart Lists	<None>
Enable for Dynamic Children	☐
Number of Possible Dynamic Children	10
Access Granted to Member Creator	Inherit

8. Add the following "children" members to 4001 (Total Revenue):

Member Name	Alias	Account Type	Source Plan Type	Data Storage	Consolidation	Data Type
4110	Hardware Revenue	Revenue	Sales	Store	Addition	Currency
4120	Support Revenue	Revenue	Sales	Store	Addition	Currency
4130	Consulting Revenue	Revenue	Sales	Store	Addition	Currency
4140	Training Revenue	Revenue	Sales	Store	Addition	Currency
4150	Miscellaneous Revenue	Revenue	Sales	Store	Addition	Currency
4160	Payment Discount	Revenue	Sales	Store	Addition	Currency

9. Refresh the database.

I will load in Actual data by account. For Forecast, however, I will calculate revenue based on inputs from users. Now that I've added all the Account members, I'm going to go back and add some member formulas. These members will have Data Storage set to *Store* and I'll use the <Calculate Data Form> option in data forms so this will automatically calculate for users. I'm using *Store* instead of *Dynamic Calc* because I want this member formula to execute at level 0 members only and then aggregate for upper level dimensions.

10. Edit the *Average Price* member and add the following member formula:

```
"4110"/"Units";
```

11. Edit the *4110* member and add the following member formula:

```
IF (@ISMBR("Forecast"))
  "Units"*"List Price";
ENDIF
```

12. Edit the *4120* member and add the following member formula:

```
IF (@ISMBR("Forecast"))
  "4110"*.18;
ENDIF
```

Note! If a member formula is pasted in, sometimes it may not validate due to a different quotation format (or other character issue). Try manually typing in the quotes or the entire formula instead.

Now I am ready to add the Account member for the Product Manager Smart List.

13. Add an Account member named "Product Manager" with the following properties. Note the *Smart List* Data Type and the *Product_Manager* selection for the Smart Lists property:

Look Smarter Than You Are with Enterprise Planning Cloud

Name	Product Manager
Description	
Alias Table	Default
Alias	
Account Type	Revenue
Variance Reporting	Non-Expense
Time Balance	Flow
Skip	None
Exchange Rate Type	No Rate
Source Plan Type	Sales
Hierarchy Type	Not Set
Data Storage	Never Share
Two Pass Calculation	☐
Plan Type	Sales ☑ Ignore SalesRpt ☑ Ignore
Data Type	SmartList
Smart Lists	Product_Manager
Enable for Dynamic Children	☐
Number of Possible Dynamic Children	10
Access Granted to Member Creator	Inherit

14. Click *Save*.
15. Refresh the database.

The "Product Manager" Account member and Smart List will make its appearance when I build data forms later in my mission.

VIEW & ADD YEARS TO YEARS DIMENSION

Years is one of two Time dimensions. Years will contain the calendar years which were determined when the application was created.

I'm going to add an "All Years" member and go over how to add more years to the application. The "All Years" parent member allows users to view the accumulated data across multiple years – for example, an asset's total depreciation through its end date.

To view the Years dimension,
1. Navigate to *Dimensions* under *Navigator >> Administer*.
2. Select *Years* from the drop-down menu.

3. Review the Years members.
4. To add an "All Years" member, simply go to *Action >> Add "All Years"* or click ![icon] (Add "All Years"):

```
Plan Type  <All Plan Types>  Dimension  Years
Action ▼  View ▼   ➕ ✖ 📋 ✎ ⬇ 📄   ▣ Detach
Year            Alias (Default)      Description
FY10                        Add "All Years"
FY11
```

To add additional years to the Enterprise Planning Cloud application (because time does not stand still),

5. Select the *Years* dimension in the dimension editor.
6. Select *Action >> Add Years*.
7. Enter the number of years to add and click *OK*.
8. Refresh the database.

VIEW PERIOD DIMENSION & ENABLE DTS

It is standard for an Enterprise Planning Cloud application to have two Time dimensions. The second time dimension is Period, which includes periods like months, weeks, and quarters. The calendar for the Period dimension was created during the application creation wizard.

To view the Period dimension,
1. Navigate to *Dimensions* under *Navigator >> Administer*.
2. Select *Period* from the drop-down menu.
3. Explore the members and add the full month name as an alias, if desired (*Edit* member, type in Alias and *Save*).

Note! If users need to enter data into the BegBalance member (e.g., for statistical, Smart List, or free form text accounts that aren't stored by period), make sure to check *Include BegBalance as Time Period* under Scenario members properties:

Look Smarter Than You Are with Enterprise Planning Cloud 99

Edit Member : Plan

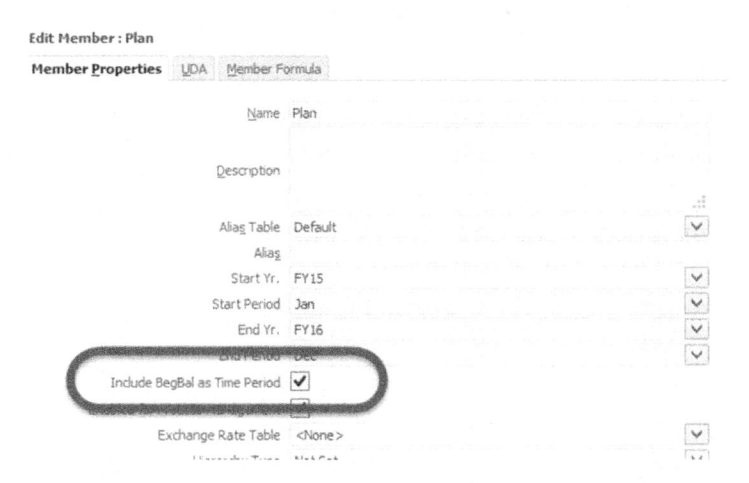

Name	Plan
Description	
Alias Table	Default
Alias	
Start Yr.	FY15
Start Period	Jan
End Yr.	FY16
End Period	Dec
Include BegBal as Time Period	✓
Exchange Rate Table	<None>

Dynamic-time-series (DTS) allows users to retrieve dynamic 'to-date' totals from the Enterprise Planning Cloud database.

To enable DTS,

1. In the Period dimension, select *Action >> DTS* or click (DTS).
2. Check the options for *YTD* and *QTD,* and assign the correct generations as follows:

Period : Dynamic Time Series

Series	Enabled	Generation	Alias Names
Y-T-D	✓	1	
H-T-D	☐	Unassigned	
S-T-D	☐	Unassigned	
Q-T-D	✓	2	
P-T-D	☐	Unassigned	
M-T-D	☐	Unassigned	
W-T-D	☐	Unassigned	
D-T-D	☐	Unassigned	

3. Click *Edit Alias Names* to add an alias, if desired.
4. Click *Save*.
5. Refresh the database.

View HSP_View Dimension

The HSP_View dimension is created when sandboxes are enabled and members are automatically created. Neither the dimension nor its members can be altered, and the members should not be reordered within the dimension.

The members in the HSP_View dimension include:

- **BaseData** – where data is stored when users are working in a non-sandbox view in a form
- **SandboxData** – where data is stored when users work in a sandbox
- **ConsolidatedData** – dynamically calculated member that retrieves data from the SandboxData member when it is available; otherwise, it retrieves the data from the BaseData member

To view the HSP_View dimension,
1. Navigate to *Dimensions* under *Navigator >> Administer*.
2. Select *HSP_View* from the drop-down menu.
3. Explore the members and their properties.

Note! For aggregations to work in the Sandbox view, sparse dimension parent members (such as Entity or custom dimensions) must be set to *Dynamic Calc*. This is also true for Hybrid Aggregation Mode once it is supported.

Because who doesn't love to play in a sandbox, I have a whole chapter dedicated to Sandboxing at the end of the book.

Create Custom Product Dimension

Enterprise Planning Cloud allows many custom dimensions for a plan type; however, it is best to limit the number of dimensions for any application. Some examples of custom dimensions include Customers, Employees, Products, and Projects. Custom dimensions can be assigned to specific plan types (meaning each plan type can have unique dimensions that don't have to belong or exist in another plan type). Once created, a dimension cannot be deleted without going through some serious gyrations.

To create a custom dimension,
1. Navigate to *Console* and in the *Application* side tab (first tab), click the *Dimensions* tab:

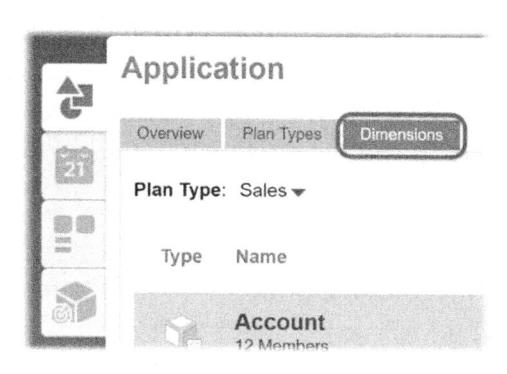

2. To the right, you will see buttons for Create, Import, and Export. Click *Create*.
3. Type in "Product" for the dimension name and check *Enabled* for both Sales and SalesRpt plan types. Leave the other options as default:

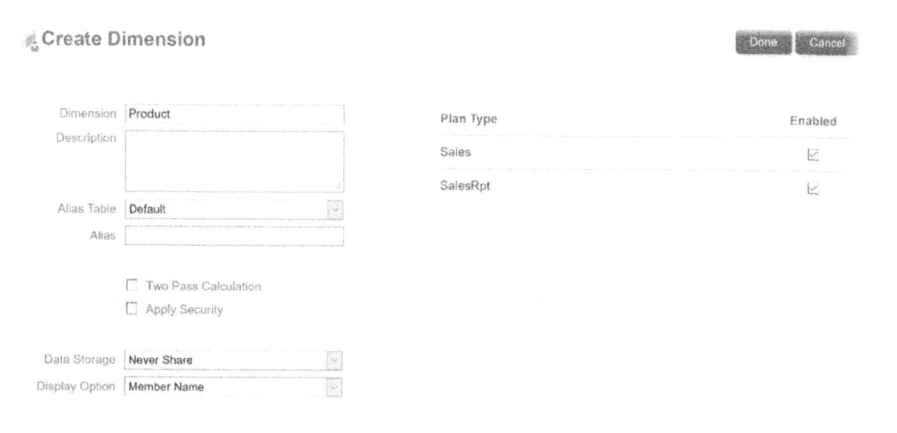

4. Click *Done*.
5. Refresh the database.

Now that the Product dimension has been created, it's time to prepare the import file.

IMPORT & EXPORT DIMENSIONS

Up until now I have defined all the dimensions manually through the dimension editor. Dimensions can be imported using the "Import Metadata" or "Export Metadata" function in the Simplified UI. So when I say "metadata", most of the time in Enterprise Planning Cloud, I mean "dimensions". Flat files are the only available source in Enterprise Planning Cloud. Data Management does not support the import or export of dimensions (yet).

Integration	Integration Option	Where	Valid Sources
Load Dimensions	Hyperion Planning format (using Outline Load Utility UI)	Simplified UI or Workspace UI (under covers Outline Load Utility)	Flat File only
Export Dimensions	Hyperion Planning format (using Outline Load Utility UI)	Simplified UI or Workspace UI (under covers Outline Load Utility)	Flat File only

Export a Dimension

You can easily create a template to help get the import file ready by exporting a dimension. You may also want to export dimensions for other purposes (for example, loading to other systems). The dimension will be exported in a "parent-child" format; generational or level exports of dimensions are not supported.

To export a dimension,
1. Navigate to *Console* and in *Application*, click the *Dimensions* tab.
2. Click the *Export* button, then *Create*.

3. Check the box next to Product and click the option for *Comma delimited* (default):

| ☑ | Product
0 Members | ● Comma delimited ○ Tab delimited ○ Other | No details are available. |

4. Click *Export*. Save the file (which normally defaults to your Downloads folder) and open (search for the most recent zip file). You should see the following in Excel:

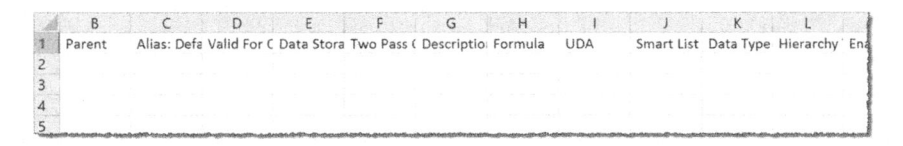

	B	C	D	E	F	G	H	I	J	K	L
1	Parent	Alias: Defa	Valid For C	Data Stora	Two Pass (	Descriptio	Formula	UDA	Smart List	Data Type	Hierarchy Ena
2											
3											
4											
5											

I can now use this file to build my Product dimension file for importing. I like to use Notepad++ or other text editors when creating these files. If I use Excel, I need to be careful with members with only numbers as the member name (e.g., "4110" as an Account member name) since those will be viewed as numeric values. Using a text editor like Notepad++ avoids that and other common CSV headaches.

Import Members for Product Dimension

Now to import members for the Product dimension,

1. Create the Product dimension by completing the template (or email info@interrel.com for a copy of the file). Save the template as a CSV file.

Once the template has been completed, it should look something like the following (not all properties are shown):

Product	Parent	Alias: Default	Valid For Consolidations	Data Storage	Two Pass Calculation	Description	Formula	UDA
P_TP		Product Total Product	FALSE	dynamic calc	FALSE		<none>	
P_000	P_TP	No Product	FALSE	store	FALSE		<none>	
P_HW	P_TP	Hardware Products	FALSE	dynamic calc	FALSE		<none>	
P_TP1	P_HW	Computer Equipment	FALSE	dynamic calc	FALSE		<none>	
P_100	P_TP1	Product X	FALSE	store	FALSE		<none>	
P_110	P_TP1	Sentinal Standard Notebook	FALSE	store	FALSE		<none>	
P_120	P_TP1	Sentinal Custom Notebook	FALSE	store	FALSE		<none>	
P_130	P_TP1	Envoy Standard Netbook	FALSE	store	FALSE		<none>	
P_140	P_TP1	Envoy Custom Netbook	FALSE	store	FALSE		<none>	
P_150	P_TP1	Other Computer	FALSE	store	FALSE		<none>	
P_160	P_TP1	Tablet Computer	FALSE	store	FALSE		<none>	
P_TP2	P_HW	Computer Accessories	FALSE	dynamic calc	FALSE		<none>	
P_200	P_TP2	Accessories	FALSE	store	FALSE		<none>	
P_210	P_TP2	Keyboard	FALSE	store	FALSE		<none>	
P_220	P_TP2	Software Suite	FALSE	store	FALSE		<none>	
P_230	P_TP2	Monitor	FALSE	store	FALSE		<none>	
P_240	P_TP2	Modem	FALSE	store	FALSE		<none>	
P_250	P_TP2	Network Card	FALSE	store	FALSE		<none>	
P_260	P_TP2	Game	FALSE	store	FALSE		<none>	

Parent members have been set to *Dynamic Calc* so I can leverage hybrid aggregation mode in our plan type (remember, when hybrid aggregation mode is supported in the future, I must tag upper level members tagged as "Dynamic Calc" to utilize the hybrid engine).

2. Navigate to *Console* and click the *Dimensions* tab.
3. Click *Import*, then *Create*.
4. Navigate to the *Product* dimension and click *Browse…*
5. Select the Product CSV file. Click *Open*.
6. Click *Import* (at the top of the screen).
7. Do not check the option to *Refresh Database if Import Metadata is successful*:

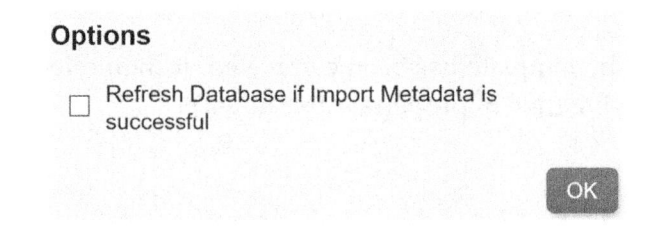

Options

☐ Refresh Database if Import Metadata is successful

OK

The *Refresh Database if Import Metadata is successful* option will force Enterprise Planning Cloud to refresh the metadata to Essbase if there are no issues with the metadata import. This is a necessary step when you change the application structure – otherwise, the changes won't be reflected to the users until the refresh has occurred. However, refreshing the database is a maintenance task and has an impact to any users that are currently connected. Therefore, I will defer the refresh of the database to later.

8. Click *OK*, then *OK* again.
9. Click *Refresh* at the top of the page and you should see the following message on the right:

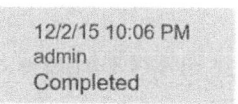

> 12/2/15 10:06 PM
> admin
> Completed

10. Click the *Completed* link. If there are errors during the import process, they will be displayed in the next screen.
11. Check out the Product dimension in the dimension editor:

Name	Alias (Default)	Data Storage
⊿ Product		Never Share
⊿ P_TP	Total Product	Dynamic Calc
P_000	No Product	Store
⊿ P_HW	Hardware Products	Dynamic Calc
⊿ P_TP1	Computer Equipment	Dynamic Calc
P_100	Product X	Store
P_110	Sentinal Standard Notebook	Store
P_120	Sentinal Custom Notebook	Store
P_130	Envoy Standard Netbook	Store
P_140	Envoy Custom Netbook	Store
P_150	Other Computer	Store
P_160	Tablet Computer	Store
⊿ P_TP2	Computer Accessories	Dynamic Calc
P_200	Accessories	Store
P_210	Keyboard	Store
P_220	Software Suite	Store
P_230	Monitor	Store
P_240	Modem	Store
P_250	Network Card	Store
P_260	Game	Store
P_270	Camera	Store
P_280	Television	Store
⊿ P_SVC	Services	Dynamic Calc
⊿ P_TP3	Computer Services	Dynamic Calc
P_291	Training_P_291	Store

12. Refresh the database to push changes to Essbase.

Using the same process as the Product dimension, let's build the Entity dimension. To follow along the build process for the Product and Entity dimension, please email info@interrel.com for sample flat files.

> **Note!** You can import and export dimensions in the Workspace UI via the Outline Load Utility over the web (*Administration >> Import and Export* menu).

Import Members for Entity Dimension

The Entity dimension differentiates between organizational entities. This dimension can be called Organizations, Cost Centers, Departments, Locations, etc. Process management (or approvals; how plans are promoted up the hierarchy) primarily follows the Entity hierarchy structure.

To build the Entity dimension with a flat file,

1. Create an Entity CSV file using the same process as the Product dimension (or email i.n.t.e.r.R.e.l for a copy of the file):

Entity	Parent	Alias: Default	Valid For Con	Data Storage	Two Pass Ca
Total Entity	Entity		FALSE	dynamic calc	FALSE
TD	Total Entity	Total Department	FALSE	dynamic calc	FALSE
0	TD	No Department	FALSE	store	FALSE
100	TD	Resources	FALSE	dynamic calc	FALSE
110	100	Facilities Resources	FALSE	store	FALSE
111	100	West Region Resources	FALSE	store	FALSE
112	100	East Region Resources	FALSE	store	FALSE
120	100	Machine Resources	FALSE	store	FALSE
130	100	Computer Resources	FALSE	store	FALSE
140	100	Communications Resources	FALSE	store	FALSE
200	TD	Other Corporate	FALSE	dynamic calc	FALSE
210	200	US Organization	FALSE	store	FALSE
220	200	CAD Organization	FALSE	store	FALSE

> **Note!** Column headers are case-sensitive and must match the template exactly.

2. Save as a CSV file.
3. Navigate to *Console* and click the *Dimensions* tab.
4. Click *Import*, then *Create*.

5. Navigate to the Entity dimension and click *Browse...*
6. Select the Entity CSV file and click *Open*.
7. Click *Import*, *OK* and *OK* again.
8. Click *Refresh* until the import is complete, then check for any errors.
9. Refresh the database.
10. Check out the Entity dimension in the dimension editor:

Entity		Never Share
⊿ Total Entity		Dynamic Calc
⊿ TD	Total Department	Dynamic Calc
> 0	No Department	Store
> 100	Resources	Dynamic Calc
> 200	Other Corporate	Dynamic Calc
> 403	Sales	Dynamic Calc
> 500	Manufacturing	Dynamic Calc
> 601	Other Departments	Dynamic Calc
> 700	Finance and Accounting	Dynamic Calc
> 800	HR and Administration	Dynamic Calc
Enterprise Global		Store
Unspecified Entity		Store
No Entity		Store

OK, the dimensions are all built. Now to explore some metadata administration options.

Export Multiple Dimensions

I already completed these steps to export a single dimension to get a file template that I can use for importing. You can choose to export more than one dimension at a time if required.

To export multiple dimensions (use the same steps discussed earlier),

1. Navigate to *Console* >> *Application*, then click the *Dimensions* tab.
2. Click the *Export* button, then *Create*.
3. Check the box next to *Account, Entity,* and *Product*.
4. Click the radio button for *Comma delimited* (or *Tab delimited* if preferred):

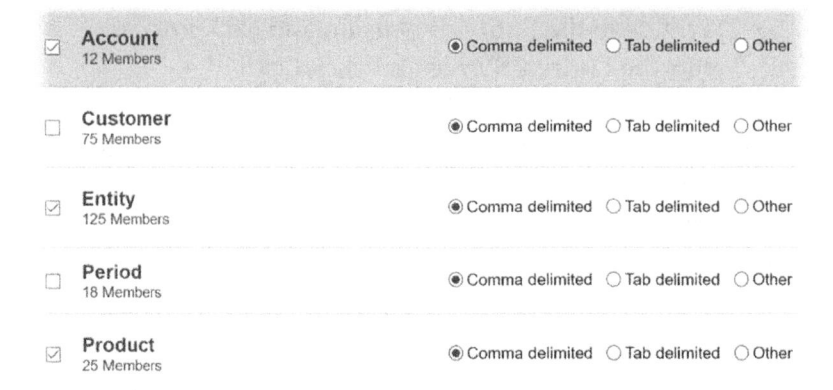

☑ **Account** 12 Members	◉ Comma delimited ○ Tab delimited ○ Other
☐ **Customer** 75 Members	◉ Comma delimited ○ Tab delimited ○ Other
☑ **Entity** 125 Members	◉ Comma delimited ○ Tab delimited ○ Other
☐ **Period** 18 Members	◉ Comma delimited ○ Tab delimited ○ Other
☑ **Product** 25 Members	◉ Comma delimited ○ Tab delimited ○ Other

5. Click *Export*.
6. Click *OK* to save files:

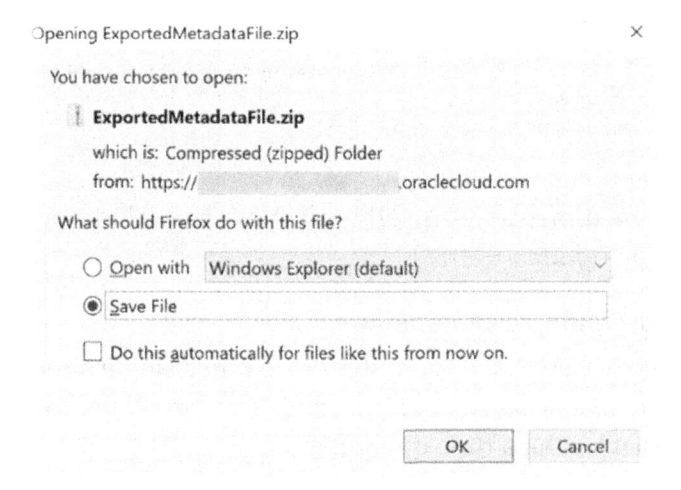

7. Open the compressed folder and open a file to view:

☑ admin_ExportedMetadata_Account
   admin_ExportedMetadata_Entity
   admin_ExportedMetadata_Product

The resulting file is as shown below:

Account	Parent	Alias: Default	Valid For (	Data Storage	Two Pass	Descri Formula
4001		Total Revenue	FALSE	dynamic calc	FALSE	<none>
4110	4001	Hardware	FALSE	store	FALSE	If(@ISMBR("Forec
4120	4001	Support	FALSE	store	FALSE	If(@ISMBR("Forec
4130	4001	Consulting	FALSE	store	FALSE	<none>
4140	4001	Training	FALSE	store	FALSE	<none>
4150	4001	Miscellaneous Reve	FALSE	store	FALSE	<none>
4160	4001	Payment Discount	FALSE	store	FALSE	<none>
Statistics	Account		FALSE	label only	FALSE	<none>
Units	Statistics		FALSE	store	FALSE	<none>
List Price	Statistics		FALSE	never share	FALSE	<none>
Average Price	Statistics		FALSE	dynamic calc	FALSE	"4110"/"Units";
Product Manag	Account		FALSE	never share	FALSE	<none>

Note! Remember, parent-child format is the only supported export option for Enterprise Planning Cloud today. This sort of stinks because Cloud products like Business Intelligence Cloud Service (BICS) and Data Visualization Cloud Service (DVCS) only support generational dimension formats.

USE EXCEL TO UPDATE DIMENSIONS

I've now updated dimensions over the web and I've imported dimensions from a flat file. I can also use Microsoft Excel! With Enterprise Planning Cloud, administrators can update metadata in Excel with the Smart View add in.

To take use Excel to update dimensions and members,
1. Go to *Navigator >> Install* and click *Smart View Add-on for Administrator*.
2. Install the utility.
3. Open Excel and go to the Smart View ribbon.

If you have an older version of Smart View installed, you might have to uninstall and reinstall the version available in Enterprise Planning Cloud. To install Smart View, go to *Navigator >> Install* and click the *Smart View for Office* link.

4. Configure Smart View to connect with the Enterprise Planning Cloud instance. Go to *Options* and type in the Shared Connections URL. A sample of the URL is below:

https://<yourPlanningCloudURLpln.pbcs.us1.oracleCloud.com>/workspace/SmartViewProviders

General	
Shared Connections URL:	oraclecloud.com/workspace/SmartViewProviders
Number of Undo Actions	9
Number of Most Recently Used items	9
Delete All MRU Items	

5. Click *OK*.
6. Connect to the instance. Click the *Panel* (very left of the Smart View ribbon), then click *Shared Connections*:

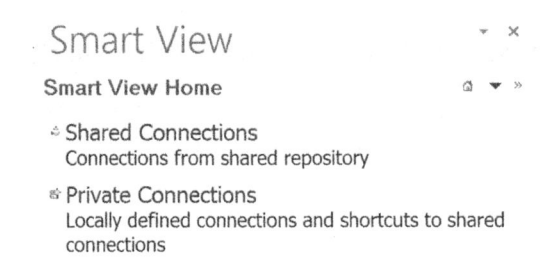

Smart View

Smart View Home

⁂ Shared Connections
Connections from shared repository

⁂ Private Connections
Locally defined connections and shortcuts to shared connections

7. You should be prompted to log into Enterprise Planning Cloud. Enter the domain and login credentials.
8. From the Panel drop-down menu, select *Oracle Hyperion Planning, Fusion Edition*.
9. Expand the server and application folder. Since I installed the administrator utility, I see a new "Dimensions" folder:

Look Smarter Than You Are with Enterprise Planning Cloud 111

```
Smart View                                        ▼ ×
Shared Connections                          ⌂ ▼ »
Oracle® Hyperion Planning, Fusion Edition    ▼  +  ▼
  ⊟ planning-            .oraclecloud.com
    ⊟ VISION
      ⊞ Dimensions
      ⊞ Forms
      ⊞ Task Lists
      ⊞ Sales
      ⊞ SalesRpt
```

10. Open the *Dimensions* folder.
11. To edit a dimension, right-click and select *Edit Dimension*. I'll edit the Account dimension.
12. Drill down the Account dimension by selecting the cell with the dimension name.
13. Navigate to the Planning Ad Hoc ribbon and *Zoom in >> All Levels*.

I can do *Zoom In* on *All Levels* because I know my dimension is pretty small; for large dimensions, I might want to zoom into specific sections of the dimension hierarchy. I can use other ribbon options like *Keep Only* or *Remove Only* to narrow my focus on the desired members.

The dimension will show in Excel with all the column properties:

Account	Parent Member	Default Data Storage	Sales Data Storage	SalesRpt Data Storage	Data Type	Sales Consol
		Never Share	Never Share	Never Share	Currency	Ignore
4001	Account	Dynamic Calc	Dynamic Calc	Dynamic Calc	Currency	Addition
4110	4001	Dynamic Calc	Dynamic Calc	Dynamic Calc	Currency	Addition
4120	4001	Dynamic Calc	Dynamic Calc	Dynamic Calc	Currency	Addition
4130	4001	Store	Store	Store	Currency	Addition
4140	4001	Store	Store	Store	Currency	Addition
4150	4001	Store	Store	Store	Currency	Addition
4160	4001	Store	Store	Store	Currency	Addition
Statistics	Account	Label only	Label only	Label only	Unspecified	Ignore
Units	Statistics	Store	Store	Store	Non-Currency	Addition
List Price	Statistics	Never Share	Never Share	Never Share	Currency	Ignore
Average Price	Statistics	Dynamic Calc	Dynamic Calc	Dynamic Calc	Currency	Ignore
Product Manager	Account	Never Share	Never Share	Never Share	Smart List	Ignore

From this worksheet, I can add and edit members and member properties. To insert a new member, simply right-click and use plain ol' Excel functionality. Type in the new member name in the blue section and then enter the member properties:

	A	B	C	D	E
1		Parent Member	Default Data Storage	Sales Data Storage	SalesRpt Data Storage
2	Account		Never Share	Never Share	Never Share
3	4001	Account	Dynamic Calc	Dynamic Calc	Dynamic Calc
4	4110	4001	Store	Store	Store
5	4120	4001	Store	Store	Store
6	4130	4001	Store	Store	Store
7	4140	4001	Store	Store	Store
8	4150	4001	Store	Store	Store
9	4160	4001	Store		Store
10	4170	4001	Store	Store	

To save changes to the dimension in Enterprise Planning Cloud, click *Submit Data*. The changes will be reflected in the application:

Submit Data has not refreshed the database or pushed changes back to Essbase yet. To refresh the database from Smart View, right-click *Dimensions* in the Smart View Panel and select *Refresh Database* to save changes to Essbase:

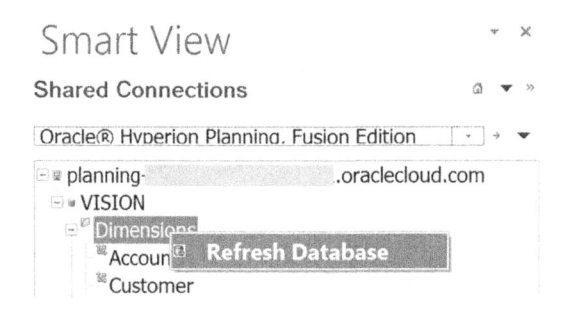

A window will appear asking what you'd like to refresh. Click *Database* and then click *Refresh*:

Refresh Database

- [✓] Database
- [ ] Update custom-defined functions
- [ ] Security Filters
  - [ ] Shared Members
- [ ] Validate Limit

[Refresh] [Cancel]

The options here relate to the various refresh options. *Database* and *Security Filters* should be used when dimension hierarchies have changed. When updating security filters, the option to refresh *Shared Members* (members that appear in more than one sub-hierarchy across a single dimension) as well as *Validate Limit* are available. As there are no shared members in this updated dimension and we're not concerned about hitting the security filters limit, these options won't be selected. Not selecting options improves performance. *Update custom-defined functions* updates Enterprise Planning Cloud custom-defined functions for the application. This option is grayed out, as it does not apply to this application.

14. A warning message will appear. Click *OK*:

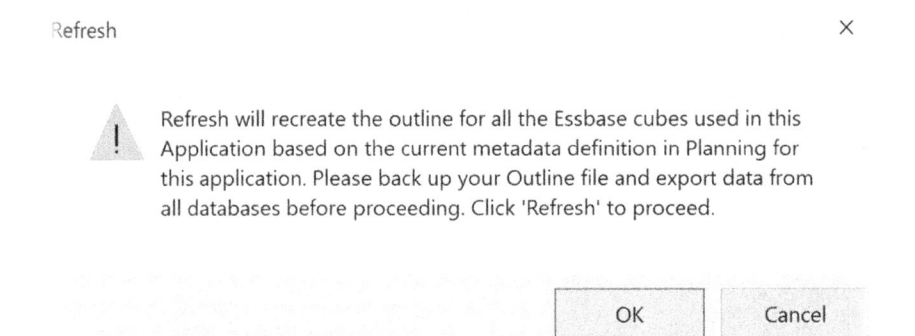

Refresh ✕

⚠ Refresh will recreate the outline for all the Essbase cubes used in this Application based on the current metadata definition in Planning for this application. Please back up your Outline file and export data from all databases before proceeding. Click 'Refresh' to proceed.

OK Cancel

15. A progress bar will appear to show you the refresh progress. When the refresh is complete click *Finish*:

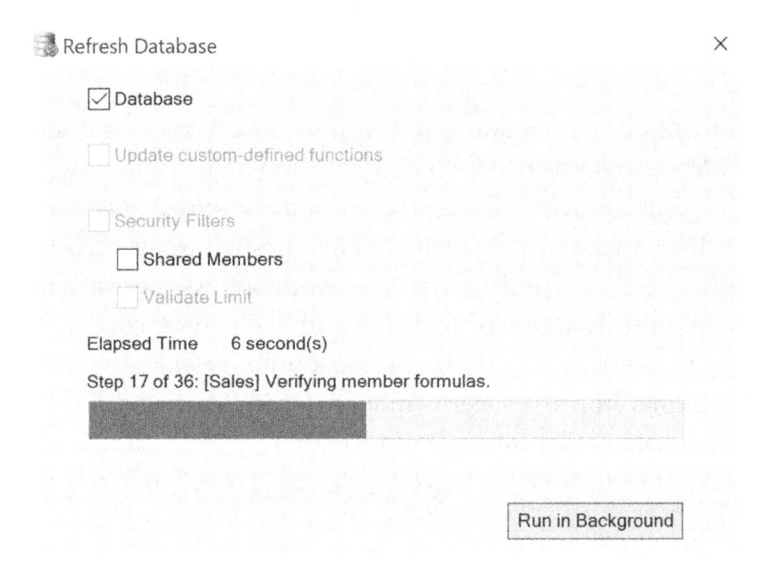

Refresh Database ✕

☑ Database

☐ Update custom-defined functions

☐ Security Filters
 ☐ Shared Members
☐ Validate Limit

Elapsed Time   6 second(s)
Step 17 of 36: [Sales] Verifying member formulas.

Run in Background

16. Upon refreshing the Smart View sheet, the new member appears as part of the Account dimension list:

Account	Parent Member	Default Data Storage	Sales Data Storage	SalesRpt Data Storage	Data Type	Sales Consol op
		Never Share	Never Share	Never Share	Currency	Ignore
4001	Account	Dynamic Calc	Dynamic Calc	Dynamic Calc	Currency	Addition
4110	4001	Store	Store	Store	Currency	Addition
4120	4001	Store	Store	Store	Currency	Addition
4130	4001	Store	Store	Store	Currency	Addition
4140	4001	Store	Store	Store	Currency	Addition
4150	4001	Store	Store	Store	Currency	Addition
4160	4001	Store	Store	Store	Currency	Addition
4170	4001	Store	Store	Store	Currency	Addition
Statistics	Account	Label only	Label only	Label only	Unspecified	Ignore
Units	Statistics	Store	Store	Store	Non-Current	Addition
List Price	Statistics	Never Share	Never Share	Never Share	Currency	Ignore
Average Price	Statistics	Dynamic Calc	Dynamic Calc	Dynamic Calc	Currency	Ignore
Product Manager	Account	Never Share	Never Share	Never Share	Smart List	Ignore

ATTRIBUTE DIMENSIONS

Block storage plan types / databases are limited in the number of dimensions that you can have per database (by practicality, if nothing else). The maximum dimensions in BSO is usually around nine to 10 dimensions, and the fewer, the better. But users complained that they needed to be able to analyze data by more dimensions.

For instance, for Vision's product dimension, they might want to also analyze Product Start Date, Product Type, and Target Group. Since all these "dimensions" are really just alternate ways of divvying up the Product dimension (in this example), attribute dimensions might be a good design choice.

Attribute dimensions are dimensions that can be placed in the rows or columns with some special considerations. Just like regular dimensions, they define characteristics about the data that is loaded to Essbase. They have hierarchies and members just like any other dimension.

One of the special qualities of attribute dimensions is that adding them to the outline does not impact the size of the Essbase database. You can add a virtually unlimited number of attribute dimensions.

You can analyze sum totals, minimums, maximums, averages and counts of members in attribute dimensions which certainly isn't possible with UDAs.

Attribute dimensions are supported in block storage and aggregate storage plan types. However, within Enterprise Planning Cloud, there are some limits with attributes in ASO plan types in the current version. An upcoming version will have full support for attribute dimensions in all of the plan types.

Varying attributes are not supported for Enterprise Planning Cloud (this is an on-premise Essbase only feature). You would use Smart Lists instead of varying attributes if the attribute varied over time.

But wait, before you get too excited, know there are performance considerations! Attribute dimensions are always dynamically calculated in block storage plan types which could mean slower performance any time an attribute is referenced in data forms and retrievals. I'll also need to watch how hybrid aggregation plan types will support attribute dimensions in the future.

In some cases, the design decisions are clear cut on when to use UDAs vs. alternate hierarchies vs. attribute dimensions vs. smart lists. In other scenarios, the answer will be less obvious. Once attributes are fully supported as a "dimension" in Oracle Enterprise Planning Cloud in an upcoming release, I will start to use attributes for analytic purposes in addition to filtering or calculation purposes. Let's review some design decision points.

When should you use Attributes?

Use when the attribute does not vary over time; it has a one-to-one relationship with its base member.

Use attributes when you need to identify a group of members for calculation purposes or you want to filter for members in a data form based on an attribute. This use case is available for both BSO and ASO plan types.

Attributes are very helpful when performing comparisons based on certain types of data or when performing calculations based on characteristics.

When not to use Attributes?

Do not use attributes when you need to define characteristics that vary over time. For example, let's say I have "Employee Status" as an attribute dimension based on the "Employee" dimension. Jack was run over by a bus in October and his employee status was changed from "Active" to "Inactive" to reflect his untimely death. If I run reports for the month of January, it will look like Jack was "inactive/no longer with us" for that month. Jack was alive and kicking for months January through September, but Oracle Enterprise Cloud has no way of knowing this because employee status is solely tied to the Employee dimension.

If you need to track how an attribute changes over time, make the attribute an account tied to a smart list. Or you could make it a stored dimension (but watch out and don't add too many dimensions).

Do not use attributes when you need to calculate a value by placing a formula on a member (member formulas aren't allowed on attribute members). Watch out for attributes when you need to improve retrieval performance (attributes are dynamically calculated and can be slow at times).

Types of Attributes

There are four types of Attribute dimensions: Text, Numeric, Boolean, and Date.

Text attributes are the default type and are used to describe text characteristics.

When AND, OR NOT, <, >, =, >=, <=, <>, !=, IN, and NOT IN operations are performed on text dimensions, Essbase makes logical comparisons for text attribute dimensions. Not always the most logical thing to do, but it's there all the same.

Numeric attribute dimensions contain numeric values at level 0. You can perform AND, OR NOT, <, >, =, >=, <=, <>, !=, IN, and NOT IN operations on numeric attribute dimensions. You can group numeric values into ranges (using the : symbol) and include these numeric values in calculations.

Boolean attribute dimensions contain exactly two members (that are defined by the user): True and False, Left and Right, Yes and No, Up and Down, Dog and Cat, or any other two members that you want. Once the two Boolean member names are defined, you must use the same names for all Boolean attribute dimensions in the database. When you perform AND, OR NOT, <, >, =, >=, <=, <>, !=, IN, and NOT IN operations on Boolean attribute dimensions, Essbase translates true to 1 and false to 0.

Date attribute members must contain date members at level-0 that are formatted properly. Valid date formats are mm-dd-yyyy or dd-mm-yyyy. All dates must be after 01-01-1970 and before 01-01-2038.

AND, OR NOT, <, >, =, >=, <=, <>, !=, IN, and NOT IN operations can be performed on Date attribute dimensions. Date values can be also included in calculations.

There are five ways to calculate attribute data: Sum, Count, Average, Minimum, and Maximum. Sum is the default when you don't specify which one to use, but you can use the other calculations as though it was yet another dimension.

There are a few rules when it comes to building attribute dimensions and members:

- Consider the implication of Dynamic Calculations as reporting on Attribute dimensions can be slow
- Define attribute dimensions on sparse dimensions only
- You cannot tag attribute members as a shared members
- You cannot tag attribute members as two-pass calculation
- You cannot assign a UDA to attribute members
- You cannot use consolidation symbols or formulas

Create an Attribute Dimension

I won't create an attribute for my Vision application but I'll show you the basic steps in case you want to add an attribute dimension to your application.

To create an attribute dimension and its members,
1. In the Simplified UI, select *Navigator >> Dimension Editor*.
2. Select the desired sparse dimension from the Dimension drop down.
3. Select the dimension member name in the Dimension Editor (if you highlight any other member in the hierarchy, the *Custom Attributes* button is disabled).
4. Select the *Custom Attributes* button:

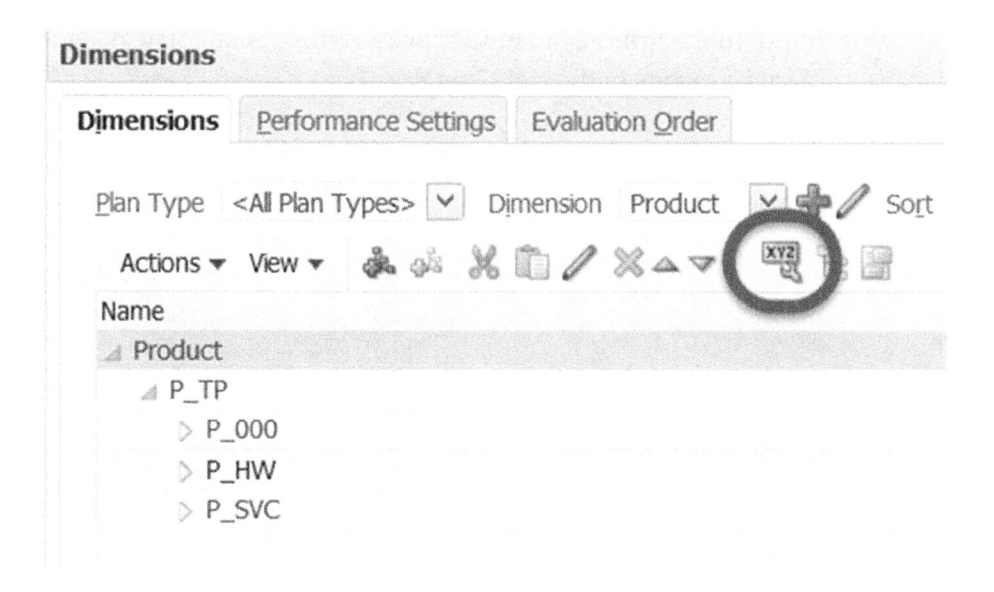

Look Smarter Than You Are with Enterprise Planning Cloud 119

5. Select the *Add* button in the left panel to create a new attribute dimension.
6. Enter the name of the custom attribute: "Quality Manager" and select *Text* as the Data Type:

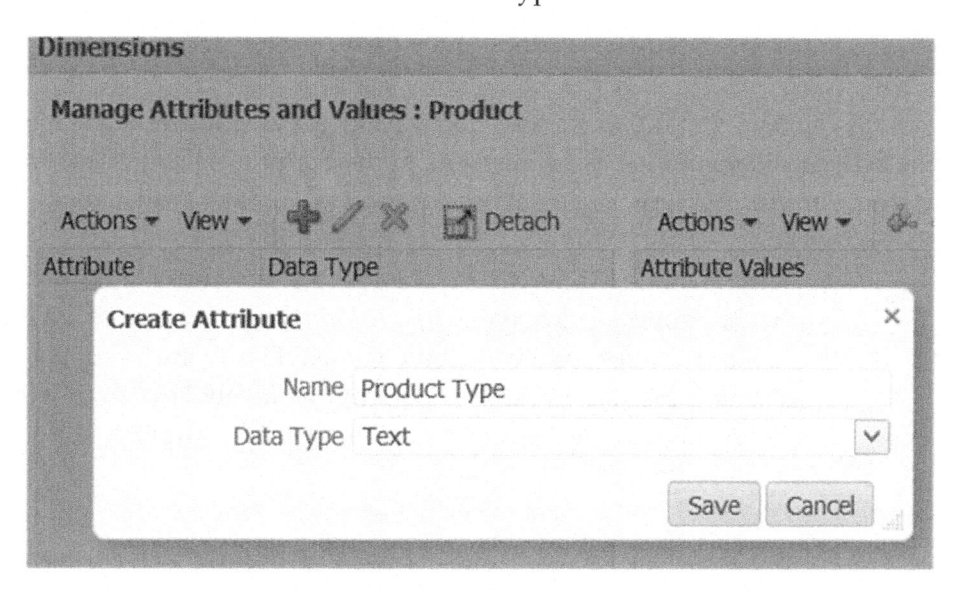

7. Click the *Save* button.

8. Add the Attribute members by selecting *Add Child* or *Add Members* icons in the right panel:

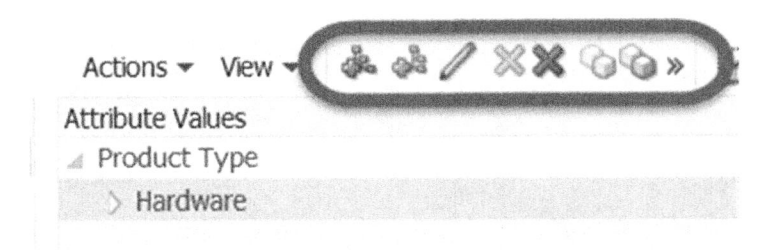

```
Actions ▼  View ▼   [icons]
Attribute Values
  ⊿ Product Type
      > Hardware
```

You can also add aliases by clicking the *Add Alias* icon:

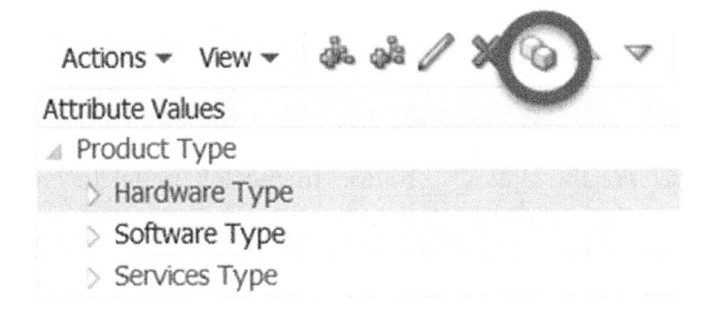

```
Actions ▼  View ▼   [icons]
Attribute Values
  ⊿ Product Type
      > Hardware Type
      > Software Type
      > Services Type
```

You can also move attribute members up and down using the arrow icons.

The next step for attributes is to associate the attribute members to the base members of the base dimension. In the example below, I need to assign a product type to the actual product.

9. Select the desired member in the Product dimension and click the *Edit* button. Select the *Attribute Values* tab.
10. Assign the appropriate attribute value ("Hardware Type") by selecting the radio button and using the arrow keys to move the member to the Assigned Attribute value window:

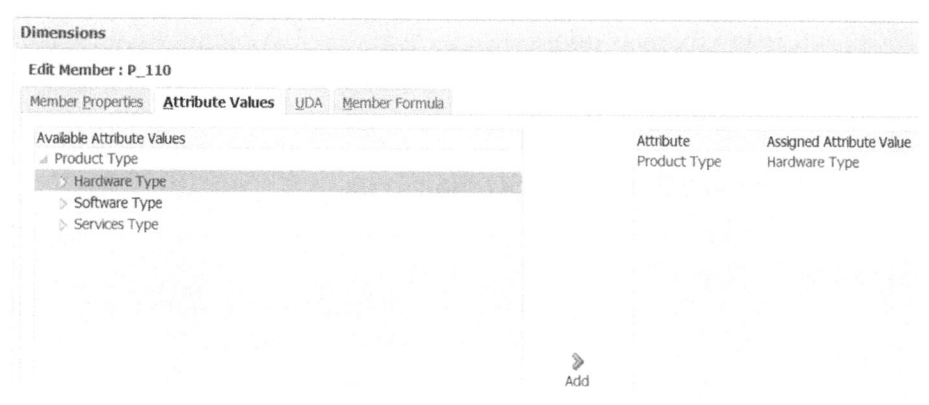

Dimensions				
Edit Member : P_110				
Member Properties **Attribute Values** UDA Member Formula				
Available Attribute Values			Attribute	Assigned Attribute Value
▲ Product Type			Product Type	Hardware Type
▷ Hardware Type				
▷ Software Type				
▷ Services Type				

≫
Add

11. Click *Save* and *Close*.
12. Repeat for the other members.
13. Finally refresh the database.

Note you can upload attribute dimensions and attribute dimension associations using the same import and export functionality of the Simplified Planning UI discussed in the previous section.

I walked through an example of creating a text attribute dimension but remember that you can create numeric, date, and Boolean attributes.

SET PLAN TYPE DEFINITIONS

Set Dimensions as Dense or Sparse

For BSO plan types, dimensions are assigned a property of dense or sparse, which impacts how the underlying database is created. This setting affects application performance.

Dense data occurs often or repeatedly across the intersection of all member combinations. You will most likely have data for all periods and most of your accounts for member combinations.

Sparse data occurs periodically or sparsely across member combinations. Dimensions like Entity or Product are usually sparse. Please review the Appendix on Essbase at the end of the book for a more comprehensive look at this topic.

To set dimensions as dense or sparse,
1. Navigate to *Console* and click the *Dimensions* tab.

2. Check the box for *Dense* for the *Account* and *Period* dimensions to tag them as dense.
3. Leave the other dimensions unchecked to tag them as sparse.
4. Refresh the database.

Dimension Order for BSO Plan Type

Dimension ordering is critical to Essbase performance in BSO plan types. Can't I just order alphabetically? NO!

First, a few definitions to understand the different types of dimensions (this will help us figure out the best order):

- **Dense dimensions** – dimensions that define the internal structure of the data block; they should reside at the top of the order
- **Aggregating Sparse dimensions** – dimensions that will be calculated to create new parent values; these dimensions should reside directly after the last dense dimension (placing these dimensions as the first sparse dimensions positions them to be the first dimensions included in the calculator cache, which gives them an ideal location for optimized calculation performance)
- **Non-Aggregating Sparse dimensions** – dimensions that organize the data into logical slices (e.g., Scenario, Version, and Years); not crucial for these dimensions to be included in the calculator cache because their members are typically isolated in FIX statements of calculation scripts for business rules

With these types of dimensions in mind, a common order is to create the "hourglass on a stick". The general starting point would be to have Period first, then Account. The aggregating sparse dimensions would go next in the outline order, followed by the non-aggregating sparse dimensions. If there is a sparse dimension that is frequently in rows, consider moving that dimension to be the first sparse dimension after the dense dimensions.

There is no one right answer. Test iterations of dense and sparse dimensions to figure out the optimal settings for your BSO plan types.

Note! Outline order only matters for BSO plan types.

Now let's actually set the dimension order using the "hourglass on a stick" method.

1. Go to *Navigator >> Administer >> Dimensions* in the Simplified UI.
2. Click the *Performance Settings* tab.
3. Choose the *Sales* plan type.
4. Using the arrows in the Position column, move the dimensions according to the following:

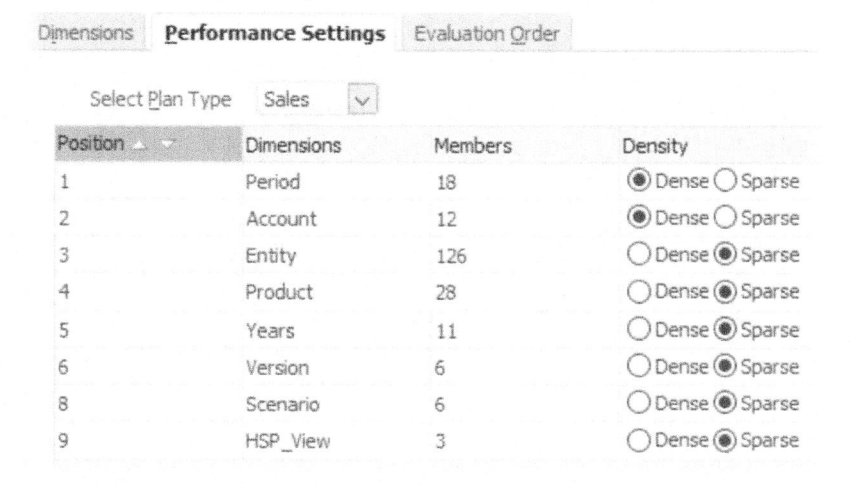

Position	Dimensions	Members	Density
1	Period	18	● Dense ○ Sparse
2	Account	12	● Dense ○ Sparse
3	Entity	126	○ Dense ● Sparse
4	Product	28	○ Dense ● Sparse
5	Years	11	○ Dense ● Sparse
6	Version	6	○ Dense ● Sparse
8	Scenario	6	○ Dense ● Sparse
9	HSP_View	3	○ Dense ● Sparse

Note that Period is listed first, then Account. Since there are no other dense dimensions, Entity, the largest sparse dimension, comes next. After that, the other sparse dimensions are listed by member size.

Set Evaluation Order

To make certain objects like Smart Lists or percentages available in data forms, you must set the evaluation order for dimensions. Evaluation order specifies which data type prevails when a data intersection has conflicting data types. Since I have a Smart List member in the Account dimension, I will set the evaluation order for Account as "1".

To set the evaluation order for dimensions,
1. Navigate to *Console* and click the *Dimensions* tab.
2. Set the Evaluation Order for Account as *1*:

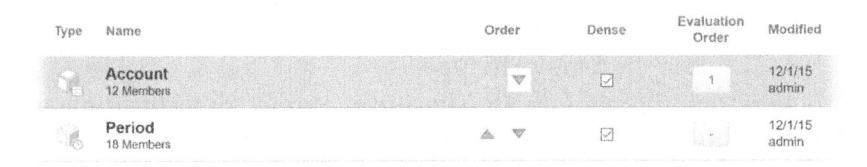

Type	Name	Order	Dense	Evaluation Order	Modified
	Account 12 Members	▼	☑	1	12/1/15 admin
	Period 18 Members	▲ ▼	☑		12/1/15 admin

3. Refresh the database.

```
LOG ENTRY: SOL 13, Entry 2
Time to see what the good Project Commander
brought for music.
90's hip hop. Darn it, McMullen.
```

Now that my BSO plan type is fully configured, I'm ready to turn my attention to ASO plan types.

ASO PLAN TYPES

About ASO Plan Types

ASO plan types function like BSO plan types for the most part. They can be used in data forms, you can load data, and you can report and analyze on ASO plan types. The key difference and why you might want to use an ASO plan type: this type of Essbase database supports much larger databases (more dimensions and more members). They are ideal for detailed actuals where you only need to aggregate or roll up the dimension hierarchies (and no complicated business rules are required).

The ASO plan type will be used in the Vision application for reporting purposes (hence the plan type name "SalesRpt"). This plan type has an extra dimension, "Customer". In this plan type users can report and analyze actuals by customer even though they do not plan at that level. I still want to push Forecast into this plan type so Vision users can do variance analysis and then drill to details on customer actuals.

ASO plan type dimensions and members have a couple of unique properties that you need to define.

Solve Order

The *Solve Order* member property tells Essbase, "here is the order to complete calculations" for ASO databases. Why is this important? You want to calculate the correct numbers in the correct order. Think order of operations for basic math. 4 + 5 * 2 does not equal (4 + 5) * 2. Solve order is the way you control the order of calculations in ASO databases.

Hierarchy Type

In ASO plan types, there are two types of hierarchies – stored and dynamic. Stored hierarchies will aggregate according to the structure of the outline. In our example, months will roll up to quarters up to a year total in the Period member. This aggregation is really fast (the nature of ASO databases), but stored hierarchies may only have the + consolidation for any member and ~ consolidation tags for members under a "Label Only" parent (other assigned consolidation tags are ignored). Also, stored hierarchies cannot have member formulas and there are a few other restrictions on Label Only assignments.

Dynamic hierarchies are calculated by Essbase (instead of being aggregated like in stored hierarchies), so all consolidation tags and member formulas are processed. The evaluation order for the calculation of members is dictated by the solve order as mentioned above. Dynamic hierarchies, as expected, do not calculate as fast as stored hierarchies.

You can also have multiple hierarchies within a single dimension. The hierarchies within a dimension can be stored, can be all dynamic, or can have one hierarchy stored and the other hierarchy dynamic.

Multiple hierarchies can contain alternate hierarchies with Shared Members or completely different hierarchies.

ASO Plan Type Considerations

A few other ASO plan type considerations include:

- Smart Lists and text measures are supported
- Predictive Analytics (discussed in the end user section) is supported
- Enterprise Planning Cloud does not generate XREFs on ASO databases (remember XREF is a function that will share data for a member from one BSO plan type to another)
- Because Enterprise Planning Cloud does not require all base dimensions on an ASO database, approvals may not apply to the ASO database if an approvals dimension is missing; if this is the case, normal security would apply
- Dynamic time series members are not supported for ASO plan types
- Attribute dimensions in Planning ASO Plan types can be trouble; because Planning treats attribute dimensions differently, you can't select attribute dimensions in data forms and reports as a "dimension"
  - Support for attributes as a dimension is coming in a future version

Build Custom Customer Dimension with Flat File

I will add a customer dimension, for just the ASO plan type, for reporting purposes. Since there are many customers for our application, I will do this using the flat file method. If you are unsure about some of the steps below, look back to the Import & Export Dimensions section of this chapter.

To build a custom, customer dimension with a flat file,
1. Back in the Home screen, navigate to *Console >> Application >> Dimensions*.
2. Click the *Create* button.
3. Type in "Customer" for the dimension name and check *Enabled* for ONLY the SalesRpt plan type. Leave other options as default.
4. Click *Done*.

Now that the Customer dimension has been created, it's time to prepare the import file. First I'll export the dimension (even though it is empty) to get the correct file format.

5. Navigate to *Console >> Application >> Dimensions*.
6. Click the *Export* button, then *Create*.
7. Check the box next to *Customer* and click the option for *Comma delimited* (default).
8. Click *Export*. Save the file and open the template.
9. Create the Customer dimension by completing the template (or email info@interrel.com for a copy of the file). Save the template as a CSV file.

Once the template has been completed, it should look something like the following (not all properties are shown):

Customer	Parent	Alias: Default	Valid For C	Data Storage	Two Pass (	Descrip	Fo
Total Customer	Customer		FALSE	never share	FALSE		<n
Large Enterprise	Total Customer		FALSE	never share	FALSE		<n
Mid Cap Enterprise	Total Customer		FALSE	never share	FALSE		<n
Small Business	Total Customer		FALSE	never share	FALSE		<n
Public Sector	Total Customer		FALSE	never share	FALSE		<n
Home and Home Office	Total Customer		FALSE	never share	FALSE		<n
A10001	Large Enterprise	WalStores	FALSE	store	FALSE		<n
A10002	Large Enterprise	Texxon Industries	FALSE	store	FALSE		<n
A10003	Large Enterprise	Clover	FALSE	store	FALSE		<n
A10004	Large Enterprise	Specific Motors	FALSE	store	FALSE		<n
A10005	Large Enterprise	Phillips 66	FALSE	store	FALSE		<n
A10006	Large Enterprise	Mustang Motors	FALSE	store	FALSE		<n
A10007	Large Enterprise	SVC Health	FALSE	store	FALSE		<n
A10008	Large Enterprise	Valerian Energy	FALSE	store	FALSE		<n
A10009	Large Enterprise	DividedHealthGroup	FALSE	store	FALSE		<n
A10010	Large Enterprise	Spherizon	FALSE	store	FALSE		<n
B10011	Mid Cap Enterprise	Circle Energy Solutions	FALSE	store	FALSE		<n
B10012	Mid Cap Enterprise	Hawk Materials	FALSE	store	FALSE		<n
B10013	Mid Cap Enterprise	ABB Educational Services	FALSE	store	FALSE		<n

Note the valid plan type columns should be for the SalesRpt plan type:

128   Chapter 4: Build an Application

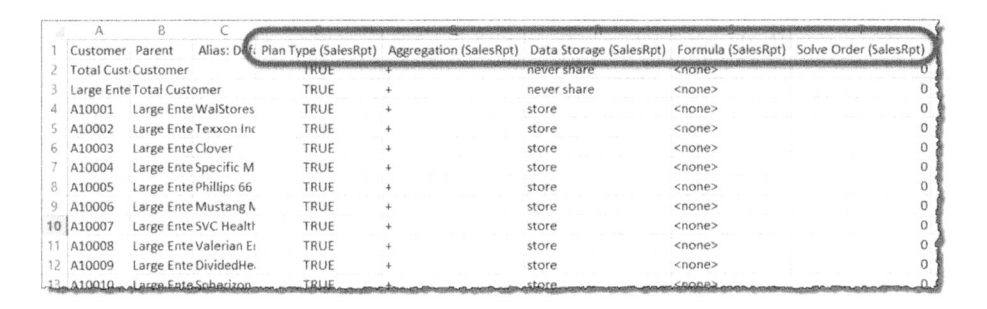

	A	B	C		Plan Type (SalesRpt)	Aggregation (SalesRpt)	Data Storage (SalesRpt)	Formula (SalesRpt)	Solve Order (SalesRpt)
1	Customer	Parent	Alias: D						
2	Total Cust	Customer		TRUE	+	never share	<none>		0
3	Large Ente	Total Customer		TRUE	+	never share	<none>		0
4	A10001	Large Ente	WalStores	TRUE	+	store	<none>		0
5	A10002	Large Ente	Texxon Inc	TRUE	+	store	<none>		0
6	A10003	Large Ente	Clover	TRUE	+	store	<none>		0
7	A10004	Large Ente	Specific M	TRUE	+	store	<none>		0
8	A10005	Large Ente	Phillips 66	TRUE	+	store	<none>		0
9	A10006	Large Ente	Mustang N	TRUE	+	store	<none>		0
10	A10007	Large Ente	SVC Health	TRUE	+	store	<none>		0
11	A10008	Large Ente	Valerian Er	TRUE	+	store	<none>		0
12	A10009	Large Ente	DividedHe	TRUE	+	store	<none>		0
13	A10010	Large Ente	Spherizon	TRUE	+	store	<none>		0

10. Navigate to *Console* and click the *Dimensions* tab.
11. Click *Import*, then *Create*.
12. Navigate to the Customer dimension and click *Browse...*
13. Select the Customer CSV file. Click *Import, OK,* and *OK* again.
14. Click *Refresh* at the top of the page until you see a "Completed" notice.
15. Click the *Completed* link. If there are errors during the import process, they will be displayed in the next screen.
16. Check out the Customer dimension in the dimension editor (*Navigator >> Administer >> Dimensions*):

Name	Alias (Default)	Data Storage
▲ Customer		Never Share
▲ Total Customer		Never Share
▲ Large Enterprise		Never Share
> A10001	WalStores	Store
> A10002	Texxon Industries	Store
> A10003	Clover	Store
> A10004	Specific Motors	Store
> A10005	Phillips 66	Store
> A10006	Mustang Motors	Store
> A10007	SVC Health	Store
> A10008	Valerian Energy	Store
> A10009	DividedHealthGroup	Store
> A10010	Spherizon	Store
> Mid Cap Enterprise		Never Share
> Small Business		Never Share
> Public Sector		Never Share
> Home and Home Office		Never Share

17. Edit the Customer member and set the hierarchy type to *Store*.
18. Refresh the database.

VARIABLES

Variables have many wonderful functions, one of which is to help reduce manual maintenance on forms, scripts, reports, etc. In addition, variables can help users by providing flexibility with member selection. In this section I'll explain two different types of variables: user variables, which users can control and change; and substitution variables, which can be used system-wide and are controlled and changed by administrators.

Create User Variables

User variables act as filters in data forms, enabling Enterprise Planning Cloud to focus on the members they are interested in. Once the user variables are created by users, they can associate a user variable with a data form so that they can plan in a data form tailored for each individual user. User variables can be "dynamic", meaning users can change their variable member selection within a data form if enabled by the administrator.

To create a user variable,
1. Go to *Navigator >> Administer >> Variables*.
2. In the User Variables tab, click ✚.
3. Select the dimension that the user variable will be associated with, then enter a name for the User Variable. I will enter "Entity" for the Dimension Name and call it "MyRegion":

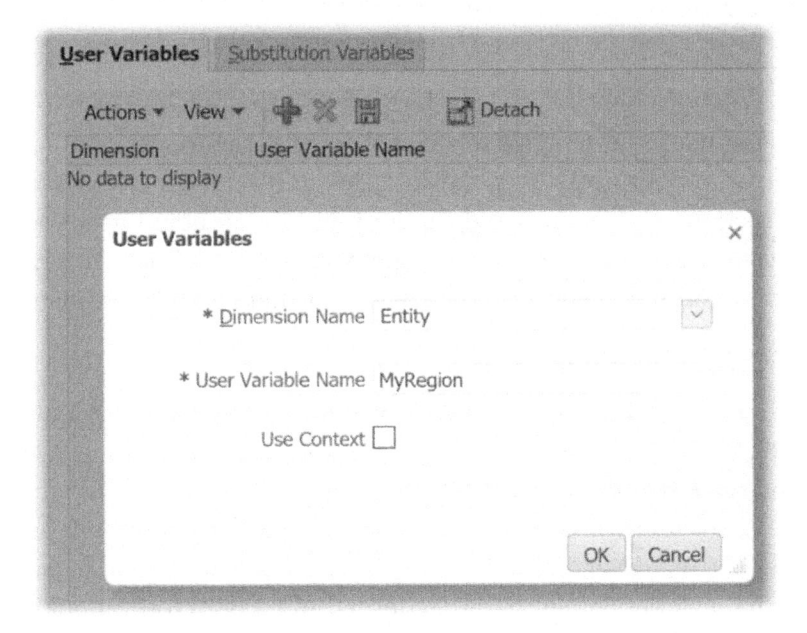

4. Click *OK*.
5. Add another user variable for the "Product" dimension and call it "ProductFamily".
6. Click *OK*.

You should have the following:

I can now select these user variables in data forms (instead of hard coding member selections). More on this when I get to the data forms section.

Select User Variable Members

In order to open forms, each user must select a member for each user variable that has been set up. This is quite simple to do.

To set your user variable in preferences,
1. Go to *Settings >> User Variables*.
2. Use the Member Selector to make selections for each user variable, or type in the member name if the exact spelling is known:

User Variables

Dimension	User Variable Name	Selected Member
Entity	MyRegion	410
Product	ProductFamily	P_100

3. Click *Save*.

Create Substitution Variables

Substitution variables are variables that serve as a placeholder for specific members. These variables can be used in data forms, calculation scripts, reporting and analysis tools, and much more. Common substitution variables include CurrentMth, CurrentYear and PriorYear. Instead of modifying 20 different months that were hardcoded into your forms or calculation scripts, you can just change the value of the substitution variable every month. The application administrator will need to change the values of the variables monthly or yearly, as they change.

To create a substitution variable,
1. Navigate to *Navigator >> Administer >> Variables*.
2. In the Substitution Variables tab, click ⊕.
3. Type in "CurrentYear" for the *Name* and "FY15" for the *Value*:

Add Substitution Variable

Application VISION

* Plan Type All Plan Types

* Name CurrentYear

* Value FY15

[OK] [Cancel]

4. Click *OK*. The substitution variable entry will appear on the screen.
5. Create another substitution variable for "PriorYear" and assign "FY14" as the value.
6. Create another substitution variable for "ForecastYear" and assign "FY16" as the value.

You can manually update substitution variables in the UI or you can automate the update of substitution variables with EPM Automate (more on this later).

```
LOG ENTRY: SOL 13, Entry 3

With the application built, I'm feeling pretty
good about this Enterprise Planning Cloud thing. Next
on my list is loading data. How hard could that be?
```

Chapter 5:
Integrate Data

Oracle Enterprise Planning Cloud provides a number of methods for both loading data into and exporting data out of applications. Data can be imported using the Simplified UI or the Workspace UI with an Essbase data format or Planning data format. A business rule can be used to export data.

Enterprise Planning Cloud data can be integrated using on-premise Financial Data Quality Management (FDMEE) beginning in release 11.1.2.4.200. FDMEE is a business users "ETL" (Extract-Transform-Load) tool. FDMEE provides a graphical interface to define sources and targets and map them together to integrate data. FDMEE has long been used with on-premise Hyperion applications and now supports integration to the Cloud. A separate license for FDMEE is required if you want to use this method.

Data can also be integrated using Data Management (which is a "lite" version of FDMEE). Data Management comes with your Enterprise Planning Cloud subscription and can be used to both import and export data to and from the Cloud.

Flat files are the only available source for Data Management and the Enterprise Planning Cloud Simplified UI. I will walk through the Data Management and Simplified UI data load methods in this portion of the mission.

While I will not cover the steps to build a data integration for FDMEE, the steps are similar to the steps addressed in the Data Management section; the main difference is that on-premise FDMEE delivers more supported sources and targets, scripting capabilities and many other features that come with the fully functional FDMEE on-premise solution.

As a warning, when you are in space and clouds, the manuals oftentimes have many tables. For example…

INTEGRATION OPTIONS OVERVIEW

The following table provides a summary of the different ways to load data to and export data from Enterprise Planning Cloud.

Integration	Integration Option	Where	Use Case	Valid Sources
Load Data	Native Essbase format	Simplified / Workspace UI	Source file can be provided in the specific / required format; good use case for moving data across Essbase databases	Flat File only
Load Data	Hyperion Planning format	Simplified / Workspace UI	Use for loading free form text and Smart List data	Flat File only
Load Data	Data load rules in Data Mgmt	Data Management (*Mgmt)	Mapping and / or drill through required; use when you don't have an Essbase or Planning data file format	Flat File only
Load Data	Data load rules in FDMEE	On Premise FDMEE	Mapping and / or drill through required; great for Hybrid Cloud/On-premise integrations	Supported FDMEE sources

Integration	Integration Option	Where	Use Case	Valid Sources
Synchronize Data	Push data between BSO and ASO Plan types	Data Mgmt	Sync data between plan types within an application	Plan type to plan type
Data Maps	Push data between BSO and ASO Plan types	Simplified UI	Sync data between plan types within an application	Plan type to plan type
Export Data	Native Essbase format	Simplified UI / Workspace UI	Move data across environments (pre-prod to prod); backup of data	Flat File only in Native Essbase format
Export Data	Hyperion Planning format	Simplified UI / Workspace UI	Export out Smart Lists and free form text intersections	Flat File only in Planning format
Export Data	Delimited data file using Data Mgmt	Data Mgmt	Export data to load to other systems	Flat File only
Export Data	Data load rules in FDMEE	On Premise FDMEE	Export data to load to other systems; great for Hybrid Cloud/On-premise integrations	Supported FDMEE targets

Integration	Integration Option	Where	Use Case	Valid Sources
Export Data	Business Rule with DATAEXPORT function	Calculation Manager	Export data to load to other systems	Flat File only
REST API	Scripted interface in conjunction with EPM Automate utility	Scripting / Programming interface	Integrate data between Cloud and other systems	Almost any source

IMPORT DATA WITH THE SIMPLIFIED UI

Load Data with Native Essbase Format

You can load data to Enterprise Planning Cloud using the native Essbase format in the Simplified UI. A good use case for this option is when you want to move entire data sets from one application to another with the exact same dimensionality (e.g., moving data from pre-production to production or on-premise to Cloud).

Free-form data loading is a simple process to load data to Essbase. The data file can be loaded as is without any explicit description of its contents (i.e. no load rule), but the data MUST be in the natural order for Essbase. So what is the natural order for Essbase? Essbase must encounter a member from every dimension before a data value. Any valid dimension / member / alias name combination is acceptable. Data is read according to the member names Essbase finds.

The steps to load the Essbase data format are mostly the same steps to load data with the Planning format.

Load Data with Planning Format

You can load data to Enterprise Planning Cloud using native Planning format in the Simplified UI. Under the covers, the Simplified UI is using the Outline Load Utility functionality from on-premise Hyperion Planning. This is a great way to load Smart List data intersections and free form text members.

This format is pretty specific. The first column is where data will be loaded to. The second column (and sometimes more) are the driver members where data is loaded (I like to use account members as the driver members). The next column is the POV which is basically the rest of the dimension members where data should be loaded. This can be tricky to create from other source systems as the POV must be enclosed in double quotes as shown in the next screen shot. It is pretty easy to create this format if have a SQL database to generate this file. The final column is the Data Load Cube name.

Here is a sample Planning Simplified UI data file displayed in Notepad++ text editor:

```
Product, Product Manager, Point-of-View, Data Load Cube Name
P_100, Rachel, "0, FY16, Actual, Jerry1_Version, BaseData, Jan", Sales
P_100, Rachel, "0, FY16, Actual, Jerry1_Version, BaseData, Feb", Sales
P_100, Rachel, "0, FY16, Actual, Jerry1_Version, BaseData, Mar", Sales
P_100, Rachel, "0, FY16, Actual, Jerry1_Version, BaseData, Apr", Sales
P_100, Rachel, "0, FY16, Actual, Jerry1_Version, BaseData, May", Sales
P_100, Rachel, "0, FY16, Actual, Jerry1_Version, BaseData, Jun", Sales
P_100, Rachel, "0, FY16, Actual, Jerry1_Version, BaseData, Jul", Sales
P_100, Rachel, "0, FY16, Actual, Jerry1_Version, BaseData, Aug", Sales
P_100, Rachel, "0, FY16, Actual, Jerry1_Version, BaseData, Sep", Sales
P_100, Rachel, "0, FY16, Actual, Jerry1_Version, BaseData, Oct", Sales
P_100, Rachel, "0, FY16, Actual, Jerry1_Version, BaseData, Nov", Sales
P_100, Rachel, "0, FY16, Actual, Jerry1_Version, BaseData, Dec", Sales
```

Be careful when updating this file. Excel can really screw this file up, removing commas, adding additional quotes, and more:

138   Chapter 5: Integrate Data

Product	Product Manager	Point-of-View	Data Load Cube Name			
P_100	Rachel	"0	FY16	Actual Final	BaseData Jan"	Sales
P_100	Rachel	"0	FY16	Actual Final	BaseData Feb"	Sales
P_100	Rachel	"0	FY16	Actual Final	BaseData Mar"	Sales
P_100	Rachel	"0	FY16	Actual Final	BaseData Apr"	Sales
P_100	Rachel	"0	FY16	Actual Final	BaseData May"	Sales
P_100	Rachel	"0	FY16	Actual Final	BaseData Jun"	Sales
P_100	Rachel	"0	FY16	Actual Final	BaseData Jul"	Sales
P_100	Rachel	"0	FY16	Actual Final	BaseData Aug"	Sales
P_100	Rachel	"0	FY16	Actual Final	BaseData Sep"	Sales
P_100	Rachel	"0	FY16	Actual Final	BaseData Oct"	Sales
P_100	Rachel	"0	FY16	Actual Final	BaseData Nov"	Sales
P_100	Rachel	"0	FY16	Actual Final	BaseData Dec"	Sales
P_110	Rachel	"0	FY16	Actual Final	BaseData Jan"	Sales
P_110	Rachel	"0	FY16	Actual Final	BaseData Feb"	Sales

To load data using the Simplified UI in Planning format,
1. Navigate to *Console*.
2. Choose *Actions >> Inbox / Outbox Explorer*.
3. Click *Upload*.
4. Browse to and upload the prepared file. Mine is called "ProductManagerLoad.csv".
5. Click *Upload File* and the file will be uploaded into the Inbox / Outbox:

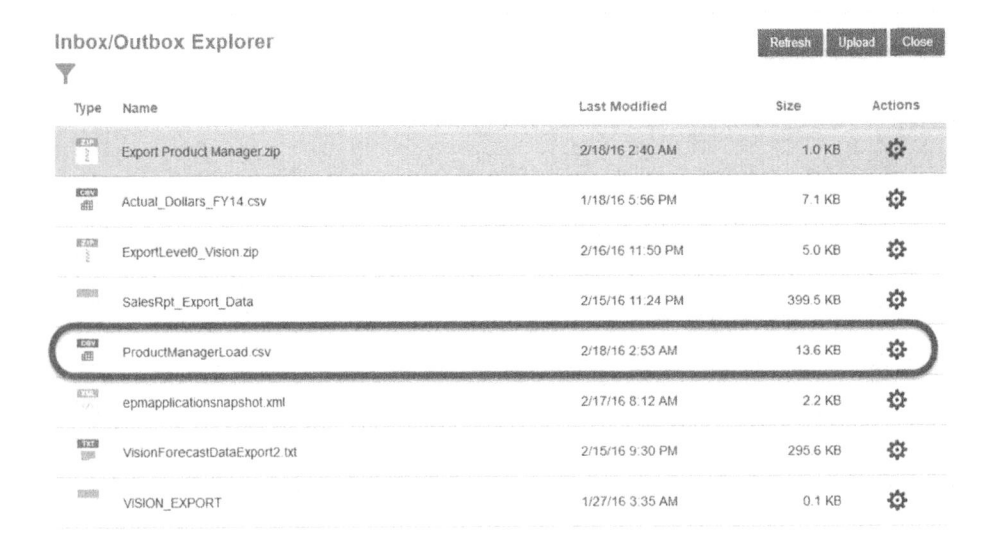

Inbox/Outbox Explorer   Refresh Upload Close

Type	Name	Last Modified	Size	Actions
ZIP	Export Product Manager.zip	2/18/16 2:40 AM	1.0 KB	⚙
CSV	Actual_Dollars_FY14.csv	1/18/16 5:56 PM	7.1 KB	⚙
ZIP	ExportLevel0_Vision.zip	2/16/16 11:50 PM	5.0 KB	⚙
	SalesRpt_Export_Data	2/15/16 11:24 PM	399.5 KB	⚙
CSV	ProductManagerLoad.csv	2/18/16 2:53 AM	13.6 KB	⚙
XML	epmapplicationsnapshot.xml	2/17/16 8:12 AM	2.2 KB	⚙
TXT	VisionForecastDataExport2.txt	2/15/16 9:30 PM	295.6 KB	⚙
	VISION_EXPORT	1/27/16 3:35 AM	0.1 KB	⚙

6. Click *Close*.
7. Choose *Actions >> Import Data*:

Look Smarter Than You Are with Enterprise Planning Cloud   139

8. Click *Create*.
9. Define the import information:

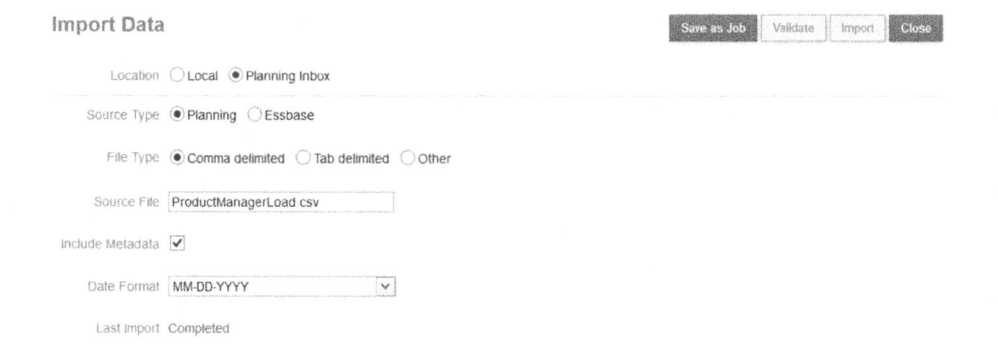

The following options are available for the Planning import type:

- **Location** – location of the file; either locally on the user's computer or on the Cloud server
- **Source Type** – format of the source file; either Planning or Essbase native format
- **File Type** – type of delimiter used in the source file; either comma, tab, or one that the user specifies
- **Source File** – name of the source file
- **Include Metadata** – specify to load metadata along with application data; this checkbox is selected by default. Deselecting this option improves performance, but you must already have the required metadata in the application. Deselecting this option also prevents members from shifting their position within the outline.
- **Date Format** – date format options if date types are used in the source file

- **Last Import** – not selectable; last date and time an import was attempted

The following options are available if the import type is Essbase:

- **Source Type** – format of the source file; either Planning or Essbase native format
- **Plan Type** – which plan type to load data to
- **Source File** – name of the source file
- **Last Import** – not selectable; last date and time an import was attempted

10. Click *Save as Job*.
11. Enter the job name "ImportProductManager", click *Save*, and then *OK*.
12. The job is created. Click *Close*.
13. Schedule the job (or run now on demand).
14. From the Console click the *Jobs* tab.
15. Click *Schedule Jobs*:

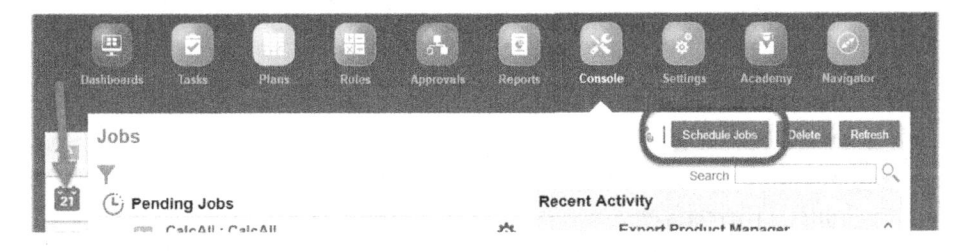

16. Enter the following job information:
    a. What type of job is this: *Import Data*
    b. When do you want to run this job: *Run Now:*

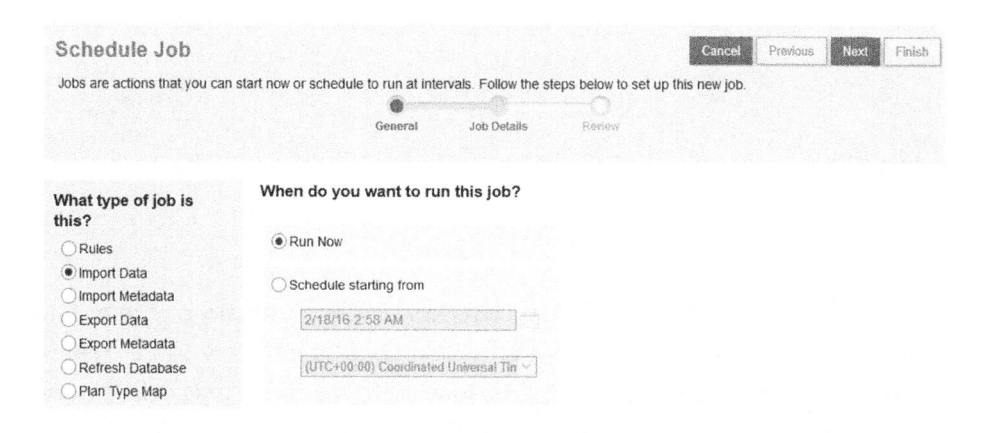

Look Smarter Than You Are with Enterprise Planning Cloud   141

17. Click *Next*.
18. View the Job Details:

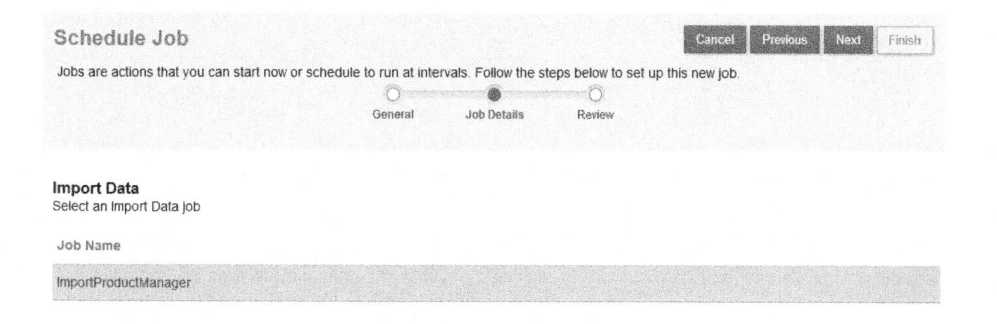

19. Click *Next*.
20. Review the job information and click *Finish*.
21. You can view the job progress in the console:

22. When the job is complete, you can select the job to view the process details:

Import and Export Status

Load Id	140	Start Time	2/18/16 3:00:51 AM
Type	Data Import	End Time	2/18/16 3:00:52 AM
Run By	errel.com	Records Read	192
Dimension	Product	Records Processed	192
Job Status	Completed	Records Rejected	0

Show Errors ▼

Category	Record Index	Message

No data to display

To check that the data load was successful, you can create a data form to view the data (I'll do this in the next chapter). Once you've created the data form, you can verify the data load with a data form (I called mine "Check Product Manager Load" data form):

[Check Product Manager Load data form showing Product Manager assignments by month (Jan-Dec) for various products including Product X, Sentinal Standard Notebook, Sentinal Custom Notebook, Envoy Standard Netbook, Envoy Custom Netbook, Other Computer, Tablet Computer, Accessories, Keyboard, Software Suite, Monitor, Modem, Network Card, Game, Camera, Television, Training_P_291, Miscellaneous_P_292, Maintenance_P_293]

EXPORT DATA WITH THE SIMPLIFIED UI

Export Data Using the "Export Data" in Simplified UI

The best way to figure out the Planning data form is to export data through the Simplified UI first to give you a template. It's also handy to know how to quickly export data.

Data can easily be exported using the Export Data function in the Simplified UI if needed.

To export data in the Simplified UI,
1. Click the *Console* icon in the main menu.
2. Go to Actions and click *Export Data*.
3. Click *Create*.

4. Keep the default options:

Export Data

Location ● Local ○ Planning Outbox

Plan Type Sales ▼

File Type ● Comma delimited ○ Tab delimited ○ Other

Smart Lists ● Export Labels ○ Export Names

Now a slice of data will need to be defined to customize the export. Click the hierarchy icon next to each dimension name to select the members.

When inside the Select Members screen:

- Click on a parent name to show its children
- To add a relationship function, click the function icon (fx) next to the appropriate member
- To select just a single member name (for the Point of View), click the box to the left of the member name

5. Make the following Slice Definition selections.
    a. **Row** – Account: Descendants ("4001")
    b. **Column** – Period: ILvl0Descendants(YearTotal)
    c. **Point of View** – BaseData, FY14, Actual, Final, Descendants(TD), Descendants(P_TP):

Row	Column	Point of View
Account	Period	Select...
Descendants("4001")	ILvl0Descendants(YearTotal)	HSP_View
		BaseData
		Years
		FY14
		Scenario
		Actual
		Version
		Final
		Entity
		Descendants(TD)
		Product
		Descendants(P_TP)

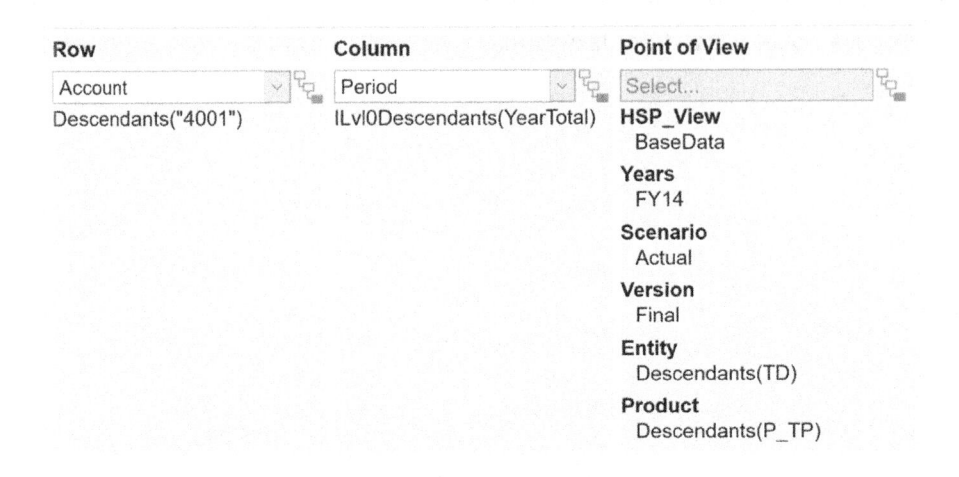

6. Click *Export* and wait for the data export to complete:

Data Export

0% —————————————— 100%

Data is currently being exported...

OK

7. Save the .zip file. Then open it and note the Planning format (remember Excel can mess up the POV column pretty easily).

Note, you cannot export data from the Simplified UI in the Essbase format. The Essbase format is used in Application Management when you take snapshots of your application (more on this later).

Export Data Using a Business Rule

You can also export data from BSO plan types using business rules and the Data Export function. Check out the Calculate Data chapter for more information.

INTRO TO DATA MANAGEMENT

As I mentioned earlier, Data Management within Enterprise Planning Cloud is another one of the ways you can load data and export data. Data Management is a "lite" version of Financial Data Quality Management Enterprise Edition (FDMEE) and is the data integration tool for Enterprise Planning Cloud (along with most future EPM Cloud products).

Data Management today can import and export flat files from any sources to and from Enterprise Planning Cloud, perform mapping translations and sync data across plan types.

Supported integrations for Data Management today include:

Data Integration	Valid Sources	Data and / or Metadata
Data Load	File based, Fusion GL and Commitment Control Files from Fusion CS	Data Only
Synchronization	Move data between BSO and ASO plan types within Enterprise Planning Cloud application	Data Only
Write Back	File based, Fusions file from Fusion CS	Data Only

Data Management is a more robust integration solution and has a few more steps than the simplified UI. With more steps, I get greater flexibility and functionality. The overall steps to load data using Data Management are as follows. Don't worry – I'll explain each of the steps in more detail as I go through this chapter / portion of the mission.

Data Management Steps to Build an Integration

#	Task / Term	Term Definition	Where to Perform the Task
1	Define System Settings	System settings are default settings (or system level profiles) that you define that will apply to the entire system	*Setup >> Configure >> System Settings*
2	Define Application Settings	Application settings are default settings (or application level profiles) that you define that will apply to target application	*Setup >> Configure >> Application Settings*
3	Define **Source** System	Where you will load data from; for Enterprise Planning Cloud this is a flat file	*Setup >> Register >> Source System*
4	Define app as a **Target** (Optionally set drill flag to *Yes*)	Where you will load data to; for Enterprise Planning Cloud this is the Enterprise Planning Cloud application or an export of the Enterprise Planning Cloud application data	*Setup >> Register >> Target Application*
5	Define **Import Format** (including defining Drill URL to source)	Determines which columns are extracted from the source system, how the data is stored in the Data Management staging table and import mapping information	*Setup >> Integration Setup >> Import Format*
6	Create a **Location**	Associates Import Format with Target Application and	*Setup >> Integration*

#	Task / Term	Term Definition	Where to Perform the Task
		combines mapping and data load rules for Target	*Setup >> Location*
7	Define **Mappings** (Data Source, Period, Category Mappings)	Map source fields to Target Application (any delimited data file can be mapped to target application; define period mappings and category mappings)	*Setup >> Integration Setup >> Period Mapping*
8	Define Logic groups (optionally)	Define Logic groups, check rule groups, and check entity groups	*Setup >> Data Load Setup >> Logic Group*
9	Create a **Data Load** Rule	Defines what file to run; if file is left blank, user is prompted at run time	*Workflow >> Data Load >> Data Load Rule*
10	**Execute** (which will load data to the Workbench and / or Target application)	Will load data to the Data Management staging tables and / or Target application)	*Workflow >> Data Load >> Data Load Rule* or *Workflow >> Data Load >> Workbench*

That is quite a few steps, so I'm going to create my own acronym to remember the steps: S_T_IF_Lo_Ma_DL_E ("*Stiflomadle*": Create Source, Create Target, Define Import Format, Define Location, Define Mappings, Define Data Load Rule, and finally Execute).

An important concept in data management is Point of View or POV. Sources are loaded for a POV which is made up of a POV Location, POV Period (month and year), and POV Category. If you are loading a single Actuals source file, you may just have one location. If you are loading files from multiple sources, you might have more than one location. Data Management is geared to load data for a single period (Period POV), but loading for multiple periods is supported. A POV category is telling Data Management – do I want to load to Actual or Budget?

> **Note!** Today's version of Enterprise Planning Cloud does NOT have all of the features and functions available in on-premise FDMEE, such as scripting, mostly due to Cloud security precautions. However, the near-term roadmap for on-premise FDMEE includes hybrid support, which will allow it to integrate with Enterprise Planning Cloud, as well as on-premise applications.

Enterprise Planning Cloud only allows one Data Management application. Because of this requirement, Data Management will perform some of the setup steps for you with Enterprise Planning Cloud:

- **Target Applications** – two application targets are automatically created as [Appname] and [Appname_Export] (so you can load data to the application and export data from the application)
- **Default Import Format** – when you create an Enterprise Planning Cloud application, a default import format is automatically created with the name [Appname_1]; use this import format to map a source data file to a Planning application
- **Default Location** – default Location is automatically created with the name [Appname_1]

Navigate to Data Management

To navigate to Data Management in the Simplified UI,
1. Go to *Navigator* >> *Manage* and click *Data Integration*.

Although "Data Integration" was originally selected through the Simplified UI, Data Management in Enterprise Planning Cloud Workspace will open. Data Management has two main sections, Workflow and Setup:

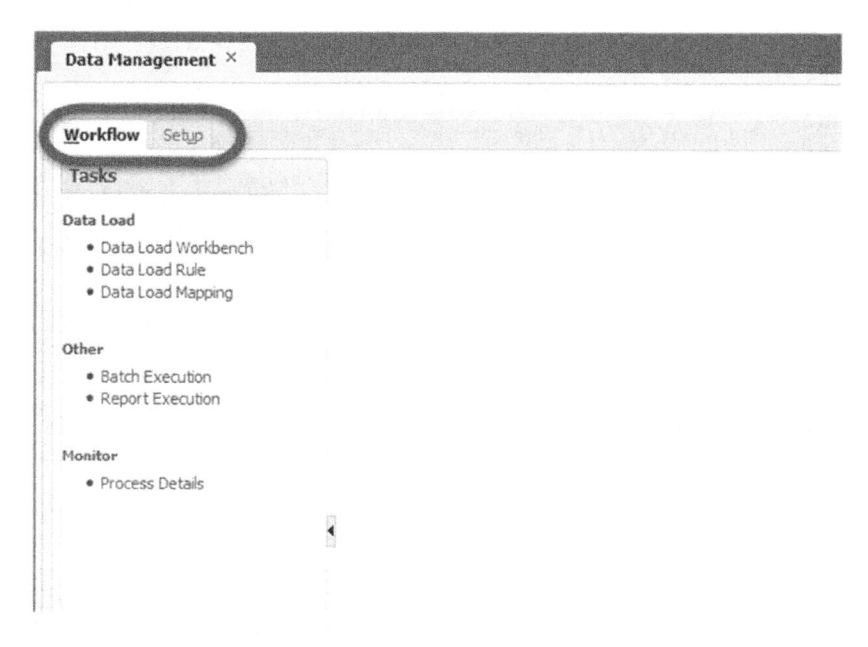

Tasks in Data Management are grouped by Workflow and Setup.

LOAD DATA FILE USING DATA MANAGEMENT

Data File Requirements

Data Management file requirements must follow these guidelines:

- Must be a CSV file
- Supported delimiters include:
    - comma (,)
    - exclamation (!)
    - semicolon (;)
    - colon (:)
    - pipe (|)
    - tab

150   Chapter 5: Integrate Data

- Enterprise Planning Cloud supports single period or multiple period load (with periods across the columns)
- Enterprise Planning Cloud does not support periods and years in the rows (although it does export data this way from EPM sources):

```
1  ACCOUNT,ENTITY,UD1,UD2,UD3,SCENARIO,YEAR,PERIOD,AMOUNT
2  Units,420,A10001,P_130,Final,Actual,FY16,Dec,10
3  Units,410,A10001,P_130,Final,Actual,FY16,Dec,10
4  4110,410,A10001,P_130,Final,Actual,FY16,Dec,5000
5  Units,420,A10002,P_280,Final,Actual,FY16,Nov,4
6  Average Price,440,D10061,P_160,Final,Actual,FY16,Dec,1600
7  List Price,440,D10061,P_160,Final,Actual,FY16,Dec,1600
8  List Price,430,D10051,P_160,Final,Actual,FY16,Dec,1600
9  List Price,450,H10001,P_120,Final,Actual,FY16,Dec,1000
10 Average Price,450,A10001,P_280,Final,Actual,FY16,Nov,400
11 Average Price,430,A10001,P_280,Final,Actual,FY16,Nov,400
```

Define System Settings

To define the System Settings,

1. Click the *Setup* tab.

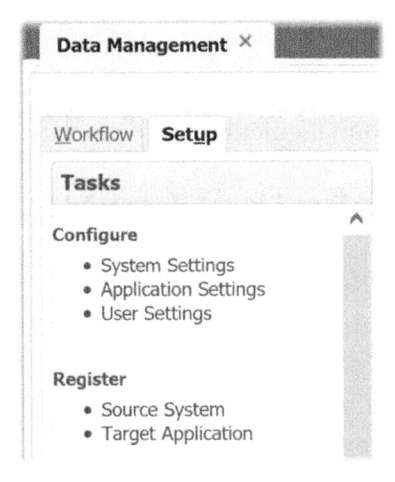

2. Click the *System Settings* link under Configure.
3. Then change the Profile Type to *All* to see all of the possible System Settings available.

System settings are default settings that apply to the entire system (all target applications in Data Management). Usually, you can leave most of the System Settings blank to accept Data Management defaults. Here are a few you should consider setting:

- **Log Level** – this setting specifies the level of detail included in the Data Management process log. Default value is "4" which is recommended for production. Set to a value of "5" for the most verbose option that should be used during development.
- **Batch Size** – this setting is used to adjust performance. When data is loaded, this setting determines how many records are stored in the cache before being committed. Set to a higher number for better performance, but avoid setting it too high as the application can become unstable.

Define Application Settings

To define the Application Settings,
1. Still within the *Setup* tab, click the *Application Settings* link under Configure.

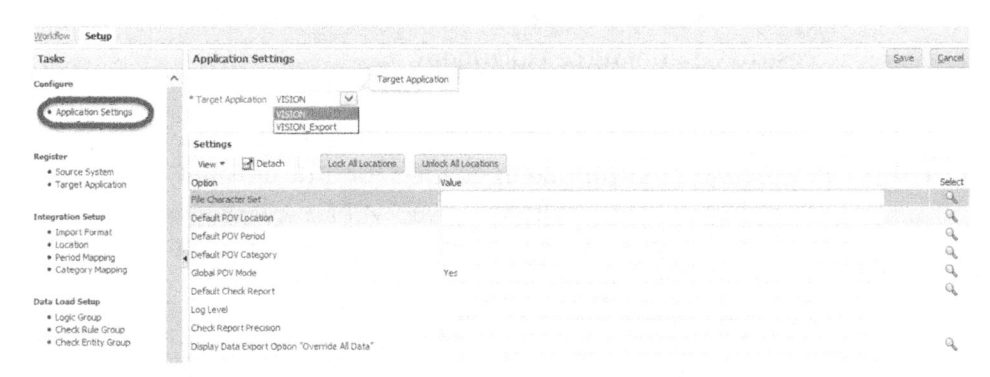

The first step in setting up data loads is to define application settings. Application settings are default settings (or application level profiles) that you define which will apply to the Target application (and override any System Settings for that particular application). You will select a Target application and then define the application settings. Since Enterprise Planning Cloud only allows one application, two application targets are automatically created as *Appname* and *Appname_Export* (so you can load data to the application and export data from the application).

You can set each of these Application Settings, or leave blank to accept Data Management defaults:

- **File Character Set** – specify method for mapping bit combinations to characters for creating, storing and displaying text (e.g., UTF-8)
- **Default POV location**
- **Default POV Period**
- **Default POV Category**
- **Global POV Mode (Yes or No)** – when this is set to *Yes*, other POVs are ignored
- **Default Check Report** – define the type of Check Report to use at the application level (either picking a pre-defined Check Report or custom report that you create)
- **Log Level** – Define level of detail to display in the log (1 = least detail and 5 = greatest detail); logs are displayed in *Process Details >> Log*
- **Check Report Precision** – number of decimals for check report
- **Display Data Export Option "Override All Data"**
- **Access to Open Source Document**

In Application Settings, you can choose to click *Lock All Locations* which will prevent data from being loaded for a designated period and category. To unlock locations, choose *Unlock All Locations*:

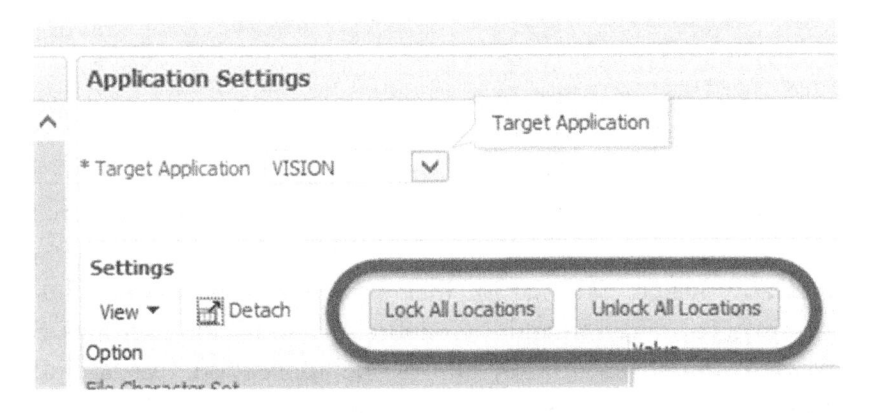

2. For example, if I wanted to prevent users from loading data for Feb-16 actuals, I could select those members and click *OK*:

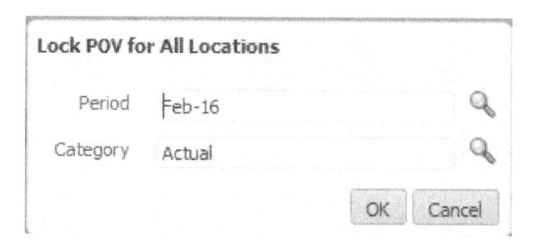

Look Smarter Than You Are with Enterprise Planning Cloud 153

Lock POV for All Locations

Period: Feb-16
Category: Actual

[OK] [Cancel]

I'll continue on and define the application settings for my Vision data load.

3. Select the application to load data to. In this case, I will select *VISION*.
4. Type "Yes" in the Global POV field:

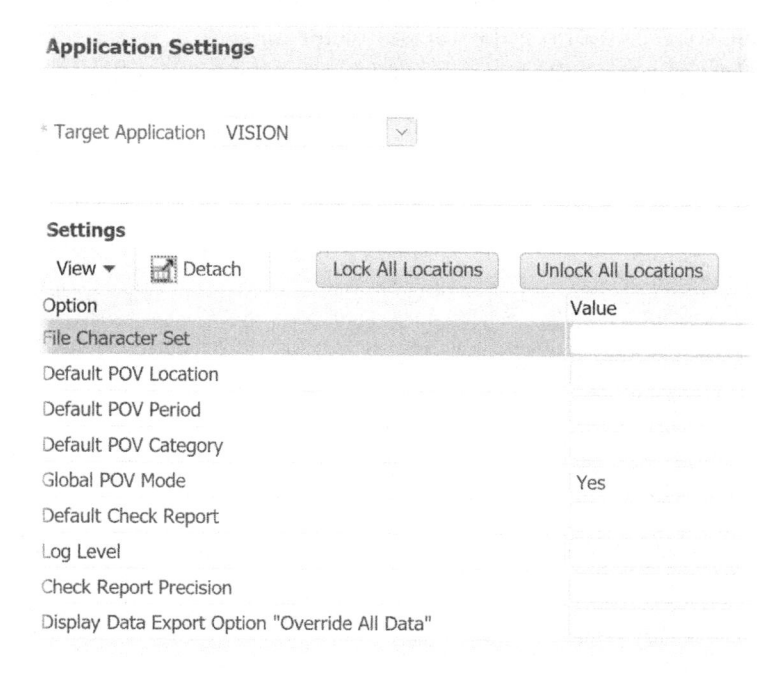

Application Settings

*Target Application: VISION

Settings

View ▼ | Detach | Lock All Locations | Unlock All Locations

Option	Value
File Character Set	
Default POV Location	
Default POV Period	
Default POV Category	
Global POV Mode	Yes
Default Check Report	
Log Level	
Check Report Precision	
Display Data Export Option "Override All Data"	

5. Click *Save*.

Define Source System

To define a source system,

1. Under the Setup tab and Register section, click *Source System*.

2. Review the *File* source system that is created by Enterprise Planning Cloud by default.

The Source System section is where I define the information about where I am loading data from. The "File" source will already exist by default since it is the only source available in Enterprise Planning Cloud (for now). If you are loading data from an Oracle Fusion ERP data file, there is an additional step to identify the file as a Fusion file.

For file-based source systems, you will see the name, type, description, and drill-through URL for the source (to learn more about drill through, check out Oracle's tutorial video – https://goo.gl/sxD6IL).

You can add new source systems, edit source system details, and delete sources. The option to *Configure Source Connection* is used for Oracle Fusion file sources (not regular file sources).

The File type will already exist by default since it is the only source available in Enterprise Planning Cloud. I could use this source system but I'm going to create a new one to show you the process from start to finish:

3. Click the + *Add* icon to add a new source system.
4. Enter *Source System Name* as "Vision Data File" with a *Source System Type* of "File":

: Details

* Source System Name: Vision Data File
* Source System Type: File
* ODI Context Code: GLOBAL

Source System Description: Vision Actual Data Load file

Drill Through URL:

5. Click *Save*.

Define Target Application

To review the setup and properties for a target application,

1. Click *Setup >> Register >> Target Application*.

The BSO application defined in Enterprise Planning Cloud (in this case, VISION) will already exist by default as a target application along with any ASO plan types.

2. Click on the *VISION* target application.

You will see the dimensions listed in the Dimension Details tab. Each dimension is assigned a *Target Dimension Class* and a *Data Table Column Name*. You can also check the option to *Create Drill Region*, as well as define the sequence.

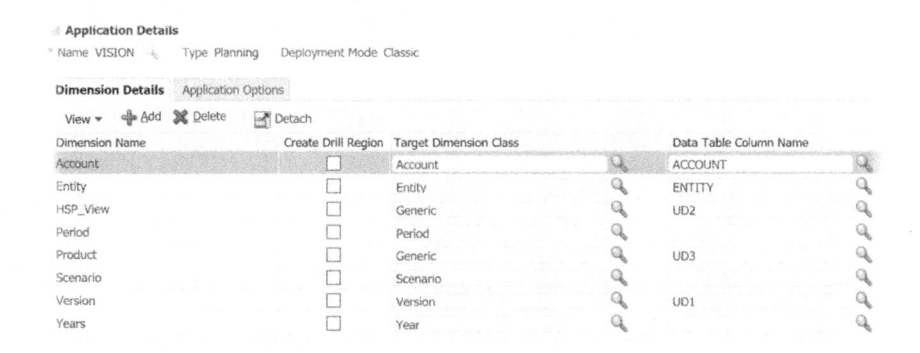

Application Details

* Name: VISION   Type: Planning   Deployment Mode: Classic

Dimension Details | Application Options

View ▼ Add Delete Detach

Dimension Name	Create Drill Region	Target Dimension Class	Data Table Column Name
Account	☐	Account	ACCOUNT
Entity	☐	Entity	ENTITY
HSP_View	☐	Generic	UD2
Period	☐	Period	
Product	☐	Generic	UD3
Scenario	☐	Scenario	
Version	☐	Version	UD1
Years	☐	Year	

3. If all dimensions are not listed in Dimension Details, add a new row to include the missing dimension. Data Management will read the dimensions from Enterprise Planning Cloud and assign the Target Dimension Class and Data Table Column Name.

4. Define or update the appropriate Target Dimension Class and Data Table Column Name using the magnifying glass icon if it doesn't match the above image.

A *Target Dimension Class* is a property that is defined by the dimension type. For example, dimensions with months rolling to quarters to Year correspond to the Period dimension class, Account dimensions to the Account dimension class, and so forth. Generic class will be used for most Custom dimensions. The dimension classes Employee, Position, Job Code, Budget Item, and Element are all used for Public Sector Budgeting (ignore these for Enterprise Planning Cloud). You can add or update the assigned Target Dimension Class. Valid Target Dimension classes are shown below:

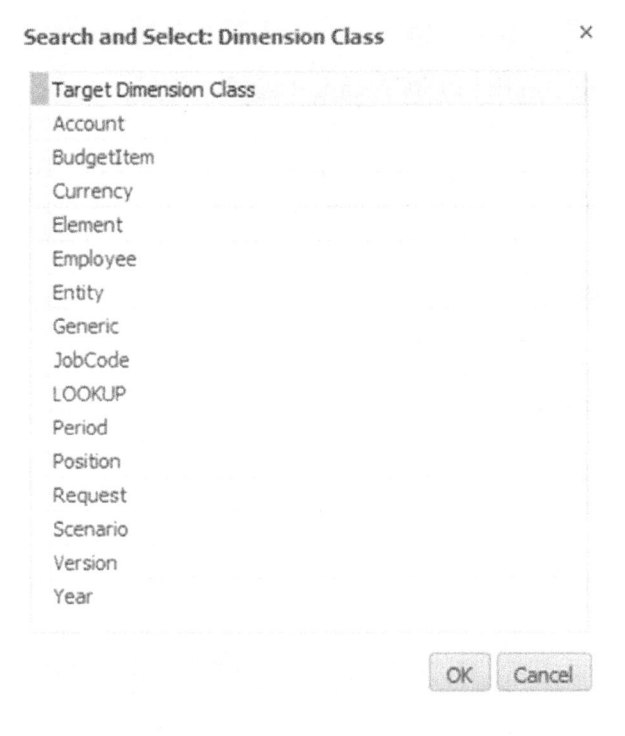

Search and Select: Dimension Class

Target Dimension Class
- Account
- BudgetItem
- Currency
- Element
- Employee
- Entity
- Generic
- JobCode
- LOOKUP
- Period
- Position
- Request
- Scenario
- Version
- Year

OK   Cancel

5. Make sure Entity is tagged as *Entity* (and not Country).
6. Make sure Years is tagged as *Year*.

The *Data Table Column Name* is the name of the column in the Data Management staging table where the dimension value is stored.

7. Set the Account dimension to *Account* for the Data Column Name, the Entity dimension to *Entity*, and the rest of the dimensions will be tagged as UDx.

ICP (Intercompany Partner) will not apply for Enterprise Planning Cloud. You can either type in the Data Column Name or click the *Search* icon to select it:

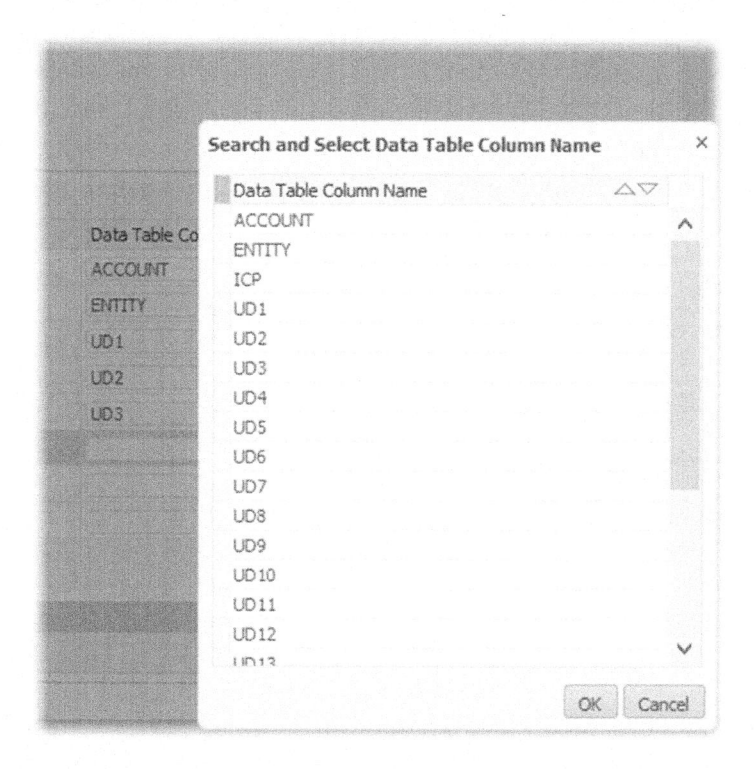

Do not specify a Data Table Column Name for Year, Period, or Scenario dimensions. These should be left blank since those members are defined by the POV.

8. Select the *Application Options* tab to review and define parameters for Batch Size, Drill Region, and Source Language (leave all as default):

Chapter 5: Integrate Data

Batch Size is the batch size used to write data to files (the default is 10,000). Batch size is covered above under System Settings. *Source Language for Member Description* is used for default language of member descriptions. *Drill Region*, if marked "Yes", is used for drill-through.

Use *Refresh Metadata* to synchronize application metadata from the target application and display any new dimensions (important if you add a new dimension), and *Refresh Members* to synchronize members from target dimensions (important when you need to update mappings):

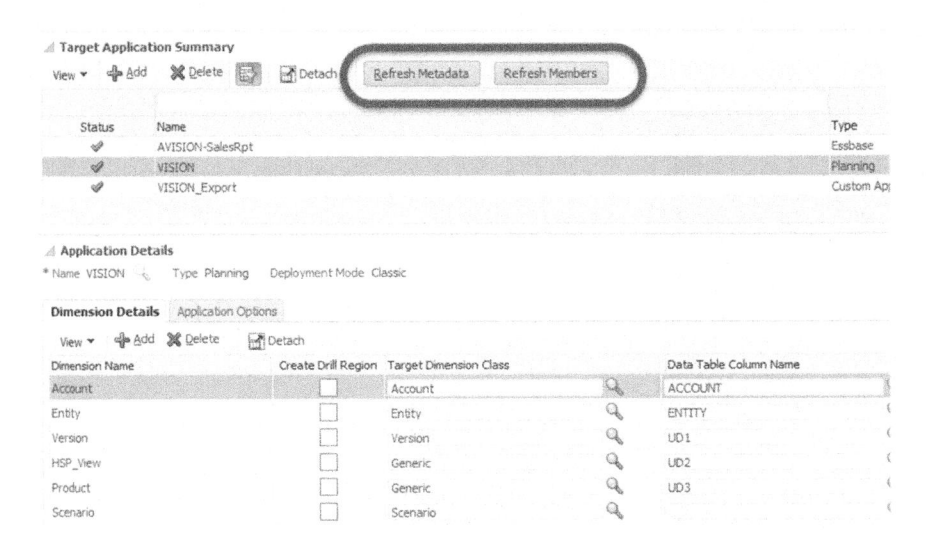

Since the Vision application has already been defined, let's create a target application for the SalesRpt ASO plan type.

Note! Target applications can only be created once per Planning plan type or Essbase database. Custom applications can have multiple target applications attached to them. If you ever need to delete a target

Look Smarter Than You Are with Enterprise Planning Cloud   159

application, select it and click ✖. All data load rules associated with it will also be deleted.

To add the SalesRpt Target application,

1. Click ✚ under Target Application Summary.
2. Select *Essbase* as the Type:

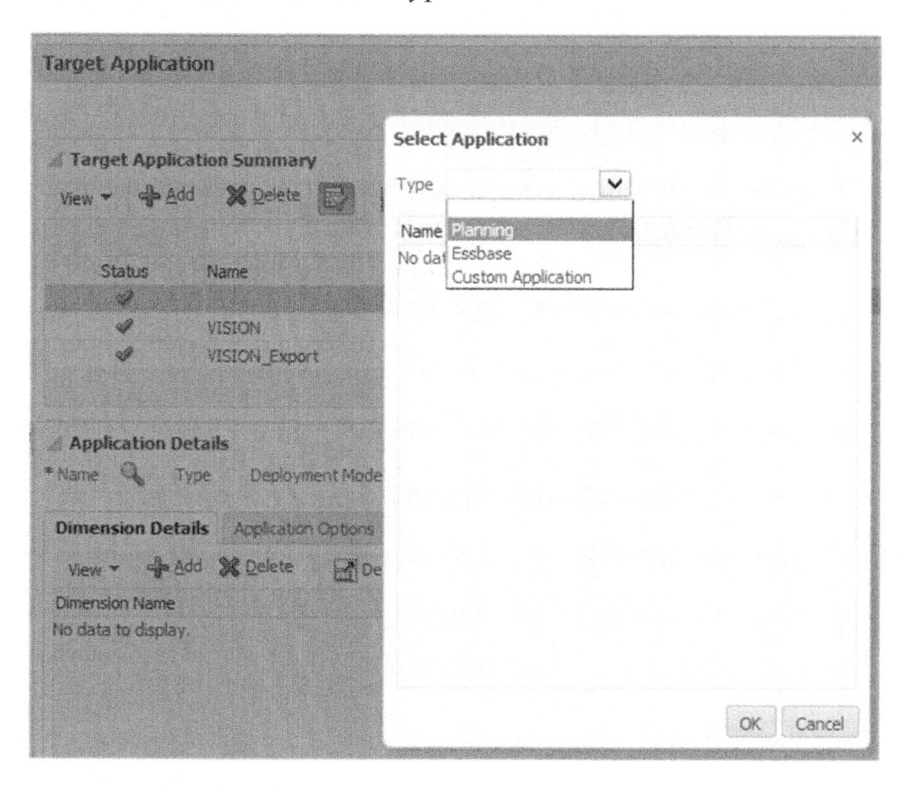

3. Select the ASO application name, *AVISION-SalesRpt*.
4. Click *OK*:

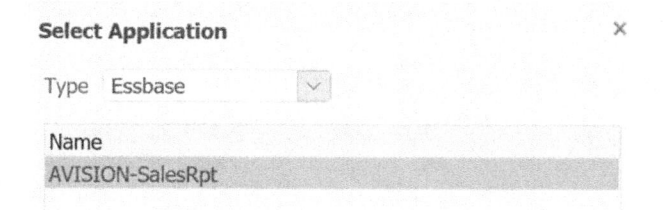

Many of the Dimension Details will populate automatically, but they may not be correct.

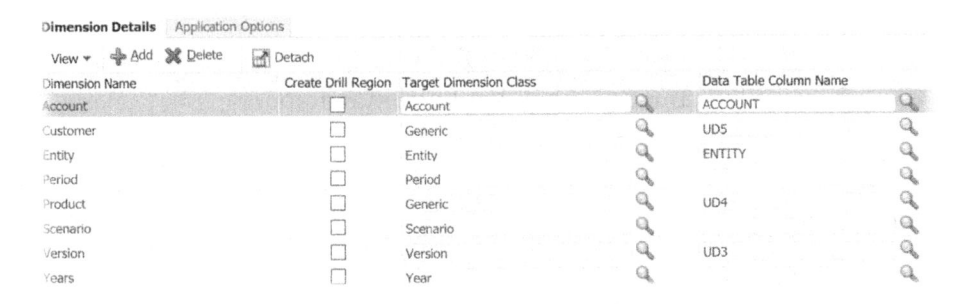

Dimension Name	Create Drill Region	Target Dimension Class	Data Table Column Name
Account	☐	Account	ACCOUNT
Customer	☐	Generic	UD5
Entity	☐	Entity	ENTITY
Period	☐	Period	
Product	☐	Generic	UD4
Scenario	☐	Scenario	
Version	☐	Version	UD3
Years	☐	Year	

5. Set *Entity* Dimension Name to *Entity* Target Dimension Class and *Entity* Data Table Column Name.
6. Set *Version* Dimension Name to *Version* Target Dimension Class and *UDx* Data Table Column Name.
7. Set *Scenario* Dimension Name to *Scenario* Target Dimension Class.
8. Ensure that Years, Period, and Scenario Dimension Names do not specify a Data Table Column Name. These should be left blank since those members are defined by the POV:

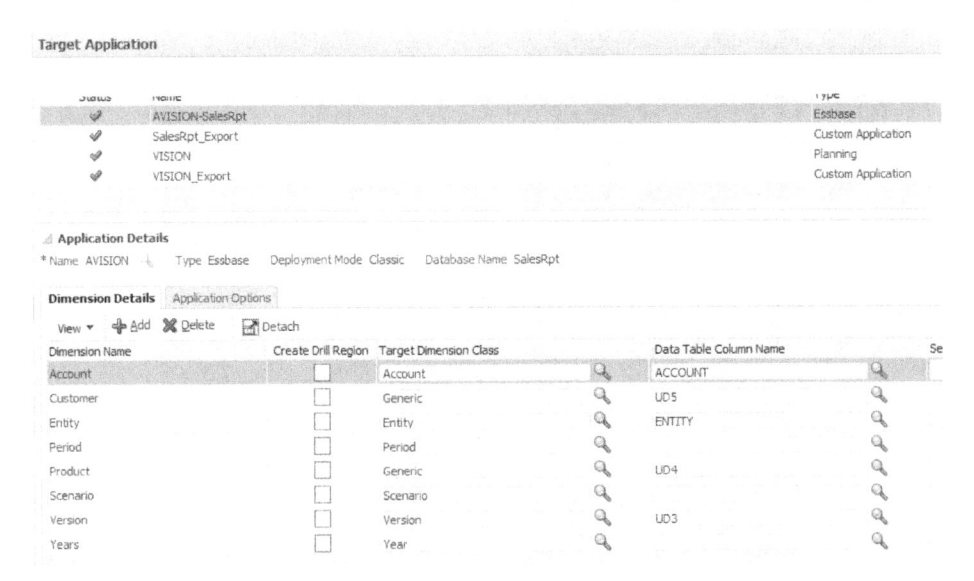

Target Application

Status	Name	Type
✓	AVISION-SalesRpt	Essbase
✓	SalesRpt_Export	Custom Application
✓	VISION	Planning
✓	VISION_Export	Custom Application

Application Details
*Name AVISION   Type Essbase   Deployment Mode Classic   Database Name SalesRpt

Dimension Name	Create Drill Region	Target Dimension Class	Data Table Column Name
Account	☐	Account	ACCOUNT
Customer	☐	Generic	UD5
Entity	☐	Entity	ENTITY
Period	☐	Period	
Product	☐	Generic	UD4
Scenario	☐	Scenario	
Version	☐	Version	UD3
Years	☐	Year	

9. Click *Save* to save the target application.

Look Smarter Than You Are with Enterprise Planning Cloud 161

One last note for now – a custom application target is used to export data from Enterprise Planning Cloud. I'll cover this in the Export section in just a bit.

Define Import Format

The import format defines which columns are extracted from the source system, how the data is stored in the Data Management staging table, and import mapping information.

To define the import format,

1. Under the Integration Setup section within the Setup tab, click *Import Format*.

The Import Format Screen consists of three sections:

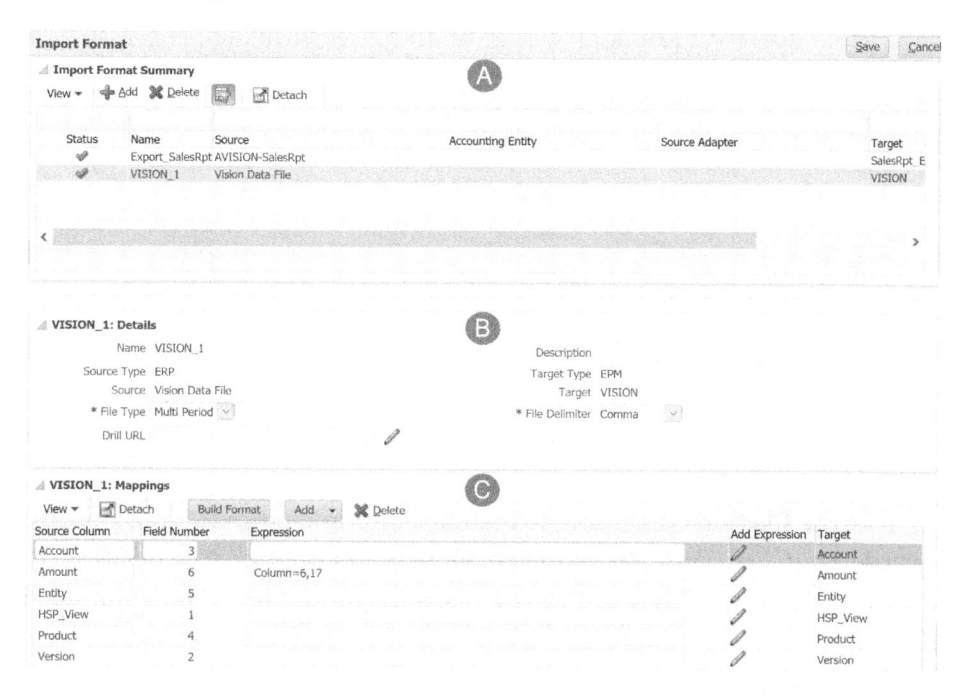

Import Format						Save	Cancel
Import Format Summary				A			
View ▼ ✚ Add ✘ Delete 📋 📋 Detach							
Status	Name	Source		Accounting Entity	Source Adapter		Target
✔	Export_SalesRpt	AVISION-SalesRpt					SalesRpt_E
✔	VISION_1	Vision Data File					VISION

VISION_1: Details — B
- Name: VISION_1
- Source Type: ERP
- Source: Vision Data File
- *File Type: Multi Period
- Drill URL
- Description
- Target Type: EPM
- Target: VISION
- *File Delimiter: Comma

VISION_1: Mappings — C
View ▼ 📋 Detach Build Format Add ▼ ✘ Delete

Source Column	Field Number	Expression	Add Expression	Target
Account	3		✎	Account
Amount	6	Column=6,17	✎	Amount
Entity	5		✎	Entity
HSP_View	1		✎	HSP_View
Product	4		✎	Product
Version	2		✎	Version

A. **Import Format Summary** – lists the import formats and details about source and target applications; new import formats are added in this pane

B. **Import Format Details** – specific import format configurations: name, source and target information, file type, drill through, etc.
C. **Import Format Mappings** – maps source file columns to target dimensions, as well as data columns

Enterprise Planning Cloud will create an import format by default for the BSO plan type. Select the *Vision_1* import format and review the import format details. I could use this import format but I'll create a new import format so you can see the process from start to finish.

2. Click ✚ to add an import format.
3. Under Details, name the import format "Load Vision Actuals".
4. For the File Type, select *Vision Data Files* from the drop-down menu.
5. Specify the File Type as *Multi Period* to match the load file format:

Load Vision Actuals: Details

Name	Load Vision Actuals
Source Type	ERP
*Source	Vision Data File
*File Type	Multi Period
Drill URL	

Description	
Target Type	EPM
*Target	VISION
*File Delimiter	Comma

6. Click *Save*. Note that until you save the new import format, Mappings will appear to be blank.

The file that I am going to load has multiple periods which is why I chose *Multi Period* for the File Type. Other valid options are *Fixed* (for set column widths to identify fields) or *Delimited* (individual data values use delimiters like quotation marks). These two options are used when loading a single period.

Supported delimiters are:

- comma (,)
- exclamation (!)
- semicolon (;)
- colon (:)
- pipe (|)
- tab

I'm going to use the Import Format Builder to help build my definition. The Import Format Builder supports both Fixed and Delimited files (though it does not support tab-delimited files).

7. Select *Build Format*.

8. Select *Upload* to upload the file.
9. Browse and select the "Vision_Actual_Dollars_FY14.csv" file.
10. Click *OK*:

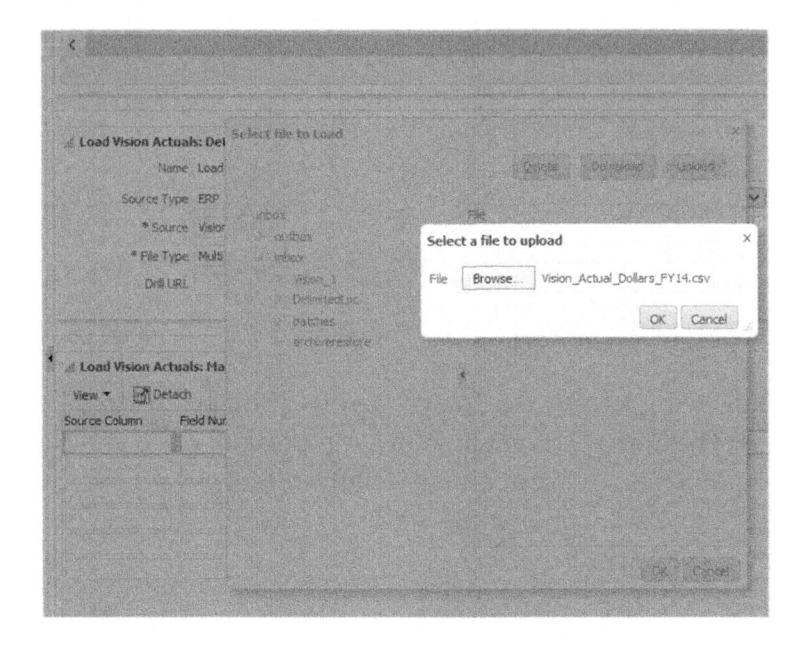

11. Select the file and click *OK*:

12. The Import Format Builder will display:

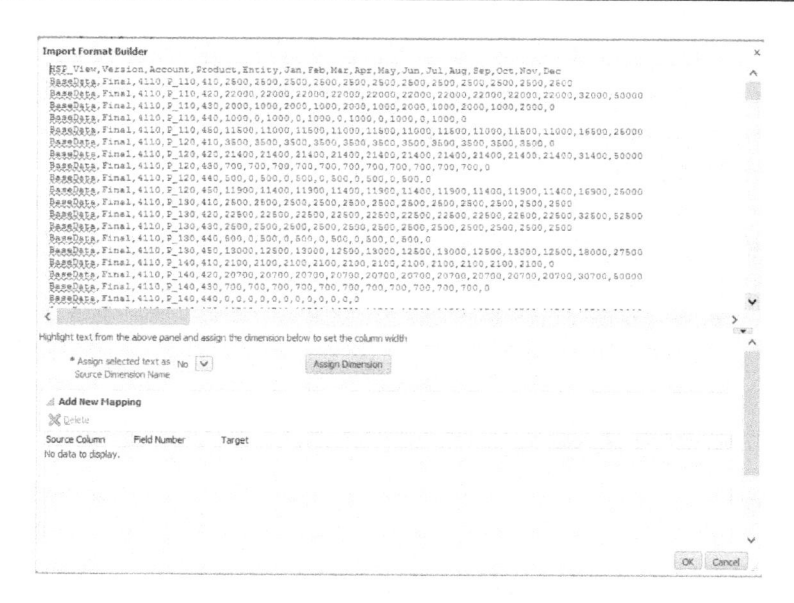

Look Smarter Than You Are with Enterprise Planning Cloud

13. Select *HSP_View* text.
14. Set *Assign selected text as Source Dimension Name* to *Yes*.
15. Click *Assign Dimension*:

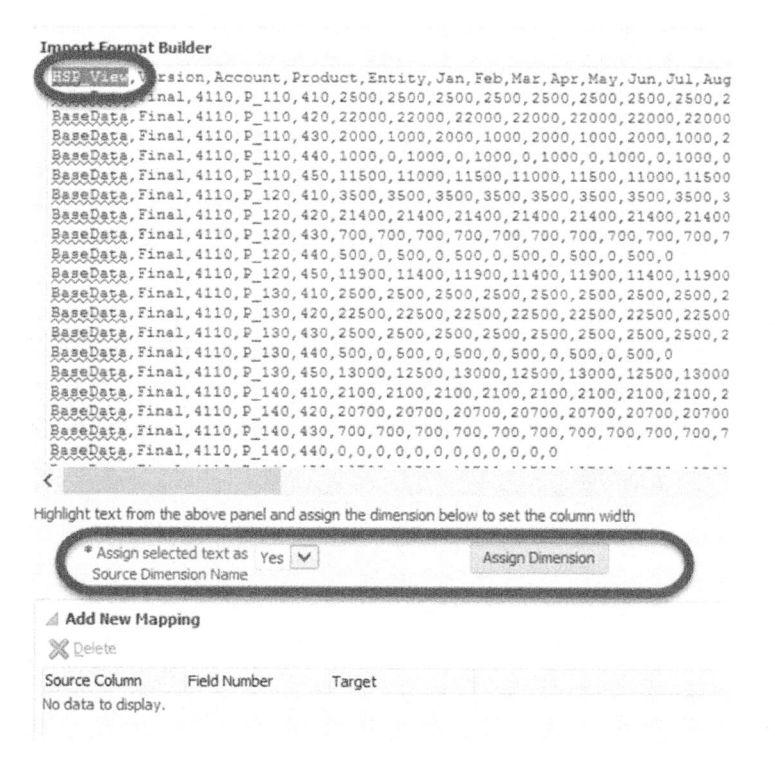

Chapter 5: Integrate Data

16. Make sure *Source Dimension Name* is set to *HSP_View*.
17. Set the *Target Dimension* to *HSP_View*.
18. Leave *Field Number* as 1.
19. Click *OK*:

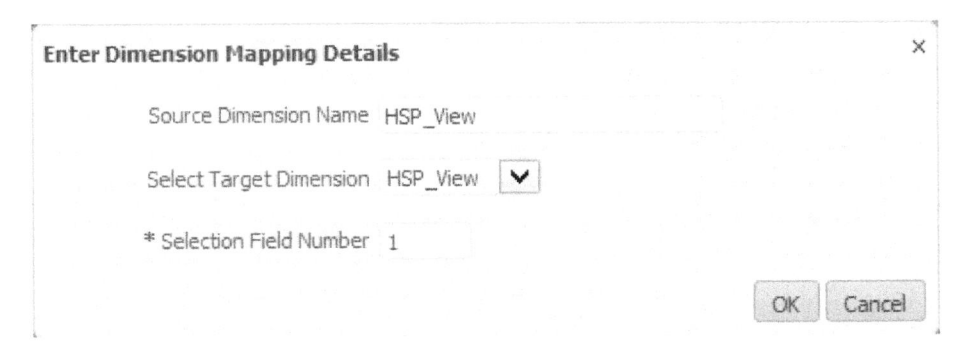

Enter Dimension Mapping Details

Source Dimension Name HSP_View

Select Target Dimension HSP_View

* Selection Field Number 1

OK Cancel

20. The first mapping row is added:

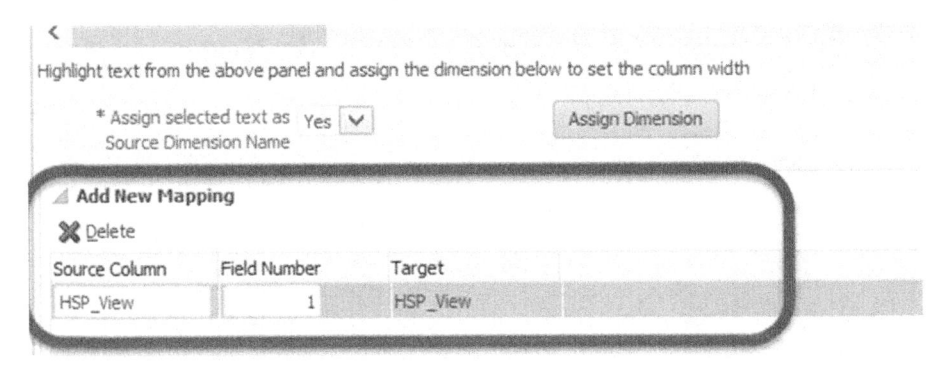

Highlight text from the above panel and assign the dimension below to set the column width

* Assign selected text as Yes
Source Dimension Name

Assign Dimension

Add New Mapping
Delete

Source Column	Field Number	Target
HSP_View	1	HSP_View

21. Select *Version* text.
22. Set *Assign selected text as Source Dimension Name* to *Yes*.
23. Click *Assign Dimension*:

Look Smarter Than You Are with Enterprise Planning Cloud 167

[Screenshot of Import Format Builder showing HSP_View data with Version column circled, and the "Assign selected text as Source Dimension Name" option circled with Assign Dimension button.]

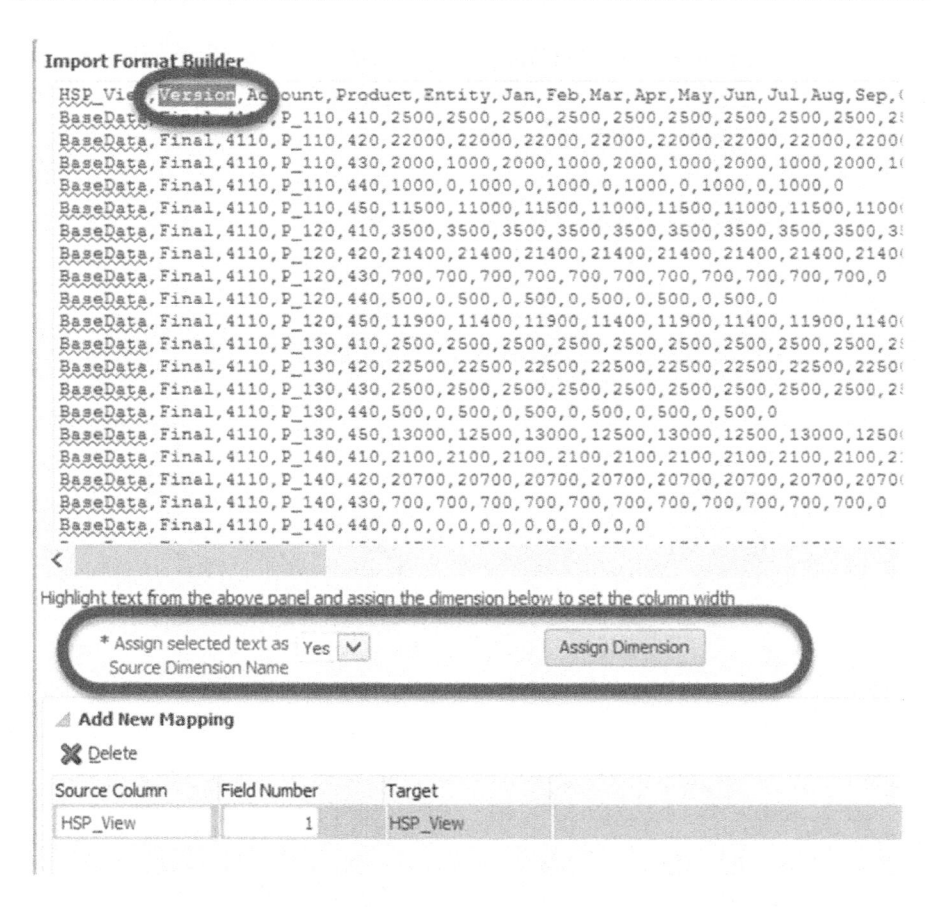

24. Make sure *Source Dimension Name* is set to *Version*.
25. Set the *Target Dimension* to *Version*.
26. Leave *Field Number* as "2".
27. Click *OK*:

[Screenshot of "Enter Dimension Mapping Details" dialog showing Source Dimension Name: Version, Select Target Dimension: Version, Selection Field Number: 2, with OK and Cancel buttons.]

28. Repeat the same steps to define the remaining mapping rows through Entity, selecting the Target Dimension that matches the Source Dimension Name for each field.

This is what things should look like so far:

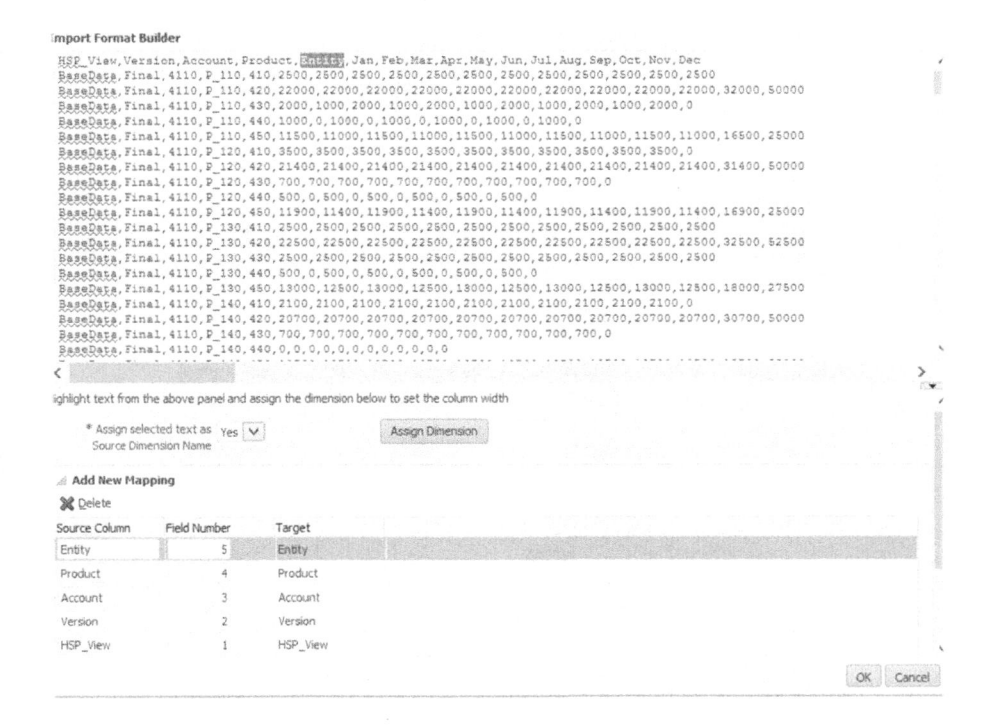

29. When you get to the columns containing the values by month, select all of the months:

30. Set *Assign selected text as Source Dimension Name* to *No*.
31. Click *Assign Dimension*.
32. Type "Amount" for the *Source Dimension Name*, set the *Target Dimension* to *Amount*, set the *Selection Field Number* to "6".
33. Click *OK*:

Enter Dimension Mapping Details

Source Dimension Name Amount

Select Target Dimension Amount

* Selection Field Number 6

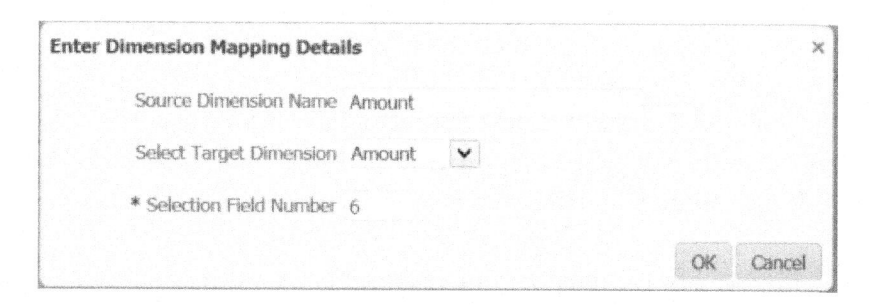

The end result should look as follows:

Source Column	Field Number	Target
Amount	6	Amount
Entity	5	Entity
Product	4	Product
Account	3	Account
Version	2	Version
HSP_View	1	HSP_View

34. Click *OK* to add the new mapping.
35. The final step is to use an expression to identify the Amount columns. Type "Column=6,17" to specify Column 6 as the first data number and Column 17 as the last data number:

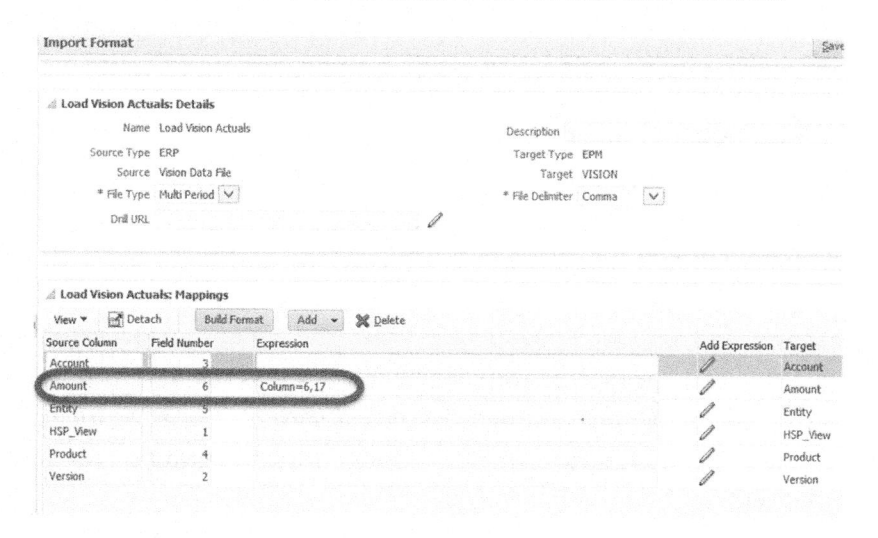

Import Format

Load Vision Actuals: Details
- Name: Load Vision Actuals
- Source Type: ERP
- Source: Vision Data File
- * File Type: Multi Period
- Drill URL
- Description
- Target Type: EPM
- Target: VISION
- * File Delimiter: Comma

Load Vision Actuals: Mappings

Source Column	Field Number	Expression	Target
Account	3		Account
Amount	6	Column=6,17	Amount
Entity	5		Entity
HSP_View	1		HSP_View
Product	4		Product
Version	2		Version

Make sure there are no spaces in your expressions or you will receive an error message.

36. Click *Save* to save the import format.

Note that I did not define Scenario, Period, or Year. Scenario will be defined in the Category mapping. Period and Year will be defined in the POV upon data load rule execution.

Import file formats support a number of expressions which are helpful for reading and parsing data files. Supported expressions include:

- Conversion of nonstandard numeric signs
- Conversion from European to US notation
- Padding fields with leading fills
- Padding fields with trailing fills
- Multiplying by whole number and decimal factors
- Disabling zero suppression

For file-based mappings you can add a mapping row to define additional specifications for the import file. You can define:

- **Skip** – to skip rows with no data or zeros or specific accounts
- **Attribute** – load up to 13 additional attributes to the staging table which can be helpful in drill through and for documentation purposes
- **Description** – load up two description columns
- **Currency** – load data in currency other than the default currency
- **Dimension** – allows you to concatenate fields for file-based data; to use this option, select the dimension, start and end positions, and the expression

You can concatenate source system fields as needed to map to a target dimension. While I did not use these features, it is good for you to know they exist. Check out the Oracle documentation for more information.

Define Location

Locations associate Import Format with Target Application, and combines mapping and data load rules for Target.

Important information about a location:

- A location will have one source system
- A location is assigned one import format
- A location is assigned one or more data load rules
- A location is assigned one data load mapping
- A location is the level at which a data load is executed
- Duplicate locations with the same source system and target application are allowed
- You can create different locations that use the same import format where the target application and dimensionality are the same
- Parent locations are supported. You can define mappings at a parent location and the related or "children" locations will use those mappings. Use this feature when you have multiple locations loading data using the same chart of accounts.
- A location can be assigned a logic account group (a logic account group contains one or more logic accounts that are generated when a source file is loaded; logic accounts are calculated accounts derived from source data)

You can also enable free form text using Data Management scripts in locations.

To set up a location,
1. Under Integration Setup in the Setup tab, click *Location:*

172   Chapter 5: Integrate Data

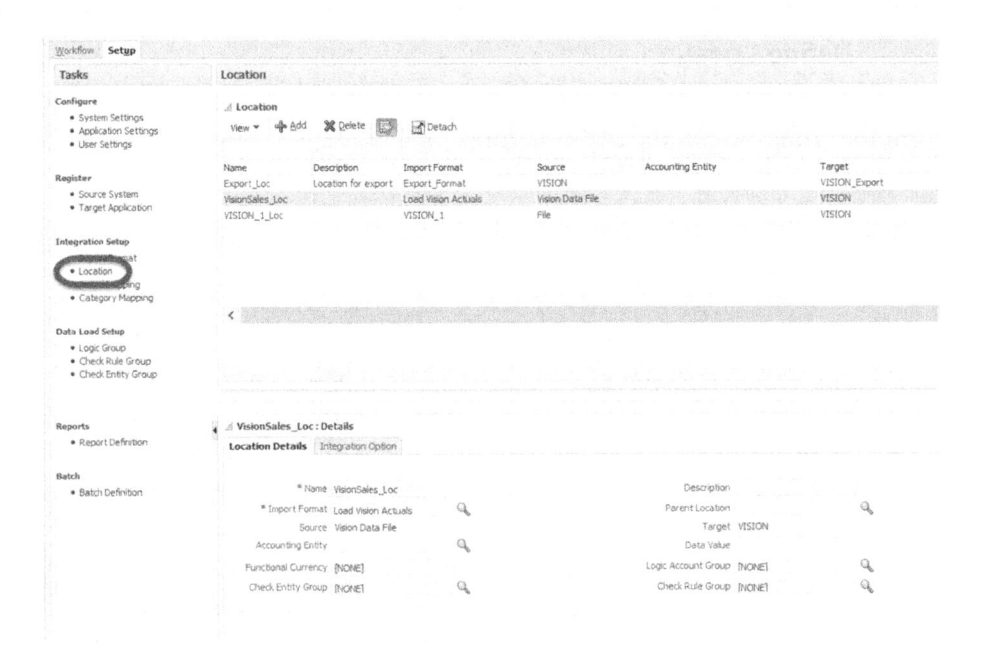

2. Click ➕ to create a new location.
3. Enter the following Location details, leaving some of these settings to default to [NONE] or blank (e.g., *Accounting Entity* is used for ERP loads from Fusion or E-Business Suite; the default behavior for *Check Entity Group* is to run for each entity):

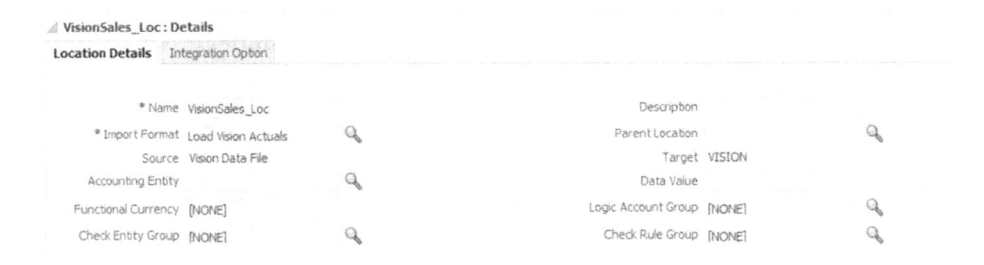

4. Click *Save*.

> **LOG ENTRY: SOL 14, Entry 1**
>
> I keep asking myself... Why is the Save button all the way at the top in Data Management? Why aren't Finn and Rachel together? Why did Notorious B.I.G. have to leave us so soon?
> I think being isolated in the Cloud with Data Management, Glee and McMullen's '90s hip hop music is getting to me.

Define Period Mapping

Period mappings define the mapping of ERP calendars, and EPM application year and periods. Period mappings may be defined in a global mapping, application mapping, or source mapping. Use *Global Mapping* when your target applications get data from sources with the calendar definitions. If you are loading data from multiple sources with varying complex calendar definitions, use *Application Mapping*. *Source Mapping* is used for adapter-based integrations, which are not available for Enterprise Planning Cloud.

To define a period mapping,
1. Under Integration Setup in the Setup tab, click *Period Mapping:*

In the Global Mapping tab, all entries should be populated with the years specified at application creation (in my case, FY10 to FY20). The Period Key and Prior Period Key fields are not relevant to Enterprise

Planning Cloud applications. I will focus on the Target Period Month and Year Target:

Period Key	Prior Period Key	Period Name	Target Period Month	Target Period Quarter	Target Period Year	Target Year Target
1/31/2010	12/31/2009	Jan-10	Jan			FY10
2/28/2010	1/31/2010	Feb-10	Feb			FY10
3/31/2010	2/28/2010	Mar-10	Mar			FY10
4/30/2010	3/31/2010	Apr-10	Apr			FY10
5/31/2010	4/30/2010	May-10	May			FY10
6/30/2010	5/31/2010	Jun-10	Jun			FY10
7/31/2010	6/30/2010	Jul-10	Jul			FY10

2. Ensure that all target months and years match up to the *Period Name*.

Define Category Mapping

Category mappings will map scenarios from source systems to targets. For example, your ERP system might use "Budget" scenario but in Enterprise Planning Cloud you have a "Plan" member. You would define a category mapping to match these two elements.

Global Mapping defines mappings that cross multiple applications (so you only have to set them once). Most of the time "Actual" from a source will map to "Actual" in a Target. This is a good candidate for a global category mapping.

Application Mapping defines category mappings that are specific for a target application.

I will define my category mappings as global.

To define a category mapping,
1. Under Integration Setup in the Setup tab, click *Category Mapping*.
2. In the Global Mapping tab, click ✛ to enter a new row.
3. Enter *Category* as "Actual", *Frequency* as "Monthly", and *Target Category* as "Actual".

4. Enter *Category* as "Forecast", *Frequency* as "Monthly", and *Target Category* as "Forecast".
5. Enter *Category* as "Plan", *Frequency* as "Monthly", and *Target Category* as "Plan".
6. If you see any other rows (e.g., "Current"), delete them. Your screen should look like the following:

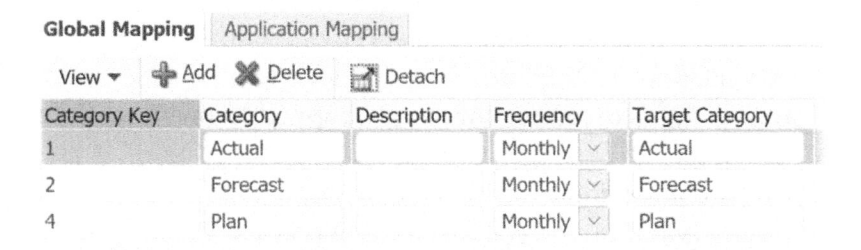

Category Key	Category	Description	Frequency	Target Category
1	Actual		Monthly	Actual
2	Forecast		Monthly	Forecast
4	Plan		Monthly	Plan

7. Click *Save* (at the top of the screen).

LOG ENTRY: SOL 14, Entry 2

Finally the setup is complete! Can I load data? No. Not yet.

Ugh. Now that I think about it, the first time I created a data load in Essbase that also seemed to have a million steps. I'll be patient as I complete this first data load.

Maybe.

Define Data Load Mapping

I now will switch to the Workflow section, where I will define member maps and data load rules.

Member maps are defined in Data Load Mapping. I must map members for all target dimensions. Member mappings are used during the data load process to load data to the appropriate members in the target dimension. This is where I can map or transform data from the source to the target (e.g., if I have five GL accounts that I would like to map into one summary Enterprise Planning Cloud account, I define that mapping here).

You will not map Period or Scenario dimensions because you already did that in the Setup section under Period Mapping and Category Mapping.

Valid member mapping types include:

- **Explicit** – source value is matched exactly and replaced with the target member value (e.g., your source file has a column with values "current" and you want to load that to "Final" version member in the Version dimension)
- **Between** – range of source values is replaced with one target member value (e.g., I want to specify accounts 6000-6999 should be loaded to "COGS" member in Enterprise Planning Cloud)
- **In** – list of source accounts to be mapped to one target member value
- **Multi-Dimension** – define a member mapping based on multiple column values (e.g., you are combining Cost Center column and Department column to map to Entity dimension members in Enterprise Planning Cloud)
- **Like** – string in the source value is matched and replaced with target member value

Special characters to be used in Like mappings:

Special Character	How to Use	Example / Use Cases
Asterisk (*) Wildcard	Represents source value; you can add a prefix or suffix	Use when source members match target members exactly – use * to *; for example, A* would take source value "6001" and load to member "A6001"
Question Mark (?) Wildcard	Strips a single character from a source value; you will probably use this in an expression	?* would take source value "A6001" and load to member "6001"

Special Character	How to Use	Example / Use Cases
<1> returns first concatenated segment, <2> returns second concatenated segment, <3> returns third concatenated segment, and so on... <4>, <5>	Processes rows that have concatenated values separated by an underscore "_" and extracts corresponding value; can use with ? but not *	<2> would take source value "A_6001" and load to member "6001"
<BLANK>	Processes only rows that contain spaces; use to map to "No_XXX" members in the target In on-premise FDMEE, <BLANK> does not recognize an actual blank; it only recognizes a space	<BLANK> as source and "No_Product" would load any rows with blank values to "No_Product" member

Multiple mappings might apply to a specific source value. Within each mapping type (except for Explicit), mapping is evaluated in alphabetical order according to Rule Name.

Format masks are also supported in Data Management mappings (available for all mapping types except Explicit). You might use #FORMAT when replacing segments from the source value, replacing segments with string operations, and replacing segments with string operations using prefixes or suffixes. For example a source value might look like "ABC-6001" and you want to load to a member, "ABC-Account-6001-Expense". Using the format mask syntax with special characters will generate this result.

To ignore a member mapping, select the source value and then in *Target Value*, enter "IGNORE". Data will not be loaded for any source values defined with IGNORE mapping.

To create a data load mapping,
1. In the Workflow tab, click *Data Load Mapping*:

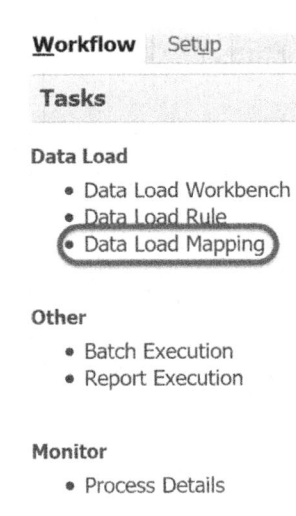

Workflow Setup

Tasks

Data Load
- Data Load Workbench
- Data Load Rule
- Data Load Mapping

Other
- Batch Execution
- Report Execution

Monitor
- Process Details

2. At the bottom of the screen, choose the Location just created, *VisionSales_Loc*. Change the period and category to match the image below:

Data Load Mapping
Save
Cancel
Dimensions Account
Data Table Column ACCOUNT
All Mappings
Explicit
Between
In
Multi Dimension
Like
View
Export
Import
Restore Mapping
Delete Mappings
Delete All Mappings
Detach
Type
Source Value
Target Value
Location VisionSales_Loc Period Dec-16 Category Actual Source Vision Data File Target VISION

Now I need to complete the appropriate mappings for each target dimension.

3. Choose the *Account* dimension from the drop-down list near the top of the Data Load Mapping screen.
4. Select the *Like* tab.

Note!

Data Management processes these mappings from left to right: *Explicit* first, then *Between, In, Multi Dimensional*, and then *Like*.

5. Click ✚ to add a row into the mapping (note that you can add multiple rows in a mapping for Like, if requirements dictate; you can also delete rows).
6. Enter "*" as both the Source Value and Target Value, and call the Rule Name "DirectMapAccount":

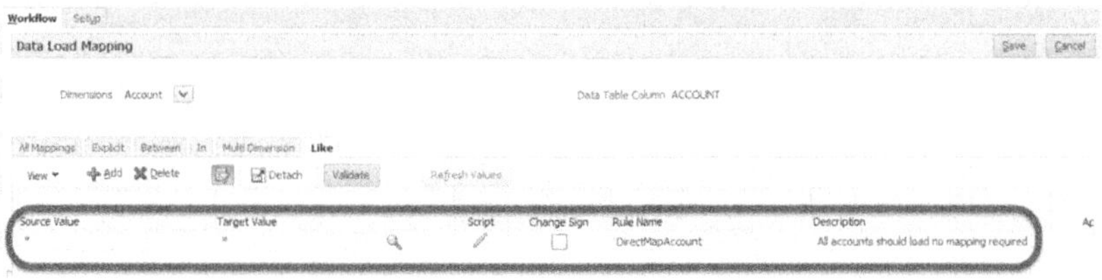

Note!

The "Rule Name" name is a misnomer in Data Management. This is actually a name for the mapping created and it is unique across locations. Data Management processes these maps in alphabetical order after left to right based on operation, so the name you choose can be critical in the mapping process. Once a match is found then it will map and move to the next record. Rule Names can handle numbers as well as text, so numbers can be used to force process order. Numbers, however, are processed as text.

7. Click *Save*.
8. Choose the *Entity* dimension from the drop-down list.
9. Select the *Like* tab.
10. Click ✚ to add a row into the mapping.
11. Enter "*" as the *Source Value* and "*" as the *Target Value* and call the *Rule Name* "DirectMapEntity":

12. Click *Save*.
13. Choose the *Product* dimension from the drop-down list.
14. Select the *Like* tab.
15. Click ✚ to add a row into the mapping.
16. Enter "*" as the *Source Value* and "*" as the *Target Value* and call the *Rule Name* "DirectMapProduct":

Look Smarter Than You Are with Enterprise Planning Cloud   181

[Data Load Mapping screenshot: Dimensions Product, Data Table Column UD1, with Source Value *, Target Value *, Rule Name DirectMapProduct, Description "All products should load no mapping required"]

17. Click *Save*.
18. Choose the *HSP_View* dimension from the drop-down list.
19. Select the *Explicit* tab.
20. Click ✛ to add a row into the mapping.
21. Add "BaseData" as the *Source Value* and "BaseData" as the *Target Value* and add a description. I could have used the Like mapping as I did earlier, but I wanted to show you the steps for a different mapping method. I would use this if the source file had "Base Data" and I needed to map to "BaseData" in the target:

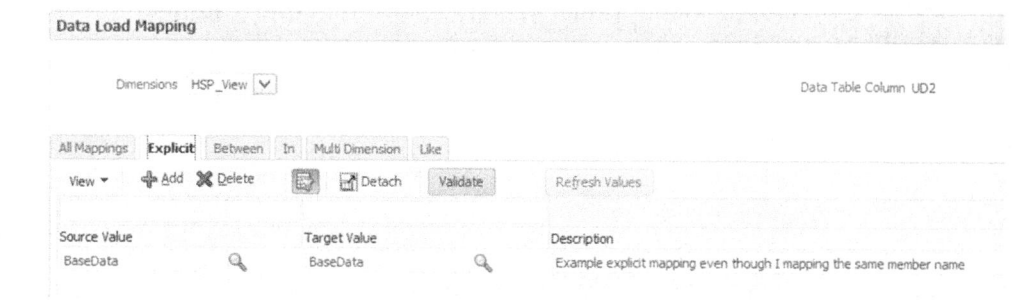

[Data Load Mapping screenshot: Dimensions HSP_View, Data Table Column UD2, Explicit tab, Source Value BaseData, Target Value BaseData, Description "Example explicit mapping even though I mapping the same member name"]

22. Click *Save*.
23. Choose the *Version* dimension from the drop-down list.
24. Select the *Explicit* tab.
25. Click ✛ to add a row into the mapping.
26. Add "Final" as the *Source Value* and "Final" as the *Target Value* and add a description. As before, I could have used the *Like* mapping. I would use this if the source file had "Current" and I needed to map to "Final" in the target:

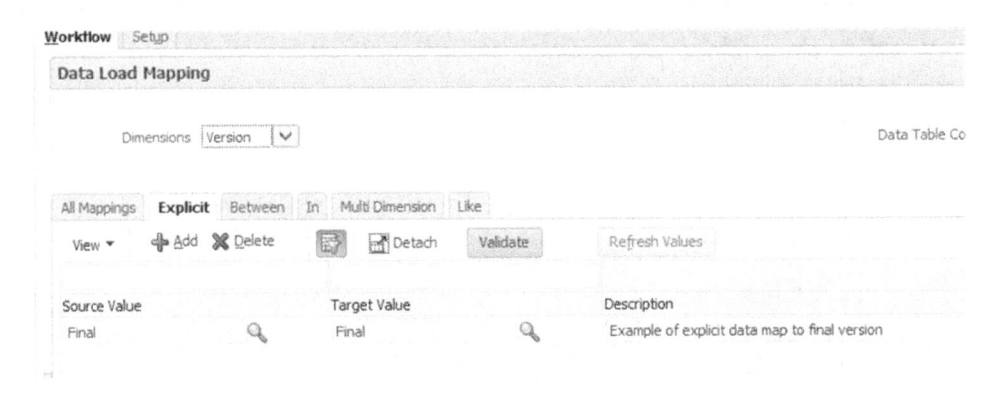

Once you're done, you can check all mappings in the *All Mappings* tab by cycling through each dimension in the drop down. All dimensions except Scenario, Period, and Years need to be mapped in this manner. This view is helpful because it is possible to combine mapping requirements (e.g., using *Explicit*, *Like* and *Between*) for a single dimension. You can only view the mappings for a single dimension at a time.

> **Note!** If you have mappings that are valid for many locations, then it's recommended that you create a parent location and then define the mappings there.

27. Click *Save*. Check that all dimensions in the drop-down are mapped.

Export & Import Excel Mappings

Mapping in particular may be updated in a more granular fashion via the Data Load Mapping interface in FDMEE, which allows exporting or importing maps for one or more dimensions.

To download an Excel Import Template, select *Import >> Download Excel Template*:

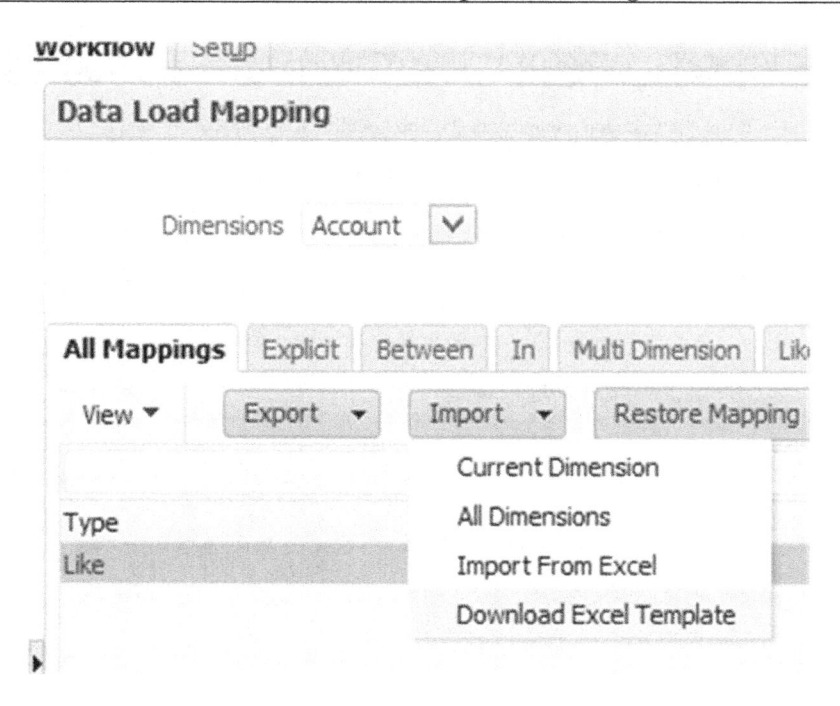

Here are some guidelines for creating the mapping template:

- Mapping templates may not have any blank lines
- Do not insert lines into the mapping template
- You may only have one mapping template per workbook
- Create a separate workbook for each dimension

Follow these additional instructions to complete your Excel mapping template:

Mapping Instructions

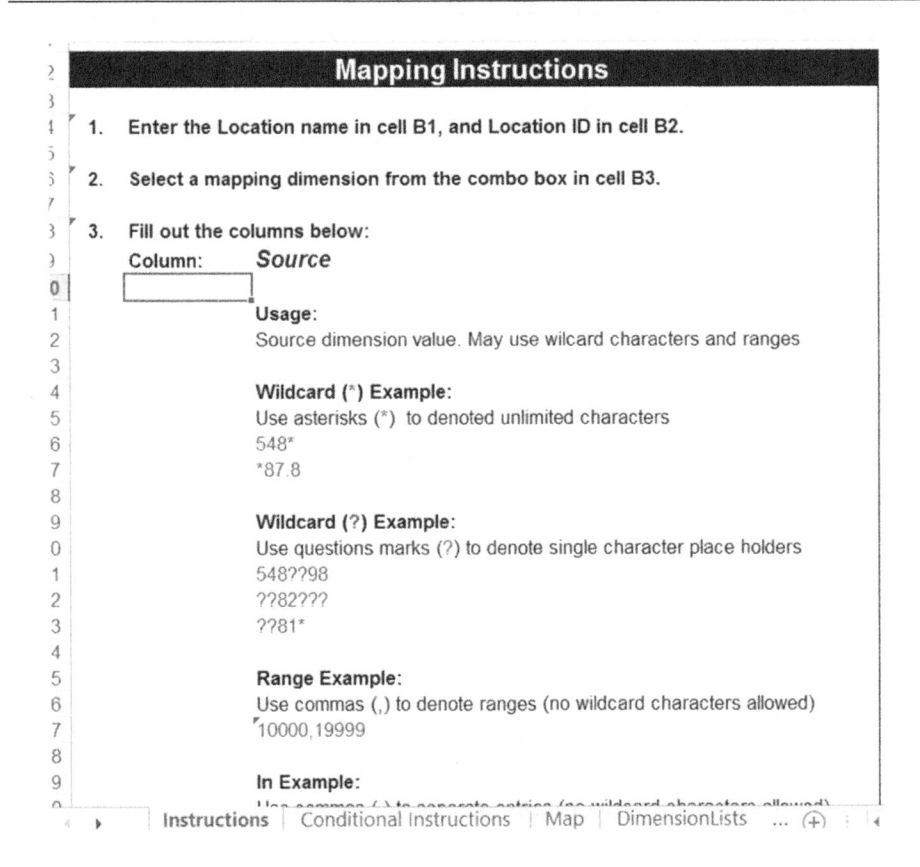

1. Enter the Location name in cell B1, and Location ID in cell B2.

2. Select a mapping dimension from the combo box in cell B3.

3. Fill out the columns below:

   Column: *Source*

   Usage:
   Source dimension value. May use wilcard characters and ranges

   Wildcard (*) Example:
   Use asterisks (*) to denoted unlimited characters
   548*
   *87.8

   Wildcard (?) Example:
   Use questions marks (?) to denote single character place holders
   548??98
   ??82???
   ??81*

   Range Example:
   Use commas (,) to denote ranges (no wildcard characters allowed)
   10000,19999

   In Example:

Once the template is ready, you can import the Excel template with all mappings. Choose the dimension from the drop-down list, then click *Import >> Import From Excel*:

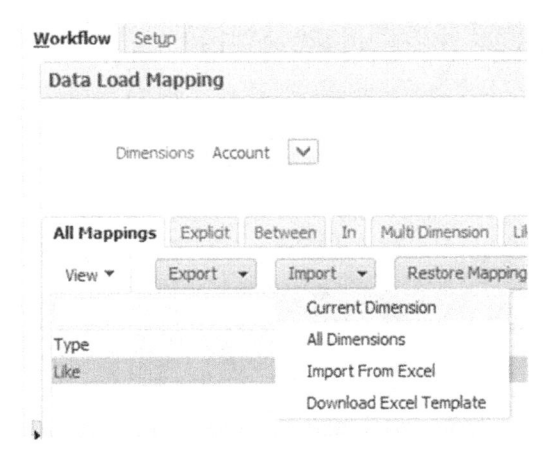

Data Load Mapping

Dimensions Account

All Mappings | Explicit | Between | In | Multi Dimension | Like

View ▼ | Export ▼ | Import ▼ | Restore Mapping

- Current Dimension
- All Dimensions
- Import From Excel
- Download Excel Template

You'll specify the file and then define options to merge or replace mappings. You can also export existing mappings for a single dimension or all dimensions.

Exporting Mapping

To export a mapping, click *Export*:

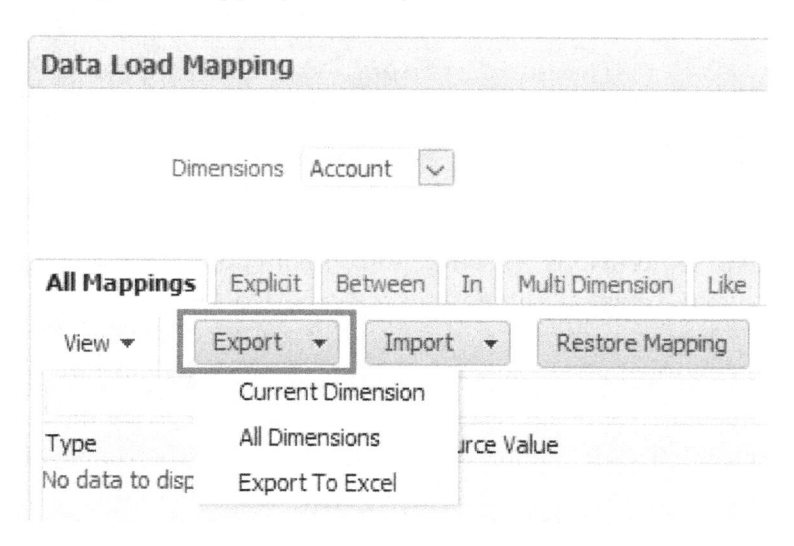

The following *Export* options are available:

- **Current Dimension** – exports the current dimension for the current location (POV) to a comma-delimited flat file in the Enterprise Planning Cloud Inbox. When prompted, enter a file name (including .txt or .csv extension) and click *OK*. Then select the file from the Inbox and click *Download* to download it locally. Other options from the Enterprise Planning Cloud Inbox include *Upload* and *Delete*:

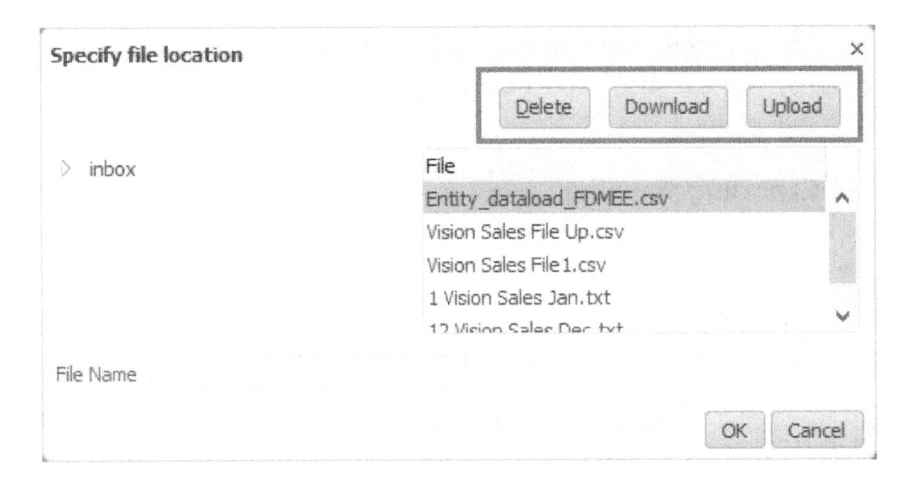

- **All Dimensions** – same functionality as Current Dimension above, except all dimensions are exported for the current location (POV)
- **Export to Excel** – exports mapping as a formatted report that is intended for business users. Prompts to open / save the Excel file locally. This is a report only. It may be used to coordinate mapping changes but may not be directly imported to FDMEE

Importing Mapping

To import a mapping, click *Import*:

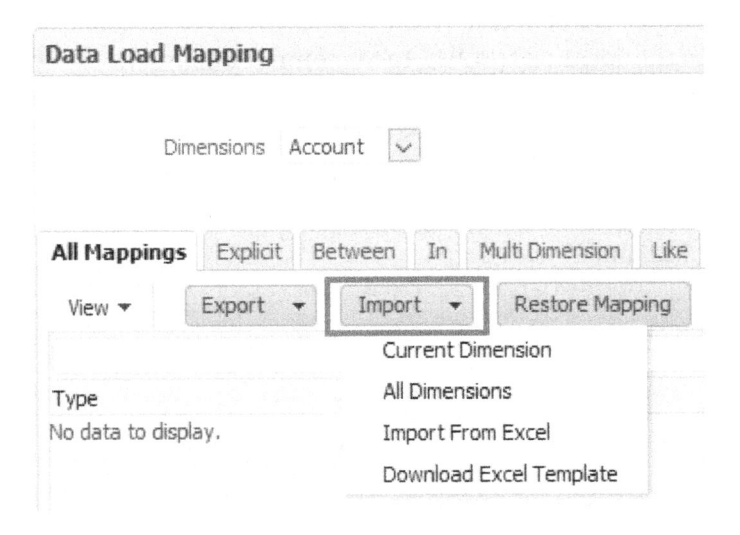

The following *Import* options are available:

- **Current Dimension** – imports mapping from a comma-delimited flat file for the current dimension and current location (POV). When prompted, click *Upload* to upload a file, or select an existing file from the Enterprise Planning Cloud Inbox, and click *OK*
- **All Dimensions** – same functionality as *Current Dimension* above, except all dimensions are imported for the current location (POV)
- **Import from Excel** – imports mapping from the Excel Template (see below)
- **Download Excel Template** – prompts to open/save the Excel Template file locally. Instructions are included in the file. This provides a user-friendly alternative to exporting / importing mapping via comma-delimited flat file

After selecting a file to import, a prompt appears with the following import mode and validation options:

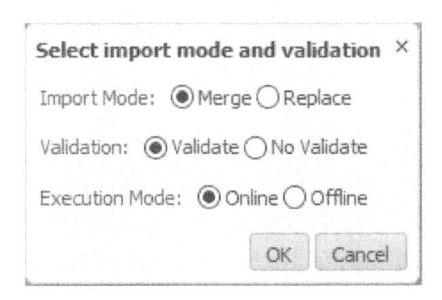

```
Select import mode and validation  ×
Import Mode:   ● Merge  ○ Replace
Validation:    ● Validate  ○ No Validate
Execution Mode: ● Online  ○ Offline
                        OK    Cancel
```

- **Import Mode**
    o **Merge** – add to (but not change) existing mapping
    o **Replace** – replace all existing mapping
- **Validation**
    o **Validate** – checks mapping for any invalid target members
    o **No Validate** – does not check mapping for invalid target members
- **Execution Mode**
    o **Online** – executes immediately (recommended)
    o **Offline** – executes in the background (check status under Process Details)

Create Data Load Rule

I'll create a data load rule now that I've completed the member mappings. A data rule is defined for a single location. You may have many data load rules that load to your target application, allowing for loads from multiple sources.

To create a data load rule,
1. Navigate to the *Data Load >> Data Load Rule* section.
2. Check that your POV at the bottom of the screen is set to the "VisionSales_Loc" Location and "Actual" Category. (Ignore Period – that will be defined in Execution because this is a multi-period file).
3. Click *Add*.
4. Enter the name "Load Vision Sales Actuals":

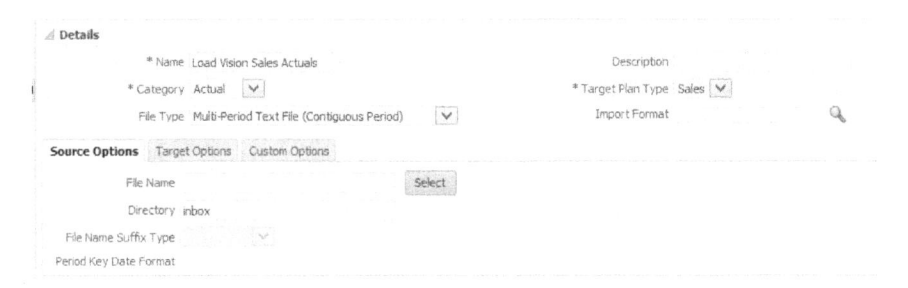

5. Select *Actual* for Category.
6. Select *Multi-Period Text File (Contiguous Period)* for File Type.
7. Select *Sales* for Target Plan Type.
8. Select *Load Vision Actuals* for Import Format:

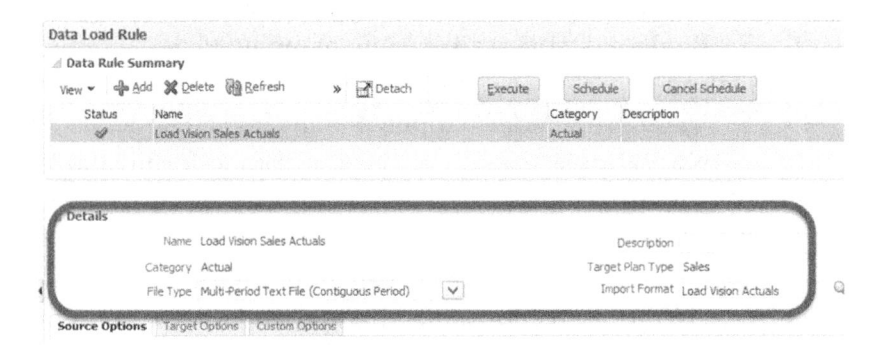

Defining the import format here is an optional step. You can choose to overwrite the import format that is defined with the location. If you do not select anything here, the default import format for the location will be used (in my case, I picked the same import format so I'm really using the same import format definition).

9. Click *Save*.
10. Under Source Options, click *Select*.
11. Click *Upload* and browse to the file *Vision_Actual_Dollars_FY14.csv*, then click *OK*.
12. Select the file *Vision_Actual_Dollars_FY14.csv* and click *OK*.
13. Leave all other options set to default.
14. Click *Save*.

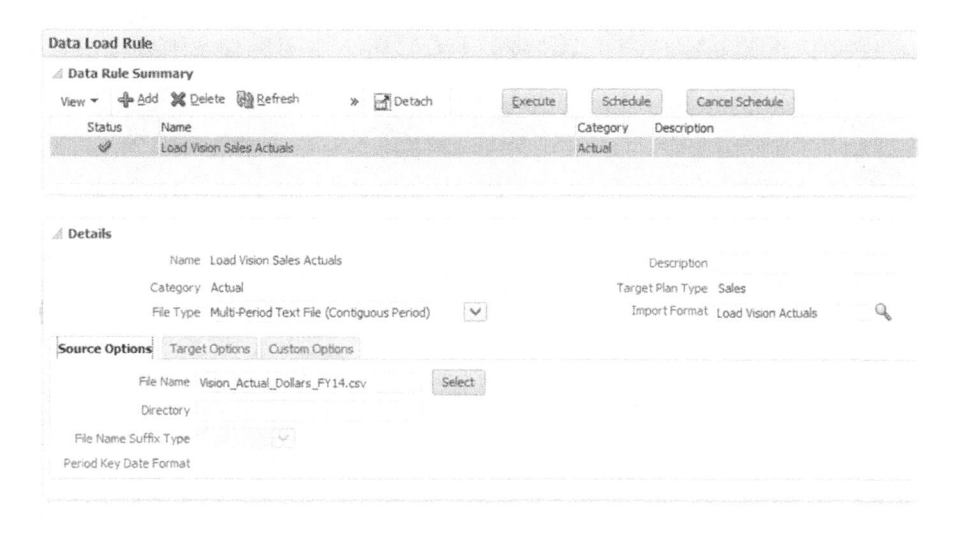

The data load rule is now saved and ready for use.

> LOG ENTRY: SOL 14, Entry 3
>
> Finally the data load rule is complete! Can I load data?
> Yes! Yes, I can.
> Boy, I never thought I would get here but here I am. Ready to load data into the Cloud with Data Management!

Execute Load Rule to Load Data

Before I run the load process, I want to revisit how Data Management loads data. Data Management will import source data to a staging table and then load to the Target. I can do this in two steps, or all in one step.

Source → Staging Table → Target

I can execute the load rule from the *Data Load Rule* section:

1. Once ready to load, select the desired load rule, in my case *Load Vision Sales Actuals*, and click *Execute*.

You have the option to *Import from Source* which will import into Data Management's staging table. You can stop there if you would like, or you can continue and export the data from the Data Management staging table and load to the Target.

2. Check the options to:
   a. *Import from Source*

b. *Export to Target*
3. Specify the Start Period and End Period (in my case I'm loading data from Jan-14 to Dec-14).
4. Set Import Mode to *Replace*.

Available import modes / load methods for files are *Append* (new rows will be appended to rows in the staging table for the POV) or *Replace* (replace all rows in the staging table for the POV). Remember that the POV is the Location, Period, Year, and Scenario. *Append* is useful when a particular location has multiple source files. The first source file may be loaded as *Replace* and subsequent source files may be loaded as *Append*.

5. Set Export Mode to *Replace Data*:

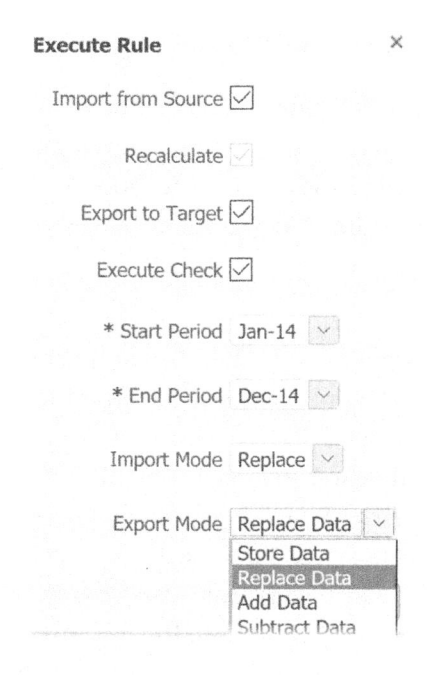

Execute Rule

- Import from Source ☑
- Recalculate
- Export to Target ☑
- Execute Check ☑
- * Start Period: Jan-14
- * End Period: Dec-14
- Import Mode: Replace
- Export Mode: Replace Data
  - Store Data
  - Replace Data
  - Add Data
  - Subtract Data

Export Mode defines how data will be exported from the staging table and loaded into the target.

Available options for Export Mode include:

- **Store Data** – inserts file from source and replaces any value that currently exists in the target
- **Add Data** – adds the value from the source to the value that exists in the target
- **Subtract Data** – subtracts the value from the source to the value that exists in the target
- **Replace Data** – clears all data in the target for the POV currently being loaded and then loads the source file

Another option, *Override All Data* (clears ALL data in the target), is available but only if it is enabled in *System Settings* or *Application Settings*.

Note!
- **Import Mode** – controls how the data is imported to the Data Management staging table
- **Export Mode** – controls how the data is exported from the Data Management staging table to the target application

The example above loads data to one set of accounts all the way from source to target. If there is a need to load multiple files, one option is to accumulate it all in FDMEE first and then load it to the target at one time. To do this, set the first load's Import Mode to *Replace* and do not select the option to *Export to Target*. This will replace all previously existing FDMEE data records with the first data file set. Then for each subsequent data file load except the last, change the Import Mode to *Append* so that records are appended to the underlying Data Management staging table only. Otherwise, the data loaded for the first set of accounts will be cleared in the Data Management staging table when each new data set is loaded. Continue to not select *Export to Target* in these subsequent loads. On the final data file load, keep the Import Mode as *Append*, finally check the option to *Export to Target*, and set the Export Mode to *Replace*. This will add the last data file's records into the staging table and then load all of the accumulated data records from the staging table to the target.

Note! When loading multiple sets of data or multiple data files, change the Import Mode to *Append* and the Export Mode to *Store Data* or *Add Data* so that records are appended to the underlying Data Management staging table. Otherwise, the data loaded for the first set of accounts will be cleared when the second data set is loaded.

6. Click *Run*. You should receive a message indicating that the process is running in the background. Make a mental note of the Process Id:

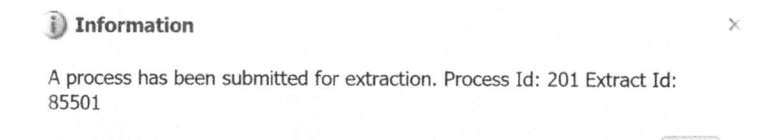

> **Information** ✕
>
> A process has been submitted for extraction. Process Id: 201 Extract Id: 85501
>
> OK

You can view the load process status in the top of the Data Load Rule window, within the *Data Rule Summary* section.

7. Click the *Refresh* button after at least 10 seconds to see the status:

> Data Load Rule
> ▲ Data Rule Summary
> View ▾   ✚ Add   ✕ Delete   🔄 Refresh   Show ▾
> | Status | Name |
> |---|---|
> | ✓ | Load Vision Sales Actuals |
> | ◎ | Load Vision Sales Actuals - FY15 |

8. For more details on the process, go to *Monitor >> Process Details*:

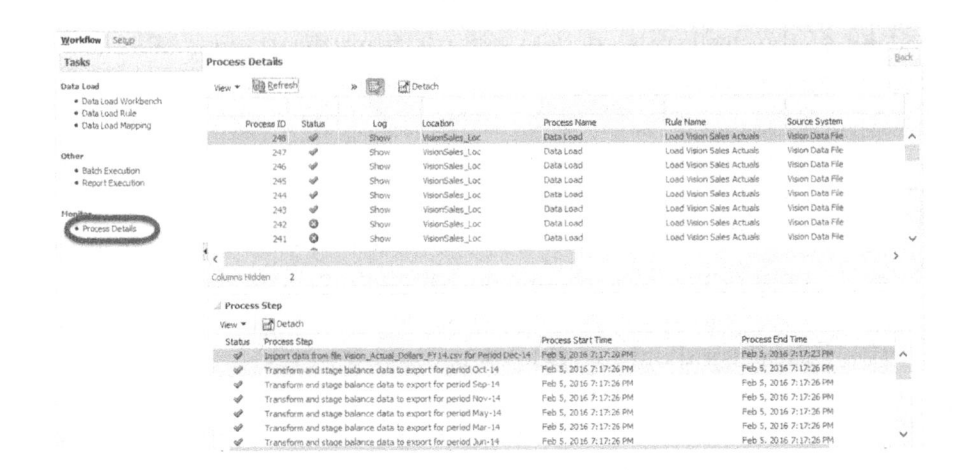

Note! Process Details will give you a lot of great information in the log file. For instance, the log file can tell you how many records go through a specific mapping.

9. View logs and search for "Error" to see if any errors have occurred (though the log file can be confusing).

Note! Data cannot be loaded to members that are tagged as Dynamic Calc or are not Level 0.

Workbench

The *Data Management Workbench* helps me monitor and view each of the stages of the Data Management load process. The Workbench allows you to interact with each of the stages (Import, Validate, Export, and Check), drill back to source details, and more. The Workbench, however, does not support multi-period loads, so you have to view data for a single period:

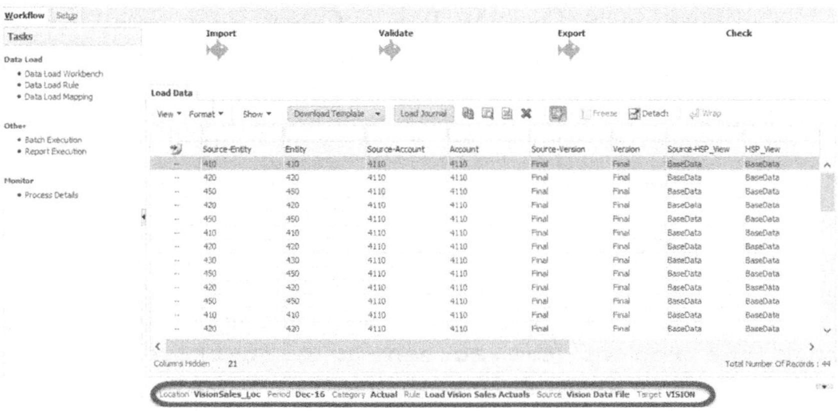
Workflow
Setup
Tasks
Data Load
Data Load Workbench
Data Load Rule
Data Load Mapping
Other
Batch Execution
Report Execution
Monitor
Process Details
Import
Validate
Export
Check
Load Data
View
Format
Show
Download Template
Load Journal
Freeze
Detach
Wrap
Source-Entity
Entity
Source-Account
Account
Source-Version
Version
Source-HSP_View
HSP_View
Columns Hidden 21
Total Number Of Records : 44
Location VisionSales_Loc Period Dec-16 Category Actual Rule Load Vision Sales Actuals Source Vision Data File Target VISION

The Workbench consists of four sections:

- Workflow grid
- POV bar
- Status
- Data grid

The workflow grid lets users process data from start to finish. The four main stages are listed as headers here. Fish icons (the illustrious "fishies" that this product is known for) mark the status of each step. If a step is completed successfully, the fish turns orange.  If the step is unsuccessful, the fish turns gray.  The four stages of processing data are as follows:

- **Import** – loads data from the source
- **Validate** – checks to ensure that all members have a valid account home
- **Export** – loads the valid members to the target application
- **Check** – verifies the accuracy of the data with user-defined rules

The POV bar is accessible at the bottom of the workbench screen.

Location VISION_1 Period Dec-20 Category Actual Rule Vision1_DLR Source Vision Data File Target VISION

This governs the Location, Period, Category (Scenario), and Data Load Rule that will process data. The status shows the current status of the data processing. The data grid allows users to import, view, verify, and export data from source systems, as well as, drill through to the source data and view mapping details.

LOG ENTRY: SOL 14, Entry 4

Did you see how Data Management uses fishies across the top of the screen to illustrate the stage of the data integration process (Import, Validate, Export, Check)? Being a huge fan of Aquaman, I love the fishies!

Once I create my data forms, I'll be able to verify and view that data in Enterprise Planning Cloud:

Check Actuals Data Load

Scenario: Actual
Entity: International Sales
Version: Jerry1_Version

Jerry1_Version

		FY14 YearTotal	FY15 YearTotal	FY16 YearTotal
Total Product	4001:Total Revenue	401720	1498358.75	

Load More Data

I need to load the rest of my data for the Vision application. Do I have to go through all of the "Stiflomadle" steps? No – I can actually reuse the same source, target applications, import formats, locations, and mappings. All I need to do is create a new data load rule that points to the new data file.

To load FY15 data,
1. Navigate to the *Data Load >> Data Load Rule* section.

2. Check that your POV is set to the *VisionSales_Loc* Location and *Actual* Category. (Ignore Period – that will be defined in Execution because this is a multi-period file).
3. Click ✚ to add a new Data Load Rule.
4. Enter the name "Load Vision Sales Actuals-FY15".
5. Select *Load Vision Actuals* for Import Format.
6. Select *Actual* for Category.
7. Select *Multi-Period Text File (Contiguous Period)* for File Type.
8. Select *Sales* for Target Plan Type.
9. Under Source Options, click *Select*.
10. Click *Upload* and browse to the file *Vision_Actual_FY15.csv*.
11. Leave all other options set to default.
12. Click *Save*:

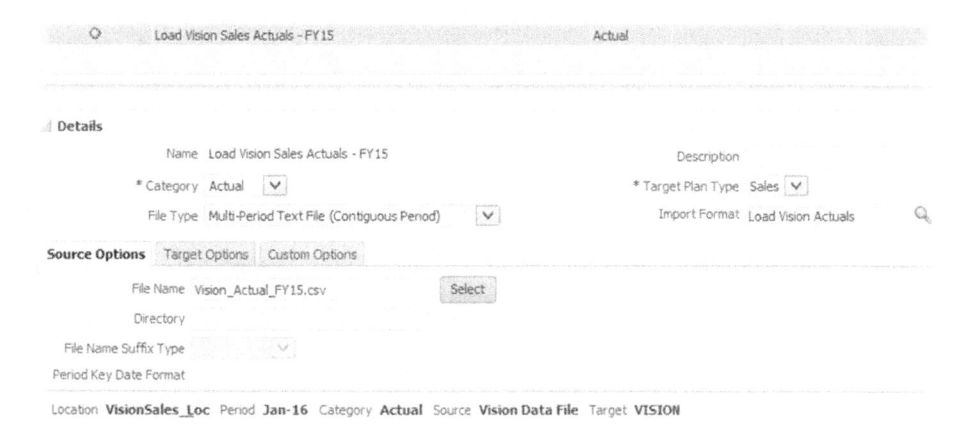

13. Click *Execute*.
14. Check the options to:
    a. *Import from Source*
    b. *Export to Target*
15. Specify the Start Period and End Period (in my case I'm loading data from Jan-15 to Dec-15).
16. Set Import Mode to *Replace*.
17. Set Export Mode to *Replace Data*.

Chapter 5: Integrate Data

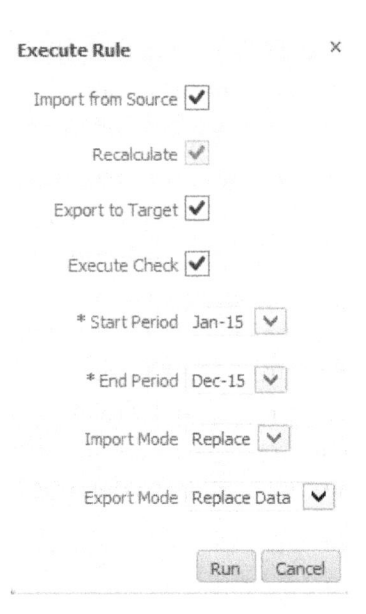

Execute Rule

- Import from Source ✓
- Recalculate ✓
- Export to Target ✓
- Execute Check ✓
- *Start Period: Jan-15
- *End Period: Dec-15
- Import Mode: Replace
- Export Mode: Replace Data

[Run] [Cancel]

18. Click *Run*. You should receive a message indicating that the process is running in the background.
19. Navigate to *Process Details* to view data load status (click *Refresh* until the load is complete):

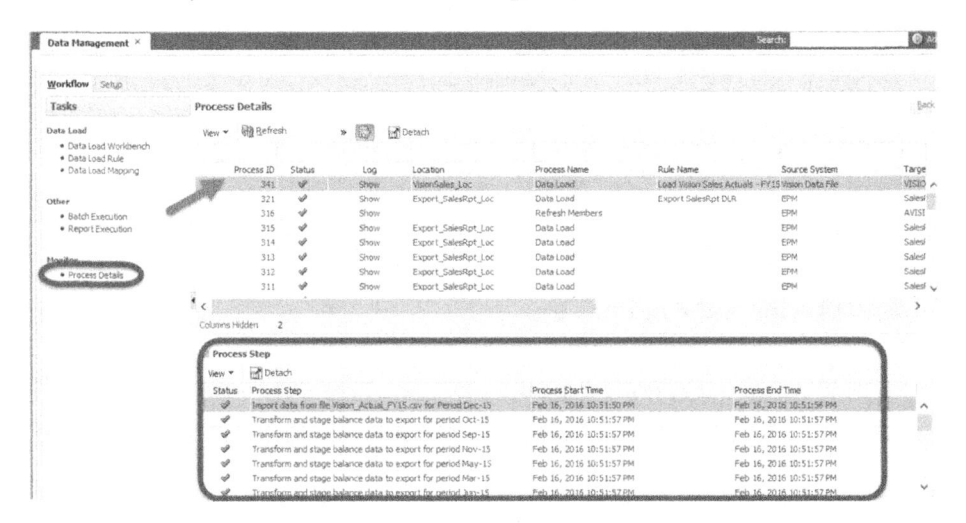

Now I need to load FY16 data. To do this,
1. Navigate to the *Data Load >> Data Load Rule* section.

2. Check that your POV is set to the *VisionSales_Loc* Location and *Actual* Category. (Ignore Period – that will be defined in Execution because this is a multi-period file).
3. Click ✚ to add a new Data Load Rule.
4. Enter the name "Load Vision Sales Actuals-FY16".
5. Select *Actual* for Category.
6. Select *Multi-Period Text File (Contiguous Period)* for File Type.
7. Select *Sales* for Target Plan Type.
8. Select *Load Vision Actuals* for Import Format.
9. Under Source Options, click *Select*.
10. Click *Upload* and browse to the file *Vision_Actual_FY16.csv*.
11. Leave all other options set to default.
12. Click *Save*:

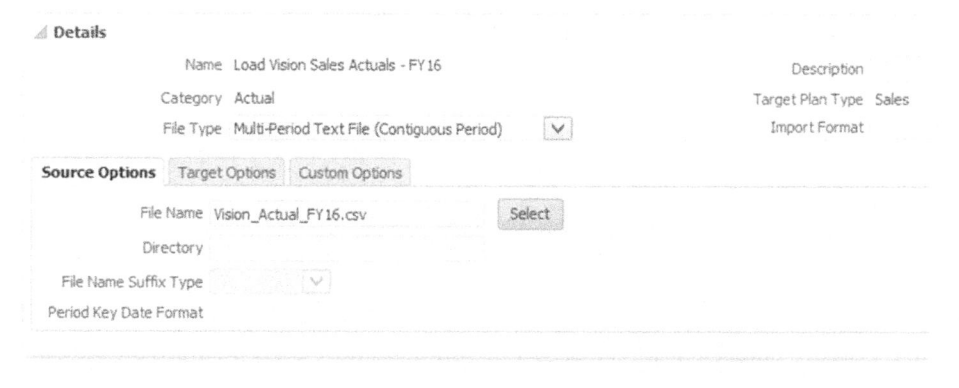

▲ Details

Name Load Vision Sales Actuals - FY16   Description
Category Actual   Target Plan Type Sales
File Type Multi-Period Text File (Contiguous Period)   Import Format

Source Options | Target Options | Custom Options

File Name Vision_Actual_FY16.csv   Select
Directory
File Name Suffix Type
Period Key Date Format

Location **VisionSales_Loc** Period **Jan-16** Category **Actual** Source **Vision Data File** Target **VISION**

13. Click *Execute*.
14. Check the Options to:
    a. *Import from Source*
    b. *Export to Target*
15. Specify the Start Period and End Period (in my case I'm loading data from Jan-16 to Dec-16).
16. Set Import Mode to *Replace*.
17. Set Export Mode to *Replace Data*.
18. Click *Run*. You should receive a message indicating that the process is running in the background.

19. Navigate to *Process Details* to view data load status (click *Refresh* until the load is complete).

Load Data to ASO Plan Type

Next I need to load data to the ASO Plan type, SalesRpt. Do I have to go through all of the "Stiflomadle" steps? This time, yes because I have a new target application to load data to.

My source "File" has already been defined so no further steps are required under source application.

To add the SalesRpt Target application (if you did not create in the section above; if AVISION-SalesRpt target exists, jump to the Import Format step),

1. Click the *Setup >> Register >> Target Application* link.
2. Click ✤ under Target Application Summary.
3. Select *Essbase* as the Type:

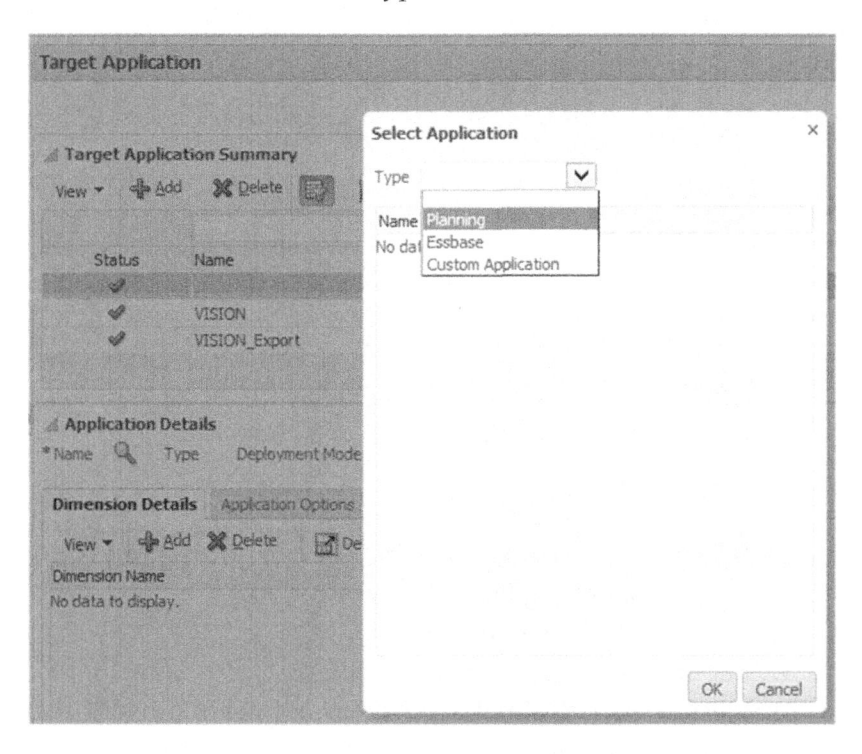

4. Select the ASO application name, *AVISION-SalesRpt*.

5. Click *OK*.

Select Application

Type Essbase

Name
AVISION-SalesRpt

Many of the Dimension Details will populate automatically. Make sure you set Entity to *Entity* for Target Dimension Class (sometimes it will default to Country).

6. Review the Dimension Details tab.
7. Set Entity to *Entity* Target Dimension Class.
8. Set Version to *Version* Target Dimension Class.
9. Set Scenario to *Scenario* Target Dimension Class:

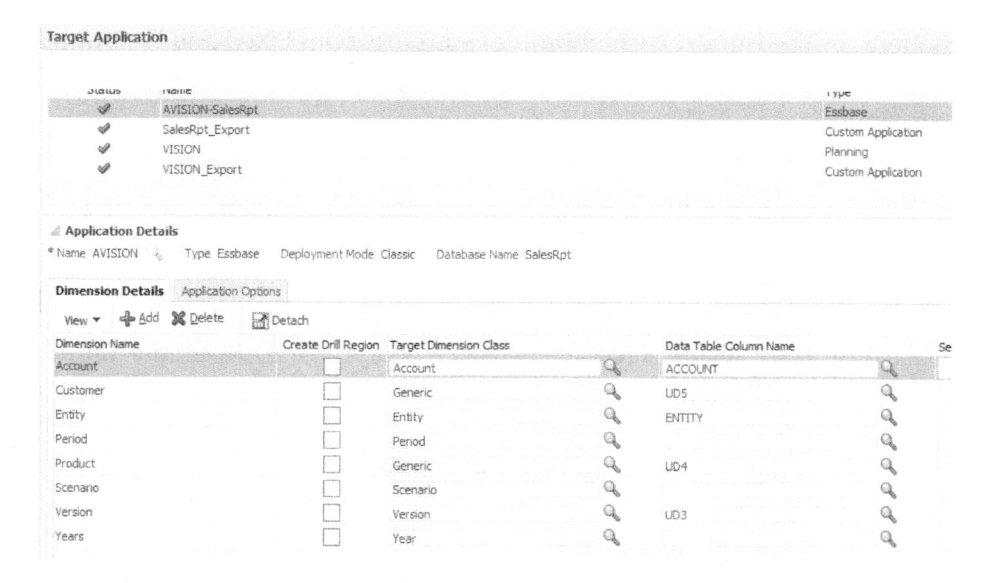

Status	Name			Type
✓	AVISION-SalesRpt			Essbase
✓	SalesRpt_Export			Custom Application
✓	VISION			Planning
✓	VISION_Export			Custom Application

Application Details
* Name AVISION   Type Essbase   Deployment Mode Classic   Database Name SalesRpt

Dimension Details | Application Options

View ▼ ✚ Add ✘ Delete ▦ Detach

Dimension Name	Create Drill Region	Target Dimension Class	Data Table Column Name	Se
Account	☐	Account	ACCOUNT	
Customer	☐	Generic	UD5	
Entity	☐	Entity	ENTITY	
Period	☐	Period		
Product	☐	Generic	UD4	
Scenario	☐	Scenario		
Version	☐	Version	UD3	
Years	☐	Year		

10. Click *Save* to save the target application.

Next I need to define the Import Format. To do this,

11. Under Integration Setup in the Setup tab, click *Import Format*.
12. Click ✚.

13. Under *Details*, enter the following information. Specify the *File Type* as *Multi Period* to match the load file format and click *Save* when done:

⊿ Load SalesRpt_IF: Details

Name	Load SalesRpt_IF		Description	
Source Type	ERP ⌄		Target Type	EPM ⌄
* Source	Vision Data File ⌄		* Target	AVISION-SalesRpt ⌄
* File Type	Multi Period ⌄		* File Delimiter	Comma ⌄
Drill URL		✎		

The file that I am going to load has multiple periods, which is why I chose *Multi Period*. Other valid options are *Fixed* (for set column widths to identify fields) or *Delimited* (individual data values use delimiters like quotation marks). These two options are used when loading a single period.

I'm going to use the Import Format Builder to help build my definition. The Import Format Builder supports both Fixed and Delimited files (though it does not support tab-delimited files). You could alternatively manually build the mapping rows.

In this step I am mapping the Source columns in the data file to the Target application dimensions.

14. Select *Build Format*.
15. Select *Upload* to upload the file.
16. Browse and select the *SalesRpt_Load_Data_FY14.csv* file. (email info@interrel.com for a copy of this file and the next two files) Click *OK*.
17. Select the file and click *OK*. The Import Format Builder will display.
18. Select *Account* text.
19. Set Assign selected text as Source Dimension Name to *Yes*.
20. Click *Assign Dimension*.
21. Make sure Source Dimension Name is set to *Account*.
22. Set the Target Dimension to *Account*.
23. Leave Field Number as "1":

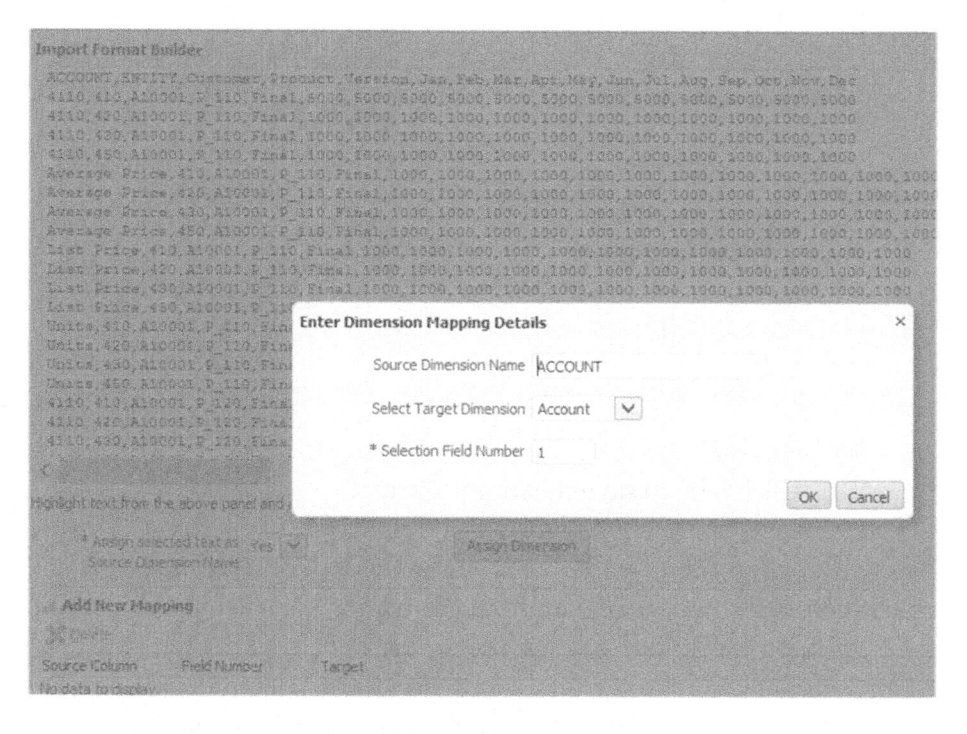

Look Smarter Than You Are with Enterprise Planning Cloud 203

24. Click *OK*. The first mapping row is added.
25. Repeat the above steps, assigning the columns / fields to the matching target dimension.
26. When you get to the columns containing the values by month, select all of the months.
27. Set Assign selected text as Source Dimension Name to *No*.
28. Click *Assign Dimension*.
29. Enter *Amount* as the Source Dimension Name, select *Amount* as the Target Dimension, and click *OK* and then *OK* again.
30. The final step is to use an expression to identify the Amount columns. Type "Column=6,17" in the Expression field and set the Field number to "6" (the first column of data numbers). The end result should look as follows:

Chapter 5: Integrate Data

Load_SalesRpt_IF: Details

Name	Load_SalesRpt_IF	Description	
Source Type	ERP	Target Type	EPM
Source	Vision Data File	Target	AVISION-SalesRpt
* File Type	Multi Period	* File Delimiter	Comma
Drill URL			

Load_SalesRpt_IF: Mappings

Source Column	Field Number	Expression	Add Expression	Target
ACCOUNT	1			Account
Amount	6	Column=6,17		Amount
Customer	3			Customer
ENTITY	2			Entity
Product	4			Product
Version	5			Version

31. Click *Save* to save the import format.

Note that I did not define Scenario, Period, or Year. Scenario will be defined in the Category mapping. Period and Year will be defined in the POV upon execution.

Next I need to define the Location to associate the import format with the target application. To do this,

32. Under Integration Setup in the Setup tab, click *Location*.
33. Click ➕ to create a new location.
34. Enter the following Location Details.
    a. *Name*: SalesRpt_Loc
    b. *Import Format*: Load SalesRpt_IF
    c. *Source*: Vision Data File
    d. *Target*: AVISION-SalesRpt:

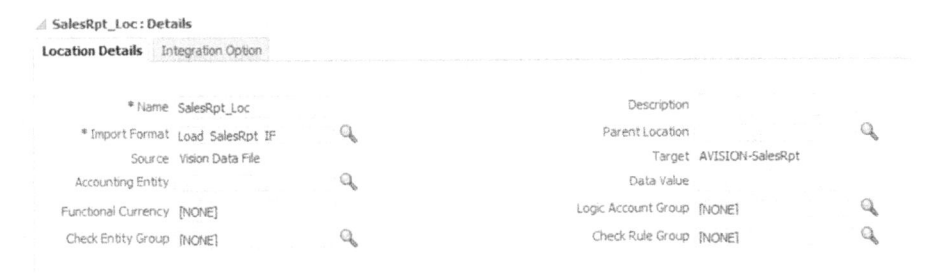

SalesRpt_Loc : Details

Location Details | Integration Option

* Name	SalesRpt_Loc	Description	
* Import Format	Load SalesRpt_IF	Parent Location	
Source	Vision Data File	Target	AVISION-SalesRpt
Accounting Entity		Data Value	
Functional Currency	[NONE]	Logic Account Group	[NONE]
Check Entity Group	[NONE]	Check Rule Group	[NONE]

35. Click *Save*.

To use the global period and category mappings,

36. Under Configure in the Setup tab, click *Application Settings*.
37. Select *AVISION-SalesRpt* and type "Yes" for *Global POV Mode*:

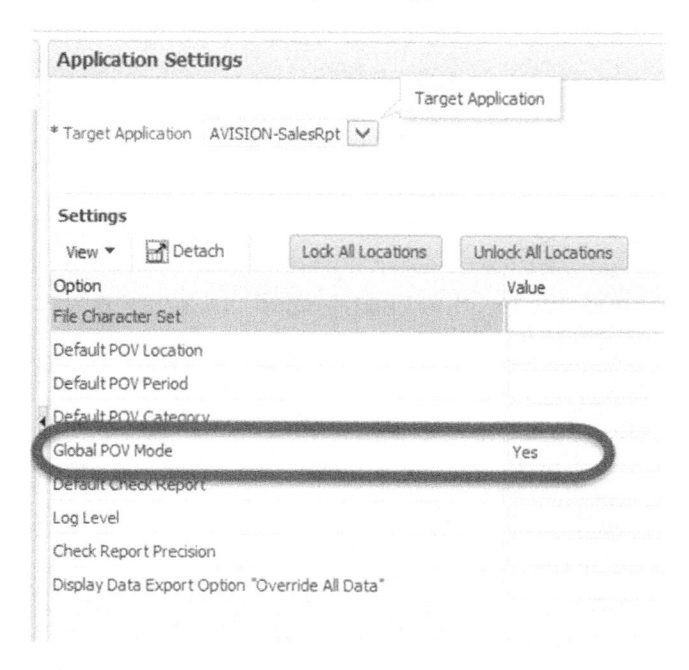

38. Click *Save*.

I now will switch to the Workflow section where I will define member maps and data load rules.

39. In the Workflow tab, click *Data Load Mapping*:

206   Chapter 5: Integrate Data

Workflow Setup

Tasks

Data Load
- Data Load Workbench
- Data Load Rule
- **Data Load Mapping**

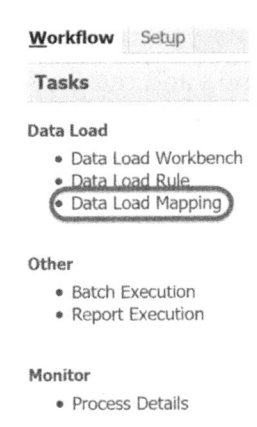

Other
- Batch Execution
- Report Execution

Monitor
- Process Details

40. Choose the location I just created, *SalesRpt_Loc*, for the POV:

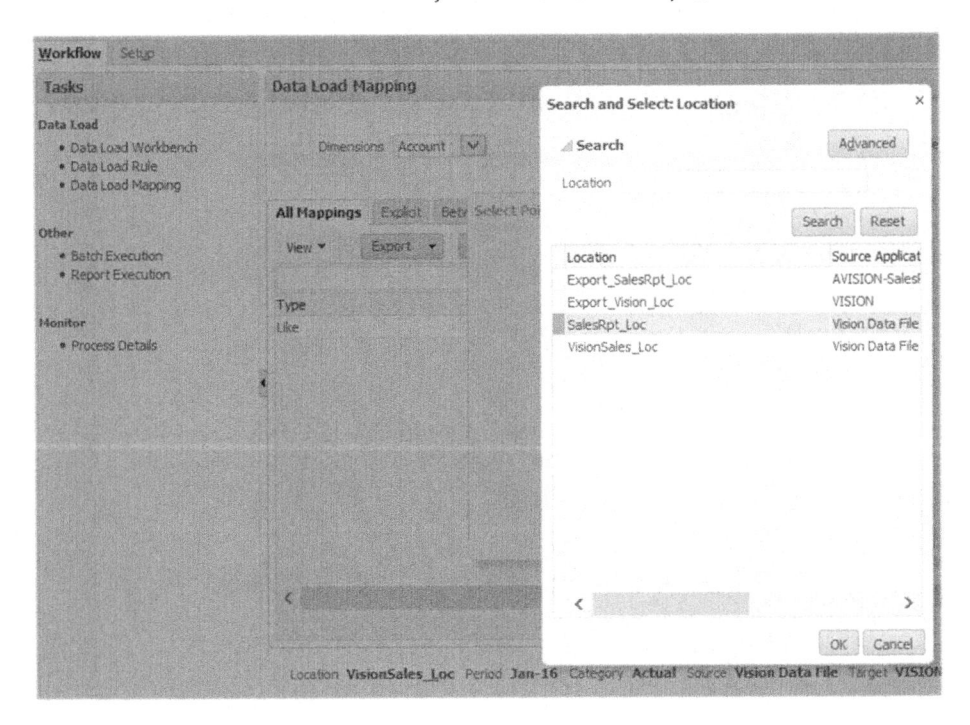

Now I need to complete the appropriate mappings for each target dimension. To do this,

41. Choose the *Account* dimension from the drop-down list.
42. Select the *Like* tab.
43. Click ✚ to add a row into the mapping.

44. Enter "*" as the Source Value and "*" as the Target Value, and call the Rule Name "DirectMapAccount":

Data Load Mapping

Dimensions: Account   Data Table Column: ACCOUNT

All Mappings | Explicit | Between | In | Multi Dimension | **Like**

View ▾ | Add | Delete | Detach | Validate | Refresh Values

Source Value	Target Value	Script	Change Sign	Rule Name
*	*			DirectMapAccount

45. Click *Save*.
46. Choose the *Entity* dimension from the drop-down list.
47. Select the *Like* tab.
48. Click ✚ to add a row into the mapping.
49. Enter "*" as the Source Value and "*" as the Target Value and call the Rule Name "DirectMapEntity".
50. Click *Save*.
51. Choose the *Product* dimension from the drop-down list.
52. Select the *Like* tab.
53. Click ✚ add a row into the mapping.
54. Enter "*" as the Source Value and "*" as the Target Value and call the Rule Name "DirectMapProduct".
55. Click *Save*.
56. Repeat these steps for the remaining dimensions so mappings are defined for every dimension.
57. Click *Save*. Check that all dimensions in the drop-down are mapped.

I'm finally ready to create my data load rule. To do this,

58. Navigate to the *Workflow >> Data Load >> Data Load Rule* section.
59. Check that your POV is set to the *SalesRpt_Loc* Location and *Actual* Category. (Ignore Period – that will be defined in Execution because this is a multi-period file).
60. Click ✚ to add a new Data Load Rule.

61. Enter the name "Load Vision SalesRpt Actuals-FY14".
62. Select *Actual* for Category.
63. Select *Multi-Period Text File (Contiguous Period)* for File Type.
64. ASO plan types will only have one database so you do not select a Target Plan Type.
65. Select *Load SalesRpt_IF* for Import Format.
66. Under Source Options, click *Select*.
67. Click *Upload* and browse to the file *SalesRpt_Load_Data_FY14*. Select this file.
68. Leave all other options set to default.
69. Click *Save*:

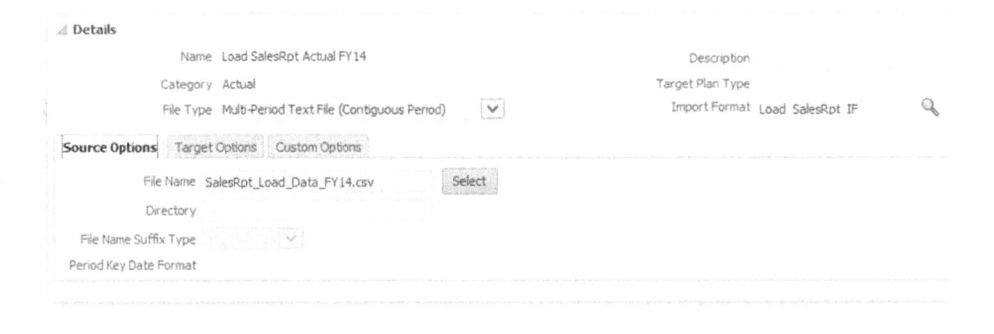

Details

Name	Load SalesRpt Actual FY 14	Description	
Category	Actual	Target Plan Type	
File Type	Multi-Period Text File (Contiguous Period)	Import Format	Load SalesRpt IF

Source Options | Target Options | Custom Options

File Name SalesRpt_Load_Data_FY14.csv [Select]
Directory
File Name Suffix Type
Period Key Date Format

Location **SalesRpt_Loc** Period **Jan-16** Category **Actual** Source **Vision Data File** Target **AVISION-SalesRpt**

70. Click *Execute*.
71. Check the Options to:
    a. *Import from Source*
    b. *Export to Target*
72. Specify the Start Period and End Period (in my case I'm loading data from Jan-14 to Dec-14).
73. Set Import Mode to *Replace*.
74. Set Export Mode to *Store Data*:

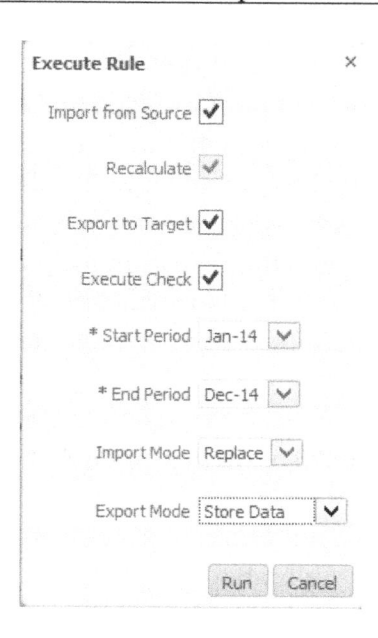

[Screenshot of Execute Rule dialog with checkboxes for Import from Source, Recalculate, Export to Target, Execute Check; Start Period Jan-14, End Period Dec-14, Import Mode Replace, Export Mode Store Data; Run and Cancel buttons.]

75. Click *Run*.
76. Navigate to *Process Details* to view data load status (click *Refresh* until the load is complete).
77. Create two more data load rules using the steps above to load data for FY15 and FY16 into the SalesRpt plan type using the respective data files.

```
LOG ENTRY: SOL 14, Entry 5

I wonder how the Texas Rangers are doing.
```

EXPORT DATA USING DATA MANAGEMENT

Data Management can also export Enterprise Planning Cloud data to a file (from both BSO and ASO plan types). I'll use the same Data Management "Stiflomadle" steps to create this integration (Create S̲ource, Create T̲arget, Define I̲mport F̲ormat, Define L̲ocation, Define M̲appings, Define D̲ata L̲oad Rule and finally E̲xecute).

Note on Source Application

Within Data Management for Enterprise Planning Cloud, by default, plan types will be available as sources.

Create a Custom Target Application

To export data out of Enterprise Planning Cloud, you first need to create a target application (actually with Enterprise Planning Cloud applications, one is created by default but I'll walk you through the steps so you understand the process from start to finish). The custom target application will be defined with the requirement dimensionality. Instead of writing data to a target, Data Management will generate a data file.

A few things to note about custom target applications and exporting data:

- Data is written to the file in this order: Account, Entity, UD1, UD2, UD3...UD20, Amount
- A few options are not valid for custom target applications
- Metadata rule is applicable
- POV category is not validated in Data Load Rules
- Target values are not validated in Data Load Mappings
- Check Rules can be created but they can't be based on target values

When the option to export the data file is enabled, Data Load Execution will create an output file named *"<Target App Name> <Process ID>.dat"*. The file will be placed in the *<APPL ROOT FOLDER>/outbox* directory. You can access the file from the Process Details page.

To create a custom target application,
1. Click *Setup >> Register >> Target Application*.
2. Click *Add*:

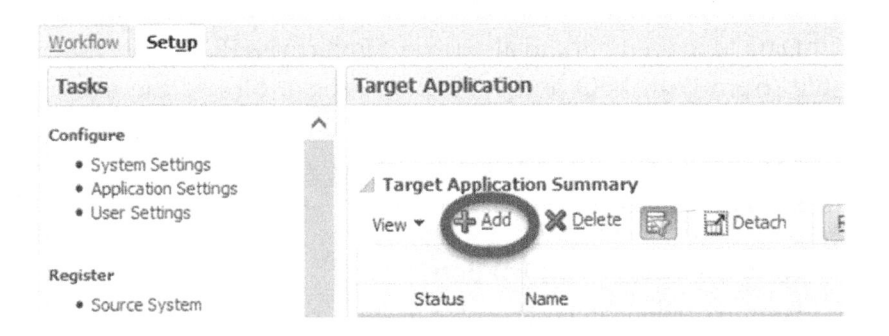

3. Choose *Custom Application*:

Look Smarter Than You Are with Enterprise Planning Cloud   211

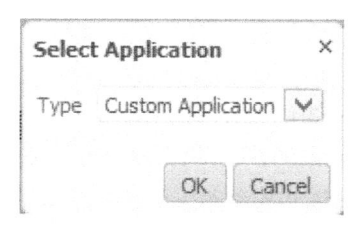

4. Click *OK*.
5. Enter the target application name "SalesRpt_Export":

6. Define the following Dimension Details including Dimension Name, Target Dimension Class, Data Table Column Name, and Sequence:

Make sure Entity dimension is set to Target Dimension Class of *Entity*, Account dimension is set to *Account* Target Dimension Class, etc. Incorrect assignments of Target Dimension Classes could cause issues down the line.

7. Click *Application Options*.
8. Set Enable export to file to "Yes".
9. Set Delimiter (available delimiters include comma, pipe, exclamation point, semi-colon and colon).

212   Chapter 5: Integrate Data

10. Enter the <File Name> to Download.

This is the name of the file that will be copied to the LCM folder. You can use EPM Automate to download the file or you can download it manually through the Simplified UI:

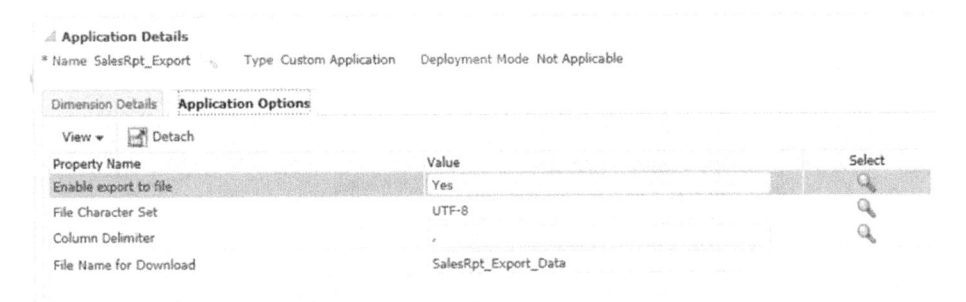

Property Name	Value	Select
Enable export to file	Yes	
File Character Set	UTF-8	
Column Delimiter	,	
File Name for Download	SalesRpt_Export_Data	

11. Click *Save* to save the target application.
12. Use Application Settings to set Global POV Mode to "Yes" and Display Data Export Option "Override All Data" to "Yes" for SalesRpt_Export:

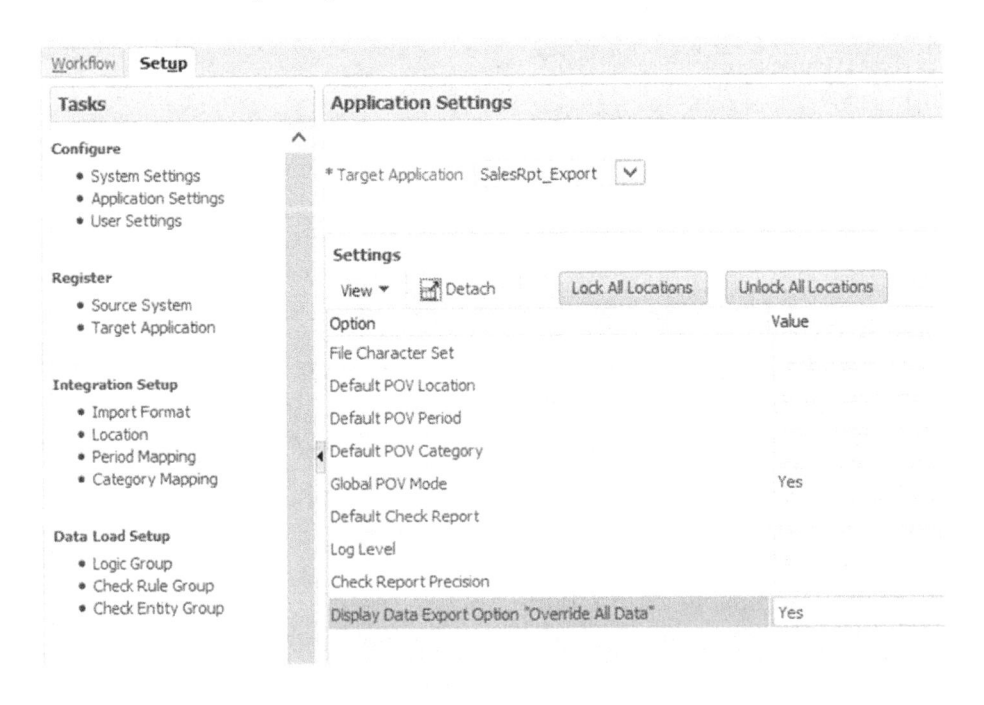

Option	Value
File Character Set	
Default POV Location	
Default POV Period	
Default POV Category	
Global POV Mode	Yes
Default Check Report	
Log Level	
Check Report Precision	
Display Data Export Option "Override All Data"	Yes

Global POV mode will ignore all other POVs. *Display Data Export Option "Override All Data"* will display the Override All Data Option from the Execute screen when I run the data load rule.

13. Click *Save* to save the application settings.

Define the Import Format

1. Select *Setup >> Integration Setup >> Import Format*.
2. Click ✚.
3. Enter the Import Format definition information:
   a. **Name**: "Export_SalesRpt_IF"
   b. **Description**: Optional
   c. **Source Type**: EPM
   d. **Source**: AVISION-SalesRpt
   e. **Target Type**: EPM
   f. **Target**: SalesRpt_Export:

Import Format			
Export_SalesRpt_IF: Details			
Name	Export_SalesRpt_IF	Description	Export SalesRpt Data
Source Type	EPM	Target Type	EPM
* Source	AVISION-SalesRpt	* Target	SalesRpt_Export
Drill URL			

4. Click *Save* to make the mappings fields appear.
5. Enter the import format mappings, selecting the source column dimensions and match to the Target application dimensions:

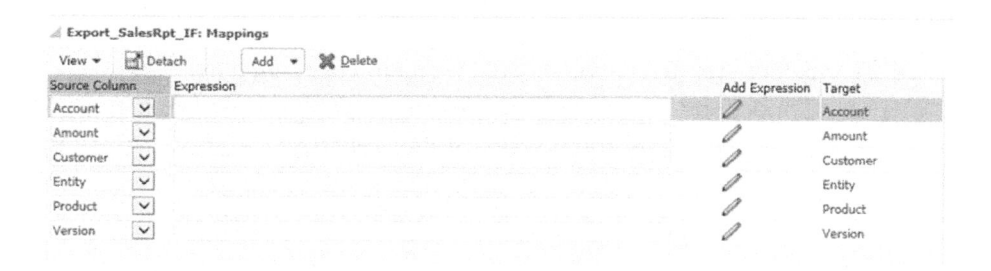

Source Column	Expression	Add Expression	Target
Account			Account
Amount			Amount
Customer			Customer
Entity			Entity
Product			Product
Version			Version

6. Click *Save* to save the import format.

Define Location

1. Select *Setup >> Integration Setup >> Location*.
2. Click ➕.
3. Enter the location information:
   a. Name: "Export_SalesRpt_Loc"
   b. Import Format: *Export_SalesRpt_IF*
4. The Source and Target will be automatically populated:

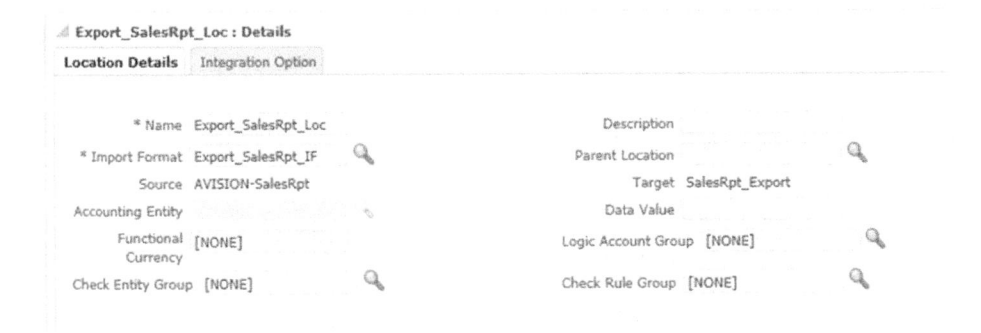

```
Export_SalesRpt_Loc : Details
Location Details   Integration Option

       * Name  Export_SalesRpt_Loc              Description
* Import Format  Export_SalesRpt_IF             Parent Location
         Source  AVISION-SalesRpt               Target  SalesRpt_Export
Accounting Entity                               Data Value
     Functional  [NONE]                         Logic Account Group  [NONE]
      Currency
Check Entity Group  [NONE]                      Check Rule Group  [NONE]
```

5. Click *Save* to save the location.

Period and Category Mappings

I can use the global mappings for Period and Category so no need to do any further steps.

Define Data Load Mappings

I do need to define the member mappings from the source to the target.

To define the member mappings,
1. Select *Workflow >> Data Load >> Data Load Mapping*.
2. Choose the Location I just created, *Export_SalesRpt_Loc*, for the POV (located at the bottom of the screen):

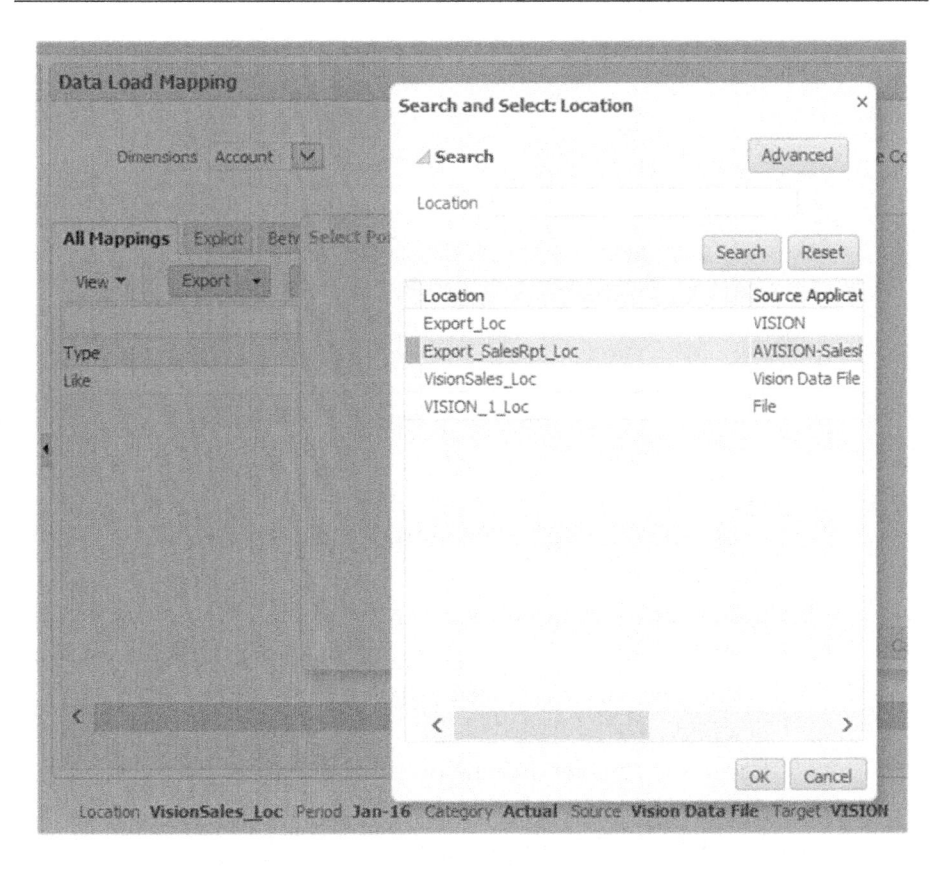

Look Smarter Than You Are with Enterprise Planning Cloud 215

[Screenshot of Data Load Mapping dialog with Search and Select: Location window showing Export_Loc, Export_SalesRpt_Loc, VisionSales_Loc, and VISION_1_Loc entries]

Now I need to complete the appropriate mappings for each target dimension.

3. Choose the *Account* dimension from the drop-down list.
4. Select the *Like* tab.
5. Click ✚ to add a mapping row.
6. Enter "*" as the Source Value and "*" as the Target Value and call the Rule Name "DirectMapAccount":

216   Chapter 5: Integrate Data

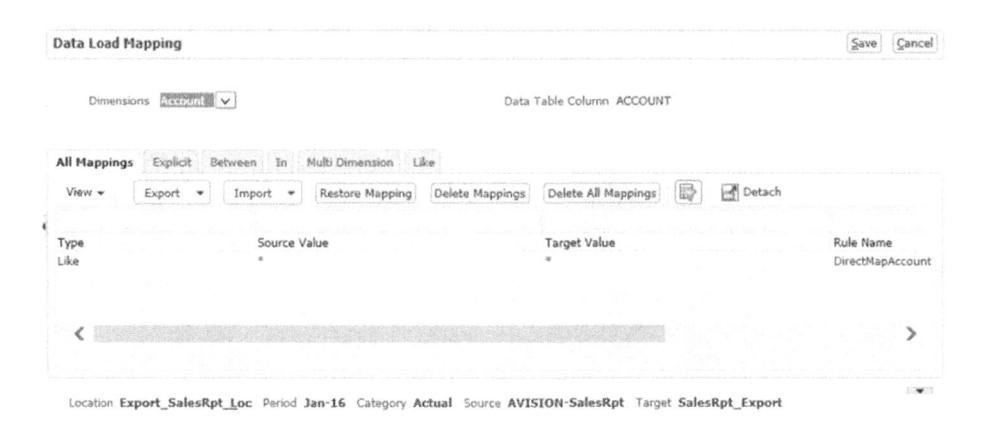

7. Click *Save*.
8. Choose the *Entity* dimension from the drop-down list.
9. Select the *Like* tab.
10. Click *Add* to add a mapping row.
11. Enter "*" as the *Source Value* and "*" as the *Target Value* and call the *Rule Name* "DirectMapEntity"
12. Click *Save*.
13. Choose the *Product* dimension from the drop-down list.
14. Select the *Like* tab.
15. Click Add to add a mapping row.
16. Enter "*" as the *Source Value* and "*" as the *Target Value* and call the *Rule Name* "DirectMapProduct".
17. Click *Save*.
18. Repeat for the rest of the dimensions (Customer, Version).

Define Data Load Rule

Now I need to define the data load rule.

1. Navigate to the *Workflow >> Data Load >> Data Load Rule* section.
2. Check that your POV is set to the *Export_SalesRpt_Loc* Location and *Actual* Category. (Ignore Period – that will be defined in Execution):

3. Click ✚.
4. Enter the name "Export SalesRpt DLR".
5. Click *Save*.
6. Select the *Source Options* tab:

Under Source Filters, you can add filters to the source (e.g., you only want to extract a specific account or set of products).

7. Optionally click ✚ under Source Filters.
8. Select the dimension and then select the "..." icon to use member selection to select members that you want to extract. For now I will export everything so I'll leave Source Filters blank.
9. Set Extract Dynamically Calculated Data to "Yes" (to allow dynamically calculated data to be extracted).
10. Optionally enter Data Precision and the Data Number of Decimal:

Details
Name Export SalesRpt DLR
Description
* Category Actual
Target Plan Type
* Period Mapping Type Default
Source Options
Target Options
Custom Options
Source Filters
View
Add
Delete
Detach
Dimension Name
Filter Condition
Select
No data to display.
Source Parameters
View
Detach
Property Name
Value
Select
Extract Dynamic Calculated Data
Yes
Data Precision
Data Number of Decimal
Location Export_SalesRpt_Loc Period Jan-16 Category Actual Source AVISION-SalesRpt Target SalesRpt_Export

- **Extract Dynamic Calculated Data:** "Yes" – include dynamically calculated values or "No" – don't include dynamically calculated values
- **Data Precision** – number of decimal places to be exported (focused on the accuracy of the data); default value is 16
- **Data Number of Decimal** – maximum number of decimal positions to be exported (focused on legibility of the number); valid values are 0 - 16. If this parameter is not specified, the Data Precision number is used

11. Select the *Target Options* tab.
12. Some of these properties should populate by default based on target application settings. Make sure the *File Name for Download* is defined (I'll find the file in our Enterprise Planning Cloud Inbox / Outbox):

Details

Name	Export SalesRpt DLR	Description
* Category	Actual	Target Plan Type
* Period Mapping Type	Default	

Source Options | **Target Options** | Custom Options

View ▼ Detach

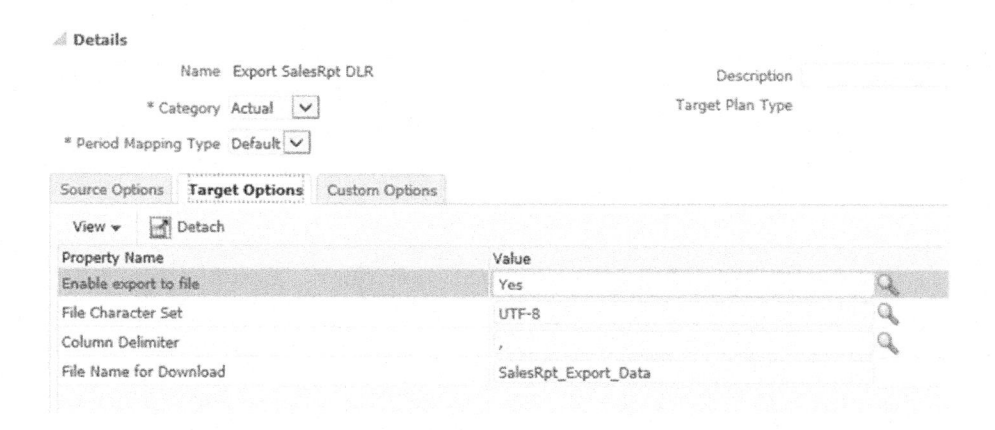

Property Name	Value	
Enable export to file	Yes	
File Character Set	UTF-8	
Column Delimiter	,	
File Name for Download	SalesRpt_Export_Data	

13. Click *Save*.

Execute Data Load Rule to Export Data to a File

Remember Data Management will import source data to a staging table and then load to the Target. I can do this in two steps or all in one step.

Source ➡ Staging Table ➡ Target

To do execute the data load rule and export data,
1. Select the *Export SalesRpt DLR* Data Load Rule and click *Execute*.
2. Check Options to *Import from Source, Export to Target*.
3. Set Start Period to *Jan-14*.
4. Set End Period to *Dec-14*.
5. Set Import Mode to *Replace*:

[Execute Rule dialog screenshot]

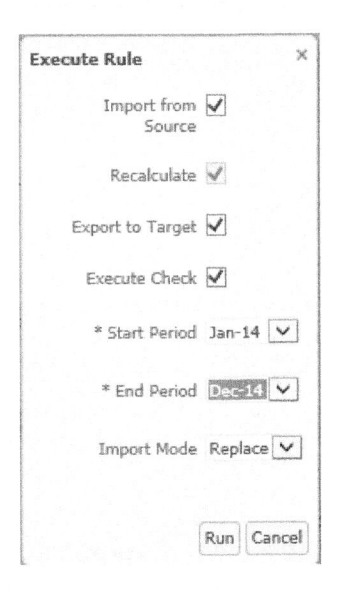

6. Click *Run*.
7. Check the data load process under *Monitor >> Process Details*:

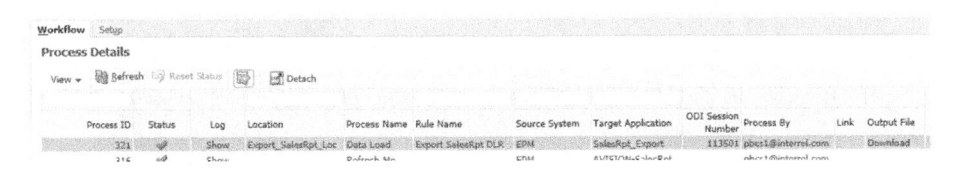

[Process Details screenshot]

8. View logs and search for "Error" to see if any errors have occurred (though the log file can be confusing).
9. Click *Download* to download the file.

Access Exported Data in Enterprise Planning Cloud

Now that the export is complete, you can access the data file in the Enterprise Planning Cloud Inbox/Outbox Explorer.

1. Navigate back to the Simplified UI for Enterprise Planning Cloud.
2. Select *Console*.
3. Select *Actions >> Inbox / Outbox Explorer*:

Look Smarter Than You Are with Enterprise Planning Cloud   221

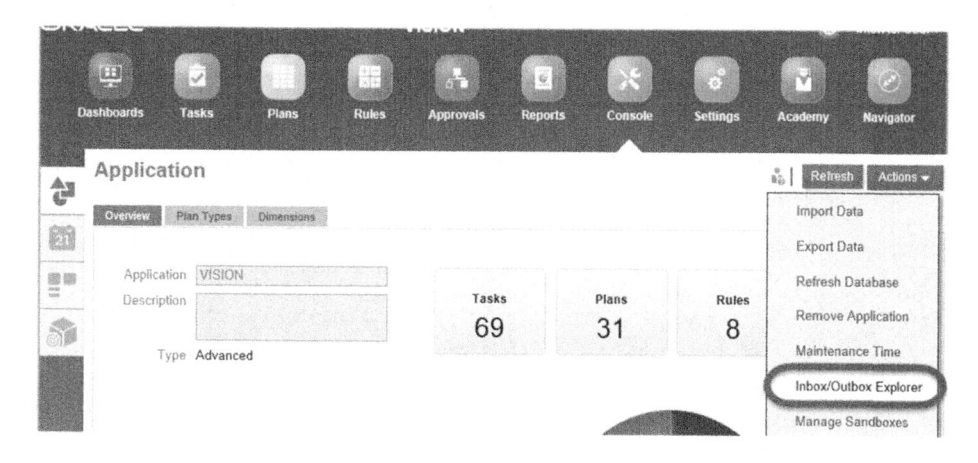

4. You can access the exported data file here (this can also be automated with EPM Automate) to download:

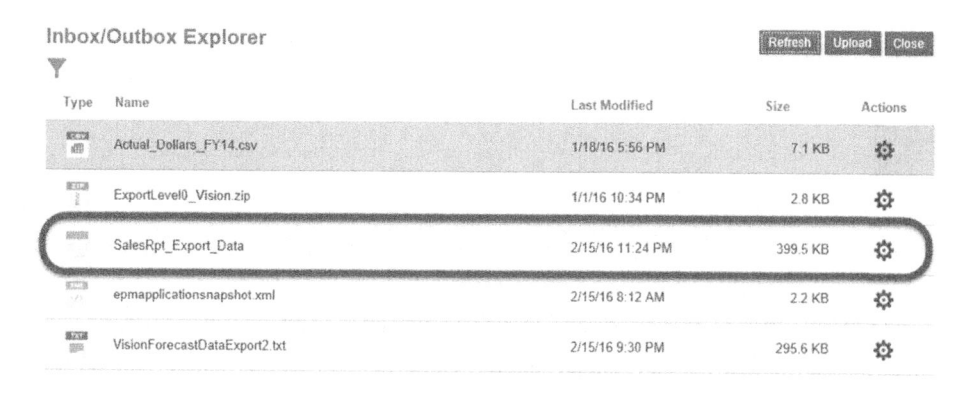

5. To download the file, select the *Gear* icon and choose *Download File*:

Voila! I have exported data from Enterprise Planning Cloud (ASO plan type):

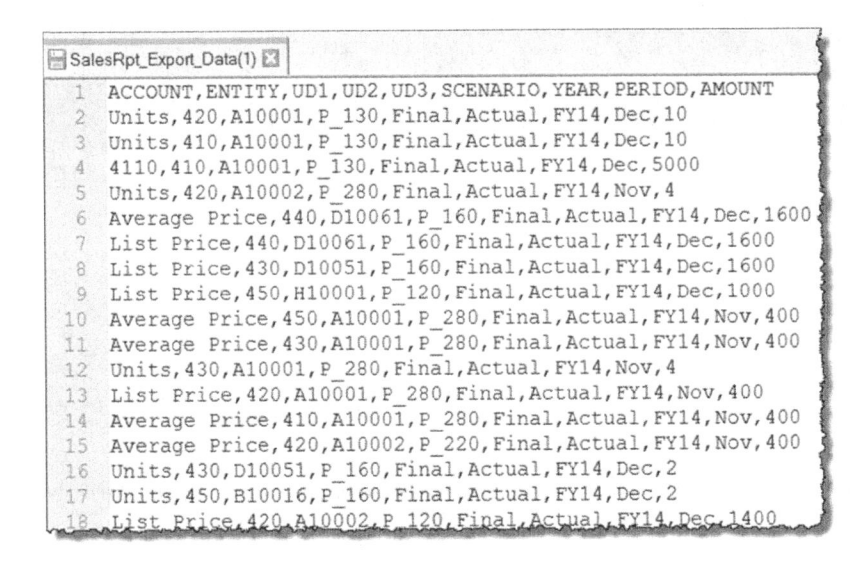

```
SalesRpt_Export_Data(1)
 1  ACCOUNT,ENTITY,UD1,UD2,UD3,SCENARIO,YEAR,PERIOD,AMOUNT
 2  Units,420,A10001,P_130,Final,Actual,FY14,Dec,10
 3  Units,410,A10001,P_130,Final,Actual,FY14,Dec,10
 4  4110,410,A10001,P_130,Final,Actual,FY14,Dec,5000
 5  Units,420,A10002,P_280,Final,Actual,FY14,Nov,4
 6  Average Price,440,D10061,P_160,Final,Actual,FY14,Dec,1600
 7  List Price,440,D10061,P_160,Final,Actual,FY14,Dec,1600
 8  List Price,430,D10051,P_160,Final,Actual,FY14,Dec,1600
 9  List Price,450,H10001,P_120,Final,Actual,FY14,Dec,1000
10  Average Price,450,A10001,P_280,Final,Actual,FY14,Nov,400
11  Average Price,430,A10001,P_280,Final,Actual,FY14,Nov,400
12  Units,430,A10001,P_280,Final,Actual,FY14,Nov,4
13  List Price,420,A10001,P_280,Final,Actual,FY14,Nov,400
14  Average Price,410,A10001,P_280,Final,Actual,FY14,Nov,400
15  Average Price,420,A10002,P_220,Final,Actual,FY14,Nov,400
16  Units,430,D10051,P_160,Final,Actual,FY14,Dec,2
17  Units,450,B10016,P_160,Final,Actual,FY14,Dec,2
18  List Price,420,A10002,P_120,Final,Actual,FY14,Dec,1400
```

The steps to export data for BSO plan types are the same steps and of course all of this can be automated with EPM Automate (more on this later).

SYNC DATA WITH DATA MANAGEMENT

Data Management supports the synchronizing and mapping of data across EPM source and targets. In the case of Enterprise Planning Cloud, this means sharing data across plan types. Sharing data between two EPM data sources is called "data sync" in Enterprise Planning Cloud Data Management.

Note! You cannot share data via Data Management directly to on-premise applications. With data management, you still must use files to navigate in a hybrid world (on-premise and Cloud). However, with Enterprise Planning Cloud release 16.04 (April 2016), on-premise FDMEE can now be used to point to Cloud EPM sources and targets.

I'll now create a Data Sync between my BSO plan type to ASO plan type (note – I can also do that through Smart Push functionality). I'll use the same Data Management "Stiflomadle" steps to create this integration

(Create Source, Create Target, Define Import Format, Define Location, Define Mappings, Define Data Load Rule and finally Execute). One difference with data sync is that I do not need to create source and target applications because they already exist.

> **Note!** Once data management objects are created, they must be deleted manually to be fully removed. Objects in Data Management will remain even after deleting the Enterprise Planning Cloud application.

When Dimensionality Differs in Source and Target

One fun new requirement is needed in this integration. I'm trying to set up data sync between my two plan types (Sales → SalesRpt). The Sales plan type has the *HSP_View* dimension which is not in the SalesRpt plan type. SalesRpt plan type has the *Customer* dimension which is not in the Sales plan type. So how to map these two dimensions?

If the source app contains a dimension that does not exist in the target app:

- Specify the dimension in the data load rule source filter and choose a default member to pull from.
- If the dimension does NOT map to any other dimension in the target app, then no other action is required

If the target app contains a dimension that does not exist in the source app, just leave the Source Column pick list empty.

Setting Up Data Sync

The Data Sync that will be created will push FY14 Actual data from the Sales plan type to the SalesRpt plan type.

To set up a data sync integration in Data Management,
1. From within the Simplified UI, navigate to *Navigator >> Manage >> Data Integration*.
2. Navigate to the *Setup* tab and then *Import Format*.
3. Create a new import format called "SyncSalesToSalesRpt" and fill in the details as shown.

a. **Name**: SyncSalesToSalesRpt
b. **Source Type**: EPM
c. **Target Type**: EPM
d. **Source**: Vision
e. **Target**: AVISION-SalesRpt:

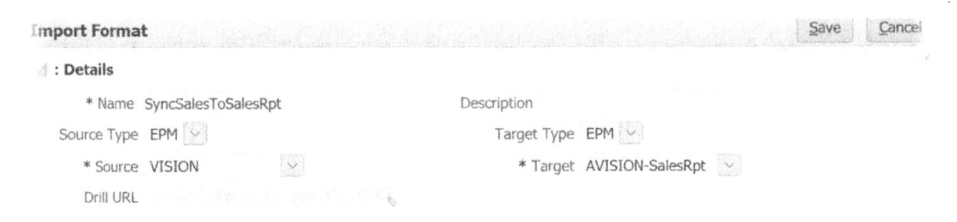

```
Import Format                                                    Save    Cancel
: Details
    * Name   SyncSalesToSalesRpt           Description
    Source Type  EPM  v                    Target Type  EPM  v
    * Source  VISION        v              * Target  AVISION-SalesRpt  v
    Drill URL
```

4. Click *Save* to save the import format.
5. Assign the mappings from the source to target as follows, leaving the target Customer dimension blank for the source application, as there is no Customer dimension within the Sales plan type:

```
SyncSalesToSalesRpt: Mappings
View ▼   Detach      Add  ▼    Delete
Source Column   Expression                      Add Expression  Target
Account    v                                         /          Account
Amount     v                                         /          Amount
           v                                         /          Customer
Entity     v                                         /          Entity
Product    v                                         /          Product
Version    v                                         /          Version
```

6. Click *Save* to save the import format again.
7. Navigate to *Location* and create a new one.
8. Name it "SalesToSalesRpt_Loc" and then fill in the details as shown below.
    a. **Name**: SalesToSalesRpt_Loc
    b. **Import Format**: SyncSalesToSalesRpt:

Look Smarter Than You Are with Enterprise Planning Cloud

SalesToSalesRpt_Loc : Details

Location Details | Integration Option

* Name	SalesToSalesRpt_Loc	Description	
* Import Format	SyncSalesToSalesRpt	Parent Location	
Source	VISION	Target	AVISION-SalesRpt
Accounting Entity		Data Value	
Functional Currency	[NONE]	Logic Account Group	[NONE]
Check Entity Group	[NONE]	Check Rule Group	[NONE]

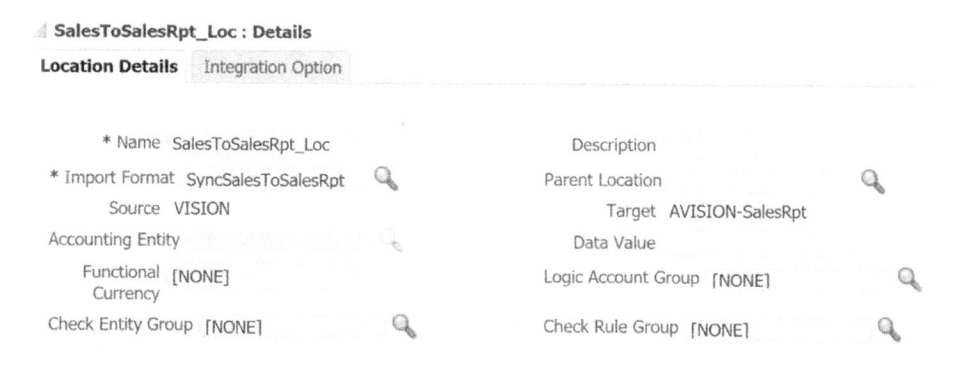

9. Click *Save* to save the location.
10. Navigate to the *Workflow* tab and then *Data Load Mapping*.
11. Change the location to the new "SalesToSalesRpt_Loc" location:

Location **SalesToSalesRpt_Loc** Period **Dec-14** Category **Actual** Source **VISION** Target **AVISION-SalesRpt**

12. For the Account, Entity, Product, and Version dimensions, do a "Like" mapping with an asterisk in both the Source Value and Target Value fields. Name each RuleName "DirectMapX" where "X" is the dimension name:

Data Load Mapping   Save   Cancel

Dimensions Account   Data Table Column ACCOUNT

All Mappings	Explicit	Between	In	Multi Dimension	**Like**
View ▼	Add Delete		Detach	Validate	Refresh Values

get Value	Script	Change Sign	Rule Name	Description
		☐	DirectMapAccount	

As there is no Customer dimension in the source, it's important to select a default member to map to in the target.

13. In the Customer dimension, add a *Like* mapping.
    a. Enter an *asterisk* in the Source Value field
    b. Enter "No Customer" in the Target Value field

c. Name the Rule Name "DirectMapCustomer":

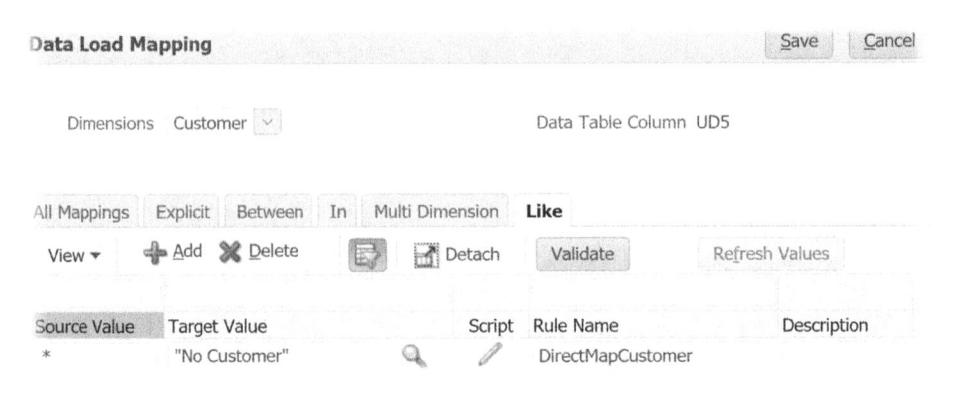

Data Load Mapping

Dimensions: Customer   Data Table Column: UD5

All Mappings | Explicit | Between | In | Multi Dimension | **Like**

Source Value	Target Value	Script	Rule Name	Description
*	"No Customer"		DirectMapCustomer	

14. Click *Save* to save the mapping.
15. Navigate to the *Data Load Rule* area.
16. Create a new data load rule and fill in the details as shown below.
    a. **Name**: SalesToSalesRpt_rule
    b. **Category**: Actual
    c. **Period**: Default
    d. **Source Plan Type**: Sales:

Details

* Name: SalesToSalesRpt_rule   Description:
* Category: Actual   Target Plan Type:
* Period: Default   * Source Plan Type: Sales
  Mapping Type:

As the Sales plan type has an HSP_View dimension and the SalesRpt plan type does not, it's important to add a source filter to map to a single member. In addition, since only Actual data is being sent over, a source filter should be added to limit to only the appropriate Actual Version member.

To set up the required source filters,
17. Navigate to the *Source Options* tab.
18. Add two source filters, as shown below.

a. Add a filter condition "BaseData" for the HSP_View dimension
b. Add a filter condition "Final" for the Version dimension:

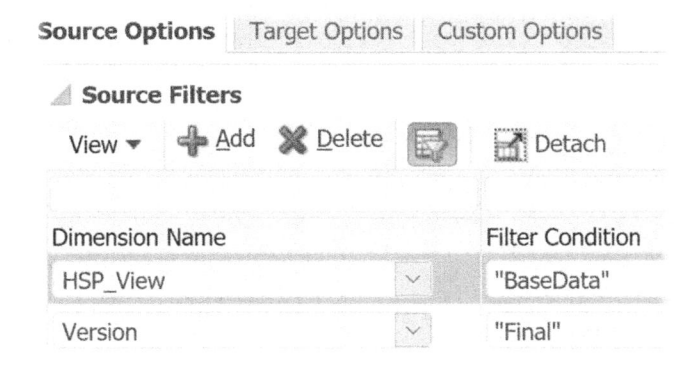

Dimension Name	Filter Condition
HSP_View	"BaseData"
Version	"Final"

19. Click *Save* to save the rule.
20. *Execute* the rule.

It should execute successfully. Once it does, verify that the Actual FY14 data matches between Sales and SalesRpt via ad hoc grid or analysis or in a data form that I create in an upcoming chapter.

OTHER DATA MANAGEMENT CONCEPTS

Batches

Batches are supported in Data Management and allow you to combine one or more data load rules in a batch and execute them at one time. Batch jobs may run in serial or parallel mode. A number of batch parameters will need to be defined, including POV settings for the batch. Period parameters can be derived based on the POV settings. Finally, batches can be grouped together. To access, go to *Setup >> Batch >> Batch Definition*:

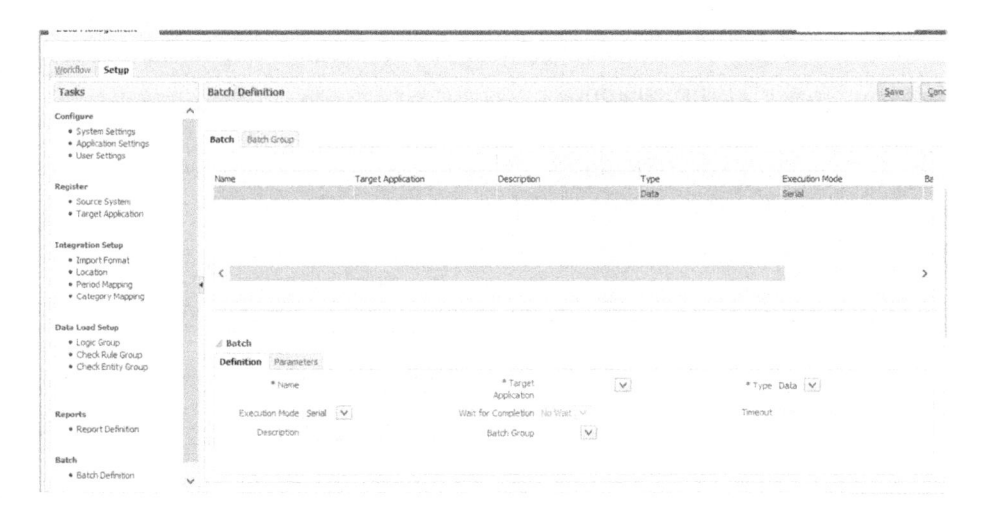

Reports Definition

Data Management has prebuilt reporting functionality to provide information and auditability about your data integrations. Go access, go to *Setup >> Reports >> Report Definition*:

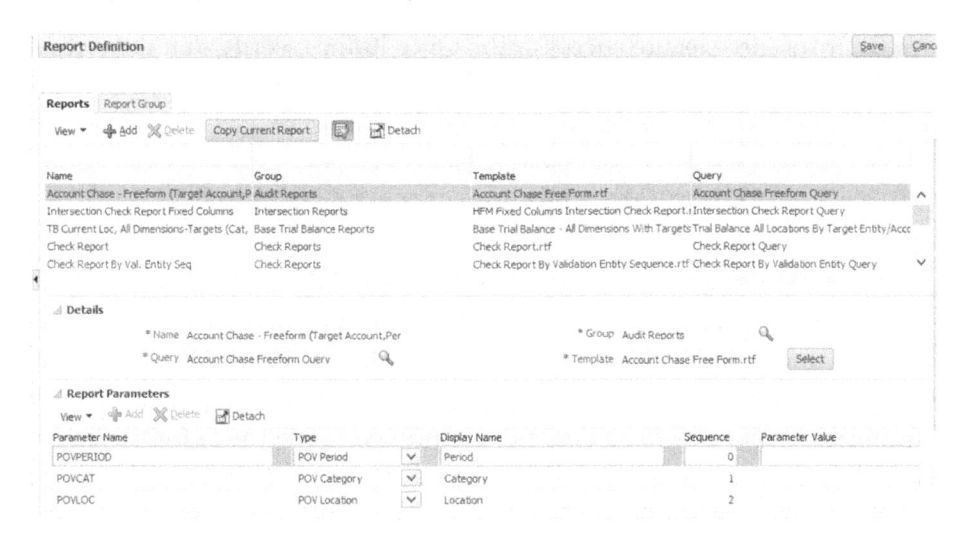

SYNC DATA WITH DATA MAPS

You can map data across plan types within your Enterprise Planning Cloud application, dimension to dimension, or Smart List to dimension. These are called "data maps" in the Simplified UI and "application mappings" in Workspace. For Vision, I want to share

Forecast data from Sales (BSO plan type) to SalesRpt (ASO plan type). Later I will see that these maps can be attached to data forms and run by the end user, if enabled. This allows users to copy data from one plan type to another without other data sharing alternatives: @XWRITE, @XREF, or partitioning.

If the dimension names are the same between the source and target databases, the mappings will automatically match up (they should in Enterprise Planning Cloud because everything is self-contained within the application). By default the members selected will be Level 0 members of the dimension selected. You can further refine the selected members by using the Member Selection – for example, if you just want to map the Forecast Scenario for the Forecast years. You can update the member selection to choose the desired slice of data to push from source plan type to the target plan type. If you are pushing data to an ASO database, you should only map level zero members in the target database.

The *Smart List to Dimension* mapping feature now allows Smart List data to be pushed to a reporting cube where that Smart List exists as a dimension. Users can slice and dice and report subtotals by the Smart List.

Create Data Maps

To create a data map,
1. Go to *Console >> Data Maps*.
2. Click *Create*.
3. Name the data map "Sales Forecast_Products".
4. Select Sales (BSO) as the Source plan type and SalesRpt (ASO) as the Target plan type:

Sales Forecast_Products
Tap description to edit

Source
VISION
Sales

Target
VISION
SalesRpt

5. In the Source column, use the following table to select members from each dimension to copy to Target:

Dimension	Members
Account	ILvl0Descendants(Account)
Entity	ILvl0Descendants (Entity)
Period	ILvl0Descendants (Period)
Product	ILvl0Descendants (Product)
Scenario	Forecast
Version	Final
Years	ILvl0Descendants (Years)
HSP_View (Unmapped)	BaseData

There are different ways to design your data map, depending on how you want to control the data push. If you're using a data map independently, then you can define it how you want. The key here is to understand the structures of the hierarchies in both the source and target. In addition, you'll want to be cognizant of the underlying architectures of the plan types. For instance, when going from a BSO cube to an ASO cube, you need to send only Level 0 member data.

Note! When using relationship functions in a data map, be careful on how many you use. Relationship functions can max out the underlying algorithm used behind the scenes, as functions are replaced with hardcoded members.

6. Dimensions that are not in common between the plan types also need mappings. In the Target column, select *No Customer* for the Customer dimension (Unmapped):

Source VISION Sales ▼		Target VISION SalesRpt ▼
IDescendants(Period)		
Product ▼ IDescendants(Product)		Product
Scenario ▼ IDescendants(Scenario)		Scenario
Version ▼ IDescendants(Version)		Version
Years ▼ IDescendants(Years)		Years

Unmapped Dimensions

HSP_View BaseData		Customer "No Customer"

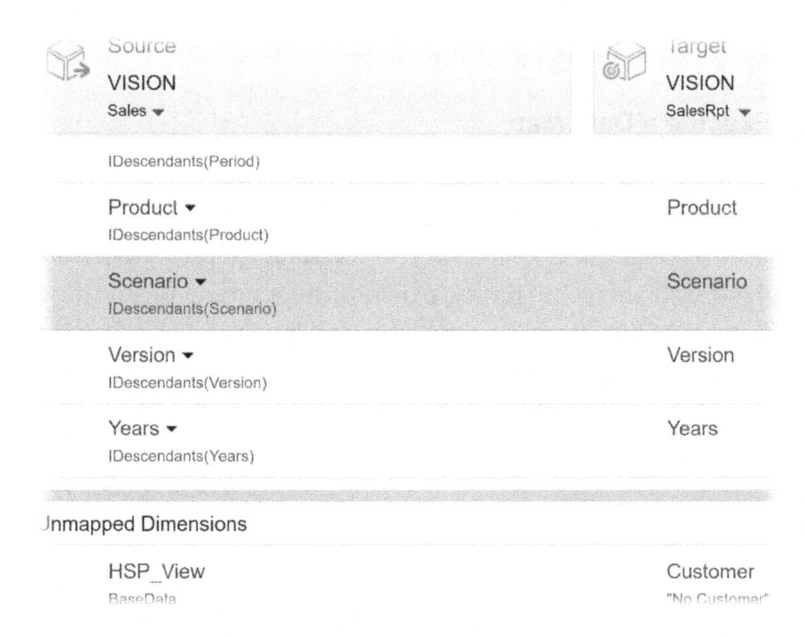

If you select *Options*, you can optionally define whether you want to copy *Comments*, *Attachments*, and / or *Supporting Detail* to a non-reporting plan type (meaning ASO reporting cubes are not applicable to this situation). The *Collate* option determines how Comments and Attachments are copied in the case when there are not one-to-one mappings between the source and target. If *Collate* is checked, then the *Comments and Attachments* are combined and then sent to the target. If *Collate* is unchecked, only the last source cell's *Comments and Attachments* are copied. In the case of *Supporting Detail*, if there is not a one-to-one mapping then Supporting Details aren't copied:

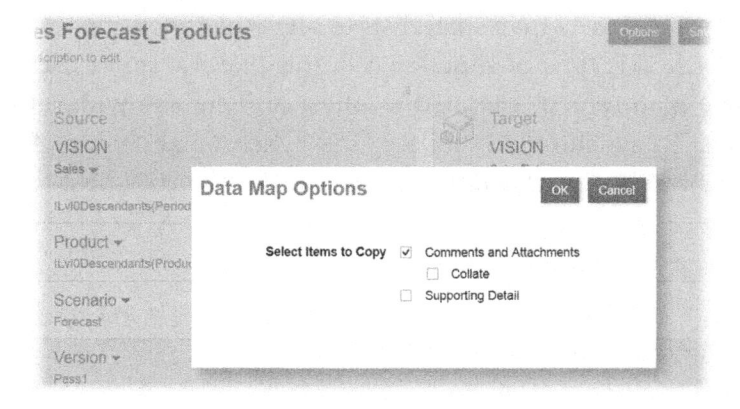

7. Review and click *Save* and *Close*.

Execute a Data Map

Now that the data map is defined, you can push all data from the source plan type to the target plan type. Click ⚙ and choose *Push Data* or *Clear and Push Data*. *Push Data* will use the data map to push data based on how the data map currently exists, independent of any additional Smart Push configurations in data forms. *Clear and Push Data* will first clear the data intersections in the target application based on the definitions in the data map, and then replace them.

Note! *Clear and Push Data* only works with member names, not member aliases.

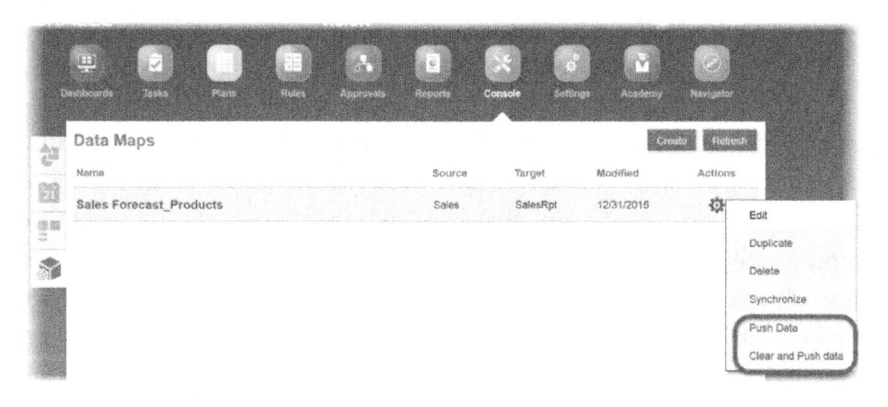

Synchronize Smart Lists in Reporting Applications

It is possible to map smart lists to physical dimensions in reporting applications. This type of situation requires that the smart list entries in the source plan type be mapped to physical members within the target plan type. To synchronize the two, the Synchronize feature should be used. This can be found within the same Actions menu next to the data map:

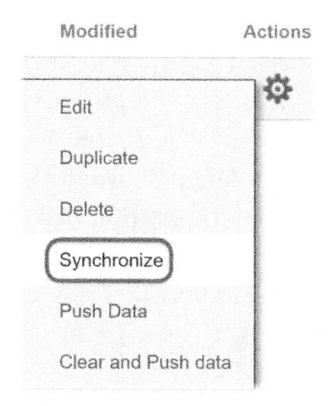

Look Smarter Than You Are with Enterprise Planning Cloud   233

Once clicked, this will add all reporting dimension members to the smart list. Smart List members are never deleted as a result of this action.

Check Job Status

You can always view the status of push reporting jobs in the Job Console. More on the Job Console in the Automation chapter / mission:

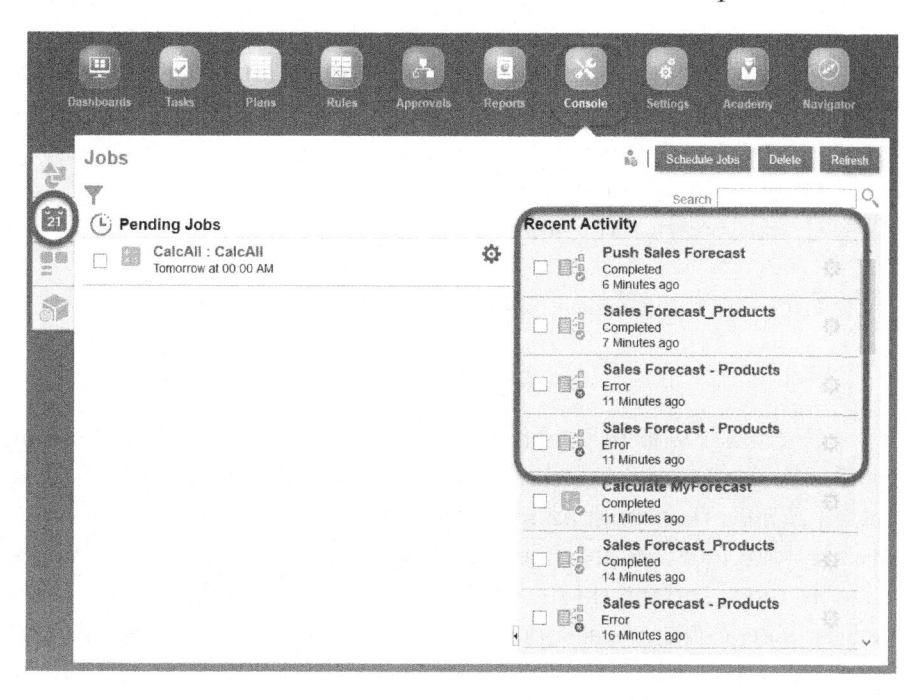

AUTOMATE DATA INTEGRATION

You can automate all of these steps with EPM Automate. The EPM Automate Utility may be downloaded from Enterprise Planning Cloud. This utility allows you to remotely perform tasks in Cloud instances. You can automate a number of data integration tasks including:

- Import and export metadata
- Import and export data
- Run business rules on data
- Copy data from one database to another; typically from a block storage database to an aggregate storage database, or from a block storage database to another block storage database
- Upload files into service instance
- Upload files into the Planning Inbox / Outbox
- Upload files into Data Management folders and initiate import process by running data load rules
- Run a Data Management batch rule and get the output log file
- Download files from the Planning Inbox / Outbox and from Data Management folders
- List the files in the Inbox / Outbox
- Delete files from the Inbox / Outbox
- Update one or more substitution variables

For more information, see the Automation chapter / mission.

REST API

One other way to integrate data with Oracle Enterprise Planning Cloud is to use the more technical / programming route of REST APIs. First, an Application Program Interface (API) by definition is one piece of software that talks to another software based upon certain routines, protocols, tools, and interfaces. The REST API is an API that falls in to the category of an architectural style or a concept that is a simple interface that transmits data using the already established HTTP methods without using any additional messaging layer such as SOAP. It works similar to how the communication happens between a Web Server hosting a web site and a client over the http protocol.

REST is short for **Re**presentational **S**tate **T**ransfer and can work with many of the EPM Automate Utility commands to integrate data between Oracle Enterprise Planning Cloud and other systems. A few basics about REST API:

- It is a Client-Server architecture
- It is Resource based vs. Action based (as in SOAP). The resources are identified by URIs
- All communications are performed via representation in XML format or JSON format
- HTTP Methods or verbs are used (GET, PUT, POST, DELETE)
- In REST, everything is a resource. Every resource is identified by a unique identifier thus making it easy to focus and request a specific piece of information. The request is in form of a uniform resource identifier (URI) that identified the resource, such as a file or folder on which to operate

REST API clients and browser add-ins are feely available on the web. The REST API add-in for Firefox is very easy and simple to use.

REST API works with EPM Automate to integrate data. EPM Automate is essentially a tool that wraps around and makes calls to the REST APIs. Nothing more, really. It's the least technically complex (and thus least powerful) way to make REST API calls. Other ways from Oracle to use writing programs or scripts include Java, cURL, or Groovy.

For more information on using REST API with Oracle Enterprise Planning Cloud, see the Oracle documentation.

```
    Meanwhile, back on earth...

    They decided to announce the tragedy on the
regularly scheduled Tuesday webcast. i.n.t.e.r.R.e.l
had been having these webcasts every Tuesday and
Thursday for years, delivering tips and tricks
information on all of the Hyperion products. They'd
```

never had to deliver bad news (well, maybe a few times when Oracle made a strategic change in direction, like no more support for ODI). What could be worse than losing Edward Roske? Oracle announcing they would stop selling Hyperion products?

Danielle White, Marketing and Press Director for i.n.t.e.r.R.e.l delivered the agreed upon statement: It was a sad day. We lost Edward Roske and the Vision EPM project today...

Immediate weeping could be heard across the Tuesday i.n.t.e.r.R.e.l webcast (well that was what Danielle imagined because on GoToWebinar everyone was muted). No more snarky jokes from Roske? It was impossible to imagine.

Chapter 6: Calculate Data

> **LOG ENTRY: SOL 15, Entry 1**
>
> I need to calculate data and I have an idiotically dangerous plan for this requirement. And boy, do I mean dangerous. But I really don't have much choice. I'm going to build business rules in Calculation Manager.

Enterprise Planning Cloud, much like its counterpart, on-premise Hyperion Planning, offers a variety of ways to calculate data. The combination of inherent member properties and member formulas to custom business rules in Calculation Manager allows Enterprise Planning Cloud to create intelligent calculations primed for consumption by administrators and business users. Common business rules in Enterprise Planning Cloud include:

- Aggregate and consolidate data
- Allocations
- Clear data
- Copy data
- Seed forecasts based on actuals
- Driver based calculations
- Data validation and checks

This section will cover one of the more powerful ways to calculate data via business rules in Calculation Manager. I'll cover some very basic business rule examples. Note, there is so much more you can do with business rules and Calculation Manager.

INTRO TO CALCULATION MANAGER

Simply put, a business rule calculates Enterprise Planning Cloud data with a series of commands, functions, and equations. In Enterprise Planning Cloud, rules can only be created in Calculation Manager since

EAS, Essbase Administration Services, is not available (for any legacy Hyperion admins out there).

In Calculation Manager, you can design rules in a graphical environment that supports calculation ranges, conditions, scripts, and loops; displays the calculation flow in a graphical way; provides pre-defined templates for standard calculations; allows custom templates definition; and supports the design and use of variables and run time prompts. You can copy or share rules across Planning applications, as well as share components across rules. Objects are organized in the calculation library by objects, or in a tree structure.

Note! Once a rule is created in Calculation Manager, it must be deleted manually to remove. Objects in Calculation Manager will remain even after deleting the Enterprise Planning Cloud application.

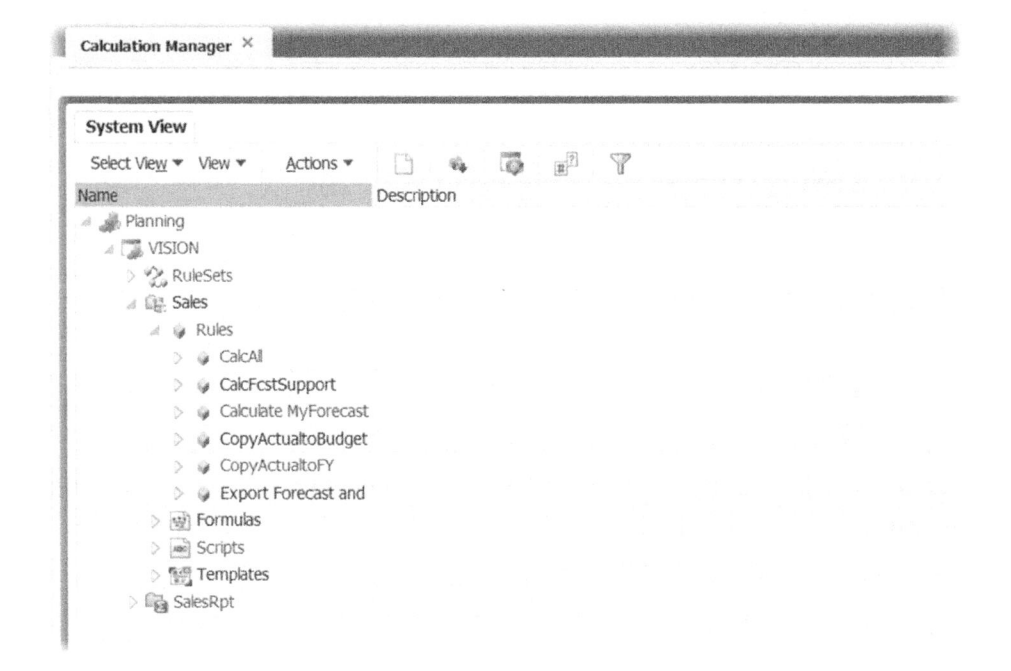

Calculation Manager	
System View	
Select View ▼ View ▼ Actions ▼	
Name	Description
▲ Planning	
▲ VISION	
> RuleSets	
▲ Sales	
▲ Rules	
> CalcAll	
> CalcFcstSupport	
> Calculate MyForecast	
> CopyActualtoBudget	
> CopyActualtoFY	
> Export Forecast and	
> Formulas	
> Scripts	
> Templates	
> SalesRpt	

Look Smarter Than You Are with Enterprise Planning Cloud   239

The System View is where you can view and manage your business rules (Open, Debug, Delete, Print, Export, Refresh, Validate, Deploy, Compare Scripts, Copy, Create Shortcut, and Save as Template):

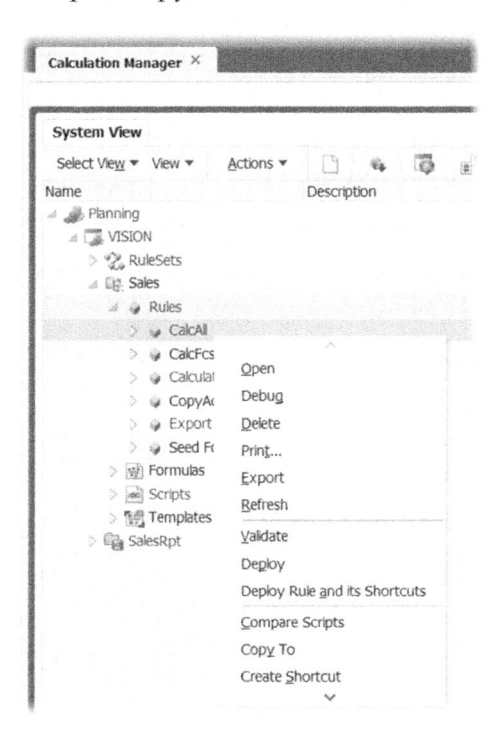

When you create and edit a business rule, the following layout will display:

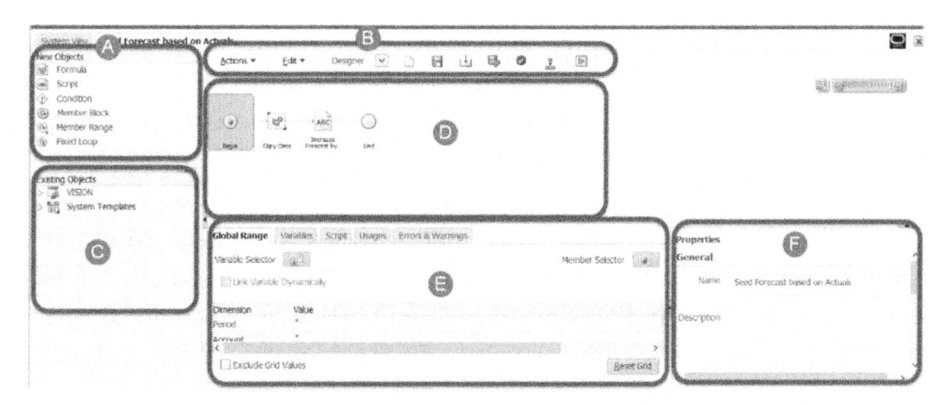

A. **New Objects** – pre-defined objects that you can drag into the main business rule layout; you'll be prompted to enter the parameters for the object
B. **Business Rule menu bar** – all of the available actions for the business rule like Save, Save As, Validate, Debug (helpful when troubleshooting), Analyze (to see if you've written an optimized script or not), Deploy, and more
C. **Existing (System) Objects** – you can save components for reuse in other scripts; access those saved objects in this section along with pre-defined templates from Oracle including:

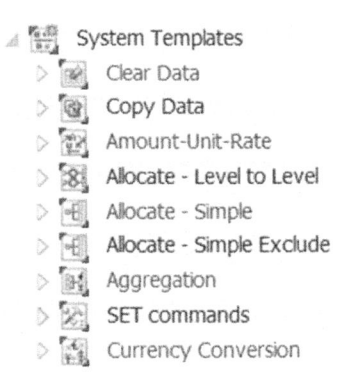

- System Templates
  - Clear Data
  - Copy Data
  - Amount-Unit-Rate
  - Allocate - Level to Level
  - Allocate - Simple
  - Allocate - Simple Exclude
  - Aggregation
  - SET commands
  - Currency Conversion

D. **Main layout** – visual data flow of the business rule; make sure to add captions for each component so the graphical flow is easy to read
E. **Details section** – displays the details for the selected component in the main layout
F. **Properties** – context-sensitive information panel to define properties for the selected component

There are two methods of creating rules: Graphical Mode and Script Mode. Graphical Mode is suitable for those less experienced in scripts, due to the templates and script wizards that it provides. Script Mode is for more experienced developers who do not need a visual of the script or any step-by-step guidance.

Once a rule is created and saved in Calculation Manager, you must deploy the rule for launch in Enterprise Planning Cloud. Business rules and rule sets are run from the Enterprise Planning Cloud web or Smart View client by users.

CREATE BUSINESS RULE IN GRAPHICAL MODE

For the Vision application, I'm going to create a simple business rule to show you how to use the graphical interface. I'm going to use the pre-defined templates to create a script that aggregates everything because this is a rule most BSO plan types need. I technically don't need this script in my Vision application because I've set all upper levels of dimensions to dynamic because I'm eagerly anticipating hybrid aggregation support in this sales forecasting application. However, until hybrid is supported in Enterprise Planning Cloud, admins will want to leverage aggregation rules like this one and tag upper level sparse members to store.

To create a business rule in graphical mode,
1. Go to *Navigator* >> *Administer* >> *Rules*. The Calculation Manager will appear.
2. In System View, expand *Planning* >> *VISION*.
3. Expand the *Sales* database and right-click on *Rules*.
4. Click *New* to create a new business rule:

Chapter 6: Calculate Data

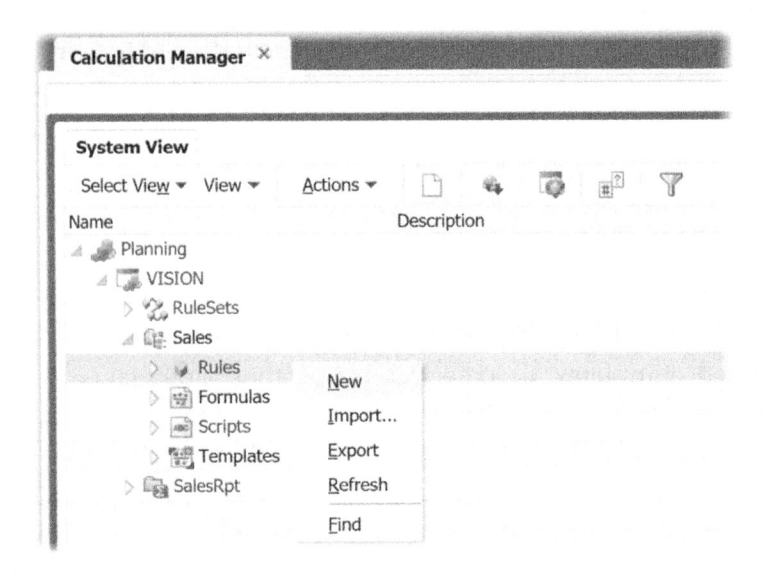

```
Calculation Manager  x

System View
Select View ▼   View ▼   Actions ▼
Name                    Description
▲ Planning
   ▲ VISION
      > RuleSets
      ▲ Sales
         > Rules          New
         > Formulas       Import...
         > Scripts        Export
         > Templates
         > SalesRpt       Refresh
                          Find
```

5. Name the rule "CalcAll". Leave other properties at their default values:

New Rule

Name	CalcAll
Application Type	Planning
Application	VISION
Plan Type	Sales

6. Click *OK*.
7. Explore the Existing Objects panel under System Templates:

Existing Objects
- VISION
- System Templates
  - Clear Data
  - Copy Data
  - Amount-Unit-Rate
  - Allocate - Level to Level
  - Allocate - Simple
  - Allocate - Simple Exclude
  - Aggregation
  - SET commands
  - Currency Conversion

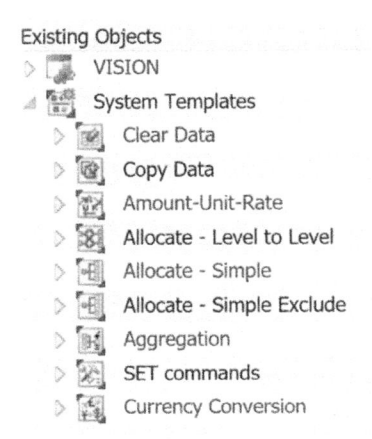

8. Drag *SET commands* to the graphical representation of the business rule, between "Begin" and "End":

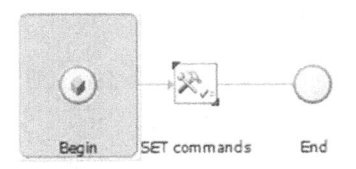

Note! If you can't view the graphical interface due to the "a plugin is needed to display this content" error, then download and install Adobe Flash Player version 10 or later.

9. In the Data Volume section, select *Calculates all data blocks* for the UPDATECALC property. This will turn off intelligent calculation, which only calculates data that has been changed after the last calculation:

1. Data Volume

(UPDATECALC) Specify whether to calculate only dirty blocks, such as updated data blocks and their dependent parents, or all data blocks	Calculates all data blocks
(CLEARUPDATES) Specify when data blocks are marked as clean	Default
(EMPTYMEMBERSETS) Specify whether to stop the calculation within a FIX command if the FIX evaluates to an empty member set	Default
(FRMLBOTTOMUP) Specify whether to optimize the calculation of complex formulas on sparse dimensions in large database outlines	Default

10. Click *Save*, then *Exit*.
11. Click the *Script* tab to see the code:

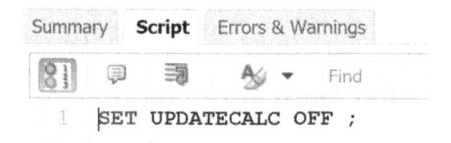

```
SET UPDATECALC OFF ;
```

12. Drag the *Aggregation* template icon to the graphical interface for the business rule, between "SET commands" and "End".
13. Double-click on the *Aggregation* icon in the graphical interface and click *Next* until the "Full dense Aggregation" section appears.
14. In the Full dense Aggregation section, select *Account* for Dense dimension 1 and *Yes* for the property following:

Full dense Aggregation

Select the dense dimensions to aggregate fully

Dense dimension 1	Account
Does dense dimension 1 have stored, non-level 0 members?	Yes
Dense dimension 2	
Does dense dimension 2 have stored, non-level 0 members?	No

If you have stored, non-level 0 members, a CALC DIM is generated for that dense dimension.

15. Click *Next*.

16. In the Full sparse Aggregation section, select *Entity* for Sparse dimension 1 and select *No* for the property following. Select *Product* for Sparse dimension 2 and select *No* for the property following:

Full sparse Aggregation

Select the sparse dimensions to aggregate fully

Sparse dimension 1	Entity
Does sparse dimension 1 have member formulas that need to be calculated?	No
Sparse dimension 2	Product
Does sparse dimension 2 have member formulas that need to be calculated?	No
Sparse dimension 3	
Does sparse dimension 3 have member formulas that need to be calculated?	No

If you want to calculate member formulas, this template generates a CALC DIM, otherwise it generates an AGG.

17. *Save* and *Exit*.
18. Click the *Script* tab to see the written code:

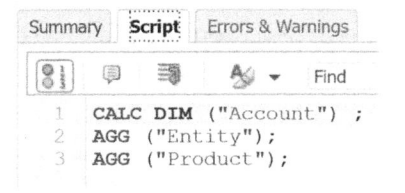

```
1  CALC DIM ("Account") ;
2  AGG ("Entity");
3  AGG ("Product");
```

Note! Remember that in our Vision application build, I don't really need this calc script to roll up data because upper members in the BSO plan type are set to dynamic. In your real life application, until hybrid is supported, this calc would make sense.

19. Click the *End* icon in the graphical representation and click the *Script* tab to view the entire script:

```
 1  FIX ("BaseData")
 2     /* Start Template:SET commands*/
 3     SET UPDATECALC OFF ;
 4     /* End Template:SET commands*/
 5     /* Start Template:Aggregation*/
 6     CALC DIM ("Account") ;
 7     AGG ("Entity");
 8     AGG ("Product");
 9     /* End Template:Aggregation*/
10  ENDFIX
```

Note! Note that if you have sandboxing enabled for the application, Calculation Manager will automatically insert a "FIX" statement at the very beginning of the rule. Most of the times this is good…sometimes it can be tricky if you're trying to write in script mode.

20. Use the menu bar to *Validate* then *Save* the rule:

Save does not automatically perform the *Validate* step – you need to *Validate* as a separate action step. You can use the *Validate and Save* option instead to tackle both actions in one step.

CREATE GRAPHICAL RULE WITH A SCRIPT COMPONENT

Now let's create a graphical rule that I do need in our Vision application. Vision would like to seed its forecast based on actuals data. I can use a business rule to do that. This time I'm still going to create a graphical rule and use a pre-defined Calc Manager template. But I'm also going to insert a script component (where I can write the logic directly); this is sort of a hybrid approach to business rule writing. You can take advantage of many of the Calc Manager features (like the flow diagrams, captions, printing, etc.), but still write your own logic if you prefer.

To create a graphical business rule,

1. Create a new business rule. Call it "Seed Forecast based on Actuals".
2. Drag the *Copy Data* template into the blank rule area.
3. Enter the following POV.
   a. *Period*: @RELATIVE(Period,0)
   b. *Account*: Units, "List Price"
   c. *Entity*: @RELATIVE(Entity,0)
   d. *Product*: @RELATIVE(Product,0)
   e. *Version*: Final
   f. *HSP_View*: BaseData:

Copy Data Wizard
Point of View

Point of View

Define the Point of View to use for copying data

Select members to restrict the data copy

Use Predefined Selection

Dimension	Value
Period	"@RELATIVE(Period, 0)
Account	"Units", "List Price"
Entity	"@RELATIVE(Entity, 0)
Product	"@RELATIVE(Product, 0)
Years	"
Scenario	"
Version	"Final
HSP_View	"BaseData"

4. Copy data from *FY15, Actual*:

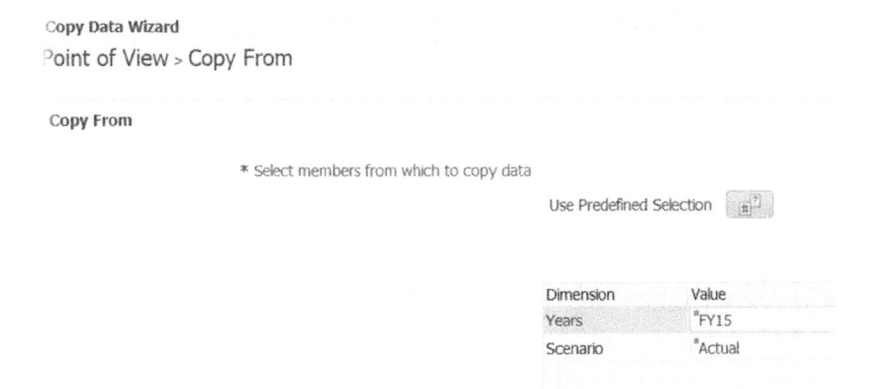

Copy Data Wizard
Point of View > Copy From

Copy From

* Select members from which to copy data

Use Predefined Selection

Dimension	Value
Years	"FY15
Scenario	"Actual

5. Copy data to *FY16, Forecast*:

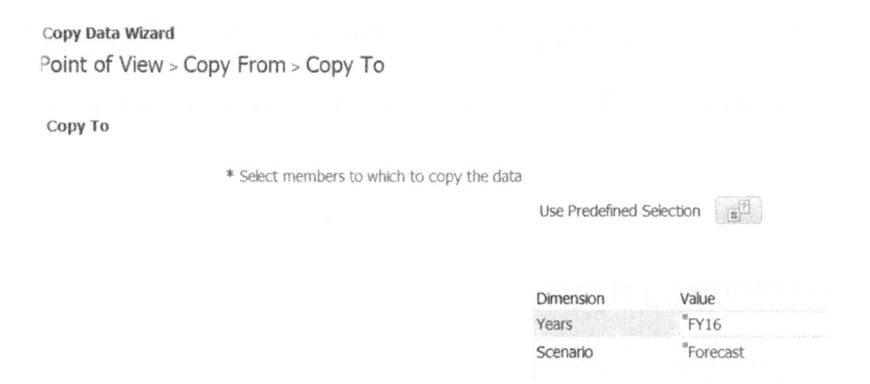

Copy Data Wizard
Point of View > Copy From > **Copy To**

Copy To

* Select members to which to copy the data

Use Predefined Selection

Dimension	Value
Years	"FY16
Scenario	"Forecast

6. Click *Yes* to create the blocks (otherwise data might not copy properly; only say no if you are certain blocks already exist for the data intersections being copied to):

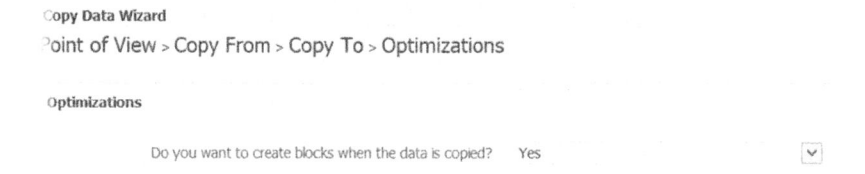

Copy Data Wizard
Point of View > Copy From > Copy To > **Optimizations**

Optimizations

Do you want to create blocks when the data is copied?   Yes

7. Note that at any time I can go back and edit the entered parameters for the template:

Summary Script Errors & Warnings

Point of View
Select members to restrict the data copy
Period   @RELATIVE(Period, 0)
Account "Units", "List Price"
Entity   @RELATIVE(Entity, 0)
Product @RELATIVE(Product, 0)
Version Final
HSP_View "BaseData"

Copy From
Select members from which to copy data
Years FY15
Scenario Actual

Copy To
Select members to which to copy the data
Years FY16
Scenario Forecast

8. Click *Finish*.

Look Smarter Than You Are with Enterprise Planning Cloud   249

9. Now drag a *Script* component into the rule after the Copy Data component:

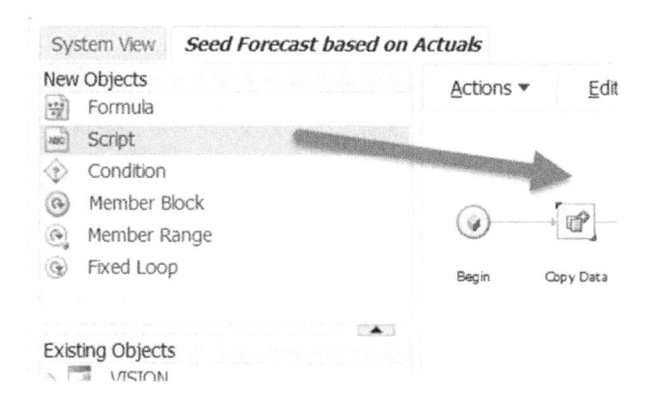

10. Type in the following logic into the script area:

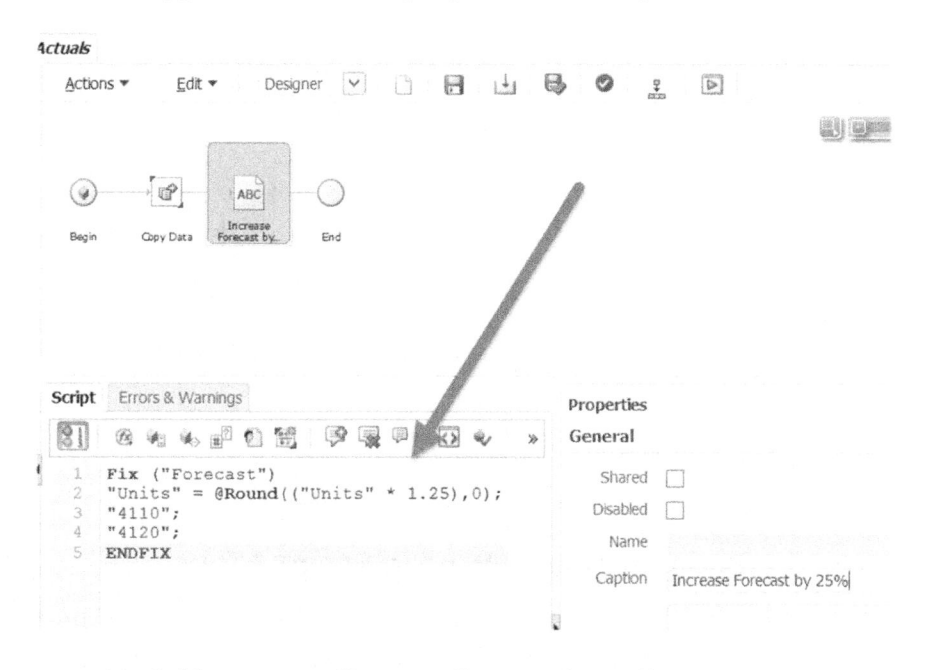

```
Fix ("Forecast")
"Units" = @Round(("Units" * 1.25),0);
"4110";
"4120";
ENDFIX
```

11. Add a caption "Increase Forecast by 25%".

Notice that the business rule calculates the two account members "4110" and "4120" which have member formulas associated with them. "4110" is based on units and price:

Dimensions

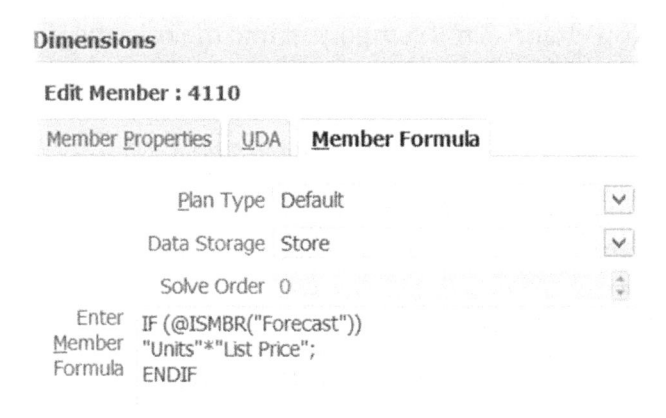

Edit Member : 4110

Member Properties | UDA | **Member Formula**

Plan Type   Default
Data Storage   Store
Solve Order   0
Enter Member Formula   IF (@ISMBR("Forecast"))
"Units"*"List Price";
ENDIF

12. "4120" is based on the "4110" revenue:

Edit Member : 4120

Member Properties | UDA | **Member Formula**

Plan Type   Default
Data Storage   Store
Solve Order   0
Enter Member Formula   If (@ISMBR("Forecast"))
"4110"* .18;
ENDIF

13. Use the menu bar to *Validate* then *Save* the rule (or you can also choose *Validate and Save* icon in one step):

CREATE BUSINESS RULE IN SCRIPT MODE

Experienced Hyperion administrators might prefer to write the business rule scripts and skip the graphical user interface. If you choose to write the business rule in script mode, there are a few simple rules to follow (these same rules apply to script objects like the one I inserted in the previous business rule):

- End every statement with a semicolon

- You can break a statement onto multiple lines, but the end of the statement must have a semicolon
- If a member name contains spaces or starts with a number, surround it with "double quotes". Spaces between member names, commands, and functions do not matter.
- Start comments with /*
- End comments with */
- Calc scripts are not case-sensitive

There are many more rules, but these are the important ones that people tend to forget, causing them to wonder for hours why their business rule scripts aren't working.

You can switch to edit in script mode by switching the drop-down box from "Designer" to "Edit Script". Thankfully when writing scripts, Calc Manager has several icons / functions / tools to help you build your logic (mouse over each icon to see the available options):

```
FIX ( Forecast )
"Units" = @Round(("Units" * 1.25),0);
"4110";
"4120";
AGG("Product", "Entity");
ENDFIX
```

Because I have to finish this in a few hours, I can't spend any more time on all of the Calc Manager features (that could be its own separate mission and book). Many online resources and your helpful partner, i.n.t.e.r.R.e.l, can provide more information on business rules and Calculation Manager.

Until hybrid aggregation is supported, you will likely want to create a business rule for users that will calculate forecast for just the entity (or product) that the user is entering data. Why re-calculate the whole database? Shouldn't I just calculate that entity and any impacted entities? Yes. You should only calculate what you have to; this will have big performance benefits for users during the planning cycle.

I will create a business rule that runs a focused aggregation using run time prompt variables to prompt users for their department and desired version and a substitution variable to focus the rule for a specific year. I'll create the run time prompt variables first, and then write the business rule script.

Variables

Before I move forward, let me explain a little more on variables. Variables are like placeholders in a business rule for a specific purpose. They can be defined at the global, application, plan type or business rule level. Calculation Manager supports two types of variables: execution and replacement variables. Supported variables include numeric, string, dimension, member or members, cross-dimension, percent, integer, member range, string as a number, date as a number, and array. A common variable is a run time prompt variable which will prompt users to enter a value to put into the variable. In Vision's case, I am going to prompt the users to select a department member and version member.

To create variables for business rules,
1. Go to *Navigator >> Administer >> Rules*. The Calculation Manager will appear.
2. Within the System View tab, navigate to *Actions >> Variable Designer*:

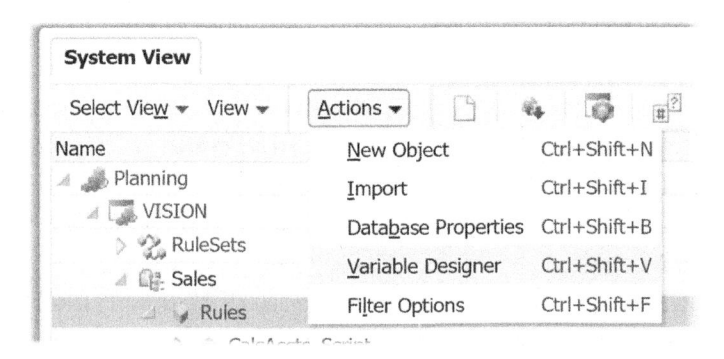

3. In the left panel, right-click the *VISION* application and click *New*:

Look Smarter Than You Are with Enterprise Planning Cloud 253

4. In the Properties section, name the variable "Department_Var".
5. Select *Member* for Type.
6. Click the radio button for *Dimension Type* and select *Entity* in the drop-down menu:

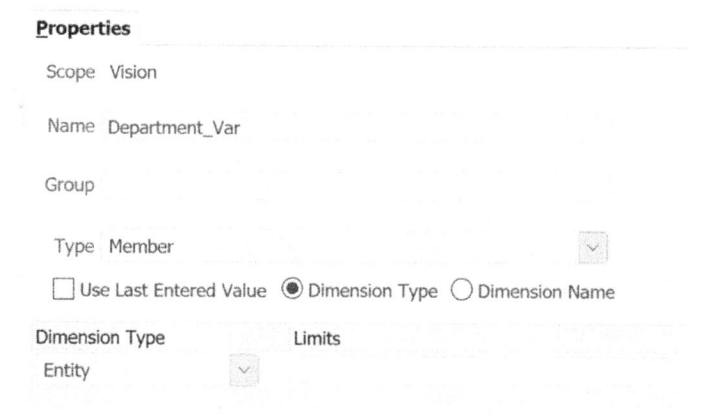

7. Check the box for *RTP* (runtime prompt) and type "Select Department" for the RTP Text:

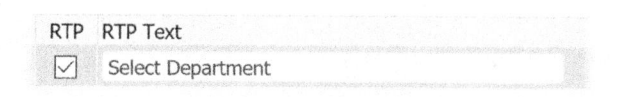

8. Create a "Version_Var" and "Year_Var" using the same principles.

The following variables should be listed in the Variable Designer:

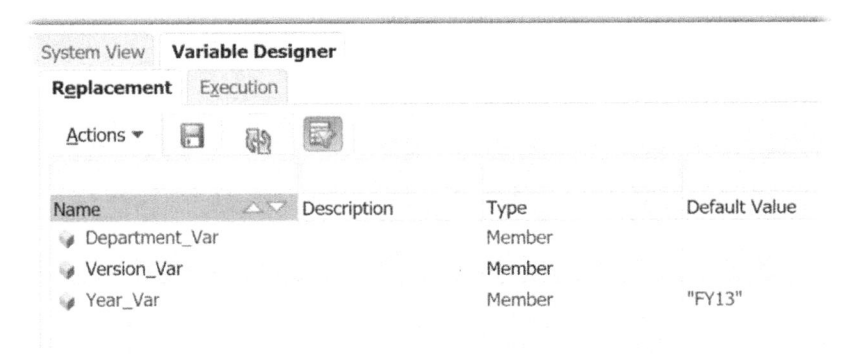

Name	Description	Type	Default Value
Department_Var		Member	
Version_Var		Member	
Year_Var		Member	"FY13"

Note! Notice "FY13" was selected as Year_Var's Default Value. Default values can be selected to make selecting runtime prompts a little easier.

Now that the variables are done, on to writing a business rule using the script mode!

To create a business rule in script mode,
1. In the Calculation Manager, expand the *Sales* database and right-click on *Rules*.
2. Click *New* to create a new business rule.
3. Name the rule "Calculate MyForecast". Leave other properties as default.
4. Click *OK*.
5. Before doing anything else, in the menu bar, change the drop-down value to *Edit Script*:

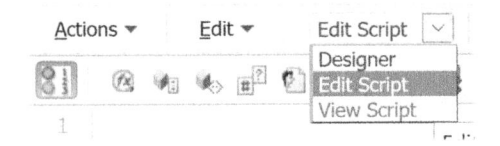

6. When the screen changes, type the following:

Look Smarter Than You Are with Enterprise Planning Cloud   255

```
FIX ("Forecast", &ForecastYear, {Version_Var})
   FIX ({Department_Var})
      "4110";
      "4120";
      AGG("Product");
   ENDFIX
   @IANCESTORS({Department_Var});
ENDFIX
```

Notice the use of the RTP variables I created earlier. The syntax for referencing a Calc Manager variable is to enclose the variable name with "{}". The syntax for referencing a substitution variable is to prefix "&" before the substitution variable name.

The line of code that says @IANCESTORS ({Department_Var}) will only calculate the entity passed to it from the data form and any ancestor members, making this a much faster business rule.

7. Click the *Script* tab to review the final code:

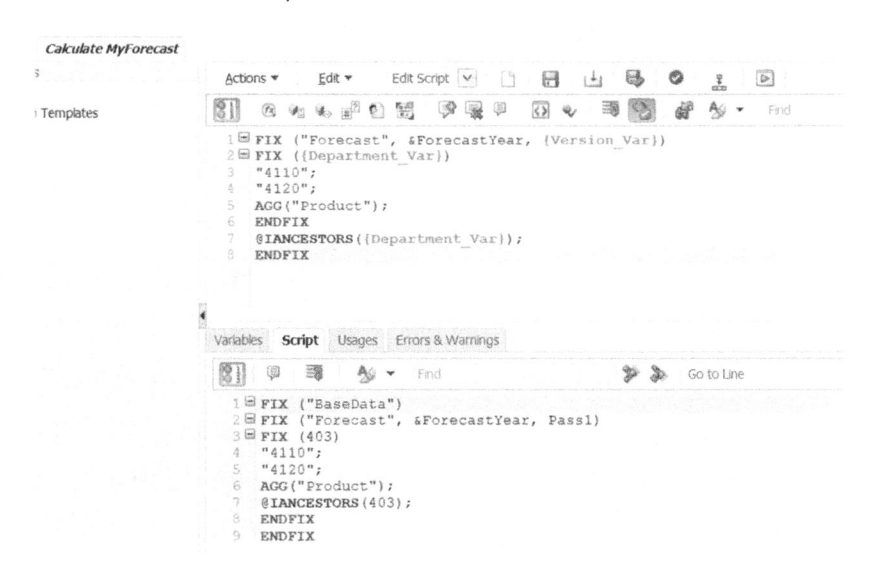

Calculate MyForecast

```
1  FIX ("Forecast", &ForecastYear, {Version_Var})
2  FIX ({Department_Var})
3     "4110";
4     "4120";
5     AGG("Product");
6  ENDFIX
7  @IANCESTORS({Department_Var});
8  ENDFIX
```

Variables | Script | Usages | Errors & Warnings

```
1  FIX ("BaseData")
2  FIX ("Forecast", &ForecastYear, Pass1)
3  FIX (403)
4     "4110";
5     "4120";
6     AGG("Product");
7     @IANCESTORS(403);
8  ENDFIX
9  ENDFIX
```

Note! Again, if you have sandboxing enabled for the application, Calculation Manger will automatically insert a FIX statement at the very beginning of the rule.

Most of the times this is good... sometimes it can be tricky if you are trying to write in script mode.

Note! The FIX statement containing BaseData should be in every rule or script when user sandboxes are enabled. See the section on HSP_View in the Build Dimensions section for more information.

8. Click the *Variables* tab and enter or select values for *Department_Var* and *Version_Var*.
9. *Validate*, then *Save*.
10. Now update the substitution variables to list the rolling forecast variables since this business rule will be attached to the rolling forecast data forms:

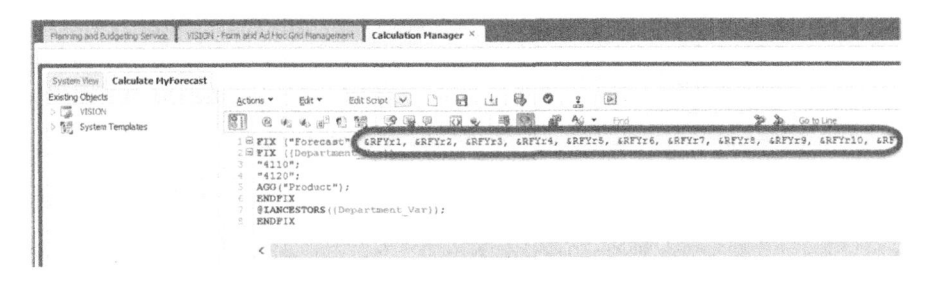

```
FIX ("Forecast", &RFYr1, &RFYr2, &RFYr3, &RFYr4, &RFYr5, &RFYr6, &RFYr7, &RFYr8, &RFYr9, &RFYr10, &RF
FIX ({Department
"4110";
"4120";
AGG("Product");
ENDFIX
@IANCESTORS({Department_Var});
ENDFIX
```

DEPLOY BUSINESS RULE

Once a business rule has been created, it must be deployed to be available in Enterprise Planning Cloud. I'll deploy the business rules I created.

To deploy the business rule,
1. In Calculation Manager, control-click the desired rules (to multi-select), right-click and select *Deploy*:

Look Smarter Than You Are with Enterprise Planning Cloud 257

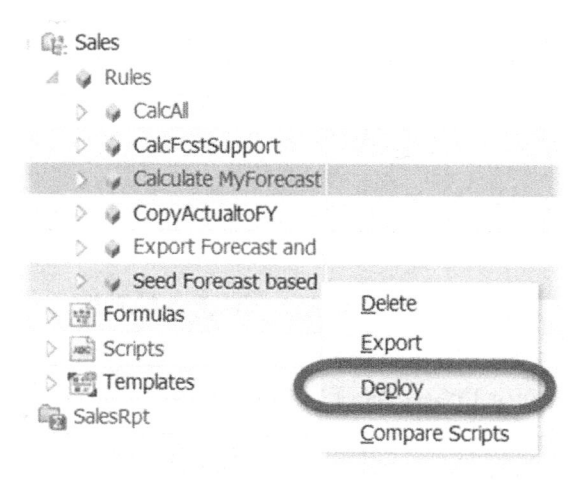

2. When the following message shows, click *OK*:

> ⓘ **Deployment Status**
> The deployment was successful.

Once deployed, the rule can be assigned to a form and launched in the Enterprise Planning Cloud application.

LAUNCH BUSINESS RULE

To launch business rules you must be in the Enterprise Planning Cloud application. You cannot launch from Calculation Manager.

To launch the business rule,
1. In the main menu, click the *Rules* icon.
2. The complete listing of business rules and for which users have access will display. Administrators see every rule.
3. Click the arrow icon for *Launch* next to the business rule you'd like to execute:

Launch

VIEW BUSINESS RULE STATUS

The Job Console provides a way to view the status of business rules that are run for Enterprise Planning Cloud.

To access the Job Console,
1. Navigate to *Console >> Jobs* (second icon on the left).

Here you can view pending and recently completed jobs within Enterprise Planning Cloud such as business rule launches and database refreshes:

Jobs

Pending Jobs
No data to display.

Within Enterprise Planning Cloud, it is also quite simple to schedule jobs using the Jobs Console. I will schedule the *CalcAll* business rule to run nightly at 12AM.

To schedule a rule,
1. In the Jobs Console, click *Schedule Jobs*:

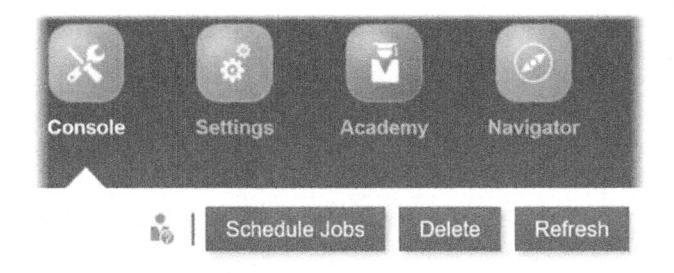

Look Smarter Than You Are with Enterprise Planning Cloud 259

2. Select the type of job, give the job a name, then designate when and how often the job should run:

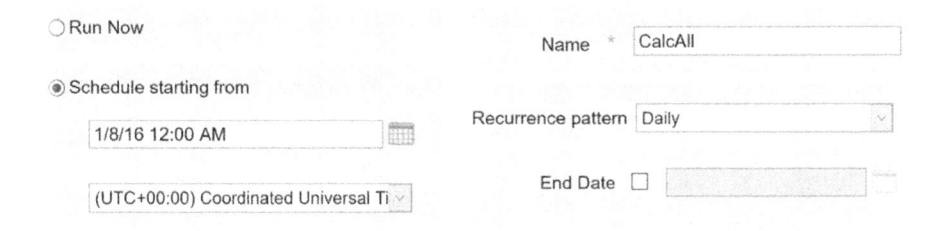

3. Click *Next*.
4. Select the rule by clicking *Select* to the right of the business rule of your choice. Click *Next*.
5. Review the scheduled job and click *Finish*.

The scheduled job will appear in the Jobs Console:

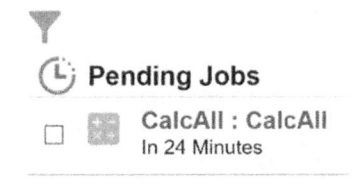

Pending Jobs

CalcAll : CalcAll
In 24 Minutes

If an error occurs, you can view the error details by clicking the job name:

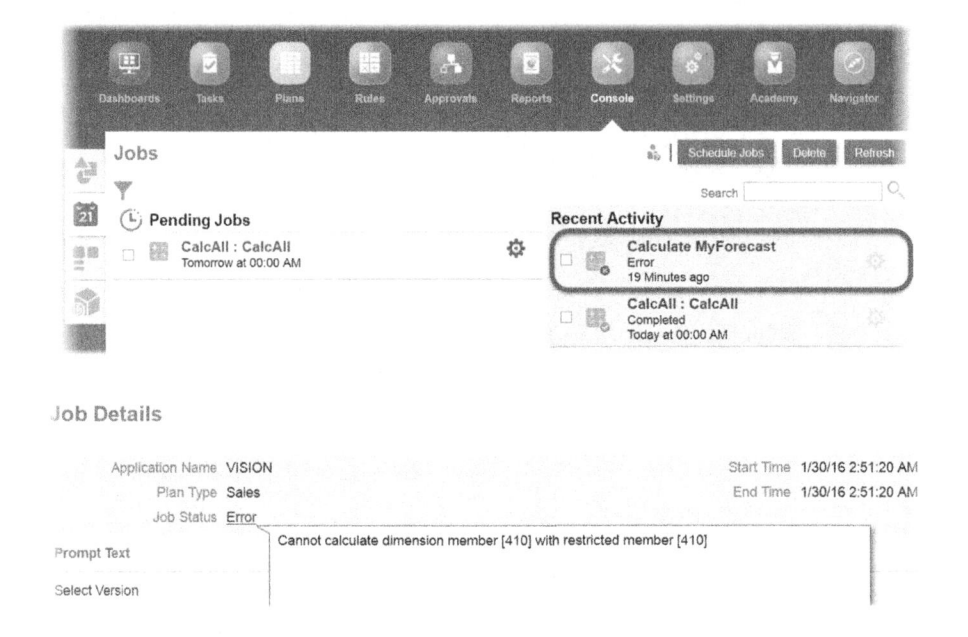

I'll come back to the Job Scheduler later on other types of automation.

ASSIGN BUSINESS RULE TO FORM

The "Calculate Form" business rule is automatically created for every form. It calculates subtotals for the members on the data form (more on data forms in just a bit). Note, if every member on your data form is stored input or dynamically calculated, you do not have to "Calculate Form".

You can also assign custom business rules to a data form, using the arrows to move over the desired business rule to the "Selected Business Rules" section. For the assigned business rule, you can specify the following:

- **Run on Load** – runs the business rule when the user opens the data form
- **Run on Save** – runs the business rule when the user clicks the save button on the data form
- The user may be prompted if a runtime prompt is included in the business rule. You can select the option, **Use Members on Data**

Look Smarter Than You Are with Enterprise Planning Cloud   261

Form, to pass the members on the data form through to the run time prompt and then optionally *Hide Prompt* to hide the run time prompt from the user.

While I haven't created a data form yet, I want to show you the steps to assign business rules in data forms.

To assign a business rule to a data form,
1. Go to *Navigator >> Administer >> Forms* and edit the *Sales Forecast – Products* data form.
2. Navigate to the *Business Rules* tab:

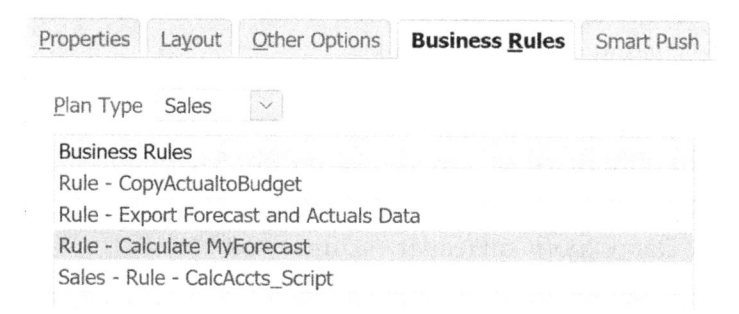

```
Properties   Layout   Other Options   Business Rules   Smart Push

Plan Type   Sales   v

Business Rules
Rule - CopyActualtoBudget
Rule - Export Forecast and Actuals Data
Rule - Calculate MyForecast
Sales - Rule - CalcAccts_Script
```

3. Add the *Calculate MyForecast* business rule to the right panel:

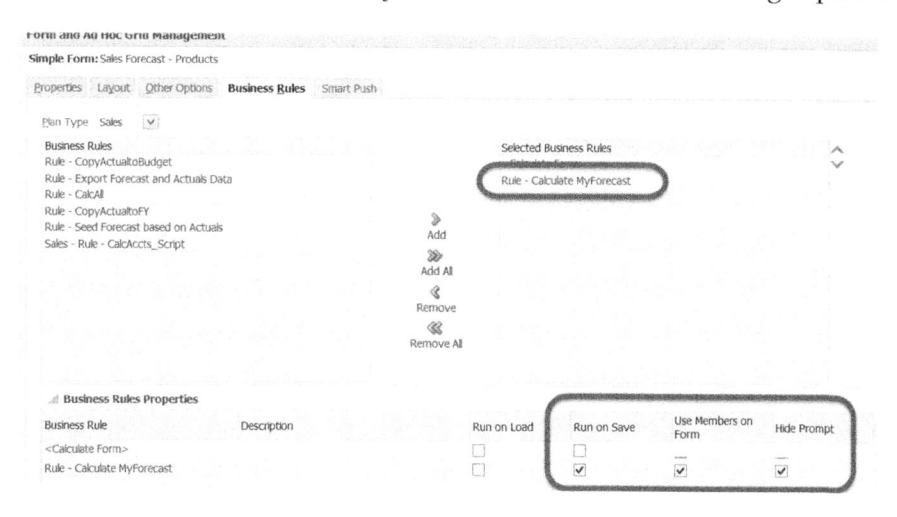

```
Form and Ad Hoc Grid Management
Simple Form: Sales Forecast - Products
Properties  Layout  Other Options  Business Rules  Smart Push

Plan Type  Sales   v

Business Rules                                    Selected Business Rules
Rule - CopyActualtoBudget                         Rule - Calculate MyForecast
Rule - Export Forecast and Actuals Data
Rule - CalcAll
Rule - CopyActualtoFY
Rule - Seed Forecast based on Actuals    Add
Sales - Rule - CalcAccts_Script          Add All
                                         Remove
                                         Remove All

Business Rules Properties
Business Rule              Description    Run on Load   Run on Save   Use Members on Form   Hide Prompt
<Calculate Form>                               □              □
Rule - Calculate MyForecast                    □              ✓              ✓                    ✓
```

4. In Business Rule Properties, check the *Run on Save*, *Use Members on Form*, and *Hide Prompt* boxes for the rule.

5. Click *Finish*.

Export Data Using a Business Rule

While I am on the topic of exporting data, I'll cover one last way to export data from Enterprise Planning Cloud. You can create a business rule and use the DATAEXPORT calculation script command. This command allows you to extract data to a text file or relational table. Placing this command within FIX statements and IF statements allows you to isolate the desired data to be pulled. You can then load the extracted data to a source cube. The full process can be automated with the Job Scheduler and scheduled to run as needed.

There are Data Export Options, a number of set commands that define information for the export, like:

- SET DataExportDecimal <n>;
- SET DataExportLevel "ALL" or "LEVEL" or "INPUT";
- SET DataExportColFormat ON or OFF;
- SET DataExportColHeader "<Dimension Name>";
- SET DataExportDynamicCalc ON or OFF;
- SET DataExportOverwriteFile ON or OFF;
- SET DataExportDimHeader ON or OFF;

Review the example export business rule script below that exports Forecast and Actual data to a file in the Inbox / Outbox Explorer called "VisionForecastDataExport2.txt".

```
FIX ("BaseData")
SET DataExportOptions
{
            DataExportLevel "ALL";
             DataExportColFormat ON;
              DataExportColHeader "Account";
             DataExportDynamicCalc ON;

      DataExportOverwriteFile ON;
                       DataExportDimHeader OFF;
            };
FIX("Forecast", "Actual",
@Relative("Years",0),
@Relative("Entity",0),
@Relative("Product",0),
"BegBalance":"Dec",
"Units",
@Relative("4001",0),
"4001",
@Relative("Version",0))

DATAEXPORT "File" ","
"/u03/lcm/VisionForecastDataExport2.txt" "NULL";

ENDFIX
ENDFIX
```

Create the business rule in the Enterprise Planning Cloud application and call it "Export Forecast and Actuals Data". Use the Job Scheduler to schedule the business rule if desired.

Whenever the business rule is run, it will create a TXT file that can be viewed and downloaded in the Inbox / Outbox Explorer. To go to the Inbox / Outbox Explorer, go to *Console >> Application >> Actions >> Inbox / Outbox Explorer*:

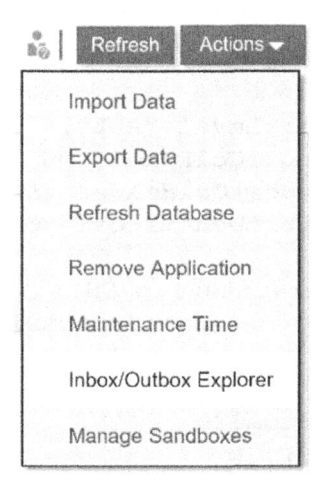

Since the business rule script specifies to overwrite the file, the file will be replaced every time the rule is launched:

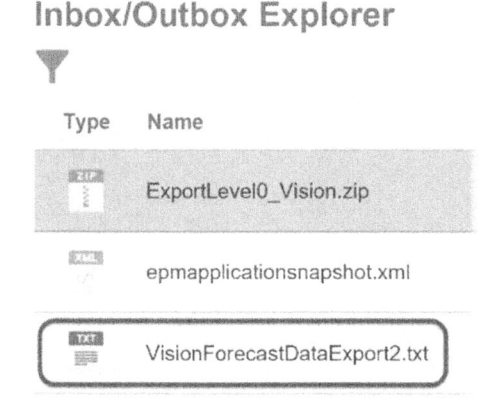

ASO PLAN TYPE BUSINESS RULES

Business rules are supported for ASO plan types with some considerations and limitations. You follow the same steps to create a business rule for an ASO plan type in the graphical interface.

The graphical interface is the only supported interface for ASO plan types (scripting is not supported). There are three pre-defined templates that you can use to build business rules for your ASO plan type: Point of View, Allocation, and Formula. The Point of View template

Look Smarter Than You Are with Enterprise Planning Cloud   265

defines the focus for the business rule. The Allocation template allocates values from a source to a destination based on a driver. This template supports single dimension allocation. The Formula template allows you to build a simple formula calculation:

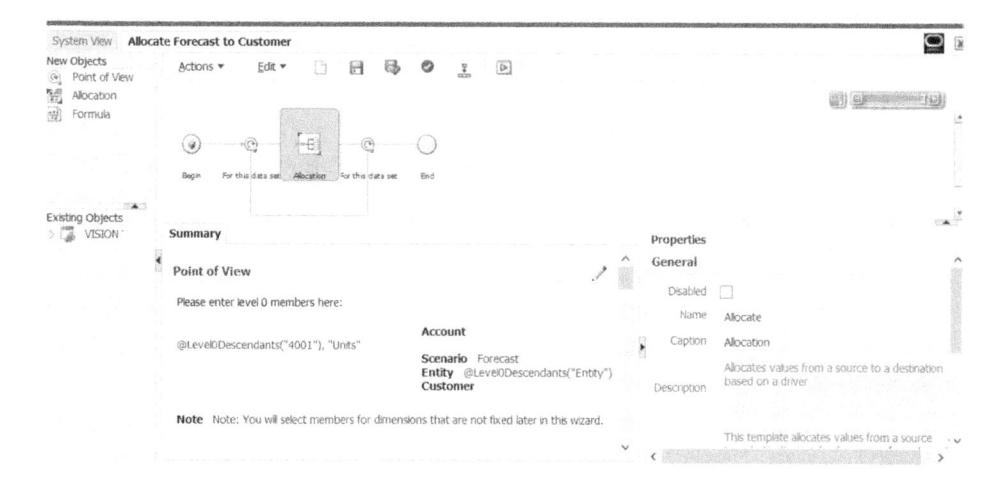

[screenshot of Calculation Manager showing "Allocate Forecast to Customer" template with Point of View, Allocation, and Formula objects, and a Summary panel showing Account, Scenario Forecast, Entity @Level0Descendants("Entity"), Customer; Properties panel with General settings: Name Allocate, Caption Allocation, Description "Allocates values from a source to a destination based on a driver"]

One other handy task that you will need to do for your ASO plan types: partial data clears. At some point you will want to clear part of the data in an ASO plan type but not all of the data.

To perform a partial data clear in an ASO plan type,
1. Open Calculation Manager.
2. Click the icon for *Database Properties*.
3. Right click on the desired plan type and select *Clear >> Partial Data*.
4. Enter the MDX expression defining the data slice that you would like to clear; for example:

```
{([Actual],[Final])}
```

MDX is the syntax that is used with ASO plan types. For more information on MDX and ASO, check out the Oracle documentation.

5. Choose the option: *Physical* or *Logical*.

A *Physical* clear will actually clear the data (which may take a little longer) and the *Logical* clear will create an offsetting slice of data (which goes a little faster). If you have time, choose *Physical*. If clearing data during the day (while users are in the system), choose *Logical* and then come back at night and run a physical clear.

6. Click *OK* and the data should clear for the specified slice.

As I mentioned at the beginning of the chapter, I've only skimmed the surface with the foundations of Calculation Manager and business rules. For more information and examples, check out the Oracle documentation and i.n.t.e.r.R.e.l.'s webcasts and Play It Forward videos.

LOG ENTRY: SOL 15, Entry 2

Well, the implementation is still going! Calculation Manager worked and it wasn't dangerous at all! Really easy in fact and it met all of my calculating, aggregating and allocating needs.

Chapter 7: Create User Interfaces

> **LOG ENTRY: SOL 16, Entry 1**
>
> Finally! Something users can see and touch and love.
> Wait. That sounded a bit awkward. What I meant to say is… I'm excited to finally create the user interfaces in Enterprise Planning Cloud.
> It is a little lonely in the Cloud by myself…

DATA FORMS

Data forms are the mechanisms for users to enter and review plan data. Data forms can be accessed over the web or in Excel via Smart View:

			Oct FY15	Nov FY15	Dec FY15	Jan FY16	Feb FY16	Mar FY16	Apr FY16
P_100:Product X		Units	12						
		List Price							
		4110:Hardware Revenue							
P_110:Sentinal Standard Notebook		Units	13	13	13	13	13	13	
		List Price	1200	1200	1200	1200	1200	1200	
		4110:Hardware Revenue	15600	15600	15600	15600	15600	15600	
P_120:Sentinal Custom Notebook		Units	13	13		13	13	13	
		List Price							
		4110:Hardware Revenue							
P_130:Envoy Standard Netbook		Units	13	13	13	13	13	13	
		List Price	500	500	500	500	500	500	
		4110:Hardware Revenue	6500	6500	6500	6500	6500	6500	
P_140:Envoy Custom Netbook		Units	8	8		8	8	8	
		List Price	700	700	700	700	700	700	
		4110:Hardware Revenue	5600	5600		5600	5600	5600	
P_150:Other Computer		Units	13	13	13	13	13	13	
		List Price	500	500	500	500	500	500	
		4110:Hardware Revenue	6500	6500	6500	6500	6500	6500	
P_160:Tablet Computer		Units	8	8	8	8	8	8	
		List Price							

Manage Form Folders

Data forms may be organized into Form Folders, and security may be applied at the folder or form level.

To create a form folder,
1. Go to *Navigator* and click *Forms* (under Administer).
2. Create a Form Folder in the left panel by clicking ✚.
3. Call the Form Folder "Vision Users". Click *OK*.

Create   ×

* Enter the name for the new folder   Vision Users

                                                        OK   Cancel

Data Form Basics

A data form is a structured interface that administrators create for end users. There are two types of data forms: Simple and Composite. A simple form is created against a single plan type with members assigned to the rows, columns, pages (drop-down menu), and point of view (POV). A composite form is comprised of two or more simple forms.

When you create a simple data form, the first tab allows you to define and update data form properties:

- Data form name
- Description
- Source plan type
- Data form instructions

You can add detailed instructions for the data form and use formatting, URLs and more to create a helpful guide to end users.

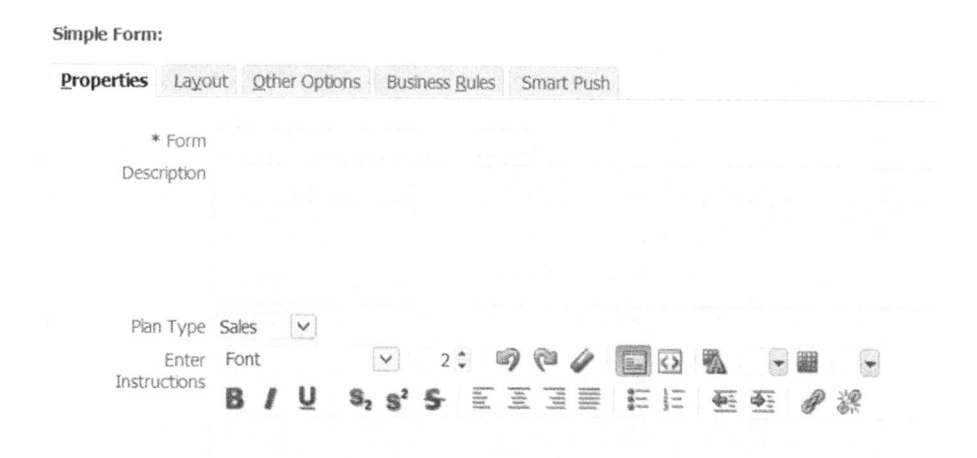

Look Smarter Than You Are with Enterprise Planning Cloud 269

Simple Form:

Properties | Layout | Other Options | Business Rules | Smart Push

* Form
Description

Plan Type Sales

Enter Font   2
Instructions
B I U S₂ S² S

On the Layout tab, you must have at least one dimension and member in a row and column. A dimension can exist in one place only – the row, column, page, or point of view. The Point of View section will select one member only from the dimensions assigned to this section. You can use the member selection icons to select members for the point of view or manually type the member name in:

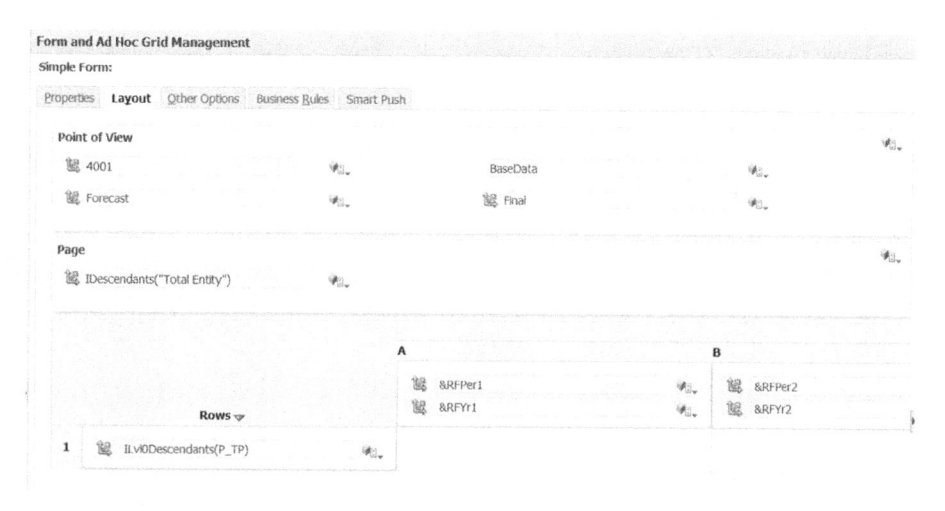

Form and Ad Hoc Grid Management

Simple Form:

Properties | **Layout** | Other Options | Business Rules | Smart Push

Point of View

4001   BaseData
Forecast   Final

Page
IDescendants("Total Entity")

		A	B
		&RFPer1	&RFPer2
	Rows	&RFYr1	&RFYr2
1	ILvl0Descendants(P_TP)		

The Page section may house one or more dimensions. These dimensions will display the selected members at the top of data forms in the form of a drop-down menu. The rows and columns of a data form are the "meat" of the form. You can define one or more rows / columns. You may place one or more dimensions in a row section or column section. Drag and drop to move dimensions around the Layout definition.

You may insert additional columns or rows into a data form (each column / row is also known as a "segment". You can also add a data column / row or a formula column / row:

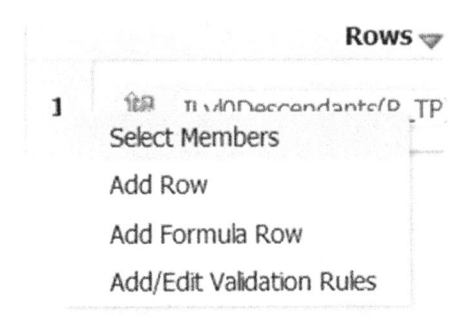

```
                        Rows ▽

    1       ቱቋ   ILvInNoccondontc/D  TP
            Select Members
            Add Row
            Add Formula Row
            Add/Edit Validation Rules
```

Member Selection

When you choose to use Member Selection to define members in the Point of View, Page, Row, and Column sections, click ▼. The Member Selection window will display:

Member Selection

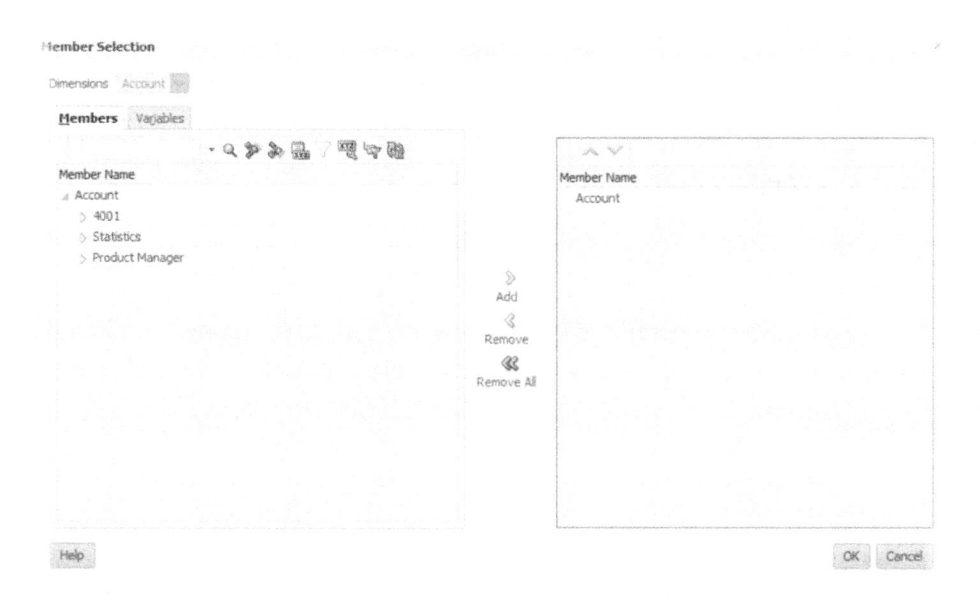

[Screenshot of Member Selection dialog showing Dimensions/Account tabs, Members/Variables tabs, Member Name list with Account, 4001, Statistics, Product Manager, Add/Remove/Remove All buttons, and OK/Cancel buttons]

From this window, you can navigate the dimension to select members. You can choose whether you want to search by member name, alias or different combinations of member name and alias by selecting the *Display* icon:

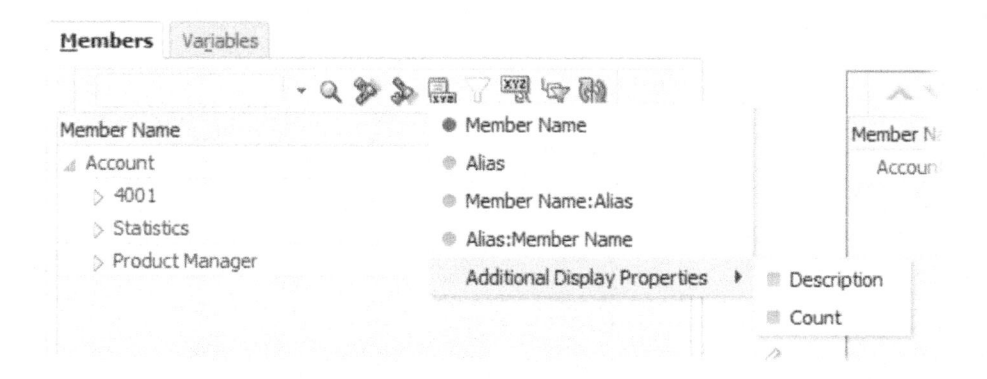

[Screenshot showing Display icon menu with options: Member Name, Alias, Member Name:Alias, Alias:Member Name, Additional Display Properties > Description, Count]

Type in the search bar and click the magnifying glass icon to search for members:

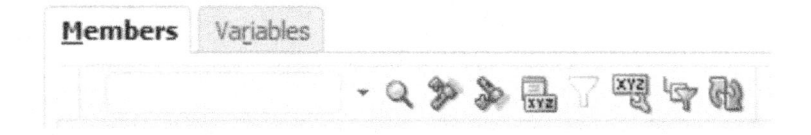

[Screenshot of Members tab with search bar and toolbar icons]

Other options include "keeping" or retaining member selections by Attributes or Level:

Instead of specific members, you can also insert applicable substitution variables, user variables, or filter members by associated attributes on the Variables tab in the Member Selection window:

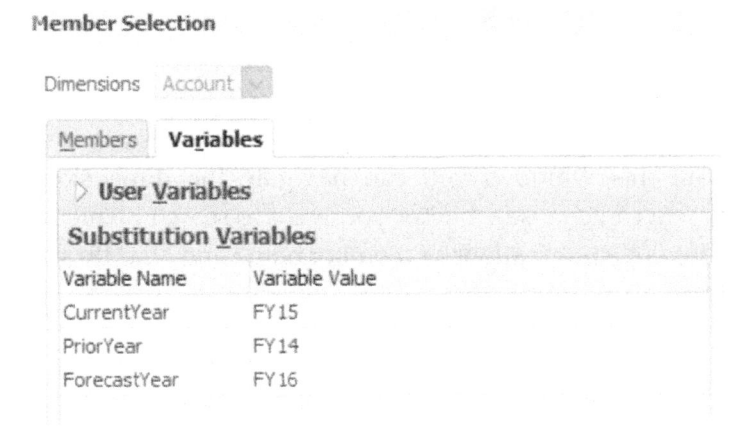

Use the arrow keys to move members between the dimension and variables list and Selected Members section:

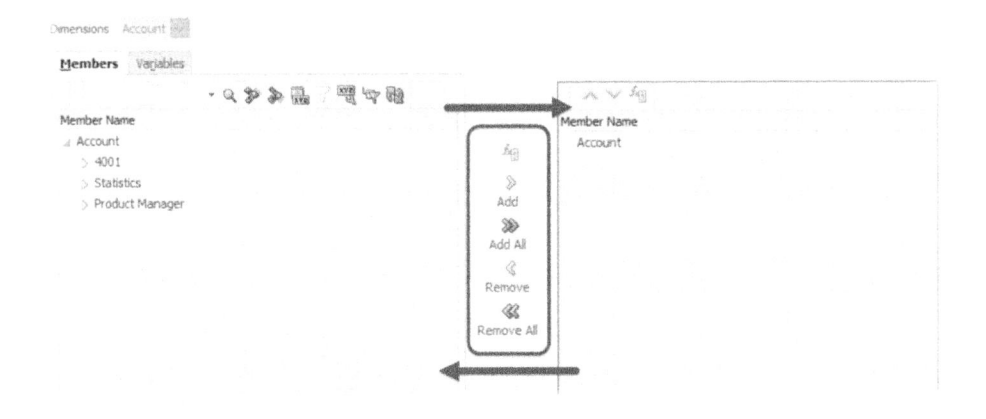

Before moving the selected member, you can also choose whether to move the member itself, or children of the member, or descendants of the member (or other available functions):

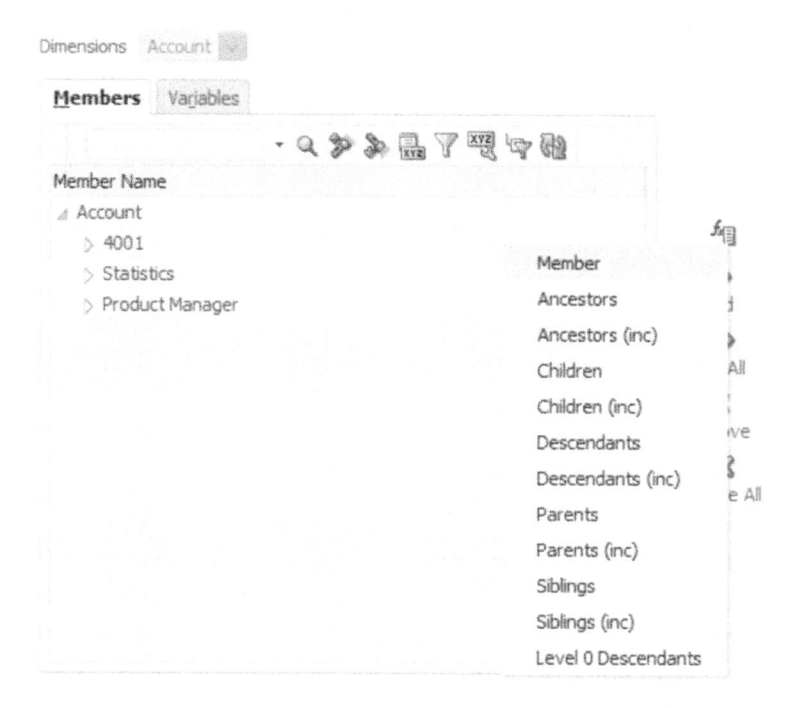

```
Dimensions  Account
Members  Variables

Member Name
▲ Account
  > 4001
  > Statistics                    Member
  > Product Manager               Ancestors
                                  Ancestors (inc)
                                  Children              All
                                  Children (inc)
                                  Descendants           ive
                                  Descendants (inc)
                                                        e All
                                  Parents
                                  Parents (inc)
                                  Siblings
                                  Siblings (inc)
                                  Level 0 Descendants
```

Functions provide two benefits:

- A faster way to pick a list of members
- They make the data form dynamic

As the dimension evolves over time (as members are added or removed), the form will automatically display the correct list.

An example of a function may be pulling in the children of Product (so that you have a dynamic list of the product categories displayed on the form) or Level 0 Descendants of Revenue (so that you always have a complete list of Level 0 revenue accounts listed in the data form).

Data Form Options

Most of the data form options are defined on the Layout tab on the collapsible right panel:

Grid Properties

The Grid Properties apply to the entire grid:

- **Suppress missing blocks** – will suppress entire blocks that do not have data. This setting can help with performance when suppressing a large number of rows, such as 90% or more. This option can degrade performance if few or no rows are suppressed.
- **Suppress missing data – Rows** – will suppress any rows that do not have data
- **Suppress invalid data – Rows** – will suppress any rows with invalid data
- **Default row height** – allows you to choose the row height displayed
    - o **Medium** – default option
    - o **Size-to-Fit** – force all text to fit in the displayed space
    - o **Custom** – enter a custom value
- **Suppress missing data – Columns** – will suppress any columns that do not have data
- **Suppress invalid data – Columns** – will suppress any columns with invalid data
- **Default column width** – allows you to choose the column width displayed

- **Small** – display 7 decimal places on the data form
- **Medium** – display 10 decimal places on the data form
- **Large** – display 13 decimal places on the data form
- **Size-to-Fit** – force all column headings to fit in the displayed space
- **Custom** – display over 13 decimal places on the data form; can enter a value up to 999

Dimension Properties

You can also set options for each dimension. Simply select a dimension and the dimension properties display:

- **Member name and Alias** – choose whether the data form should display the member name or alias (or both if the dimension is in the rows)
- **Member Formula** – choose to display the icon that will allow users to view member formulas
- **Hide dimension** – hide the dimension on a data form (helpful to "clear" real estate on the data form)
- **Show consolidation operators** – show consolidation operators
- **Start Expanded** – if you have a hierarchy selected for the dimension (e.g., IDescendants of "YearTotal"), you can decide whether you want the hierarchy to start expanded or collapsed

Once you have the settings defined you can choose the option to *Apply to all [column, row, POV] dimensions,* which applies the settings to all columns / rows / POV members (saving you some time in the data form definition process).

Segment Properties

For each dimension, you can create multiple segments (which really means that you can have multiple rows and columns in a data form). For each row or column, you can define the properties.

The following Segment properties are available:

- **Hide** – hide the segment so it is not displayed on the data form

- **Read-only** – create a read-only segment in the data form to allow comparing old, read-only data with new, editable data
- **Show separator** – create a bold border before the segment to visually distinguish parts of the data form
- **Suppress hierarchy** – for columns, do not display line breaks
- **Suppress missing data** – suppress missing data for the selected segment only
- **Apply to all [rows, columns]** – apply these settings to all columns in segments

Once you have the segment settings defined you can choose the option to *Apply to all rows / columns* (saving you some time in the data form definition process).

Display Properties

The Display properties control the overall display of the data form. You can choose to:

- **Make form read-only** – the entire form will be "grayed out" with no data entry possible by users
- **Hide Form** – hides the forms from end user access – helpful for simple forms that are used in composite forms
- **Display missing values as blank** – use this option when you don't want to see #MISSING
- **Enable account annotations** – allow users to enter account annotations (aren't used as frequently now that Planning has Smart Lists and free-form text measures so you probably won't ever check this option)
- **Allow multiple currencies per entity** – applicable for applications that use the out of the box currency logic
- **Enable Mass Allocate** – carefully consider this option; do not enable for the end-user masses (behind the scenes, Mass Allocate runs business rules)
- **Enable Grid Spread** – enable grid spreading (only enable this feature on data forms that are set up for "grid spread")

- **Enable cell-level document** – allow users to view and attach documents
- **Message for forms with no data** – enter a custom message to tell users what they should do if no data displays when the form opens

Printing Options

You can define the default printing options for the data form including whether supporting detail or comments should print; also for defining formatting, precision options, and more.

Validation Rules

You can also define validation rules for grids, rows, columns, or cells within a data form. These rules evaluate user input using condition logic.

Other Options

Back in the Data Form Designer, once you've finished the Point of View, Page, Row, and Column member selections, and have defined the data form options, you are ready for the Other Options tab. Click *Next* to move to Other Options or choose the Other Options tab. You can define options for precision, context menus, and dynamic user variables (I'll cover menus and user variables later in the book).

Business Rules

You can assign one or more business rules to a data form. The "Calculate Data Form" business rule is automatically created for every form. It calculates subtotals for the members on the data form. (Note: if every member on your data form is stored or dynamically calculated, you do not have to use "Calculate Data Form".)

You can also assign custom business rules to a data form using the arrows to move over the desired business rule to the Selected Business Rules section. For the assigned business rule, you can specify the following:

- **Run on Load** – runs the business rule when the user opens the data form
- **Run on Save** – runs the business rule when the user clicks the save button on the data form
- The user may be prompted if a runtime prompt is included in the business rule.
- You can select the option **Use Members on Data Form** to pass the members on the data form through to the runtime prompt. You can also optionally select **Hide Prompt** which hides the runtime prompt from the user

Now that I have the Data Form basics down, I'm going to build a simple form that allows users to enter forecast data for the Sales entities of Vision Company.

Build Simple Form

In order to build a simple form,
1. Click the *Vision Users* folder.
2. Then explore the options in the *Actions* menu:

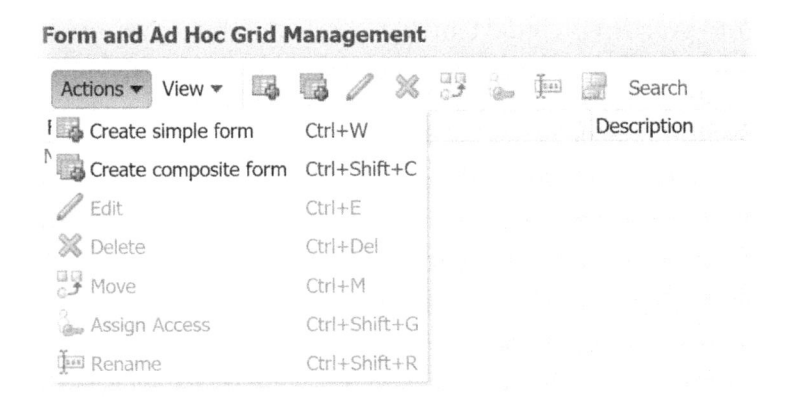

Form and Ad Hoc Grid Management

Actions ▼ View ▼		Search
Create simple form	Ctrl+W	Description
Create composite form	Ctrl+Shift+C	
Edit	Ctrl+E	
Delete	Ctrl+Del	
Move	Ctrl+M	
Assign Access	Ctrl+Shift+G	
Rename	Ctrl+Shift+R	

3. Click *Create simple form*.
4. Name the form and add a description if desired. I'm going to call this one "Sales Forecast – Products".
5. Note the Plan Type and make sure *Sales* is selected.
6. Add instructions for form users if desired:

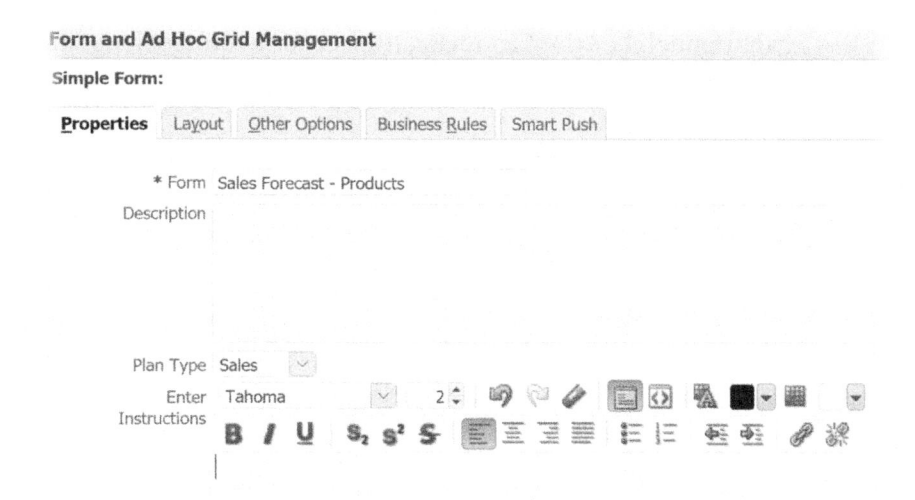

Look Smarter Than You Are with Enterprise Planning Cloud 279

Form and Ad Hoc Grid Management

Simple Form:

Properties | Layout | Other Options | Business Rules | Smart Push

* Form Sales Forecast - Products
Description

Plan Type Sales
Enter Instructions Tahoma

Note! All kinds of formatting options are available for form instructions including font type, font color, indentation, bullets, and alignment. You can also add dynamic URL links.

7. Click *Next* to move on to the Layout tab.

In the Layout tab, I will drag dimensions to the Row, Column, or Page from the Point of View. I can select the members I want through the Member Selector and also adjust Dimension and Segment properties in the right panel.

8. Click and drag the icon to the left of the dimension names to move Period and Years to the Columns section of the layout:

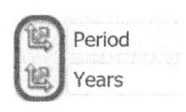

Period
Years

Note! Click the column (e.g., "A") or row (e.g., "1") identifier to view the Segment Properties.

9. Drag *Product* and *Account* to the Rows. Click on one of these dimension names to explore the Dimension Properties in the

right panel. For the Products and Accounts dimensions, make sure that the properties for *Member Name* and *Alias* are checked.

10. Drag *Version* to the Page section.
11. Leave HSP_View member *BaseData, Entity,* and *Scenario* in the Point of View:

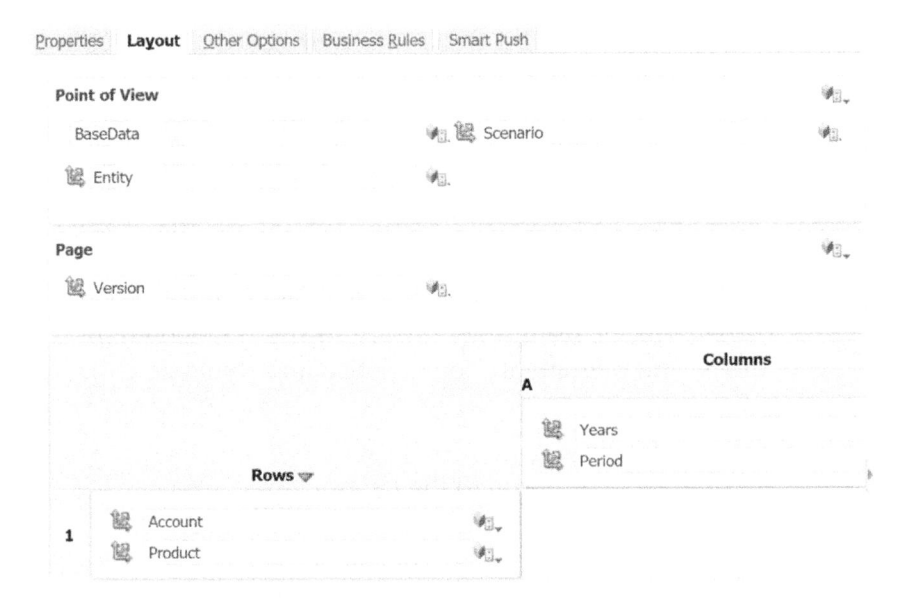

Properties	**Layout**	Other Options	Business Rules	Smart Push	
Point of View					
BaseData			Scenario		
Entity					
Page					
Version					

				Columns
				A
				Years
				Period
	Rows			
1	Account			
	Product			

The next step is to select members for each dimension.

Select Members in Data Form

I'll now select the other members for the remaining dimensions in the Sales Forecast – Products data form,

12. Click next to the *Account* dimension in the Rows section. The Member Selector will open:

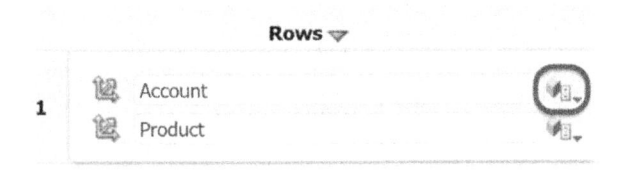

	Rows	
1	Account	
	Product	

13. Change the display in the Member Selection so you can view aliases by selecting the *Display Properties* icon. Switch to *Alias*:

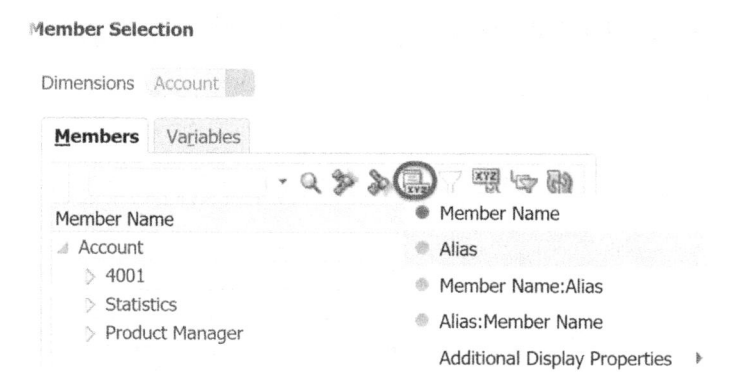

Member Selection

Dimensions Account

Members Variables

Member Name
- Account
  - 4001
  - Statistics
  - Product Manager

- Member Name
- Alias
- Member Name:Alias
- Alias:Member Name
- Additional Display Properties ▶

On the Members tab icon menu, several options are available to assist form developers with selecting and finding members for forms. The search text box allows developers to search for specific members within the hierarchy:

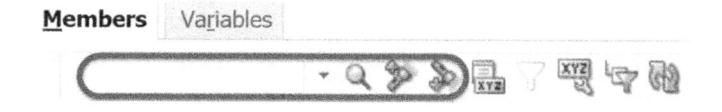

Members Variables

A search term can be entered into the search field. Once the magnifying glass is pressed, the term will be searched on in the current dimension. The drop-down next to the search field allows for more refined searches within: member names, aliases, descriptions, and / or UDA's. The flashlight icons will also search up or down (based on the placement of the green plus sign) from the current member highlighted within the dimension. Searches include shared members. In addition, they are not case sensitive and searches can be restricted to exact matches, word searches, multiple word searches, and / or wildcard characters.

The next icon is the *Display Properties*, explained previously:

Members Variables

The *Keep Only by Functions* icon activates once a member is selected within the dimension. This allows a developer to pinpoint on a specific subset of dimension members using the keep only feature with relationship functions:

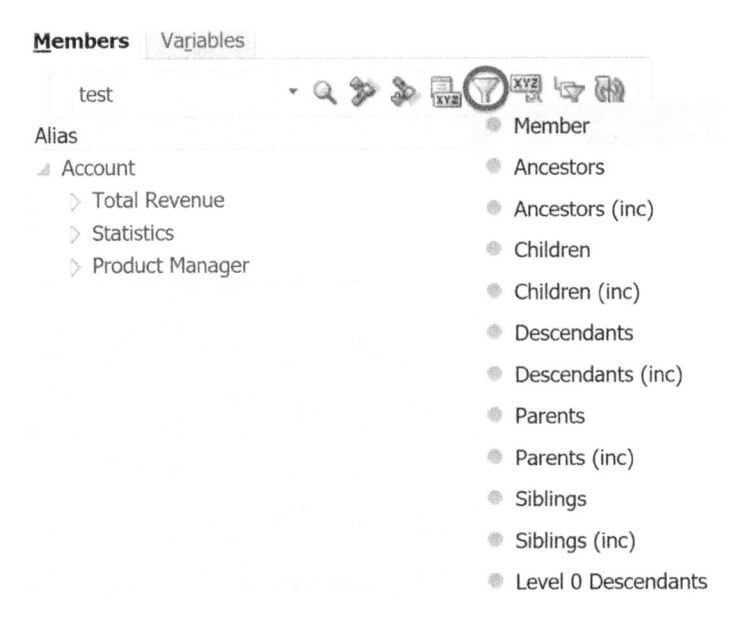

The *Keep Only by Attributes* icon only applies to attributes. If attributes are part of the design, the attribute, an operator, and a value can be used in conjunction to filter to specific members:

The *Keep Only by Levels or Generations* icon allows member filtering by either level or generation. Once Level or Generation is selected, a corresponding number is selectable:

Finally, the *Refresh* icon will remove the filters and then refresh the display:

Now you can see the aliases instead of the member names:

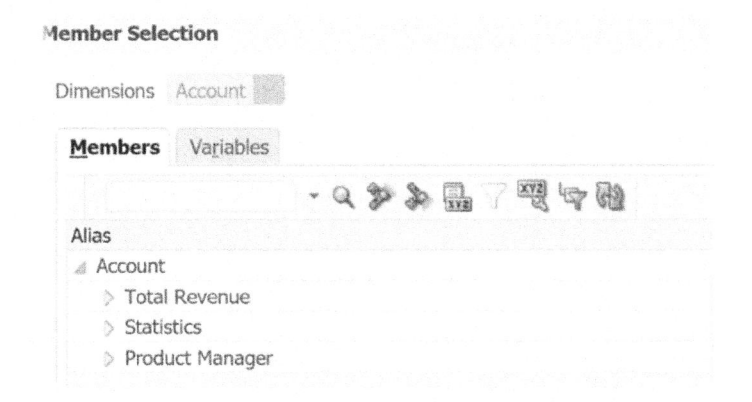

14. Drill down the *Account* hierarchy and select *Units, List Price,* and *Hardware Revenue* by clicking on them and moving them to the right. Alternatively, search for the Account names in the search bar.

For the Product dimension, I will display all the Level 0 members of "Computer Equipment" (member name "P_TP1") to display all the Computer Equipment products.

15. Click next to the Product dimension and click *Computer Equipment* on the left panel.

16. Click ƒ▤ :

```
  ƒ▤
  ≫
  Add
  ⋙
  Add All
  ≪
  Remove
  ⋘
  Remove All
```

17. Select *Level 0 Descendants*.

"ILvl0Descendants("Computer Equipment")" will appear in the right panel. This function will return all of the lowest level members under "Computer Equipment":

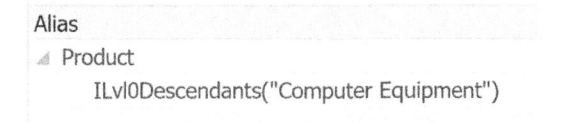

```
Alias
⊿ Product
      ILvl0Descendants("Computer Equipment")
```

18. Click *OK*.

Computer Equipment and its Level 0 descendants will appear on the data form. Next, I want to create a row that will give me the total Hardware Revenue for all Computer Equipment. I'll have to create another row to do this.

19. Right-click the row number (if there is only one row, click the "1").
20. When the menu appears, select *Add Row*:

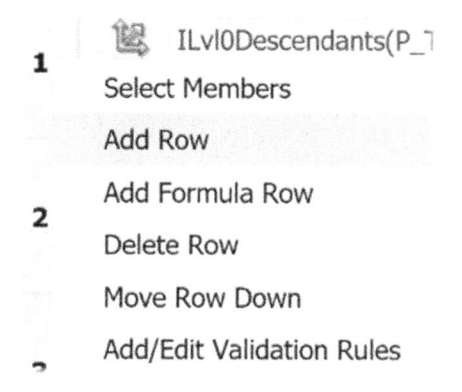

Look Smarter Than You Are with Enterprise Planning Cloud   285

1	🏛 ILvl0Descendants(P_] Select Members Add Row
2	Add Formula Row Delete Row Move Row Down Add/Edit Validation Rules

A new row with the same members as the previous row will appear.

21. Click next to the Account dimension. Change the display property to *Member Name*:

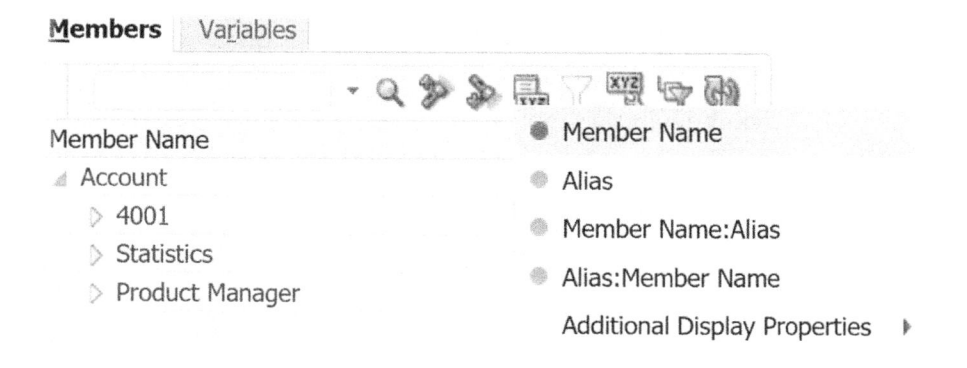

Members   Variables

Member Name
⊿ Account
　▷ 4001
　▷ Statistics
　▷ Product Manager

● Member Name
● Alias
● Member Name:Alias
● Alias:Member Name
　Additional Display Properties ▶

22. Select *4110* as the Account and *Computer Equipment (P_TP1)* as the Product.
23. Add two more rows until there are a total of four rows.
24. Select the members for each row according to the following (first two rows should be defined already):

	Rows	
1	ILvl0Descendants(P_TP1) Units,List Price,4110	
2	P_TP1 4110	
3	ILvl0Descendants(P_TP2) Units,List Price,4110	
4	P_TP2 4110	

For the Entity dimension in the POV, I will display all the members selected as the MyRegion user variable.

25. Click located in the Point of View section.
26. Choose *Entity* from the Dimensions drop-down list.
27. Click the *Variables* tab:

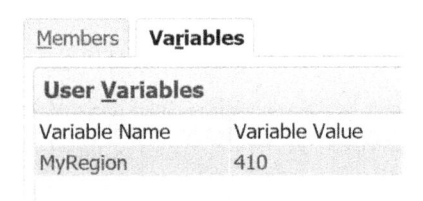

Members	**Variables**
User Variables	
Variable Name	Variable Value
MyRegion	410

28. Add the *MyRegion* variable to the right panel.
29. Choose *Scenario* from the Dimensions drop-down list.
30. Add the *Forecast* member to the right panel.
31. Click *OK*.
32. Finally, click for the Page.
33. Add all the descendants of Version using .
34. The end result should be the following:

Simple Form: Sales Forecast - Products

Properties **Layout** Other Options Business Rules Smart Push

Point of View

BaseData   Forecast

&MyRegion

Page

IDescendants(Version)

35. Click *Save*.

Enable Dynamic User Variables in Data Form

Now that I've defined the user variable MyRegion in the data form, the form will automatically filter based on what the user has specified in their preferences. This means that the user would have to go back to Preferences to change their selected member if they don't want what's currently set for MyRegion. To save the user some clicking, you can enable *Dynamic user variables* on a data form and let the user change the value within the form (so they don't have to navigate back to preferences). Once you enable dynamic user variables, users can change the user variable member within the form.

Dynamic user variables create flexible data forms that users can tailor for their desired sections of the database, reducing the number of data form objects to create and administer (vs. the administrator creating multiple data forms for multiple data groups).

To enable dynamic user variables,
1. In the Sales Forecast – Products data form, select the *Other Options* tab.
2. Towards the bottom right corner, check *Enable dynamic user variables*.
3. Move the *MyRegion* user variable to the right panel:

Dynamic User Variables

Available User Variables	Selected User Variables
ProductFamily	MyRegion

Now I'll define the Years and Period dimensions by setting up a rolling forecast.

Create Rolling Forecast

Rolling forecasts are continuous forecasts that continue past the annual fiscal period end. The periods within the rolling forecast period should roll up together even when they cross fiscal or annual years. Companies typically forecast for 12 month, 18 month, or 24 month cycles.

When allowing for rolling forecast forms, the required substitution variables are created on the fly and the values assign to them automatically. These and other substitution variables can be controlled and managed within Enterprise Planning Cloud.

Note! In the current version of Enterprise Planning Cloud, once you enable rolling forecast, all new forms will automatically place the rolling forecast variables for period and year in the columns. You can update / change the period and year columns if desired, changing members, deleting columns and / or moving to the POV or page.

To set up a rolling forecast in a form,
1. Go back to the *Layout* tab and right-click *Column A* to select *Rolling Forecast Setup*:

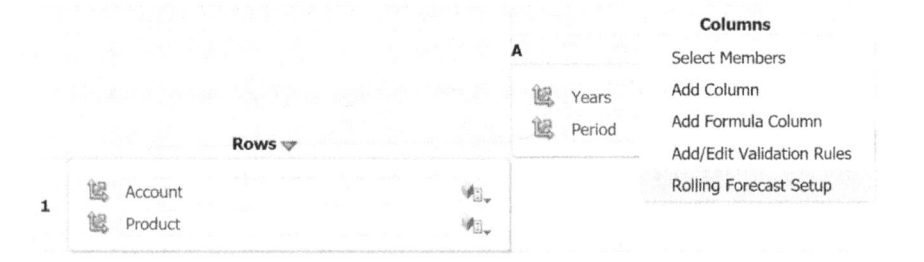

	A	**Columns**
		Select Members
	Years	Add Column
	Period	Add Formula Column
Rows		Add/Edit Validation Rules
1 Account		Rolling Forecast Setup
Product		

Look Smarter Than You Are with Enterprise Planning Cloud 289

2. Type "RF" as the prefix for the substitution variables that will be generated for the rolling forecast.
3. Select Start Year, Start Period, and Number of Periods, which I will select as *FY15*, *Oct*, and *18* respectively:

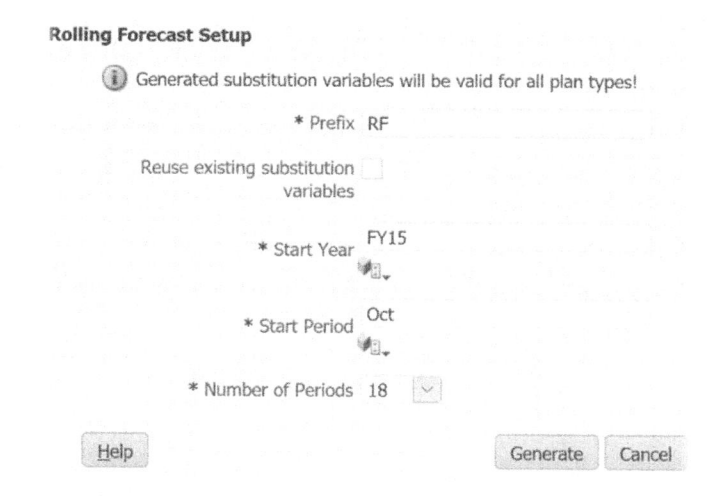

Rolling Forecast Setup

Generated substitution variables will be valid for all plan types!

* Prefix RF

Reuse existing substitution variables

* Start Year FY15

* Start Period Oct

* Number of Periods 18

Help   Generate   Cancel

4. Click *Generate*.

Substitution variables &RFPer1 through &RFPer18 and &RFYr1 through &RFYr18 will appear in the columns.

5. Click *Preview* to visually see the data form:

Scenario Forecast	MyRegion 410	Version Final				
				Oct FY15	Nov FY15	Dec FY15
P_100:Product X			Units			
			List Price			
			4110:Hardware Revenue			
P_110:Sentinal Standard Notebook			Units	13	13	13
			List Price	1200	1200	1200
			4110:Hardware Revenue	15600	15600	15600
P_120:Sentinal Custom Notebook			Units	13	13	

6. Click *Save*, then *Finish* to complete the form.

Shift Rolling Forecast Periods

When shifting rolling forecast periods, the shift is auto-generated for all forms which have been set up for rolling forecast using the same variables.

When you are ready to "shift" the variable values to the next forecast period,
1. Go to *Plans* in the main menu and open one of the data forms using the rolling forecast variables. I will open the *Sales Forecast – Products* form.
2. Click the first column containing the variable.
3. Go to *Actions* and select *Set Rolling Forecast Variables*:

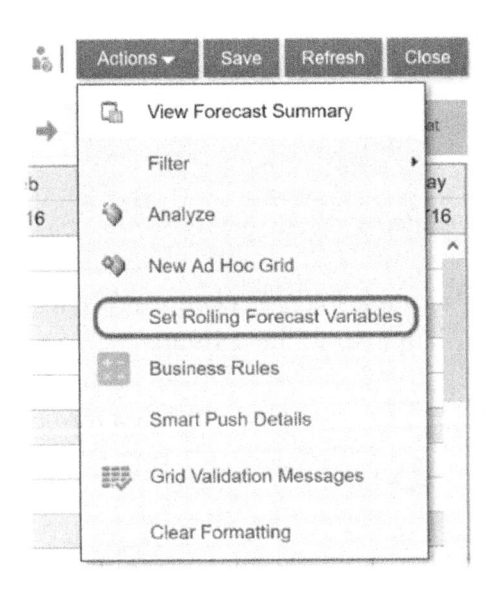

4. Towards the bottom, select "1" where it says *Shift Values By*:

5. Click *Apply*.

Years and Periods will shift by one. You can review the substitution variables created during the rolling forecast form design by going to *Navigator >> Administer >> Variables*. The values of the variables can be edited manually there.

Use Save As to Create Data Form

The *Save As* button can be used to easily create a form similar to an existing form. I'll create two data forms using Save As.

To create the second data form,
1. Open the *Sales Forecast – Products* data form and click *Save As*.
2. Name the new form "Sales Forecast – Services & Other".
3. Select members according to the following Layout:

Simple Form: Sales Forecast - Services & Other

Properties | **Layout** | Other Options | Business Rules | Smart Push

Point of View

BaseData   Forecast

&MyRegion

Page

IDescendants(Version)

	Rows	A
		&RFPer1
		&RFYr1
1	P_291	
	4140	
2	P_292	
	4150	
3	P_294	
	4130	

4. *Preview* the form, *Save,* and then *Finish.*

Sales Forecast - Services & O...

Scenario	MyRegion	Version
Forecast	410	Pass1

		Oct	Nov
		FY15	FY15
Training_P_291	4140:Training Revenue	5000	7000
Miscellaneous_P_292	4150:Miscellaneous Revenue	2000	6000
Consulting_P_294	4130:Consulting Revenue	18000	20000

To create the third data form,
1. Open the *Sales Forecast – Products* data form and click *Save As.*
2. Name the new form "Sales Forecast – Support".
3. Select members according to the following Layout:

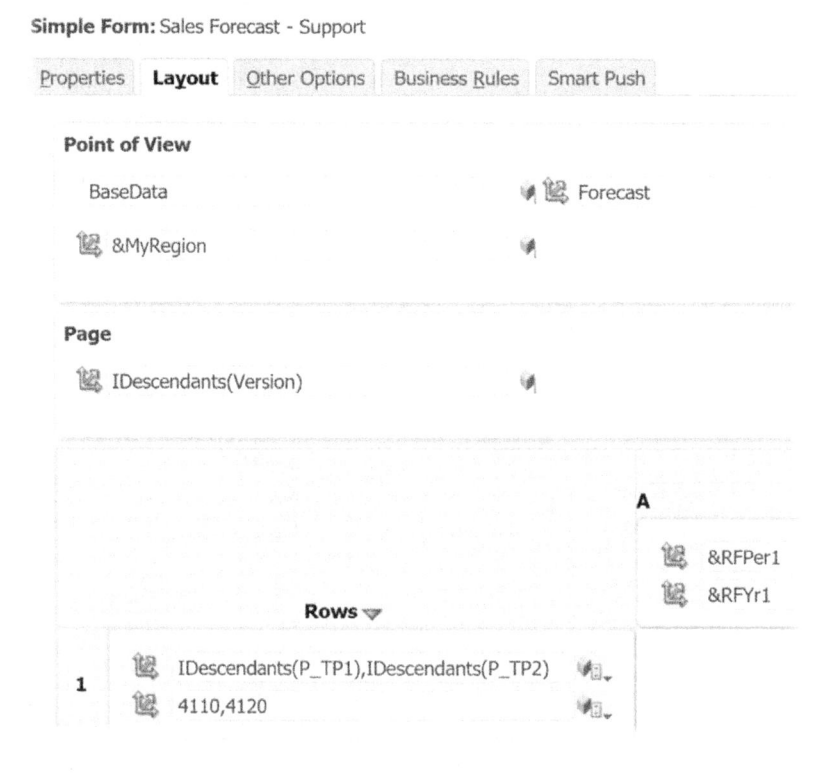

Simple Form: Sales Forecast - Support

Properties | **Layout** | Other Options | Business Rules | Smart Push

Point of View

BaseData   Forecast

&MyRegion

Page

IDescendants(Version)

A

&RFPer1
&RFYr1

Rows

1   IDescendants(P_TP1),IDescendants(P_TP2)
    4110,4120

4. In addition, for the Product Dimension Properties, check the boxes for *Alias* and *Start expanded*.
5. Check the Account Dimension Property options for *Member Formula* and *Alias*.
6. *Preview* the form, *Save*, and then *Finish*.

Sales Forecast - Support

Scenario	MyRegion	Version
Forecast	410	Pass1

		Oct FY15	Nov FY15	Dec FY15
⊞ Computer Equipment	4110:Hardware Revenue *f*	77430	78030	
	4120:Support Revenue *f*	13937.4	14045.4	
⊞ Computer Accessories	4110:Hardware Revenue *f*	33450	45350	
	4120:Support Revenue *f*	6021	8163	

Note! Any rows with members that include member formulas or are tagged as Dynamic Calc will appear gray, to indicate *Read Only*. You can tell that the ability to view member formulas has been enabled on this data form because of the function symbols displayed.

Note! In the *Sales Forecast – Support* data form, Computer Equipment and Computer Accessories can be expanded to display all their descendants. Simply click the + icon to the left of the member names.

Create Summary Form

Next, I'm going to create a summary form to view the aggregation of the Accounts entered in the other Sales Forecast forms.

1. Open one of the previous forms and use *Save As* to create a form with the following layout (call the form *Sales Forecast Summary*):

Simple Form: Sales Forecast Summary

| Properties | **Layout** | Other Options | Business Rules | Smart Push |

Point of View

   BaseData   Forecast

   &MyRegion

Page

   IDescendants(Version)

		A
	Rows	&RFPer1 &RFYr1
1	P_TP1 4110	
2	P_TP2 4110	
3	P_TP3 4130,4140,4150	
4	P_TP 4110,4120,4130,4140,4150,4160,4001	

2. Open *Grid Properties* and check *Suppress missing blocks* and *Suppress missing data – Rows*:

Grid Properties

Rows

Suppress missing blocks	☑
Suppress missing data - Rows	☑
Suppress invalid data - Rows	☐
Default row height	Medium

Columns

Suppress missing data - Columns	☐
Suppress invalid data - Columns	☐
Default column width	Medium

Other

Global Assumptions Form	☐
Enable Autosave	☐

3. *Preview* the form, *Save*, and then *Finish*:

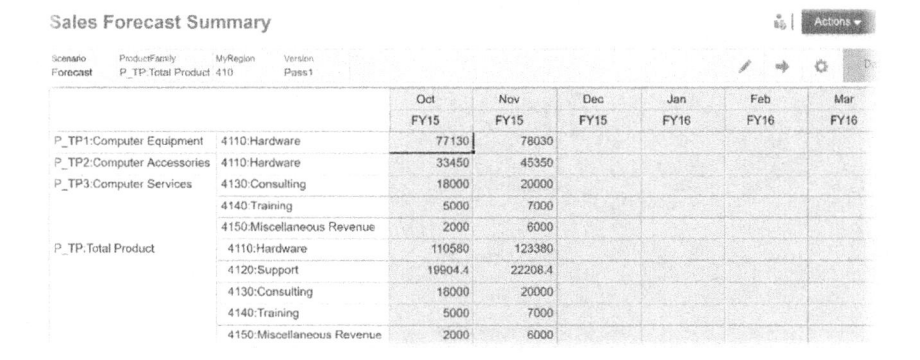

Sales Forecast Summary

Scenario: Forecast   ProductFamily: P_TP:Total Product   MyRegion: 410   Version: Pass1

		Oct FY15	Nov FY15	Dec FY15	Jan FY16	Feb FY16	Mar FY16
P_TP1:Computer Equipment	4110:Hardware	77130	78030				
P_TP2:Computer Accessories	4110:Hardware	33450	45350				
P_TP3:Computer Services	4130:Consulting	18000	20000				
	4140:Training	5000	7000				
	4150:Miscellaneous Revenue	2000	6000				
P_TP:Total Product	4110:Hardware	110580	123380				
	4120:Support	19904.4	22208.4				
	4130:Consulting	18000	20000				
	4140:Training	5000	7000				
	4150:Miscellaneous Revenue	2000	6000				

Note! Since the Sales Forecast Summary form does not contain Level 0 members, the members will be shaded gray to indicate *Read Only*. Users will not be able to enter data.

Use Smart Lists in Data Forms

The last form I will create will be used to assign Product Managers to all the products at Vision Company. Remember the Product Manager smart list I created earlier? I will use the Product Manager account for this data form.

To create a data form containing a smart list,

1. Create a new simple form and name it "Assign Product Manager".
2. Drag *Account* and *Period* to the Columns.
3. Drag *Product* to the Rows.
4. Drag *Years* to the Page.
5. Leave *HSP_View, Entity, Scenario* and *Version* in the POV.
6. Using , select *Pass1* for Version, *Plan* for Scenario and *0*, or *No Department*, for Entity.
7. For Years, select *FY15* to *FY20*.
8. For Account, select the *Product Manager* member.
9. For Period, select all Level 0 members (months).

There are many methods to select Level 0 members for any dimension, but the easiest method is to click the desired dimension, then click the *Keep Only by Functions* icon . Click the very last option that appears which reads *Level 0 Descendants*:

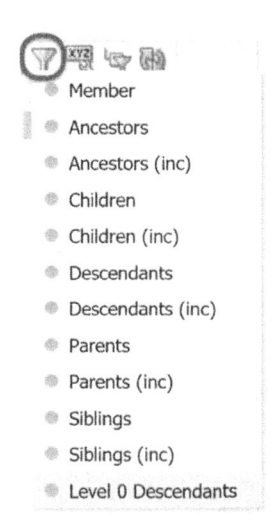

- Member
- Ancestors
- Ancestors (inc)
- Children
- Children (inc)
- Descendants
- Descendants (inc)
- Parents
- Parents (inc)
- Siblings
- Siblings (inc)
- Level 0 Descendants

Only Level 0 members will appear on the left panel. Highlight all members by clicking the first and last member while holding the *Shift* key. Move the members to the right panel.

10. For Product, select all Level 0 products.

Look Smarter Than You Are with Enterprise Planning Cloud 297

11. In the Product Dimension Properties, check *Member name* and *Alias*.

The Columns and Rows should resemble the following:

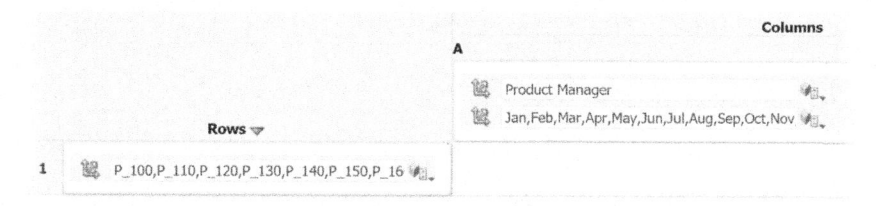

	A	Columns
		Product Manager
		Jan,Feb,Mar,Apr,May,Jun,Jul,Aug,Sep,Oct,Nov
	Rows ▽	
1	P_100,P_110,P_120,P_130,P_140,P_150,P_16	

12. Click *Save*, and then *Finish* (though I could just click Finish which will perform a Save and then close the form).

Open a Data Form

To view all the forms I have created,
1. Go to the main menu and click *Plans*.
2. Change the drop-down box to display the forms within the Vision Users folder.

Simple: Vision Users ▼
Name

Assign Product Manager

Sales Forecast - Products

Sales Forecast - Services & Other

Sales Forecast - Support

Sales Forecast Summary

3. Select the *Assign Product Manager* data form and the form will open
4. The result should look similar to the following:

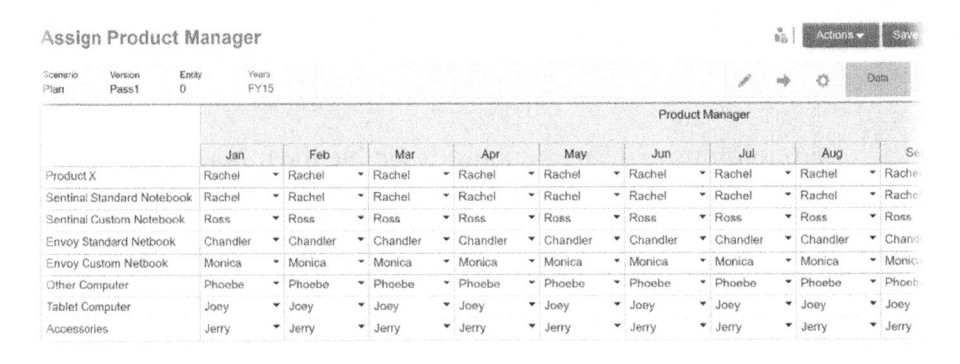

Assign Product Manager

	Jan	Feb	Mar	Apr	May	Jun	Jul	Aug	Se
Product X	Rachel	Rachel	Rachel	Rachel	Rachel	Rachel	Rachel	Rachel	Rache
Sentinal Standard Notebook	Rachel	Rachel	Rachel	Rachel	Rachel	Rachel	Rachel	Rachel	Rache
Sentinal Custom Notebook	Ross	Ross	Ross	Ross	Ross	Ross	Ross	Ross	Ross
Envoy Standard Netbook	Chandler	Chandler	Chandler	Chandler	Chandler	Chandler	Chandler	Chandler	Chand
Envoy Custom Netbook	Monica	Monica	Monica	Monica	Monica	Monica	Monica	Monica	Monic
Other Computer	Phoebe	Phoebe	Phoebe	Phoebe	Phoebe	Phoebe	Phoebe	Phoebe	Phoeb
Tablet Computer	Joey	Joey	Joey	Joey	Joey	Joey	Joey	Joey	Joey
Accessories	Jerry	Jerry	Jerry	Jerry	Jerry	Jerry	Jerry	Jerry	Jerry

Create Composite Form

Now that all the simple forms have been created, let's use a few of them to create a composite form. A composite form is a data form that combines two or more data forms into a single object. Data forms can be from the same or different plan types. You can choose to combine Page and Point of View member selections so that users select a member from a drop-down once and both data forms within the composite are updated. When combining data forms, you can choose a horizontal, vertical, or tabular orientation.

To create a composite form,

1. Go to *Navigator >> Administer >> Forms*.
2. Select the *Vision Users* folder. Then from Actions, select *Create composite form*.
3. Name the form "Sales Forecast – Composite".
4. Navigate to the *Layout* tab. In Section Properties, click ✚, check all the Sales Forecast forms and click *OK*:

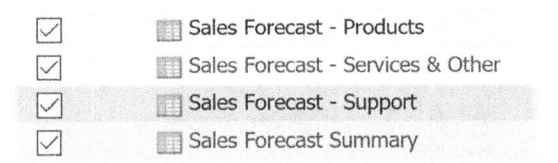

   ☑ Sales Forecast - Products
   ☑ Sales Forecast - Services & Other
   ☑ Sales Forecast - Support
   ☑ Sales Forecast Summary

5. Click ▢ in Section Properties to display forms as tabs within the composite:

Look Smarter Than You Are with Enterprise Planning Cloud 299

6. Check the option to *Set scope for all common dimensions as global*. This will allow any POV and Page settings to persist across the tabs.
7. Select *Preview*, then click *Finish*. The form should look similar to this:

Sales Forecast - Composite

| | | Oct | Nov | Dec | Jan |
		FY15	FY15	FY15	FY16
P_100:Product X	Units	86	106		
	List Price	30	30		
	4110:Hardware Revenue	2580	3180		
P_110:Sentinal Standard Notebook	Units	151	151		
	List Price	250	250		
	4110:Hardware Revenue	37750	37750		
P_120:Sentinal Custom Notebook	Units	106	106		

Enable Autosave for a Data Form

Administrators have the option to enable *Autosave* when creating data forms. Autosave is a neat, new feature in the Simplified UI that saves data input into a cell when a user tabs out of the cell. If a user mistakenly saves data by tabbing out of a cell, a Ctrl+Z shortcut will undo the mistake.

If Autosave is enabled, the cells will turn green to indicate a saved cell:

		Oct FY15	Nov FY15	Dec FY15
Training_P_291	4140:Training Revenue	500	700	750
Miscellaneous_P_292	4150:Miscellaneous Revenue			
Consulting_P_294	4130:Consulting Revenue			
Total Product	4120:Support Revenue	9895.5	9895.5	6606

Additionally, an option to *Run Form Rules* on Autosave can be enabled by the Administrator to update dynamically calculated cells that depend on the autosaved cell values that were input by the user. If rules were run, *Ctrl+Z* undoes any input and rules that were run as a part of the Autosave.

To enable autosave on a data form,
1. Create a new form by clicking *Save As* on the Sales Forecast – Products form and name it "Sales Forecast – Products Autosave":

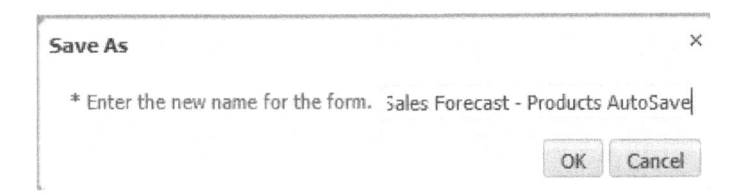

```
Save As                                                    ×

   * Enter the new name for the form.  Sales Forecast - Products AutoSave|

                                              OK     Cancel
```

2. On the *Layout* tab, under Grid Properties, check the option to *Enable Autosave* and *Run Form Calc on Autosave*:

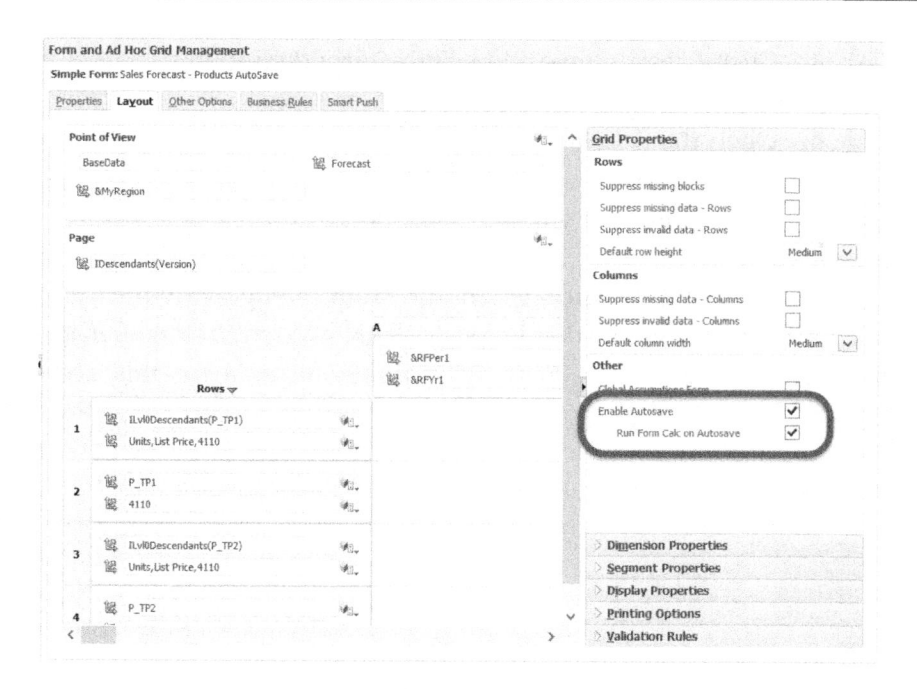

3. In the *Business Rules* tab, make sure the *<Calculate Form>* business rule is selected and checked for *Run on Save*:

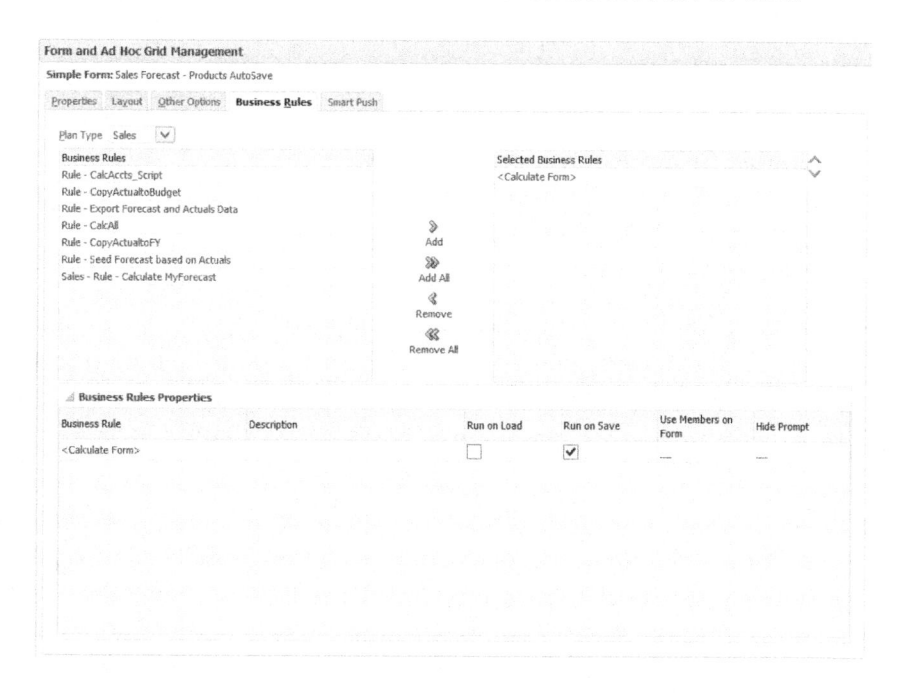

Chapter 7: Create User Interfaces

4. Click *Finish* to save and exit the form definition.
5. Navigate back to *Plans* in the Home screen.
6. Open the *Sales Forecast – Products Autosave* form and test out my very favorite, new feature.
7. Enter values for Units for product P_110.

The cell should turn green for Units along with the cell for 4110:Hardware Revenue (this is a calculated account; remember in the dimension definition, I defined the member formula for this account member):

Sales Forecast - Products Aut...

Scenario	MyRegion	Version
Forecast	410	Final
Final		

		Oct FY15	Nov FY15	Dec FY15	Jan FY16
P_100:Product X	Units				
	List Price				
	4110:Hardware Revenue				
P_110:Sentinal Standard Notebook	Units	5	5	5	5
	List Price	1000	1000	1000	1200
	4110:Hardware Revenue	5000	5000	5000	6000
P_120:Sentinal Custom Notebook	Units	13	13		13
	List Price				

Enable Smart Push on a Data Form

A recent feature called Smart Push allows users to push data from a data form, executing the data map I created earlier. It's meant to provide a quick update to reporting cubes based on planning data entry. Smart Push works in the Enterprise Planning Cloud Workspace as well as the Simplified UI. It can be used on both simple and composite data forms.

There are some rules that you'll need to play by when using Smart Push:

- Smart Push has to use at least one data map
- You can use Smart Push to push data from a BSO plan type to either a ASO or BSO plan type only
- Smart Push honors metadata and approvals security

- At least one of the dense dimensions (Account or Period, generally) needs to be set as a dimension-to-dimension mapping in the data map
- If the target plan type dimensionality changes, you need to synchronize the data in the data map

To enable the Smart Push of data from Sales to SalesRpt, I'll need to attach the data map I created previously to a form.

To attach a data map to a form,
1. Go to *Navigator >> Administer >> Forms*.
2. Edit the *Sales Forecast – Products* form.
3. Navigate to the *Smart Push* tab.
4. Click ✚ and select the *Sales Forecast_Products* data map.
5. Optionally you can check the option to *Run on Save.*

Now it's time to configure the Smart Push settings on the data form. There are three main options that are relevant here. The first two allow you to overwrite the original data mapping dimension selections:

- **Use Form Context** – push data for all members on the data form
- **Overwrite Selection** – overwrite the list of members on the data form as the source of the data with your own dimension definition; this can't be used when the Use Form Context option is checked
- **Run on Save** – when checked, this will kick off a data push once the data form is formally saved by the user. If unchecked, then the data push must occur manually by the user through the *Actions >> Smart Push Details* menu option for the form. The data map will not appear under Smart Push Details if this option is checked

If you choose to leave the defaults for *Use Form Context*, what will happen is that data from all members on the form will be attempted to be pushed, regardless of what's specified in the data map. Since data from a BSO cube is being pushed to an ASO cube, this is problematic, as ASO cubes are set up to accept Level 0 data. Therefore, *Use Form Context* shouldn't be used for the Products dimension, as the form contains upper level members.

If you choose to overwrite the selection, be careful here – the syntax within the Overwrite section is not validated. Therefore, you can accidentally reference the wrong dimension, which will lead to an error.

> **Note!** Oracle recommends Smart Push be used strategically, and on summary forms that consolidate data. Automatic push should also be limited, as users may tend to push incomplete data.

6. Change the settings so that they match the following:

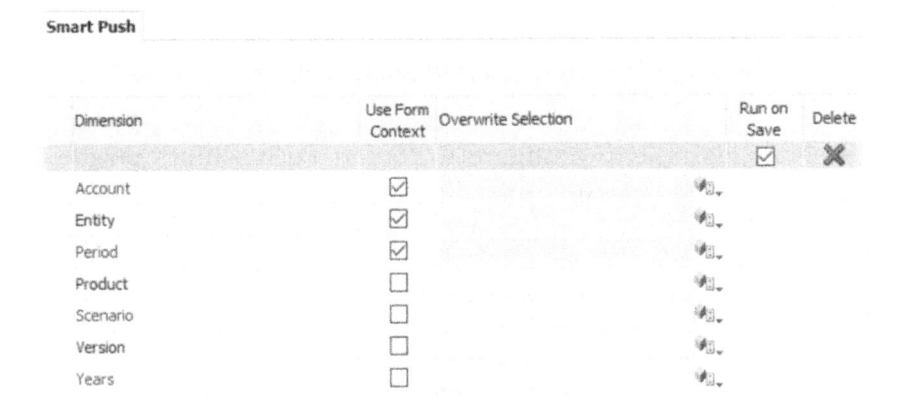

Smart Push

Dimension	Use Form Context	Overwrite Selection	Run on Save	Delete
			☑	✖
Account	☑			
Entity	☑			
Period	☑			
Product	☐			
Scenario	☐			
Version	☐			
Years	☐			

7. Click *OK*.

You should have the following:

Form and Ad Hoc Grid Management

Simple Form: Sales Forecast - Products

Properties | Layout | Other Options | Business Rules | **Smart Push**

Action ▼ View ▼ ➕ Detach

Map Reporting Application   Dimension

> Sales Forecast_Products

Look Smarter Than You Are with Enterprise Planning Cloud   305

As I mentioned above, if you don't want to use the members in the form as the focus for the data push, you can change the *Overwrite Selection* to Level 0 products. You'll need to uncheck the option *Use Form Context* first:

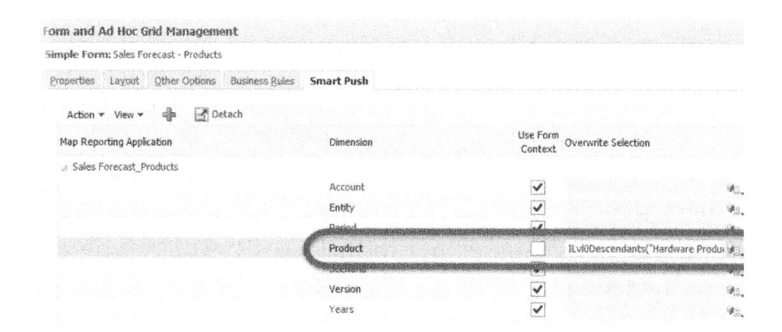

Note!

Finally, it's time to execute copy data from Sales to SalesRpt using Smart Push within a form.

To execute the Smart Push,
1. In the Simplified UI, click *Plans* from the main menu.
2. Open the *Sales Forecast – Products* form.
3. Go to *Actions >> Smart Push Details*:

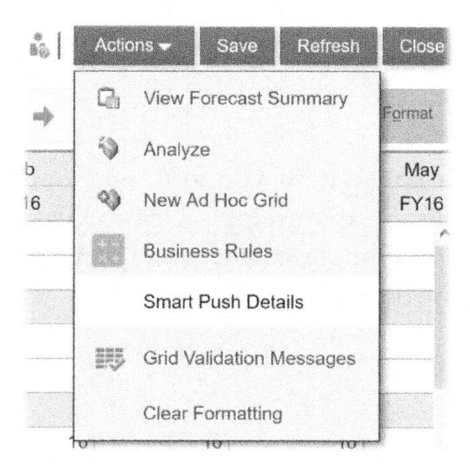

4. Click the *Sales Forecast_Products* data map to execute the Smart Push:

Chapter 7: Create User Interfaces

Smart Push　　　　　　　　　　　　　　　[Close]

Sales Forecast_Products

The following image will appear if the Smart Push was successful:

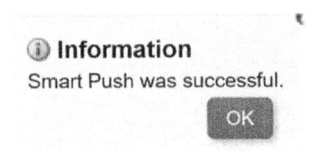

ⓘ Information

Smart Push was successful.

[OK]

Check that the data was transferred from the Sales plan type to the SalesRpt plan type by connecting to the SalesRpt plan type and viewing the data in Smart View with ad hoc analysis. The following shows the copied data in Smart View:

	A	B	C	D	E	F	G	H	I	J	K	L
12	Product X	Units	#Missing	#Missing	#Missing	#Missing	#Missing	#Missing	#Missing	#Missing	#Missing	#Missi
13	Product X	List Price	#Missing	#Missing	#Missing	#Missing	#Missing	#Missing	#Missing	#Missing	#Missing	#Missi
14	Product X	Hardware	#Missing	#Missing	#Missing	#Missing	#Missing	#Missing	#Missing	#Missing	#Missing	#Missi
15	Sentinal Standard	Units	10	10	10	10	10	10	10	10	10	10
16	Sentinal Standard	List Price	500	500	500	500	500	500	500	500	500	500
17	Sentinal Standard	Hardware	5000	5000	5000	5000	5000	5000	5000	5000	5000	5
18	Sentinal Custom I	Units	10	10	10	10	10	10	10	10	10	10
19	Sentinal Custom I	List Price	700	700	700	700	700	700	700	700	700	700
20	Sentinal Custom I	Hardware	7000	7000	7000	7000	7000	7000	7000	7000	7000	7
21	Envoy Standard N	Units	10	10	10	10	10	10	10	10	10	10
22	Envoy Standard N	List Price	500	500	500	500	500	500	500	500	500	500
23	Envoy Standard N	Hardware	5000	5000	5000	5000	5000	5000	5000	5000	5000	5
24	Envoy Custom Ne	Units	10	10	10	10	10	10	10	10	10	10
25	Envoy Custom Ne	List Price	700	700	700	700	700	700	700	700	700	700
26	Envoy Custom Ne	Hardware	7000	7000	7000	7000	7000	7000	7000	7000	7000	7

Or you can create a new data form that would capture the data that was pushed over (in my example below, I created a master detail composite form that has simple form for Sales plan type on top and simple form for SalesRpt on bottom):

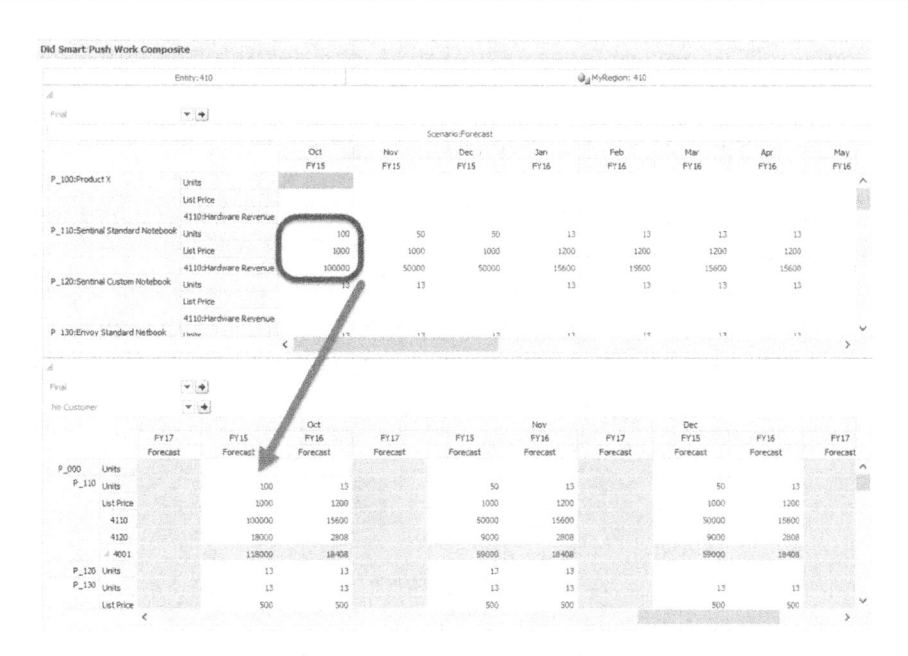

Sometimes this feature can behave a little wonky. It seems to be a little finicky when you use functions in the member selection. Hardcoded definitions, though not ideal, are the most consistent. Make sure to synchronize mappings after metadata changes to dimensions:

Other workaround tips (for now, if you have issues) are to update data forms that need Smart Push to have members match the definitions in the data map (with no references to upper level dynamic members).

Master Composite Forms

Master Composite forms are supported in Enterprise Planning Cloud. These composite forms allow you to define dimension members in one source or master form and have it apply to the target forms. The target forms need to have the dimensions for which context is being passed in the Page or POV area of the target form. Master detail forms provide two significant advantages:

1) You can visualize the source and target forms within the same content area.

2) You can see the immediate impact on several dependent forms within the same composite form.

To tag a form as the master form, edit the form and go to the *Layout* tab. Right-click the desired form and click *Tag as Master Composite Form*:

Note! The master form dimensions apply to the entire composite form; therefore, there can only be one master form.

Other Form Options

I've just highlighted the possibilities with data forms, but there are many more features I have not fully covered. Other form features include defining validation rules for grids, rows, columns, or cells within a data form:

The options to enable account annotations, print supporting details, automatically save data entry with Autosave, mass allocate, grid spread, and attach cell-level documents are also available in data forms:

Display Properties

Make form read-only	☐
Hide Form	☐
Display missing values as blank	☑
Enable account annotations	☐
Allow multiple currencies per entity	☐
Enable Mass Allocate	☐
Enable Grid Spread	☑
Enable cell-level document	☑
Message for forms with no data	

Additionally, member name / alias display, the ability for users to see member formulas in data forms and other dimension properties can also be enabled:

Dimension Properties

Account

Apply to all row dimensions	☐
Member name	☑
Alias	☑
Member Formula	☑
Hide dimension	☐
Show consolidation operators	☐
Start expanded	☑

Manage Data Forms

Click *Navigator >> Forms* to manage data forms. From the *Forms and Ad Hoc Grid Management* section, you can edit, move, rename, assign access, or delete data forms folders or data forms by selecting the appropriate task from the *Actions* drop-down menu or icon from the menu bar. You can also Search for a particular form:

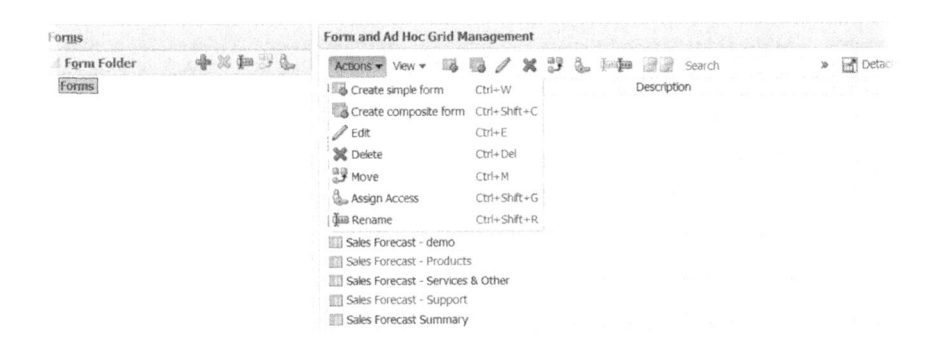

Some of the options mentioned above are discussed further in the End User Activities section of this chapter. For more information on data forms, view Oracle documentation or reach out to info@interrel.com for tips, tricks & design best practices on data forms.

Finally, the data forms are complete.

SMART FORMS

About Smart Forms

Smart Forms are a new feature to the Oracle planning and budgeting world. They are data forms based on ad hoc grids that use Excel formulas and calculate data on the client side rather than in Essbase. Oracle calls these Excel formulas "business calculations". These calculations do not affect metadata within the application and can be executed both in the web and in Smart View.

You will assign a grid label (a custom header) to the Excel formula header row or column in the Smart Forms. These required grid labels replace member names in the ad hoc grid.

Smart Form features include:

- Support Excel formulas with most Excel functions
- Support Excel formatting
- Support Excel cell merging
- Created in Smart View
- Can be used by end users like any old data form in the web or Smart View
- A sandbox may be created from a Smart Form

Administrators and power users can create Smart Forms in Smart View. They must provision access to the Smart Forms for users. Users may access Smart Forms either within the Simplified UI or Smart View.

Why would users want to use Smart Forms? If the calculations on a form are done directly on a form, users may experience better performance and a more enjoyable user experience. Formulas use a syntax that everyone is familiar with – Excel!

Create a Smart Form

To define a Smart Form,
1. Connect to the application with Smart View.
2. Select a form in the Panel and click *Ad hoc analysis* at the bottom. Alternatively, open an ad hoc grid.
3. Add grid labels and Excel formulas as desired. The example below is using the SUM Excel formula to add up quarters:

Q1	Q2	Q3	Q4	Q1+Q2	Q3+Q4
474	474	474	352	948	826
27240	27240	27240	27240	54480	54480
259200	259200	259200	219200	518400	478400

4. In the Planning Ad Hoc ribbon, click *Save As Smart Form*:

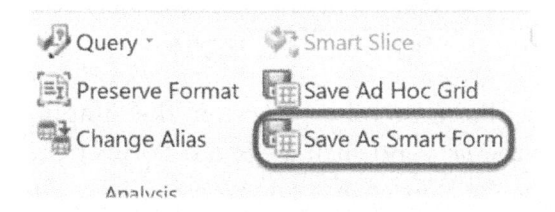

5. Name the grid "FY14_Actual_Smart Form", keep the default Forms root folder, and add a description if desired:

Once the Smart Form has been saved, it can be seen in the Smart View Panel, under the root Forms folder:

```
⊟ VISION
  ⊞ Dimensions
  ⊟ Forms
    ⊟ Vision Users
        Assign Product Manager
        Sales Forecast - Composite
        Sales Forecast - Products
        Sales Forecast - Products Autosave
        Sales Forecast - Services & Other
        Sales Forecast - Support
        Sales Forecast Summary
      (FY14_Actual_Smart Form)
```

This Smart Form can also be seen in the Simplified UI. To access Smart Forms, go to *Plans* and click the Smart Forms tab:

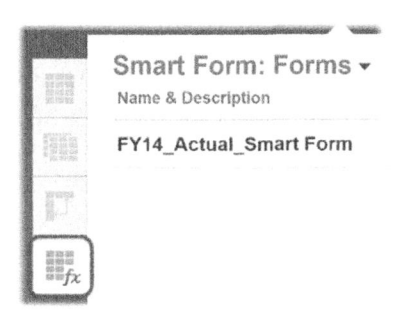

Smart Form: Forms ▾
Name & Description

FY14_Actual_Smart Form

The grid labels and the Excel calculations can be seen in the Smart Form. Hover over the calculated cells to see the formulas:

Q1+Q2	Q3+Q4		
948	826		
54480	54480		

Row Total ProductList Price Column Q1+Q2 54480 This cell is read-only
Formula:=SUM(D3:E3)

You have to follow a few rules when it comes to Smart Forms:

- You must enter grid labels in order to save the business calculations in the Smart Form; expect wonky behavior if empty space is entered instead of a grid label
- Grid labels may be entered at any dimension location for an axis
- Grid label names may not match any member name or alias
- Member functions are not supported in the Smart Form definition

You can view Smart Forms in the Form definition area, but you cannot edit the form.

VALID INTERSECTIONS

Valid intersections allow administrators to define rules, called valid intersection rules, to restrict invalid data entry for users. Cells in data forms containing invalid intersections are shown as read-only. This restriction speeds the planning process and optimizes the information available to users. This is a new feature available in the Simplified UI or Smart View.

For this application, I'm going to create a rule that allows users to enter data for accounts related to Computer Services while preventing users from entering units for Computer Services members in the *Forecast Sales – Products* form, since forecast for this product is entered in dollars. I'm also going to make sure users enter data for the matching product – account combinations.

Create Valid Intersection Rule

To create valid intersections,

1. From the Simplified UI go to *Console >> Valid Intersections*.

> **Valid Intersections**
> Order Name
> No data to display

2. Click *Create*.
3. Name the valid intersection rule "Services&Other _Accounts" and add a description:

Services&Other_Accounts

To allow users to enter data into the Support, Consulting, Training and Misc. Revenue accounts for Services & Other products. Data entry into the Units and List Price accounts disabled.

4. Select *Product* as the Anchor dimension.
5. Next, click *Add Dimension* and select *Account*.

Note! Depending on which dimension is designated as the Anchor dimension, the valid intersections of data will vary. In our case, Product is the Anchor dimension and Account is the Non-Anchor dimension, which means that only the selected accounts will be valid for the selected products. All accounts will be valid for products that were not selected.

6. Click *Add Rule*.
7. Click the drop-down arrow for Product and select *Edit*:

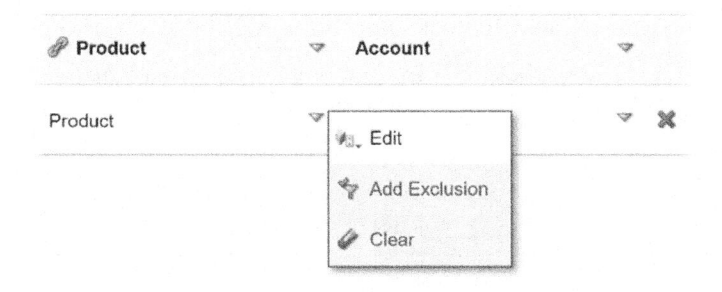

Look Smarter Than You Are with Enterprise Planning Cloud   315

8. Select ⚙ in the upper right-hand corner and choose to *Show Alias*.
9. Navigate to *Computer Services* then select the member "Training_P_291":

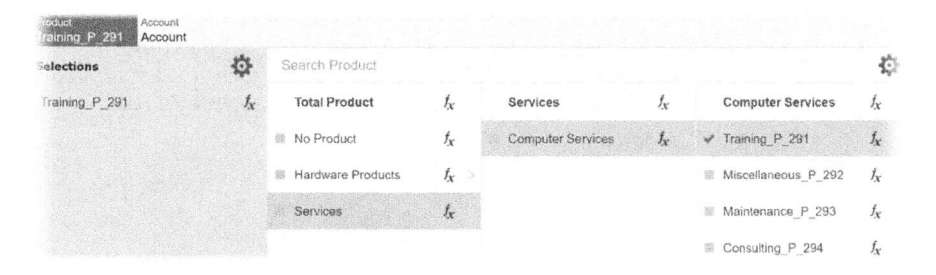

10. Click the *Account* tab.
11. Select *Total Revenue* (4001) to open its children and select *Training Revenue* (4140):

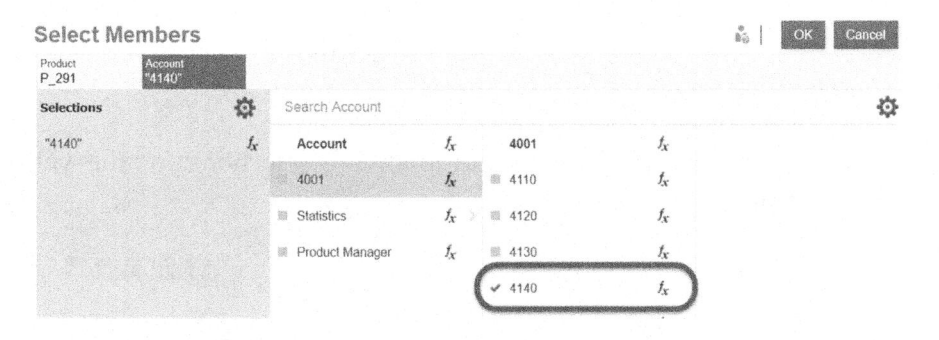

12. Click *OK*.

Note! To remove or uncheck members: highlight the member to remove, click ⚙ in the Selections panel and click *Remove*:

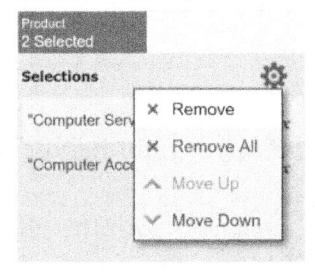

Note! If you would like to add a filter or show the alias instead of the member name, more setting options are available in Settings (⚙ located in the right-most panel of the Member Selector):

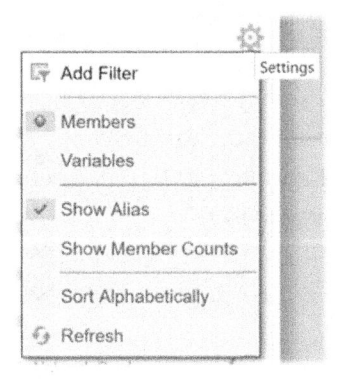

13. Check that you have the following selections for the valid intersection rule:

14. Add additional rules and type in the member names for both Product and Account, as shown below:

Services&Other_Accounts

To allow users to enter data into the Support, Consulting, Training and Misc. Revenue accounts for Services & Other products. Data entry into the Units and List Price accounts disabled.

Product	Account	
P_291	4140	✖
P_292	4150	✖
P_293	4120	✖
P_294	4130	✖

The purpose of the rule is to ensure that inputs are entered at the correct intersections of Product and Account (e.g., the Training Product member is valid for only the Training Revenue account and the Consulting Product member is only valid for the Consulting Revenue account).

15. Click *Save and Close* at the top right.

Note! To Edit, Duplicate, Delete, or Move a valid intersection, click ⚙ in the main Valid Intersections page:

318   Chapter 7: Create User Interfaces

16. Ensure that the rule is enabled with a ✓ (disabled valid intersections will have a grey check mark).
17. Check that the Valid Intersection Rule has been correctly set up using the Analyze capabilities in Enterprise Planning Cloud Simplified UI or in Smart View (see sections *Analyze* and *Ad Hoc Grids* – located in End User Activities).

Valid Intersections & Data Forms

I created a form to check if the valid combinations worked. It worked! This Enterprise Planning Cloud stuff is awesome:

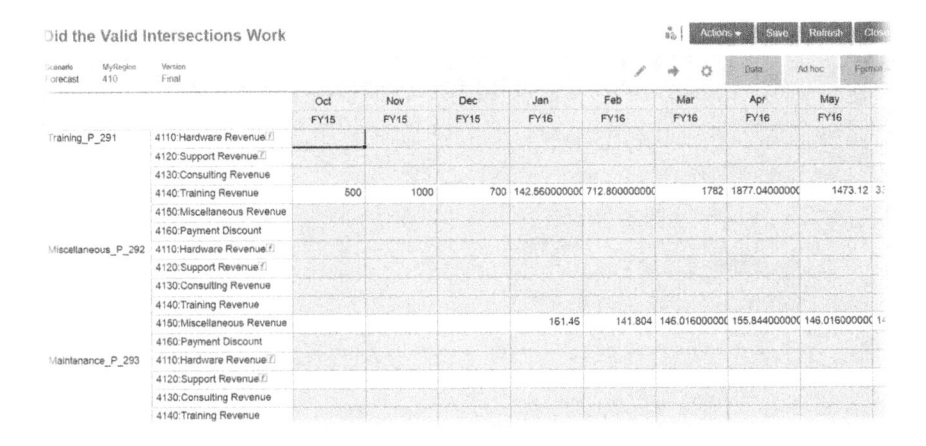

A few notes about data forms and valid intersections:

- Invalid sections will be displayed as read only
- If you mouse over an invalid section, a tool tip displays:

> Row Miscellaneous_P_2924110:Hardware Revenue Column Dec FY15 This cell is read-only because it is defined as an invalid intersection.

- If invalid intersections are in the POV and / or page, a warning will display
- Valid intersections will apply to run time prompts launched within Enterprise Planning Cloud web or Smart View (but not Smart Forms)

ACTION MENUS

Another handy set of tools that you can add to data forms are menu items for the Action Menu. These objects provide users a quick way to launch related data forms, business rules and URLs.

Create Action Menu

To create an action menu,
1. Go to *Navigator >> Administer >> Action Menus*.
2. Click ✚ to create a new menu.
3. Name the menu. I'm going to call it "Sales Forecast".
4. Once it has been created, edit the menu (✎).
5. Click (Add Child) while in the Sales Forecast menu. (Adding a "child" really just means creating a menu.)
6. Name the Menu Item and Label "View Forecast Summary".
7. Select *Form* as the Type and click ✚ to select the *Sales Forecast Summary* form.

Edit Menu Item : View Forecast Summary

* Menu Item	View Forecast Summary
* Label	View Forecast Summary
Icon	
Type	Form
Required Parameters	None

Form

* Form	Sales Forecast Summary

8. Click *Save*.

Assign Action Menu to Form

To assign the action menu to a form,

1. Go to *Navigator >> Administer >> Forms*.
2. Edit the Sales Forecast – Products form and go to the *Other Options* tab.
3. In the Context Menus section, move the Sales Forecast menu to the right panel:

Context Menus

Available Menus	Selected Menus
	Sales Forecast

4. Click *Finish*.
5. Back in the Home screen, go to *Plans* and open the *Sales Forecast – Products* form.
6. Click the *Action* menu. I can see the Menu Item that I created at the top of the drop-down list:

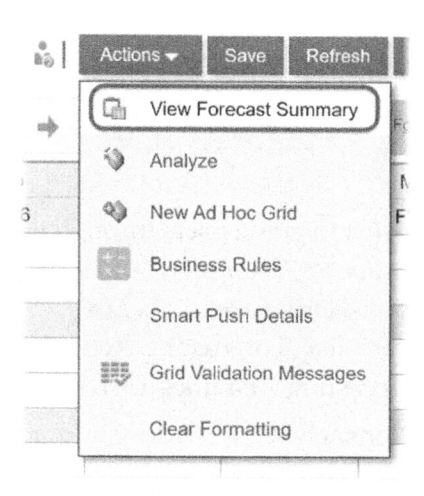

Tasks

Budgeting and forecasting often require users to perform multiple activities or tasks to complete the process. Tasks are lists of Enterprise Planning Cloud steps to guide users through the planning process, listing the tasks to be completed with instructions and due dates. Administrators and power users can create and manage tasks and task lists.

A task list can include the following in Enterprise Planning Cloud Simplified UI:

- URL
- Form
- Business Rule
- Manage Approvals
- Descriptive

The following task list types are available for use in the Enterprise Planning Cloud Workspace, but not the Simplified UI:

- Copy Version
- Job Console
- Dimension Editor
- Security Management
- Process Management

- Refresh Application
- Import and Export
- Form Management

Create Tasks

To create a task list to guide users through the forecasting process,
1. Go to *Navigator >> Administer >> Tasks*.
2. Under Actions, click *Create Task List*.
3. Name the task list "Forecasting Activities".
4. *Edit* the Forecasting Activities Task List.
5. Under Actions, click ⚘. (Add Child adds a new item to an existing task list.)
6. Enter a name for the task, in our case, "Enter Sales Forecast – Products".
7. Select *Form* as the Type and use ➕ to select the radio button to the left of the appropriate form.
8. Set a Start Date, End Date, and Alerts:

Edit Task List - Forecasting Activities

Task - Enter Sales Forecast - Products

Task Enter Sales Forecast - Products

Type Form

Form Sales Forecast - Products
☐ Set Page Member Defaults

Duration 0

Start Date ☑ 12/14/15 12:00 AM

End Date ☑ 12/26/15 12:00 AM
☐ Repeat Every 0 Hour(s)

Alert ☑ 12/21/15 9:00 AM
☑ Repeat Every 1 Day(s)

Dependency

Alerts will display: Green = On Schedule, Yellow = Approaching End Date, Red = Overdue. If End Date is checked, you can send emails when a task is not completed by the due date. Optionally, you can select the Dependency check box if the completion of this task is dependent upon completing the primary task.

9. Add instructions for users to provide more guidance.
10. Click *Save*.
11. Repeat steps 5-10, but for the Sales Forecast – Services & Other form. Add Sibling instead of child for step 5.
12. Repeat steps 5-10 again for the Sales Forecast Summary form. Add Sibling instead of child for step 5.

The completed task list should look as follows:

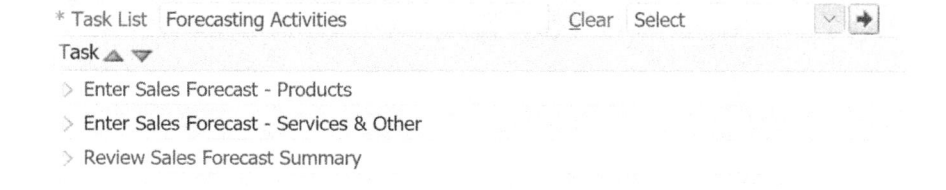

```
* Task List   Forecasting Activities                    Clear   Select
Task ▲ ▼
> Enter Sales Forecast - Products
> Enter Sales Forecast - Services & Other
> Review Sales Forecast Summary
```

13. Click *Save*.

To view or go through the task list, click *Tasks* in the Enterprise Planning Cloud main menu.

Note! To save some time, you can also use *Save As* to duplicate an entire task list.

Update Tasks

To manage existing task lists through Workspace,
1. Open up Workspace. Launch the application and then expand *Manage Task Lists*.
2. The Manage Task Lists section will display:

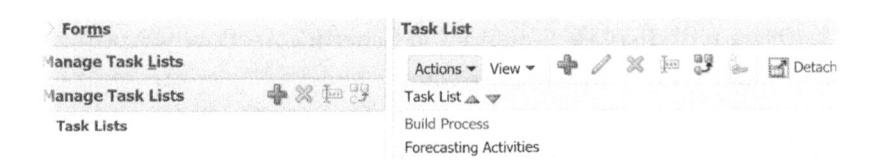

From this screen, you can create, edit, move, or delete task lists and task list folders. This is also where you assign user access for specific task lists.

Monitor Tasks

As an administrator you will want to monitor the status of a specific task list, understanding what steps have been completed and what tasks are outstanding. To view task list status, simply click Tasks from the Simplified UI:

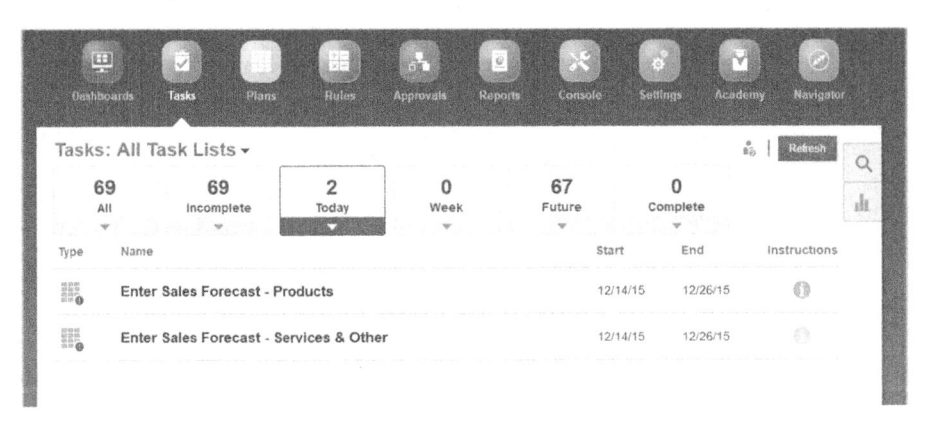

You can filter, sort, and view all of the tasks for which you are provisioned.

DASHBOARDS

Dashboards are a new feature available in the Enterprise Planning Cloud Simplified UI. These interactive dashboards allow users to visually analyze the information they need in one place. Objects included in the dashboards include: dashboard header, forms, charts, webpages, and commentary text. Charts are based on existing forms. In future versions, you'll be able to edit data directly in the Dashboard.

The forms that I have created so far are not ideal for displaying in dashboards due to the number of rows / columns included.

Let's create a simple form that will display the data that I want to see in a dashboard.

Create a Form for Dashboard

To create a dashboard,
1. Create a simple form called "Prior Year Actual Sales".
2. Create the layout of the form according to the following table:

Dimension	Layout	Members
Scenario	POV	Actual
Version	POV	Final
Account	POV	4001 (Total Revenue)
Entity	Page	Descendants of Total Entity
Product	Rows	P_TP1, P_TP2
Period	Columns	&RFPer1, &RFPer2, &RFPer3
Years	Columns	&PriorYear

You should have the following result:

Prior Year Actual Sales

Scenario	Version	Account	Entity
Actual	Final	4001:Total Revenue	410

	Oct	Nov	Dec
	FY14	FY14	FY14
Computer Equipment	227032	227032	130980
Computer Accessories	105067.2	105067.2	5947.2

Now that I'm ready, time to create the dashboard.

Create Dashboard

To create a dashboard in Enterprise Planning Cloud,

1. In the Home screen, go to *Dashboards*.
2. Click *Create*.
3. Enter a Dashboard Name.
4. Enter a Dashboard Header (click ⚙ to type in and format the header).
5. Drag the *Prior Year Actual Sales* form to the top-left quadrant of the dashboard:

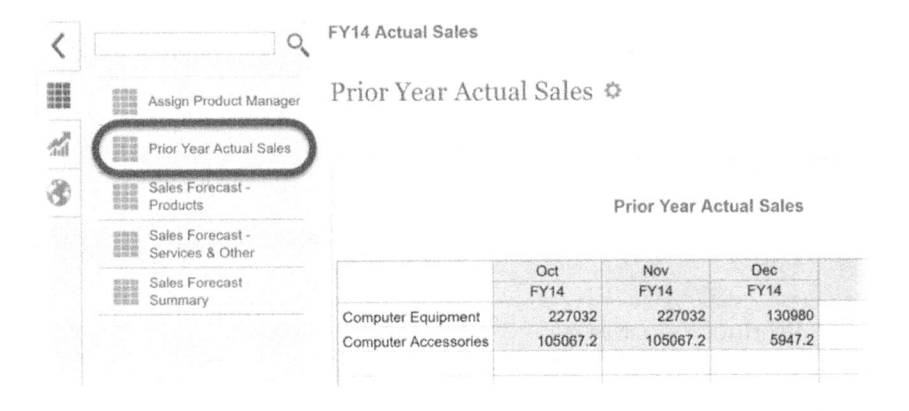

6. Click the *Chart Types* icon on the left:

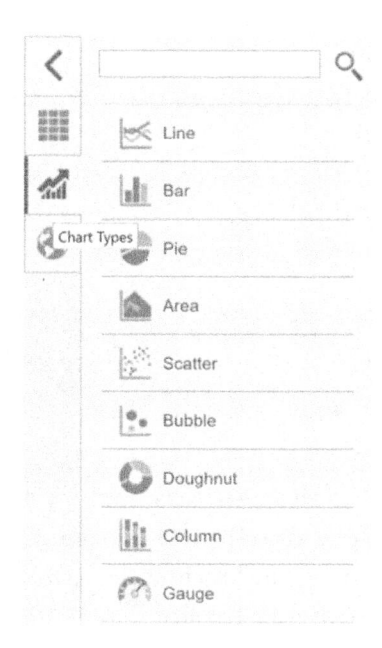

Look Smarter Than You Are with Enterprise Planning Cloud   327

- Line
- Bar
- Chart Types — Pie
- Area
- Scatter
- Bubble
- Doughnut
- Column
- Gauge

7. Drag the *Pie* chart to the top-right quadrant.
8. Click ⚙.
9. Change the chart properties to match those below. Switch over to the *Forms* tab and select the *Prior Year Actual Sales* form and then click *OK*:

Header	Prior Year Actual Sales
Chart Type	Pie
3D Graph	☐
Background Fill	◉ No Fill ○ Solid Fill ○ Gradient Fill
Legend Position	◉ Right ○ Bottom ○ Left ○ Top

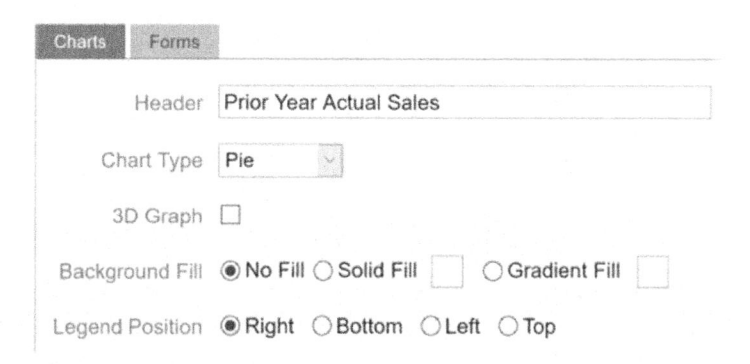

10. Drag the *Line* chart to the bottom-left quadrant.
11. Click ⚙ and change the chart properties to match those below. Switch over to the *Forms* tab and select the *Prior Year Actual Sales* form and then click *OK*:

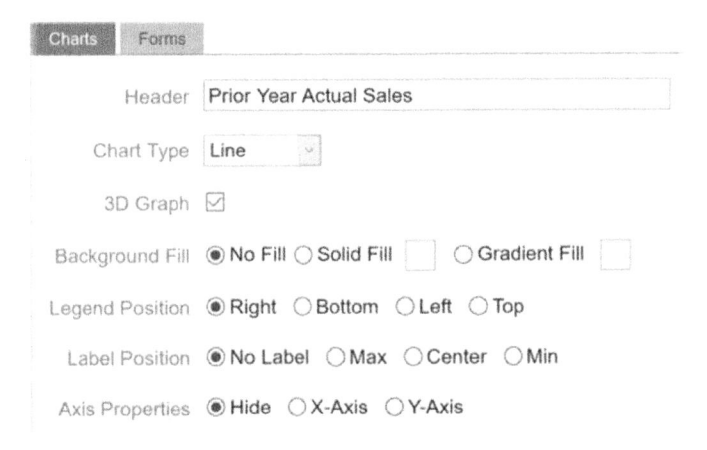

12. Open the *External Artifacts* tab on the left and drag the *Commentary* object to the last quadrant.
13. Add commentary and format the text.
14. Review the entire dashboard:

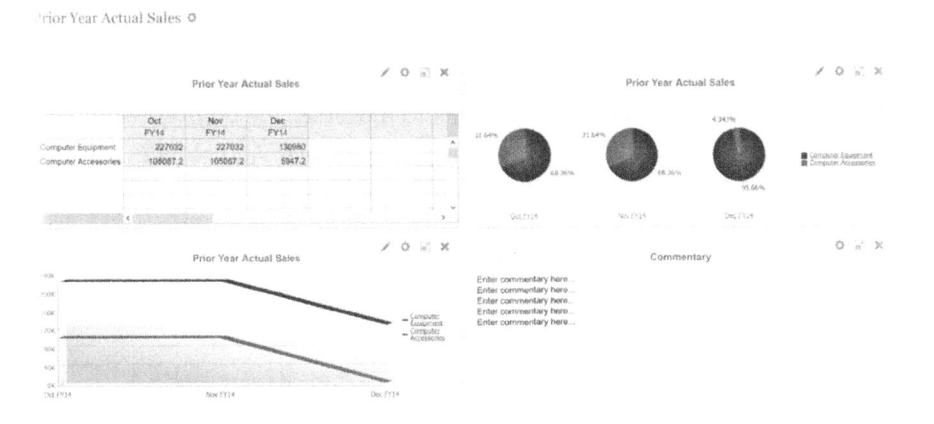

FINANCIAL REPORTS

Financial Reporting Studio is a reporting solution for Oracle EPM to create nicely formatted, printable reports. Report designers build and define reports. When reports are executed, they retrieve information from the database as it currently exists, including any recent data changes. Therefore, a report could display different values each time it is run if the data changes frequently.

It is often desirable to keep a copy of a report that is run at a specific point in time, similar to a photograph or a Polaroid snapshot. This records the data as it existed at that point in time. Financial Reporting accomplishes this by creating "Snapshots". Snapshots are essentially reports with stored data values that can be viewed at any time. Since the data is stored, the report is not rerun against the database and data values remain static. After a snapshot is created, changes to the data in the database will not be reflected in that snapshot. Snapshots are created in Application Management within Workspace.

Books are a collection of reports. A book can include both reports and snapshots, though they typically contain one or the other, and offer an easy way to work with multiple reports. Other artifacts from the Workspace repository, such as text, HTML, PDFs, and Microsoft Word, Excel and PowerPoint files, can be included in the book with the reports and snapshot reports. Books are created by following this path in Workspace: *File >> New >> Document*.

Note! Both Snapshots and Books can only be created in Enterprise Planning Cloud Workspace by the Administrator. The Simplified UI does not provide these features.

The Oracle EPM Smart View Add-in provides integration with Financial Reporting. You can import report images from Financial Reporting into Word or PowerPoint and report grids from Financial Reporting into Word, PowerPoint, or Excel. This is sometimes helpful for standard presentations or documents where you need to pull EPM Cloud information with external information.

Standardized, formatted reports are created using Financial Reporting Studio (FRS). The original FRS can be installed from the Simplified UI by going to *Navigator >> Install >> Financial Reporting Studio*. It can also be installed from Workspace under *Tools >> Install >> Financial Reporting Studio*. The new Reporting Web Studio can be launched from the Simplified UI (*Navigator >> Manage >> Reporting Web Studio*) or Workspace (*Tools >> Launch Reporting Web Studio*).

Note! A new web studio for Financial Reports was released in March 2016. Most of the same Financial Reporting Studio concepts will apply with the new user interface. In fact, you can open existing FR reports with the new Reporting Web Studio.

I'll first be creating a Sales Revenue by Product report in the FR desktop studio to explore the neat functionality FRS has to offer. Then I'll create a similar report in Reporting Web Studio to compare and contrast reports development. Finally, I'll show how to create a book using reports from both. This is not a comprehensive guide for FRS. For full documentation, please refer to Oracle's Financial Reporting Studio User's Guide or the Oracle Cloud "Designing with Financial Reporting Web Studio for Oracle Planning and Budgeting Cloud" guide.

Note! In March 2016, Oracle released a new UI to create Financial Reporting documents. The steps below use the traditional desktop UI which is still supported.

Create Report in Financial Reporting Studio (Desktop)

To create a new report in FR Desktop,
1. Open Financial Reporting Studio.
2. Log in with a username, password, and the Server URL.

To log into FRS by connecting to an Enterprise Planning Cloud server, the username must include the domain name and a period before the username.

Note! For example: domain.username

Sample Enterprise Planning Cloud Server URL below:

https://test-cloud-pln.pbcs.us1.oraclecloud.com

Look Smarter Than You Are with Enterprise Planning Cloud   331

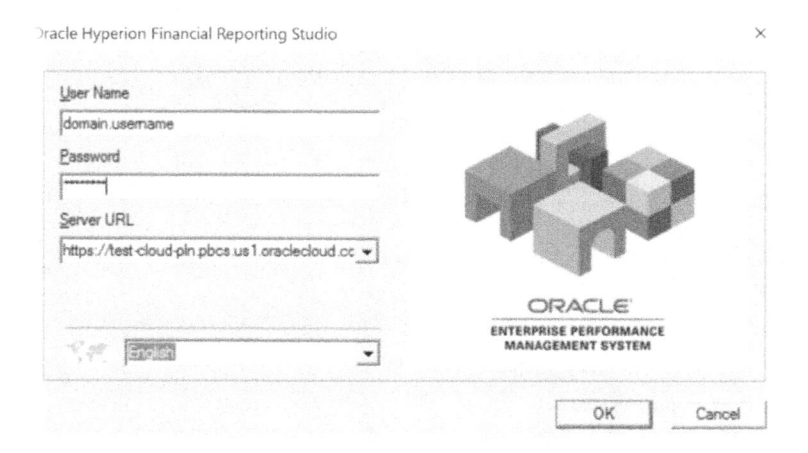

3. Click the first icon to create a *New Report*:

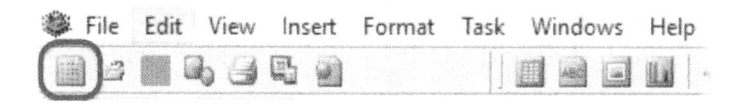

There are basically four objects that can be added to a Financial Reporting report. In the order that they appear on the tool bar, they are:

- Grids
- Text objects
- Images
- Charts

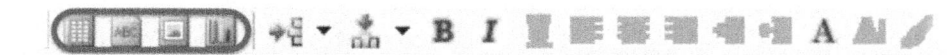

Create a Grid

To create a grid,
4. Click the icon on the left, *Insert Grid*, and create the size of the grid with a click, drag and release on the report.
5. To create a Grid, I need to create a database connection. Click *New Database Connection...*
6. Type in the Database Connection Name, User Name, Password, Application, and Database:

Database Connection Properties

Database Connection Name
SalesRpt

User Name
admin

Password
****

Application
VISION

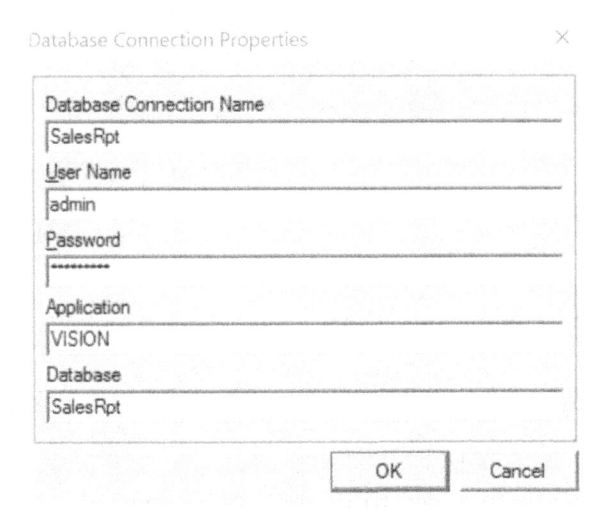

Database
SalesRpt

[OK] [Cancel]

---

7. Click *OK*. The Dimension Layout will open.
8. Click and drag the following dimensions from the POV to the Pages, Columns, or Rows:

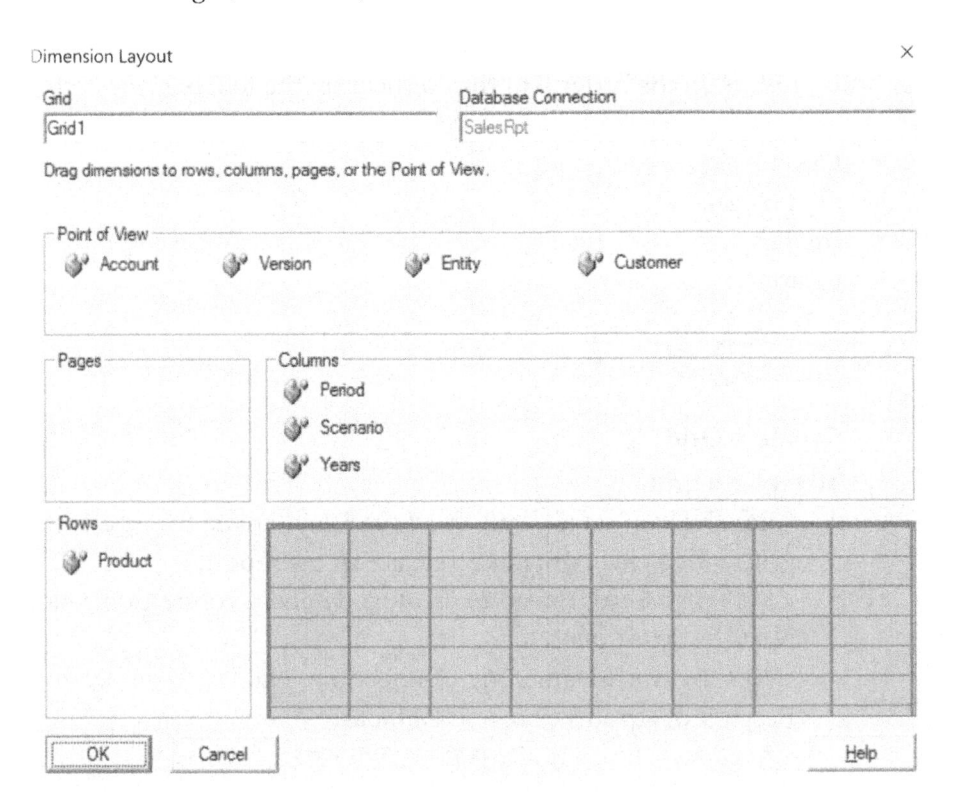

Dimension Layout

Grid: Grid1

Database Connection: SalesRpt

Drag dimensions to rows, columns, pages, or the Point of View.

Point of View:
- Account
- Version
- Entity
- Customer

Pages:

Columns:
- Period
- Scenario
- Years

Rows:
- Product

[OK] [Cancel] [Help]

Look Smarter Than You Are with Enterprise Planning Cloud   333

9. Click *OK*.
10. Double-click each dimension in the grid to select the desired members. Double-click *Product*.
11. Remove the default *Product* member.
12. Select *Total Product* and *Descendants of Computer Equipment* and *Descendants of Computer Accessories* using the *Add Relationship* function icon highlighted below:

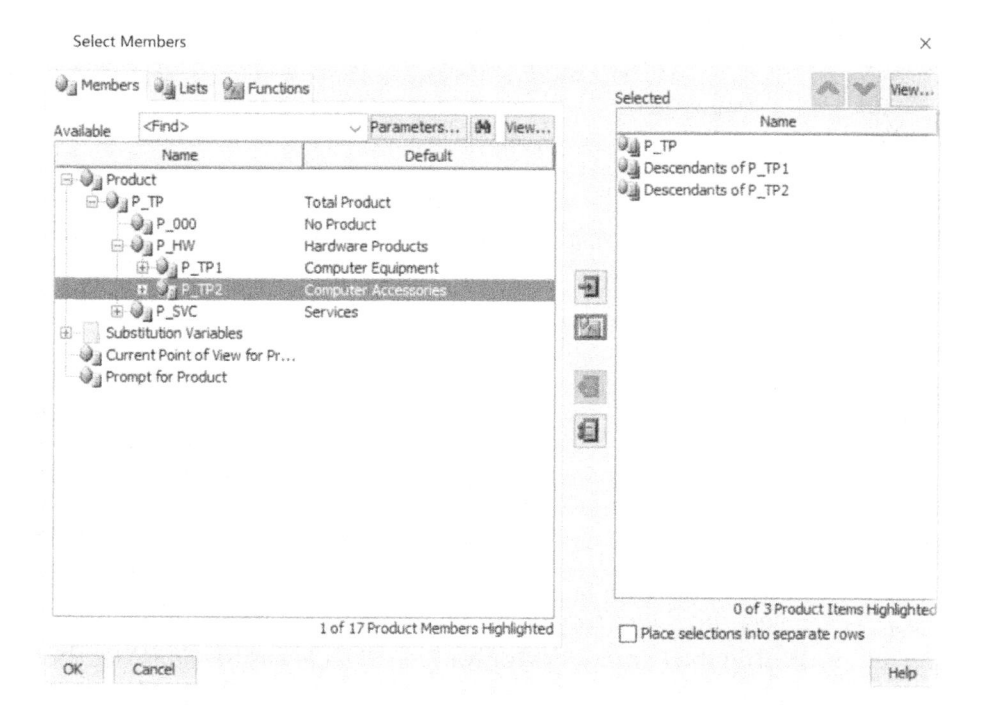

13. Click *OK*.
14. I'm going to display Actual data and Forecast data for an entire year. Double-click *Scenario* and select *Actual* and *Forecast*.
15. Remove the default *Scenario* member.
16. Check the box for *Place selections into separate columns*:

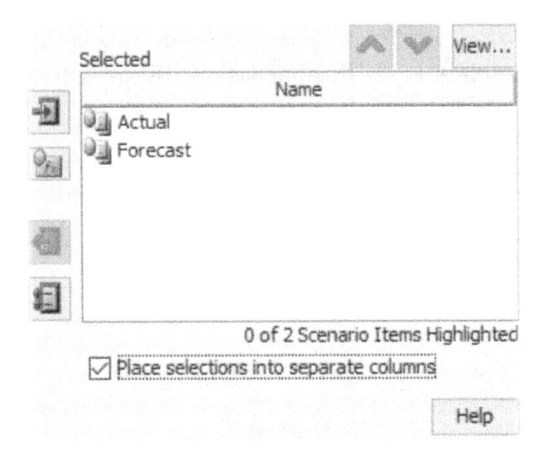

17. Click *OK*.
18. Double-click *Period* in Column A. Remove the default *Period* member. Navigate to the *Functions* tab:

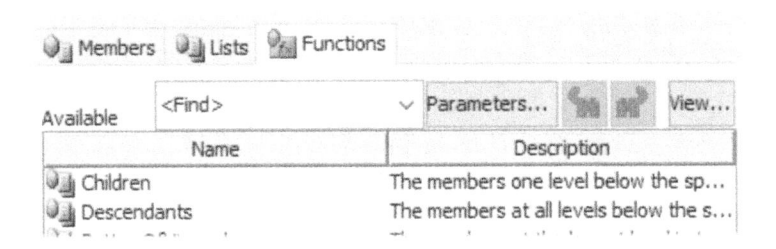

19. Select the *Range* function.
20. Within the Parameters for Range, select *Jan* as the StartMember and *$RFPer1* as the EndMember:

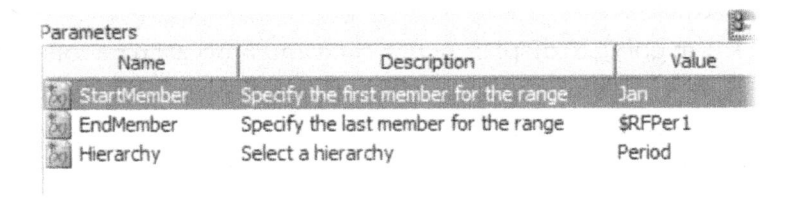

21. Click *OK* and *OK* again.
22. Double-click *Period* in Column B. Remove the default *Period* member.

23. Select the *Range* function and specify StartMember as *$RFPer2* and EndMember as *Dec*.

Note! The $ symbol indicates a substitution variable in Financial Reporting Studio.

24. Click *OK* and then *OK* again.
25. For both Columns A and B double-click *Years*. Remove the default *Years* member and select *Prompt for Years*.

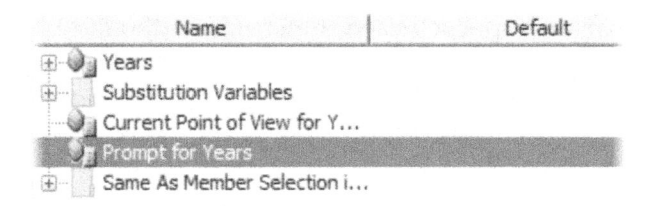

Name	Default
Years	
Substitution Variables	
Current Point of View for Y...	
Prompt for Years	
Same As Member Selection i...	

26. Define the prompt parameters. For Column A, choose *$CurrentYear* as the default. For Column B, choose *$ForecastYear* as the default.
27. You are left with the following for the grid:

		A	B
		Range from Jan to $RFP	Range from $RFPer2 to Dec
		Actual	Forecast
		Prompt for Years	Prompt for Years
1	P_TP, Descendants of P_TP1, Desc	#	#

Note! The default grid name for the first grid in any report will be "Grid1". To change the grid name, right-click the top left corner of the grid, click *Dimension Layout...* and change the name there:

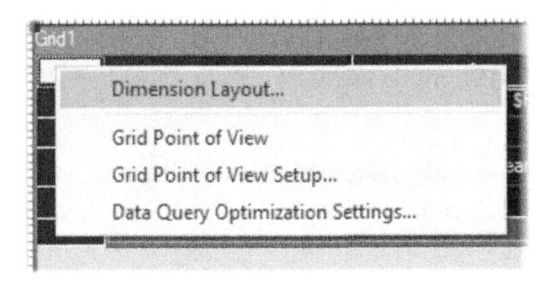

Now that the grid dimensions have been defined, I still need to define the dimensions in the POV.

28. Near the top, click each dimension in the POV and make the following selections:

   Account:4001 | Version:Final | Entity:403 | Customer:Total Customer

Now let's format the grid. To do this,

29. Click the row that contains *Prompt for Years* so that the entire row is highlighted.
30. In the Row Properties on the right, check the box for *Hide Always*.
31. Highlight the cells you would like to format:

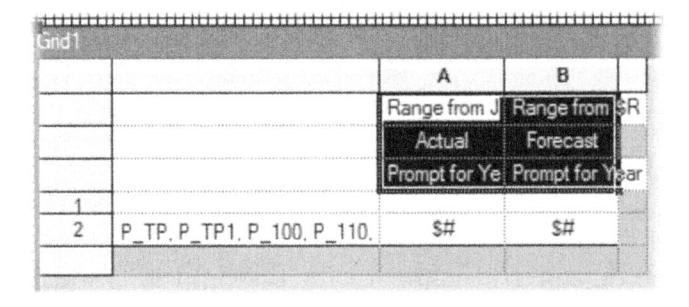

32. Right-click the cells and click *Format*.
33. Explore the formatting tabs and change cells as desired (bold, center, add prefixes to data, create borders, etc.):

Look Smarter Than You Are with Enterprise Planning Cloud   337

Note! You can also insert more rows of data, text, or even formulas in the report grids. Column and Row Properties allow more formatting options as well.

Create a Text Box

To create a text box,

34. Click the *Insert Text* icon at the top:

35. Click, drag, and release in the report to create the size of the text box.
36. Type in a title for the report and format the font and alignment.
37. Insert text functions, like *Member Name*, to make text more dynamic.

You should have something like the following:

Total Revenue by Products - <<MemberName("Grid1", 1/A/1, "Years")>>
(Report in Thousands)

Note! Images, such as company logos and charts that are based on report grids, can also be inserted into reports.

Save and View the Report

To save and view the report,

38. Select *File >> Save As,* navigate to the desired directory folder, name your report, then *Save* the report as a *Reports type.*
39. Click the *PDF icon* to run the report and view as a PDF:

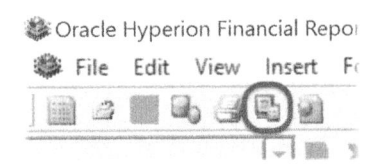

40. Specify the Years to view in the report then click *OK.*
41. View the report output:

Total Revenue by Products - FY14
(Report in Thousands)

	Jan Actual	Feb Actual	Mar Actual	Apr Actual	May Actual	Jun Actual	Jul Actual	Aug Actual	Sep Actual	Oct Actual	Nov Forecast	Dec Forecast
Total Product	594,617	580,752	588,077	580,752	594,617	580,752	594,617	574,212	594,617	574,212	-	-
Product X	-	-	-	-	-	-	-	-	-	-	-	-
Sentinal Standard Notebook	39,000	36,500	39,000	36,500	39,000	36,500	39,000	36,500	39,000	36,500	-	-
Sentinal Custom Notebook	38,000	37,000	38,000	37,000	38,000	37,000	38,000	37,000	38,000	37,000	-	-
Envoy Standard Netbook	41,000	40,000	41,000	40,000	41,000	40,000	41,000	40,000	41,000	40,000	-	-
Envoy Custom Netbook	34,200	34,200	34,200	34,200	34,200	34,200	34,200	34,200	34,200	34,200	-	-
Other Computer	4,000	4,000	4,000	4,000	4,000	4,000	4,000	4,000	4,000	4,000	-	-
Tablet Computer	65,600	65,600	61,600	65,600	65,600	65,600	65,600	61,600	65,600	61,600	-	-
Accessories	6,120	5,940	6,120	5,940	6,120	5,940	6,120	5,940	6,120	5,940	-	-
Keyboard	360	360	360	360	360	360	360	360	360	360	-	-
Software Suite	61,200	59,400	61,200	59,400	61,200	59,400	61,200	59,400	61,200	59,400	-	-
Monitor	6,800	6,800	6,800	6,800	6,800	6,800	6,800	6,800	6,800	6,800	-	-
Modem	-	-	-	-	-	-	-	-	-	-	-	-
Network Card	-	-	-	-	-	-	-	-	-	-	-	-
Same	-	-	-	-	-	-	-	-	-	-	-	-
Camera	32,800	31,800	32,800	31,800	32,800	31,800	32,800	31,800	32,800	31,800	-	-
Television	34,600	33,600	34,600	33,600	34,600	33,600	34,600	33,600	34,600	33,600	-	-

Create Report in Financial Reporting Studio (Web)

With the Enterprise Planning Cloud release in March 2016, FR web studio was added to the set of tools available to users on the Cloud interface. The web studio requires no client installation and offers most of the same functionality as the desktop software. This is the first release of this cloud offering, so it's important to keep your lines of communication open with Oracle Support in case any issues are encountered.

To create a new report in FR Web Studio (note, there are a lot of steps in this task),

1. Within the Simplified UI, go to *Navigator >> Manage >> Reporting Web Studio*:

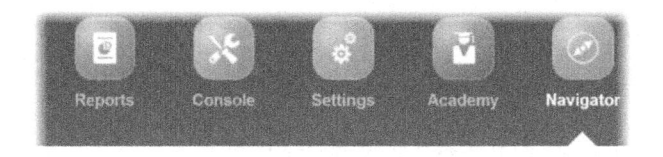

Look Smarter Than You Are with Enterprise Planning Cloud 339

Manage
Application Management
Clear Cell Details
Copy Data
Copy Versions
Data Integration
Document Repository
(Reporting Web Studio)

Workflow
Planning Unit Hierarchy
Scenario and Version Assignment
Manage Approvals

2. Click the first icon, *New Document*, to create a new report:

New Document

The same four objects for reports available in the FR desktop studio are also available in the FR web studio:

- Grids
- Text objects
- Images
- Charts

Create a Grid

3. Click the *Grid* icon and create the shape of the grid with a click, drag, and release on the report.
4. To create a Grid, I need to connect to a database connection. The database connections available to the FR desktop studio are also available here, as they are managed centrally. Point to

the same *SalesRpt* connection and then type in the login credentials:

Database Connection Properties
Data Sources
SalesRpt
New Connection
User Name
admin
Password
••••••••
OK   Cancel

5. Click *OK*. The Dimension Layout will open.
6. Click and drag the following dimensions from the POV to the Pages, Columns, or Rows:

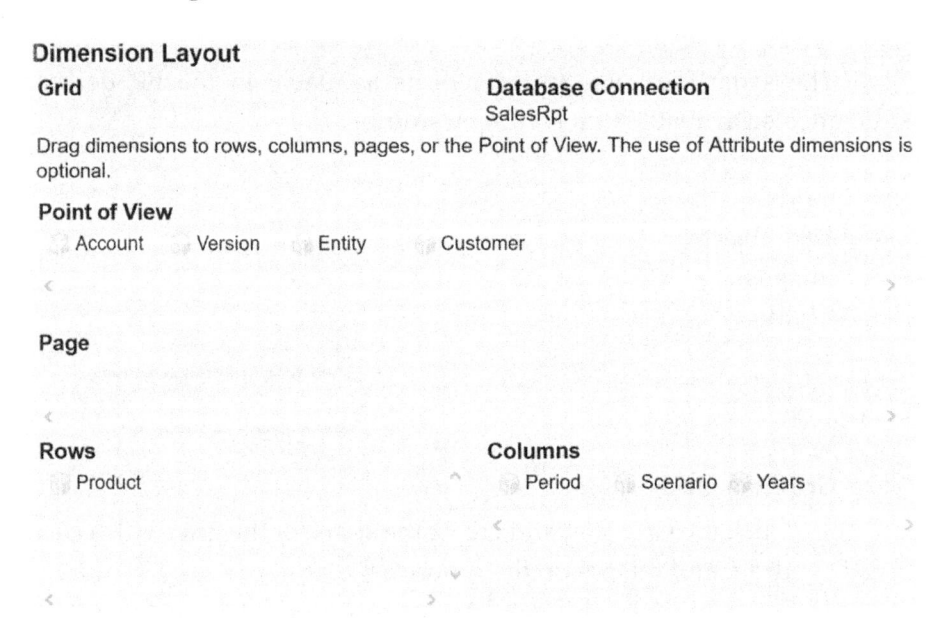

Dimension Layout

Grid **Database Connection**
SalesRpt

Drag dimensions to rows, columns, pages, or the Point of View. The use of Attribute dimensions is optional.

Point of View
Account   Version   Entity   Customer

Page

Rows **Columns**
Product   Period   Scenario   Years

7. Click *OK*.

8. Double-click each dimension in the grid to select the desired members. Double-click *Product*. Expand the dimension and then check the box next to the Services member ("P_SVC"). Then click the member function drop-down at the top and select *Descendants (Inclusive)*:

Select Members

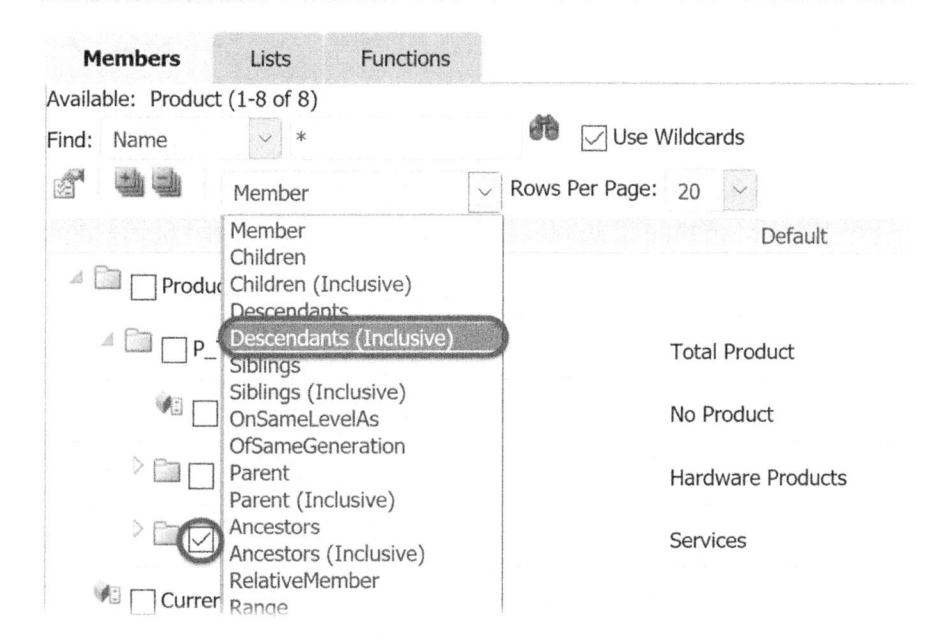

Members	Lists	Functions

Available: Product (1-8 of 8)

Find: Name ∨ *   ☑ Use Wildcards

Member ∨   Rows Per Page: 20 ∨

	Default
Produ☐ Member / Children / Children (Inclusive) / Descendants	
☐ P_ **Descendants (Inclusive)** / Siblings	Total Product
☐ Siblings (Inclusive) / OnSameLevelAs	No Product
☐ OfSameGeneration / Parent / Parent (Inclusive)	Hardware Products
☑ Ancestors / Ancestors (Inclusive)	Services
☐ Currer RelativeMember / Range	

9. Move the selection to the right. Then remove the previously default-selected *Product* selection.

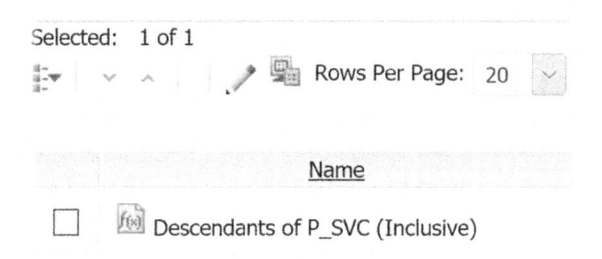

Selected: 1 of 1

Rows Per Page: 20 ∨

Name
☐ Descendants of P_SVC (Inclusive)

10. Click *OK*.
11. I'm going to display Actual data for an entire year. Double-click *Scenario* and select *Actual*.

12. Double-click *Period* in Column A and remove the default *Period* member.
13. Navigate to the *Functions* tab:

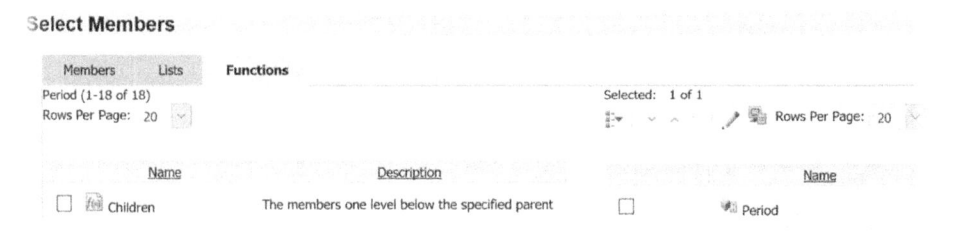

Select Members

Members	Lists	**Functions**				
Period (1-18 of 18)				Selected: 1 of 1		
Rows Per Page: 20						Rows Per Page: 20

	Name	Description		Name
☐	Children	The members one level below the specified parent	☐	Period

14. Check the box next to the *Range* function. Then move it to the right pane.
15. Within the Parameters for Range, select *Jan* as the StartMember and *Dec* as the EndMember:

Select Members

Range

	Name	Description	Value
	StartMember	Specify the first member for the range	Jan
	EndMember	Specify the last member for the range	Dec
	Hierarchy	Select a hierarchy	Period

16. Click *OK*.
17. In addition to your Range from Jan to Dec, add the *YearTotal* member.
18. Click *OK*:

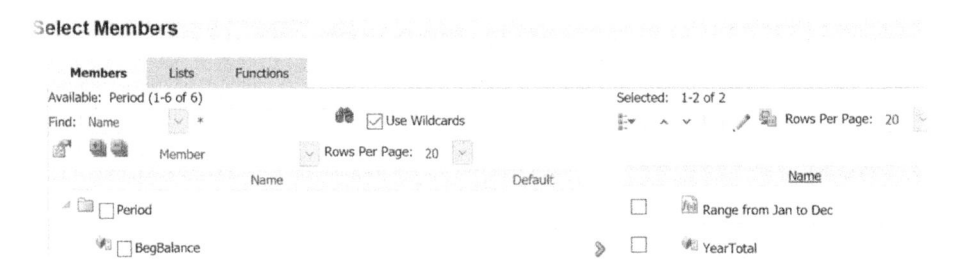

Select Members

Members	Lists	Functions				
Available: Period (1-6 of 6)				Selected: 1-2 of 2		
Find: Name	*		☑ Use Wildcards			Rows Per Page: 20
	Member		Rows Per Page: 20			

	Name	Default		Name
▲ ☐ Period			☐	Range from Jan to Dec
☐ BegBalance			☐	YearTotal

19. Double-click *Years* in Column A and remove the default Years member.

Look Smarter Than You Are with Enterprise Planning Cloud 343

20. Select the checkbox next to *Prompt for Years* and move it over:

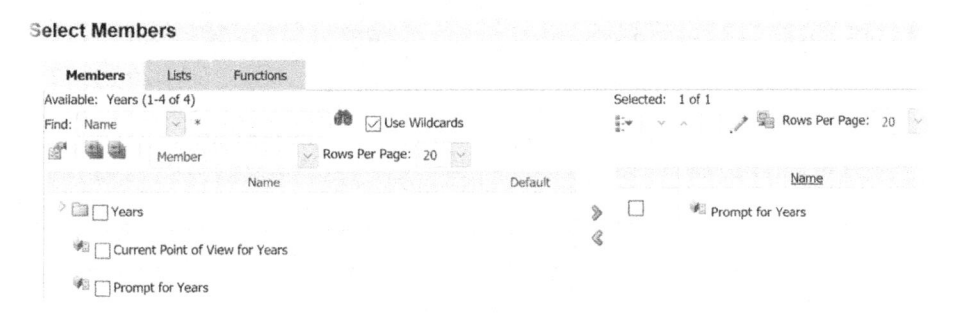

Select Members

Available: Years (1-4 of 4)		Selected: 1 of 1
Years		Prompt for Years
Current Point of View for Years		
Prompt for Years		

21. Click *OK*. Fill in the details of the prompt and click *OK*:

Define Prompts

Title: Enter Years

Default Member: $CurrentYear

Choices List:

Member Name

OK Cancel

22. Your report build should now be designed as follows:

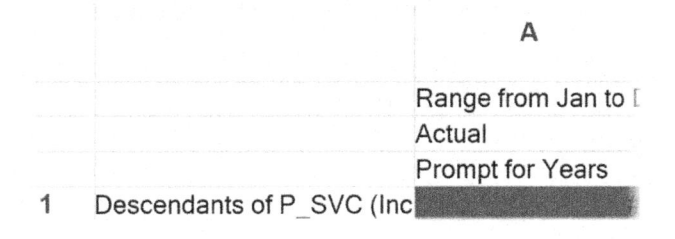

	A
	Range from Jan to [
	Actual
	Prompt for Years
1	Descendants of P_SVC (Inc

Note! The default grid name for the first grid in any report will be "Grid1". To change the grid name, click the top left corner of the grid, and change the name in the *Grid Properties* pane to the right:

Grid Properties - [SalesRpt_G

SalesRpt_Grid

Database Connection
SalesRpt

Dimension Layout

Now that the grid dimensions have been defined, I still need to define the dimensions in the POV.

23. Near the top, click each dimension in the POV and make the following selections:

Account: 4001 | Version: Final | Entity: Total Entity | Customer: Total Customer

Now let's format the Grid. To do this,

24. Click the row that contains *Prompt for Years* so that the entire row is highlighted:

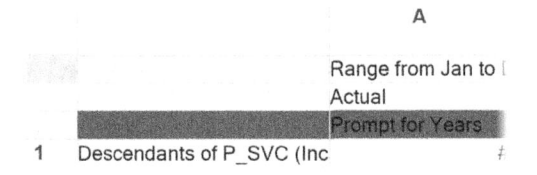

		A
		Range from Jan to
		Actual
		Prompt for Years
1	Descendants of P_SVC (Inc	

25. In the Row Properties on the right, check the box for *Hide Always*:

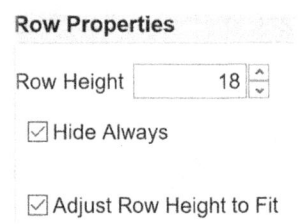

Row Properties

Row Height   18

☑ Hide Always

☑ Adjust Row Height to Fit

Look Smarter Than You Are with Enterprise Planning Cloud   345

26. Highlight the cells you would like to format:

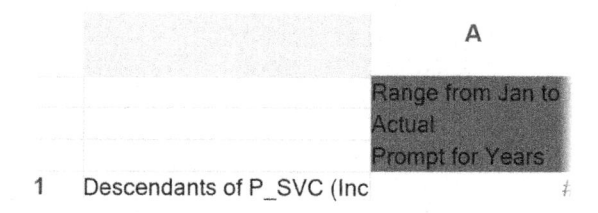

	A
	Range from Jan to Actual Prompt for Years
1	Descendants of P_SVC (Inc

27. Right-click the cells and click *Format*.
28. Explore the formatting tabs and change cells as desired (bold, center, add prefixes to data, create borders, etc.):

Format Cells

Number   Alignment   Font   Borders & Shading   Inherit Formatting

Note! You can also insert more rows of data, text, or even formulas in the report grids. Column and Row Properties allow more formatting options as well.

Create a Text Box

Now's a good time to save the report. To do this,

29. Click the *Save* icon, name it, and save it in the *Vision >> Sales* workspace folder. It should be saved as *Reports* type:

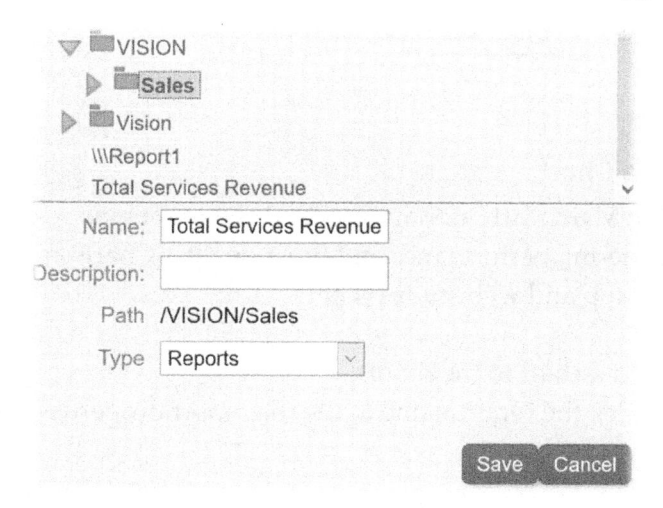

```
▼ VISION
    ▷ Sales
    ▷ Vision
      \\\Report1
      Total Services Revenue

        Name:  Total Services Revenue
 Description:  
        Path   /VISION/Sales
        Type   Reports

                              Save   Cancel
```

30. Navigate back to the *Report Properties* by clicking on the report name in the left pane:

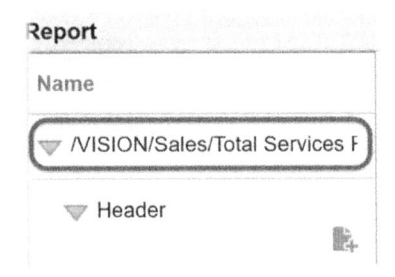

```
Report
Name
   ▼ /VISION/Sales/Total Services F
      ▼ Header
```

31. Click the *Text* icon at the top:

32. Click, drag, and release in the report header to create the shape of the text box.
33. Type in a title for the report and format the font and alignment.
34. Insert text functions, like *Member Name*, to make text more dynamic.

You should have something like the following:

Total Services Revenue - <<MemberName("SalesRpt_Grid", 1/A/1, Scenario)>> <<MemberName("SalesRpt_Grid", 1/A/1, Years)>>

(Report in Thousands)

Add a Chart

In the March 2016 update for FR, the chart engine was updated to improve rendering performance and functionality. Charts are available to both the desktop and web studio clients.

To add a chart to the report,
35. Click the report name to see the report properties.

Now I'll be able to move around objects on the report to make space for a chart. I'm going to keep the header at 0.5 inches. I'm also going to move down the grid, as I want the chart at the top of the report.

36. Click the *Chart* icon on the menu bar and then draw a chart box above the grid:

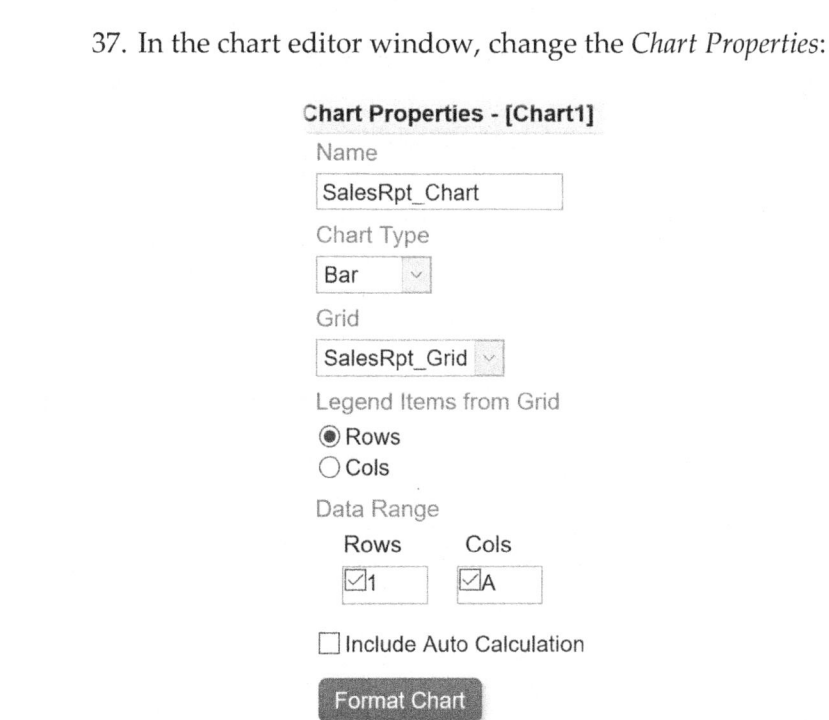

37. In the chart editor window, change the *Chart Properties*:

Chart Properties - [Chart1]

Name
[SalesRpt_Chart]

Chart Type
[Bar ▾]

Grid
[SalesRpt_Grid ▾]

Legend Items from Grid
◉ Rows
○ Cols

Data Range
  Rows   Cols
  ☑1   ☑A

☐ Include Auto Calculation

[Format Chart]

☐ Page Break Before

38. Click *Format Chart* to change specific aspects of the chart. In the *Appearance* tab, add a chart title:

348   Chapter 7: Create User Interfaces

Format Chart
Appearance | Legend | Axes | Element Style | Bar Options

Chart Title

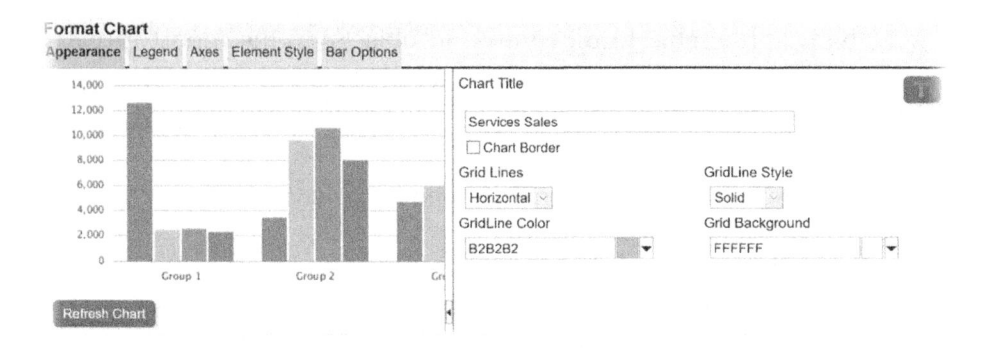

Services Sales
☐ Chart Border

Grid Lines   GridLine Style
Horizontal   Solid

GridLine Color   Grid Background
B2B2B2   FFFFFF

39. Play with whichever other settings make sense for this report.
40. Click *OK*.
41. Back in the main Chart Properties, change the position of the chart so that it's vertically aligned to the top and horizontally centered. To get to the position settings, use the expander next to Position:

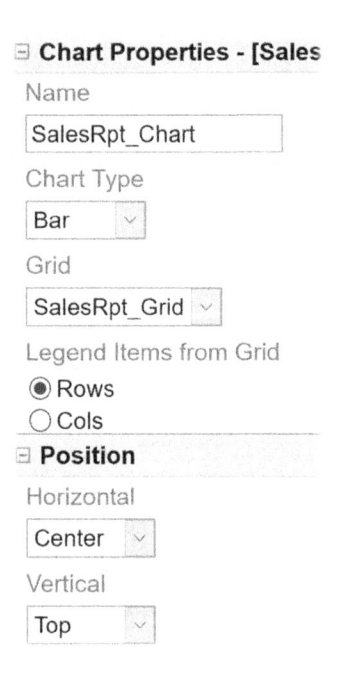

⊟ **Chart Properties - [Sales**

Name
SalesRpt_Chart

Chart Type
Bar

Grid
SalesRpt_Grid

Legend Items from Grid
● Rows
○ Cols

⊟ **Position**

Horizontal
Center

Vertical
Top

42. Do the same for the grid, but change the Vertical alignment to *Relative*.

Save and View the Report

43. *Save* the report.
44. Click the *PDF Preview* icon to run the report and view as a PDF:

45. Specify the Year to view in the report and click *OK*.
46. View the report:

Total Services Revenue - Actual FY14

(Report in Thousands)

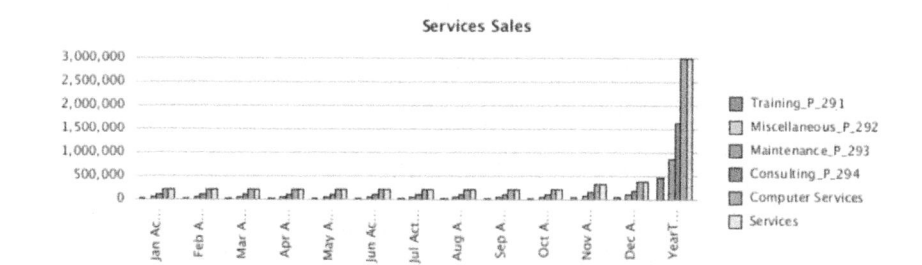

Services Sales

	Jan	Feb	Mar	Apr	May	Jun	Jul	Au
Training_P_291	36,368	35,520	35,968	35,520	36,368	35,520	36,368	3
Miscellaneous_P_292	1,818	1,776	1,798	1,776	1,818	1,776	1,818	
Maintenance_P_293	65,462	63,936	64,742	63,936	65,462	63,936	65,462	6
Consulting_P_294	127,288	124,320	125,888	124,320	127,288	124,320	127,288	12
Computer Services	230,937	225,552	228,397	225,552	230,937	225,552	230,937	22
Services	230,937	225,552	228,397	225,552	230,937	225,552	230,937	22

Comparing the Desktop FR Studio to the Web Studio

Regardless of which studio is used to develop report objects, they are stored centrally and can be accessed through either interface. However, there are a handful features are not available through the web studio yet. Some notable ones include:

- Row and column templates
- Conditional formatting
- Butterfly reports

However, never fear – these features can be accessed through the desktop client.

Combining Reports into a Book

Financial Reporting supports the creation of books. A book is a single object/report package that contains one or more Financial Reporting documents. I'm going to create a book in Enterprise Planning Cloud Workspace UI that includes both of the reports created above.

To create a Financial Reporting book,
1. Navigate to the Enterprise Planning Cloud Workspace URL.
2. Click the *Explore* button to navigate to the Workspace repository:

3. Go to *File >> New >> Document*:

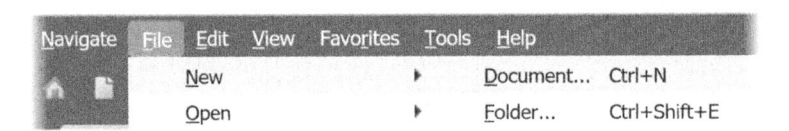

4. Keep the default of *Collect Reports into a Book*.
5. Click *Next*:

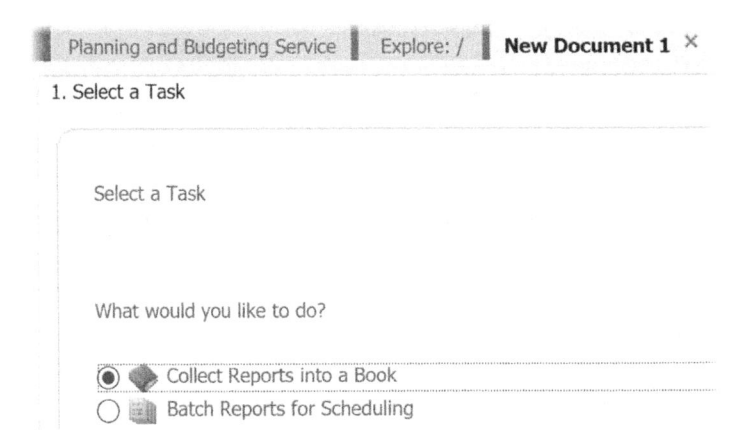

Look Smarter Than You Are with Enterprise Planning Cloud 351

6. Add the two reports created in the above sections and then click *Finish*.
7. Change the drop-down to *Book Setup* and make changes as necessary:

8. Save the object as a *Financial Reporting Book*:

9. Choose to preview the book to ensure that it's working correctly.

And there you have it! Both reports are now combined into a single Financial Reporting book.

I've only skimmed the surface with the functionality in Financial Reporting. Make sure to check out the Oracle documentation and/or attend one of i.n.t.e.r.R.e.l.'s training classes.

AD HOC GRIDS & DYNAMIC REPORTS

Ad Hoc Grids

Ad hoc grids are focused data slices created by users that are saved for reuse within the Enterprise Planning Cloud application. Users choose the dimensions and members that they want to see in the rows, columns and page section and are not confined to the data form definition and layout. The user interface is a "grid" vs. a "data form". Users can still update data in ad hoc grids.

To create an ad hoc grid,
1. Open up a data form. Go to *Actions >> New Ad Hoc Grid*:

Or within the ad hoc grids, click *Create*.

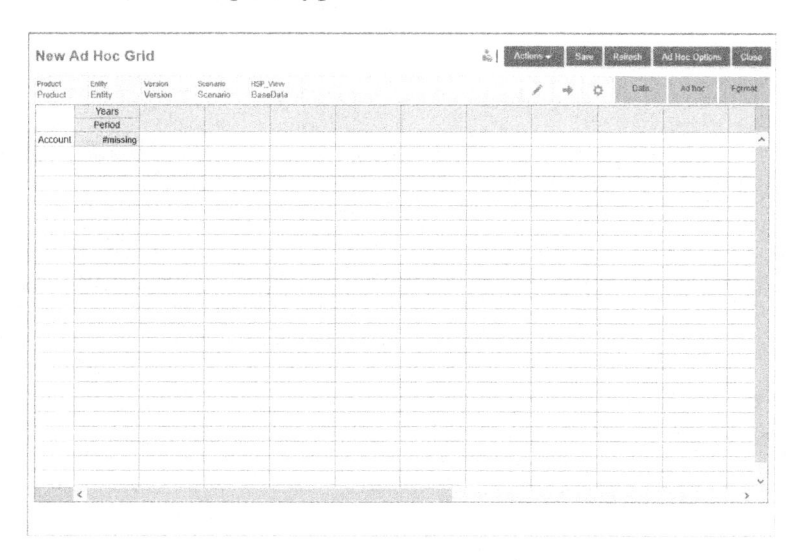

Look Smarter Than You Are with Enterprise Planning Cloud   353

2. Choose the plan type *Sales* and click *Create*:

New Ad Hoc Grid										
Product	Entity	Version	Scenario	HSP_View		Actions ▼	Save	Refresh	Ad Hoc Options	Close
Product	Entity	Version	Scenario	BaseData				Data	Ad hoc	F-grmat
	Years									
	Period									
Account	#missing									

Analyze to Build the Ad Hoc Grid Layout

With the blank grid, users can select members for each dimension and use the *Ad Hoc* menu to zoom, move and pivot dimensions however they wish. However, you might find it helpful to use the UI to build your ad hoc grid.

3. Click the *Ad Hoc* icon to show the Ad hoc panel:

354   Chapter 7: Create User Interfaces

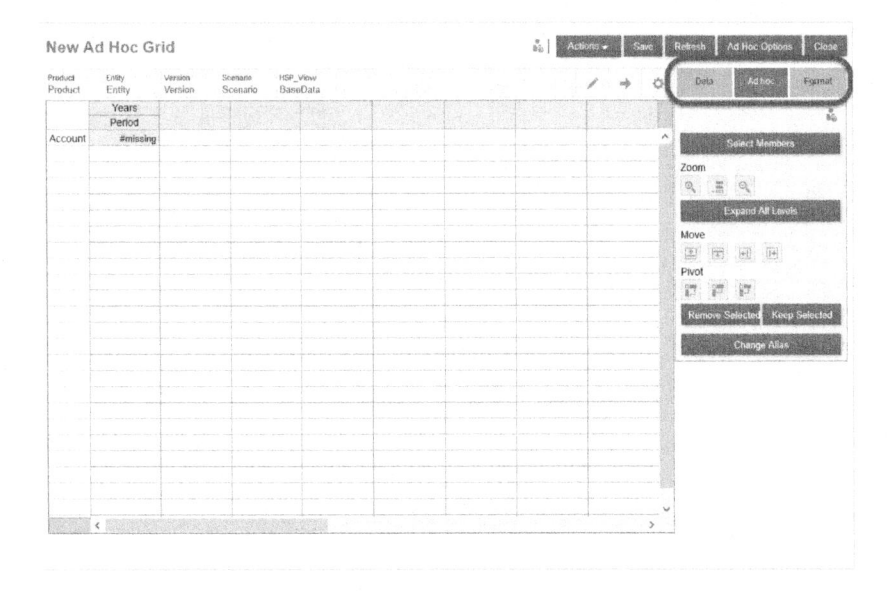

4. Drag *Product* from the POV to the columns.
5. Select *Years* and click the *Page Pivot* icon. This will actually pivot to the POV.
6. Select *Period* and click the *Page Pivot* icon. This will actually pivot to the POV:

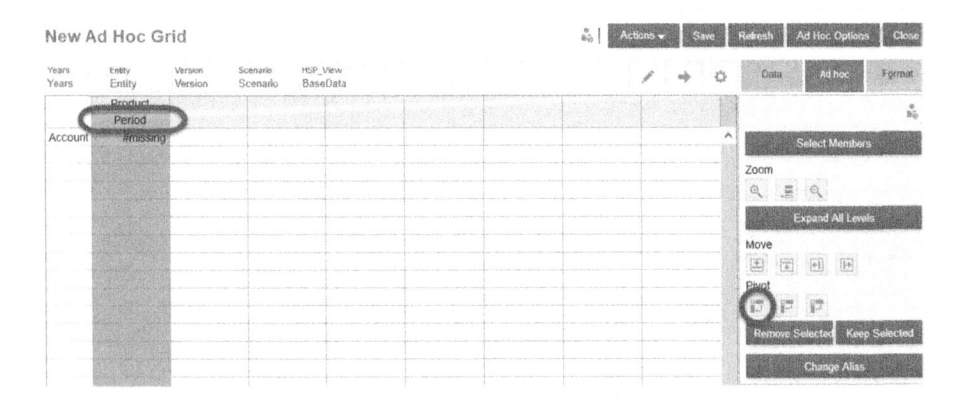

7. Drag *Entity* into the Rows.
8. Pivot *Account* into the Page. This will actually pivot to the POV.

The result should look as follows:

New Ad Hoc Grid

	Account	Period	Years	Version	Scenario	HSP_View
	Account	Period	Years	Version	Scenario	BaseData
		Product				
Entity		#missing				

9. Update the POV member selections by selecting the dimension in the POV and choosing the member through the member selection process, or click ✎ and select each member through the member selection icon there:

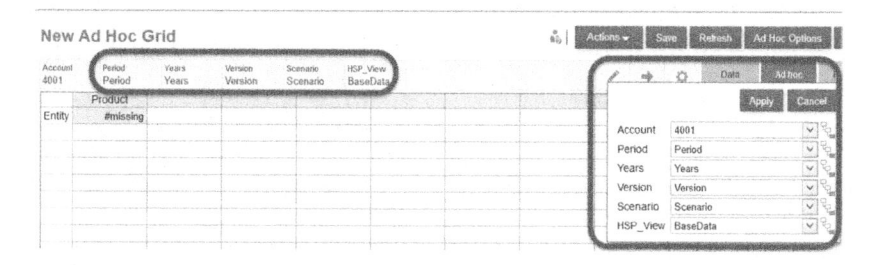

10. Update the POV to:
   a. Account = 4001 (Total Revenue)
   b. Period = YearTotal
   c. Years = FY16
   d. Versions = Final
   e. Scenario = Forecast
   f. HSP_View = BaseData

Period	Years	Account	Version	Scenario	HSP_View
YearTotal	FY16	4001	Final	Forecast	BaseData
Final					

	Product				
Entity	17882846.64800				

11. Double-click on *Entity* within the grid to zoom down. Zoom until you get to Sales numbers "403" (and then choose the option to *Keep Selected*):

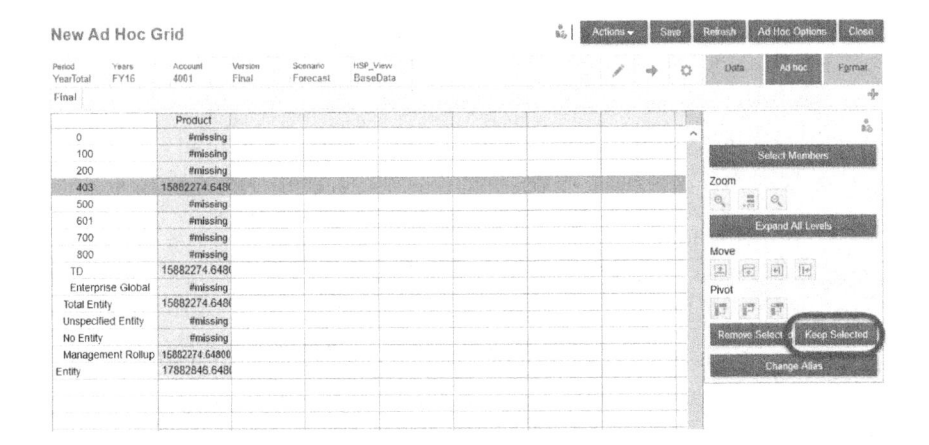

12. Now zoom in on product, using the *Zoom in* icon in the Ad hoc panel. Click it twice.

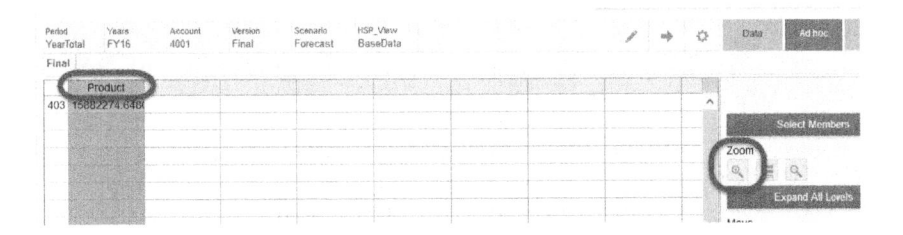

13. Choose *Product* and *Remove Selected*.
14. Click on the *Data* icon:

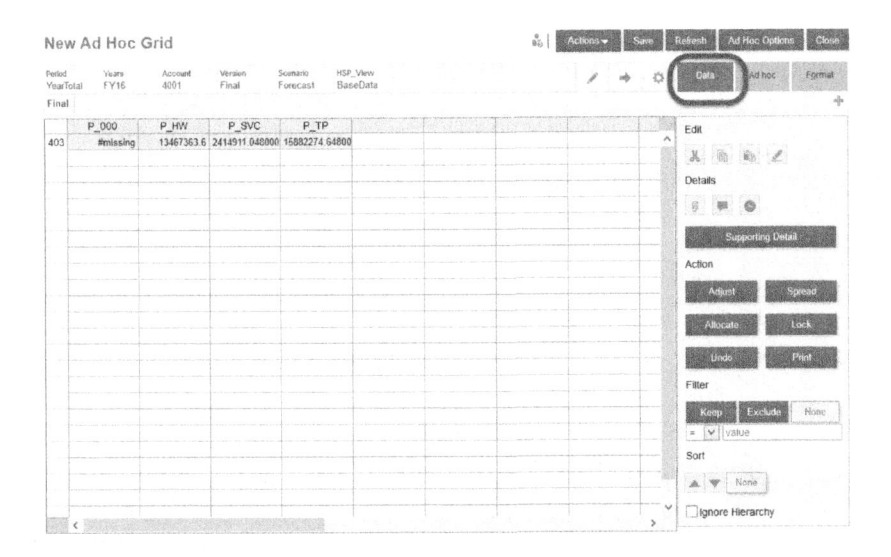

Look Smarter Than You Are with Enterprise Planning Cloud 357

Notice many of the actions that you perform within data forms are available in ad hoc grids, like: entering and viewing supporting detail, viewing change history, adjusting, spreading, locking, and printing:

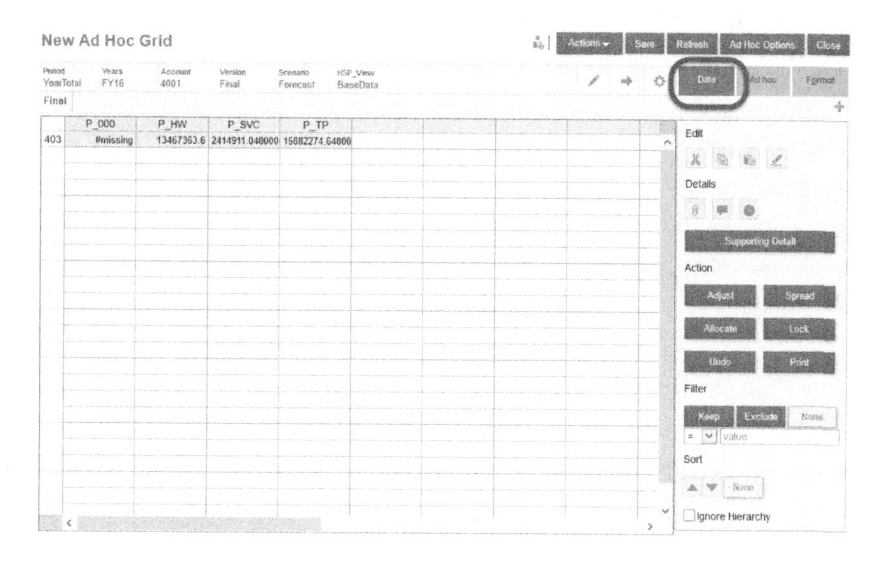

15. Click on the *Format* icon. Drill down on member "403".

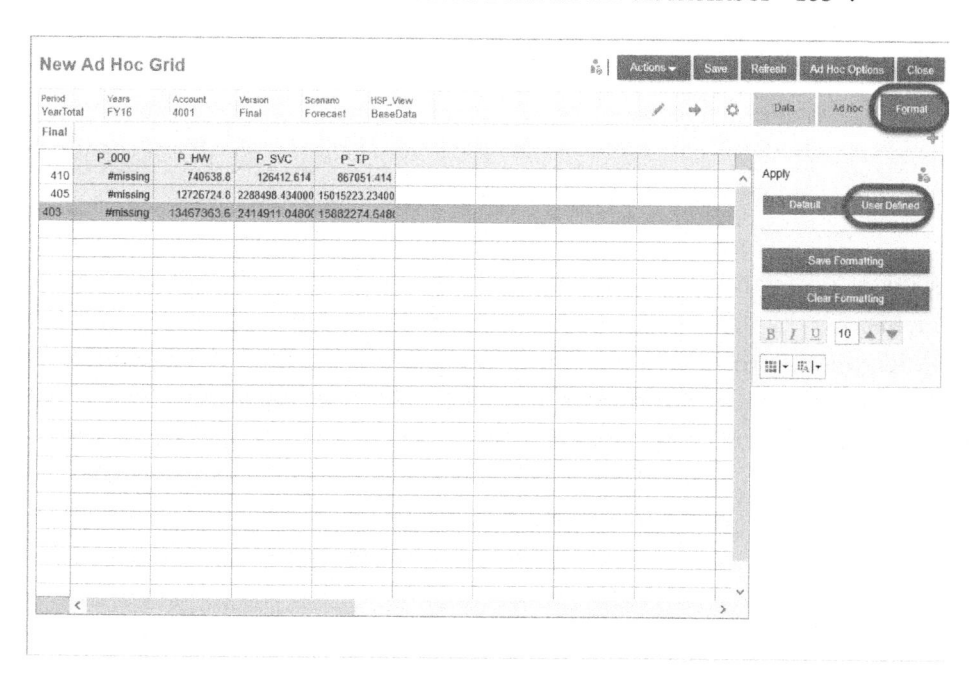

Chapter 7: Create User Interfaces

16. Select *User Defined*.
17. Apply formatting to the total rows and columns. Make sure to click *Save Formatting* as you go.
18. Click *Ad Hoc Options*.
19. Change the options to match the following and click *Save*:

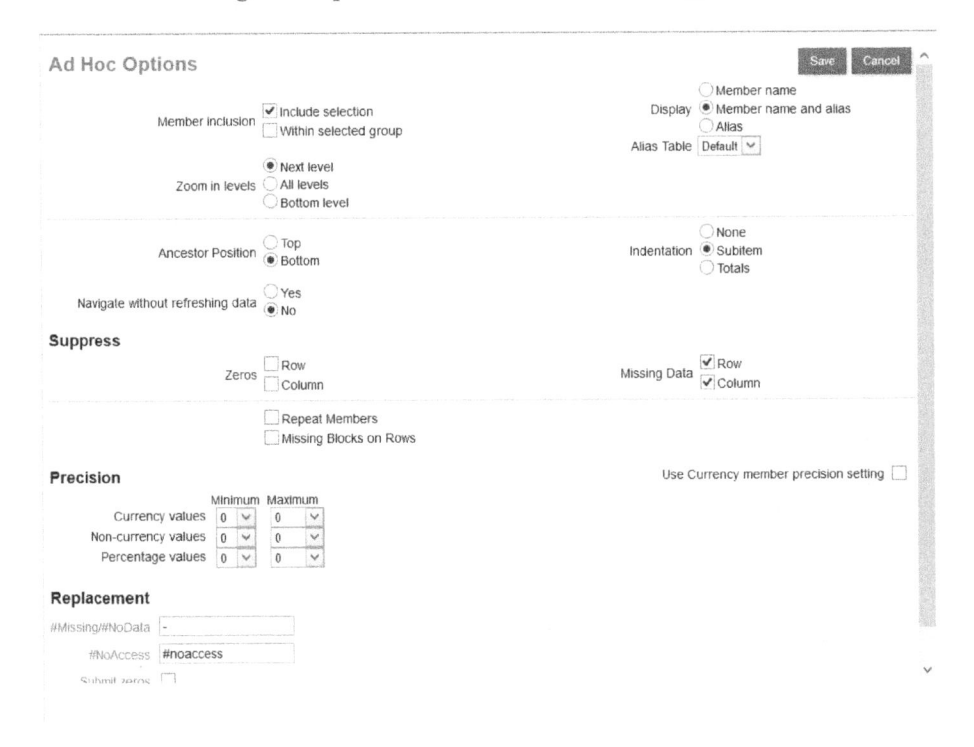

Ad Hoc Options	Save Cancel
Member inclusion: ☑ Include selection / ☐ Within selected group	Display: ○ Member name / ● Member name and alias / ○ Alias
	Alias Table: Default
Zoom in levels: ● Next level / ○ All levels / ○ Bottom level	
Ancestor Position: ○ Top / ● Bottom	Indentation: ○ None / ● Subitem / ○ Totals
Navigate without refreshing data: ○ Yes / ● No	
Suppress	
Zeros: ☐ Row / ☐ Column	Missing Data: ☑ Row / ☑ Column
☐ Repeat Members	
☐ Missing Blocks on Rows	
Precision	Use Currency member precision setting ☐
	Minimum / Maximum
Currency values	0 / 0
Non-currency values	0 / 0
Percentage values	0 / 0
Replacement	
#Missing/#NoData	-
#NoAccess	#noaccess
Submit zeros	☐

These same Ad Hoc Options are also covered in the Analyze section, you can set the default options for ad hoc actions for member inclusion, display of member name and / or alias, zoom behavior, indentation, ancestor position, navigation with / without data, suppression, precision and replacement. As with all forms and grids, formatting options are also available.

20. Click *Actions* >> *Save Ad Hoc Grid*:

Current Year Forecast Summary

Period YearTotal Final	Years FY16	Account 4001 : Total Revenue	Version Final	Scenario Forecast	HSP_View BaseData		
		P_HW Hardware Prod	P_SVC Services	P_TP Total Product			
410:International Sales		740639	126413	867051			
405:Domestic Sales		12726725	2288498	15015223			
403:Sales		13467364	2414911	15882275			

Actions menu: Filter, Ad Hoc, **Save Ad Hoc Grid**, Ad Hoc Options, Business Rules, Smart Push Details, Sandbox, Clear Formatting

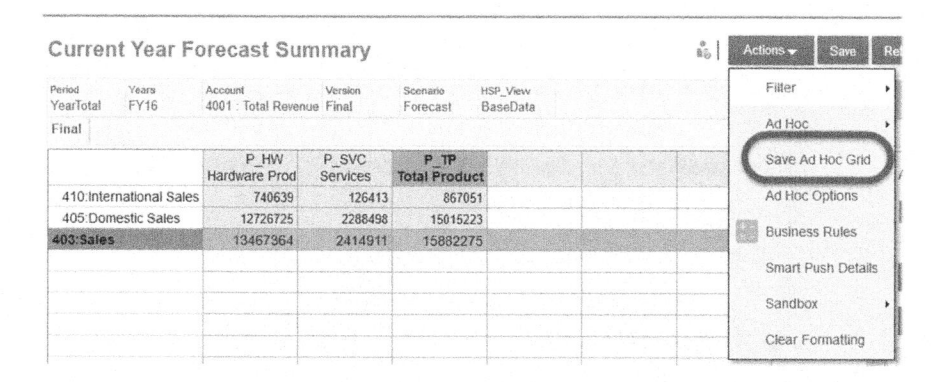

21. Save the grid as "Current Year Forecast Summary". Choose *Ad Hoc Form* and click *Save*:

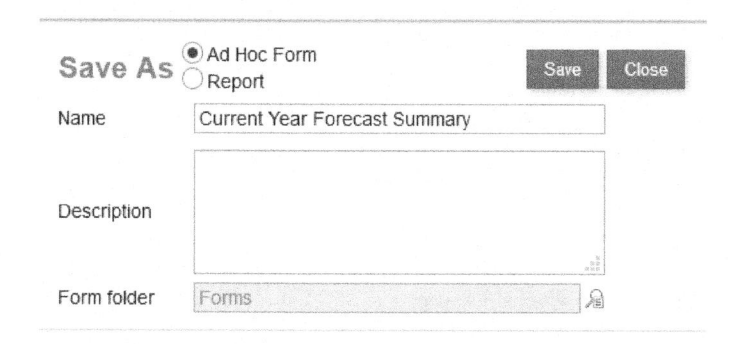

Save As: ● Ad Hoc Form ○ Report

Name: Current Year Forecast Summary

Description:

Form folder: Forms

22. Go to *Plans >> Ad Hoc: Forms* to navigate back to the grid.

Manage Ad Hoc Grids

Click *Navigator >> Forms* to manage ad hoc grids (along with data forms). From the Forms and Ad Hoc Grid section, you can move, rename, assign access, or delete ad hoc grids by selecting the appropriate task from the *Actions* drop-down menu or icon from the menu bar. You can also Search for a particular form.

Note! You cannot edit the ad hoc grid from this section.

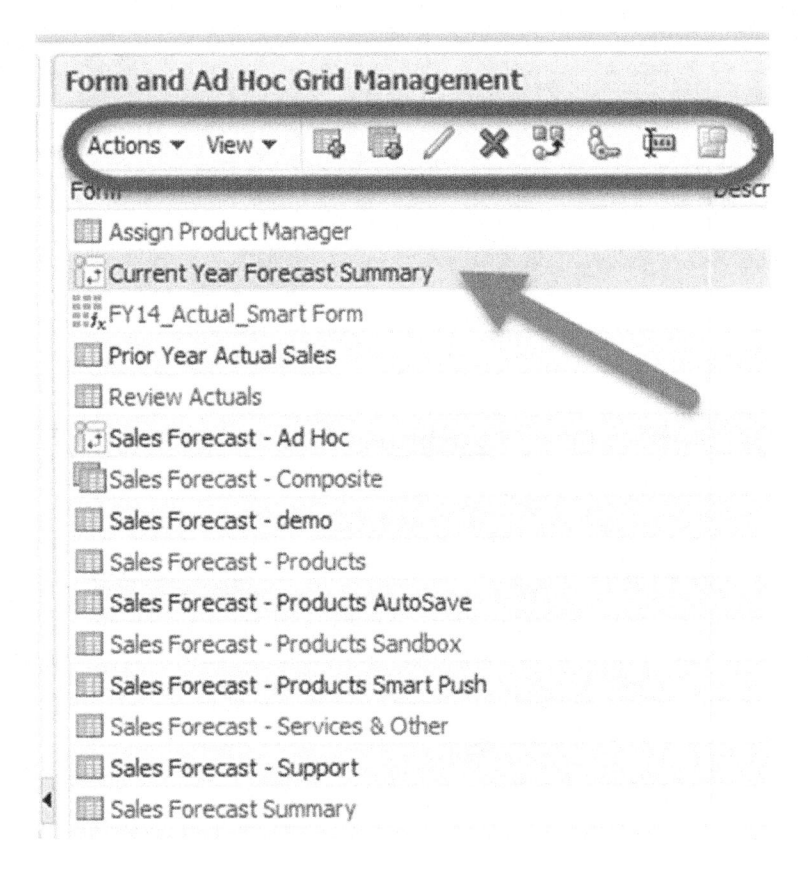

Form and Ad Hoc Grid Management

Actions ▼ View ▼

- Assign Product Manager
- Current Year Forecast Summary
- FY14_Actual_Smart Form
- Prior Year Actual Sales
- Review Actuals
- Sales Forecast - Ad Hoc
- Sales Forecast - Composite
- Sales Forecast - demo
- Sales Forecast - Products
- Sales Forecast - Products AutoSave
- Sales Forecast - Products Sandbox
- Sales Forecast - Products Smart Push
- Sales Forecast - Services & Other
- Sales Forecast - Support
- Sales Forecast Summary

Dynamic Reports

Essentially, dynamic reports are ad hoc grids saved as a report. These reports are dynamic because the data shown depends on the dimension members selected from the Page menu.

To create a Dynamic Report,

1. In *Plans >> Ad Hoc: Forms*, open the *Current Year Forecast Summary* ad hoc grid (if not open).
2. Click *Actions >> Save Ad Hoc Grid*:

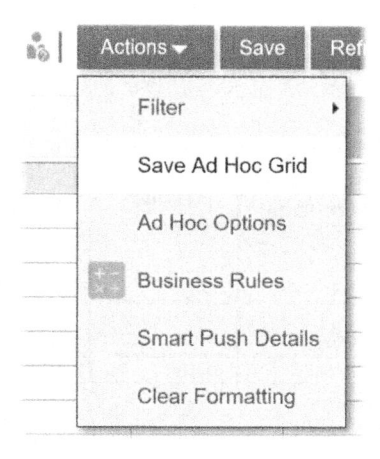

Look Smarter Than You Are with Enterprise Planning Cloud   361

[Menu screenshot showing: Actions, Save, Ref buttons with dropdown containing: Filter, Save Ad Hoc Grid, Ad Hoc Options, Business Rules, Smart Push Details, Clear Formatting]

3. The *Save As* window will open. Click the radio button for *Report*, name the report "Current Year Forecast Summary Dynamic Report", and click *Save*:

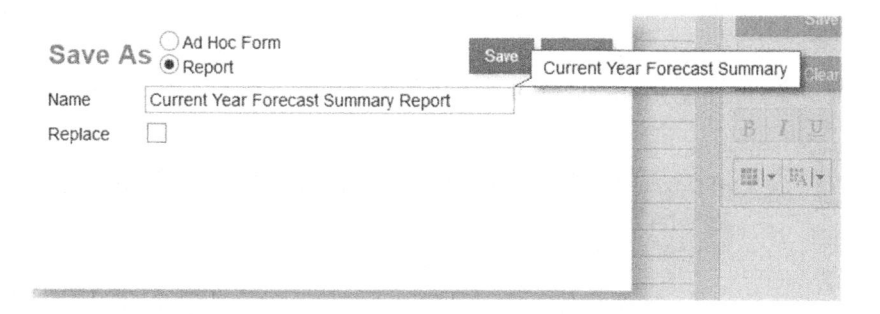

[Screenshot of Save As dialog with Ad Hoc Form / Report radio buttons, Name field "Current Year Forecast Summary Report", Replace checkbox]

The dynamic report will be saved in *Reports* from the main menu:

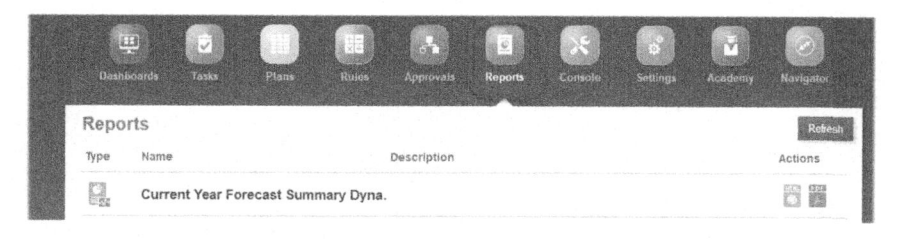

[Screenshot of main menu bar: Dashboards, Tasks, Plans, Rules, Approvals, Reports, Console, Settings, Academy, Navigator; Reports listing showing Type, Name, Description, Actions columns with "Current Year Forecast Summary Dyna."]

4. Click the *HTML* view to see dimension options:

Current Year Forecast Summary Dynamic Report

Page: YearTotal, FY16, 4001 Total Revenue, Final, Forecast, BaseData

	P_HW Hardware Products	P_SVC Services	P_TP Total Product
410 International Sales	740,639	126,413	867,051
405 Domestic Sales	12,726,725	2,288,498	15,015,223
403 Sales	13,467,364	2,414,911	15,882,275

Export In Query-Ready Mode

Page 1

Current Year Forecast Summary Dynamic Report   Confidential   Tuesday, February 02, 2016

Data will change depending on the page option selected. Our example had a single page selection because all dimensions were defined in the POV or the rows and columns.

Note! The page options will vary depending on how the ad hoc grid was set up.

Ad hoc grids and dynamic reports may be opened in Smart View by switching to the *Reporting Settings* drop-down option within Shared Connections:

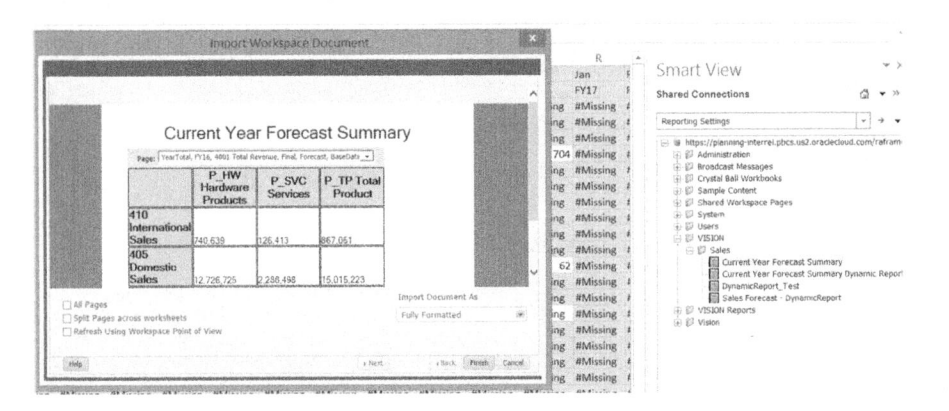

> **LOG ENTRY: SOL 19, Entry 1**
>
> Holy moly! The project might make it! I have an application with dimensions, data, business rules and interfaces. This is awesome. Holy moly!! Okay. Stay calm.

Chapter 8: Assign Security

```
LOG ENTRY: SOL 19, Entry 2

The implementation is going to explode!
```

```
LOG ENTRY: SOL 19, Entry 3

Just kidding. Things were going along so well, I
thought I would add some drama into this mission.
    Everything is going according to plan and my next
step is to set up security.
```

Users can't get into the system until you assign access. That is a pretty important step. The overall flow of setting up security in the Oracle Enterprise Planning Cloud is as follows:

1. Create users in My Services and provision their role.
2. Create native groups in Application Management and assign users to those groups.
3. Assign application access to users or groups within the Enterprise Planning Cloud application.

Users can only be created and provisioned by the Identity Domain Administrator through Oracle Cloud My Services. I did this step in chapter 2, creating the users and assigning their roles. Users cannot be created within the Enterprise Planning Cloud Workspace or within the Simplified UI nor can their roles be assigned. This is different from on-premise Hyperion Planning where you create users and provision them in Shared Services.

Within Enterprise Planning Cloud there are only five different roles. The table below briefly describes the roles available.

Role	Description
Identity Domain Administrator	Creates users and assigns roles in Oracle Cloud My Services
Service Administrator	Functional administrator for an application
Power User	Grants some functional administrator rights such as creating and maintaining forms, Smart View worksheets, business rules, task lists and FRS reports; controlling approvals process
Planner	Enters data through forms and Smart View, performs ad hoc analysis and drills through to source system
Viewer	Grants view-only access through forms and Smart View

Jump back to Chapter 2 to learn the step to create users in My Services and provision their roles.

NATIVE GROUPS

The next step in the security process is to define native groups. Using group access will save you time when creating and maintaining application security.

Application Management in Oracle Enterprise Planning Cloud is the place where you will perform a couple of different administrative tasks for your applications. Relevant to the current phase of this mission, this is where I can create and manage native security groups for assigning application security. I can do other things like migrating applications in Application Management but I'll get to that later.

The navigation panel on the left portion of the window controls the main content area. For example, if you select "User Directories", the main content area will allow you to search, add, and display the native directory containing any native groups. The *User Directories* section groups native groups for security assignments:

Chapter 8: Assign Security

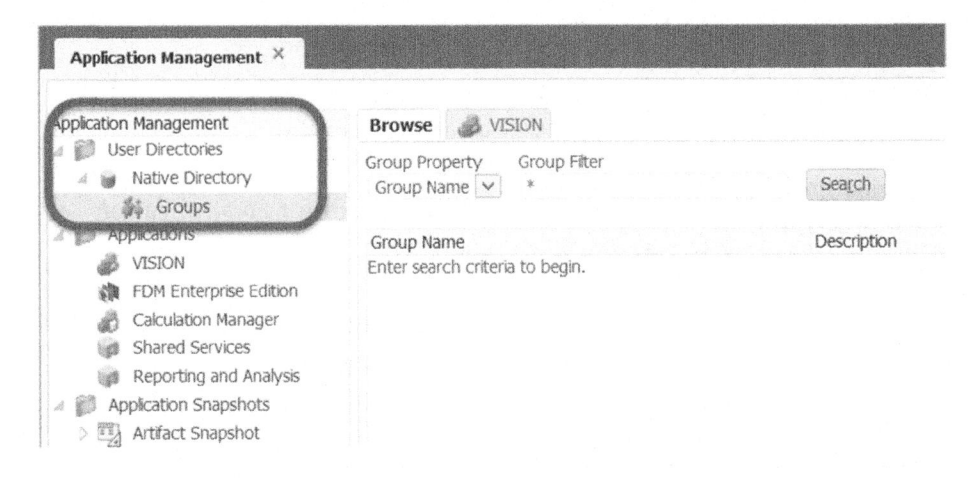

```
Application Management  X
Application Management         Browse    VISION
  User Directories
    Native Directory           Group Property   Group Filter
      Groups                   Group Name  v    *                    Search
    Applications
      VISION                   Group Name                             Description
      FDM Enterprise Edition   Enter search criteria to begin.
      Calculation Manager
      Shared Services
      Reporting and Analysis
  Application Snapshots
    Artifact Snapshot
```

Oracle Enterprise Planning Cloud supports native user groups for security assignments. You can assign a group of users to native groups and then assign application security to a group level or user level. Native groups can also be imported.

As I mentioned, you want to use group security assignments as much as possible. Groups reduce the overall maintenance for your security application. You define security once and as users come and go, they can be added to and removed from groups. If security requirements change, you update the group security once vs. many times for individual users. Native groups that can contain other groups are called nested groups.

You might create different user groups based on what the user can do. For example, you might create a group called "Planner" for most end users and common security definitions across all users and a group called "Power" for the budget and financial planning office. You will likely create different security groups for your entity dimension so that users can only enter plans for their specific department or division.

To create a native security group,
1. Within Application Management, select *User Directories >> Native Directory >> Groups*.
2. Right-click on Groups and select *New Group*:

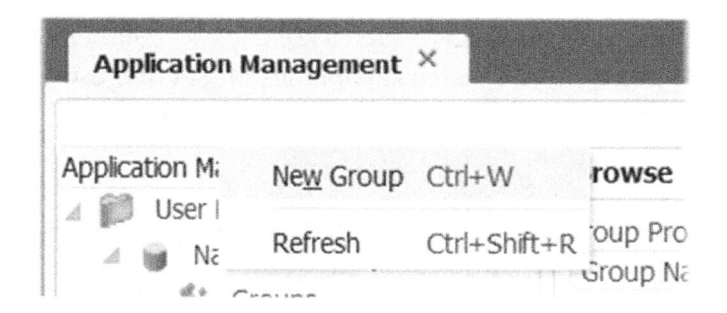

Look Smarter Than You Are with Enterprise Planning Cloud   367

[screenshot: Application Management menu showing New Group Ctrl+W, Refresh Ctrl+Shift+R]

The *Create Group* window displays.

3. Type in the group name "International_Sales_Grp" and optionally add a description:

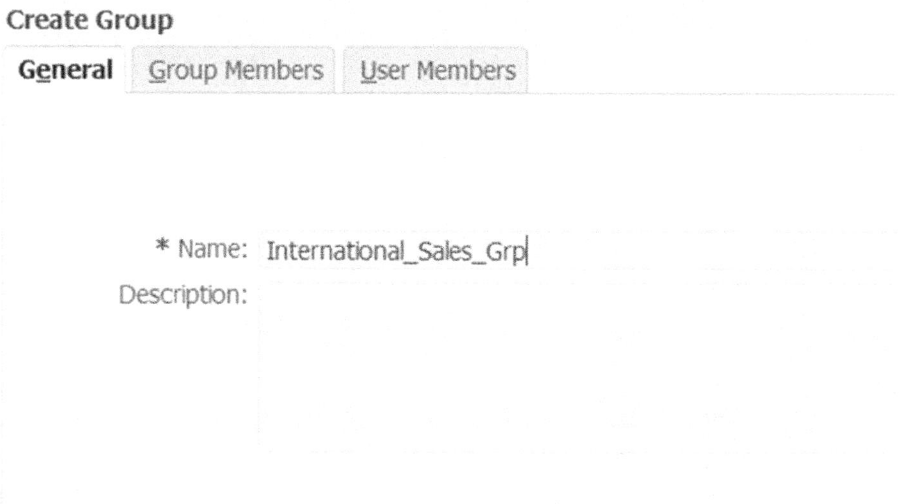

Create Group

General | Group Members | User Members

* Name: International_Sales_Grp
Description:

4. Click the *Next* button to advance to the Group Members tab.

On this tab, you can select desired available groups (either native or external) to assign (nested group security). You can search for specific groups or search for all groups. Next just check the group and use the arrow icons to move into the "assigned" section.

5. Click the *Next* button to advance to the User Members tab.

On the final tab, you select desired available users (either native or external). You have the same search capabilities for specific users as you did for groups. Use the arrow icons to assign the selected users:

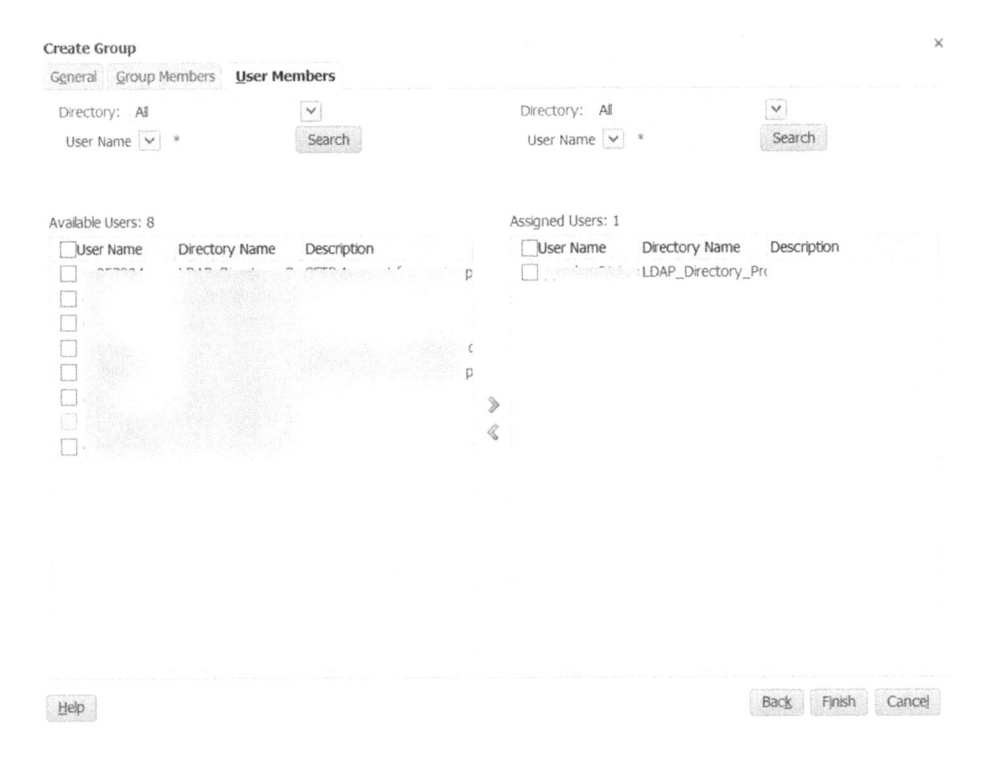

6. Click *Save* to create the group and click *OK* to close the Create Group window.
7. Repeat the above steps to create a group called "Vision Planners".

SET ENTERPRISE PLANNING CLOUD APPLICATION SECURITY

After the users and roles have been created in My Services and the native groups created in Application Management, the final part of Enterprise Planning Cloud security is to assign access to all of the components. You will assign member-specific security for the Account, Entity, Version, Scenario, and User-Defined Dimensions (Product). You also need to assign security to data form folders, data forms, business rules, and task lists. Thankfully the steps to do so are the same for all objects. You can perform these steps in Enterprise Planning Cloud Workspace or the Simplified UI.

When assigning application security you will, select the Users or Groups tab. Select the desired User/Group and choose *Read, Write* or *None* and choose *Member, Children, Children (Inclusive), Descendants,* or *Descendants (Inclusive)*:

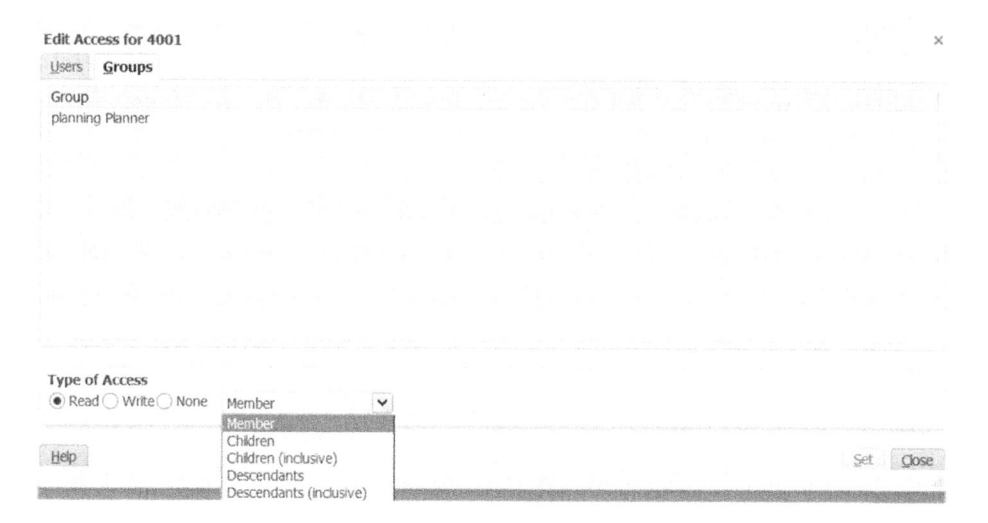

Edit Access for 4001

Users Groups

Group
planning Planner

Type of Access
○ Read ○ Write ○ None   Member
                         Member
                         Children
   Help   Children (inclusive)   Set   Close
                         Descendants
                         Descendants (inclusive)

Member security will be assigned for the selected object or in the case of dimensions, member. *Children* security will be assigned for the children of the member in the dimension but not the member. *Children (Inclusive)* security will be assigned for the member and its children in the dimension. *Descendants* and *Descendants (Inclusive)* are similar to Children / Children (Inclusive) except that all members below the selected member will be assigned access.

If you need to edit or delete security, you will still select *Action* menu option. Click *Edit Access* or *Remove*:

Assign Access for 4001

Users Groups

Action ▼ View ▼ ➕ ✏ ✖ Detach

		Access Rights	Relation
Add Access	Ctrl+W	Write	Descendants (inclusive)
Edit Access	Ctrl+E	Write	Descendants (inclusive)
Remove Access	Ctrl+Del	Read	Descendants (inclusive)

Security Design Best Practices

Inheritance may determine the user or group's access permissions. Access permissions assigned to members take precedence over inherited access permissions. You can include or exclude the member from the access permissions setting.

To save time in the security definition process, you may want to create a Planner group for all Planners (as I mentioned above). Assign common security like Scenario and Version members in the Planner group. Then create entity specific or account specific security groups may be created and assigned for more granular security. The entity specific or account specific groups should be assigned to the Planner group to inherit the common security assignments.

Why isn't security assigned by Fiscal Periods or Years? All users have access to all periods and years. You control write access for periods by defining the Start Yr., Start Period, End Yr. and End Period in the member properties.

ASSIGN MEMBER ACCESS

To assign metadata (or dimension and member) access,
1. Go to *Navigator >> Administer >> Dimensions*.
2. While in the Dimension Editor for Account, click the parent member whose descendants users will need access to. I'm first going to grant access to Account member *4001*:

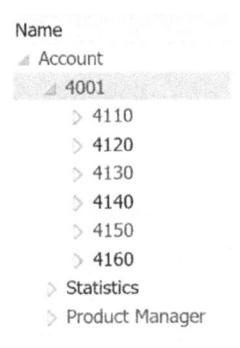

```
Name
▲ Account
   ▲ 4001
      > 4110
      > 4120
      > 4130
      > 4140
      > 4150
      > 4160
   > Statistics
   > Product Manager
```

3. Click the *Assign Access* icon:

4. Open the *Groups* tab.
5. Click the *Add icon*.
6. Select the *Vision Planner* group:

7. Click the radio button for *Write* and select *Descendants (inclusive)* from the drop-down menu:

8. Click *Add*.

Security for the 4001 member is complete.

9. Using the steps above, complete metadata security according to the following table:

Member	Security Access	Group / User
Account – 4001, Statistics, Product Manager	Write – Descendants (inclusive)	Group: Vision Planner
Account – 4110	Read – Member	Group: Vision Planner
Account – 4120	Read – Member	Group: Vision Planner
Account – Average Price	Read – Member	Group: Vision Planner
Entity – 410	Write – Descendants (inclusive)	Group: International Sales Grp
Entity – 405	Write – Descendants (inclusive)	Users: Elaine, Larry
Scenario – Plan, Forecast	Write – Member	Group: Vision Planner
Scenario – Actual	Read – Member	Group: Vision Planner
Version – Pass1, Pass2, Final	Write – Member	Group: Vision Planner

Access must be granted to the Account, Entity, Scenario, and Version dimensions. Why isn't security assigned by Periods or Years? All users have access to all periods and years. You control write access for periods by defining the Start Yr., Start Period, End Yr., and End Period in the Scenario dimension.

You'll notice that certain account members such as 4110 and 4120 have Read access for Planner rather than Write access. This is because those accounts have member formulas that calculate the value and I don't want any users inputting data where it should be calculated.

In a few cases above, I assigned access to a specific user. A better design principle would be to use a security group instead like I did for the International Sales group.

> **Note!** Security cannot be edited for the Sandboxes Version members (children for this member are created by users).

By now you're familiar with refreshing the database to save changes to Essbase. The security information you've just assigned is only stored in the relational database. The refresh to Essbase will create security filters required for the Essbase database. Essbase must be in sync with the security information stored in the underlying Enterprise Planning Cloud relational repository.

10. Refresh the database by going to *Console >> Actions >> Refresh Database*.

> **Note!** Service Administrators will always have access to everything, therefore, access does not need to be granted again.

ASSIGN FORM ACCESS

You can assign security at the form folder or individual data form level. All data forms will inherit the form folder security definition, so if you can apply security there it is definitely more efficient to do so.

To assign form folder or data form access,
1. Go to *Navigator >> Administer >> Forms*.
2. Assign access to either the *Forms* or *Vision Users* folder. Assign *Read* access to the "Vision Planner" group:

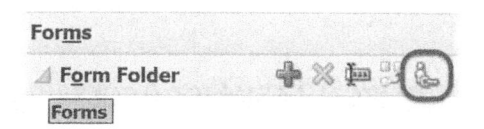

You can also apply security at the form level. If you need to assign unique data form security, select the form and click :

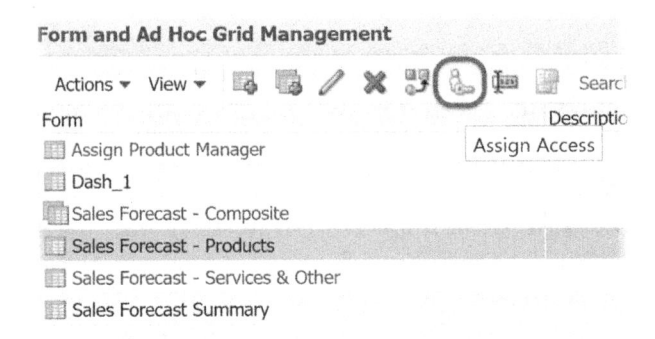

Form and Ad Hoc Grid Management

Assign Access

Open the *Groups* tab and assign the correct access. *Read* access will allow users to view the form. *Write* access will allow the user to change the data form definition and layout if they are provisioned as a Power User role in My Services.

ASSIGN BUSINESS RULE ACCESS

To assign business rule access to the Planner role,
1. Go to *Navigator >> Administer >> Rules Security*.
2. Click the Business Folder *CalcMgrRules* and click :

3. Grant *Launch* access to the "Vision Planner" group.

You will assign either *Launch* or *No Launch* access. You can apply security at the individual business rule level. If you need to assign unique business rule security, select the desired rule and assign the appropriate access using the steps above.

ASSIGN TASK LIST ACCESS

To assign task list access,

1. Go to *Navigate >> Administer >> Tasks*.
2. Highlight the desired Task List and click:

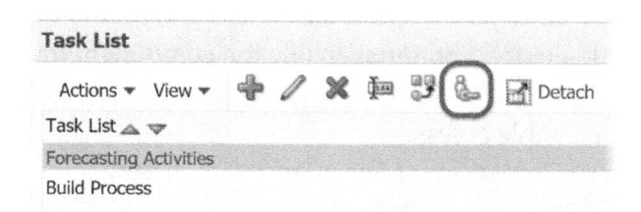

```
Task List
   Actions ▼  View ▼  ✚  ✎  ✖  ▦  ▦  (👤)  ▦ Detach
   Task List ▲ ▼
   Forecasting Activities
   Build Process
```

3. Grant the *Assigned* access to the "Vision Planner" group:

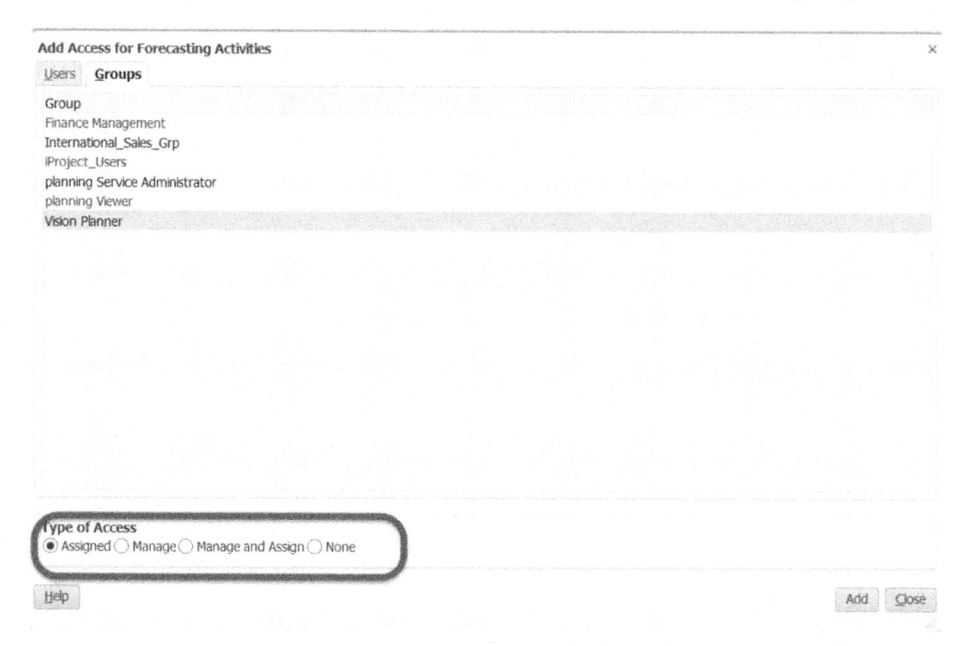

```
Add Access for Forecasting Activities                                    ✖
  Users  Groups
  Group
  Finance Management
  International_Sales_Grp
  iProject_Users
  planning Service Administrator
  planning Viewer
  Vision Planner




  Type of Access
  ⦿ Assigned ◯ Manage ◯ Manage and Assign ◯ None

  Help                                                          Add    Close
```

4. Click *Add*.

Assigned access allows users to view and follow the task list. *Manage* allows the user to update the task list, adding new tasks, removing tasks or setting due dates. *Manage and Assign* lets the user both use and manage the task list. You can also remove security (if inherited) by using *None* access.

ALLOW TABLET ACCESS

Forms, Tasks, and Rules are not available on mobile or tablet devices by default. If you want to allow users to access a form, task, or rule on a mobile device, you must enable the component for tablet access.

To enable table access,
1. Go to *Navigator >> Manage >> Tablet Access*.
2. Click to assign a form with tablet access:

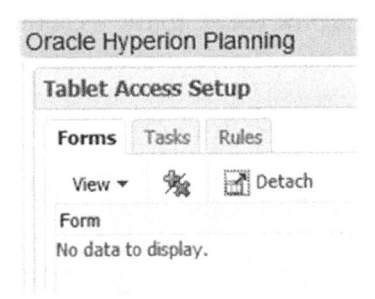

3. Select the desired forms and click *OK*:

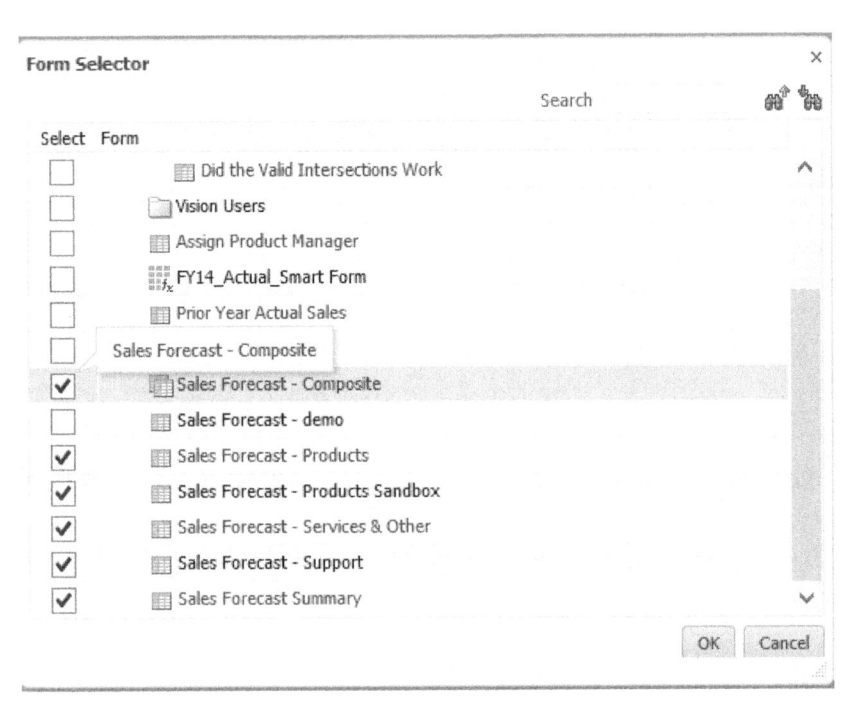

Look Smarter Than You Are with Enterprise Planning Cloud 377

4. Select the *Tasks* tab and repeat the steps to select the *Forecasting Activities* tasks for tablet access.
5. Select the *Rules* tab and repeat the steps to select all business rules for tablet access.

And those are the steps to give users access to the application!

LOG ENTRY: SOL 20, Entry 1

I think I'm done. Done.

Looking back to when I thought the project would die and what I've accomplished since then. It was actually pretty easy. Much easier than saying being stranded on Mars.

Now how do I let the folks back on Earth know that the sales forecasting application is ready?

Meanwhile, back on earth…

After the webcast, Rockstar i.n.t.e.r.R.e.l. Consultant Cathy Son stared at the ceiling, monitoring Cloud access. Implementing EPM solutions at i.n.t.e.r.R.e.l had sounded exciting when Director Glen Chang had recruited her out of school. But it turns out the Cloud monitors itself. Her job turned out to be sending emails.

As she scrolled through the logs, she saw something that made her heart stop. A login for roske@interrel.com. But that project was dead! However if he logged into the Cloud, that could only mean one thing. The project was still alive and Edward was trying to implement in the Cloud.

"I need Director Glen Chang's contact information now," she thought to herself. Director Chang was in charge of i.n.t.e.r.R.e.l operations and would know what to do next.

Chapter 9: Automate & Migrate

> LOG ENTRY: SOL 20, Entry 2
>
> While I'm trying to figure out how to communicate with Vision and i.n.t.e.r.r.e.l., I guess I'll go ahead and automate some of the Enterprise Planning Cloud processes.

JOB SCHEDULER

The Enterprise Planning Cloud Simplified UI has a Job Scheduler to run many of the Enterprise Planning Cloud jobs (now or at a future time). Job Scheduler is not available in the Workspace UI.

Supported jobs include:

- **Launch Business Rule** – run a business rule
- **Import Data** – import data with the Simplified Planning UI
- **Import Metadata** – import metadata with the Simplified Planning UI
- **Export Data** – export data with the Simplified Planning UI
- **Export Metadata** – export metadata with the Simplified Planning UI
- **Refresh the Database** – refresh the database, pushing changes from UI to the underlying Essbase databases
- **Plan Type Map** – execute the map to reporting feature, pushing data from one plan type to another

To schedule a job within Enterprise Planning Cloud, you must first save tasks as jobs. As an example, I will save an Export Data task as a job. Data files must also be uploaded into the Inbox / Outbox for some tasks (you can automate this step with EPM Automate; more on this in just a moment).

Save Tasks as Jobs

I'm going to create a job that exports the Product Manager assignments from Enterprise Planning Cloud.

To create and save a job,
1. Back in the Home screen, navigate to *Console >> Application*. A majority of the jobs that can be scheduled will be found in the *Actions* menu of the Overview, Plan Types and Dimensions tabs.
2. Go to *Actions >> Export Data*:

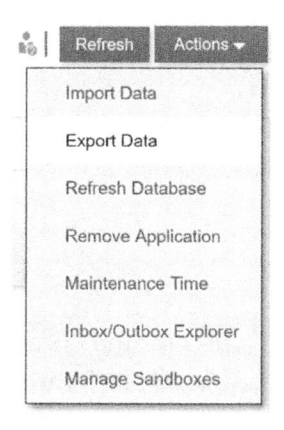

```
Refresh    Actions ▼
           Import Data
           Export Data
           Refresh Database
           Remove Application
           Maintenance Time
           Inbox/Outbox Explorer
           Manage Sandboxes
```

3. Click *Create* and the following window will display:

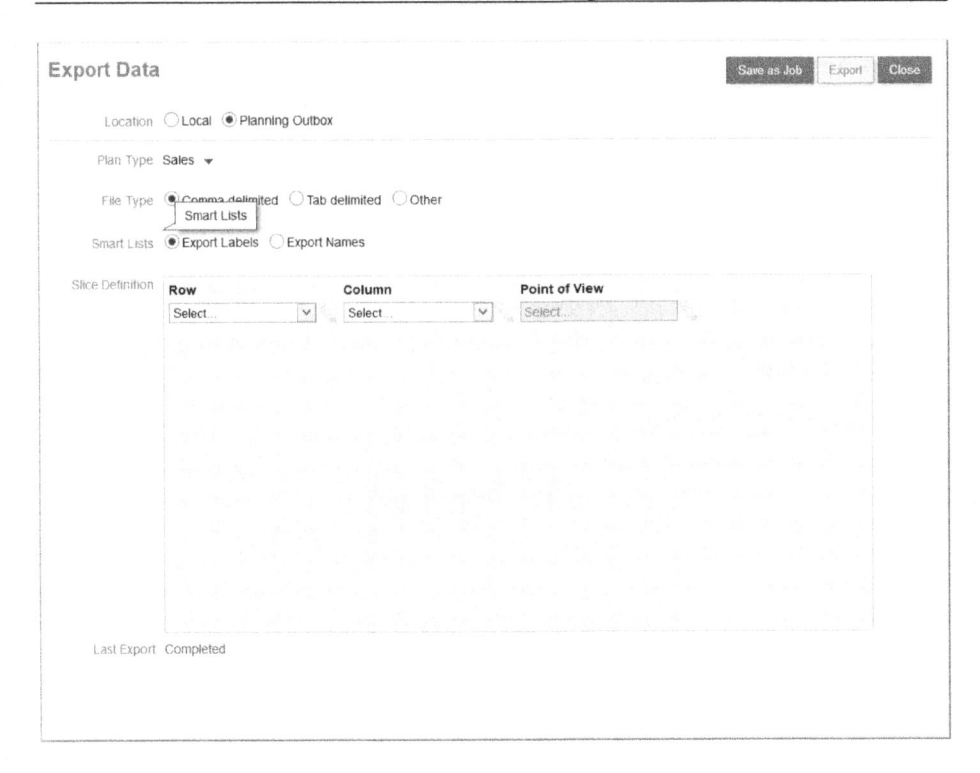

4. Select *Planning Outbox* for the Location (this is a requirement if you want to schedule this task through Job Scheduler).

Local will allow immediate save of the file to your local computer. *Planning Outbox* will place the file in the Enterprise Planning Cloud Inbox / Outbox.

5. Select the desired plan type to export data from. Choose the *Sales* plan type.
6. Choose the delimiter and for Smart Lists, whether you want export the names or the labels. Select *Comma delimited* and *Export Labels*.
7. Complete the Slice Definition section. Here, select dimensions and members for the Row, Column, and POV:
    a. **Rows**: Level 0 Products
    b. **Columns**: Product Manager for Account
    c. **POV**: Level 0 members under YearTotal
    d. **POV**: Basedata

Look Smarter Than You Are with Enterprise Planning Cloud   381

    e. **POV**: FY15
    f. **POV**: Plan
    g. **POV**: Pass1
    h. **POV**: The Entity "0" which is located in *Total Entity >> TD*):

8. Click *Save as Job*.
9. From this screen, you can select the task to edit (e.g., select *Export Product Manager* and you can update the export task parameters and member selections):

Now that the task job has been created, I am ready to schedule it!

Schedule a Job

To schedule a job,

1. Go to *Console* >> *Jobs*. You will see any upcoming jobs along with recently run jobs.
2. Click *Schedule Jobs*:

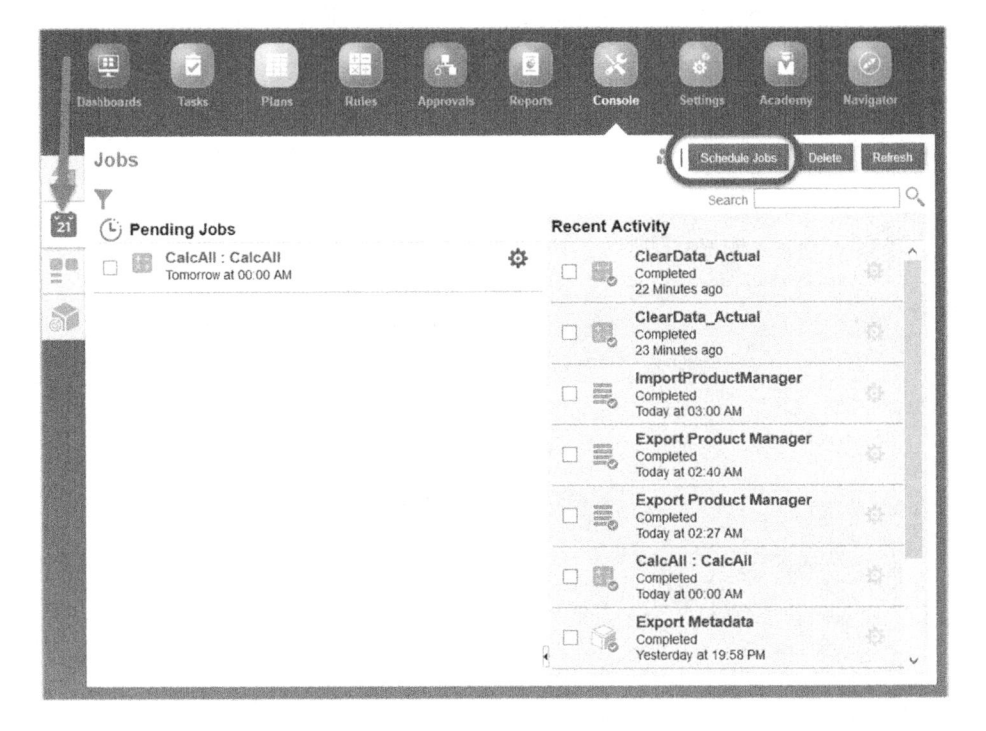

3. Below is a list of available jobs types. Click the radio button for *Export Data*:

4. Click *Next*. Enter the scheduled job parameters:

Look Smarter Than You Are with Enterprise Planning Cloud 383

a. When do you want to run the job? Run now or schedule to start from a selected day and time.
b. How often do you want to run the job? Define a name, reoccurrence pattern, and optional end date:

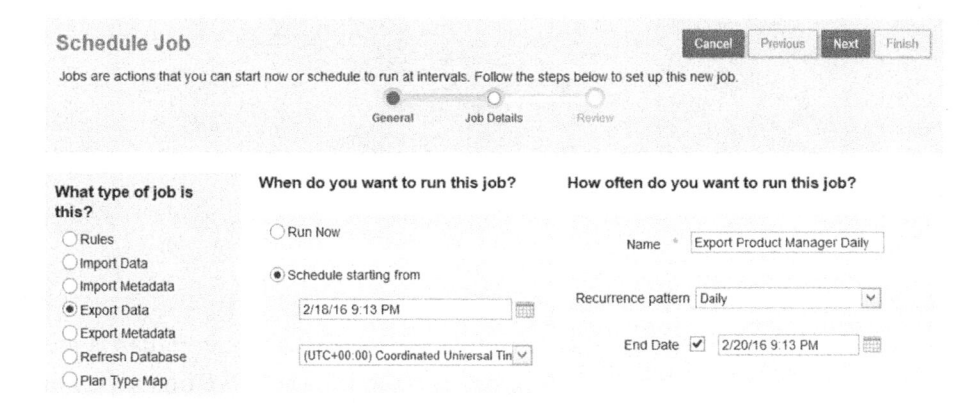

5. Click *Next*.
6. Select the Export Data job to schedule. Highlight the *Export Product Manager* job that I created in the Simplified UI:

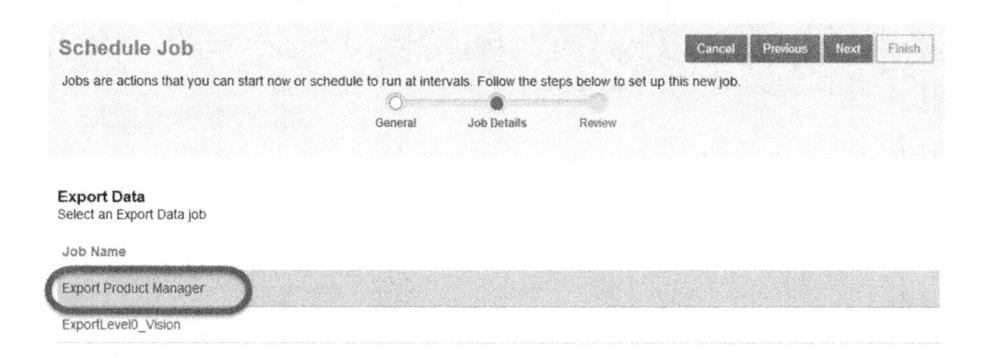

7. Click *Next*.
8. Review and click *Finish*:

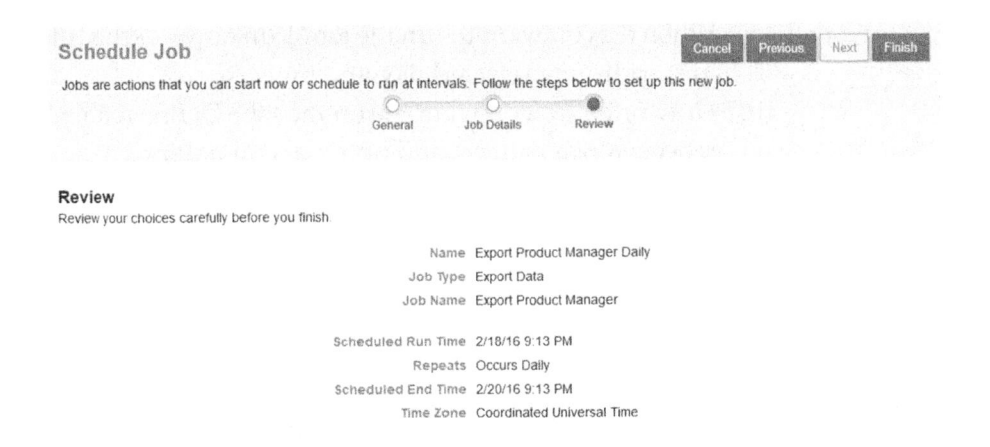

384   Chapter 9: Automate & Migrate

Schedule Job

Jobs are actions that you can start now or schedule to run at intervals. Follow the steps below to set up this new job.

General — Job Details — **Review**

Review
Review your choices carefully before you finish.

Name	Export Product Manager Daily
Job Type	Export Data
Job Name	Export Product Manager
Scheduled Run Time	2/18/16 9:13 PM
Repeats	Occurs Daily
Scheduled End Time	2/20/16 9:13 PM
Time Zone	Coordinated Universal Time

Job Console

As I mentioned earlier, from the Job Console, you can view pending and recently run jobs. Jobs are retained in the Job Console for 90 days. You will see jobs from the scheduler along with other non-scheduled jobs from Enterprise Planning Cloud activity (remember in the Workspace UI, I used to get to the Job Console via *Tools >> Job Console*):

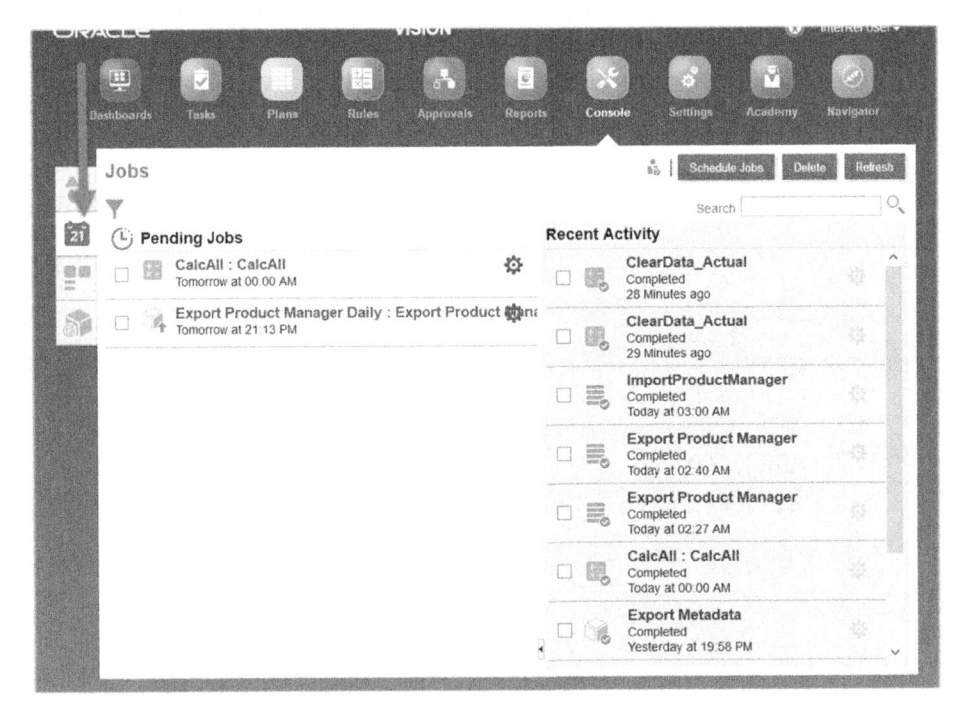

Look Smarter Than You Are with Enterprise Planning Cloud 385

Select any job in the Recent Activity pane to view the details including the job type, who it was run by, status, start and end times, and some other job specific details (e.g., if it was an Export Data job, you would see how many records were read and written and also be able to download the exported data file). You can also change the level of messages that you see:

You can filter jobs by using the *Filter* icon:

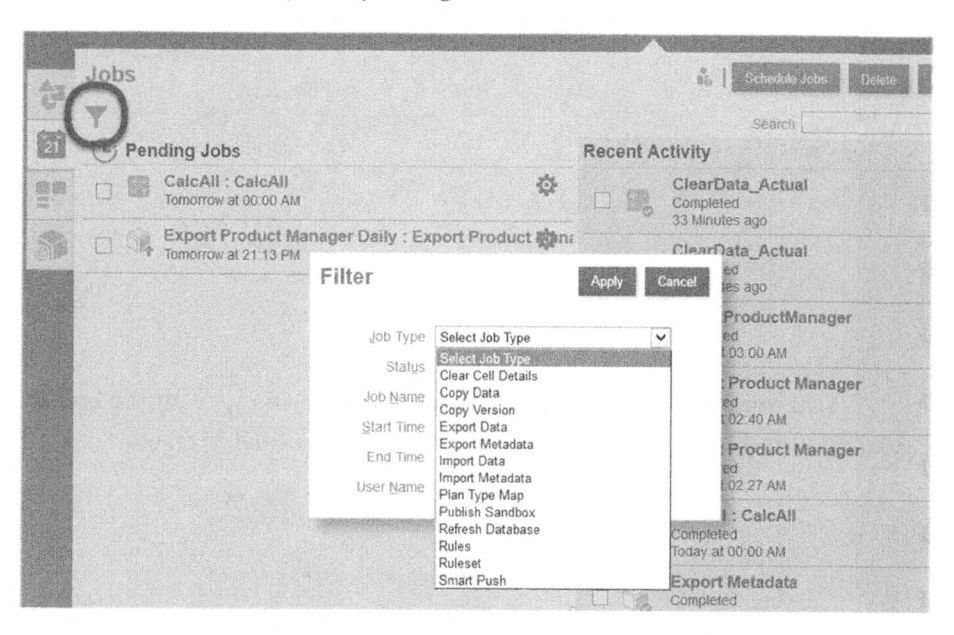

Note! You'll see a lot more job types here in the filter than what you are allowed to schedule.

I'll choose to filter Job Type by Rules and I see all of the recently run Business Rules from Enterprise Planning Cloud (which were run from the UI and not scheduled). The big thing to remember is that the Job

Console will show you both scheduled jobs and jobs run from Enterprise Planning Cloud Simplified UI:

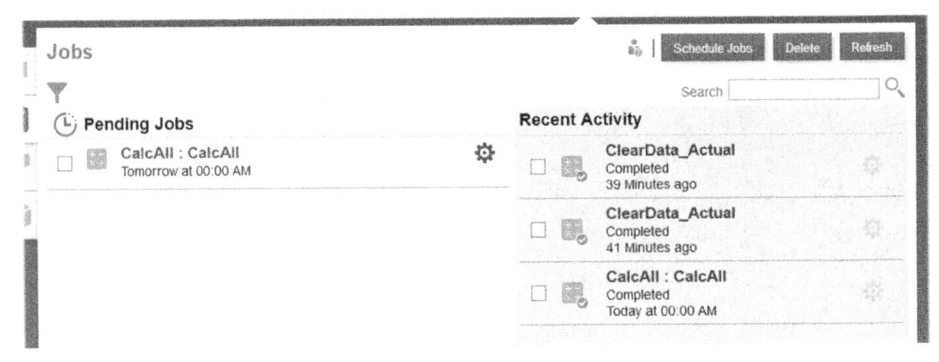

You can also search the Job Console activity. In my example below, I searched for all jobs containing a reference to "Product Manager":

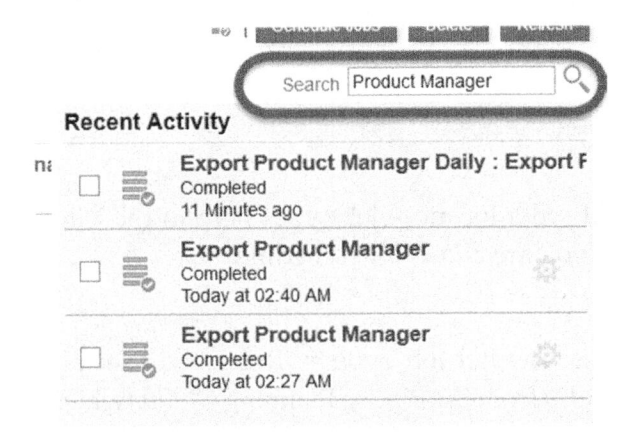

You can manage, edit, and delete jobs from the Job Console.

You also have the option to cancel Rules and RuleSets Jobs if they are in a processing state. You cannot cancel import, export, mapping, or refresh jobs.

Inbox / Outbox Explorer

You can export, upload, and download files to the Inbox / Outbox Explorer, a central place where files are stored within the Enterprise Planning Cloud application. To access the Inbox / Outbox Explorer, go to *Console >> Application >> Actions >> Inbox / Outbox Explorer*:

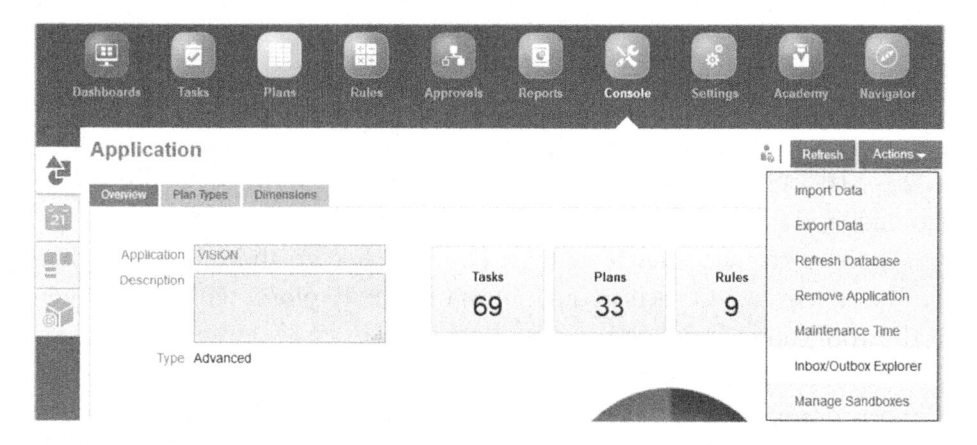

Note! The Inbox / Outbox Explorer is only available in the Simplified UI.

The Inbox / Outbox Explorer will display with any currently uploaded files:

Inbox/Outbox Explorer

Type	Name	Last Modified	Size	Actions
ZIP	Export Product Manager.zip	2/18/16 9:17 PM	1.0 KB	⚙
CSV	Actual_Dollars_FY14.csv	1/18/16 5:56 PM	7.1 KB	⚙
ZIP	ExportLevel0_Vision.zip	2/16/16 11:50 PM	5.0 KB	⚙
	SalesRpt_Export_Data	2/15/16 11:24 PM	399.5 KB	⚙
CSV	ProductManagerLoad.csv	2/18/16 2:53 AM	13.6 KB	⚙
XML	epmapplicationsnapshot.xml	2/18/16 8:13 AM	2.2 KB	⚙
TXT	VisionForecastDataExport2.txt	2/15/16 9:30 PM	295.6 KB	⚙
	VISION_EXPORT	1/27/16 3:35 AM	0.1 KB	⚙

To upload a file, simply click *Upload* and browse to the file to upload, and to download a file, go to *Actions >> Download File*.

You can also delete files (it is good to keep the Inbox / Outbox Explorer "clean"). Objects in the Inbox / Outbox Explorer will remain even if the application is deleted.

Calculation Manager will place files here if you use the Data Export command within a rule to export a slice of data. The syntax for this type of rule looks like the following (see the Business Rule section for more detail):

```
DATAEXPORT "File" ","
"/u03/lcm/VisionForecastDataExport2.txt" "NULL";
```

The complete rule looks as follows:

```
FIX ("BaseData")
SET DataExportOptions
{
            DataExportLevel "ALL";
             DataExportColFormat ON;
              DataExportColHeader "Account";
             DataExportDynamicCalc ON;

     DataExportOverwriteFile ON;
                         DataExportDimHeader OFF
             };
FIX("Forecast", "Actual",
@Relative("Years",0),
@Relative("Entity",0),
@Relative("Product",0),
"BegBalance":"Dec",
"Units",
@Relative("4001",0),
"4001",
@Relative("Version",0))

DATAEXPORT "File" ","
"/u03/lcm/VisionForecastDataExport2.txt" "NULL";

ENDFIX
ENDFIX
```

Data Management also uses the Inbox / Outbox Explorer to place export files when exporting data from an Enterprise Planning Cloud plan type.

So if I can automate jobs with Enterprise Planning Cloud using the Job Scheduler, why would I ever need a utility like EPM Automate? Job Scheduler can automate tasks within Enterprise Planning Cloud but if you need to create a complete lights out script that requires upload of files or download of files or scripting a series of steps together (e.g., upload data file, load data file, calculate data, export data, download file), you have to use EPM Automate.

EPM AUTOMATE

EPM Automate is the automation utility of Enterprise Planning Cloud (and other Cloud products) that allows the Administrator to remotely perform many administrative tasks. Administrators create scripts using the utility that can then be automated using the Windows Scheduler. You must be a Service Administrator to run the EPM Automate Utility.

> **Note!** EPM Automate is only supported on 64-bit operating systems.

The following tasks can be scripted and executed with EPM Automate:

- Import and export metadata and data
- Refresh the application
- Run business rules
- Copy data from one database to another
- Upload file into the Enterprise Planning Cloud Inbox / Outbox Explorer
- Upload file into Data Management folders
- Run a Data Management rule or batch and get the output log file
- Download files from the Inbox / Outbox and from Data Management folders
- Export and import application and artifact snapshots using Application Management
- List the files in the Inbox / Outbox
- Delete files from the Inbox / Outbox
- Take a snapshot of the entire instance
- Run a provisioning report
- Run an audit report to see who has logged in and for how long
- Update substitution variables

Install EPM Automate via the Enterprise Planning Cloud Simplified UI by going to *Navigator >> Install >> EPM Automate* (separate links for Windows and Linux / Unix).

You may install multiple instances of EPM Automate (especially if you need to run tasks in Production and Pre-Production at the same time). If you need to do this, execute the utility from separate directories:

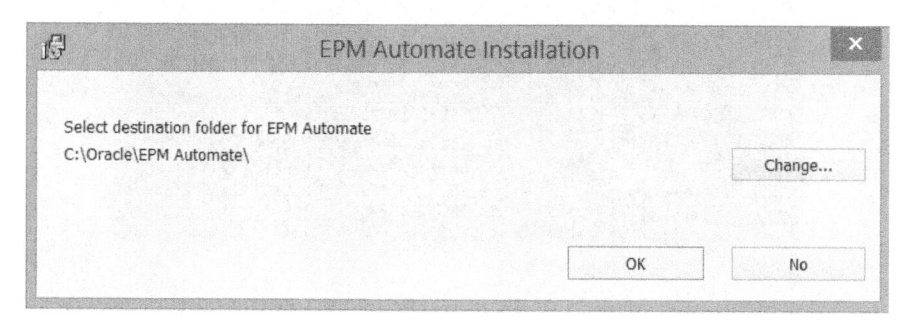

EPM Automate Installation

Select destination folder for EPM Automate
C:\Oracle\EPM Automate\

[Change...]   [OK]   [No]

Launch the EPM Automate client on your computer and log in. Use the following as a guideline for logging in:

```
C:\Oracle\EPM Automate\bin>epmautomate login username password PBCSURL domain
```

Note! To receive guidance directly from the tool, type "epmautomate help" and press *Enter*. You can also use this in conjunction with specific commands. For example, for help logging in you can type "epmautomate login help".

Type "epmautomate listcommands" to see the entire list of tasks possible:

```
List of all EPM Automate commands:

login              Log in to a service instan
logout             Log out of the service ins
uploadfile         Upload a file into a Data
downloadfile       Download a file from a Dat
importdata         Import data from a file in
exportdata         Export application data in
refreshcube        Refresh the Planning appli
runbusinessrule    Launch a business rule
listfile           List the files in the Plan
deletefile         Delete a file or applicati
folder
exportsnapshot     Repeat a previous export
importsnapshot     Import the contents of a
importmetadata     Import metadata from a fil
exportmetadata     Export Planning applicatio
runplantypemap     Copy data from a BSO to an
```

To automate tasks, create a script to run commands and use the Windows Task Scheduler to schedule them.

Where Do I Put the Data Files?

Files that are used to import / export data and metadata are placed in the Simplified UI Inbox / Outbox Explorer. Files uploaded to the Data Management Inbox and Outbox are accessible in Data Management (not in the Simplified UI Inbox / Outbox). One thing that is a little confusing is that if you create a data load rule in Data Management to export data from an EPM application, that export file will be placed in the Simplified UI Inbox / Outbox. Application Snapshots created using EPM Automate are stored in the Application Snapshots node of Application Management.

Note! On Windows-based machines, the EPM Automate commands are not case sensitive. In addition, quotes are not necessary unless spaces are used in the directory / file names.

EPM Automate Commands

Command	Description	Syntax and Parameters
help	List supported commands or display information on specific command	epmautomate help
encrypt	Uses AES to encrypt password and store it in a file (one time process)	epmautomate encrypt PASSWORD KEY PASSWORD FILE
login	Log into Enterprise Planning Cloud	epmautomate login USERNAME PASSWORD URL IDENTITYDOMAIN
logout	Logout of Enterprise Planning Cloud	epmautomate logout
uploadfile	Upload file from local computer to Planning Simplified UI Inbox / Outbox	epmautomate uploadfile *"DIRECTORY/DATAFILE"* epmautomate uploadfile "C:/pbcsdat/monthlydata.csv"
uploadfile	Upload file from local computer to Data Management folder; you add the [DATA_MANAGEMENT_FOLDER] parameter at the end	epmautomate uploadfile *"DIRECTORY/DATAFILE"* [DATA_MANAGEMENT_FOLDER] epmautomate uploadfile "C:/DataManagementdat/monthlydata.csv" inbox/repository

Command	Description	Syntax and Parameters
downloadfile	Download file from the Planning Simplified UI Inbox / Outbox	epmautomate downloadfile "FILE_NAME" epmautomate downloadfile "ExportProductManager.zip"
downloadfile	Download file from Data Management folder	epmautomate downloadfile "[FILE_PATH]/FILE_NAME" epmautomate downloadfile outbox.csv
importmetadata	Import metadata from Inbox / Outbox into the Enterprise Planning Cloud application using a Planning Job Filenames must match file names in the job OR follow this format "metadata_DIMENSIONNAME.csv"	epmautomate importmetadata JOB_NAME [FILE_NAME] epmautomate importmetadata importAccount importAccount.zip

Command	Description	Syntax and Parameters
exportmetadata	Export metadata to Inbox / Outbox into the Enterprise Planning Cloud application using a Planning Job; Will export in ZIP file only	epmautomate exportmetadata epmautomate exportmetadata dailyAccountexport Accountexport.ZIP
refreshcube	Refresh the database	epmautomate refreshcube
importdata	Import data from Inbox / Outbox into the Enterprise Planning Cloud application using a Planning Job Filenames can be ZIP, CSV For Essbase Cloud format, use TXT	epmautomate importdata JOB_NAME [FILE_NAME] epmautomate importdata dailydataload dailydata.zip
exportdata	Export data to Inbox / Outbox into the Enterprise Planning Cloud application using a Planning Job; Will export in ZIP file only	epmautomate exportdata JOB_NAME [FILE_NAME] epmautomate exportdata dailydataexport dailyData.zip

Command	Description	Syntax and Parameters
rundatarule	Run Data Management load rule; Valid import modes are: APPEND, REPLACE, NON Valid export modes are: STORE_DATA, ADD_DATA, SUBTRACT_DATA, REPLACE_DATA, NONE	epmautomate rundatarule RULE_NAME START_PERIO DEND_PERIOD IMPORT_M ODE EXPORT_MODE [FILE_ NAME] *Multi-period* *Import*: epmautomate rundatarule VisionActual Mar-15 Jun-15 REPLACE STORE_DATA inbox/Vision/GLActual.dat *Single-period* *Import*: epmautomate rundatarule "Vision Actual" Mar-15 Mar-15 REPLACE STORE_DATA inbox/Vision/GLActual.dat
runbatch	Run Data Management batch	epmautomate runbatch BATCH_NAME
runbusinessrule	Run business rule; Optionally define values for run time prompts using PARAMETER	epmautomate runbusinessrule RULE_NAME [PARAMETER = VALUE]
runplantypemap	Runs a Planning job to copy data from one plan type to another	epmautomate runplantypemap JOBNAME [clearData=true l false]

Command	Description	Syntax and Parameters
listfiles	List file in Planning simplified UI Inbox / Outbox	epmautomate listfiles
deletefile	Delete a file from Planning simplified UI Inbox / Outbox	epmautomate deletefile FILE_NAME
exportsnapshot	Export a previously run snapshot to create snapshot in Application Management	epmautomate exportsnapshot SNAPSHOT_NAME
importsnapshot	Imports a snapshot into the instance, updating / overwriting artifacts	epmautomate importsnapshot
resetservice	If you see severe performance issues, this command will restart the service instance	epmautomate resetservice
feedback	Send feedback to oracle	epmautomate feedback "comment"
recreate	CAUTION – this will restore service to a clean slate and delete everything!	epmautomate recreate-f

EPM Automate Status Codes

EPM Automate will return a status code of a particular operation. You are looking for "0"!

0	Operation completed without errors
1	Operation failed to execute because of an error
2	Cancel pending
3	Operation is terminated by the user
4	Incorrect parameters
5	Insufficient privileges
6	Service is not available
7	Invalid command
8	Invalid parameter
9	Invalid user name, password or identity domain
10	Expired password
11	Service is not available

Now that I've introduced EPM Automate, I'm ready to write some scripts! To follow along, I will be using the Windows version. Check out the Oracle documentation for details on Linux scripting.

Encrypt the Password

First I want to encrypt my password and create a password file. To do this,

1. Launch EPM Automate (go to *Start >> Programs >> EPM Automate* or launch a DOS command prompt).
2. The EPM Automate screen will display:

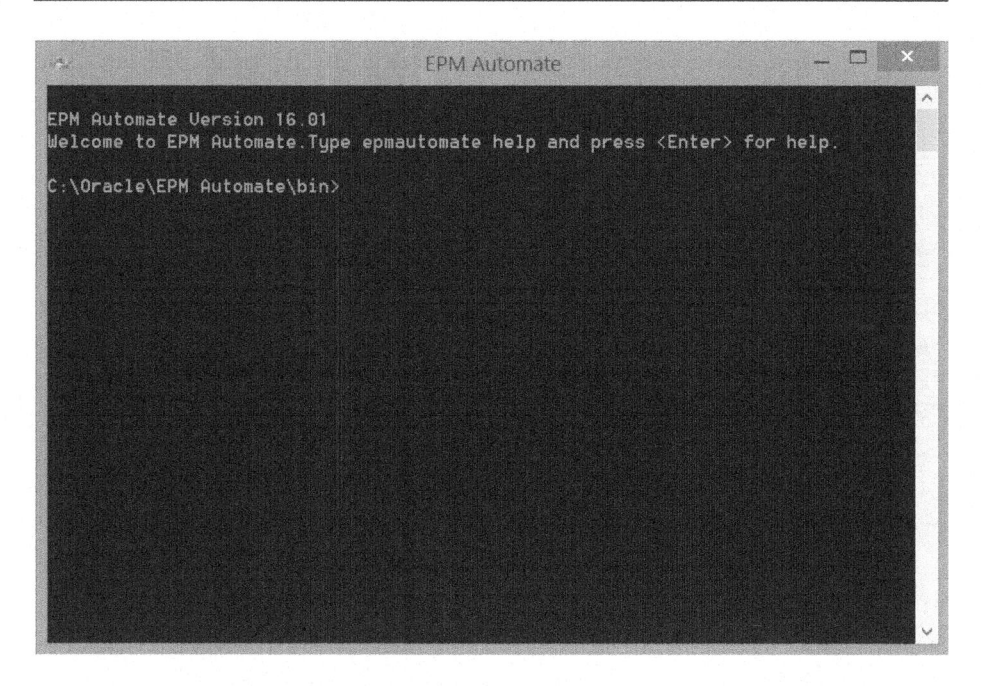

[Screenshot of EPM Automate command prompt showing:
EPM Automate Version 16.01
Welcome to EPM Automate. Type epmautomate help and press <Enter> for help.
C:\Oracle\EPM Automate\bin>]

3. I can optionally navigate to any desired directory where I plan to perform operations. I will stay here in the *Oracle\EPM Automate\bin* directory.
4. Type "epmautomate encrypt *password* myKey C:\EPMAutomateFiles\password.epw":

[Screenshot showing:
C:\Oracle\EPM Automate\bin>epmautomate encrypt H······3 myKey C:\EPMAutomateFiles\password.epw
encrypt completed successfully]

Automate a Planning Job

I just reviewed how to create a Planning job in the previous section. Many EPM Automate Utility commands require jobs to be created within the application such as import data jobs, export of data jobs, and "Plan Type Map" jobs (aka, copy data from one plan type to another).

To automate an Enterprise Planning Cloud job,
1. In the EPM Automate interface, type the following using your own username, domain, Enterprise Planning Cloud URL, and file name (step by step is recommended). Remember the first

line of the script should be all one line through the identity domain:

```
epmautomate login ServiceAdmin
C:\EPMAutomateFiles\password.epw PBCSURL
myIdentityDomain

epmautomate exportdata ExportProductManager
epmautomate listfiles
epmautomate downloadfile ExportProductManager.zip
epmautomate logout
```

Note in the above example, you should have no character returns in the first three lines.

This will execute the ExportProductManager job and place the file in your EPM Automate / Bin folder.

Now let's compare Job Scheduler and EPM Automate. Note that the Job Scheduler allows me to automate the export of the Product Manager data just as EPM Automate Utility did. The difference is the EPM Automate Utility has additional commands that will allow you to download the exported file (to be picked up by another process if dictated by requirements):

Name	Date modified	Type	Size
.prefs	2/21/2016 9:07 AM	PREFS File	1 KB
epmautomate.bat	12/17/2015 7:40 A...	Windows Batch File	2 KB
ExportProductManager.zip	2/21/2016 9:06 AM	zip Archive	2 KB

2. Save the syntax / commands as a script batch file in the *C:\Oracle\EPM Automate\bin* directory:

Look Smarter Than You Are with Enterprise Planning Cloud 401

Name	Date modified	Type	Size
.prefs	2/21/2016 9:07 AM	PREFS File	1 KB
epmautomate.bat	12/17/2015 7:40 A...	Windows Batch File	2 KB
ExportProductManager.zip	2/21/2016 9:06 AM	zip Archive	2 KB
exportproductmanager_script.bat	2/21/2016 9:47 AM	Windows Batch File	1 KB
Vision_Actual_FY17.csv	2/16/2016 4:34 PM	Microsoft Excel Co...	16 KB

```
epmautomate login         @interrel.com C:\EPMAutomateFiles\password.epw https://planning-
epmautomate exportdata ExportProductManager
epmautomate listfiles
epmautomate downloadfile ExportProductManager.zip
epmautomate logout
```

Automate a Nightly Process

Now let's take things up a notch by creating a more robust script. Here is an example of what an entire nightly process script might look like: logging in, updating a dimension, refreshing the cube, loading data, running a business rule, and then logging out.

```
@echo off
REM Nightly script for EPM Automate
REM Created by: interRel Consulting
REM Created on: March 9, 2016

SET url=https://servicename-
domain.pbcs.usx.oraclecloud.com
SET user=admin
SET pwd=C:\EPMAutomateFiles\password.epw
SET domain=MyServicesDomain
SET returnvalue=0

ECHO Logging In
call epmautomate login %user% %pwd% %url% %domain%
@echo off
IF %ERRORLEVEL% NEQ 0 (
echo Login failed with error %ERRORLEVEL%.
goto :END
)

ECHO Updating Product dimension
call epmautomate importmetadata ImportProduct
@echo off
IF %ERRORLEVEL% NEQ 0 (
echo Product dimension failed with error
%ERRORLEVEL%.
goto :END
)

ECHO Refresh cube
call epmautomate refreshcube RefreshCube
@echo off
IF %ERRORLEVEL% NEQ 0 (
echo Refresh cube failed with error %ERRORLEVEL%.
goto :END
)

ECHO Load sales data
call epmautomate importdata LoadSalesFY16
@echo off
IF %ERRORLEVEL% NEQ 0 (
echo Loading of sales data failed with error
%ERRORLEVEL%.
```

```
goto :END
)

ECHO Run CalcAll business rule
call epmautomate runbusinessrule CalcAll
planType=Sales
@echo off
IF %ERRORLEVEL% NEQ 0 (
echo Run business rule failed with error
%ERRORLEVEL%.
goto :END
)

ECHO Logging Out
call epmautomate logout
@echo off
IF %ERRORLEVEL% NEQ 0 (
echo Logout failed with error %ERRORLEVEL%.
goto :END
)

:END
ECHO Return code: %ERRORLEVEL%
SET returnValue=%ERRORLEVEL%
EXIT /B %returnValue%
```

This script is based on the Oracle documentation and is written for MS-DOS batch. Statements like "REM" are used for commenting the code, "SET" creates and assigns variables, and "ECHO" writes comments out to the command window / log file. Special statements for error trapping (e.g., "IF %ERRORLEVEL% NEQ 0...") have also been included to show a more realistic example. This script uses variables (e.g., %user%) to make maintenance easier. It is called by another file in order to capture the actions to a log file that can be reviewed after the fact. The following steps will cover the basics of the each EPM Automate command.

I need to set up the objects referenced from the EPM Automate commands. Most formal processes called by this script, such as importing metadata, refreshing the cube, and loading data, require an official job in Enterprise Planning Cloud.

I'll set up these jobs in order. First, I'll upload all the files that I'll need to run these jobs.

To upload job files,
1. Navigate to *Console* >> *Actions* >> *Inbox / Outbox Explorer*.
2. I have not previously uploaded the Product dimension source file, so I'm going to upload it now.
3. Click *Upload*.

Note! In order to save metadata and data imports as jobs, the source files must be located in the Planning Inbox. Refreshed files can be uploaded through EPM Automate.

4. Browse to the local file, select it, and then click *Upload File*.
5. Now I need to upload the FY16 Actuals data file. Repeat the previous two steps to upload this data file as well.
6. *Close* out of the Inbox / Outbox Explorer.

Next, I'll set up the "ImportProduct" job, which updates the Product dimension by importing metadata for it.

To set up a job,
1. Navigate to *Console* >> *Application* >> *Dimensions*.
2. Click *Import*.
3. Click *Create*.
4. Select *Planning Inbox* at the top of the screen since the file is already on the server.

Location ○ Local ● Planning Inbox

5. Next to the Products dimension, select a delimiter type – in my case I'll keep the default of *Comma delimited* since my file is of CSV type.
6. Type in the name of the newly uploaded file on the server.

Product
27 Members | Product.csv | ● Comma delimited

7. Ignore the option to the right to *Clear Members*. This option would clear the members first, prior to uploading the new metadata file.

This step is recommended if there are significant changes to the sort order and it's OK to delete the data associated with any deleted members.

8. Click *Save as Job* to save this import as a formal job process.
9. Name the job. I'm going to call this "ImportProduct".
10. Keep the option to *Refresh Database if Import Metadata is successful* unchecked.

This option will refresh the dimension within the underlying Essbase database only if the metadata import is successful. I'm going to handle this in a separate step in EPM Automate.

11. Click *Save* and then *OK* at the confirmation window.
12. *Close* out of the screen and you'll see the new job listed in the Import Metadata screen.
13. *Close* out of this screen as well.

Now I need to create the job to refresh the Essbase cube,
1. Navigate to *Actions >> Refresh Database*.
2. Click *Create* to create a new process.
3. Now select the options that relate to actions before and after the refresh. This is job-dependent. I have made the following selections:

Refresh Database

Before Refresh Database

Enable Use of the Application for
○ All users ⦿ Administrators

☑ Log off all users

☑ Kill all active requests

After Refresh Database

Enable Use of the Application for
⦿ All users ○ Administrators

4. Click *Save as Job*.
5. Name the job. I'm going to call this "RefreshCube":

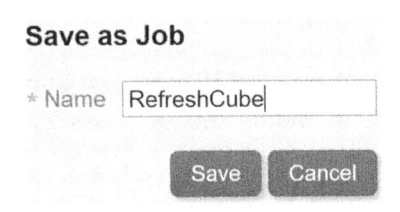

Save as Job

* Name RefreshCube

Save   Cancel

6. Click *Save*.
7. Click *OK* at the confirmation window.
8. Click *Close* and then *Close* again.

Next, I need to create one last job to load data.
1. Navigate to *Actions >> Import Data*.
2. Click *Create*.
3. Change the location at the top to *Planning Inbox*.

Note! In order to save a data import as a job, the source file must be located in the Planning inbox.

4. Choose the other options that make sense for this data load.
   a. **Location** – Planning Inbox
   b. **Source Type** – Planning
   c. **File Type** – Comma delimited
   d. **Source File** – Actual_Sales_FY16.csv
   e. Do not check *Include Metadata*

This data file is based on a Planning data file export, so it is in the native Planning format. It's also comma delimited. Since there is no new metadata in the file, for performance reasons I have chosen to uncheck *Include Metadata*:

Import Data

Location	○ Local ● Planning Inbox
Source Type	● Planning ○ Essbase
File Type	● Comma delimited ○ Tab delimited ○ Other
Source File	Actual_Sales_FY16.csv
Include Metadata	☐
Date Format	MM-DD-YYYY
Last Import	Completed

5. Click *Save as Job*.
6. Name the job and click *Save*. Click *OK* at the confirmation window.
7. Click *Close*.

You'll now see the new job in the Import Data list:

Import Data

Type	Name
	LoadSalesFY16

8. Click *Close* again.

Now that the formal jobs have been created and I know that I'm using an existing business rule, I'm ready to write my EPM Automate script and test it.

```
@echo off
REM Nightly script for EPM Automate
REM Created by: interRel Consulting
REM Created on: March 9, 2016

SET url=https://servicename-domain.pbcs.usx.
oraclecloud.com
SET user=admin
SET pwd=C:\EPMAutomateFiles\password.epw
SET domain=MyServicesDomain
SET returnvalue=0
```

The first part of the script (above), sets up the housekeeping part. Header commentary and variables are set.

```
ECHO Logging In
call epmautomate login %user% %pwd% %url% %domain%
@echo off
IF %ERRORLEVEL% NEQ 0 (
echo Login failed with error %ERRORLEVEL%.
goto :END
)
```

The next part of this script logs into the server. Parameters for the "login" command include the username, password, Enterprise Planning Cloud URL, and Enterprise Planning Cloud domain. This script uses the basic EPM Automate login command and the parameters are filled in by the variables set at the top of the script.

I've embedded some generic error trapping logic that's used in each command section. The "IF" logic checks for an error after the command runs. If there is an error (it knows this by checking to see if the error code is not equal to zero, which is a successful code), the script skips to the ":END" section (described later in this section).

```
ECHO Refresh cube
call epmautomate refreshcube RefreshCube
@echo off
IF %ERRORLEVEL% NEQ 0 (
echo Refresh cube failed with error %ERRORLEVEL%.
goto :END
)
```

Now that the dimension has been updated, I need code to do a database refresh. Otherwise, there could be a disconnect between Enterprise Planning Cloud and Essbase during the data loading step (since I elected to not check the option to include metadata on the data load). I could have skipped this step, but I chose not to use the inherent option in the import metadata job. This was done for error trapping purposes. Parameters for the "refreshcube" command include the name of the job that does the database refresh.

```
ECHO Load sales data
call epmautomate importdata LoadSalesFY16
@echo off
IF %ERRORLEVEL% NEQ 0 (
echo Loading of sales data failed with error %ERRORLEVEL%.
goto :END
```

Now that Planning and Essbase are in sync, I can load data into Essbase. Parameters for the "importdata" command include the job name and then an optional parameter to override the job's data file.

```
ECHO Run CalcAll business rule
call epmautomate runbusinessrule CalcAll
planType=Sales
@echo off
IF %ERRORLEVEL% NEQ 0 (
echo Run business rule failed with error %ERRORLEVEL%.
goto :END
)
```

If I'm loading data into a BSO plan type, I need to aggregate my data after loading it (unless I'm using hybrid aggregation). I have a nifty business rule called CalcAll that will take care of this. The "runbusinessrule" command has several parameters. The first parameter is the business rule name in Calculation Manager. The next parameter is the plan type that the rule needs to be run against. Finally, there are optional parameters for any run time prompts called by the business rule (which don't apply in this example).

```
ECHO Logging Out
call epmautomate logout
@echo off
IF %ERRORLEVEL% NEQ 0 (
echo Logout failed with error %ERRORLEVEL%.
goto :END
)
```

The final, formal command involves logging out. The "logout" command is simple and has no parameters.

```
:END
ECHO Return code: %ERRORLEVEL%
SET returnValue=%ERRORLEVEL%
EXIT /B %returnValue%
```

The last section of the code is for housekeeping purposes. It figures out the current error code (if there is one) and then returns it.

Here is the final sequence of commands resulting from this script:

Look Smarter Than You Are with Enterprise Planning Cloud 411

```
Logging In
Login successful
Updating Product dimension
Processing...
Retrieving status...
importmetadata completed successfully
Refresh cube
Processing...
Retrieving status...
refreshcube completed successfully
Load sales data
Processing...
Retrieving status...
importdata completed successfully
Run CalcAll business rule
Processing...
runbusinessrule completed successfully
Logging Out
logout completed successfully
Return code: 0
```

Automate a Data Load in Data Management

EPM Automate can run data load rules and batches that are created in Data Management.

To automate a data load in Data Management,
1. First place the *Vision_Actual_FY17.csv* file in your c:\EPMAutomateFiles directory. (email info@interrel.com for a copy of the file)
2. In the EPM Automate interface, type the following (step by step recommended) and hit *Enter*:

```
epmautomate uploadfile
c:\EPMAutomateFiles\Vision_Actual_FY17.csv inbox

epmautomate rundatarule LoadVisionSalesFY17 Jan-17
Dec-17 REPLACE STORE_DATA
inbox/Vision_Actual_FY17.csv
```

```
C:\Oracle\EPM Automate\bin>epmautomate uploadfile Vision_Actual_FY17.csv inbox
Processing...
100% completed
uploadfile completed successfully

C:\Oracle\EPM Automate\bin>epmautomate rundatarule LoadVisionSalesFY17 Jan-17 De
c-17 REPLACE STORE_DATA inbox/Vision_Actual_FY17.csv
Processing...
Retrieving status...
rundatarule completed successfully

C:\Oracle\EPM Automate\bin>
```

The rule shows a successful execution in Data Management:

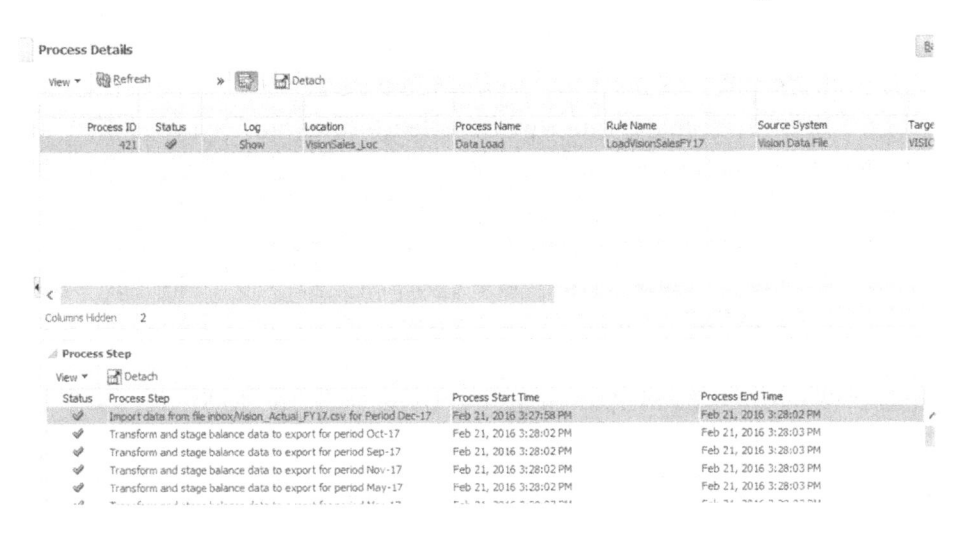

Adding Scripts to the Windows Task Scheduler

It's possible to schedule EPM Automate scripts through Windows Scheduler on a Windows-based computer.

Note! The following screen shots are from Windows 10.

To schedule EPM Automate scripts to run in a Windows Task Scheduler,

1. On the computer where you wish to schedule tasks using Windows Task Scheduler, launch the Control Panel and navigate to *Administrative Tools*.
2. Open *Task Scheduler*.
3. Select *Action >> Create Basic Task*:

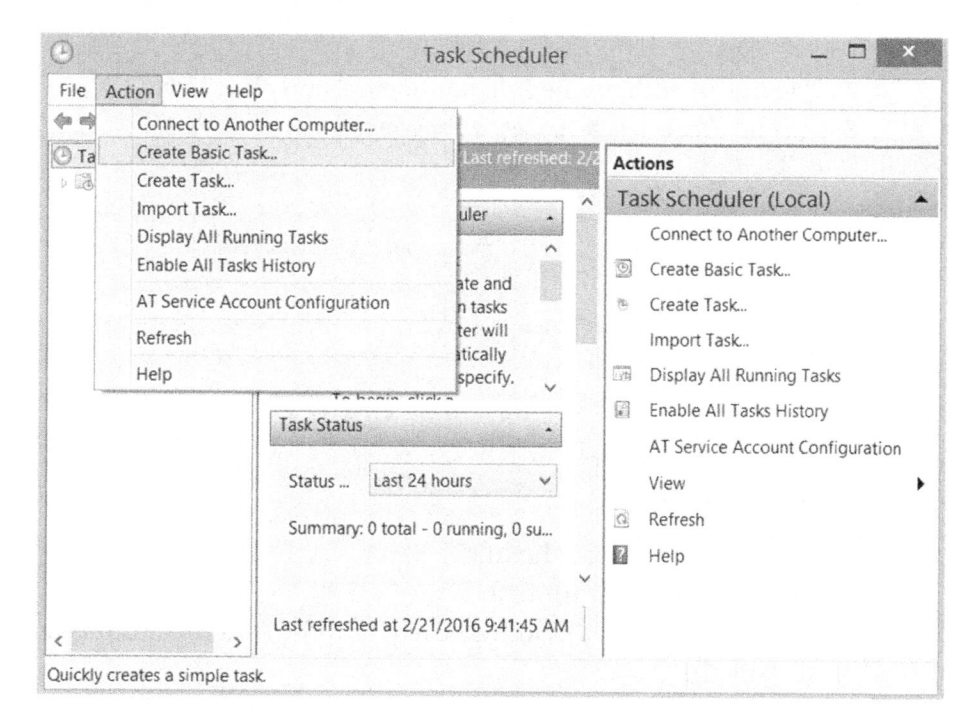

4. Enter the task name.
5. Click *Next*.
6. Under Task Trigger, select the schedule and click *Next*:

Chapter 9: Automate & Migrate

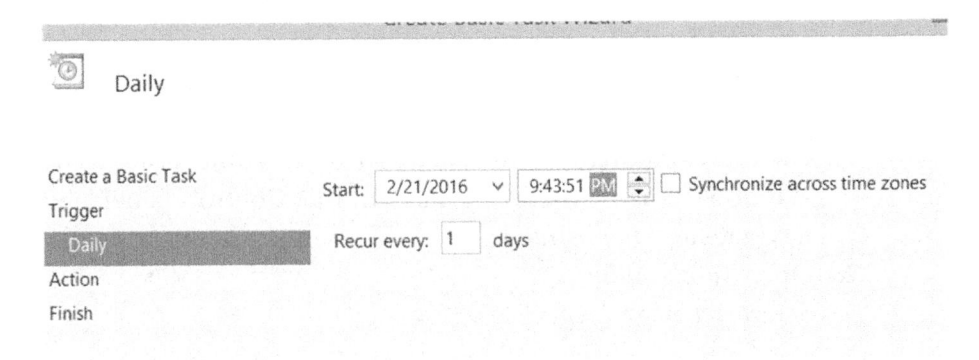

Daily

Create a Basic Task
Trigger
Daily
Action
Finish

Start: 2/21/2016   9:43:51 PM   ☐ Synchronize across time zones

Recur every: 1 days

7. Define any other schedule parameters and click *Next*.
8. Under Action, select *Start a Program*:

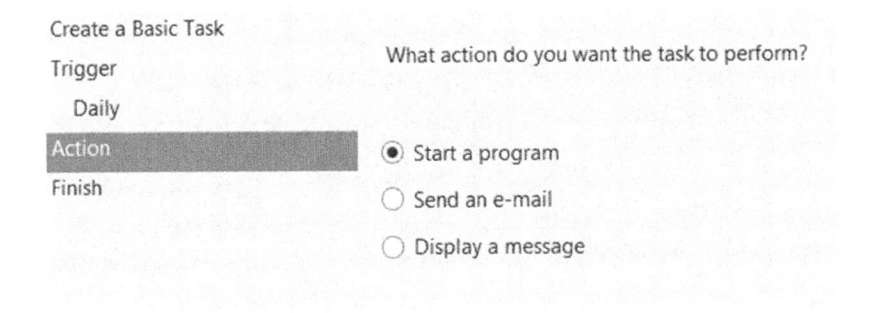

Create a Basic Task
Trigger
Daily
Action
Finish

What action do you want the task to perform?

● Start a program
○ Send an e-mail
○ Display a message

9. Select the script to schedule.
10. Optionally add arguments.
11. In *Start in*, enter the location where EPM Automate utility is installed:

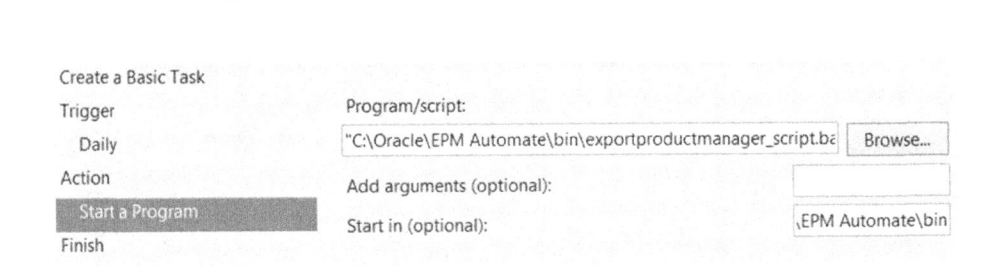

Start a Program

Create a Basic Task
Trigger
Daily
Action
Start a Program
Finish

Program/script:
"C:\Oracle\EPM Automate\bin\exportproductmanager_script.ba   Browse...

Add arguments (optional):

Start in (optional):   \EPM Automate\bin

12. Click *Next*.

13. Check the option "Open the Properties dialog for this task when I click Finish".
14. Click *Finish*.
15. Under the General tab in task properties, define security options for running the script when a user is logged in or not, and whether or not to run with highest privileges:

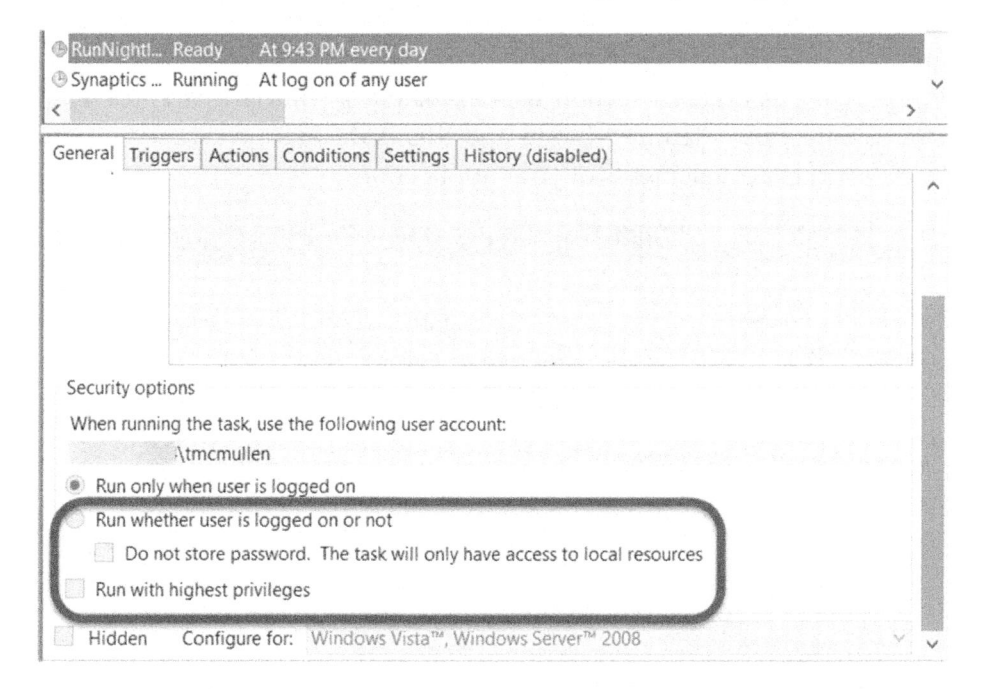

Voila! I now have a fully automated nightly process that run each night to my Enterprise Planning Cloud application.

APPLICATION MANAGEMENT

As I mentioned earlier, Application Management in Oracle Enterprise Planning Cloud is the place where you will perform a couple of different administrative tasks for your applications. You will create and manage native security groups for your application. You can export or import application artifacts (basically any object or component in your application but it sounds cooler when you use the term "artifact") or the entire application. Application snapshots are uploaded and downloaded from Application Management. You can also run provisioning reports and migration reports. For any on-premise Hyperion Planning administrators, Application Management is essentially a version of the on-premise Life Cycle Management.

The navigation panel on the left portion of the window controls the main content area. For example, if you select "User Directories", the main content area will allow you to search, add, and display the native directory containing any native groups. The *User Directories* section groups native groups for security assignments.

The *Applications* section lists all of the products that come with Oracle Enterprise Planning Cloud and this is the section where you can import and export elements of your application:

Application Management		
Application Management	Browse VISION	
▲ User Directories	Application: VISION	
▲ Native Directory		
Groups	**Artifact List** Selected Artifacts Search Artifacts	
▲ Applications	Name ▲	Type
VISION	> ☐ Configuration	Folder
FDM Enterprise Edition	> ☐ Essbase Data	Folder
Calculation Manager	> ☐ Global Artifacts	Folder
Shared Services	> ☐ Plan Type	Folder
Reporting and Analysis	> ☐ Relational Data	Folder
▲ Application Snapshots	> ☐ Security	Folder
> Artifact Snapshot		

- **<Application Name>** – contains the core Oracle Enterprise Planning application; in my case, Vision
- **FDM Enterprise Edition** – contains all of the Data Management components
- **Calculation Manager** – contains all of the Calculation Manager objects like rules, rule sets and variables
- **Shared Services** – contains the native group definition and assigned users to those groups
- **Reporting and Analysis** – contains all of the Financial Reporting objects like reports, books and batches

The *Application Snapshots* section contains all of the imported and exported snapshots. You can rerun an export snapshot from this section or it can be scheduled to run with EPM Automate. You can also delete and rename snapshots.

APPLICATION MIGRATION

> Meanwhile, back on Earth...
> When Project Commander McMullen had first heard that Roske and the implementation were still alive from Director Chang, she was flooded with relief. Of course, Roske would find a way!
> So now she had to see what she could do to help Roske. His application was in good shape. Still, she could improve a few things. Let's import this baby to our on-premise environment and see if any "tweaking" is needed.

Application Management is the place to be to import and export Oracle Enterprise Planning applications and objects. You can choose to export the entire application or individual artifacts (a.k.a. objects). You will import / export some components in separate steps. As I mentioned earlier, the Applications section in Application Management will allow you to import or export each the following components: the main application and artifact set (including application definition, dimensions, data, data forms, task lists), Calculation Manager artifacts, Data Management artifacts (which are found under FDM Enterprise Edition), native groups (which are found under Shared Services), and Financial Reporting artifacts (which are found under Reporting and Analysis):

```
· User Directories                Application: VISION
    · Native Directory
        · Groups                  Artifact List  Selected Artifacts  Search
· Applications                    Name
    · VISION                        > ☐ Configuration
    · FDM Enterprise Edition        > ☐ Essbase Data
    · Calculation Manager           > ☐ Global Artifacts
    · Shared Services               > ☐ Plan Type
    · Reporting and Analysis        > ☐ Relational Data
· Application Snapshots             > ☐ Security
```

Why would I want to import or export to Oracle Enterprise Planning Cloud? Oh, let me count the reasons. You want to move an on-premise application to the Cloud or vice versa. You want to move application from pre-production instance to the production instance of Oracle Enterprise Planning Cloud. You have an issue and Oracle Support requests a copy of your application. You want to make a backup or snapshot of the application. In short, you will definitely need to do this at some point in your Oracle Enterprise Planning Cloud administrator life.

Export Enterprise Planning Cloud Application

To export an Enterprise Planning Cloud application from a Cloud instance,

1. In the Simplified UI, go to *Navigator >> Manage >> Application Management*. The Application Management tab in Enterprise Planning Cloud Workspace will open.

Application Management in Enterprise Planning Cloud is very similar to Shared Services in on-premise Hyperion Planning.

2. Drill into the *Applications* folder and click the application name, in this case, *VISION*:

Look Smarter Than You Are with Enterprise Planning Cloud 419

> Application Management
> - User Directories
> - Applications
>   - VISION
>   - FDM Enterprise Edition
>   - Calculation Manager
>   - Shared Services
>   - Reporting and Analysis

3. Check the boxes next to the artifacts to export:

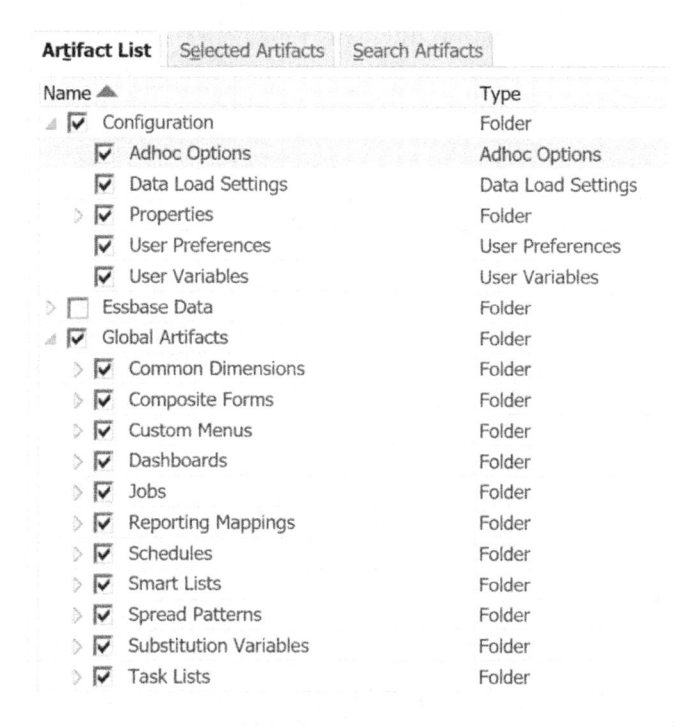

Artifact List | Selected Artifacts | Search Artifacts

Name	Type
▼ Configuration	Folder
Adhoc Options	Adhoc Options
Data Load Settings	Data Load Settings
Properties	Folder
User Preferences	User Preferences
User Variables	User Variables
☐ Essbase Data	Folder
▼ Global Artifacts	Folder
Common Dimensions	Folder
Composite Forms	Folder
Custom Menus	Folder
Dashboards	Folder
Jobs	Folder
Reporting Mappings	Folder
Schedules	Folder
Smart Lists	Folder
Spread Patterns	Folder
Substitution Variables	Folder
Task Lists	Folder

4. Verify selected artifacts by going to the *Selected Artifacts* tab:

	Browse VISION	
	Application: VISION	
	Artifact List **Selected Artifacts** Search Artifacts	
	Name ▲	Type
	☑ Configuration	Folder
	☑ Global Artifacts	Folder
	☑ Plan Type	Folder
	☑ Relational Data	Folder
	☑ Security	Folder

5. Click *Export*, name the export and click *Export* again:

Folder Name: admin 16-01-15

Help   Export   Cancel

6. View the Migration Status report. Look in the Status column to verify whether or not the migration is completed.
7. You can click the *Refresh* button at the bottom of the screen to check its progress:

User	Source	Destination	Start Time	Completed Time	Duration	Status
admin	VISION	admin 16-01-15/HP-VISION	January 15, 2016 12:14:13	January 15, 2016 12:14:16	00:00:03	Completed
	Shared Services	Artifact Snapshot/HSS-Shared S				
	Reporting and Analysis	Artifact Snapshot/RnA-Reporting				
epm_default_clx	VISION	Artifact Snapshot/HP-VISION	January 15, 2016 00:12:59	January 15, 2016 00:14:04	00:01:05	Completed
	Calculation Manager	Artifact Snapshot/CALC-Calculat				
	FDM Enterprise Edition	Artifact Snapshot/FDMEE-FDM E				
	Shared Services	Artifact Snapshot/HSS-Shared S				
	Reporting and Analysis	Artifact Snapshot/RnA-Reporting				
epm_default_clx	VISION	Artifact Snapshot/HP-VISION	January 14, 2016 00:12:53	January 14, 2016 00:13:51	00:00:58	Completed
	Calculation Manager	Artifact Snapshot/CALC-Calculat				
	FDM Enterprise Edition	Artifact Snapshot/FDMEE-FDM E				
	Shared Services	Artifact Snapshot/HSS-Shared S				
	Reporting and Analysis	Artifact Snapshot/RnA-Reporting				
epm_default_clx	VISION	Artifact Snapshot/HP-VISION	January 13, 2016 00:13:02	January 13, 2016 00:14:00	00:00:58	Completed

8. Check for the exported folder containing the exported application in the Application Snapshots folder:

```
Application Management
  User Directories
  Applications
    VISION
    FDM Enterprise Edition
    Calculation Manager
    Shared Services
    Reporting and Analysis
  Application Snapshots
    admin 16-01-15
    Artifact Snapshot
    VISION 15-12-03
```

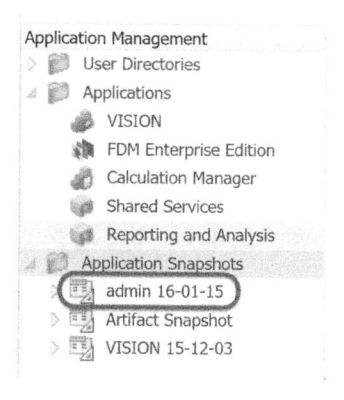

The Enterprise Planning Cloud application export is complete. This export contains all of the Enterprise Planning Cloud artifacts within the application. Note this did not export the Calculation Manager business rules, Shared Services native groups, or the Data Management (it is referred to as FDM Enterprise Edition) objects. You must repeat the same steps above for both Calculation Manager, Data Management, Shared Services, and Reporting Analysis to export the entire set of application artifacts.

Import Enterprise Planning Cloud Application

The Administrator can import an application and its artifacts once it is located in Application Snapshots.

To import an application snapshot into on-premise Planning Application Management,

1. In the Simplified UI, go to *Navigate >> Manage >> Application Management*.
2. Select the *Application Snapshots* folder.
3. Right click and select *Upload*.
4. Browse to the snapshot zip file containing the artifacts (for example the zip file created when I exported the Enterprise Planning Cloud application in the earlier section).

To import an application snapshot into Enterprise Planning Cloud,

1. In the Simplified UI, go to *Navigate >> Manage >> Application Management*.
2. Drill into the *Application Snapshots* folder and find the application you want to import to a new Enterprise Planning Cloud application.
3. Right-click the snapshot of the application to import and click *Import*:

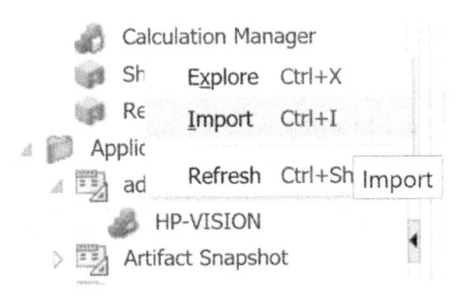

```
    Calculation Manager
    Sh    Explore   Ctrl+X
    Re    Import    Ctrl+I
  Applic
    ad    Refresh   Ctrl+Sh  Import
        HP-VISION
        Artifact Snapshot
```

4. Select the artifacts to import:

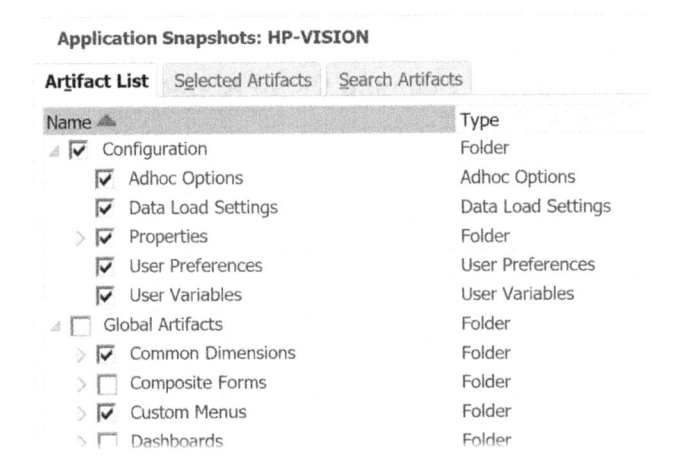

Application Snapshots: HP-VISION

Name	Type
☑ Configuration	Folder
☑ Adhoc Options	Adhoc Options
☑ Data Load Settings	Data Load Settings
☑ Properties	Folder
☑ User Preferences	User Preferences
☑ User Variables	User Variables
☐ Global Artifacts	Folder
☑ Common Dimensions	Folder
☐ Composite Forms	Folder
☑ Custom Menus	Folder
☐ Dashboards	Folder

5. Go to the *Selected Artifacts* tab and review.
6. Click *Import* and *Import* again:

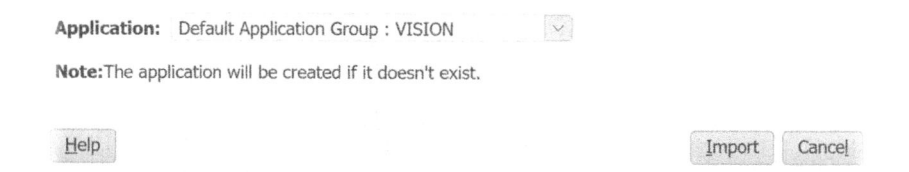

Application: Default Application Group : VISION

Note: The application will be created if it doesn't exist.

[Help] [Import] [Cancel]

Note! Since Enterprise Planning Cloud allows one application at a time, the existing application will be overwritten. If an application does not exist, a new one will be created with the imported artifacts.

7. Verify the migration and make sure everything you need has been imported.

Export On-Premise Application

If you have an on-premise Hyperion Planning environment and would like to migrate to Cloud, you will likely need to move your on-premise application to the Cloud. The steps to export an application from on-premise Hyperion Planning is similar to the export steps in Enterprise Planning Cloud but there are a few slight differences. One main difference is that you will work in "Life Cycle Management" or the "Shared Services Console" (vs. Application Management, though most of the user interface and actions are the same).

Note there are some on-premise artifacts that are not supported in Oracle Enterprise Planning Cloud like Essbase calc scripts and Essbase data load rules. You will receive errors for any non-supported artifacts when you try to import into the Cloud. Also, depending on your on-premise version (e.g., in version 11.1.2.3.500, you might have issues exporting data via Life Cycle Management. Uncheck the data option if you run into issues and use an Essbase data export to load via the Simplified UI).

To export an on-premise Planning application,
1. Go to *Navigate >> Administer >> Shared Services Console*:

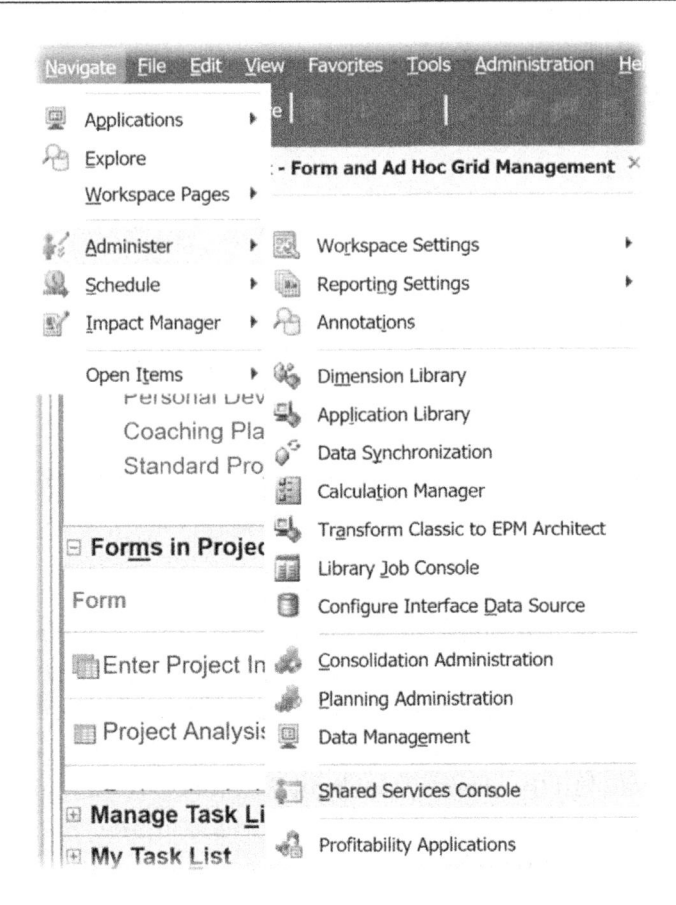

2. Go into the *Application Groups* folder, then find the application to export in the Planning folder.
3. Select the artifacts to export:

4. Click *Export* and name the File System Folder.
5. Click *Export* again. Wait for a "Completed" status in the Migration Status Report:

Look Smarter Than You Are with Enterprise Planning Cloud					425

User	Source	Destination	Start Time	Completed Time	Duration	Status
admin	iProject	ADMIN 16-01-22\HP-iProject	January 22, 2016 13:46:55	January 22, 2016 13:47:00	00:00:05	Completed
admin	Calculation Manager	RACE-TDABC admin 16-01-19\CAL...	January 19, 2016 08:49:51	January 19, 2016 08:49:53	00:00:02	Completed
admin	Shared Services	RACE-TDABC - ALL SS Export admin...	January 19, 2016 08:46:18	January 19, 2016 08:46:20	00:00:02	Completed
admin	TDABC3	RACE-TDABC3 admin 16-01-19\HP...	January 19, 2016 08:44:44	January 19, 2016 08:45:02	00:00:18	Completed
admin	Calculation Manager	TDABC3 Calc Mgr admin 16-01-16\...	January 16, 2016 17:12:22	January 16, 2016 17:12:24	00:00:02	Completed

Once completed, the application export will be located in the File System folder of Shared Services. Right-click the exported folder for the following options:

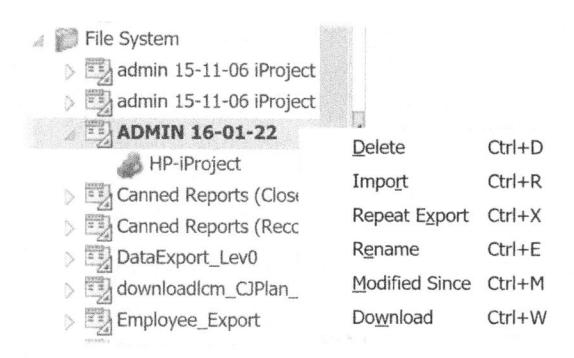

- File System
  - admin 15-11-06 iProject
  - admin 15-11-06 iProject
  - **ADMIN 16-01-22**
    - HP-iProject
    - Canned Reports (Close
    - Canned Reports (Recc
    - DataExport_Lev0
    - downloadlcm_CJPlan_
    - Employee_Export

Delete	Ctrl+D
Import	Ctrl+R
Repeat Export	Ctrl+X
Rename	Ctrl+E
Modified Since	Ctrl+M
Download	Ctrl+W

Note! To import an on-premise Planning application to Enterprise Planning Cloud, download the file to your computer so that it can be uploaded to Enterprise Planning Cloud.

Import On-Premise Application

You can import your on-premise applications to Oracle Enterprise Planning Cloud. As I mentioned before, there are some on-premise artifacts that are not supported in Oracle Enterprise Planning Cloud like Essbase calc scripts and Essbase data load rules. You will receive errors for any non-supported artifacts when you try to import into the Cloud.

To import an on-premise Hyperion Planning application to Enterprise Planning Cloud,
1. In the Simplified UI, go to *Navigate >> Manage >> Application Management*.
2. Right-click the *Application Snapshots* folder and click *Upload*:

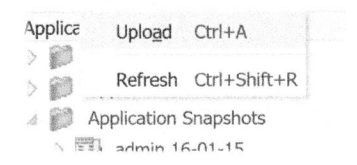

```
Applica    Upload   Ctrl+A
           Refresh  Ctrl+Shift+R
    Application Snapshots
       admin 16-01-15
```

3. Browse for the on-premise application zip file and click *Upload*.

The folder will appear in the Application Snapshots section of Application Management.

4. Open the uploaded folder and select the application name.
5. Select artifacts to import and click *Import*.
6. Verify the import.

Easy as pie to move import and export applications to and from the Cloud!

```
LOG ENTRY: SOL 20, Entry 3

    My email works. Huh?! So I can communicate with
i.n.t.e.r.R.e.l. Guess I should have checked that first
thing.
    After pondering how I was going to communicate my
success at getting the Enterprise Planning Cloud
application up and going, I received an email from
Project Commander McMullen. They could access the
application!
    Now that I can communicate with i.n.t.e.r.R.e.l,
Project Commander McMullen thinks she can build a
better sales forecasting application than me. I figure
out how to do this all by myself in the Cloud and now
she's taken my application and changed it! She exported
my application using LCM to her instance and now has
some "tweaks".
    I think I'm having some interference and her email
just isn't coming across. (Really I'm going to just
ignore her comments for this phase and turn this
application over to the end users).
    Time to go live!
```

Chapter 10:
End User Activities

> LOG ENTRY: SOL 21, Entry 1
>
> Now that I've successfully completed the sales forecasting application, the users are ready to enter their sales forecast data. I'll turn it over to End User Specialist, Opal Alapat, to help users enter their plans in the Enterprise Planning Cloud.
> What's next for me? It's time for some well-earned R&R. Surprisingly, Glee is growing on me. Maybe it is because I don't have any other option. I wonder if the New Directions glee club will finally make it to Nationals?

NAVIGATE SIMPLIFIED UI

The Simplified UI is a streamlined UI for users of Enterprise Planning Cloud. In order to provide ease of use for tablets, this interface does not have any right-click options and everything is large enough to click with a finger.

To make things easy, all the end user functions will be explained according to the order of the main menu:

Alright, let's get started!

REVIEW DASHBOARDS

Dashboards are great to see the big picture of things. They are created by the Administrator and can be viewed by users (if they have security access to the specific intersection of data represented in the dashboard). Four quadrants are available and each quadrant contains one dashboard object. Dashboard objects include a variety of charts, URLs and commentary text:

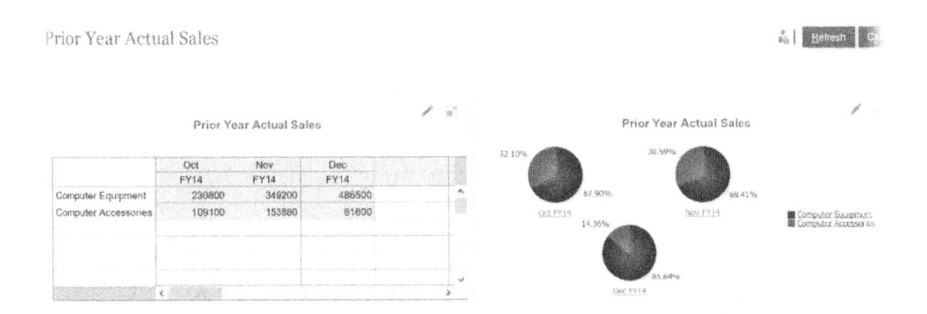

FOLLOW TASKS

As it is with most things in life, a little bit of guidance and support can go a long way. You've already seen that data form instructions help you in your planning process. Think of task lists as having your own personal tour guide through the budgeting and forecasting process.

The wizard-like task list will itemize the steps users need to complete as they work through the budget. It even has helpful instructions and due dates for those who do not spend their entire lives strapped to a computer doing budgeting. Administrators and power users can create and manage tasks and task lists.

This brings you to the Task List summary view where you see the task list steps, their status (complete or incomplete), due date, completed date, and any defined instructions:

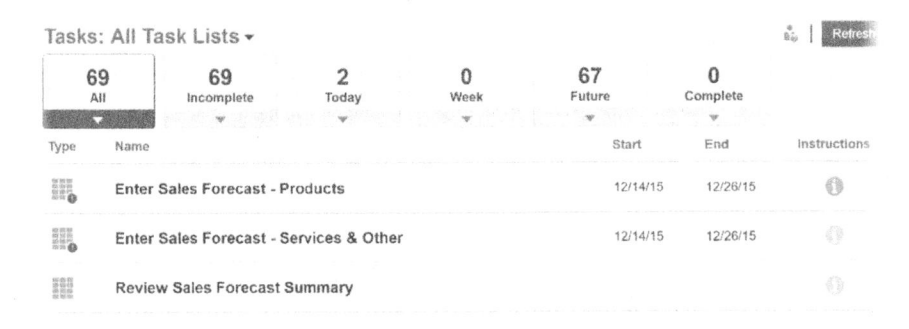

According to the task list dashboard pictured above, no one at the company is very productive because not a single item has been completed.

To complete a task,

1. Click on an incomplete task and perform the task (if the task opens a form, input data and save the form – more on inputting data to a form very shortly).
2. When the task is complete, check the box for *Complete*:

3. *Close* the task. You'll notice that there is a pleasant green check mark next to the completed task:

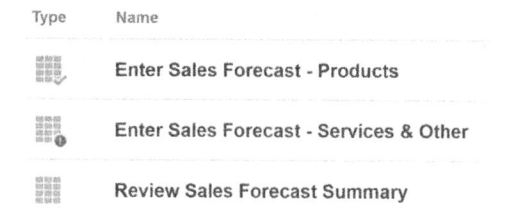

Move on to other tasks created by the Administrator to complete the entire task list.

View Form Instructions

Before you get in too much of a hurry to input data in the forms, it might be helpful to view some instructions created by the Administrator. To view instructions for a form, simply click *Plans* and click the *Instructions* icon:

INPUT PLANS

From the Simplified UI, click *Plans* to jump directly to data forms:

[Simplified UI icon grid showing: Dashboards, Tasks, Plans, Rules, Approvals, Reports, Console, Settings, Academy, Navigator]

Before you enter data, let's review some of the data form components:

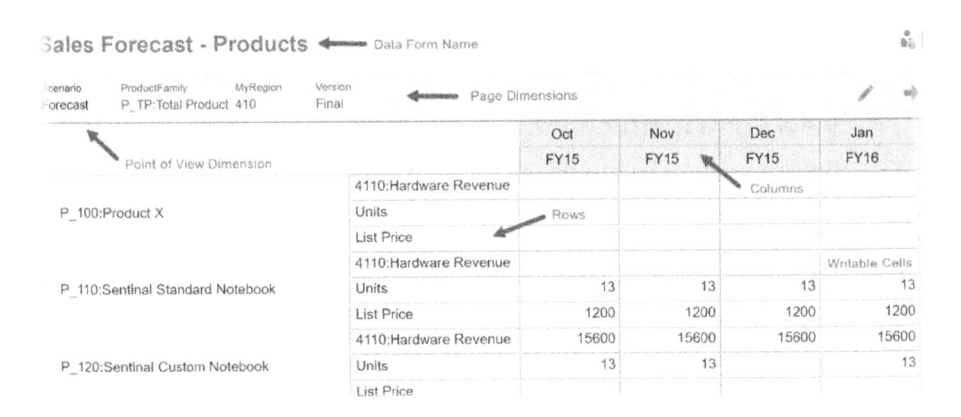

[Screenshot of a data form "Sales Forecast - Products" with annotations pointing to Data Form Name, Page Dimensions, Point of View Dimension, Rows, Columns, and Writable Cells]

		Oct	Nov	Dec	Jan
		FY15	FY15	FY15	FY16
	4110:Hardware Revenue				
P_100:Product X	Units				
	List Price				
	4110:Hardware Revenue				
P_110:Sentinal Standard Notebook	Units	13	13	13	13
	List Price	1200	1200	1200	1200
	4110:Hardware Revenue	15600	15600	15600	15600
P_120:Sentinal Custom Notebook	Units	13	13		13
	List Price				

Scenario: Forecast; ProductFamily: P_TP:Total Product 410; MyRegion; Version: Final

A data form will contain one or more dimensions in the rows and columns of the form. You may see a list of members or a hierarchy of members that you can collapse or expand, allowing you to view and plan data at a summary or detailed level:

	4110:Hardware Revenue	1000	1000
⊟ P_TP2:Computer Accessories	Units	81	81
	List Price	835	835
	4110:Hardware Revenue	14375	14375
⊞ P_TP3:Computer Services	Units		
	List Price		
	4110:Hardware Revenue		
⊟ P_TP:Total Product	Units	149	149

A data form has a Point of View, which as I've mentioned is a fixed set of members for dimensions that are not in the Page, Rows, or Columns. For example, if the data form should always use the Forecast scenario, you will probably add it to the Point of View. In general, users can't change Point of View (often called POV, for short) selections. One exception is when dynamic user variables have been configured for the form.

A data form may also contain one or more Page drop-down boxes. A Page component is a drop-down list of members from a dimension. In the Forecast Sales – Products data form, the Page dimensions include: Product, Entity, and Version. You can choose the desired member from the Page drop-down by checking the box next to the member name:

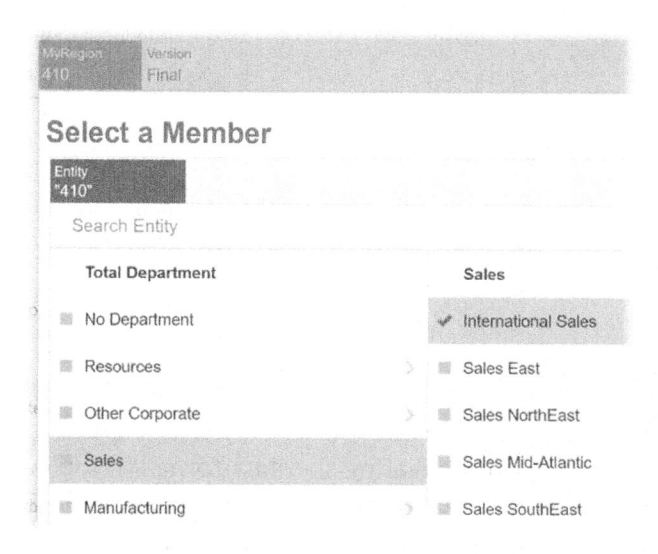

Select a Member

Entity
"410"

Search Entity

Total Department	Sales
No Department	✓ International Sales
Resources	Sales East
Other Corporate	Sales NorthEast
Sales	Sales Mid-Atlantic
Manufacturing	Sales SouthEast

You'll notice the data hasn't changed. You have to click the arrow button (a.k.a. the *Go* button) to refresh the form:

432   Chapter 10: End User Activities

Once you've selected the page options, you are ready to enter data into valid data cells by typing some numbers (or in some cases, text) into the data form.

You will see that there are four primary types of cells in a data form, each indicated by a different shade of color (although hard to distinguish in the screen shot – darned black and white printing!):

White Cells	Valid data cells available for input
Yellow Cells	"Dirty" cells; A cell that is "dirty" indicates that data has been changed but not saved
Gray Cells	Read-only cells. You cannot edit or input data into these cells
Green Cells	Cells that have been recently changed and auto-saved

		FY15	FY15	FY15
	List Price	700	700	700
	4110:Hardware Revenue	5600	5600	
P_150:Other Computer	Units	13	13	13
	List Price	500		500
	4110:Hardware Revenue	6500	Writable Cell	6500
P_160:Tablet Computer	Units	9	8	8
	List Price		80	80
	4110:Hardware Revenue	64 Dirty Cell	640 Read Only Cell	0
P_TP1:Computer Equipment	Units	80	68	47
	List Price	3700	3700	3700

A quick note on navigating the data forms: if you want to move horizontally, say from "Jan" to "Feb" to "Mar" while in the same row, then click *Tab*. If you want to move vertically, down the month of Jan for each row, then press *Enter*. Tab moves you from left to right, and Enter moves you from top to bottom when in the data entry mode.

Look Smarter Than You Are with Enterprise Planning Cloud   433

EVERYTHING'S UNDER A MENU

First things first: with the Simplified UI, there are no right-click menus like you see in on-premise Planning (although I hear this is coming in a future version). The one exception is right-clicking on the Page or POV area of a web form and accessing the Action Menu.

Because the Simplified UI is tablet friendly, I am provided with context-sensitive Action menus; the items under the Action menus depend on what screen the user is in. In a data form, users can analyze with ad hoc analysis, create new ad hoc grids, run business rules, execute smart push, view validation messages, or clear the form's formatting:

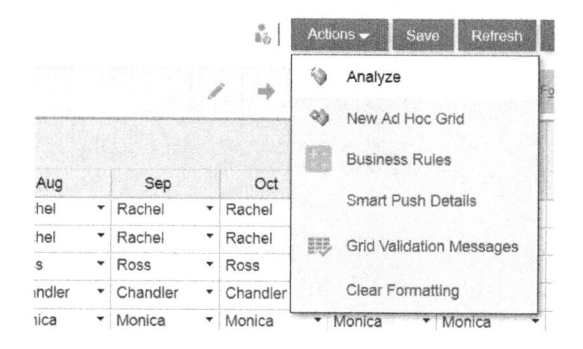

Enterprise Planning Cloud provides options for users to interact with the data in in data forms. There are menus for editing data, performing ad hoc analysis, and formatting:

Below are the options available under the *Data*, *Ad Hoc*, and *Format* menus respectively:

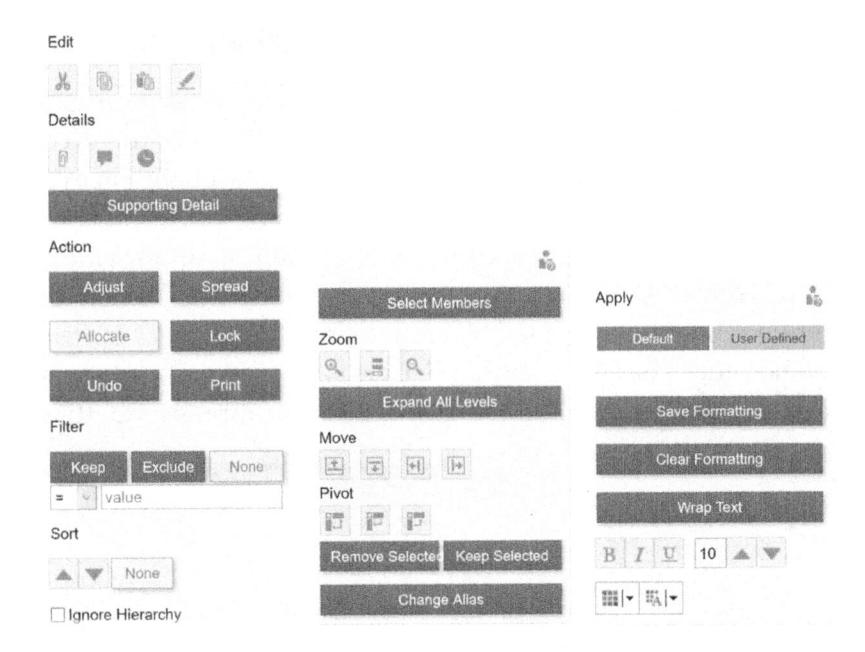

In addition to standard menu items within Enterprise Planning Cloud, the Administrator may design some custom menu items under the Actions menu to help guide users through the planning process. Refer to the Actions Menus section to read how a Administrator can add additional Action menu items for data forms.

Apply Filtering in a Data Form

Through the Data menu, you can apply filtering on data and metadata. Simply click the *Data* menu and go to the Filter section to keep or exclude certain values or records:

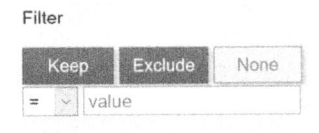

Filters are session-specific. If you navigate away from the data form, you will lose the filter.

Look Smarter Than You Are with Enterprise Planning Cloud   435

Apply Sorting in a Data Form

You can also apply sorting in the hierarchy for data or metadata. Go to *Data >> Sort* and click the arrow for *Sort Ascending* or *Sort Descending*:

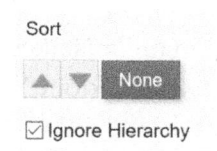

Sorting is session-specific. If you navigate away from the data form, you will lose the filter.

SELECT SMART LIST VALUES

Users can choose text values from pre-defined drop-down lists within a data form. These pre-defined lists are called Smart Lists and are created by the Administrator. See the example below in which a user can select a Product Manager for each Product and Period:

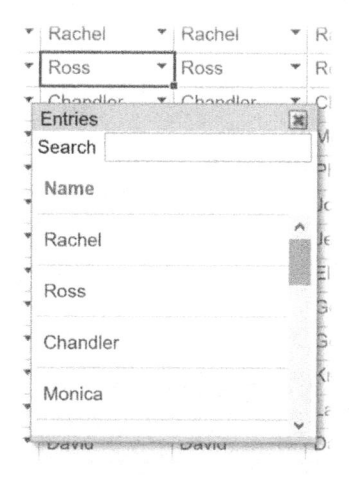

You can use Smart List values in business rules and reports.

ENTER TEXT & DATES

You can also enter free form text values or dates in data forms if enabled by the Administrator (done by creating members with the "Text"

Data Type). Simply type in the empty cell. Be aware, keep it brief because display options are not optimized for text cells.

REFRESH A DATA FORM

Let's face it, we've all made mistakes. What if you enter data but you don't want to save what you've done? Should you delete all of the values that you typed in? Try this and notice how the cells are still marked as "dirty" even though I deleted all of the data. If you want to make these cells "clean" again or go back to the original data values in the form without saving, one option is to refresh the data form.

> **Note!** If the Autosave feature is turned on for the form, the best way to clean your cells is to undo your changes by pressing Ctrl-Z.

To refresh a data form (and not save data changes),
1. With the data form opened, click *Refresh*.
2. The window below will appear. Click *OK*:

Warning
There is unsaved data. If you proceed, this data will be lost. Do you wish to continue?

[OK] [Cancel]

3. If you click *OK*, the form's data will revert back to the original values.

SAVE A DATA FORM

To save data, all you need to do is click *Save* (next to the Actions menu). In general, Save will re-calculate the form's subtotals and possibly run business rules associated to the form (this depends on how the Administrator designed the form). If you have changed data and you try to leave the form without saving, you will receive a prompt to save. Click *OK* to save and *Cancel* to discard.

If the Autosave feature is turned on (explained in more detail shortly), users don't need to manually save their form multiple times (unless business rules set to run on save need to be launched). The Autosave feature will save data once the user clicks off of their current cell.

SHORTCUT KEYS

Users are granted further ease of use when inputting data into forms with the availability of shortcut keys in the Simplified UI. Shortcut keys can be used in simple forms and on the desktop only (not on a tablet).

The shortcut keys provided below are a combination of shortcuts that were available prior to Enterprise Planning Cloud and shortcuts that are new with the Enterprise Planning Cloud Simplified UI:

Shorcut Keys	Description
Ctrl+Home	Move to the first cell of the form
Ctrl+Z	Undo previous action(s) – can undo multiple actions at a time
Tab	Move to the next cell to the right
Enter	Move down one cell
K	Indication of a number in the thousands. For example, entering "5K" will result in 5,000
Up / Down arrow	Move up one cell / down one cell
Ctrl+Alt+B	Bold a value

AUTOSAVE & UNDO

Administrators have the option to enable Autosave when creating data forms. Autosave is a neat, new feature in the Simplified UI that saves data input into a cell when a user tabs out of the cell. If a user mistakenly saves data by tabbing out of a cell, a Ctrl+Z shortcut will undo the mistake.

If Autosave is enabled, the cells will turn green to indicate a saved cell (this would look really cool if the book was printed in color):

		Oct	Nov	Dec
		FY15	FY15	FY15
Training_P_291	4140:Training Revenue	500	700	750
Miscellaneous_P_292	4150:Miscellaneous Revenue			
Consulting_P_294	4130:Consulting Revenue			
Total Product	4120:Support Revenue	9895.5	9895.5	6606

Additionally, an option to *Run Form Rules* on Autosave can be enabled by the Administrator to update dynamically calculated cells that depend on the autosaved cell values that were input by the user. If rules were run and Ctrl+Z is used, the rules that were run as a part of the Autosave will be undone as well.

ADJUSTMENTS & DATA SPREADING

Adjust

Have you ever finished your budget only to be told by someone above you in the org chart that you need to increase revenue or decrease expenses? Rather than go back to the beginning every time you need to revise, Planning provides the ability to adjust data in cells by either a specific amount or a percentage. In the Simplified UI, only one cell can be adjusted at a time. Enterprise Planning Cloud Workspace allows adjustments to multiple cells; simply highlight all the cells to adjust. Let's go through an example in the Simplified UI.

To adjust a cell,
1. Select the cell to adjust.
2. Open the *Data* menu and click *Adjust* (under Action section).
3. Type in the number or percentage to adjust by:

Adjust Data

Cell Value	76
Adjust By	20 +/- %
New Value	91.2

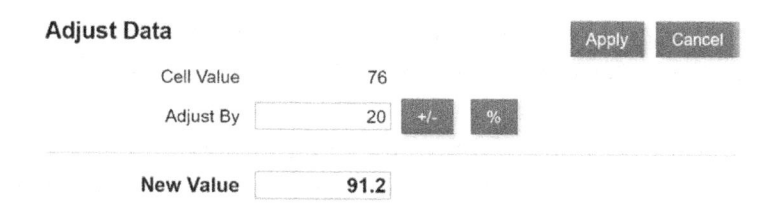

[Apply] [Cancel]

4. Review the new value.
5. Click *Apply* to adjust the data.

Time Spreading

Time Spreading allows you to enter data at a summary level (like at the quarter or year level) and then have Enterprise Planning Cloud automatically push the data down to the time periods underneath. Let's explore time spreading in more detail.

While working in a data form, you can:

- Spread the value in a summary time period back to its base time periods
- Spread values among members based on the proportional values of existing data
- Spread values based on a calendar's weekly distribution in a quarter: 4-4-5, 5-4-4, 4-5-4, or None (this depends on how the Administrator set up the application)

To spread, or distribute, data based on the Periods dimension,
1. On the data entry form, select the cell for the summary time period whose new value you want to spread.
2. Enter the new value.
3. When you leave the cell, the new values should spread to the time periods beneath the summary time period.

So how will the data values spread? It depends on the type of account or measure for which you are planning. For Revenue, Expense, and Saved Assumption Accounts (Flow), values entered at upper levels are spread to the children based on a percentage of the values already there. It sort of goal-seeks in a way. If there are no existing values, values are spread evenly or based on weekly seasonal distributions (4-4-5, 5-4-4, or 4-5-4).

For Asset, Liability, Equity Accounts, and Saved Assumption with Time Balance First, values entered at upper levels are placed in the first child. Other children remain unchanged. For example, if you change Qtr 1 from "30" to "50", January will change to "50". February and March will remain unchanged. If there are no existing values in any of a member's children, values entered at upper levels will be placed in all children.

For Asset, Liability, Equity, and Saved Assumption Accounts with Time Balance Last, values entered at upper levels are placed in the last child. Other children remain unchanged. For example, if you change Qtr 1 from "30" to "50", March will change to "50". January and February will remain unchanged. If there are no existing values in any of a member's children, values entered at upper levels will be placed in all children.

Let's see an example of Time Spreading in action. Notice below I have January through March, rolling up to Q1:

	Jan	Feb	Mar	Q1
Units	500	400	400	1300
List Price				

Enter a new value into Q1. Once applied, the values are spread proportionally based on the existing data distribution:

	Jan	Feb	Mar	Q1
Units	600	480	480	1560
List Price				

You can temporarily lock a cell so that it is not impacted by spreading (Enterprise Planning Cloud will ignore the locked cell) by selecting *Data >> Action >> Lock*.

Note! Months that have already been locked by administrators cells with supporting detail and other read-only cells will also be skipped.

Grid Spread

Grid Spread allows you to increase or decrease cell values in your form by number or percentage. When using Grid Spread, the calculations are performed right then and there on your computer (the client), and you're able to see the calculation results so you can decide whether to save or not to save (to paraphrase Hamlet). Grid Spread in Enterprise Planning Cloud is available for users if enabled by the Administrator.

There are three types of spreads: Regular, Chunky, and Extra Creamy. Wait, those are for peanut butter. There are three types of *Grid Spreads* – Proportional Spread, Evenly Split, and Fill:

- **Proportional** – divides a value across members and dimensions in proportion to the values that are already there
- **Evenly Split** – divides a value evenly across the base level members
- **Fill** – fills the base members with a specified value

To perform a grid spread in a data form,
1. Select the upper level cell to adjust.
2. Click the *Data* button near the top right of the data form.
3. Under Actions, click *Spread*.
4. Adjust the cell by a number or percentage and select a spread method:

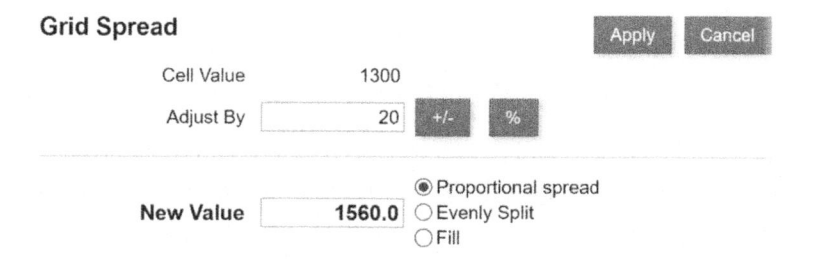

Grid Spread

			Apply	Cancel
Cell Value	1300			
Adjust By	20	+/- %		

		● Proportional spread
New Value	1560.0	○ Evenly Split
		○ Fill

5. Click *Apply* and review.
6. Click *Save* to save changes.

> **Note!** The Simplified UI only allows one cell to be selected at a time. As a result, Grid Spread in the Simplified UI can be done one cell at a time. Enterprise Planning Cloud Workspace does not have this restriction.

ATTACHMENTS, COMMENTARY, & DETAIL

Add Attachments to Data Forms

Sometimes you have some supporting information in the form of reports and you'd like to attach them to your planning data. In Enterprise Planning Cloud, users can attach reference documents in a cell on a form by inputting a reference URL.

I'll walk through a basic example to show you how to attach a URL in an Enterprise Planning Cloud data form cell.

To add an attachment to a data form,
1. Select a cell in a data form to add an attachment to.
2. Go to *Data >> Details >> Attachment* (paper clip icon):

3. Enter a Reference URL and click *Post*:

Attachments

admin
1/13/16 11:54 PM
/workspace/browse/get/VISION%20Reports
/Total%20Revenue%20by%20Product
Edit Delete

[Enter Reference URL]

Post Close

Note! The report URL can be copied by going to *Explore* (in Enterprise Planning Cloud Workspace), right-clicking the report, going to *Properties,* then copying the *SmartCut* URL segment:

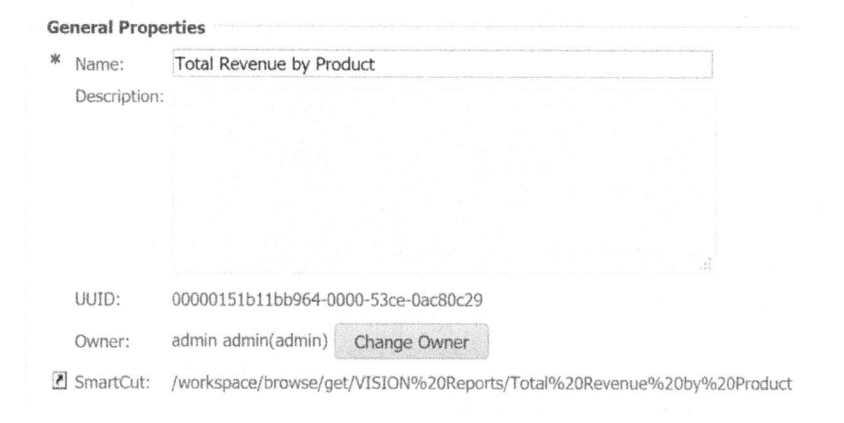

General Properties

* Name:	Total Revenue by Product
Description:	
UUID:	00000151b11bb964-0000-53ce-0ac80c29
Owner:	admin admin(admin) Change Owner
SmartCut:	/workspace/browse/get/VISION%20Reports/Total%20Revenue%20by%20Product

To open the attachment, click the cell containing the attachment, click the *Attachments* icon and click the URL. Since the URL links to a Financial Reporting Studio report in HTML view, you may need to enter some additional information, such as run time prompt entries, to view the report.

Add Supporting Details

What you shouldn't do is come up with your budget outside of Enterprise Planning Cloud and then copy the summary values in. If you want to show where a summary number comes from, Supporting Detail allows you list out your assumptions and drivers you used to calculate the required number on the form.

Some people refer to Supporting Detail as "line item detail" because it allows end users to provide detail below the bottom-level in the Enterprise Planning Cloud model. For example, there may be an account called "Travel" and you want to include details for each trip that makes up the travel account. You can build a hierarchy of supporting detail under a cell or cells using different methods for aggregation (+ - * / ~).

To enter or view Supporting Detail,
1. Select the desired cell and go to *Data >> Supporting Detail*:

The Supporting Detail window will display.

2. Click *Actions* and use the following actions (*Add Child* adds a line below the selected line, *Add Sibling* adds a line next to the selected line, etc.) to enter supporting detail lines:

Look Smarter Than You Are with Enterprise Planning Cloud 445

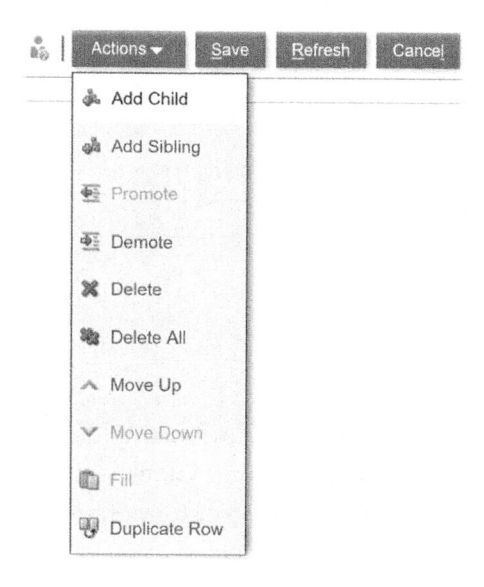

> Actions ▼ | Save | Refresh | Cancel
> - Add Child
> - Add Sibling
> - Promote
> - Demote
> - Delete
> - Delete All
> - Move Up
> - Move Down
> - Fill
> - Duplicate Row

3. Once the lines are added in the supporting detail window, you can add text to label the details, select an operator and enter the amount:

Supporting Detail

	Operator	Oct
Base	+	70.0
Additional	+	16.0
Total		86.0

4. Click *Save*.

The form will save and the cell with the supporting details will be shaded a deep, blue color:

	Oct	Nov
Units		
List Price		
4110:Hardware Revenue		
Units	86	106
List Price	30	30
4110:Hardware Revenue	2580	3180
Units	151	151
List Price	250	250

Print Supporting Details

You might want to print the supporting details included on a data form. You can do this in the Simplified UI, as well as, in Workspace. The option to print supporting details is set by default by the Administrator during form creation, or it can be selected at the time of printing.

Administrators can include supporting details in printed forms by default by simply checking the *Include supporting detail* option under Printing Options in the form Layout tab.

To enable supporting details at the time of printing,
1. Go to *Plans* and select the form to print.
2. Go to *Data >> Print*:

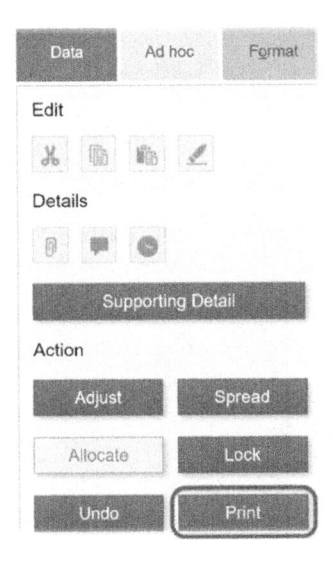

3. Check *Include supporting detail* under Printing Options:

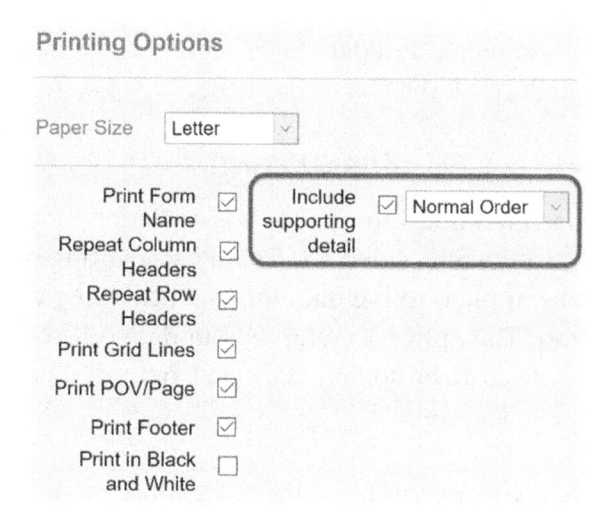

Printing Options

Paper Size: Letter

- [x] Print Form Name
- [x] Repeat Column Headers
- [x] Repeat Row Headers
- [x] Print Grid Lines
- [x] Print POV/Page
- [x] Print Footer
- [ ] Print in Black and White

- [x] Include supporting detail — Normal Order

4. Click *Print Preview*, then *Open* or *Save* the file to do what you wish with it.

Add Comments

Once in a while, you'll want to comment on an individual value in your form. Maybe a variance is off and you want to explain why or maybe you need to explain why "Going to Cabo" is a legitimate business expense.

Comments let you add commentary to your plan. Cell-level text comments can be added to any intersection at any level in a data form:

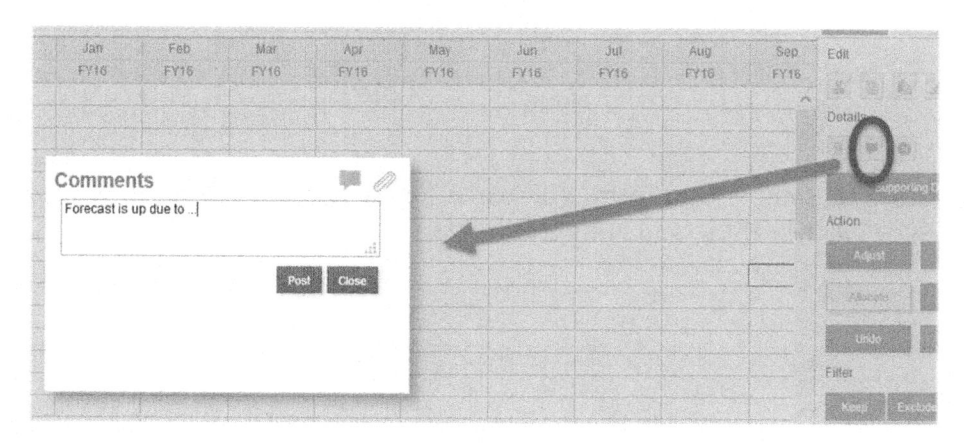

All users who have read access to the cell can read the cell text comment. The comment can be printed within the data form.

To enter comments in a data form, simply click on a cell and go to *Data*. Under Details, click the *Comments* icon.

FORMATTING

Enterprise Planning Cloud allows user-defined formatting for all forms and grids in the Simplified UI. Default formatting or user-defined formatting can be applied to the data forms. Formatting can be saved or cleared, if desired. The option to wrap text in data cells is also available. Form numbers or text can be bolded, italicized, or underlined, and the font sizes can be adjusted as well.

To format a form, simply click the *Format* menu and add your desired formatting options:

A sample of a form with some formatting is shown below (cell color, cell text color, and bolded values):

Look Smarter Than You Are with Enterprise Planning Cloud 449

		Jan	Feb	Mar	Q1
P_000:No Product	Units	500	400	400	1300
	List Price				
	4110:Hardware Revenue.f				
P_100:Product X	Units				
	List Price				
	4110:Hardware Revenue.f				
P_110:Sentinal Standard Notebook	Units	13	13	13	39
	List Price	1350	1200	1200	3750
	4110:Hardware Revenue.f	17550	15600	15600	48750
P_120:Sentinal Custom Notebook	Units	13	13	13	39
	List Price				
	4110:Hardware Revenue.f				
P_130:Envoy Standard Netbook	Units	13	13	13	39

As an added bonus, users can adjust the height and width of a column or row with a click and a drag, or by right-clicking a row or column and entering in a pixel value:

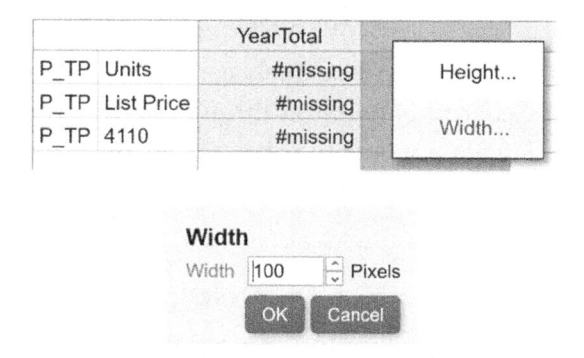

		YearTotal
P_TP	Units	#missing
P_TP	List Price	#missing
P_TP	4110	#missing

Height...
Width...

Width
Width 100 Pixels
OK Cancel

VIEW MEMBER FORMULAS

Have you ever wondered, "Where in the heck did this number come from?" The Enterprise Planning Cloud Administrator will usually create a number of calculations for the Planning application that automatically derive numbers based on your plan inputs. In many cases, this is done using member formulas. You can view the logic behind the member formula calculations. In the example below, the administrator has enabled *Member Formula* on the Sales Forecast – Products data form.

Once the administrator has enabled the Member Formula option for a specific row or column, users can view the formulas in the data forms.

Click the *Formula* icon to view:

P_120:Sentinal Custom Notebook	Units		106	106
	List Price		350	350
	4110:Hardware Revenue [f]		37100	37100
P_130:Envoy Standard Netbook	Units			
	List Price			
	4110:Hardware Revenue [f]			

The member formula will appear in a box:

Member Formula
If (@ISMBR("Forecast"))
"Units"*"List Price";
ENDIF

ANALYZE

Users can perform ad hoc analysis within a data form with the Analyze feature. Security is honored through ad hoc grids so users can still read and update data where they have been assigned access.

Users can perform the following ad hoc actions:

Ad Hoc Option	Description
Pivot	Move a dimension from and to Page, Row or Column
Move	Move a dimension Up, Down, Left or Right when more than one dimension is listed in a Row, Column or Page
Zoom In Next Level	Drill down into the next level of a hierarchy of a dimension
Zoom In Bottom Level	Zoom into all Level 0 members of a specified parent member

Ad Hoc Option	Description
Zoom Out	Drill up a hierarchy to the parent of the selected member
Expand All Levels	Expand the entire hierarchy of the selected member
Keep Selected	Keep the selected member(s) and remove all other members in that dimension
Remove Selected	Remove the selected member(s) and keep all other members in that dimension
Select Members	Launch a member selection window for the member selected
Change Alias	Toggle between alternate alias tables for an application

To use the Analyze feature in a data form, go to *Actions >> Analyze*:

Once in Analyze mode, users can use typical analytic functions like zooming, pivoting, and selecting members by going to the *Ad hoc* menu:

Users can save the form definition for future use by selecting *Actions >> Save Ad Hoc Grid*:

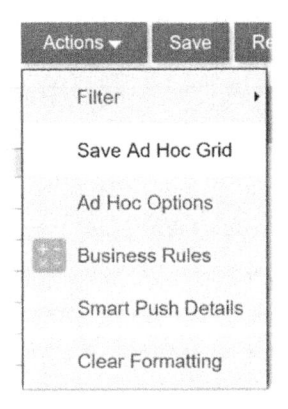

You will enter a name for the definition:

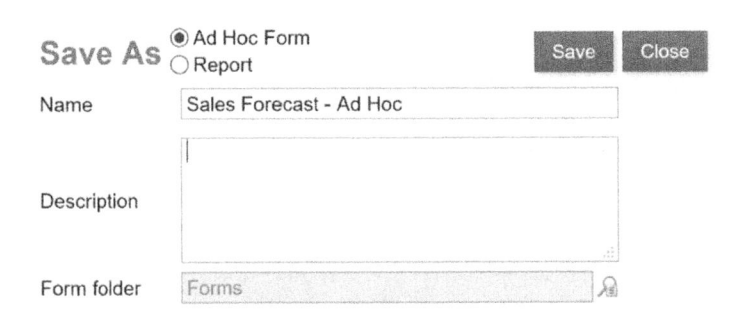

By default, the ad hoc grid will be saved under *Plans >> Ad Hoc* tab and then the *Ad Hoc: Forms* folder:

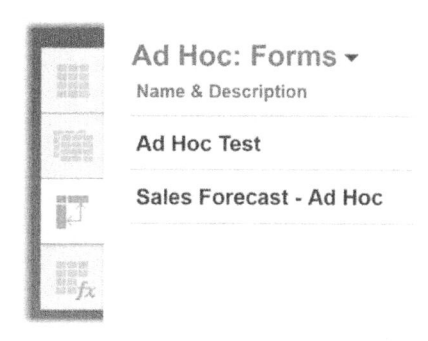

Ad Hoc: Forms ▼

Name & Description

Ad Hoc Test

Sales Forecast - Ad Hoc

Note! *Save* will not save the ad hoc definition such as the POV. *Save* only saves any data changes that you made in ad hoc mode.

You can change the default ad hoc options to support your analyzing experience. Click *Ad Hoc Options* within an ad hoc form:

| Actions ▼ | Save | Refresh | Ad Hoc Options | Close |

The Ad Hoc Options window will open with various property options (not all options are shown below):

Ad Hoc Options

Member inclusion
- ☑ Include selection
- ☐ Within selected group

Zoom in levels
- ◉ Next level
- ○ All levels
- ○ Bottom level

Ancestor Position
- ○ Top
- ◉ Bottom

Navigate without refreshing data
- ○ Yes
- ◉ No

Suppress

Zeros
- ☐ Row
- ☐ Column

- ☐ Repeat Members
- ☐ Missing Blocks on Rows

Precision

	Minimum	Maximum
Currency values	0	None
Non-currency values	0	None
Percentage values	0	None

Under Ad Hoc Options, you can choose the drill behavior – do you want to keep the member that you zoom on or not? Do you want to show the member name, the alias, or both? Do you want to suppress missing data? You can set options for these under Ad Hoc Options.

Available Ad Hoc Options include Member inclusion, display of member names and aliases, ancestor position, indentation, suppression (including suppression of data for columns), precision, and replacement options for missing or no-access data cells.

The Analyze feature is great for taking an existing data form's structure and then going to "ad hoc" mode. To create a grid completely from scratch, users can create ad hoc grids.

USE SMART FORMS

Simply put, Smart Forms are saved ad hoc grids that allow Excel formulas and grid labels that are not defined in the application. Smart Forms are available in the Simplified UI and in Smart View.

> **Note!** Smart Forms can be seen in Enterprise Planning Cloud Workspace, but don't be fooled – they cannot be opened in Workspace.

In the Simplified UI, Smart Forms can be found under *Plans* in the Smart Form tab:

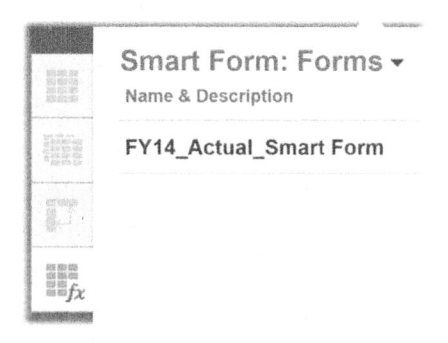

Smart Form: Forms
Name & Description

FY14_Actual_Smart Form

Hover over the calculated cells to view the formulas:

Q1+Q2	Q3+Q4			
948	826			
54480	54480			
518400	478400			

Row Total ProductHardware Revenue Column Q1+Q2 518400 This cell is read-only
Formula:=SUM(D4:E4)

To view Smart Forms in Smart View, connect to the application and open the form. Then double-click the form to open. Grid labels will show as orange and the calculated cells will show as light green:

	A	B	C	D	E	F	G	H	I
1			-YearTotal					Q1+Q2	Q3+Q4
2		Units	1774	474	474	474	352	948	826
3	Total Prod	List Price	108960	27240	27240	27240	27240	54480	54480
4		Hardware	996800	259200	259200	259200	219200	518400	478400

RUNNING BUSINESS RULES

If you need to run either simple or complex calculations on your Planning data, then business rules are going to be your weapon of choice. Business rules perform calculations on data like aggregating data from detail levels to summary levels, allocating data from summary levels to detailed levels, copying data, clearing data, and more. Business rules, in most cases, are created by the Enterprise Planning Cloud administrator.

Some business rules are attached to data forms and will automatically run when you save a data form. You can also launch a business rule associated with a data form by going to *Actions >> Business Rules*.

Some business rules may not be associated with a specific data form. Go to *Rules* from the main menu to select and run any business rule in the Enterprise Planning Cloud application by clicking the *Launch* arrow. The list of business rules that the current user has access to is shown. Users have the option to filter business rules by Plan Type or Rule Type:

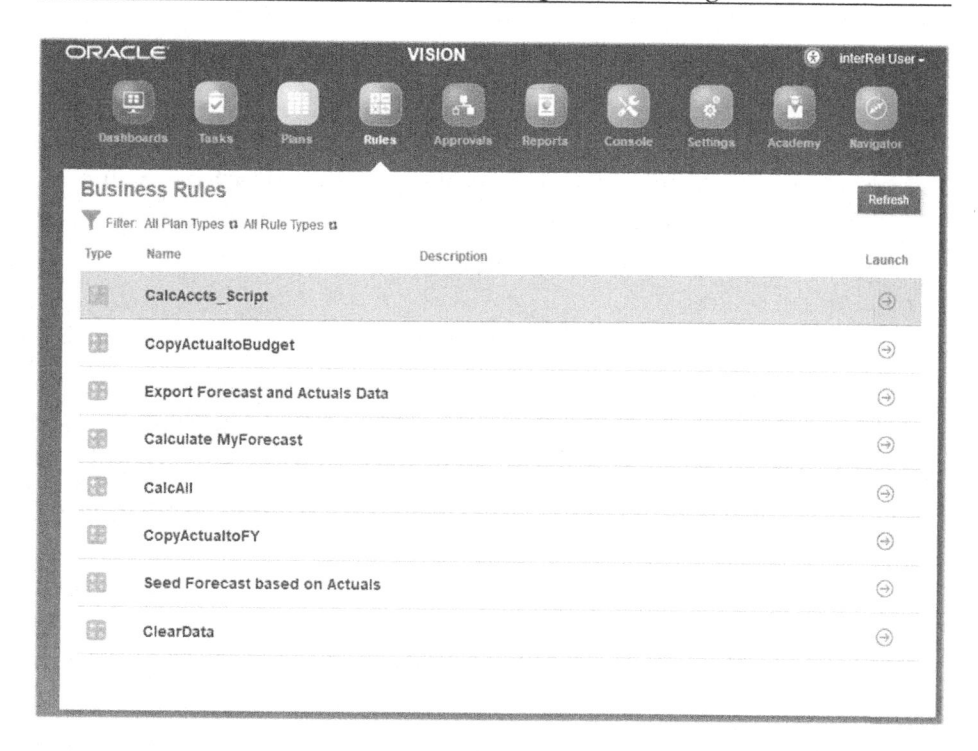

	CalcAccts_Script		
	CopyActualtoBudget		
	Export Forecast and Actuals Data		
	Calculate MyForecast		
	CalcAll		
	CopyActualtoFY		
	Seed Forecast based on Actuals		
	ClearData		

Depending on the rule, it may run a few seconds or a few minutes. A message will display letting you know the business rule has run successfully (or if it failed in misery with errors).

Runtime Prompts

Sometimes you may be prompted to enter some information for the business rule. What market should be calculated? What period should be calculated? What percent should be used in the bonus calculation?

Business rules have the ability to prompt users for values when they are launched. This is conveniently called a "run time prompt". Say you needed to re-calculate your department budget after submitting data. A single business rule is created for all the departments, and all you have to do is select your specific department when prompted by the business rule. The rule will run for your department.

For example, you may create a business rule that prompts users to select a Scenario, Version, and Segment. A *Member Search* icon is available to search the dimensions for a specific member or members. If you know the desired member name exactly, simply type it in. Click the *Launch* icon to run the business rule.

The administrator dictates the rules for run time prompts. They can be single or multiple members, numeric value, Smart List value, or text value. Members available for runtime prompts are limited by your security and limitations further defined by the administrator.

APPROVALS

Approvals can be used as a mechanism for reviewing, tracking, and approving plans via the Enterprise Planning Cloud Workspace, Simplified UI, or Smart View. The administrator may define approval paths for plans, set validations to highlight exceptions, view audit information for plans and comment, and annotate the plans.

Approvals are managed by Planning Units. The Planning Unit consists of the Entity, Scenario, and Version dimensions. Once Planning Units are initiated, users enter their plans in the data forms and run business rules, then submit their plans for review and approval.

Under Approvals, users can view the status of approvals and sort through them by Approvals Status, Current Owner, or Planning Unit Name.

The administrator must complete several steps before you are ready to use approvals. Check out the Oracle documentation for more information on approvals.

RUN REPORTS

Reports that were created in Financial Reporting Studio or Ad Hoc Grids saved as reports will be saved in the Reports section of the Simplified UI. Simply click the *Reports* icon from the Simplified UI main menu:

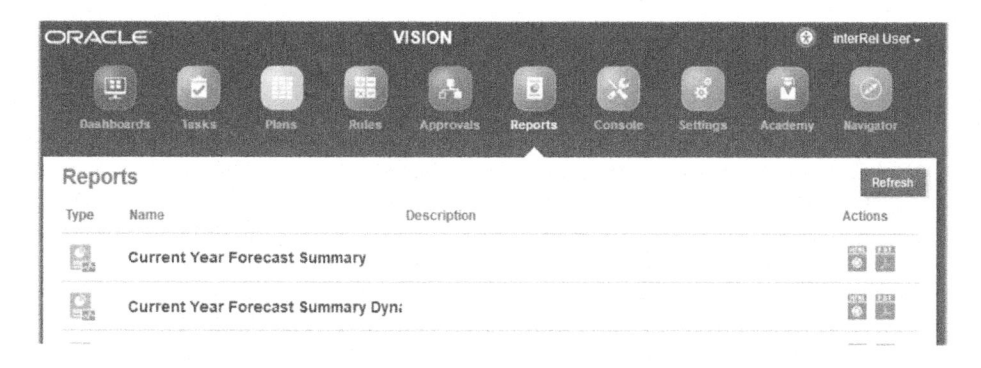

Look Smarter Than You Are with Enterprise Planning Cloud   459

The reports can be viewed in HTML or PDF view:

Some reports will require users to specify the members for each dimension for the user point of view:

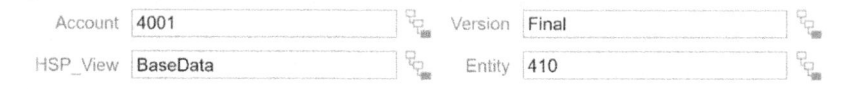

Other reports may be designed to use report prompts. End users will answer prompts and the report will be displayed:

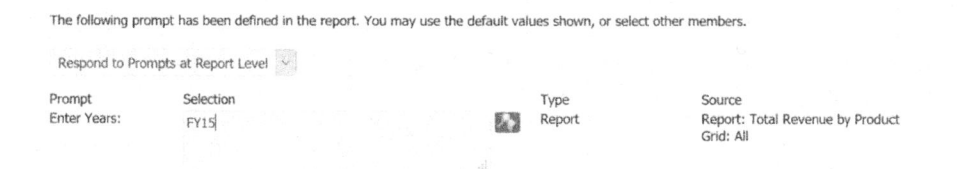

Finally, the report opens in another window:

| Account: 4001 | HSP_View: BaseData | Version: Final | Entity: 410 |

Total Revenue by Products - FY15

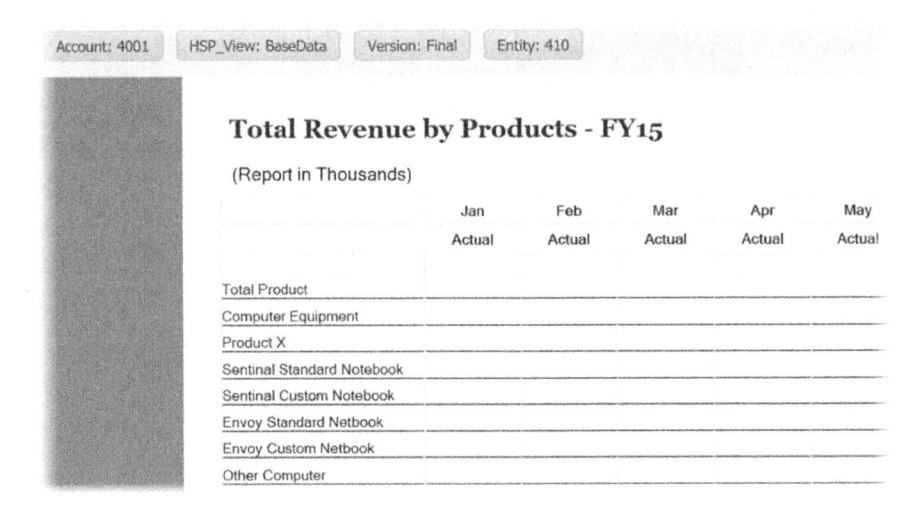

(Report in Thousands)

	Jan	Feb	Mar	Apr	May
	Actual	Actual	Actual	Actual	Actual
Total Product					
Computer Equipment					
Product X					
Sentinal Standard Notebook					
Sentinal Custom Notebook					
Envoy Standard Netbook					
Envoy Custom Netbook					
Other Computer					

> **Note!** In HTML view, POV members can be changed; simply click the blue dimension buttons at the top of the report.

SETTINGS

Define Application Settings

Users can also select a number of settings to make Enterprise Planning Cloud behave like it's your own personal budgeting product. The Application Settings tab is where you can access and make changes to several preference options. You can enable e-mail notification so that you automatically receive e-mail notifications when you become the new owner of a planning unit. You can also control display of member names or their aliases, set number formatting options, or change the time zone. The Simplified UI provides minimal setting options compared to Enterprise Planning Cloud Workspace in order to stick with the minimalist approach.

To access user preferences, click *Settings* from the Simplified UI main menu:

Look Smarter Than You Are with Enterprise Planning Cloud 461

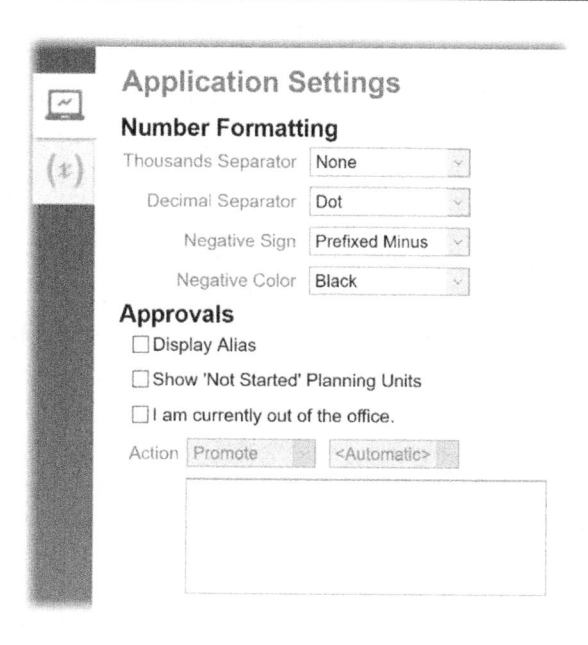

Users have the option to stick with the application defaults (defined by the Enterprise Planning Cloud administrator) or define their own application settings. Be sure to click *Save* once settings have been defined:

Set User Variables

The second tab users will see in Settings is the User Variable Options. User Variables allow data forms to be filtered for just the members end users want to see. For example, an end user may have read access to all entities but write access for the International Sales entity. When he inputs the sales forecast, he really only cares about International Sales. So the administrator sets up a User Variable called "MyRegion" and designs the Sales Forecast – Products form to select this variable. The end user sets his MyRegion variable to "International Sales" and the form only shows International Sales and not the other entities.

The Sales Forecast – Products data form was created to contain one user variable: MyRegion. If you open the data form without defining a user variable for MyRegion, you will get an error message that states that user variables members must be selected before the form can be opened. You cannot open a data form that contains a user variable if you haven't selected a member for that variable.

To set the user variables,
1. Click *Settings* from the main menu.
2. Click the *User Variables* tab:

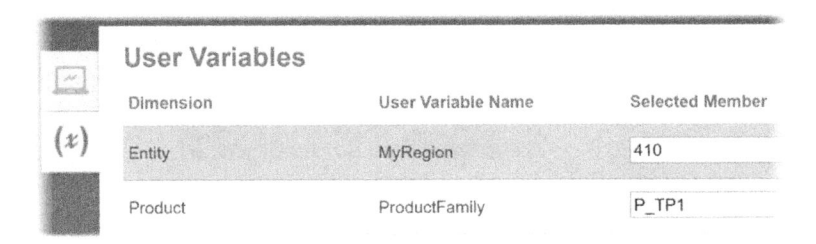

User Variables

Dimension	User Variable Name	Selected Member
Entity	MyRegion	410
Product	ProductFamily	P_TP1

3. Use the Member Selector to designate a member for both user variables:

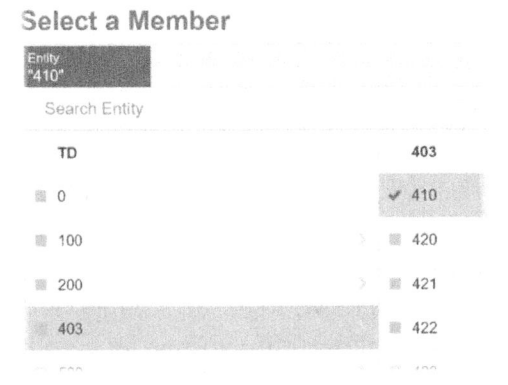

Select a Member

Entity
"410"

Search Entity

TD	403
☐ 0	✓ 410
☐ 100	☐ 420
☐ 200	☐ 421
403	☐ 422

Note! You can type "P_TP1" or any other member name into the text box if you know the exact spelling of the member name.

4. Click *Save*.
5. Open the Sales Forecast – Products form and notice the form defaults to the member that was selected for MyRegion:

Sales Forecast - Products

Scenario	MyRegion	Version			
Forecast	410	Pass1			
				Oct	Nov
				FY15	FY15
P_100:Product X			Units	86	106
			List Price	30	30
			4110:Hardware Revenue	2580	3180

As you can see, user variables provide huge time savings when it comes to data form development for power users and administrators.

ALLOW USERS TO ADD MEMBERS ON THE FLY

A new feature was added in the 11.1.2.3 on-premise Planning release that allows users to dynamically "add new members on the fly". If enabled and configured by the administrator, end users can add new sparse dimension members through data forms and enter data for those new members (without performing a database refresh). This same functionality is available in Enterprise Planning Cloud.

The administrator can manage this process by setting boundaries on how many members can be added, identifying the parent of the new members, and performing the initial configuration for this feature. Placeholder members are created under the covers and not visible to users until they've added their new sparse member. Users can add a single new member at a time on the data form.

To set this up properly, settings need to be set properly in the sparse dimension of choice, business rules, and the data forms. I'll start by some initial configuration steps in the desired dimension.

To allow for dynamic "members on the fly" within a dimension for a specific parent,

1. In the Simplified UI, go to *Navigator >> Administer >> Dimensions*.
2. Select a sparse dimension from the drop-down. I'm going to choose *Product*.
3. Create a new parent for these dynamic members or select an existing one. I'm going to add a new parent to the root called "New Products".

There are a few settings specific to enabling dynamic members.

4. Check *Enable for Dynamic Children*.
5. Select how many maximum children you'll allow users to add to it, as well as the type of access rights. I'm going to allow 25 maximum children members and *Inherit* permissions:

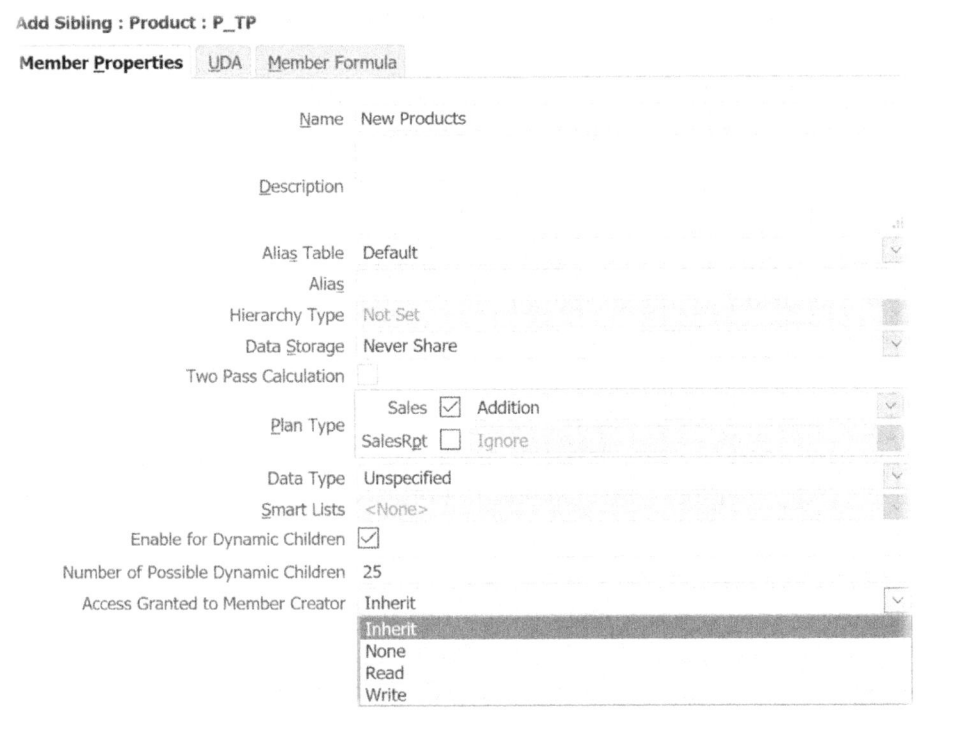

Add Sibling : Product : P_TP

Member Properties UDA Member Formula

Name	New Products
Description	
Alias Table	Default
Alias	
Hierarchy Type	Not Set
Data Storage	Never Share
Two Pass Calculation	
Plan Type	Sales ☑ Addition / SalesRpt ☐ Ignore
Data Type	Unspecified
Smart Lists	<None>
Enable for Dynamic Children	☑
Number of Possible Dynamic Children	25
Access Granted to Member Creator	Inherit

Inherit
None
Read
Write

Now I'll need to refresh the database to create the placeholders for the dynamic members in the database. To do this,
6. Go to *Console* >> *Actions* >> *Refresh Database* and refresh the database.
7. Once the refresh is complete and successful, click *Finish*.
8. Click *Close* and then *Close* again to get completely out of the Refresh Database screens.

Next, it's time to create the Calculation Manager rule that will prompt users for the member name and optionally other information for the new member.

To create the Calc Manager business rule for users to use to add dynamic members,
1. In the Simplified UI, go to *Navigator* >> *Administer* >> *Rules*.
2. Choose *Actions* >> *New Object*.
3. Make the selections necessary to create a new business rule within the Sales plan type of the Vision app.
    a. **Application Type**: Planning
    b. **Application**: Vision
    c. **Plan Type**: Sales
    d. **Object Type**: Rule
    e. **Name**: "AddDynamicProducts":

New Object

Application Type	Planning
Application	VISION
Plan Type	Sales
Object Type	Rule
Name	AddDynamicProducts

Help　　　　　　　　　　　　　　　　　　　　　　　OK　Cancel

4. Click *OK*.

The new business rule editor will open. Now I need to set up the new business rule so that it allows for the creation of dynamic members.

5. The "Begin" step in the graphical interface should be highlighted by default. While highlighted, on the bottom right-hand side, find the Properties window and check the option to *Create dynamic members*:

Properties

Location

Application   VISION
Plan Type   Sales

Options

Create dynamic members ☑
Delete dynamic members ☐
Enable Notifications   ☐

Next, a variable needs to be added. This will need to be a run-time prompt that accepts the new product names.

6. Within the *Global Range* tab, select the *Variable Selector* button:

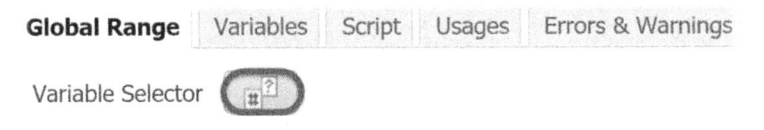

Global Range | Variables | Script | Usages | Errors & Warnings

Variable Selector

7. Click *Create* to create a new variable:

Look Smarter Than You Are with Enterprise Planning Cloud   467

Select Variable

Scope Plan Type [v]   Create

Replacement Execution

Variable   Description   Group   Type
No data to display

Type
Value

Help   OK   Cancel

8. In the left-hand pane, navigate down the Planning tree until the *Sales* plan type is highlighted:

```
System View   AddDyna
Variable Navigator
▲ 🌐 Planning
   ▷ 🌐 <Global>
   ▲ 🗂 VISION
       ▷ 📄 Sales
       ▷ 📄 SalesRpt
```

9. Then within the Variable Designer tab, select *Actions >> New* to create a new variable:

Variable Designer

Replacement | Execution

Actions ▾

New — Ctrl+Shift+V
Save — Ctrl+S
Refresh — Ctrl+Shift+R

10. Enter the properties of the new variable, as shown below.
    a. **Dimension**: Product
    b. **Limits**: @RELATIVE("New Products",0)
    c. **RTP**: Checked
    d. **RTP Text**: Add New Products
    e. **Dynamic Member Parent**: "New Products"

It's critical that the parent of the new dynamic members be specified in the "Dynamic Member Parent" field:

Properties					
Scope VISION.Sales		Description			
Name AddProducts					
Group					
Type Member					
☐ Use Last Entered Value					
Dimension	Limits	Default Value	RTP	RTP Text	Dynamic Member Parent
Product	"@RELATIVE("New Products", 0)"		☑	Add New Products	"New Products"

11. Click the *Save* icon to save the variable.
12. Navigate back to the rule.
13. Within the Global Range window, specific the new variable as the range of the Products dimension:

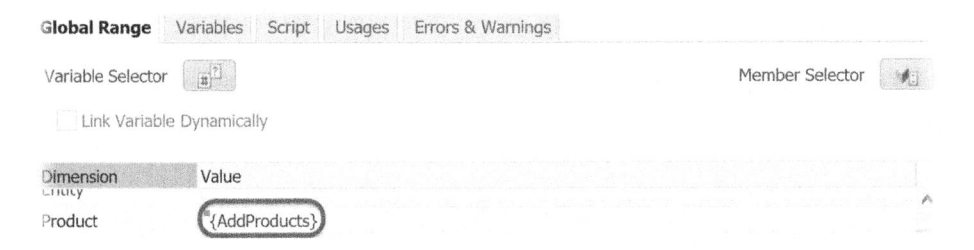

Global Range	Variables	Script	Usages	Errors & Warnings

Variable Selector   Member Selector

☐ Link Variable Dynamically

Dimension	Value
Entity	
Product	{AddProducts}

14. Save the rule. Click *OK* when you receive the confirmation.

15. Validate and deploy the rule.
16. You should receive a message that the deployment was successfully.

> **ⓘ Deploy**
> The deployment was successful.

17. Close out of Calculation Manager.

This rule will simply add the new product member. You may also want to add additional prompts to collect information from users in this step, prompting them to enter the forecast units and average price.

Now let's create an action menu that will be assigned on a data form that will run this business rule. This will be the construct that allows users to add members dynamically.

1. Within the Simplified UI, go to *Navigator >> Administer >> Action Menus*.
2. Create a new menu by selecting the green plus symbol or going to *Actions >> Create Menu*.
3. Name the menu "Products Menu":

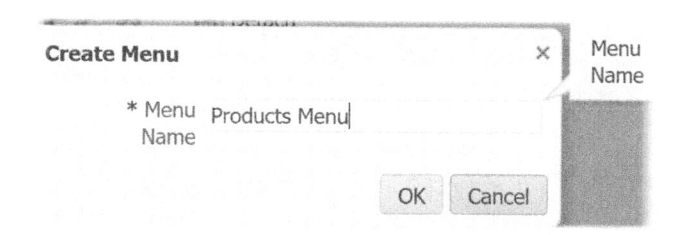

Create Menu　　　　　　　　　　　　　× | Menu Name
* Menu Name　Products Menu
OK　Cancel

4. Edit the menu.
5. Click the *Add a child* icon to add the first menu item:

470   Chapter 10: End User Activities

Menus

Edit Menu : Products Menu

6. Enter the properties of the new menu item.
   a. **Menu Item**: Add New Products
   b. **Label**: Enter new product members
   c. **Type**: Business Rule
   d. **Required Parameters**: None
   e. **Plan Type**: Sales
   f. **Business Rules**: AddDynamicProducts
   g. **View Type**: Classic View:

7. Save the menu item and then close out of the Actions Menu window.

Next, it's time to create a Planning data form that attaches to the business rule. This is the vehicle through which users will add members dynamically.

1. Within the Simplified UI, go to *Navigator >> Administer >> Forms*.
2. Go to *Actions >> Create simple form* or click.
3. Set the name of the form and add an optional description:

Form and Ad Hoc Grid Management

Simple Form:

Properties | Layout | Other Options | Business Rules | Smart Push

* Form   Add Product Members
Description   This form allows users to add up to 25 new products

Since the primary goal of this data form is to add new products, a simple form will be created.

4. Select the Layout tab and define the dimension layout so that it matches the following:
   a. **POV Account**: Units
   b. **POV Scenario**: Forecast
   c. **POV Entity**: No entity
   d. **POV HSP_View**: BaseData
   e. **POV Version**: Final
   f. **POV Month**: &CurMth
   g. **Rows**: IDescendants(New Products)
   h. **Columns**: &ForecastYear:

5. Add the menu in the *Other Options* tab:

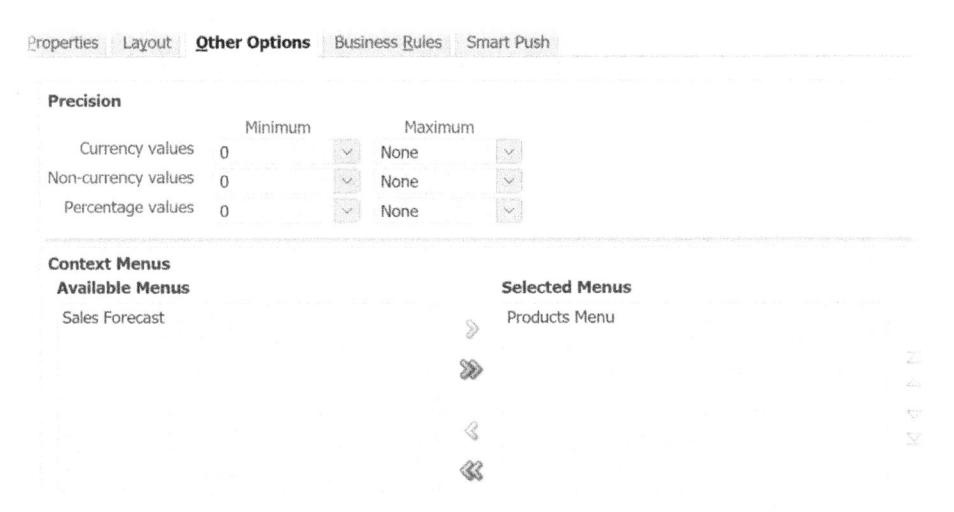

6. Save the form and then close it.

Finally, let's test out the final product. Can an end user really add a member on the fly and enter data? Yes!

To add members on the fly,
1. From the Simplified UI, navigate to *Plans >> Add Product Members* data form and open it.

2. Right-click on one of the dimension members in the POV bar. You will see the newly created action menu. Click on it.

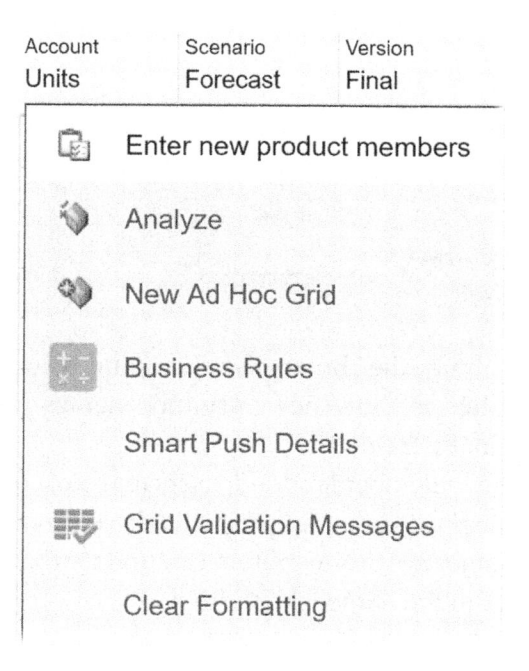

Account	Scenario	Version
Units	Forecast	Final

- Enter new product members
- Analyze
- New Ad Hoc Grid
- Business Rules
- Smart Push Details
- Grid Validation Messages
- Clear Formatting

3. Enter a new product "External Hard Drive":

AddDynamicProducts

* Product Name: External Hard Drive

4. Click *Launch* to launch the rule. If the rule launches successfully, a confirmation message will show:

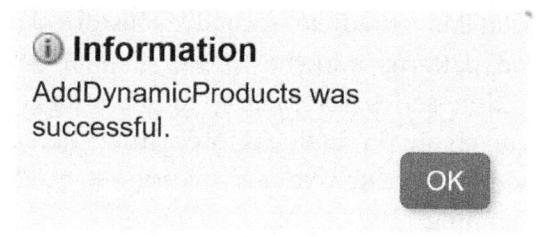

ⓘ Information

AddDynamicProducts was successful.

OK

Up to 25 new products can be added under the New Products member, based on the criteria originally set in the member properties. The new products will be listed in the data:

Add Product Members

Account Units	Scenario Forecast	Version Final	Entity No Entity	Period Apr
		FY16		
External Hard Drive				
⊟ New Products				

The next time the Enterprise Planning Cloud administrator refreshes the database, the new product names will replace the placeholders originally created.

Once the new member is added, users may not change the member name. If the business rule is set up properly, there are options to let users delete the new member. Administrators can update the member name or delete the member in the Dimension Editor.

PREDICTIVE ANALYTICS

Enterprise Planning Cloud supports Predictive Analytics, a statistical forecasting feature that is accessible to all Enterprise Planning Cloud users. Predictive Analytics provides the following features and benefits:

- Utilize statistical prediction scenarios
- Enables sanity check during forecast cycles
- Ability to compare accuracy of forecasts vs. statistical predictions
- Uses Crystal Ball's Predictor to analyze historical data and projects trends and patterns into the future. Crystal Ball Predictor is a powerful time-series forecasting tool that leverages Microsoft Excel. It can create professional forecasting charts and reports
- Users review forecasted values, override if needed, then submit back to Planning
- Automatically forecast best and worst case scenarios in addition to base case

PLAN IN EXCEL USING SMART VIEW

Good news! Smart View and all the neat things you can do with it are also available with Enterprise Planning Cloud. If you are not familiar with Smart View, it is NOT just another Excel add-in for Oracle EPM. Its capabilities are far greater than any other Hyperion Excel add-in you've seen to date. Smart View provides a common Microsoft Office interface to multiple tools including Essbase, Financial Management, on-premise Planning, Financial Reporting, and more. This means you can use Microsoft Excel to input data and Microsoft Excel, Word, or PowerPoint to view, manipulate, report, and share data.

Combining the powers of Enterprise Planning Cloud and Smart View allows planners to update data in forms, calculate data using business rules, and utilize most of the other features available through the Enterprise Planning Cloud web client, all through Microsoft Excel (if you are a financially minded individual, you know that Excel is as valuable as your left hand). The chart below shows the similarities between the Enterprise Planning Cloud web client and Smart View (everything you can do in the web from an end user perspective you can do in Smart View):

Feature	Enterprise Planning Cloud Web Client	Smart View
Web	Yes	No
Enter Data	Yes	Yes
Launch Business Rules	Yes	Yes
Supporting Detail	Yes	Yes
Cell Text	Yes	Yes
Adjust	Yes	Yes
Mass Allocate, Grid Spread	Yes	Yes

Feature	Enterprise Planning Cloud Web Client	Smart View
Linked Excel Formulas	No	Yes
View Instructions	Yes	Yes
Workflow	Yes	Yes
Copy / Paste	Yes	Yes
Client Install Required	No	Yes
Composite Forms	Yes	Yes
Update User Variables	Yes	Yes
Smart Form	Yes (but not editing)	Yes
Task List	Yes	Yes
Cascade Data	No	Yes

As you can see, almost everything that you can do in the Enterprise Planning Cloud web client can be done in Smart View. You may have noticed that Smart View requires a client install. To do this, open *Navigate* and under Install, click *Smart View for Office*. Follow the installation process and you will notice a Smart View ribbon in Excel.

Note! Always download the latest version of Smart View. If there is an older version installed on your computer, uninstall it first then install the current version through Enterprise Planning Cloud.

Let's go over how do use some of these awesome Smart View features, starting with connecting to the VISION application with Smart View.

To connect to an application in Smart View,
1. Open Microsoft Excel.
2. Click the *Smart View* ribbon:

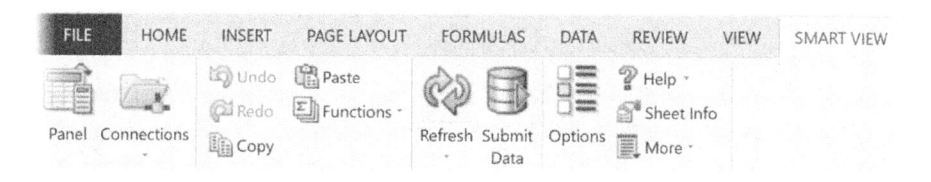

3. Click *Options* and click the *Advanced* tab.
4. In Shared Connection URL, enter the connection URL. A sample URL is below:

https://servicename-test-domainname.PBCS.Cloud.us1.oraclecloud.com/workspace/SmartViewProviders

Note! The Shared Connections URL only needs to be input once for each instance. If you want to connect to another instance (say you want to change from Test to Production), a new Shared Connections URL must be entered.

5. Click *OK*.
6. Click the *Panel* icon (to the very left).
7. When the Panel appears, click *Shared Connections*:

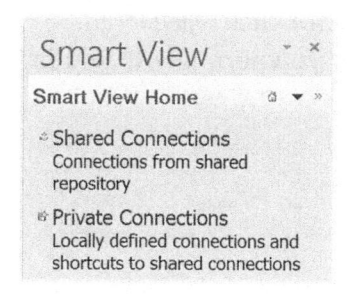

8. Enter the domain. Click *OK*.

9. Enter your username and password. Click *OK*.
10. In the Panel, select *Oracle Hyperion Planning, Fusion Edition* from the server drop-down menu.
11. Expand the server and VISION application folder:

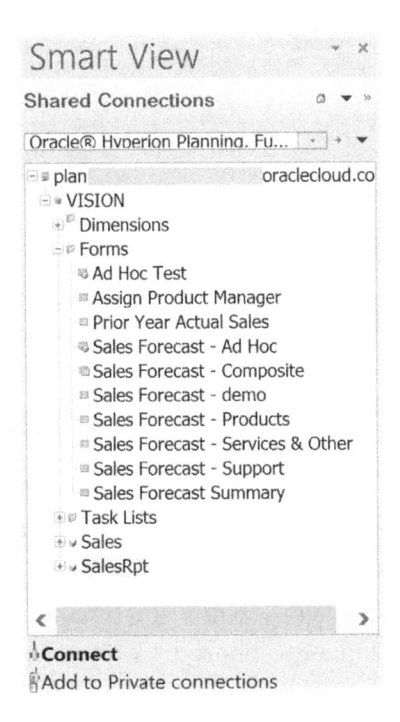

```
Smart View
Shared Connections
Oracle® Hyperion Planning. Fu...
  plan                        oraclecloud.co
    VISION
      Dimensions
      Forms
        Ad Hoc Test
        Assign Product Manager
        Prior Year Actual Sales
        Sales Forecast - Ad Hoc
        Sales Forecast - Composite
        Sales Forecast - demo
        Sales Forecast - Products
        Sales Forecast - Services & Other
        Sales Forecast - Support
        Sales Forecast Summary
      Task Lists
      Sales
      SalesRpt

Connect
Add to Private connections
```

Connection to the application is complete.

To open a data form, input data, and save data in Smart View,

1. In the Panel, expand the *Forms* folder and double-click on the desired form (or click *Open form*).
2. Enter data as you normally would in Excel:

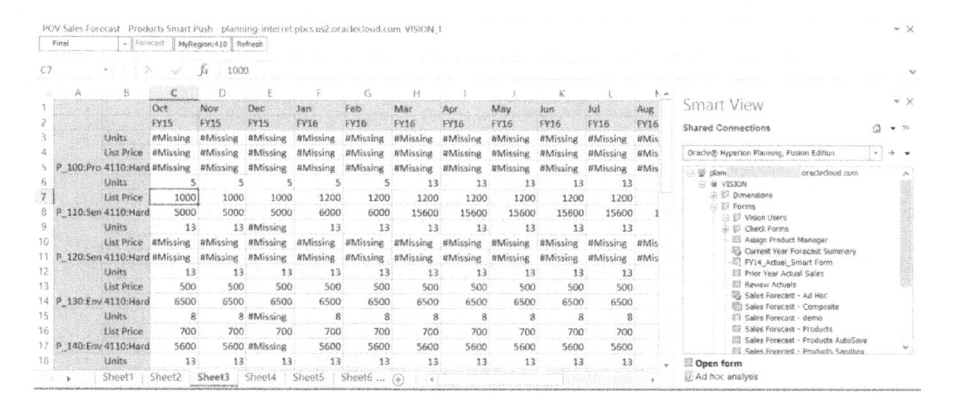

Look Smarter Than You Are with Enterprise Planning Cloud 479

3. To save the data back to Enterprise Planning Cloud, click *Submit Data* in the Planning ribbon (this ribbon appears when you open a data form):

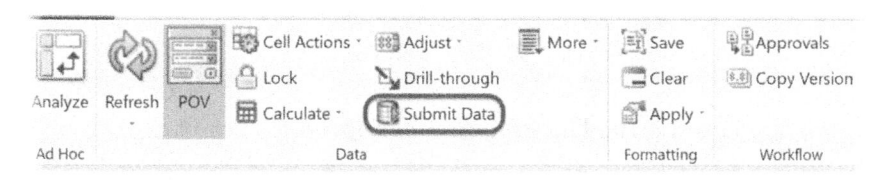

Using the Planning panel, users can also add comments, supporting detail, and attachments, calculate data by running business runs, and adjust data.

In the Panel, users can access and perform Task List activities by opening the Task List folder and double-clicking on a task:

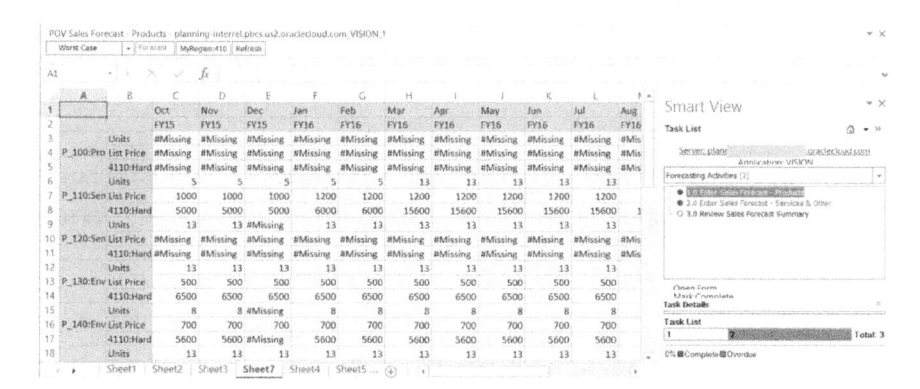

To perform ad hoc analysis in Smart View,
1. Click on a database (a.k.a., plan type or cube):

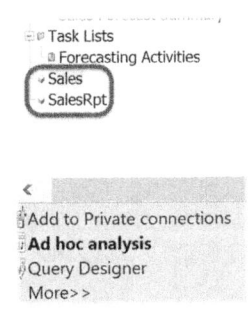

2. Click *Ad hoc analysis* to open a blank ad hoc grid:

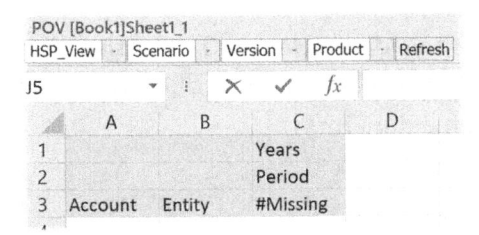

The Planning Ad Hoc ribbon will appear:

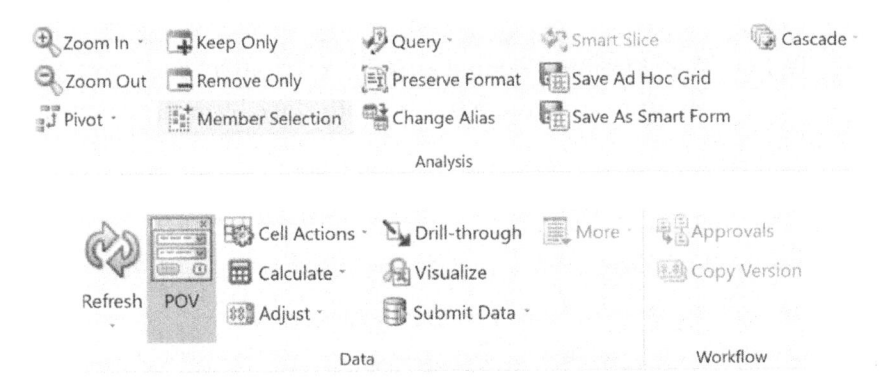

3. Select dimension members (or type them in if you are sure of the exact spelling) and zoom in, zoom out, pivot, and cascade to analyze away!

Look Smarter Than You Are with Enterprise Planning Cloud 481

(screenshot of Smart View ad hoc grid in Excel showing POV BaseData, Forecast, International Sales, Final, with columns Oct FY15 through Nov FY16 and rows for Product X and Sentinal St/C Hardware with Units, List Price, Hardware values, and Envoy Star/Cus Hardware data)

> **Note!** To perform ad hoc analysis on a data form, click *Analyze* in the Planning ribbon while the form is open in Smart View. Alternatively, you can select a form in the Panel and click *Ad hoc analysis*.

Ad hoc grids can be saved by users for later use.

RETAIN EXCEL FORMATTING / CUSTOM STYLES

You can apply formatting to data forms and ad hoc grids in Smart View by choosing the Save icon under formatting (note this is not available in Analyze mode):

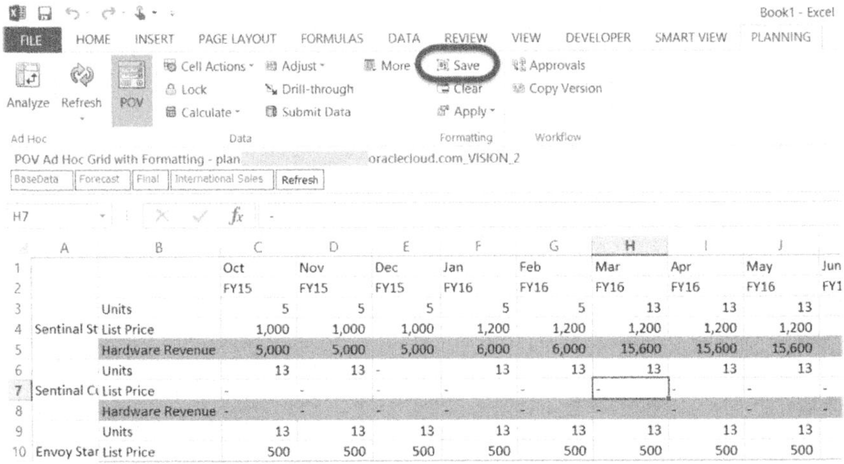

If saving an ad hoc grid, you can choose to *Submit Formatting*:

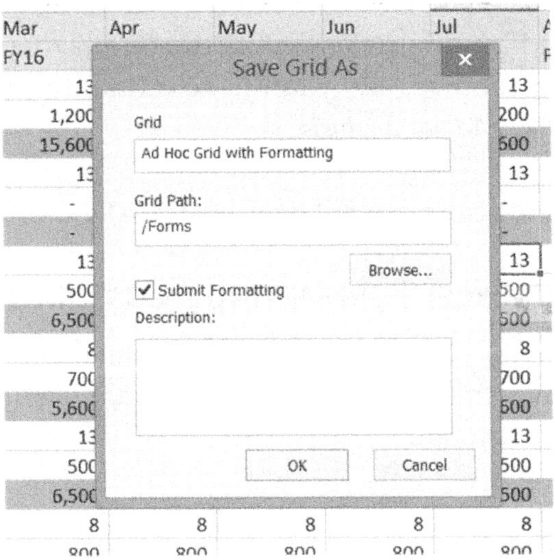
Save Grid As
Grid
Ad Hoc Grid with Formatting
Grid Path:
/Forms
Browse...
Submit Formatting
Description:
OK
Cancel

Now when you reopen the data form or ad hoc grid in Smart View, you can reapply the custom formatting. By default, cell styles will be applied. Select *Apply >> Custom Styles*:

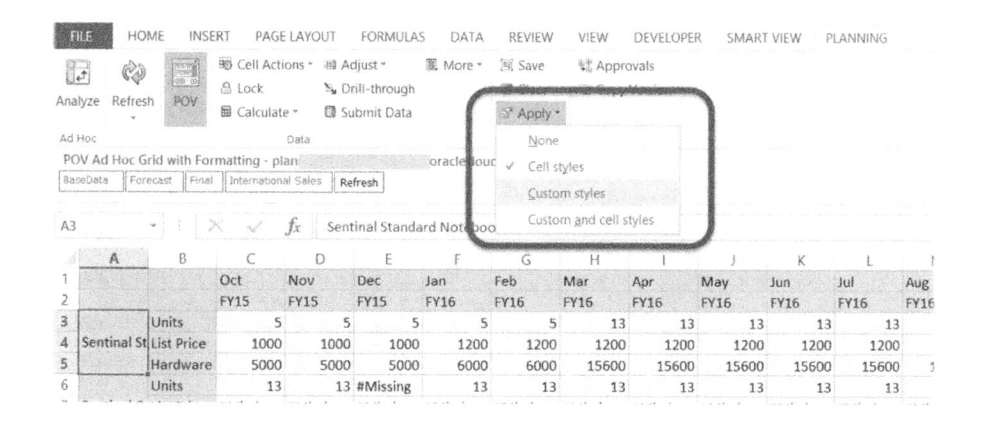

Look Smarter Than You Are with Enterprise Planning Cloud

And the formatting is reapplied:

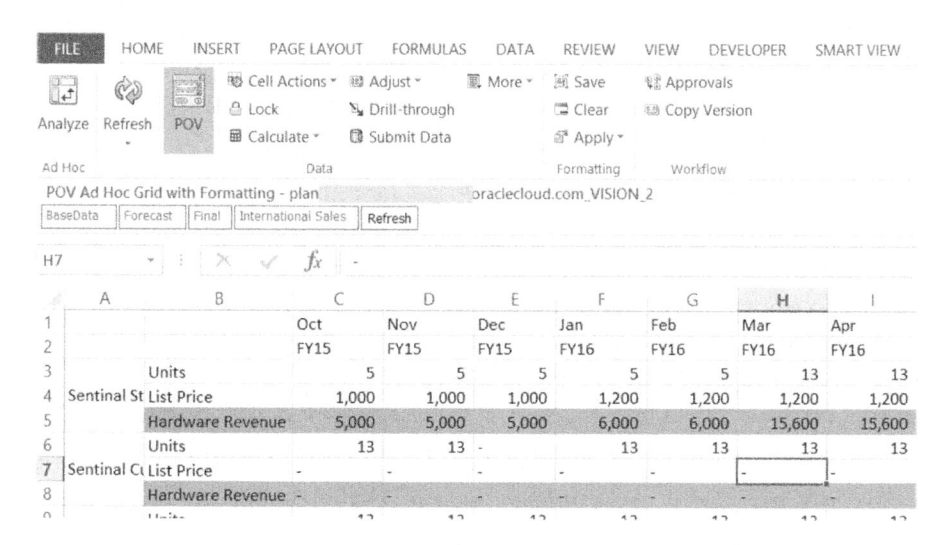

The formatting is also applied in the Simplified UI:

Ad Hoc Grid with Formatting												
HSP_View BaseData	Scenario Forecast	Version Final	Entity 410									
	Oct FY15	Nov FY15	Dec FY15	Jan FY16	Feb FY16	Mar FY16	Apr FY16	May FY16	Jun FY16	Jul FY16	Aug FY16	Sep FY16
P_110 Units	5	5	5	5	5	13	13	13	13	13	13	13
P_110 List Price	1000	1000	1000	1200	1200	1200	1200	1200	1200	1200	1200	1200
P_110 4110	5000	5000	5000	6000	6000	15600	15600	15600	15600	15600	15600	15600
P_120 Units	13	13	#NumericZero	13	13	13	13	13	13	13	13	13
P_120 List Price	#NumericZero	#NumericZero	#NumericZero	#NumericZero	#NumericZero	#NumericZero	#NumericZero	#NumericZero	#NumericZero	#NumericZero	#NumericZero	#NumericZero
P_120 4110	#NumericZero	#NumericZero	#NumericZero	#NumericZero	#NumericZero	#NumericZero	#NumericZero	#NumericZero	#NumericZero	#NumericZero	#NumericZero	#NumericZero
P_130 Units	13	13	13	13	13	13	13	13	13	13	13	13
P_130 List Price	500	500	500	500	500	500	500	500	500	500	500	500
P_130 4110	6500	6500	6500	6500	6500	6500	6500	6500	6500	6500	6500	6500
P_140 Units	8	8	#NumericZero	8	8	8	8	8	8	8	8	8
P_140 List Price	700	700	700	700	700	700	700	700	700	700	700	700
P_140 4110	5600	5600	#NumericZero	5600	5600	5600	5600	5600	5600	5600	5600	5600
P_150 Units	13	13	13	13	13	13	13	13	13	13	13	13
P_150 List Price	500	500	500	500	500	500	500	500	500	500	500	500
P_150 4110	6500	6500	6500	6500	6500	6500	6500	6500	6500	6500	6500	6500
P_160 Units	8	8	8	8	8	8	8	8	8	8	8	8
P_160 List Price	800	800	800	800	800	800	800	800	800	800	800	800
P_160 4110	6400	6400	6400	6400	6400	6400	6400	6400	6400	6400	6400	6400
P_200 Units	5	5	5	58	58	58	58	58	58	58	58	58
P_200 List Price	15	15	20	20	20	20	20	20	20	20	20	20
P_200 4110	75	75	100	1160	1160	1160	1160	1160	1160	1160	1160	1160

You can toggle back and forth between custom styles and default cell styles.

A few considerations for this formatting feature:

- Formatting can affect performance and is not recommended for large forms
- Not all Excel formatting options are supported
- Administrators can define formatting for a form, then users with access can overwrite the formatting and save the changes on the form
- Composite forms are not supported

For more information regarding all the features and functionalities of Smart View, check out the *Look Smarter Than You Are with Smart View* book or view the Oracle Smart View documentation.

MOBILE SUPPORT

Enterprise Planning Cloud supports many, many tasks on mobile devices. Users can review and enter plans, follow tasks, launch business rules, and run reports. To access Enterprise Planning Cloud content on a mobile device, make sure you have tagged the object with Tablet Access (*Navigator >> Tablet Access*). See the security section for more details.

Additionally, there is an EPM mobile app (called "Oracle EPM Mobile App") that is available at the App Store to support the approvals process:

> LOG ENTRY: SOL 23, Entry 1
>
> The Vision users love the Oracle Enterprise Cloud. Their planning cycle was shorter. The forecasts were more accurate and enabled better, faster decision making.
> Yeah! Feel my EPM Cloud power!

> LOG ENTRY: SOL 23, Entry 2
>
> So I just received an email from Cloud Specialist Alapat. I'm not quite finished! Users are requesting more functionality around sandboxes.
> Whaaaaaat?

Chapter 11: Sandboxing

> LOG ENTRY: SOL 23, Entry 3
>
> In high school I used to be a board game fanatic. (And maybe I still am.) You may not have guessed this, but I used to be a bit of a nerd. My favorite card and board games were Risk (Lord of the Rings version, of course), Settlers of Catan, and Werewolf. I also liked the Who Wants to be a Millionaire board game version. What I wouldn't give to have a lifeline right now for Vision's last requirement.
>
> Users want more flexibility in creating sandboxes. Thankfully Oracle Enterprise Planning Cloud has a lifeline built in with a new feature called sandboxing. I enabled this feature when I initially set up the application. Just a few more configuration steps away from completing this mission.

SANDBOXING

Sandboxes allow users to analyze and perform impact analysis on data without affecting the plans of other users. Sandboxes are private to the users and the changes made in the sandbox are not saved to the application and cannot be viewed by other users.

Enable Sandboxes on Application Creation

Sandboxing must be enabled when the application is created. I did this what seems like forever ago:

Look Smarter Than You Are with Enterprise Planning Cloud 487

Our planning frequency is	Weekly / **Monthly** / Quarterly
Select a start and end year	2010 To 2020
Fiscal Year First Month	January
Weekly Distribution	Even Distribution
	☐ Enable rolling forecast for this application
Rolling Forecast Period Duration	1
Our main currency is	USD United States of America dollar
We use more than one currency	☐
Enable Sandbox	☑
Plan Type : BSO	Sales
Plan Type : ASO	SalesRpt

Enable Version for Sandboxing

You must enable the desired versions for sandboxing. Remember back in the dimension build section, I enabled sandboxing for Final and Pass1:

Understand the Version Dimension & the Sandbox Members

Once you've enabled Sandboxes for a version, a corresponding sandbox member is created for that version:

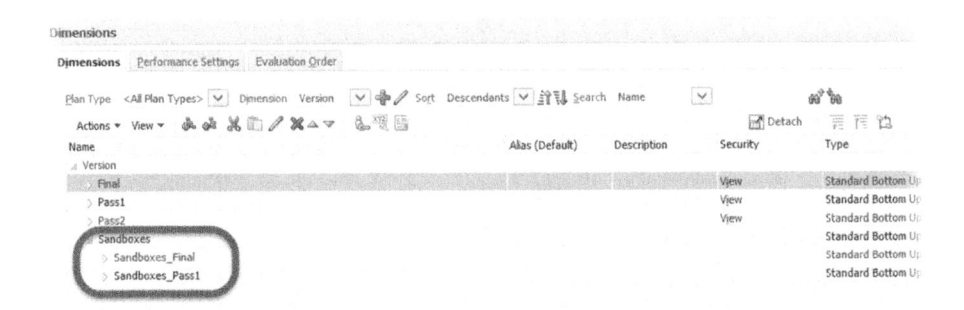

```
Dimensions
Dimensions  Performance Settings  Evaluation Order

Plan Type <All Plan Types>  Dimension Version     Sort Descendants    Search Name                              Detach
Actions ▼ View ▼

Name                                                         Alias (Default)    Description    Security        Type
▲ Version
    Final                                                                                      View            Standard Bottom Up
    > Pass1                                                                                    View            Standard Bottom Up
    > Pass2                                                                                    View            Standard Bottom Up
    Sandboxes                                                                                                  Standard Bottom Up
    > Sandboxes_Final                                                                                          Standard Bottom Up
    > Sandboxes_Pass1                                                                                          Standard Bottom Up
```

Understanding the HSP_View Dimension

The HSP_View dimension is created when sandboxes are enabled during application creation. The dimension or its members cannot be altered and should not be reordered. The members below are created along with it:

- **BaseData** – where data is stored when users are working in a non-sandbox view in a form
- **SandboxData** – where data is stored when users work in a sandbox
- **ConsolidatedData** – retrieves data from the SandboxData member when it is available; otherwise, it retrieves the data from the BaseData member; this member is dynamically calculated

By default, forms and ad hoc grids will use the *BaseData* member. When users enter data in a sandbox, the data is housed in *SandboxData* of the HSP_View dimension rather than *BaseData*. Users can publish the data in a sandbox to BaseData so that it can be seen by others and be saved to the application.

Per the Oracle Enterprise Planning Cloud documentation, Administrators need to update the member formula for the ConsolidatedData member to make sure that the proper sandbox member is referenced. I tried to update the member formula for this member and was not able to actually save the formula.

The documentation recommends adding the following member formula to ConsolidatedData in the HSP_View dimension:

```
IF(@ISLev("Product",0))
IF(@ISLev("Entity",0))
IF (@ISLev("Period", 0))
IF(NOT (@ismbr(@relative("Sandboxes",0))))
BaseData;
ELSE
        IF (SandboxData== #MISSING )
IF(@ISCHILD("Sandboxes_Final"))
                    "Final"->BaseData;
ELSEIF(@ISCHILD("Sandboxes_Pass1"))
                    "Pass1"->BaseData;
ENDIF
        ELSE
SandboxData;
        ENDIF
ENDIF   ENDIF   ENDIF   ENDIF
```

The formula validates which is good:

But I'm unable to save:

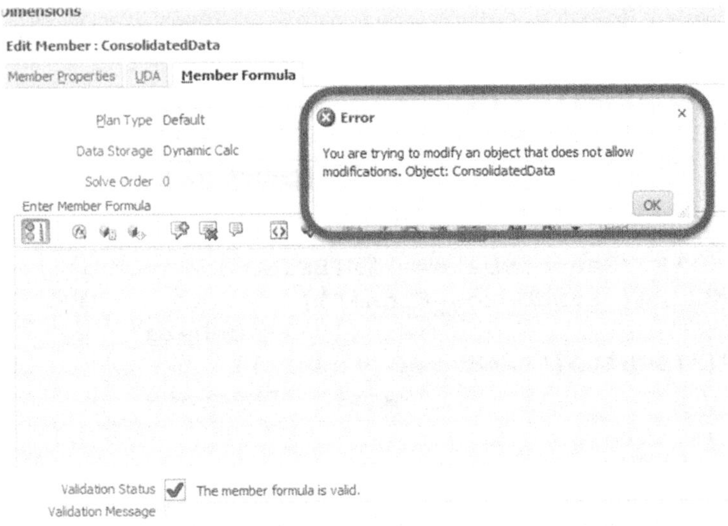
Dimensions
Edit Member : ConsolidatedData
Member Properties
UDA
Member Formula
Plan Type Default
Data Storage Dynamic Calc
Solve Order 0
Enter Member Formula
Error
You are trying to modify an object that does not allow modifications. Object: ConsolidatedData
OK
Validation Status
The member formula is valid.
Validation Message

Huh? So this is either a bug or the documentation is wrong. I'll just keep going and see if I can MacGyver this to work. What I'll find out shortly is that this step is no longer necessary. ConsolidatedData will automatically show BaseData + Sandbox data appropriately.

Update Member Formulas to Support Sandboxing

You do need to do this step! When you use sandboxing, you need to create or modify member formulas to support sandbox views by referencing the ConsolidatedData member. Otherwise, data will not calculate properly for sandbox views.

To update the member formulas to support sandboxing,

1. Update the member formula for 4110 to point to the ConsolidatedData member in the HSP_View dimension:

```
IF (@ISMBR("Forecast"))
IF( (@ISMBR(@relative("Sandboxes",0))))
"Units"->"ConsolidatedData" * "List Price" -
>"ConsolidatedData";
ELSE
"Units"*"List Price";
ENDIF
```

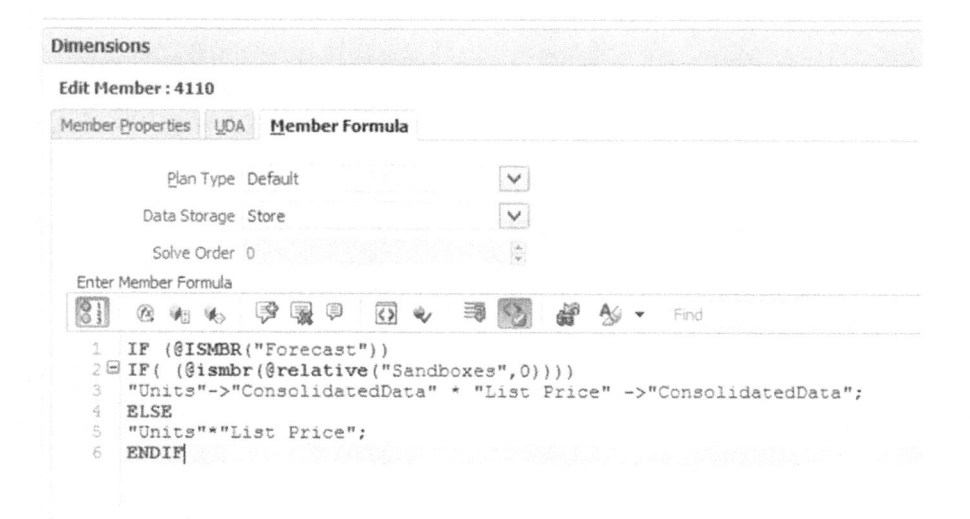

2. Save the member.
3. Refresh the database.

Only the Calculate Data Form Business Rule Works

The only business rule that will work with sandbox views is the "Calculate Data Form" business rule (and "Calculate Currencies", but I'm not using multiple currencies in this application). Thankfully for me, I designed the calculations as member formulas (a recommended practice in Enterprise Planning Cloud when possible for this very reason).

To verify this,
1. Edit *Sales Forecast – Products* and then *Save As* to a new form called "Sales Forecast - Products Sandbox".
2. Remove the Rule – *Calculate MyForecast*.
3. Add *<Calculate Form>* to the Selected Business Rule pane (if not already there) and check the option to *Run on Save*:

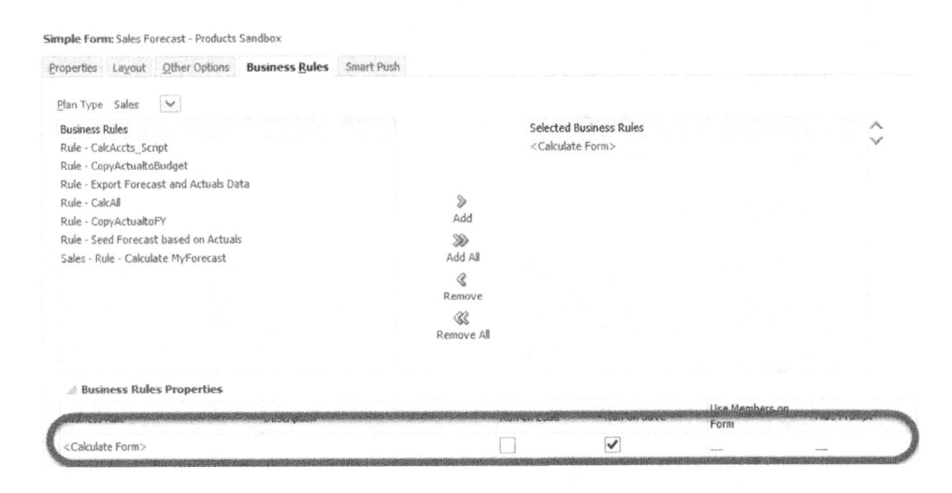

4. Click *Finish* to save and close the form.

Set Sparse Upper Level Members Dynamic

In order for aggregations to work for sandbox versions, upper level members of sparse dimensions must be dynamic if shown on the data form.

Finally, users are ready to create a sandbox.

Create a Sandbox

To create a sandbox through a form or an ad hoc grid,

1. While in a data form, click ✚ to create a new sandbox:

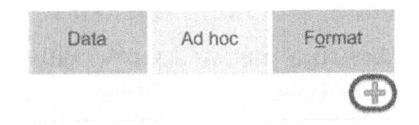

Note! The administrator must check the *Enable Sandboxes* box in Version member properties for ✚ to appear for users.

2. Name the sandbox "Worst Case":

Create Sandbox

Name: Worst Case

3. Click *Create*. The sandbox will appear as a new tab next to the original form:

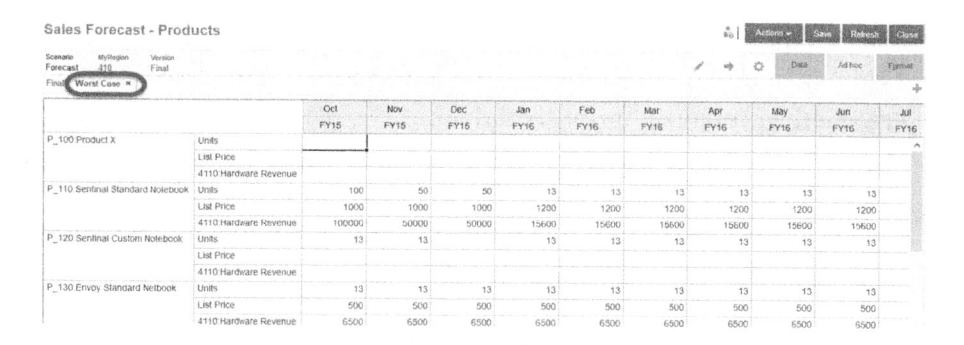

4. Enter data in the sandbox and view the impact on other accounts or forms. Woo hoo! It worked. The golden yellow cells indicate data in my sandbox that have been calculated:

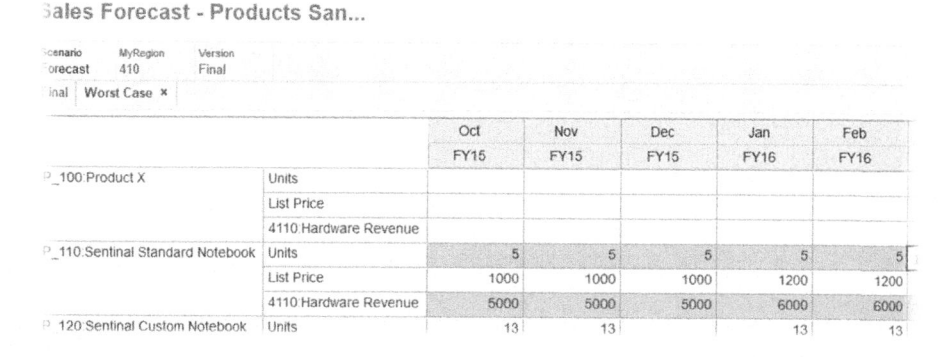

		Oct FY15	Nov FY15	Dec FY15	Jan FY16	Feb FY16
P_100 Product X	Units					
	List Price					
	4110 Hardware Revenue					
P_110 Sentinal Standard Notebook	Units	5	5	5	5	5
	List Price	1000	1000	1000	1200	1200
	4110 Hardware Revenue	5000	5000	5000	6000	6000
P_120 Sentinal Custom Notebook	Units	13	13		13	13

All other forms will have the sandbox tab until the data is published.

Note! Any Supporting Detail cells previously created in the non-sandbox version cannot be removed in a sandbox version. It allows you to go through the steps, but the supporting detail will come back.

Publish a Sandbox

To publish data from a sandbox to other users, the *Publish* action will move the sandbox data back to the BaseData member. All modified data from the sandbox will be published (across different POVS or pages, and across different forms). If multiple planners publish sandbox data to the same member in the base view, the most recently published data will overwrite the previously published data.

To publish a sandbox,
1. When ready to publish the data in the sandbox, go to *Actions >> Sandbox >> Publish*:

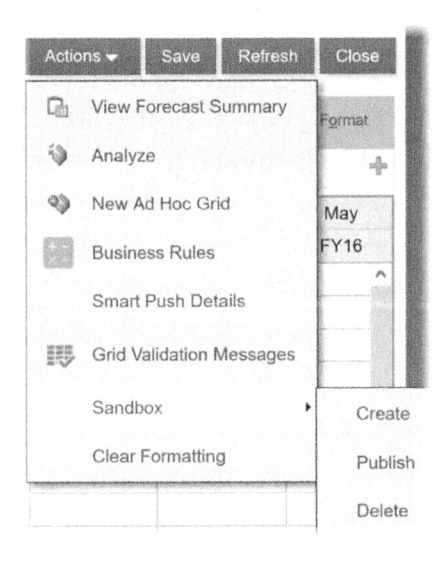

Once the sandbox is published, it will disappear and its data will be saved to Essbase under the BaseData member.

Other Rules about Sandboxing

A few rules about sandboxing:

- All security is still in effect when users sandboxes
- Planners may have multiple sandboxes and switch between them
- Planners won't impact other planners when sandboxing
- You might need to update member formulas so they calculate properly when viewing base data and sandboxes; to do this you reference the "ConsolidatedData" member
- For a form to support sandboxing, Version must be on the page or in the POV as a user variable
- The only supported business rules for sandboxes are the default "Calculate Form" and "Calculate Currencies" rules
- Some sandboxing functionality is supported in Smart View (update data in a sandbox):

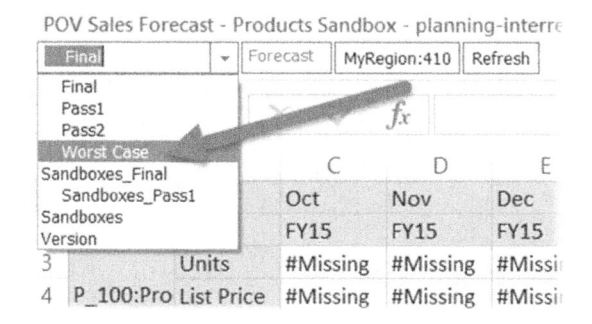

- You can't create, delete, or publish data from Smart View

If you don't see the sandbox options in a data form, it is likely because you broke one of the above rules.

Manage Sandboxes

Administrators can manage all sandboxes that were created by all users and can see the following information:

- Data in all sandboxes
- Which version member the sandbox is based on
- Who created each sandbox
- When the sandboxes were last modified

Administrators can also delete anyone's sandbox. To manage sandboxes, go to *Console >> Actions >> Manage Sandboxes*:

Manage Sandboxes			Refresh Delete Close
▼ Filter:			
Sandbox Name	Base Version	Created By	Last Modified
Worst Case	Final	pbcs1@interrel.c	2/2/2016

```
LOG ENTRY: SOL 23, Entry 4

   The Vision users love the Oracle Enterprise Cloud
with sandboxing. Their planning cycle was shorter. The
forecasts were more accurate and enabled better, faster
decision making. And now they can what-if and sandbox
to their hearts content.
   Yeah! Feel my EPM Cloud power! Again.
```

Chapter 12: Maintain & Support

> LOG ENTRY: SOL 24, Entry 1
>
> Before I can move on to my next Cloud mission, I need to document some of the maintenance steps for the Enterprise Planning Cloud for the Vision admin. What if something stops working? What if users are in the middle of a process and everything freezes?
>
> I'm using this log entry to document some of these helpful administrative tips.

MANAGE PLAN TYPES

Create and Edit Plan Types

You can create new plan types after the application creation in the Simplified UI. Simply go to *Console >> Application*. In the *Plan Types* tab, click *Create*:

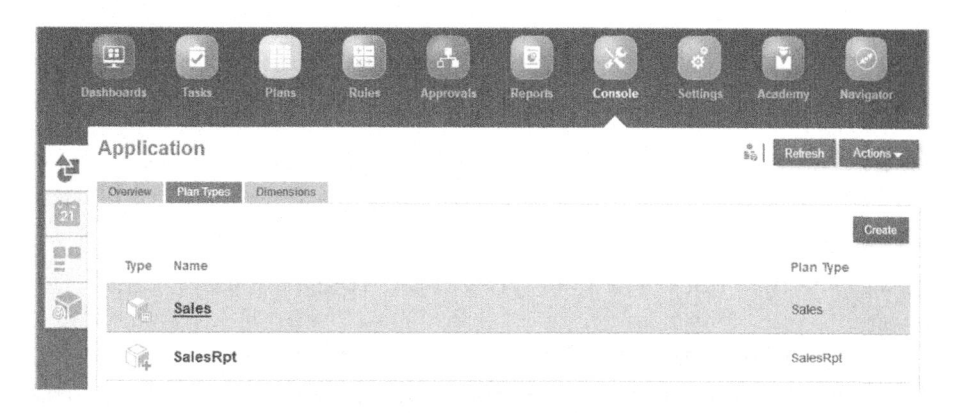

In the Workspace UI, you can navigate to the plan type editor by going to *Administration >> Manage >> Plan Types*. Here, you can view and create new plan types. You can also select *Actions >> Edit Reporting Cube* to refresh the reporting application and sync the mapped reporting application:

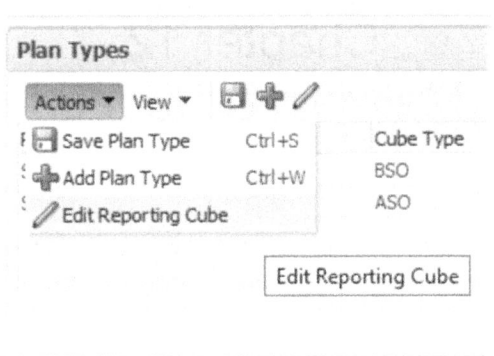

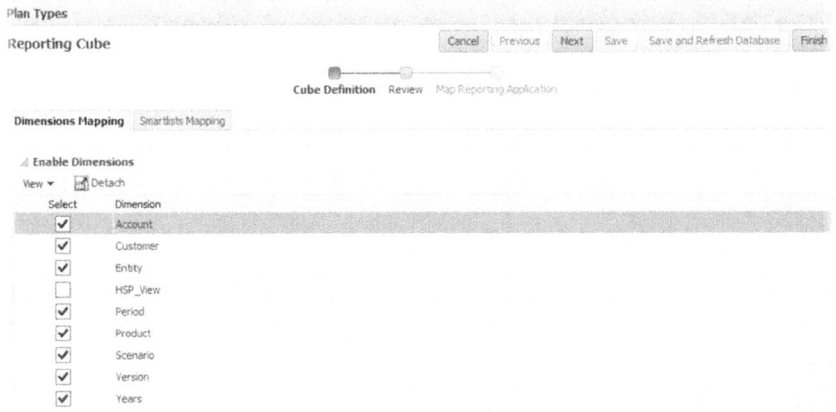

There are a couple of rules governing plan type creation:

- You may add up to three BSO plan types and the number of BSO plan types +1 ASO plan types (four total ASO plan types) in Enterprise Planning Cloud
- You may not delete plan types in Enterprise Planning Cloud

View and Set Underlying Plan Type Properties

It is possible to edit some of the traditional Essbase properties. This has to be done in Calculation Manager.

To view Plan Type database properties (traditional Essbase database properties),
1. Within the Simplified UI, go to *Navigator >> Administer >> Rules*. This will launch Calculation Manager.
2. In the System View, navigate to *Actions >> Database Properties*:

Look Smarter Than You Are with Enterprise Planning Cloud   499

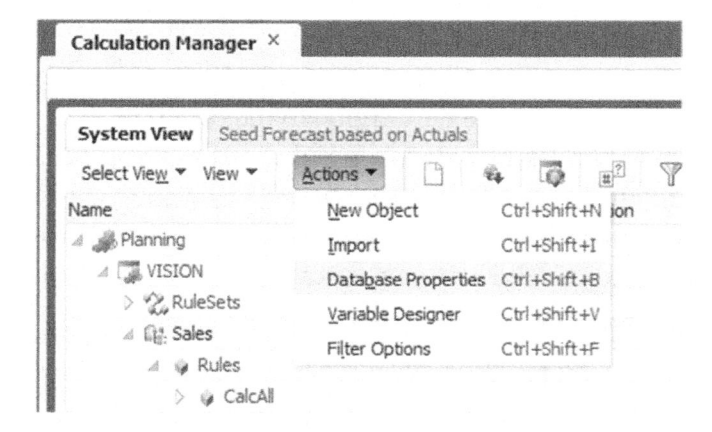

3. In the Database Properties tab, highlight a plan type. The properties will appear:

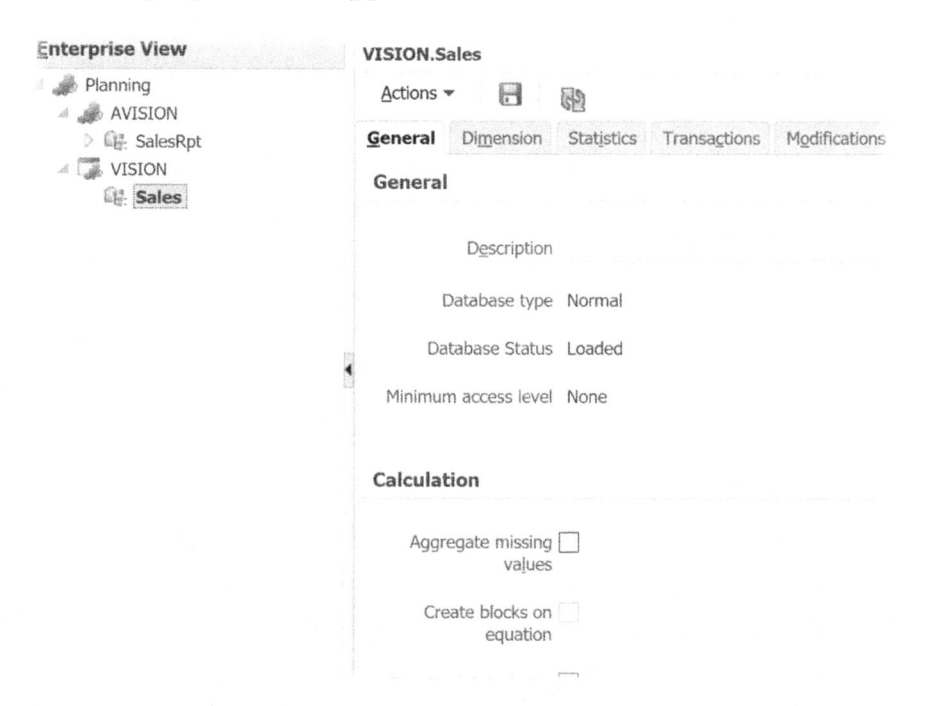

You can modify some of properties in Calculation Manager.

In the General tab:

- **Description** – adds a description to the plan type
- **Aggregate missing values** – a global setting to aggregate missing values during database calculation
- **Two-pass Calculation** – a global setting of two-pass calculation; members tagged with two-pass calculation are recalculated after a database default calculation:

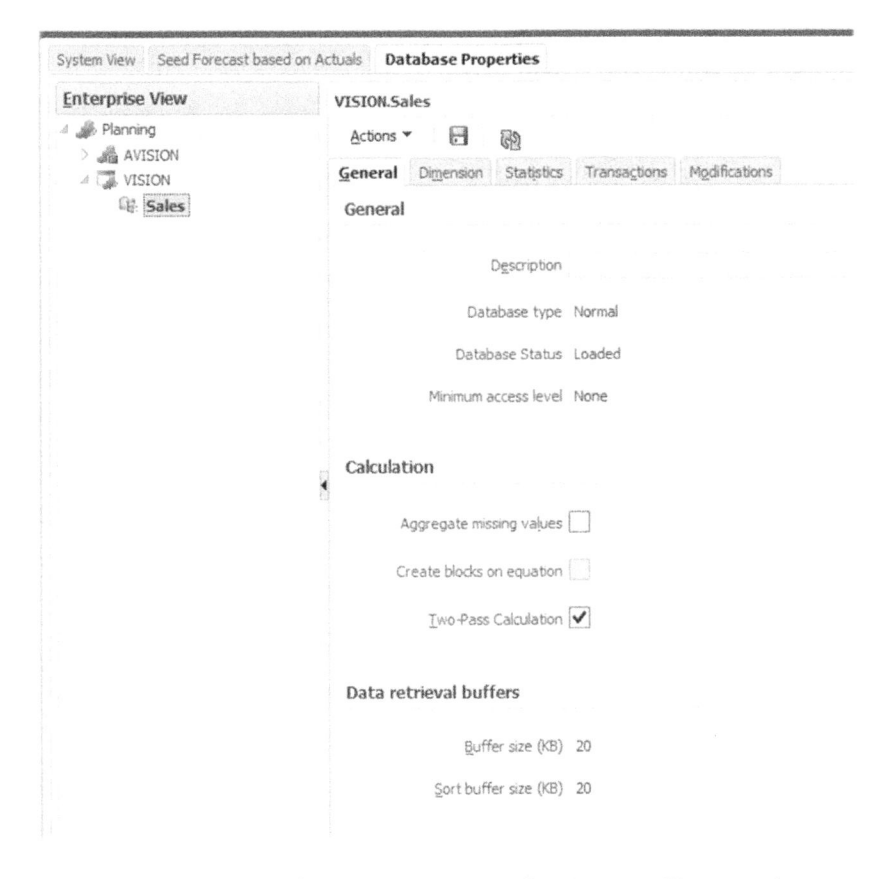

![Database Properties screenshot showing General tab with VISION.Sales selected, displaying Description, Database type Normal, Database Status Loaded, Minimum access level None, Calculation section with Aggregate missing values unchecked, Create blocks on equation unchecked, Two-Pass Calculation checked, and Data retrieval buffers with Buffer size (KB) 20 and Sort buffer size (KB) 20.]

Properties in the Dimension, Statistics, Transactions, and Modifications Tabs cannot be modified here. They are for display purposes only. You can view dimension statistics:

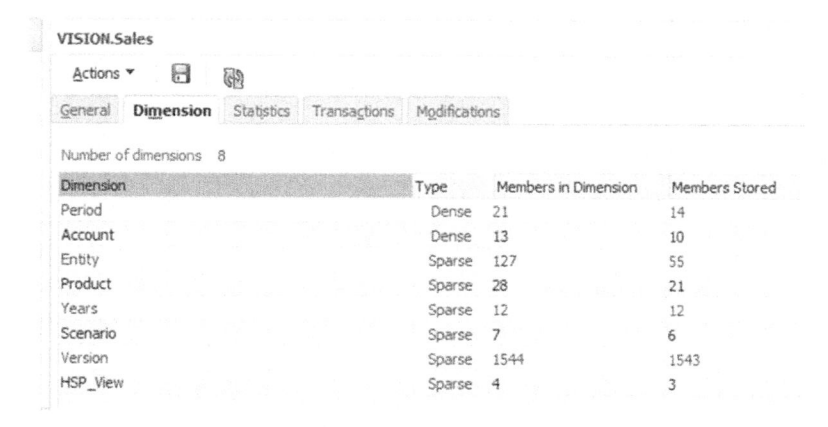

VISION.Sales

Actions ▼

General **Dimension** Statistics Transactions Modifications

Number of dimensions 8

Dimension	Type	Members in Dimension	Members Stored
Period	Dense	21	14
Account	Dense	13	10
Entity	Sparse	127	55
Product	Sparse	28	21
Years	Sparse	12	12
Scenario	Sparse	7	6
Version	Sparse	1544	1543
HSP_View	Sparse	4	3

You can view database statistics like block size and number of blocks:

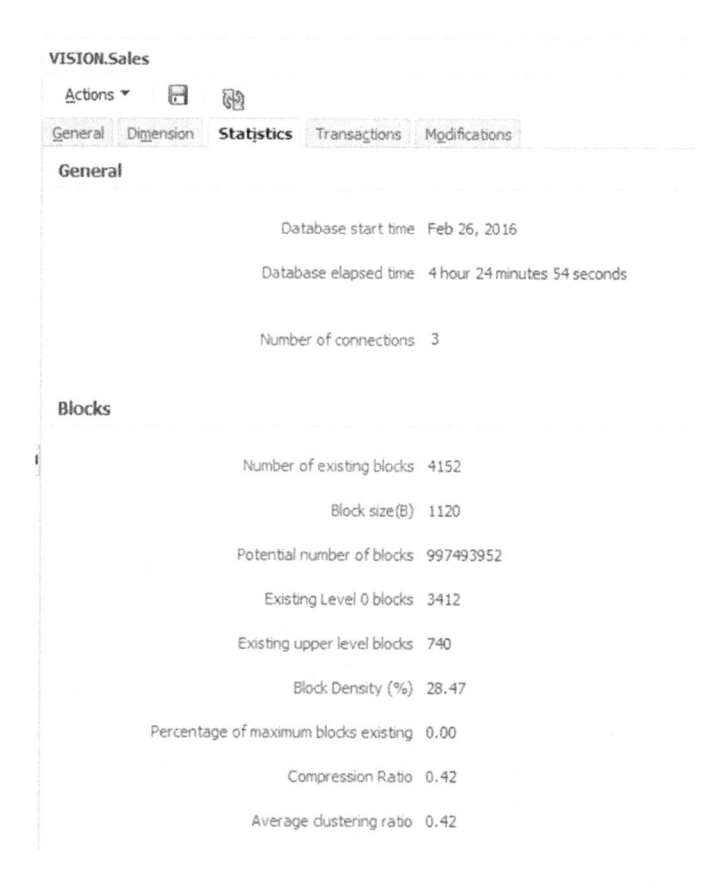

VISION.Sales

Actions ▼

General Dimension **Statistics** Transactions Modifications

General

Database start time Feb 26, 2016

Database elapsed time 4 hour 24 minutes 54 seconds

Number of connections 3

Blocks

Number of existing blocks 4152

Block size(B) 1120

Potential number of blocks 997493952

Existing Level 0 blocks 3412

Existing upper level blocks 740

Block Density (%) 28.47

Percentage of maximum blocks existing 0.00

Compression Ratio 0.42

Average clustering ratio 0.42

You can view transaction settings:

VISION.Sales

General | Dimension | Statistics | **Transactions** | Modifications

Options Uncommitted access

Synchronization point

Commit blocks 3000

Commit rows 0

You can view information on when the plan type was last loaded and calculated:

VISION.Sales

General | Dimension | Statistics | Transactions | **Modifications**

Operation	User	Start Time	End Time
Data Load	epm_default_cloud_admin@Native Direct Feb 24, 2016		Feb 24, 2016
Calculation	epm_default_cloud_admin@Native Direct Feb 26, 2016		Feb 26, 2016
Outline Update	epm_default_cloud_admin@Native Direct Feb 16, 2016		Feb 16, 2016

The ASO database properties vary some. You can view the data retrieval buffers:

Look Smarter Than You Are with Enterprise Planning Cloud 503

AVISION.SalesRpt

Actions ▼

General | Dimension | Statistics | Compression | Modifications

General

Description

Database type   Aggregate storage

Database Status   Loaded

Minimum access level   None

Data retrieval buffers

Buffer size (KB)   20

Sort buffer size (KB)   20

You can view compression information which may be helpful in performance tuning:

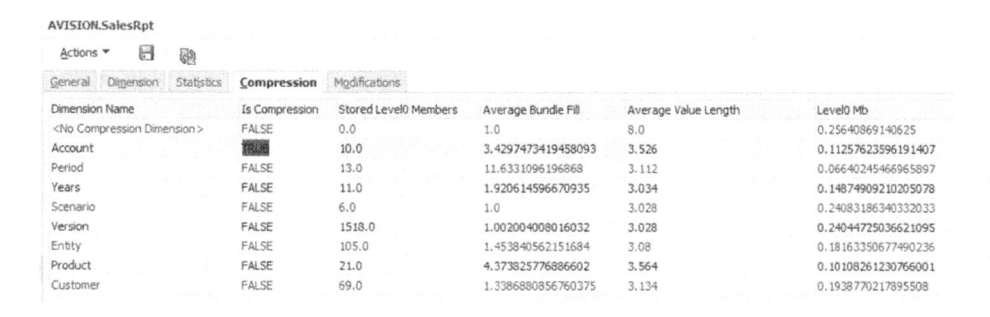

AVISION.SalesRpt

Actions ▼

General | Dimension | Statistics | **Compression** | Modifications

Dimension Name	Is Compression	Stored Level0 Members	Average Bundle Fill	Average Value Length	Level0 Mb
<No Compression Dimension>	FALSE	0.0	1.0	8.0	0.25640869140625
Account	TRUE	10.0	3.4297473419458093	3.526	0.11257623596191407
Period	FALSE	13.0	11.6331096196868	3.112	0.06640245466965897
Years	FALSE	11.0	1.9206145966670935	3.034	0.14874909210205078
Scenario	FALSE	6.0	1.0	3.028	0.24083186340332033
Version	FALSE	1518.0	1.002004008016032	3.028	0.24044725036621095
Entity	FALSE	105.0	1.453840562151684	3.08	0.18163350677490236
Product	FALSE	21.0	4.373825776886602	3.564	0.10108261230766601
Customer	FALSE	69.0	1.3386880856760375	3.134	0.1938770217895508

For more information on all of these properties, I recommend you check out our *Look Smarter Than You Are with Essbase* book.

CHANGE HISTORY / AUDIT TRAIL

Auditing for data, business rule launches, approvals, dimension administration, task lists, etc., can be enabled in the Enterprise Planning Cloud Workspace. Open the application and go to *Tools >> Reports*. Click the *Auditing* tab and check the actions to audit. Check *Data* to see change history in data forms:

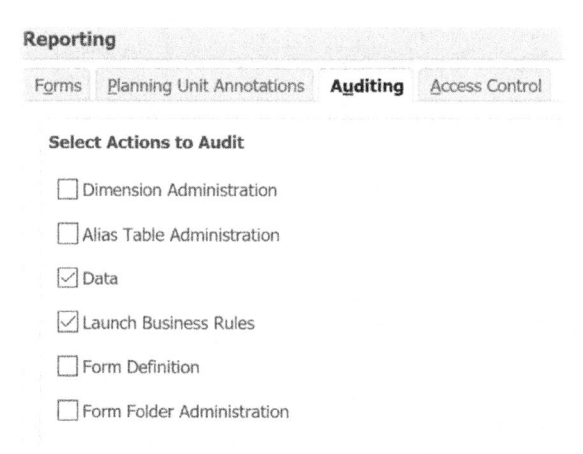

Reporting

Forms | Planning Unit Annotations | **Auditing** | Access Control

Select Actions to Audit

☐ Dimension Administration
☐ Alias Table Administration
☑ Data
☑ Launch Business Rules
☐ Form Definition
☐ Form Folder Administration

All data changes will now be tracked including who made the data change, when, the old value, and the new value.

To view the change history for a data cell, open a form and click the *Show Change History* icon under the Data menu:

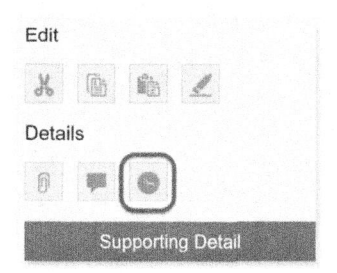

The User, Date, Old Value, and New Value will appear in a window. Cell history is also available through the History option in Smart View. Simply click a cell to view, then go to *Cell Actions >> History*:

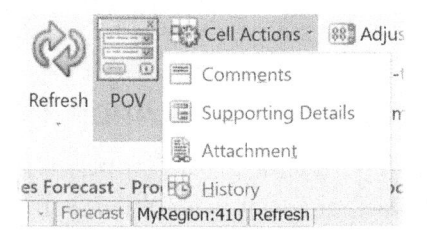

The Change History window will appear with a record of the changes.

MAINTENANCE AND NOTIFICATIONS

Scheduling the Maintenance Time

The administrator can schedule the maintenance time by going to *Console >> Actions >> Maintenance Time*:

Maintenance Time
Backup Schedule: Select the hour when the system needs to be backed up every day

Select Time Zone	(UTC-06:00) Chicago - Central Time (CT)
Maintenance Time	2:00

Note: Maintenance duration is 1 hour

⚠ Warning: You must perform a Refresh Database, either manually or as a job, before the scheduled maintenance time. Keep in mind that the refresh duration is affected by the application size and/or changes that were made since the last refresh, so you must ensure the Refresh Database is completed before the scheduled maintenance time.

Last Patch Applied   PBCS_16.01.49 at **2016/01/18 02:08:47 CT**

[Save] [Cancel]

During the maintenance window, the system will be backed up and it will normally take about one hour. To ensure that no changes are lost, refresh the database before the scheduled backup time.

Restarting the Enterprise Planning Cloud Application

There may be instances where the Planning application needs to be restarted. Now that the backend components are not as easily available in the cloud, a different process is required for restarts. Oracle has created steps to "reboot" (reset) the Enterprise Planning Cloud environment.

Why would one ever need to do this? There are a couple of important reasons: runaway processes and performance issues to start with. Oracle recommends that this command be used only when severe performance degradation is witnessed or if error messages pop up, indicating that the instance is unusable. Service resets do not affect application customization (for example, locale change, settings related to theme and currency, etc.) and it can take up to 15 minutes to fully reset.

To perform a reset with EPM Automate,
1. Open a command prompt. You'll use the `resetservice` command within EPM Automate.

2. Navigate to the EPM Automate install location. Example: `CD C:\Oracle\EPM Automate`

```
C:\Windows\system32\cmd.exe
Microsoft Windows [Version 6.1.7601]
Copyright (c) 2009 Microsoft Corporation. All rights reserved.

C:\Users\       >CD C:\Oracle\EPM Automate
C:\Oracle\EPM Automate>
```

3. Log in to the Cloud instance. Example of the generic syntax: `epmautomate login username password/<password file> url identitydomain`

Comments can also be used to track the reasons for restart. Comments must be enclosed within double quotation marks.

4. Type: `epmautomate resetservice "Import Metadata processing is stuck"`

```
C:\Oracle\EPM Automate\bin>epmautomate resetservice "Import metadata processing is stuck"
Are you sure you want to restart the service instance (yes/no): no ?[Press Enter]
yes
Processing...
Retrieving status...
resetservice completed successfully
```

A batch file can also be generated from the above commands to make processing easier in the future.

Environment Notifications

There are different types of notifications that Oracle allows administrators to receive. In Enterprise Planning Cloud, administrators can set up their personal notifications for specific types of events, such as outages.

To set up notifications,
1. Log into the Cloud home page at https://cloud.oracle.com/home:

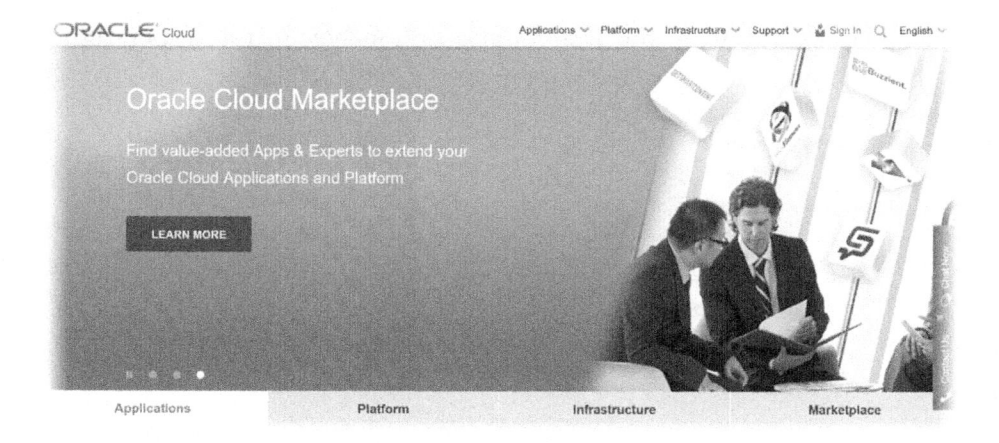

Look Smarter Than You Are with Enterprise Planning Cloud 507

2. Select *Sign In* in the top right-hand corner.
3. Under *My Services*, select the appropriate Data Center/Region for your instance and then click *Sign In to My Service*:

My Services

For service and identity domain administrators with an active Oracle Cloud service:

- Administer cloud services
- Monitor utilization and uptime details
- Manage users and roles for cloud services
- Obtain a list of your accounts from here

Select Data Center/Region

US Commercial 1 (us1)

Sign In to My Services >

4. Sign in with the appropriate credentials.

5. Navigate to the *Notifications* option box in the upper right-hand corner of the screen:

Dashboard　　Users　　Notifications

6. Under the *Notification Preferences* tab, take a look at the Categories for notification.
7. Click the checkbox next to the notifications you'd like to receive:

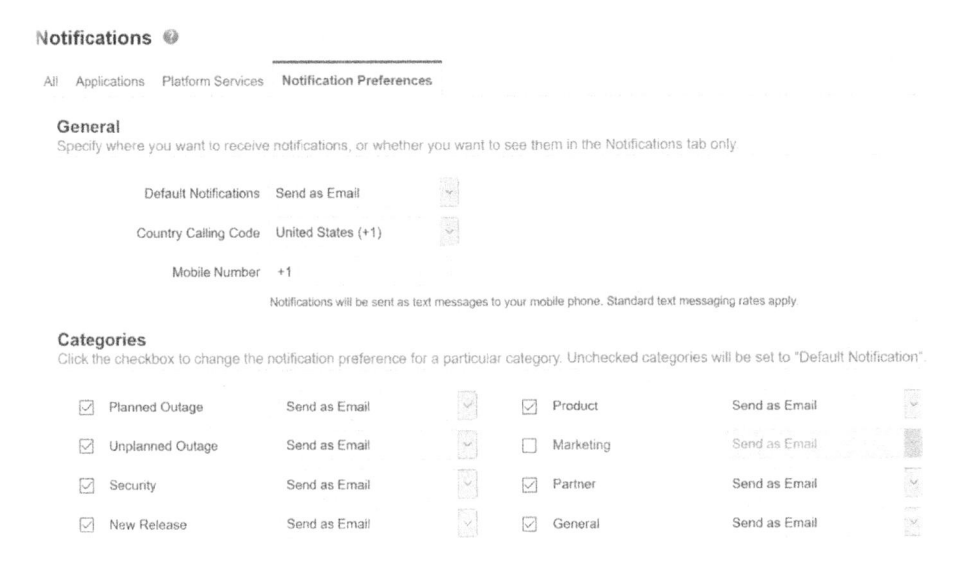

Notifications

All　Applications　Platform Services　**Notification Preferences**

General
Specify where you want to receive notifications, or whether you want to see them in the Notifications tab only.

Default Notifications	Send as Email
Country Calling Code	United States (+1)
Mobile Number	+1

Notifications will be sent as text messages to your mobile phone. Standard text messaging rates apply.

Categories
Click the checkbox to change the notification preference for a particular category. Unchecked categories will be set to "Default Notification".

☑	Planned Outage	Send as Email	☑	Product	Send as Email
☑	Unplanned Outage	Send as Email	☐	Marketing	Send as Email
☑	Security	Send as Email	☑	Partner	Send as Email
☑	New Release	Send as Email	☑	General	Send as Email

8. Click *Save*.

DELETE APPLICATION

Oracle Enterprise Planning Cloud supports a single application. To create a new application, you will need to delete an existing application.

To delete an application,
1. Navigate to *Console*.
2. In the Application Overview tab, go to *Actions >> Remove Application*:

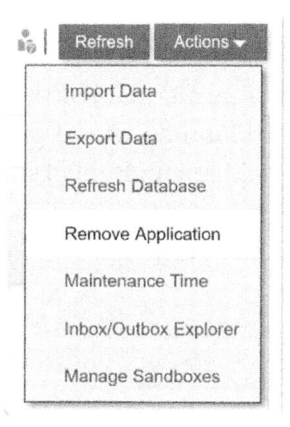

3. Click *Yes*. It will take a few seconds for the application to delete.

APPLICATION SETTINGS

A number of application settings can be defined by the administrator including enabling or disabling the application for use by users and setting application defaults.

To define application settings and defaults,
1. Select *Navigate >> Application Settings*.
2. Update the settings accordingly:

For more information on each of these settings, check out the Oracle documentation.

ACADEMY & LEARNING MORE

The Academy is an educational starting page for Users to get an overview of the Enterprise Planning Cloud product itself. The first page of the Academy section provides a high-level summary of what Enterprise Planning Cloud can do and how to do it. The second page of Academy provides a link to the Oracle Enterprise Planning Cloud Help Center:

Getting Started for Users

Designed for busy planners, this mobile-friendly user interface offers easy-to-navigate pa This quick guide shows you the basics, including:

- Reviewing key indicators using dashboards
- Organizing planning tasks
- Working with and analyzing data
- Launching calculations
- Structuring the process for approving plans
- Viewing reports that summarize data
- Setting number formatting, notifications, user variables, and so on
- Accessing learning tools such as videos and instructions

Note: This simplified interface supports only Landscape mode for iPad and Android table

Dashboards

Want to quickly compare your business unit's current revenue against last year's revenu graphically compare the numbers. The Dashboards' **Layout** page lets you drop forms, c

---

LOG ENTRY: SOL 24, Entry 2

Well, the project didn't die. This Oracle Enterprise Planning Cloud thing really works! I wonder what my next mission will be. Enterprise Performance Reporting Cloud? Business Intelligence Cloud?

For now it's time to celebrate with a little Naughty by Nature and Hip Hop Hooray, "Ho, Hey, Ho ..."

Epilogue: The EPM Martian

Meanwhile, back on earth...

"Crap," Danielle said. "Edward Roske and the project are still alive and we haven't communicated it out to anyone besides i.n.t.e.r.R.e.l and Vision? You've got to be kidding me."

Director Chang glared across the room and said, "Not helping, Danielle."

"You don't have to face those darn i.n.t.e.r.R.e.l supporters like Mike Reed and Scot Martin. We should have told them when we first knew the project was alive."

This was going to be rough and Danielle knew it. Not only did she have to deliver the biggest mea culpa in i.n.t.e.r.R.e.l.'s history, every second would be remembered for forever (well maybe thirty minutes). She was confident that none of the concern showed in her voice as she leaned into the computer microphone on i.n.t.e.r.R.e.l.'s regularly-scheduled, free webcast.

"Thank you all for attending today. We have an important announcement to make. We have viewed recent Oracle EPM Cloud logs and have confirmed that Consultant Edward Roske and the Vision implementation are, currently, alive. In fact, he has successfully implemented Oracle Enterprise Planning Cloud in just a few sols."

After one full second of utter silence, the webcast chat session exploded with questions.

Appendix: *Look Smarter Than You Are with Essbase* Highlights

```
LOG ENTRY: Note to Self

    Because many of the Cloud applications sit on top
of Essbase, I'll review my Look Smarter Than You Are
with Essbase refresher manual to help define some of
the basic Essbase definitions and concepts that will
be helpful to implementing the Cloud solutions.
```

INTRO TO ESSBASE

Essbase is currently produced by a company named Oracle. Prior to the earthshaking acquisition by Oracle, Essbase was produced by a company named Hyperion Solutions Corporation. Although Hyperion was founded in 1981, the Essbase product came along in the early 1990's – compliments of a company whose only product was Essbase: Arbor Software. Up until 1998 when Hyperion and Arbor "merged", the two companies were fierce competitors who were just as likely to spit on each other in waiting rooms as work together (I am kidding, but only slightly).

Good terms to describe these databases: OLAP (On-Line Analytical Processing) or Multi-dimensional databases. There were several features that Essbase offered that no previous database could handle.

Multi-Dimensional Databases

First of all, Essbase was a multi-dimensional database (MDDB or MDB, for short). What did the good doctor mean when he said Essbase was multi-dimensional? Simply that any of the dimensions set up in a database could be put in the rows or the columns (or applied to the whole page / report).

Relational databases are two-dimensional: records and fields. Essbase had no theoretical dimension limit (though there was certainly a practical limit).

While any relational database can be set up to give the appearance of having multiple dimensions, it takes a lot of upfront work by developers. Essbase and other OLAP databases have dimensionality built-in.

Essbase databases were also optimized for retrieval at any level of the hierarchy – even the very topmost number that might represent every dollar the company has ever made in its history. OLTP databases (relational databases) were nicely optimized for retrieval of detailed records but definitely not hierarchical information. By pre-saving summarized information, Essbase allows analysis to happen from the top-down with no decrease in performance.

For OLAP databases, the hierarchy is native to the database itself. This is far different from relational databases that store the data in one table and then have one or more other tables that can be joined in to view data in a rolled-up fashion. For Essbase, the hierarchy is the database. When you change the hierarchy logic in Essbase on how a product is grouped or how a market rolls-up, you actually change where the data is stored.

Because hierarchy is inherent to OLAP databases, drill-down (sometimes known as "slicing and dicing" but never known as "making julienne data") is inherent as well. Essbase is great at doing Ad hoc analysis because it knows that when a user double-clicks on Qtr1, she wants to see Jan, Feb, and Mar. This is because the roll up of months to quarters is pre-defined back on the server.

Dimensions

Data is organized within an Essbase database (or plan type if you are using Enterprise Planning Cloud) into dimensions or groupings of related data elements grouped into a hierarchical format. To oversimplify, a *dimension* is something that can be put into the rows or columns of your report or data form (or it applies to the whole page). Different databases have different dimensions.

Have a look at this really simple Profit & Loss Statement:

	Actual	Budget
Sales	400,855	373,080
COGS	179,336	158,940
Margin	221,519	214,140
Total Expenses	115,997	84,760
Profit	**105,522**	**129,380**

It only has two dimensions. Down the rows, I have our "Measures" dimension (often called "Accounts"). Across the columns, I have our "Scenario" dimension – the dimension that contains Actual, Budget, Forecast, and the like.

The only two dimensions so far are Scenario and Measures. The more detailed breakdowns of Measures (Sales, COGS, Margin, etc.) are the members of the Measures dimension. Actual and Budget are members in the Scenario dimension. A *member* identifies a particular element within a dimension.

If I pivot the Measures up to the columns and the Scenario dimension over to the rows, our report will now look like this:

	Sales	COGS	**Margin**	Total Expenses	**Profit**
Actual	400,855	179,336	221,519	115,997	105,522
Budget	373,080	158,940	214,140	84,760	129,380

While it doesn't look very good, it does illustrate a couple of important points. First, a dimension can be placed into the rows, the columns, or the page (as I'll see in a second). If it's really a dimension (as Scenario and Measures both are), there are no restrictions on which dimensions can be down the side or across the top. Second, notice that the values in the second report are the same as the values in the first report. Actual Sales are 400,855 in both reports. Likewise, Budgeted Profit is 129,380 in both reports. This is not magic.

A spreadsheet is inherently two dimensional (as are most data forms and reports for Planning). It has rows and columns. This is great if your company only produces a Profit & Loss Statement one time and then files for bankruptcy, but most companies will tend to have profit (be it positive or negative) in every month. To represent this in Excel, I use the spreadsheet tabs (one for each month):

All Products and Markets.xls		
	Actual	**Budget**
Sales	31,538	29,480
COGS	14,160	12,630
Margin	17,378	16,850
Total Expenses	9,354	6,910
Profit	8,024	9,940

Jan / Feb / Mar / Apr / May / Jun / Jul / Aug / Sep / Oct / Nov / Dec

I've now introduced a third dimension, Time. It could be across the columns (if you wanted to see a nice trend of twelve months of data) or down the rows, but I've put it in the pages. That is, if you click on the "Jan" tab, the whole report will be for January.

If you're looking for Actual Sales of 400,855, you won't find it now because that was the value for the whole year. I could get it by totaling the values of all twelve tabs onto a summary tab.

Right now, this spreadsheet is not broken down by product or market. Within Excel, it's problematic to represent more than three dimensions (since I've used the rows, columns, and tabs). One way is to have a separate file for each combination of product and market:

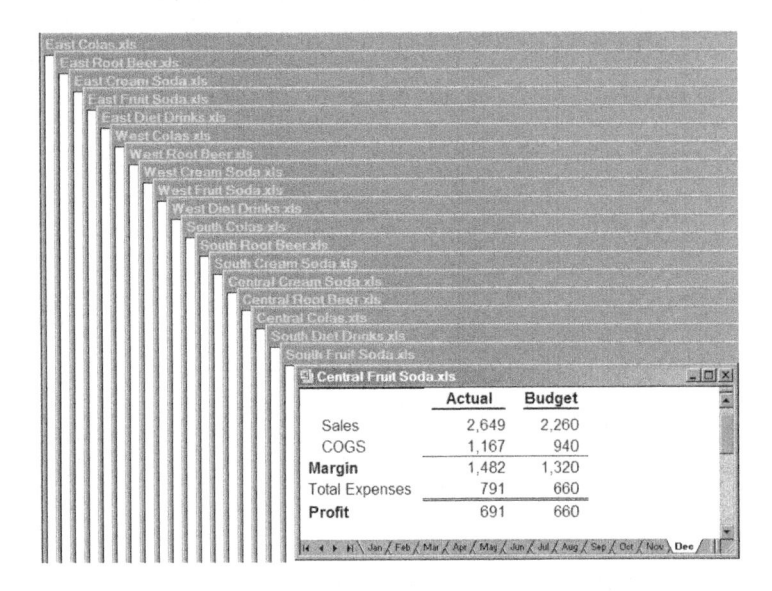

	Actual	Budget
Sales	2,649	2,260
COGS	1,167	940
Margin	1,482	1,320
Total Expenses	791	660
Profit	691	660

As you can see, this is getting ridiculous. What if I want to pivot our market dimension down to our columns to compare profitability across different regions? To do this, I'd either have to have a series of linked spreadsheet formulas (which would break as soon as I added or deleted a new product or market) or I could hire a temporary employee to print out all the spreadsheets and type them in again with the markets now in the columns.

Now that you understand what a dimension is, let's discuss some terms related to the elements within a dimension. A member or member name is the short, computery name for the member of an Essbase dimension (like "100-10"). An alias is the longer, more descriptive name for a member (like "Cola"). Members are grouped into hierarchies within a dimension.

Dimension Member References

Since I'm discussing dimensions, I'll also cover some "family" topics. The most common way to refer to members in a dimension relative to each other is by using "family tree" relationships:

```
- Product
    - 100 (+) (Alias: Colas)
        100-10 (+) (Alias: Cola)
        100-20 (+) (Alias: Diet Cola)
        100-30 (+) (Alias: Caffeine Free Cola)
    - 200 (+) (Alias: Root Beer)
        200-10 (+) (Alias: Old Fashioned)
        200-20 (+) (Alias: Diet Root Beer)
        200-30 (+) (Alias: Sasparilla)
        200-40 (+) (Alias: Birch Beer)
    - 300 (+) (Alias: Cream Soda)
        300-10 (+) (Alias: Dark Cream)
        300-20 (+) (Alias: Vanilla Cream)
        300-30 (+) (Alias: Diet Cream)
    - 400 (+) (Alias: Fruit Soda)
        400-10 (+) (Alias: Grape)
        400-20 (+) (Alias: Orange)
        400-30 (+) (Alias: Strawberry)
    - Diet (~) (Alias: Diet Drinks)
        100-20 (+) (Alias: Diet Cola)
        200-20 (+) (Alias: Diet Root Beer)
        300-30 (+) (Alias: Diet Cream)
```

The members directly below a member are called its children. For example, a Product dimension has five children: Colas, Root Beer, Cream Soda, Fruit Soda, and Diet Drinks. If I ever wanted to refer to those members on a report or data form without hard coding them, I could say "give us all the children of Product."

The advantage to this (aside from the saving in typing) is that if a new product line needs to be added (say, "Water"), I don't have to modify our reports and data forms. Any report or data form designed to display the children of Product will pick up the new "Water" product and add it to the list automatically.

If Colas, Root Beer, and the other rug rats are all the children of Product, what relation is Product to its children? Assuming you didn't fail "Birds and the Bees 101," you'll know that Product must be the *parent* of Colas, Root Beer, and the rest. In other words, the parent of any member is the one that the member rolls-up into. Qtr2 is the parent of May. Year is the parent of Qtr2.

Since Colas and Root Beer are both the children of Product, Colas and Root Beer are siblings. This is simple, but what relationship do January and May have? Well, their parents are siblings so that makes them... cousins. Correct, but "cousins" while technically correct isn't used that often. In general, people say that January and May are at the "same level."

What if you want to refer to all the members into which May rolls (not just the one right above)? Well, those are its ancestors, which in this case would be Qtr2 and Year. Correspondingly, the descendants of Year would include all four quarters and all twelve months.

Note that there are members that don't have any children. If our database doesn't go below the month level, May is barren. I refer to childless members as being "Level 0". If you want all bottom, child-less members of a dimension, just ask for the Level 0 members. For example, the Level 0 members of the Year dimension are the months.

Level 0 (bottom level) members also are sometimes referred to as "leaves," because they're at the edges of the family tree. I sometimes refers to Level 0 members as "the ones who have to sit at the little table in the living room on Thanksgiving," but I think he is the only one, because that's rather a lot to say.

All of the parents of the Level 0 members are referred to as Level 1. Since the Level 0 members of the Year dimension are the months, then the Level 1 members are the quarters. For the Market dimension, the Level 1 members are the regions: East, West, South, and Central.

Just as the parents of the Level 0 members are Level 1 members, the parents of Level 1 members are Level 2 members, their parents are level-3 members, and so on up the hierarchy. There are many places in Essbase that you can specify, for example, "All the Level 2 members of the Product dimension," so remember that levels count up from the bottom of a dimension starting at 0.

If you want to count down the hierarchy, use generations instead of levels. The dimension itself is considered Generation 1 (or "Gen1," for short). Its children are Gen2. For the Year dimension, the Gen2 members are the quarters.

Yes, the quarters are both Level 2 and Generation 2. Why do I need both levels and generations? Well, in some dimensions with many, many levels in the hierarchy, you'll want to count up from the bottom or down from the top depending on which is closer. I've seen a dimension with 17 levels in the hierarchy, and it was nice definitely to have both options available. The children of gen2 members are gen3 and so on down the hierarchy.

Note! Why do generations start counting from 1 and levels from 0? It's because Generation 0 is considered to be the outline itself making its children, the dimensions, Generation 1.

While counting with generations is pretty straight-forward, levels can sometimes be a bit tricky. Look at this portion of the Measures dimension:

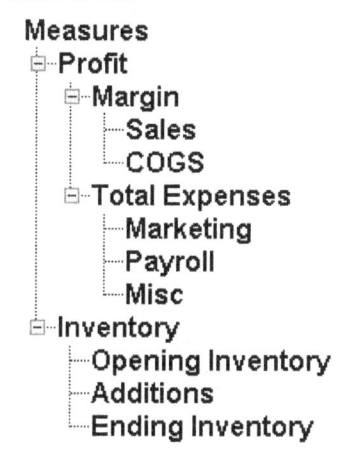

Measures
- **Profit**
  - **Margin**
    - Sales
    - COGS
  - **Total Expenses**
    - Marketing
    - Payroll
    - Misc
- **Inventory**
  - Opening Inventory
  - Additions
  - Ending Inventory

For this dimension, Gen1 is Measures. Gen2 is Profit and Inventory. Gen3 is Margin, Total Expenses, Opening Inventory, Additions, and Ending Inventory.

So far this is looking pretty easy, but let's switch our focus to the levels. The Level 0 members are Sales, COGS, Marketing, Payroll, Misc, Opening Inventory, Additions, and Ending Inventory. The Level 1 members are Margin, Total Expenses, and Inventory. What are the Level 2 members? Profit (because it's the parent of Level 1 members Margin and Total Expenses) and Measures (because it's the parent of Level 1 member Inventory).

The trickiness is that Measures is *also* a Level 3 member because it's the parent of Profit, a Level 2 member. This means that if you ask Essbase for Level 2 members, you'll get Measures, but you'll also get Measures if you ask for Level 3 members. Notice that this counting oddity does not occur with generations.

BLOCK STORAGE DATABASE

Dense & Sparse

Before defining dense and sparse, I'll start with defining a member combination. A member combination is the intersection of members from each dimension. See the following examples of member combinations for the following sample outline:

```
Year Time (Active Dynamic Time Series Members: H-T-D, Q-T-D) (Dynamic Calc)
    Qtr1 (+) (Dynamic Calc)
    Qtr2 (+) (Dynamic Calc)
    Qtr3 (+) (Dynamic Calc)
    Qtr4 (+) (Dynamic Calc)
Measures Accounts (Label Only)
    Profit (+) (Dynamic Calc)
    Inventory (~) (Label Only)
    Ratios (~) (Label Only)
Product {Caffeinated, Intro Date, Ounces, Pkg Type}
    100 (+) (Alias: Colas)
    200 (+) (Alias: Root Beer)
    300 (+) (Alias: Cream Soda)
    400 (+) (Alias: Fruit Soda)
    Diet (~) (Alias: Diet Drinks)
Market {Population}
    East (+) (UDAS: Major Market)
    West (+)
```

Example member combinations:

- Qtr1 -> Profit -> 100 -> East -> Actual
- Year -> Profit -> 100 -> East -> Actual
- Jan -> Sales -> 100-10 -> New York -> Budget
- Jan -> Sales -> 100 -> New York -> Budget

Note! The symbol "->" is known as a cross dimensional operator in Essbase (more on this later). For now, when you see the "->", think of the word "at". I am referencing the data value at Qtr1 at Profit at 100 at East at Actual.

Dense data is data that occurs often or repeatedly across the intersection of all member combinations. For example, you will most likely have data for all periods for most member combinations. You will most likely have data for most of your accounts for member combinations. Time and accounts are naturally dense.

Sparse data is data that occurs only periodically or sparsely across member combinations. Product, Market, and Employee dimensions are usually sparse:

	Products				
Markets	X				
				X	
	X				
		X			
					X

Sparse

	Time				
Measures	X	X		X	
	X	X	X	X	X
	X	X	X		X
		X	X	X	X
	X		X	X	X

Dense

You, as the administrator, will assign a dense / sparse setting to each dimension. This will dictate how the Essbase database is structured.

Why can't you see the dense / sparse setting for the Product Manager dimension or any other attribute dimensions? If you answered "attribute dimensions are always sparse", pat yourself on the back.

Block Structure

The Essbase database is composed of a number of blocks. A block is created for each intersection of the sparse dimensions. In the example below, Market and Product are sparse. See a block for each sparse member combination in the example below:

Cola->East

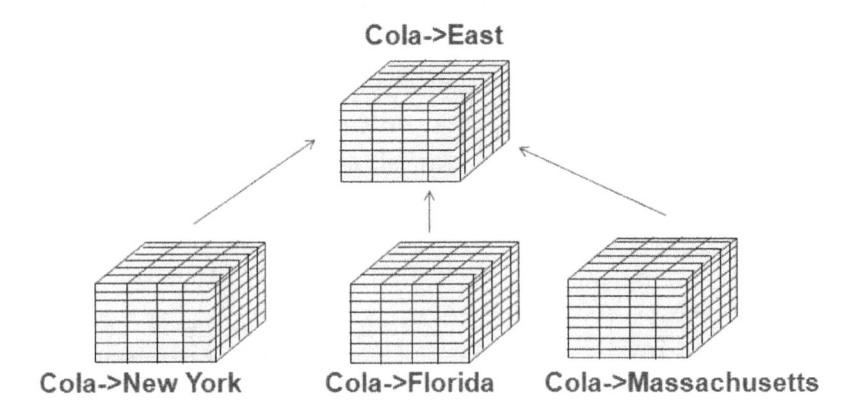

Cola->New York **Cola->Florida** **Cola->Massachusetts**

There are four types of blocks:

- Input blocks are blocks where data is loaded or input.
- Calculated blocks are blocks that are created through consolidation or calculation.
- Level zero blocks are blocks that are created from the level zero members of all dimensions.
- Upper-level blocks are all blocks that contain at least one upper level member (non-level zero).

Each block is made up of cells. These cells are created for each intersection of the dense dimensions. In the example below, Time, Measures, and Scenario are dense dimensions. See the cells for each dense member combination in the example below (I've highlighted one specific cell "Profit" at "Jan" at "Actual"):

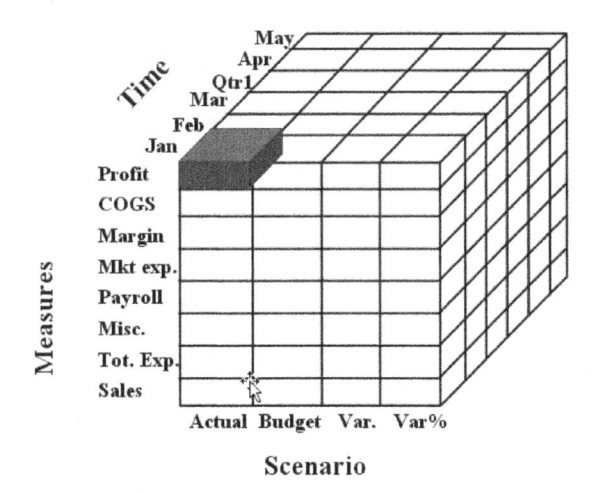

Outline Consolidation

Essbase is built to perform outline consolidations. You assigned a consolidation attribute to each member that tells Essbase how to perform the consolidation, whether it should add to the total, subtract from the total, and so forth. Unary operators include +, -, *, /, %, and ~. The consolidation will use these operators and follow the path of the hierarchies for each dimension.

So what do outline consolidation and dense / sparse have to do with each other? Essbase will perform dense calculations first and then sparse calculations.

The default calculation order for Essbase is the following:

- First, Accounts
- Second, Time
- Third, remaining dense dimensions
- Fourth, remaining sparse dimensions
- Finally, Two Pass Calculation (as applicable)

Let's follow the path of an Essbase consolidation to help you better understand. In the example below, the highlighted cells indicate cells loaded with data:

524   Appendix

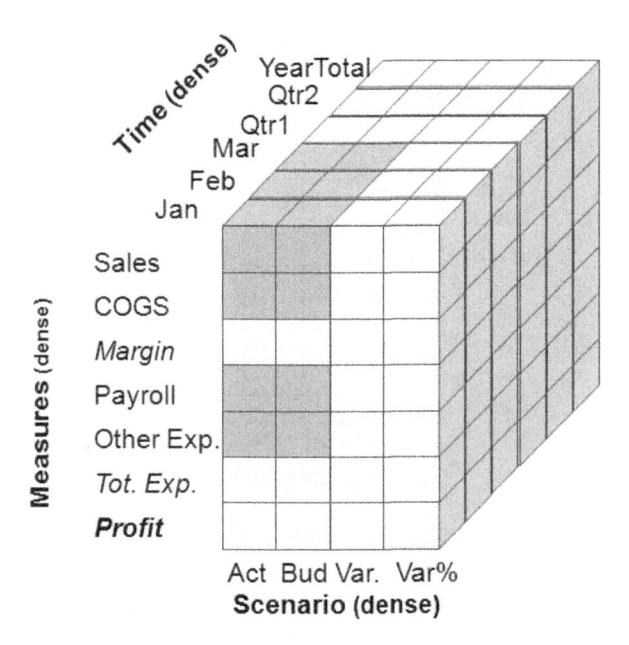

Next, you see those cells populated with the Accounts dimension calculation (see Profit, Margin, Tot. Exp):

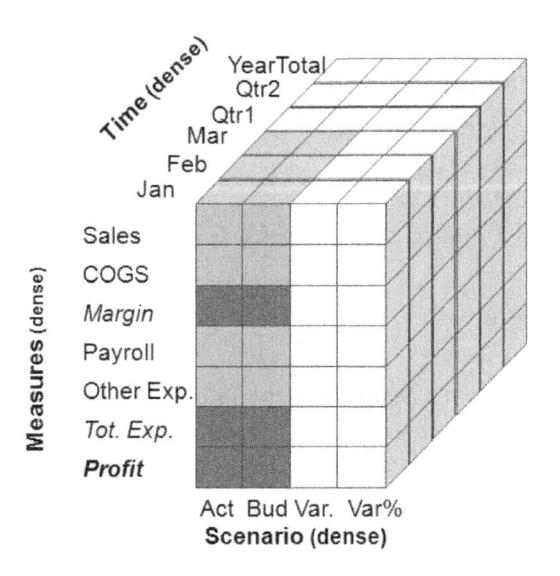

Finally, the cells in the upper portion of the block represent those cells populated with the Time dimension calculation (Qtr1, Qtr2, YearTotal):

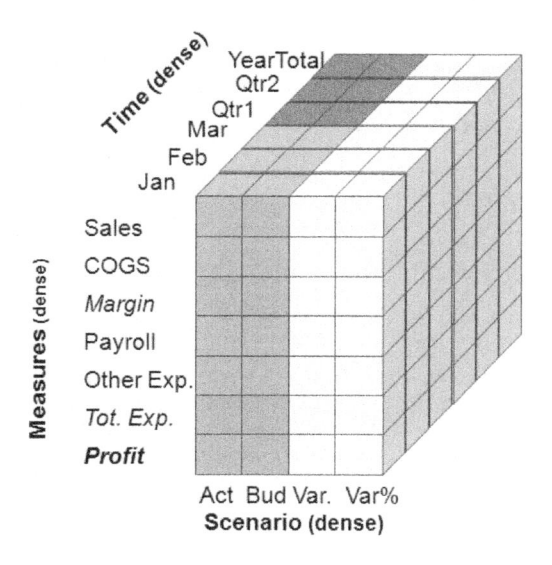

Why don't the variance and variance % members show calculated data values? 99% of the time you will tag these two members with the dynamic calc property so data will never be stored and in most cases, you won't need to calculate the Scenario dimension (and in most cases, this is a sparse dimension instead of a dense dimension; but I'm getting a bit ahead of ourselves).

Here is another view of this dense calculation. Data is loaded to Sales and COGS members for each month. I am looking at the block for Vermont, Cola, and Actual (there's that cross dimensional symbol that means "at"):

Vermont -> Cola -> Actual

Accounts	Jan	Feb	Mar	Qtr1
Sales	124.71	119.43	161.93	
COGS	42.37	38.77	47.28	
Margin				

First I consolidate the Accounts dimension, calculating the Margin member:

Vermont -> Cola -> Actual

Accounts	Jan	Feb	Mar	Qtr1
Sales	124.71	119.43	161.93	
COGS	42.37	38.77	47.28	
Margin	82.34	80.66	114.65	

Next I consolidate the Time dimension, calculating the Qtr1 member:

Vermont -> Cola -> Actual

Accounts	Jan	Feb	Mar	Qtr1
Sales	124.71	119.43	161.93	406.07
COGS	42.37	38.77	47.28	128.42
Margin	82.34	80.66	114.65	277.65

Once the Dense calculation is complete, the sparse calculation is next. The Vermont -> Cola -> Actual block and the New York -> Cola -> Actual block are added together to create the East -> Cola -> Actual block:

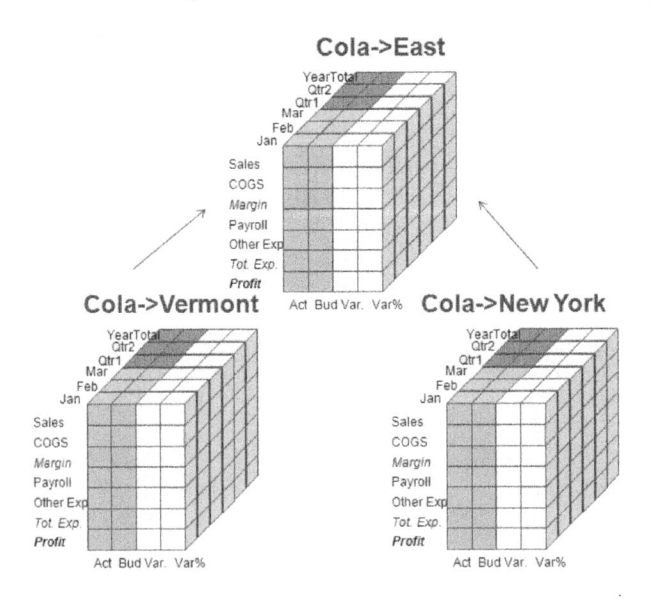

Note! This unevenness of some dimensions is also known as a ragged hierarchy.

AGGREGATE STORAGE DATABASE

Essbase allows two database types: aggregate storage databases (ASO) and block storage databases (BSO). ASO databases are designed to handle more dimensions and members, smaller batch windows for loads and aggregations of sparse data, and smaller database footprints.

Benefits of an ASO plan type in Enterprise Planning Cloud applications include unified dimension maintenance and security for BSO and ASO planning and reporting. No aggregation is required for ASO databases so results at upper levels are available immediately.

Users can use ASO plan types to provide write back to databases with larger number of dimensions and members. ASO plan types provide a higher level of granularity for requirements that dictate detailed planning.

In ASO databases, there are three types of hierarchies: stored, dynamic, or multiple hierarchies ("Hierarchies Enabled"). Stored hierarchies will aggregate according to the structure of the outline. For example, months will roll up to quarters up to a year total in the Period member. This aggregation is really fast (the nature of ASO databases); however, stored hierarchies may only have the + for any member and ~ consolidation tags for members under a label only parent (other assigned consolidation tags are ignored). Also, stored hierarchies cannot have member formulas; there are a few other restrictions on label only assignments.

Dynamic hierarchies are calculated by Essbase (versus aggregated like in stored hierarchies) so all consolidation tags and member formulas are processed. The evaluation order for the calculation of members is dictated by the solve order. Dynamic hierarchies, as expected, do not calculate as quickly as stored hierarchies.

The Solve Order member property tells the ASO database the order to complete calculations. Why is this important? You want to calculate the correct numbers in the correct order. Think about the order of operations for basic math. $4 + 5 * 2$ does not equal $(4 + 5) * 2$. Solve order is the way you control the order of calculations in ASO databases. This is a property specific to ASO plan types and does not apply to BSO.

You can also have multiple hierarchies within a single dimension. The hierarchies within a dimension can be stored, all dynamic, or have one hierarchy stored and the other hierarchies dynamic. Multiple hierarchies can contain alternate hierarchies with Shared Members or completely different hierarchies.

Hybrid Aggregation

Hybrid aggregation databases were introduced in Essbase 11.1.2.3.500 as a new alternative to BSO databases and are supported in on-premise versions of Hyperion Planning and Essbase. Hybrid aggregation databases are not supported for Enterprise Planning Cloud yet but I anticipate this feature coming soon!

With the latest on-premise version, 11.1.2.4, hybrid aggregation supports many common functions, and it's a good candidate for your plan types unless you have a valid reason for using either straight BSO or ASO.

Design considerations for hybrid aggregation cubes are very much the same as the design considerations for a Block Storage application. Users can write back to stored dimensions at any level, and the same calculation engine in BSO is still available to hybrid aggregation applications; however, dynamic dimensions in a hybrid aggregation application benefit from lightning-fast aggregations like an ASO application. On the downside, the dimensions are somewhat constrained still, like a BSO application, although larger BSO applications are possible if they use dynamic dimensions.

Hybrid aggregation applications are truly a blend of both ASO and BSO, which makes them perfect for reporting applications or Planning applications where there is a desire to see the latest aggregated numbers as fast as possible.

Hybrid will be the default setting for many Cloud Essbase based products in the future (I think).

Comparing Essbase Database Options

First, a quick disclaimer: this chapter was written mainly for Essbase 11.1.2.4. The hard working developers have enhanced the ASO engine dramatically in versions 9, 11.1.1.x, and 11.1.2.x, so comparing the two database types has been a rapidly moving target. If you are on Essbase 7x or an early version of System 9, you will see more differences than noted in the discussion below.

Let's start with the most important point – what does the user see? The beauty of ASO, BSO and hybrid aggregation databases is that front-end tools like the Excel Add-In, Smart View, and OBIEE really don't care if the database is BSO or ASO or a combination of both (even MaxL sees only minor differences between the two). The three types seem like multidimensional databases that have Zoom In and Zoom Out and Keep Only and Remove Only and Pivot and all that nice stuff. There are some minor differences, but for the most part the database type is pretty much transparent to the end-user.

What else is the same? The three types of databases are defined by their outline. Most dimension and member properties like dimension type, data storage (store, never share, label only), consolidation tags, and aliases are consistent for all three application types. How you build dimensions and load data is essentially the same. Certain rule files properties are database type specific, but the overall interface and steps are the same.

Calculating the databases is where I really begin to see the differences between them. In ASO databases, after data values are loaded into the level 0 cells of an outline, *the database requires no separate calculation step*. From any point in the database, users can retrieve and view values that are aggregated for only the current retrieval. ASO databases are smaller than block storage databases, enabling quick retrieval of data. For even faster retrieval, administrators can pre-calculate data values and store the pre-calculated results in aggregations. You can add in calculated members with member formulas in ASO. The syntax for the formulas is MDX.

On the other side of the house, BSO databases also have member formulas, but they use a different syntax: Essbase calc script syntax. In most cases, you will need to aggregate the BSO database after performing a data load. You will use the default calc script or one that you manually create to roll up all of the values for the dimensions in the database. These BSO calc scripts can perform complex business logic and allocations.

For hybrid aggregation applications, once data is loaded there may or may not be a need to aggregate the database depending on the dimensions and member properties of the Sparse dimensions. If not all Sparse dimensions are dynamic, a more limited aggregation script may need to be run. In hybrid applications, member formulas and calculation scripts are available just like BSO apps, and hybrid aggregation uses the same syntax as the BSO Essbase calculator engine.

Write back is another differentiator. For block storage databases, users can write back to any level in the database if they have permissions, while aggregate storage databases only allow write back to level zero members. Hybrid applications allow write back to any level as long as the dimension is stored and not dynamically calculated. If most dimensions are marked as dynamic in a hybrid app, then write back at level zero would be permitted like an ASO application.

Under the covers, the types of databases are radically different. ASO outlines have two types of hierarchies: stored and dynamic. BSO outlines define dense and sparse dimensions. Hybrid applications also have dense and sparse dimensions, but some sparse dimensions can be dynamically aggregated. ASO databases are stored in a series of tablespaces while BSO databases are stored in a series of index and page files and hybrid applications are a combination of both. How you tune each database is very different.

All of these concepts are covered in much greater detail in the *Look Smarter Than You Are with Essbase* book, but I wanted to have one place to summarize the great ASO vs. BSO vs. hybrid aggregation debate.

Note! General guideline – use ASO when requirements dictate large numbers of dimensions and members that simply "roll up" (i.e. minimal complex calculations are required).

General guideline – Use BSO for applications that require complex calculations and write back capabilities to any level.

General guideline – Use hybrid aggregation to achieve the best of both worlds. This will likely become the default option.

DIMENSION ORDER FOR BSO PLAN TYPE

Dimension order is critical for Essbase performance. The administrator may want to test different iterations of dimension order to determine the optimal structure. The hourglass methodology involves the largest dense dimensions to the smallest dense dimension to be ordered first, then the smallest sparse dimension to the largest sparse dimension to be ordered last. The hourglass format works well when parallel calculations is not utilized. If parallel calculations are being used, a different dimension order would be more optimal.

First, a few definitions:

- **Dense dimensions** – dimensions that define the internal structure of the data block; they should reside at the top of the order
- **Aggregating Sparse dimensions** – dimensions that will be calculated to create new parent values; these dimensions should reside directly after the last dense dimension. Placing these dimensions as the first sparse dimensions positions them to be the first dimensions included in the calculator cache, which gives them an ideal location for optimized calculation performance.
- **Non-Aggregating Sparse dimensions** – dimensions that organize the data into logical slices (e.g., Scenario, Version and Years); it is not crucial for these dimensions to be included in the calculator cache because their members are typically isolated in FIX statements

With these types of dimensions in mind, you can create the optimal dimension order. This method is sometimes called an "hourglass on a stick". The general starting point would be to have Period first, then Account. If there is a sparse dimension that is frequently in rows, consider moving that dimension to be the first sparse dim after the dense dimensions.

What was just presented is a basic guideline for dimension ordering; for best results, test iterations of dense and sparse dimensions to figure out the optimal settings for your application.

INDEX

Academy, 510
Account, 67, 84, 92
Account Administrator, 19, 22
Account Annotations, 308
Account Reconciliation Cloud, 12
Account Reconciliation Manager, 12
Account Type, 88
Action Menu, 319, 320, 433
Ad Hoc Analysis, 450, 479
Ad Hoc Grid, 352
Ad Hoc Options, 454
Adjust, 438
Advanced Planning, 63
Aggregate Storage Database, 58, 527
Aggregating Sparse Dimension, 122, 531
Aggregations, 529
Alias, 67
Alias Display, 309
All Years, 97, 98
Alternate Hierarchy, 72
Analyze, 352, 450, 454
Application, 57
Application Creation Wizard, 62
Application Management, 365, 415, 418

Application Management (Shared Services), 53
Application Settings, 460
Approvals, 458
ASO, 58, 65, 124, 527
Assign security, 368
Attachment, 442
Attribute dimension, 126
Attributes, 72
Audit Trail, 503
Autosave, 299, 308, 437

BaseData, 100, 256, 488
BI, 3
BICS, 9
Block Storage Database, 58
Blocks, 521, 522
Bottom Up Version, 81
BSO, 58, 65
BSO Calc Functions, 73
BSO Dimension Order, 122, 531
Business Rule, 59, 237, 256, 257, 260, 374, 456

Calculate Data Form, 260
Calculate Data Form business rule, 277
Calculation Manager, 54
Capital Assets Planning, 8, 58
Cell Color, 432
Cell Text, 447
Cells, 522

Change History, 496, 503
Chart Type, 326
Cloud, 5
Cloud Support Case, 39
Cloud.oracle.com, 15
Comments, 447
Composite Form, 268, 298
ConsolidatedData, 100, 488
Consolidation Operators, 70
Context Sensitive Menu, 433
Continuous Forecast. *See* Rolling Forecast
Copy Scenario, 76
Country, 67
Create custom dimension, 101
Create Users, 29
Cross-Dimensional Operator, 520
Ctrl+Z, 299, 437
Custom ASO Dimension, 126
Custom Dimension, 67, 100
Customer Support ID, 28

Dashboard, 324, 326, 427
Data Center, 3
Data form, 430
Data Form, 59, 267, 373
Data Integration (Data Management), 54
Data Management, 145
Data Management (Data Integration), 54
Data Management Application Settings, 146, 151
Data Management file requirements, 149

Data Management Steps to Build an Integration, 146
Data Map, 229, 303
Data Storage, 68
Data Type, 68, 88
Data Visualization Cloud Service, 9
Data Visualization Cloud Service (DVCS), 10
DATAEXPORT, 262
Date Cell, 435
DBaaS, 9
Default BSO Calculation Order, 523
Default Value, 254
Delete application, 53, 508
Dense, 520, 530
Dense Data, 121
Dense Dimension, 122, 531
Desktop installs, 53, 54
Dimension, 59, 66, 109, 513, 514
Dimension Editor, 66
Dimension Management Cloud, 13
Dimension Properties, 275, 279, 309
Dimension Template for Import, 102
Dimensions, 464
Dirty Cell, 432
Display properties, 276
DMCS, 13
Download a file, 387
DTS. *See* Dynamic Time Series
DVCS, 9
Dynamic Calc, 69, 525

Dynamic Hierarchies, 125, 527, 530
Dynamic report, 360
Dynamic Time Series, 99
Dynamic User Variable, 287
Dynamically add members on the fly, 463

E-mail Notifications, 460
Enter data, 430
Enterprise Performance Reporting Cloud, 11
Enterprise Planning, 8
Enterprise Planning Budgeting Cloud Service, 8
Enterprise Planning Cloud, 41
Enterprise Planning pricing option, 8, 58
Entity, 106
EPBCS, 8
EPM, 3
EPM Automate, 212, 390
EPM Automate Utility, 234
EPM Cloud, 13
EPRCS, 11
error trapping, 408
Essbase, 3, 68
Essbase Administration Services, 238
Essbase Cloud, 13
EssCS, 13
Evaluation Order, 123
Exchange Rate Type, 89
Expense Reporting, 85
Explore, 54
Export data, 142, 209, 262

Export Metadata, 107
Export On Premise Application, 425
Export PBCS Application, 418, 508

Family tree relationships, 516
FCCS, 12
FDMEE, 14, *See* Financial Data Quality Management, *See* Financial Data Quality Management, *See* Financial Data Quality Management
Filter Data Form, 434
Financial Consolidation and Close Cloud, 12
Financial Data Quality Management, 145
Financial Planning, 84
Financial Reporting, 458
Financial Reporting Studio, 328, 329, 458
Financial Reports, 330
Financials, 8
Flat File, 102, 133
Flying Cars, 4
Focused aggregation, 252
Form Folder, 267, 268
Form Instructions, 429
Form Layout, 279
Format Forms, 448
Formatting, 460, 481
FR Desktop Studio, 330, 350
FR Web Studio, 330, 338, 350
Free Form Text, 435
Frozen, 4

FRS, 329

Generations, 518, 519
Graphical business rule, 241, 246
Graphical Mode, 240
Grid, 331, 339
Grid properties, 274
Grid Spread, 441

HSP_View, 66, 82, 100, 488
HTML View, 443
Human Capital Planning, 85
Hybrid, 13
Hybrid aggregation, 58, 65
Hybrid Aggregation, 528, 529, 530, 531
Hybrid Aggregation Mode, 100
Hyperion, 512

Identity Domain, 20, 24
Identity Domain Administrator, 19, 20, 22, 30, 364
Ignore, 71
Implicit Sharing, 69
Import data, 136, 149
Import PBCS Application, 421
Import users, 34
Inbox / Outbox Explorer, 263, 387
interRel, 6
Inventory Planning, 84

Job Console, 258
Job Scheduler, 378, 381

Label Only, 69
Launch Business Rules, 458

Level-0 member, 518
Levels, 518, 519
Lock Cell, 440

Maintenance time, 53, 505
Mark Watney, 3
Master Composite Form, 307
MaxL, 529
MDX, 529
Measures, 514, 519
Member, 514
Member Formula, 72, 80
Member Name Display, 309
Member Properties, 67
Member search, 49, 50
Member selection, 49
Member selection filters, 51
Member Selector, 280
Members on the fly, 463
Metadata Access, 370
Microsoft Office, 41, 475
Microsoft Office Integration, 329
Migration, 418, 421, 508
Mobile support, 484
Monitor Service status, 36
Monitor usage metrics, 37
Multi-Dimensional Databases, 512
My Account, 19
My Services, 20, 29, 364

Native Essbase format, 136
Native Planning format, 137
Navigator, 90
Never Consolidate, 71
Never Share, 69

Non-Aggregating Sparse Dimension, 122, 531
Notifications, 38, 506

OBIEE, 9
OLAP, 512
On-Premise, 7
Oracle, 512
Oracle Business Intelligence Enterprise Edition, 9
Oracle Enterprise Planning Cloud, 7
Oracle Enterprise Planning Cloud Version for this book, 62
Outline, 519
Outline Consolidations, 523
Outline Load Utility, 102

PaaS, 9
Page, 431
Partial Data Clear, 265
PBCS, 7, 41
PCMCS, 13
PDF View, 459
Performance, 121
Period, 98
Plan type, 57, 121, 124, 497
Plan Type, 498
Planner, 31, 365
Planning and Budgeting Cloud Service, 7
Plans, 430
Point of View, 431
Power User, 31, 365
Predictive Analytics, 474

Profitability & Cost Management Cloud, 13
Project Financial Planning, 8

Read Only, 293, 295
Refresh, 436
Refresh Database, 78
Refresh the database, 77
Refresh the Database, 77
Report Book, 329
Reports, 328, 458
Restarting Instance, 505
Roles, 365
Rolling Forecast, 64, 288, 290
RTP. *See* Run Time Prompt
Run time prompt, 457

SaaS, 8
Sales Planning, 84
Sample Application, 63
Sandbox, 65, 81, 100, 488
SandboxData, 100, 488
Sandboxes, 486
Save Tasks, 379
Scenario, 74, 514
Schedule Jobs, 258
Script business rule, 250
Script Mode, 240, 250, 254
Security, 368
Segment Properties, 275
Select Level 0 Members, 296
Servers, 3
Service Administrator, 19, 22, 23, 30, 365
Shared Connection URL, 477
Shared Services, 418

Shortcut Keys, 437
Simple Form, 268, 278
Simple Planning, 63
Simplified Interface, 41, 62
Simplified UI, 427
Skip Missing, 87
Slice Definition, 143
Smart Form, 310
Smart list, 90, 126
Smart List, 89, 295, 435
Smart Push, 229, 305
Smart View, 109, 329, 475, 476
Smart View Panel, 477
SmartCut, 443
Snapshot, 329
Solve Order, 125, 527
Sort Data Form, 435
Source Plan Type, 85
Sparse, 65, 521, 530
Sparse Data, 121
Sparse Dimension, 69
Store, 69
Stored Hierarchies, 125, 527, 530
Subscription ID, 28
Substitution Variable, 131
Substitution Variables, 289
Supported Data Sources for PBCS, 133
Supporting Detail, 308, 443, 446
Sync data, 222
System 9, 3

Tablespaces, 530
Tablet access, 484
Tablet Access, 376
Target Version, 81

Task, 321, 428
Task list, 321, 428
Task List, 59, 374, 479
Task List Alerts, 323
Tax Provisioning & Reporting Cloud, 13
Time, 67
Time Balance, 86, 87
Time Spreading, 439
TPRCS, 13
Two Pass, 71

UDA, 72
Undo, 299, 437
UPDATECALC, 243
Upload a file, 387
User Defined Attribute, 72
User Interfaces, 41
User Preferences, 460
User Variable, 129, 461

Valid for Plan Type, 70
Valid Intersection, 313
Validation Rule, 308
Validation Rules, 277
Variable Designer, 252
Variance, 72, 79
Variance Reporting, 85, 86
Version, 81
View Member Formulas, 309, 449
Viewer, 31, 365
Visual Analyzer, 9, 10

Web Client vs. Smart View, 475
Wildcard search, 50
Workforce Planning, 8, 58

Workspace, 41, 62
Workspace user interface, 52

Years, 97

XREF, 85, 126

Made in the USA
Coppell, TX
24 November 2019